PRAISE FOR *NEW WORLDS*

"*New Worlds* is a clear, concise textbook . . . **the best textbook on th**

—Lisa Mizes, *St. Louis Community College at Meramac*

"New Worlds is **a first-rate text** for an introductory college reading class. Students find the selections interesting and relevant."

—Lori Murphy, *Westchester Community College*

"The main strengths within this text are its focus on the interconnectivity between reading and writing and understanding, its strong visuals, and especially its **keen attention to student success.**"

—Tondalaya VanLear, *Dabney S. Lancaster Community College*

"A **thorough, step-by-step approach** that introduces college-level reading, creating a user-friendly avenue."

—Tanya Masso, *South Texas College*

"*New Worlds* **will help students comprehend whole new worlds** while developing necessary reading skills."

—Gerardo Mechler, *Palo Alto College*

"The features, reading selections, online support, maps, glossaries, and overall design provide **an appealing, inclusive environment** for learners to improve their reading ability."

—Julie Rae Zimmerman-Kelly, *St. Johns River Community College*

"New Worlds **takes our students step by step** through the whys and hows of effective college reading **and prepares them to become successful students.**"

—Victoria Covington, *Isothermal Community College*

About the Authors

Joe Cortina

Janet Elder

Joe Cortina and **Janet Elder** began their writing collaboration as colleagues in the Human and Academic Development Division at Richland College, a member of the Dallas County Community College District. Professor Elder now writes full time; Professor Cortina currently teaches both developmental reading and honors English courses at Richland, and serves as the developmental reading program coordinator. Both are trained reading specialists and are highly experienced in teaching basic and advanced reading improvement and study skills courses. Their combined teaching experience spans elementary, secondary, and undergraduate levels, as well as clinical remediation.

Dr. Cortina and Dr. Elder began collaborating in 1985. Their first textbook was *Comprehending College Textbooks: Steps to Understanding and Remembering What You Read.* Their intermediate-level textbook, *Opening Doors: Understanding College Reading,* is now in its sixth edition. Dr. Elder is also the author of an introductory-level text, *Entryways into College Reading and Learning,* and an intermediate- to upper-level college reading improvement textbook, *Exercise Your College Reading Skills: Developing More Powerful Comprehension,* now in its second edition. Both authors are long-standing members of the College Reading and Learning Association (CRLA) and the National Association for Developmental Education (NADE). Dr. Cortina is also a member of the Texas counterparts of these national organizations, Texas-CRLA and TADE, and Dr. Elder has given numerous presentations at their conferences over the years.

Joe Cortina earned his B.A. degree in English from San Diego State University and his master's degree and doctoral degree in curriculum and instruction in reading from the University of North Texas. He has taught undergraduate teacher education courses in reading at the University of North Texas and Texas Woman's University. In 1981 he was selected to represent the Dallas County Community College District as a nominee for the Piper Award for Teaching Excellence. In addition, Dr. Cortina was selected as his division's nominee for Richland's Excellence in Teaching Award in 1987, 1988, 1993, and 2008. In 1992 he was selected as an honored alumnus by the Department of Elementary, Early Childhood and Reading Education of the University of North Texas, and in 1994 and 2009 he was a recipient of an Excellence Award given by the National Institute for Staff and Organizational Development. In addition to teaching, Dr. Cortina conducts in-service training and serves as a mentor to both new full-time and adjunct faculty at Richland College.

Janet Elder was graduated summa cum laude from the University of Texas in Austin with a B.A. in English and Latin, and is a member of Phi Beta Kappa. She was the recipient of a government fellowship for Southern Methodist University's Reading Research Program, which resulted in a master's degree. Her Ph.D. in curriculum and instruction in reading is from Texas Woman's University where the College of Education presented her the Outstanding Dissertation Award. After teaching reading and study skills courses at Richland for several years, she implemented the college's Honors Program and directed it for six years before returning to teaching full time. She was a three-time nominee for excellence in teaching awards. Disability Services students also selected her three times as the recipient of a special award for "exceptional innovation, imagination, and consideration in working with students with disabilities." She is a recipient of the National Institute for Staff and Organizational Development's Excellence Award. In the fall of 2004 she left teaching in order to write full time, but she continues her affiliation with Richland as a professor emerita. A frequent presenter at professional conferences and in-service workshops, she has a deep interest and expertise in "brain-friendly" instruction.

ANNOTATED INSTRUCTOR'S EDITION

New Worlds

An Introduction to College Reading

FOURTH EDITION

Joe Cortina
Professor

Janet Elder
Professor Emerita

Richland College
Dallas County Community College District

The McGraw·Hill Companies

This book is printed on acid-free paper.
1 2 3 4 5 6 7 8 9 0 WVR/WVR 0

ISBN: 978-0-07-340717-3 (student edition)
MHID: 0-07-340717-8 (student edition)
ISBN: 978-0-07-735076-5 (instructor's edition)
MHID: 0-07-735076-6 (instructor's edition)

Vice President, Editorial: *Michael Ryan*
Publisher: *David S. Patterson*
Sponsoring Editor: *John Kindler*
Marketing Manager: *Allison Jones*
Developmental Editor: *Barbara Conover*
Production Editor: *Regina Ernst*
Manuscript Editor: *Margaret Moore*
Design Manager: *Allister Fein*
Text Designer: *Kay Lieberherr*
Cover Designer: *Allister Fein*
Photo Researcher: *Sonia Brown*
Art Editor: *Sonia Brown*
Production Supervisor: *Louis Swaim*
Composition: *10.5/12 Times Roman by MPS Limited, A Macmillan Company*
Printing: *45# Publishers Thinbulk, World Color, Inc*

Cover Image: © David McNew/Getty Images

Photo Credits: p. 1: David McNew/Getty Images; **p. 3:** AP Photo; **p. 14:** Purestock/SuperStock; **p. 27:** © 2003 Baltimore Sun Company; **p. 36:** © Adam Crowley/Getty Images; **p. 49:** Bill Aron/PhotoEdit; **p. 59:** Royalty-Free/Corbis; **p. 62:** © MIXA/Getty Images; **p. 106:** © Les Stone/Sygma/Corbis; **p. 116:** © Digital Vision/Getty Images; **p. 125:** David McNew/Getty Images; **p. 127:** © Wilfried Krecichwost/Getty Images; **p. 130:** BananaStock/JupiterImages; **p. 158:** © Reuters/Corbis; **p. 177:** © Comstock Images; **p. 180:** The McGraw-Hill Companies, Inc./Christopher Kerrigan, photographer; **p. 200:** © NBAE/Getty Images; **p. 210:** (c) Andy Bernhauf/ Photo Researchers; **p. 220:** © AP Photo; **p. 231:** © Photodisc/Getty Images; **p. 233:** © PhotoAlto/SuperStock; **p. 256:** © Brand X Pictures/PunchStock; **p. 257:** Paul Margolies; **p. 279:** © BananaStock/JupiterImages; **p. 291:** © Royalty-Free/Corbis; **p. 294:** © Tetra Images/Getty Images; **p. 327:** Kurt Scholz/SuperStock; **p. 339:** © AP Photo; **p. 349:** © Pixtal/SuperStock; **p. 398:** © Royalty-Free/Corbis; **p. 408:** Library of Congress, #LC-DIG-ggbain-02466; **p. 421:** © Mark Richards/PhotoEdit; **p. 431:** David McNew/Getty Images; **p. 433:** (c) Masterfile/Royalty-Free; **p. 475:** Kristi A. Rines for Hobbs Studio; **p. 495:** McGraw-Hill Companies, Inc./Gary He, photographer; **p. 528:** © Photodisc/Gety Images; **p. 536:** © Digital Vision/PunchStock; **p. 555:** David McNew/Getty Images; **p. 557:** The McGraw-Hill Companies, Inc./Christopher Kerrigan, photographer; **p. 573:** © Photodisc Collection/Getty Images; **p. 574:** © Bettmann/Corbis; **p. 615:** Getty Images/Digital Vision; **p. 638 (top left):** © AP Photo; **p. 638 (top right):** Courtesy of Gateway, Inc.; **p. 638 (bottom left):** Courtesy of Wacom; **p. 638 (bottom right):** Courtesy of HP; **p. 641 (left):** Courtesy of Research in Motion; **p. 641 (middle):** Courtesy of Nokia; **p. 641 (right):** Courtesy of Nokia

Library of Congress Cataloging-in-Publication Data

Cortina, Joe.
New worlds : an introduction to college reading / Joe Cortina ; Janet Elder. — 4th ed.
p. cm.
Includes bibliographical references and index.
ISBN-13: 978-0-07-340717-3 (alk. paper)
ISBN-10: 0-07-340717-8 (alk. paper)
1. Reading (Higher education) 2. College readers. I. Elder, Janet. II. Title.
LB2395.3.C68 2009
428.6—dc22

2009043312

www.mhhe.com

Brief Contents

Contents

To the Instructor: Getting Started in *New Worlds*

Welcome to the fourth edition of *New Worlds: An Introduction to College Reading*. This text is designed to help students move toward a college reading level. It presents a systematic way of approaching college textbook material that can make students more efficient in their reading and studying. The heart of the text is Part Two, "A New World of Understanding: Using Core Comprehension Skills When You Read College Textbooks" (Chapters 3 through 7).

The scope of this book is broad, but the focus is always on comprehension. Moreover, the skills are integrated, and there is continual application of skills once they have been introduced. Although this text emphasizes comprehension of essential main ideas and supporting details (Part Two, "A New World of Understanding"), it includes skills that range from study skills and developing a college-level vocabulary (Part One, "A New World of Learning: Reading and Studying in College"), to reading critically and evaluating material you are reading (Part Three, "A New World of Reading and Thinking Critically"), to selecting, organizing, and rehearsing textbook material to be learned for a test (Part Four, "A New World of Studying: Effective and Efficient Study Techniques"). In Part Four, students learn to use textbook features to full advantage, to underline and annotate textbook material, and to organize material several ways in writing so that it can be mastered for tests.

Although *New Worlds* is designed for developing readers, we have chosen to use only college textbook excerpts and other materials students would be likely to encounter in college. The reading selections were chosen on the basis of field-testing with hundreds of our students in order to identify selections that are interesting, informative, and appropriate. Field-testing also revealed that *with coaching and guidance from the instructor, students can comprehend all of the selections.* Equally important is the fact that students like dealing with "the real thing"—actual college textbook material—since that is what they will encounter in other college courses. This type of practice enables them to transfer skills to other courses and avoid the frustration and disappointment of discovering that their reading improvement course did not prepare them for "real" college reading. Finally, these passages help students acquire and extend their background knowledge in a variety of subjects.

College textbook material contains many words students do not know, but need to learn. However, underprepared students and English-as-a-second-or-other-language students tend to focus on *words* rather than ideas. Therefore, we present vocabulary-in-context exercises throughout the text. It will also be important for you, the instructor, to help students view words as a means of accessing content rather than as ends unto themselves. We hope *New Worlds* will help you accomplish this.

Vocabulary words are from the chapter reading selections and are, as noted above, presented in context. The practice exercises in *New Worlds* are extensive. Comprehension questions are the same type that content-area teachers ask on tests (rather than "The main idea of the selection is . . ." etc.). There are also word-structure questions and reading skill application questions. Single paragraphs and short excerpts are used to introduce and illustrate skills. "Test Your Understanding" exercises containing paragraph-length excerpts follow the chapter review cards in Chapters 2 to 10. Exercises include both objective and short-answer questions. Fifty-seven mini-exercises are integrated into the chapters for on-the-spot practice. Additionally, students are given the opportunity to apply the skills presented in each chapter to full-length selections by completing the annotation practice exercises within each reading selection. Despite our continued, long-held belief that having students "write out" their responses to questions over a selection is the most complete way to assess their comprehension, we realize that students need practice with traditional multiple-choice items as well.

PROVEN FEATURES

- An extensive **Comprehension Core** as the heart of the text (Part Two, Chapters 3 to 7).
- Introduces the skills of **Reading and Thinking Critically** (Part Three, Chapters 8 and 9).
- Clear explanations and understandable examples of each comprehension skill.
- Numerous textbook excerpts for application of reading and study skills.
- **Chapter Review Card Exercises** following each chapter.
- Eighteen **Test Your Understanding Exercises** in Chapters 2 to 10 requiring objective (multiple-choice) responses as well as exercises requiring written responses.
- Twenty-seven **Full-length Reading Selections** (three in each of the first nine chapters).
- Two **Chapter-length Reading Selections** (in Chapters 10 and 11).
- **Comprehension and Vocabulary Quizzes** are included for the 27 reading selections in Chapters 1 to 9. These 20-question quizzes contain four parts:

  Comprehension This part of the Comprehension and Vocabulary Quiz contains five questions much like those that a content-area instructor (such as a psychology professor) would expect students to be able to answer after reading this selection.

  Vocabulary in Context This part of the Comprehension and Vocabulary Quiz contains five questions that test the ability to determine the meaning of a word by using context clues.

  Word Structure This part of the Comprehension and Vocabulary Quiz contains five questions that test the ability to use word-structure clues to help determine a word's meaning. In these exercises, students will learn the meaning of a word part (root) and use it to determine the meaning of the several other words that have the same root.

  Reading Skills Application This part of the Comprehension and Vocabulary Quiz contains five questions that test the student's ability to apply certain reading skills to the material in this selection. These are the types of questions that appear on standardized reading tests, exit tests, and state-mandated basic skills tests.

- **Annotation Practice Exercises** and **Responding-in-Writing Exercises** that integrate writing and reading and call for written responses and the formulation of overall main ideas of reading selections.
- Twenty-question **Practice Chapter Quiz** accompanying the chapter-length reading selection 11-1, "Information Technology, the Internet, and You." This practice quiz provides students with an opportunity to test their comprehension (and retention) of material presented in the selection.

- Websites for each reading selection so that students can read more about the topic or the author of the selection, and suggested keywords to guide students as they search online for more information about a selection's topic on their own.
- Cumulative review and continued application of skills taught in the comprehension core.
- Presentation of vocabulary and study skills as they relate to learning from college textbooks and other college-level materials.
- **Comprehension Monitoring Questions** (for reading comprehension and critical reading and thinking) are featured throughout the book in the margins.
- A substantive ***Student Online Learning Center*** replete with supplemental exercises, quizzes, and other resources.
- An extensive ***Instructor's Online Learning Center (OLC)*** that contains answer keys, chapter practice tests, chapter comprehension review tests, and supplemental reading selections with accompanying tests.
- Flexibility, allowing instructors to adapt assignments to the specific needs of their own students.
- Skills typically included on state-mandated reading competency tests are addressed.
- Consistency in philosophy and approach with our other reading textbooks, *Entryways into College Reading and Learning* (Elder); *Opening Doors: Understanding College Reading* (Cortina and Elder); and *Exercise Your College Reading Skills: Developing More Powerful Comprehension* (Elder).

ENHANCEMENTS AND NEW FEATURES IN THE FOURTH EDITION

- Eight new and updated reading selections with accompanying activities, exercises, and quizzes:

  3-2: Giving a Speech? If You're Nervous, You're Normal! *(Speech Communication)*
  4-1: Good Boss? Bad Boss? Three Leadership Styles *(Business)*
  5-2: Avian Flu: A Coming Pandemic *(Biology)*
  6-1: "Hold It! You Can Recycle That!" Recycling: A Twenty-First Century Necessity *(Environmental Science)*
  6-3: The New Immigrants: Asian Americans and Latinos *(History)*
  8-1: Excerpt from *For One More Day (Literature)*
  8-2: I Never Made It to the NFL *(Literature)*
  9-2: Planet Under Stress: Curbing Population Growth *(Biology)*

- Fifty-seven brief **within-chapter exercises** in Chapters 2 to 10, providing immediate application and practice of skills presented.

Chapter 2: Context Clues; Word-Structure Clues; Figurative Language	9 Exercises
Chapter 3: Topic	5 Exercises
Chapter 4: Stated Main Idea	3 Exercises
Chapter 5: Implied Main Idea	4 Exercises
Chapter 6: Major and Minor Supporting Details	3 Exercises
Chapter 7: Relationships within/between Sentences; Writing Patterns	16 Exercises
Chapter 8: Author's Point of View, Purpose, Tone, Intended Audience	4 Exercises

Chapter 9: Distinguishing Facts from Opinions; Drawing Logical Inferences 8 Exercises
Chapter 10: Interpreting Visual Aids; Interpreting Graphic Aids 5 Exercises

- **Revised Chapter 1, Introduction to Reading and Studying: Being Successful in College.** This chapter now emphasizes a variety of study skills including sections on

  The Reading and Studying Process
  Keys to Studying College Textbooks
  The SQ3R Study System
  Adjusting Your Reading Rate When You Study
  Setting Goals
  Learning Styles

- New **"It's Your Call"** feature within Chapter 1 that refers users to more complete discussions of study skills and test-preparation skills that appear later in the book.
- New section on **transition words that signal the relationship of ideas within sentences and between sentences** in Chapter 7.
- Enhanced and reformatted section on **authors' writing patterns** in Chapter 7, including additional writing patterns and sample diagrams and examples.
- New section on **propaganda devices** in Chapter 9 with an accompanying exercise for immediate application and practice.
- New material on **interpreting visuals and graphic aids** in Chapter 10 that helps students understand how to interpret and evaluate information presented in this form.
- Many new photographs, graphics, and other visuals throughout the text.

While many instructors will choose to use the eleven chapters in *New Worlds* in the order in which they are presented, others may choose an alternative sequence (three possible sequences are included in the Instructor's Guide in the Annotated Instructor's Edition) that suits their specific course. For this reason, the instructions for completing Chapter Review Cards are deliberately repeated in each chapter. Similarly, the instructions for the practice exercises that accompany each reading selection are included with each selection so that instructors may assign the reading selections in any order.

We hope that you, along with your students, will learn new and interesting things from the selections in this book. Your enthusiasm for acquiring new information, your willingness to become engaged with the material, and your pleasure in learning will serve as a model for your students.

We wish you success in using *New Worlds* to prepare your students to read textbooks effectively and to be successful in college. We hope the endeavor will be enjoyable and rewarding for both you and your students.

SUPPLEMENTS TO *NEW WORLDS*

Print Resources

- ***Annotated Instructor's Edition*** (*AIE*) (0-07-735076-6)

  The *AIE* contains the full text of the student edition with answers as well as marginal notes that provide a rich variety of teaching tips and related information.

Digital Components in *New Worlds*

- ***New Worlds* Online Learning Center** (OLC)

  A dedicated website (www.mhhe.com/newworlds4e) offers students quizzes, Internet exercises, writing prompts, a glossary, and more. Instructors have access to an Instructor's Manual, PowerPoints, and Test Bank.
- ***Connect Reading***

  This resource prepares students for success in college and beyond. An online learning environment identifies and addresses individual needs, offers the visual components today's students expect, and provides progressive learning as students advance.

Additional Value-Added Packaging Options

- **Merriam-Webster Dictionary, Thesaurus, and other resources**

  We offer a number of dictionary and thesaurus options from Merriam-Webster. Contact your McGraw-Hill representative to learn more.

ACKNOWLEDGMENTS

We are grateful to John Kindler, Senior Sponsoring Editor, for helping make this fourth edition of *New Worlds* a reality. Developmental Editor Barbara Conover, was a model of diligence, and we benefited greatly from her meticulous attention to detail. We were fortunate once again to have Senior Designer Gino Cieslik apply his talents to this new edition. Manuscript Editor Margaret Moore brought a superb eye to the manuscript. We are also indebted to Editorial Coordinator Jesse Hassenger for helping us in myriad ways throughout this project and for the effort and expertise that he has lent us throughout the years. In addition, we are grateful to Marketing Manager, Jacklyn Elkins, Production Editor Regina Ernst, Text Permissions Editor Marty Moga, and Photo Researcher Sonia Brown.

The thoughtful, constructive comments and suggestions provided by the following reviewers contributed greatly to this new edition, and we thank them.

Linda Bakian, *Passaic County Community College*
Tomekia Cooper, *Albany Technical College*
Judy Covington, *Trident Technical College*
Victoria Covington, *Isothermal Community College*
Sandra Frank, *Mount Hood Community College*
Yvonne Frye, *Community College of Denver*
Guadalupe Gutierrez, *San Antonio College*
Tanya Masso, *South Texas College*
Gerardo Mechler, *Palo Alto College*
Lisa Mizes, *St. Louis Community College at Meramac*
Lori Murphy, *Westchester Community College*
Sylvia Orozco, *Miami Dade College*
Catherine Robinson, *Hillsborough Community College–Brandon*
Dawn Sedik, *Valencia Community College*
Tondalaya VanLear, *Dabney S. Lancaster Community College*
Michael Vensel, *Miami Dade College*
Julie Rae Zimmerman-Kelly, *St. Johns River Community College*

Behind every McGraw-Hill education product is research. Thousands of instructors participate in our course surveys every year providing McGraw-Hill with longitudinal information on the trends and challenges in your courses. That research, along with reviews, focus groups and ethnographic studies of both instructor and student workflow, provides the intensive feedback that our authors and editors use to assure that our revisions continue to provide everything you need to reach your course goals and outcomes.

Some KEY FINDINGS from our Developmental Reading Course Survey

87% of Developmental Reading instructors want a text with student oriented pedagogy. 67% said they want high interest, discipline specific readings.

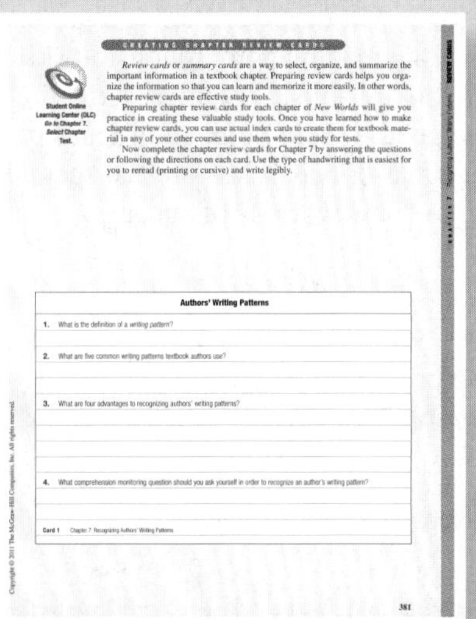

CREATING CHAPTER REVIEW CARDS

Student Online Learning Center (OLC) *Go to Chapter 7. Select Chapter Test.*

Review cards or *summary cards* are a way to select, organize, and summarize the important information in a textbook chapter. Preparing review cards helps you organize the information so that you can learn and memorize it more easily. In other words, chapter review cards are effective study tools.

Preparing chapter review cards for each chapter of *New Worlds* will give you practice in creating these valuable study tools. Once you have learned how to make chapter review cards, you can use actual index cards to create them for textbook material in any of your other courses and use them when you study for tests.

Now complete the chapter review cards for Chapter 7 by answering the questions or following the directions on each card. Use the type of handwriting that is easiest for you to reread (printing or cursive) and write legibly.

Authors' Writing Patterns

1. What is the definition of a *writing pattern*?
2. What are five common writing patterns textbook authors use?
3. What are four advantages to recognizing authors' writing patterns?
4. What comprehension monitoring question should you ask yourself in order to recognize an author's writing pattern?

Card 1 Chapter 7: Recognizing Authors' Writing Patterns

381

Note cards throughout the text help students select, organize, and summarize important information.

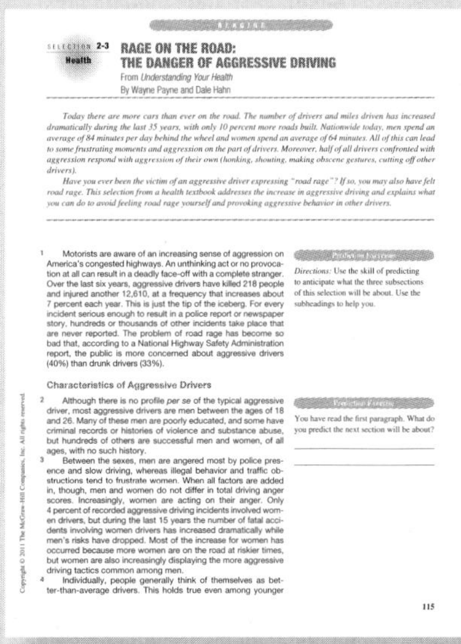

SELECTION 2-3 Health

RAGE ON THE ROAD: THE DANGER OF AGGRESSIVE DRIVING

From *Understanding Your Health*
By Wayne Payne and Dale Hahn

Today there are more cars than ever on the road. The number of drivers and miles driven has increased dramatically during the last 35 years, with only 10 percent more roads built. Nationwide today, men spend an average of 84 minutes per day behind the wheel and women spend an average of 64 minutes. All of this can lead to some frustrating moments and aggression on the part of drivers. Moreover, half of all drivers confronted with aggression respond with aggression of their own (honking, shouting, making obscene gestures, cutting off other drivers).

Have you ever been the victim of an aggressive driver expressing "road rage"? If so, you may also have felt road rage. This selection from a health textbook addresses the increase in aggressive driving and explains what you can do to avoid feeling road rage yourself and provoking aggressive behavior in other drivers.

1 Motorists are aware of an increasing sense of aggression on America's congested highways. An unthinking act or no provocation at all can result in a deadly face-off with a complete stranger. Over the last six years, aggressive drivers have killed 218 people and injured another 12,610, at a frequency that increases about 7 percent each year. This is just the tip of the iceberg. For every incident serious enough to result in a police report or newspaper story, hundreds or thousands of other incidents take place that are never reported. The problem of road rage has become so bad that, according to a National Highway Safety Administration report, the public is more concerned about aggressive drivers (40%) than drunk drivers (33%).

Directions: Use the skill of predicting to anticipate what the three subsections of this selection will be about. Use the subheadings to help you.

Characteristics of Aggressive Drivers

2 Although there is no profile *per se* of the typical aggressive driver, most aggressive drivers are men between the ages of 18 and 26. Many of these men are poorly educated, and some have criminal records or histories of violence and substance abuse, but hundreds of others are successful men and women, of all ages, with no such history.

3 Between the sexes, men are angered most by police presence and slow driving, whereas illegal behavior and traffic obstructions tend to frustrate women. When all factors are added in, though, men and women do not differ in total driving anger scores. Increasingly, women are acting on their anger. Only 4 percent of recorded aggressive driving incidents involved women drivers, but during the last 15 years the number of fatal accidents involving women drivers has increased dramatically while men's risks have dropped. Most of the increase for women has occurred because more women are on the road at riskier times, but women are also increasingly displaying the more aggressive driving tactics common among men.

You have read the first paragraph. What do you predict the next section will be about?

4 Individually, people generally think of themselves as better-than-average drivers. This holds true even among younger

115

Students gain more from readings that pertain to them.

To the Student

> *"Didn't I realize that reading would open up whole new worlds? A book could open doors for me. It could introduce me to people and show me places I never imagined existed."*
>
> Richard Rodriguez, *Hunger of Memory*

Welcome to *New Worlds.* As you work through this book, we hope that you will take advantage of all of its features and that you will discover that you are becoming a better reader. Not only will you have a clearer understanding of the reading comprehension skills, but you also will have had a great deal of practice with them, so that you are able to use these skills in your other college courses.

New Worlds is designed to help you acquire and practice the reading and study skills that will make you a success in college. Described below are the special features that will help you learn efficiently from this book and lead you to "new worlds" of success.

SPECIAL FEATURES OF *NEW WORLDS*

New Worlds is organized into four parts. Each part focuses on skills that are essential to your success.

Part 1 A New World of Learning: Reading and Studying in College

(Chapters 1–2)

This section includes information on studying, goal-setting, motivation, time management, learning styles, and developing a college vocabulary.

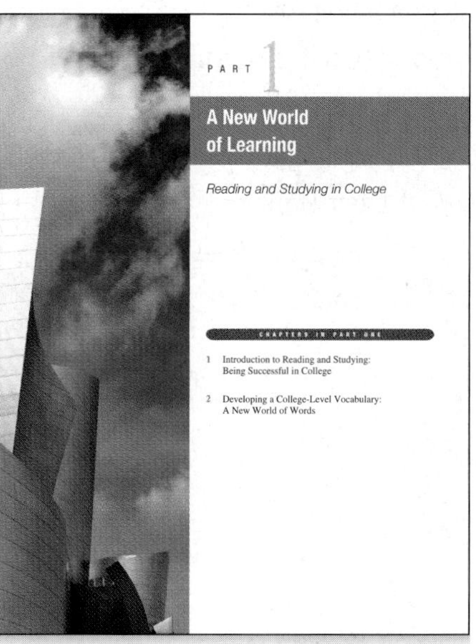

PART 1

A New World of Learning

Reading and Studying in College

CHAPTERS IN PART ONE

1 Introduction to Reading and Studying: Being Successful in College

2 Developing a College-Level Vocabulary: A New World of Words

Part 2 A New World of Understanding: Using Core Comprehension Skills When You Read College Textbooks

(Chapters 3–7)

Comprehending what you read is vital to your success as a college student. This section will help you

- Determine the topic.
- Locate the stated main idea.
- Formulate an implied main idea sentence.
- Identify supporting details.
- Recognize authors' writing patterns.

Part 3 A New World of Reading and Thinking Critically *(Chapters 8–9)*

This section will help you

- Read critically.
- Think critically.

Part 4 A New World of Studying: Effective and Efficient Study Techniques *(Chapters 10–11)*

This section will help you

- Study college textbooks and interpret visual and graphic aids.
- Prepare for tests.

BUILT-IN LEARNING AIDS

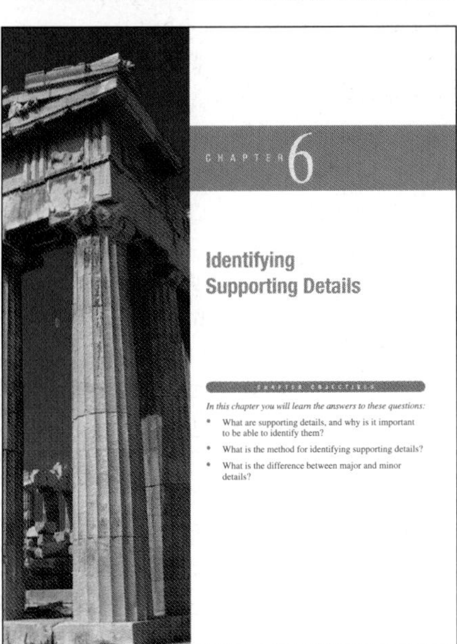

CHAPTER 6

Identifying Supporting Details

CHAPTER OBJECTIVES

In this chapter you will learn the answers to these questions:

- What are supporting details, and why is it important to be able to identify them?
- What is the method for identifying supporting details?
- What is the difference between major and minor details?

Chapter Opening Page

These pages contain chapter objectives to focus your learning.

Chapter Contents

These pages list the skills presented in the chapter. They show the material in the chapter and how it is organized. They also list the chapter reading selections.

CHAPTER CONTENTS

What Are Supporting Details, and Why Are They Important?

What Is the Method for Identifying Supporting Details?

Major and Minor Details

Other Things to Keep in Mind When Identifying Supporting Details

- Watch for clues that indicate a list of details.
- Avoid overmarking your textbook by numbering the supporting details in a paragraph rather than highlighting or underlining them.
- Listing the supporting details on separate lines in your study notes can help you learn the information efficiently.

CREATING CHAPTER REVIEW CARDS

TEST YOUR UNDERSTANDING

Identifying Supporting Details, Part One

Identifying Supporting Details, Part Two

READINGS

Selection 6-1 ***(Environmental Science)***
"'Hold It! You Can Recycle That!' Recycling: A Twenty-First Century Necessity"
from *Environmental Science: A Study of Interrelationships*
by Eldon D. Enger and Bradley F. Smith

Selection 6-2 ***(History)***
"The Life of Buddha: The Path to Nirvana"
from *The 100: A Ranking of the Most Influential Persons in History*
by Michael Hart

Selection 6-3 ***(History)***
"The New Immigrants: Asian Americans and Latinos"
from *Nation of Nations: A Narrative History of the American Republic*
by James Davidson et al.

Key Terms

Important terms appear in the margins so that the terms and their definitions are easy to locate.

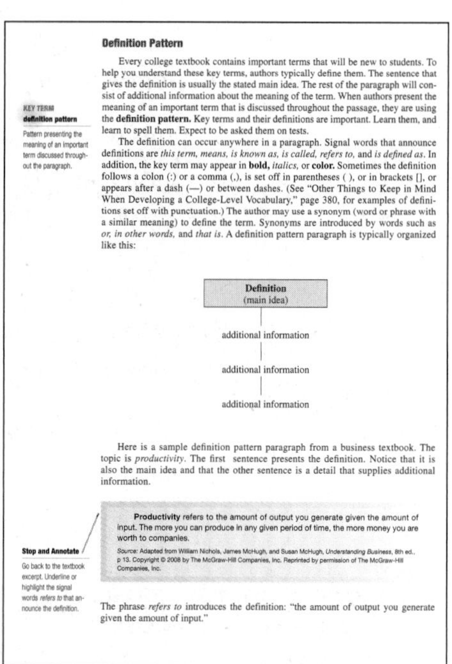

Definition Pattern

KEY TERM
definition pattern
Pattern presenting the meaning of an important term discussed throughout the paragraph.

Every college textbook contains important terms that will be new to students. To help you understand these key terms, authors typically define them. The sentence that gives the definition is usually the stated main idea. The rest of the paragraph will consist of additional information about the meaning of the term. When authors present the meaning of an important term that is discussed throughout the passage, they are using the **definition pattern.** Key terms and their definitions are important. Learn them, and learn to spell them. Expect to be asked them on tests.

The definition can occur anywhere in a paragraph. Signal words that announce definitions are *this term, means, is known as, is called, refers to,* and *is defined as*. In addition, the key term may appear in **bold,** *italics,* or **color.** Sometimes the definition follows a colon (:) or a comma (,), is set off in parentheses ( ), or in brackets [], or appears after a dash (—) or between dashes. (See "Other Things to Keep in Mind When Developing a College-Level Vocabulary," page 380, for examples of definitions set off with punctuation.) The author may use a synonym (word or phrase with a similar meaning) to define the term. Synonyms are introduced by words such as *or, in other words,* and *that is*. A definition pattern paragraph is typically organized like this:

Here is a sample definition pattern paragraph from a business textbook. The topic is *productivity*. The first sentence presents the definition. Notice that it is also the main idea and that the other sentence is a detail that supplies additional information.

Productivity refers to the amount of output you generate given the amount of input. The more you can produce in any given period of time, the more money you are worth to companies.

Source: Adapted from William Nichols, James McHugh, and Susan McHugh, *Understanding Business*, 8th ed., p 13. Copyright © 2008 by The McGraw-Hill Companies, Inc. Reprinted by permission of The McGraw-Hill Companies, Inc.

Stop and Annotate
Go back to the textbook excerpt. Underline or highlight the signal words *refers to* that announce the definition.

The phrase *refers to* introduces the definition: "the amount of output you generate given the amount of input."

Stop and Annotate Exercises

These exercises give you the opportunity to stop and annotate actual college textbook excerpts. You will learn actively by underlining or highlighting stated main idea sentences, writing formulated main ideas in the margin, or numbering the important supporting details in a passage, for example.

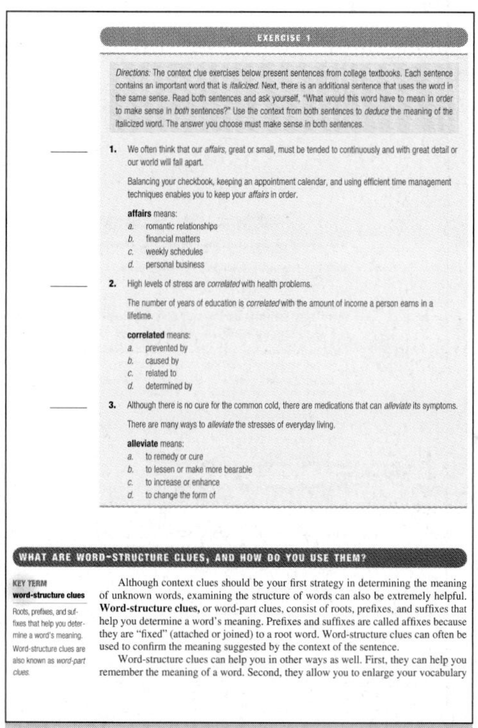

EXERCISE 1

Directions: The context clue exercises below present sentences from college textbooks. Each sentence contains an important word that is *italicized*. Next, there is an additional sentence that uses the word in the same sense. Read both sentences and ask yourself, "What would this word have to mean in order to make sense in *both* sentences?" Use the context from both sentences to *deduce* the meaning of the italicized word. The answer you choose must make sense in both sentences.

_____ **1.** We often think that our *affairs*, great or small, must be tended to continuously and with great detail or our world will fall apart.

Balancing your checkbook, keeping an appointment calendar, and using efficient time management techniques enables you to keep your *affairs* in order.

affairs means:
a. romantic relationships
b. financial matters
c. weekly schedules
d. personal business

_____ **2.** High levels of stress are *correlated* with health problems.

The number of years of education is *correlated* with the amount of income a person earns in a lifetime.

correlated means:
a. prevented by
b. caused by
c. related to
d. determined by

_____ **3.** Although there is no cure for the common cold, there are medications that can *alleviate* its symptoms.

There are many ways to *alleviate* the stresses of everyday living.

alleviate means:
a. to remedy or cure
b. to lessen or make more bearable
c. to increase or enhance
d. to change the form of

WHAT ARE WORD-STRUCTURE CLUES, AND HOW DO YOU USE THEM?

KEY TERM
word-structure clues
Roots, prefixes, and suffixes that help you determine a word's meaning. Word-structure clues are also known as *word-part clues*.

Although context clues should be your first strategy in determining the meaning of unknown words, examining the structure of words can also be extremely helpful. **Word-structure clues,** or word-part clues, consist of roots, prefixes, and suffixes that help you determine a word's meaning. Prefixes and suffixes are called affixes because they are "fixed" (attached or joined) to a root word. Word-structure clues can often be used to confirm the meaning suggested by the context of the sentence.

Word-structure clues can help you in other ways as well. First, they can help you remember the meaning of a word. Second, they allow you to enlarge your vocabulary

Within-Chapter Exercises

These exercises give you an opportunity to apply what you have just learned in a chapter by testing your understanding of a skill that has just been presented. There are numerous exercises such as these within Chapters 2 to 10. Exercises on vocabulary, topics, main idea, supporting details, authors' writing patterns, critical reading, critical thinking, and interpreting visual and graphic aids are included.

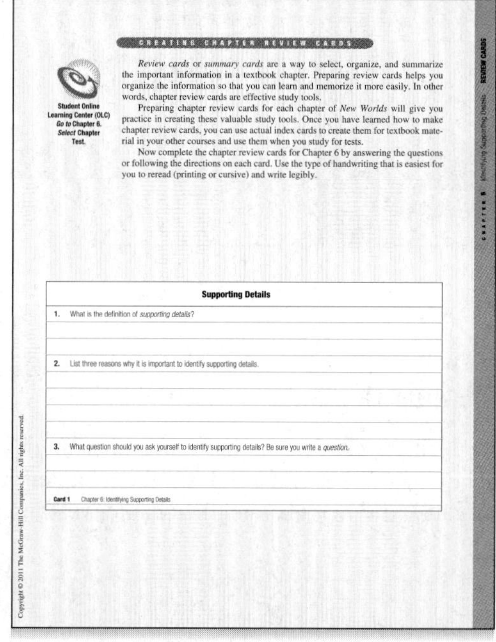

CREATING CHAPTER REVIEW CARDS

Student Online Learning Center (OLC)
Go to Chapter 6.
Select Chapter Test.

Review cards or *summary cards* are a way to select, organize, and summarize the important information in a textbook chapter. Preparing review cards helps you organize the information so that you can learn and memorize it more easily. In other words, chapter review cards are effective study tools.

Preparing chapter review cards for each chapter of *New Worlds* will give you practice in creating these valuable study tools. Once you have learned how to make chapter review cards, you can use actual index cards to create them for textbook material in your other courses and use them when you study for tests.

Now complete the chapter review cards for Chapter 6 by answering the questions or following the directions on each card. Use the type of handwriting that is easiest for you to reread (printing or cursive) and write legibly.

Supporting Details

1. What is the definition of *supporting details*?

2. List three reasons why it is important to identify supporting details.

3. What question should you ask yourself to identify supporting details? Be sure you write a *question.*

Card 1 Chapter 6: Identifying Supporting Details

CHAPTER 6 Identifying Supporting Details REVIEW CARDS

Chapter Review Cards

These simulated index cards allow you to create your own summary of the important points in the chapter. Each card includes questions and initially prompts with page numbers to direct you to the significant information.

Test Your Understanding Exercises

These comprehension and vocabulary exercise sections allow you to test yourself on the skills presented in each chapter. There are separate practice exercise sections for vocabulary, comprehension, critical reading, and thinking critically.

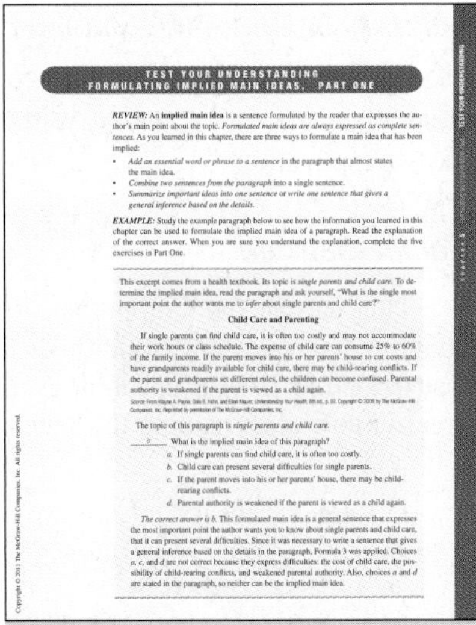

TEST YOUR UNDERSTANDING
FORMULATING IMPLIED MAIN IDEAS, PART ONE

REVIEW: An **implied main idea** is a sentence formulated by the reader that expresses the author's main point about the topic. *Formulated main ideas are always expressed as complete sentences.* As you learned in this chapter, there are three ways to formulate a main idea that has been implied:

- *Add an essential word or phrase to a sentence* in the paragraph that almost states the main idea.
- *Combine two sentences from the paragraph* into a single sentence.
- *Summarize important ideas into one sentence* or *write one sentence that gives a general inference based on the details.*

EXAMPLE: Study the example paragraph below to see how the information you learned in this chapter can be used to formulate the implied main idea of a paragraph. Read the explanation of the correct answer. When you are sure you understand the explanation, complete the five exercises in Part One.

This excerpt comes from a health textbook. Its topic is *single parents and child care.* To determine the implied main idea, read the paragraph and ask yourself, "What is the single most important point the author wants me to *infer* about single parents and child care?"

Child Care and Parenting

If single parents can find child care, it is often too costly and may not accommodate their work hours or class schedule. The expense of child care can consume 25% to 60% of the family income. If the parent moves into his or her parents' house to cut costs and have grandparents readily available for child care, there may be child-rearing conflicts. If the parent and grandparents set different rules, the children can become confused. Parental authority is weakened if the parent is viewed as a child again.

The topic of this paragraph is *single parents and child care.*

____?____ What is the implied main idea of this paragraph?

a. If single parents can find child care, it is often too costly.
b. Child care can present several difficulties for single parents.
c. If the parent moves into his or her parents' house, there may be child-rearing conflicts.
d. Parental authority is weakened if the parent is viewed as a child again.

The correct answer is b. This formulated main idea is a general sentence that expresses the most important point the author wants you to know about single parents and child care, that it can present several difficulties. Since it was necessary to write a sentence that gives a general inference based on the details in the paragraph, Formula 3 was applied. Choices *a, c,* and *d* are not correct because they express difficulties: the cost of child care, the possibility of child-rearing conflicts, and weakened parental authority. Also, choices *a* and *d* are stated in the paragraph, so neither can be the implied main idea.

Copyright © 2011 The McGraw-Hill Companies, Inc. All rights reserved.

CHAPTER READING SELECTIONS FOR CHAPTERS 1 TO 10

All the reading selections in Chapters 1 to 11 are excerpts taken from widely used introductory-level college textbooks, newsmagazines, and literary selections of the type you are likely to encounter in college. These selections provide important practice, and they will increase your background knowledge in a variety of interesting subjects. They were chosen to give you the practice, skill, and confidence you need to handle subsequent college courses successfully.

Each reading selection is accompanied by annotation exercises and follow-up exercises. In order, the exercises are described below.

Introduction to the Selection and Annotation Practice Exercises

Each selection begins with an introduction that provides helpful background information about the selection's topic. The Annotation Practice Exercises give you the opportunity to apply to the selection the reading skills you are learning.

READING

SELECTION 7-3 Health

WOULD YOU EAT "FRANKENFOOD"?

From *Understanding Your Health*
By Wayne Payne, Dale Hahn, and Ellen Mauer

Chances are you've had it for breakfast. And lunch. And dinner. It is now virtually impossible for Americans to avoid eating genetically modified, or GM, foods. British tabloid newspapers have given this new kind of food a nickname, "Frankenfood," after the literary character Frankenstein, the creature assembled from parts of dead bodies and brought to life. This passage from a health textbook presents both the risks and the advantages of GM foods and explains why many people avoid them.

1 In Britain and throughout Europe, public fears about **genetically modified** (GM) foods are running high and have even provoked a trade war with the United States. Britain's Prince Charles has said that he would never eat the stuff and won't stand for it being grown on his land. Americans, however, appear only dimly aware of GM foods. Many Americans are quite surprised to learn that GM foods are sold in most supermarkets.

2 In September of 2000 Kraft Foods recalled millions of taco-shells because they contained GM corn. This didn't prove to be the tide-turning disaster that some GM critics had hoped for. The taco shells contained traces of corn meal from StarLink, a genetically engineered variety of corn that hadn't been approved for human consumption in the United States. No one suffered any harm from eating the shells, but the episode caused many Americans to think about what would happen if allergens or other harmful substances, added to food by design or by accident, could have found their way into our stomachs.

Bioengineered Food

3 Since the mid-1990s, armed with new knowledge about genetic "code" material called DNA, scientists have been able to manipulate the genetic code of organisms that are food sources for humans. They have created new strains of plants and animals capable of growing larger in less time on less suitable soil or in less suitable conditions. Some of the new plant strains can do this while also resisting insect pests.

4 Farmers have long engaged in traditional genetics, using seeds from plants with the most desirable characteristics or crossbreeding closely related species of animals. Scientists have also tried to speed up the growth of plants by exposing them to chemicals and radiation. These ongoing experiments produce hundreds of mutations among genes, some of which may be useful.

5 Unlike traditional genetics, **genetic engineering** is very specific. It allows scientists to select a single gene for a single characteristic and insert that segment of DNA into another organism. Genetic engineers can also select a segment of DNA from one species and insert it into another species.

Annotation Practice Exercises

Directions: For each exercise below, write the topic of the main idea of the paragraph on the lines beside the paragraph. Then identify the writing pattern the authors used to organize the supporting details.

Practice Exercise

Topic of paragraph 1:

Main idea sentence of paragraph 1:

Writing pattern of paragraph 1:

Copyright © 2011 The McGraw-Hill Companies, Inc. All rights reserved.

6 The ability to alter diverse forms of plant life through genetic engineering has had a profound effect on U.S. agriculture and on the food we purchase in the grocery store. An example is the Flavr-Savr tomato, developed by Calgene to soften more slowly, meaning it can stay on the vine longer and develop a fuller taste. Because it ripens more slowly, it has a longer shelf life at the grocery store, reducing waste.

7 The use of genetically modified seed is now estimated to approach 40 to 60 percent of all U.S. planting. The seeds are modified either to make the crops resistant to weedkillers or to produce their own pesticides. Bioengineered corn and soybeans in particular are used as ingredients in a wide range of processed food, from soft drinks and beer to chips and breakfast cereal. Genetically modified organisms are fed to farm animals. Even health-food products like tofu and canola oil often contain genetically modified ingredients.

8 Genetically modified crops hold down food production costs and reduce the need for pesticides and herbicides. Modified foods being developed now are yielding more productive grains and more drought-resistant crops. Some are being developed to be more nutritious and flavorful. Caffeine-free coffee beans and even plants that produce drugs and vaccines have been developed.

What Are the Potential Health Risks?

9 While the potential benefits of higher-yielding GM food seem appealing, many people cite a number of serious health concerns about foods altered in this way. First, biotechnology foes warn that we do not know enough about the way genes operate and interact to be sure of the outcome of any genetic modification. In addition, they worry that alterations could accidentally lead to substances that are poisonous or that trigger allergies. Critics also fear that the use of DNA from plant viruses and bacteria in the modification of crops may also somehow trigger disease. Finally, they also argue that antibiotic-resistant genes could be passed to the microorganisms that make us sick, creating "superviruses" and other "superbugs" that we might not have the drugs to fight.

10 Environmental concerns are also an issue. Environmentalists are worried about genes that make crops resistant to herbicides and insects. They believe some of these genes could somehow "escape" and be transferred to other crops, resulting in the emergence of "superweeds." They fear this leakage could cause the disappearance of familiar species of insects and birds as food chains are damaged.

How Do Bioengineers Counter These Objections?

11 The biotechnology industry claims that there is no evidence of any GM food causing serious ill effects. They note that while genetic modification may result in the emergence of new allergens, so too may conventional plant breeding. Further, they claim that genetic modifications allow us to improve the flavor, texture, nutritional value, and the shelf life of food. It could boost the vitamin content

Practice Exercise

Topic of paragraph 6:

Main idea sentence of paragraph 6:

Writing pattern of paragraph 6:

Practice Exercise

Topic of paragraph 9:

Main idea sentence of paragraph 9:

Writing pattern of paragraph 9:

Comprehension and Vocabulary Quiz

This 20-question quiz contains four parts: Comprehension, Vocabulary in Context, Word Structure, and Reading Skills Application.

Comprehension

This part of the Comprehension and Vocabulary Quiz contains five questions much like those that a content-area instructor (such as a psychology professor) would expect you to know after reading the selection.

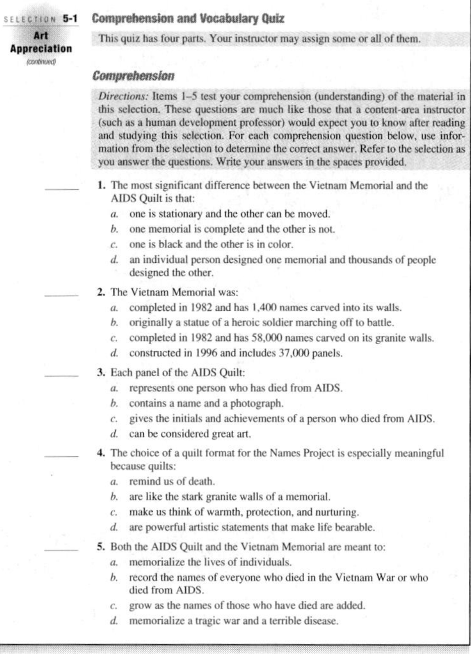

SELECTION 5-1 **Art Appreciation** *(continued)*

Comprehension and Vocabulary Quiz

This quiz has four parts. Your instructor may assign some or all of them.

Comprehension

Directions: Items 1–5 test your comprehension (understanding) of the material in this selection. These questions are much like those that a content-area instructor (such as a human development professor) would expect you to know after reading and studying this selection. For each comprehension question below, use information from the selection to determine the correct answer. Refer to the selection as you answer the questions. Write your answers in the spaces provided.

_____ **1.** The most significant difference between the Vietnam Memorial and the AIDS Quilt is that:
a. one is stationary and the other can be moved.
b. one memorial is complete and the other is not.
c. one is black and the other is in color.
d. an individual person designed one memorial and thousands of people designed the other.

_____ **2.** The Vietnam Memorial was:
a. completed in 1982 and has 1,400 names carved into its walls.
b. originally a statue of a heroic soldier marching off to battle.
c. completed in 1982 and has 58,000 names carved on its granite walls.
d. constructed in 1996 and includes 37,000 panels.

_____ **3.** Each panel of the AIDS Quilt:
a. represents one person who has died from AIDS.
b. contains a name and a photograph.
c. gives the initials and achievements of a person who died from AIDS.
d. can be considered great art.

_____ **4.** The choice of a quilt format for the Names Project is especially meaningful because quilts:
a. remind us of death.
b. are like the stark granite walls of a memorial.
c. make us think of warmth, protection, and nurturing.
d. are powerful artistic statements that make life bearable.

_____ **5.** Both the AIDS Quilt and the Vietnam Memorial are meant to:
a. memorialize the lives of individuals.
b. record the names of everyone who died in the Vietnam War or who died from AIDS.
c. grow as the names of those who have died are added.
d. memorialize a tragic war and a terrible disease.

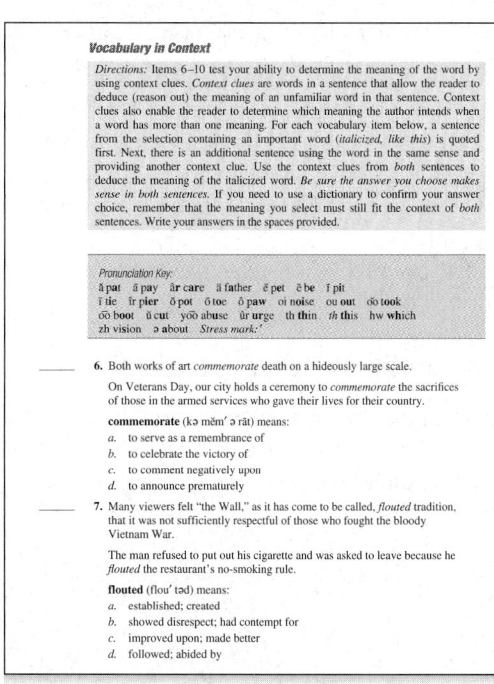

Vocabulary in Context

Directions: Items 6–10 test your ability to determine the meaning of the word by using context clues. *Context clues* are words in a sentence that allow the reader to deduce (reason out) the meaning of an unfamiliar word in that sentence. Context clues also enable the reader to determine which meaning the author intends when a word has more than one meaning. For each vocabulary item below, a sentence from the selection containing an important word (*italicized, like this*) is quoted first. Next, there is an additional sentence using the word in the same sense and providing another context clue. Use the context clues from *both* sentences to deduce the meaning of the italicized word. *Be sure the answer you choose makes sense in both sentences.* If you need to use a dictionary to confirm your answer choice, remember that the meaning you select must still fit the context of *both* sentences. Write your answers in the spaces provided.

Pronunciation Key:
ă **pat** ā **pay** âr **care** ä **father** ĕ **pet** ē **be** ĭ **pit**
ī **tie** îr **pier** ŏ **pot** ō **toe** ô **paw** oi **noise** ou **out** ŏŏ **took**
ōō **boot** ŭ **cut** yōō **abuse** ûr **urge** th **thin** *th* **this** hw **which**
zh **vision** ə **about** *Stress mark:* ′

_____ **6.** Both works of art *commemorate* death on a hideously large scale.

On Veterans Day, our city holds a ceremony to *commemorate* the sacrifices of those in the armed services who gave their lives for their country.

commemorate (kə mĕm′ ə rāt) means:
a. to serve as a remembrance of
b. to celebrate the victory of
c. to comment negatively upon
d. to announce prematurely

_____ **7.** Many viewers felt "the Wall," as it has come to be called, *flouted* tradition, that it was not sufficiently respectful of those who fought the bloody Vietnam War.

The man refused to put out his cigarette and was asked to leave because he *flouted* the restaurant's no-smoking rule.

flouted (flou′ təd) means:
a. established; created
b. showed disrespect; had contempt for
c. improved upon; made better
d. followed; abided by

Vocabulary in Context

This part of the Comprehension and Vocabulary Quiz contains five questions that test your ability to determine the meaning of a word by using context clues. *Context clues* are words in a sentence that allow you to deduce (reason out) the meaning of an unfamiliar word in that sentence. Context clues also enable you to determine which meaning the author intends when a word has more than one meaning.

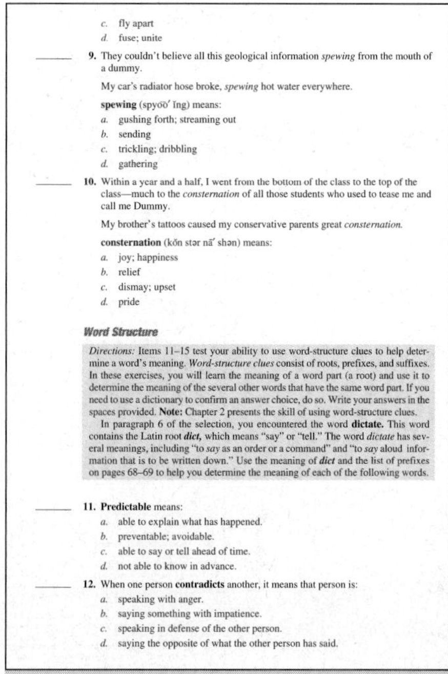

c. fly apart
d. fuse; unite

_____ **9.** They couldn't believe all this geological information *spewing* from the mouth of a dummy.

My car's radiator hose broke, *spewing* hot water everywhere.

spewing (spyōō′ ĭng) means:
a. gushing forth; streaming out
b. sending
c. trickling; dribbling
d. gathering

_____ **10.** Within a year and a half, I went from the bottom of the class to the top of the class—much to the *consternation* of all those students who used to tease me and call me Dummy.

My brother's tattoos caused my conservative parents great *consternation.*

consternation (kŏn stər nā′ shən) means:
a. joy; happiness
b. relief
c. dismay; upset
d. pride

Word Structure

Directions: Items 11–15 test your ability to use word-structure clues to help determine a word's meaning. *Word-structure clues* consist of roots, prefixes, and suffixes. In these exercises, you will learn the meaning of a word part (a root) and use it to determine the meaning of the several other words that have the same word part. If you need to use a dictionary to confirm an answer choice, do so. Write your answers in the spaces provided. **Note:** Chapter 2 presents the skill of using word-structure clues.

In paragraph 6 of the selection, you encountered the word **dictate.** This word contains the Latin root ***dict,*** which means "say" or "tell." The word *dictate* has several meanings, including "to *say* as an order or a command" and "to *say* aloud information that is to be written down." Use the meaning of ***dict*** and the list of prefixes on pages 68–69 to help you determine the meaning of each of the following words.

_____ **11. Predictable** means:
a. able to explain what has happened.
b. preventable; avoidable.
c. able to say or tell ahead of time.
d. not able to know in advance.

_____ **12.** When one person **contradicts** another, it means that person is:
a. speaking with anger.
b. saying something with impatience.
c. speaking in defense of the other person.
d. saying the opposite of what the other person has said.

Word Structure

This part of the Comprehension and Vocabulary Quiz contains five questions that test your ability to use word-structure clues to help determine a word's meaning. *Word-structure clues* consist of roots, prefixes, and suffixes. In these exercises, you will learn the meaning of a word part (root) and use it to determine the meaning of the several other words that have the same root.

Reading Skills Application

This part of the Comprehension and Vocabulary Quiz contains five questions to test your ability to apply certain reading skills to the material in this selection. These are the types of questions that appear on standardized reading tests and state-mandated basic skills tests.

Reading Skills Application

Directions: Items 16–20 test your ability to *apply* certain reading skills to information in this selection. These types of questions provide valuable practice for all students, especially those who must take standardized reading tests and state-mandated basic skills tests. You may not have studied all of the skills at this point, so these items will serve as a helpful preview. The comprehension and critical reading skills in this section are presented in Chapters 3 through 9 of *New Worlds;* vocabulary and figurative language skills are presented in Chapter 2. As you work through *New Worlds,* you will practice and develop these skills. Write your answers in the spaces provided.

_____ **16.** Based on information in the selection, which of the following represents a logical inference about Buddha and his "search for truth"?

a. Buddha regretted his decision to leave his home and family to "search for truth."
b. If Buddha had grown up in poverty, he might never have begun a "search for truth."
c. Buddha's family and friends thought his decision to "search for truth" was foolish.
d. Buddha failed in his "search for truth" and died bitter and frustrated.

_____ **17.** Which of the following represents an opinion about Buddha rather than a fact?

a. He was married at 16 to a cousin the same age.
b. He therefore resumed eating normally and abandoned asceticism.
c. By the time he died, in 483 B.C., he had made thousands of converts.
d. Buddha, as the founder of one of the world's major religions, clearly deserves a place among the most influential people in history.

_____ **18.** Which of the following is the meaning of *clouded* as it is used in paragraph 3?

a. refreshed
b. strengthened
c. confused
d. destroyed

_____ **19.** In paragraph 4 the author says "all the pieces of the puzzle seemed to fall into place" for Siddhartha, to mean that Siddhartha:

a. finally achieved the insight into human existence that he had sought for so long.
b. gave up because none of the solutions he found had worked.
c. continued to be puzzled and perplexed about the human condition.
d. became puzzled by the challenges that seemed to befall him.

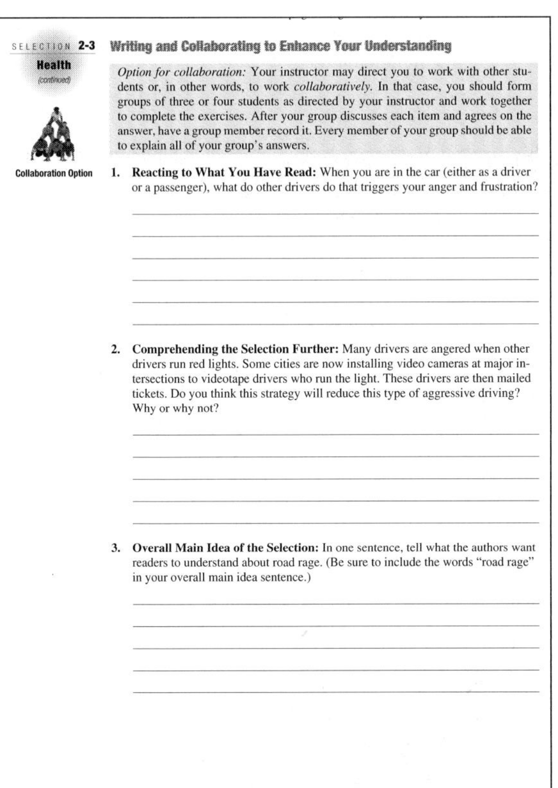

SELECTION 2-3 Health (continued)

Writing and Collaborating to Enhance Your Understanding

Collaboration Option

Option for collaboration: Your instructor may direct you to work with other students or, in other words, to work *collaboratively.* In that case, you should form groups of three or four students as directed by your instructor and work together to complete the exercises. After your group discusses each item and agrees on the answer, have a group member record it. Every member of your group should be able to explain all of your group's answers.

1. **Reacting to What You Have Read:** When you are in the car (either as a driver or a passenger), what do other drivers do that triggers your anger and frustration?

2. **Comprehending the Selection Further:** Many drivers are angered when other drivers run red lights. Some cities are now installing video cameras at major intersections to videotape drivers who run the light. These drivers are then mailed tickets. Do you think this strategy will reduce this type of aggressive driving? Why or why not?

3. **Overall Main Idea of the Selection:** In one sentence, tell what the authors want readers to understand about road rage. (Be sure to include the words "road rage" in your overall main idea sentence.)

Writing and Collaborating to Enhance Your Understanding

These short-answer and essay-type exercises ask you to write about the selection. They will help you relate the material to your own experiences. They will also give you practice in thinking critically and determining the overall main idea of the selection.

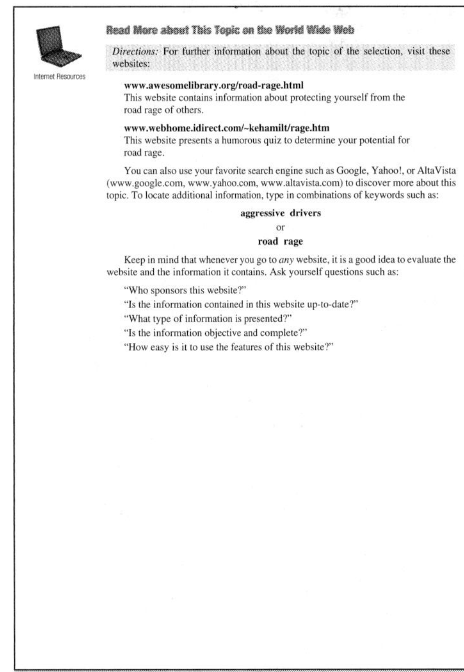

Read More about This Topic on the World Wide Web

Internet Resources

Directions: For further information about the topic of the selection, visit these websites:

www.awesomelibrary.org/road-rage.html
This website contains information about protecting yourself from the road rage of others.

www.webhome.idirect.com/~kehamilt/rage.htm
This website presents a humorous quiz to determine your potential for road rage.

You can also use your favorite search engine such as Google, Yahoo!, or AltaVista (www.google.com, www.yahoo.com, www.altavista.com) to discover more about this topic. To locate additional information, type in combinations of keywords such as:

aggressive drivers
or
road rage

Keep in mind that whenever you go to *any* website, it is a good idea to evaluate the website and the information it contains. Ask yourself questions such as:

"Who sponsors this website?"
"Is the information contained in this website up-to-date?"
"What type of information is presented?"
"Is the information objective and complete?"
"How easy is it to use the features of this website?"

Read More about This Topic on the World Wide Web

This list of websites related to the topic or author of the selection gives you an opportunity to explore the topic further. Keywords are included to guide you as you search for additional information about the selection's topic.

Practice Quiz for Chapter-Length Reading Selection

The Chapter 11 quiz differs from those in previous chapters. It is a 20-item practice quiz that consists of questions like those professors would expect you to be able to answer after you have read and studied the selection. It is designed to give you the experience of taking an actual test.

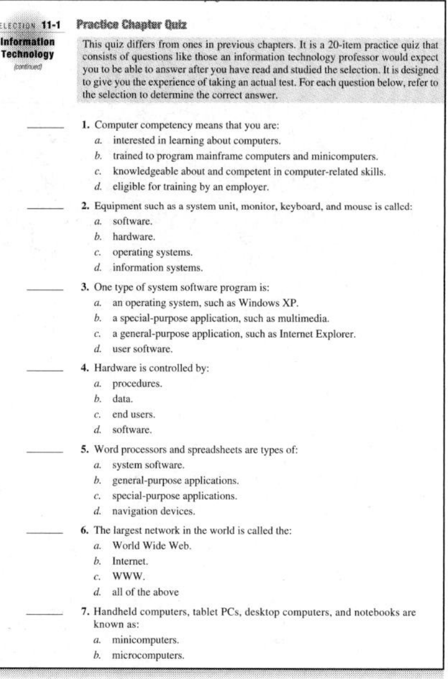

SELECTION 11-1 Information Technology (continued)

Practice Chapter Quiz

This quiz differs from ones in previous chapters. It is a 20-item practice quiz that consists of questions like those an information technology professor would expect you to be able to answer after you have read and studied the selection. It is designed to give you the experience of taking an actual test. For each question below, refer to the selection to determine the correct answer.

_____ **1.** Computer competency means that you are:
a. interested in learning about computers.
b. trained to program mainframe computers and minicomputers.
c. knowledgeable about and competent in computer-related skills.
d. eligible for training by an employer.

_____ **2.** Equipment such as a system unit, monitor, keyboard, and mouse is called:
a. software.
b. hardware.
c. operating systems.
d. information systems.

_____ **3.** One type of system software program is:
a. an operating system, such as Windows XP.
b. a special-purpose application, such as multimedia.
c. a general-purpose application, such as Internet Explorer.
d. user software.

_____ **4.** Hardware is controlled by:
a. procedures.
b. data.
c. end users.
d. software.

_____ **5.** Word processors and spreadsheets are types of:
a. system software.
b. general-purpose applications.
c. special-purpose applications.
d. navigation devices.

_____ **6.** The largest network in the world is called the:
a. World Wide Web.
b. Internet.
c. WWW.
d. all of the above

_____ **7.** Handheld computers, tablet PCs, desktop computers, and notebooks are known as:
a. minicomputers.
b. microcomputers.

SPECIAL LEARNING AIDS

In addition to the built-in learning aids that occur in each chapter, *New Worlds* offers you summary charts, diagrams, photos, cartoons, study maps, and outlines.

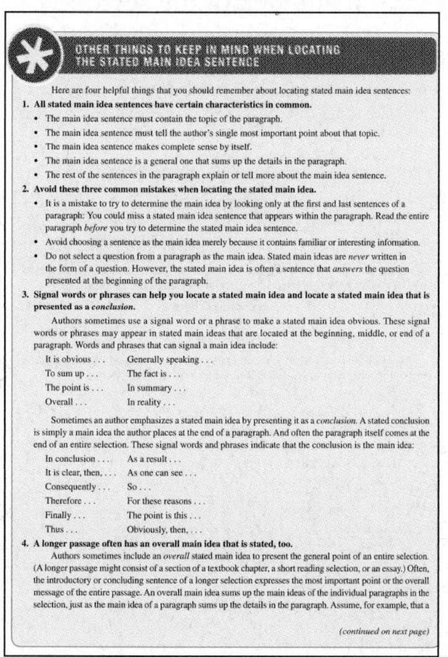

OTHER THINGS TO KEEP IN MIND WHEN LOCATING THE STATED MAIN IDEA SENTENCE

Here are four helpful things that you should remember about locating stated main idea sentences:

1. **All stated main idea sentences have certain characteristics in common.**
   - The main idea sentence must contain the topic of the paragraph.
   - The main idea sentence must tell the author's single most important point about that topic.
   - The main idea sentence makes complete sense by itself.
   - The main idea sentence is a general one that sums up the details in the paragraph.
   - The rest of the sentences in the paragraph explain or tell more about the main idea sentence.
2. **Avoid these three common mistakes when locating the stated main idea.**
   - It is a mistake to try to determine the main idea by looking only at the first and last sentences of a paragraph: You could miss a stated main idea sentence that appears within the paragraph. Read the entire paragraph *before* you try to determine the stated main idea sentence.
   - Avoid choosing a sentence as the main idea merely because it contains familiar or interesting information.
   - Do not select a question from a paragraph as the main idea. Stated main ideas are *never* written in the form of a question. However, the stated main idea is often a sentence that *answers* the question presented at the beginning of the paragraph.
3. **Signal words or phrases can help you locate a stated main idea and locate a stated main idea that is presented as a *conclusion*.**

   Authors sometimes use a signal word or a phrase to make a stated main idea obvious. These signal words or phrases may appear in stated main ideas that are located at the beginning, middle, or end of a paragraph. Words and phrases that can signal a main idea include:

   It is obvious . . . Generally speaking . . .
   To sum up . . . The fact is . . .
   The point is . . . In summary . . .
   Overall . . . In reality . . .

   Sometimes an author emphasizes a stated main idea by presenting it as a *conclusion*. A stated conclusion is simply a main idea the author places at the end of a paragraph. And often the paragraph itself comes at the end of an entire selection. These signal words and phrases indicate that the conclusion is the main idea:

   In conclusion . . . As a result . . .
   It is clear, then, . . . As one can see . . .
   Consequently . . . So . . .
   Therefore . . . For these reasons . . .
   Finally . . . The point is this . . .
   Thus . . . Obviously, then, . . .
4. **A longer passage often has an overall main idea that is stated, too.**

   Authors sometimes include an *overall* stated main idea to present the general point of an entire selection. (A longer passage might consist of a section of a textbook chapter, a short reading selection, or an essay.) Often, the introductory or concluding sentence of a longer selection expresses the most important point or the overall message of the entire passage. An overall main idea sums up the main ideas of the individual paragraphs in the selection, just as the main idea of a paragraph sums up the details in the paragraph. Assume, for example, that a

(continued on next page)

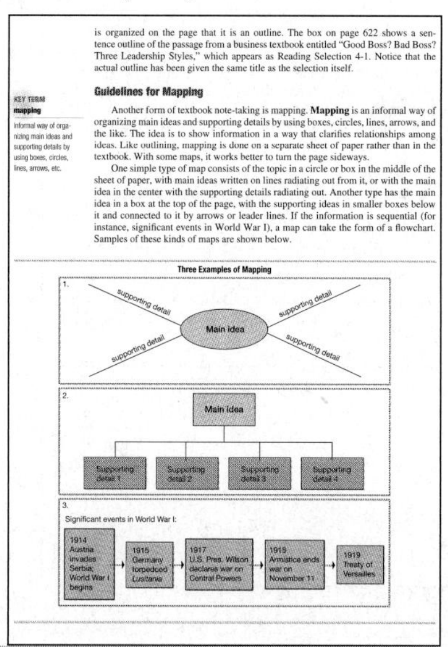

is organized on the page that it is an outline. The box on page 622 shows a sentence outline of the passage from a business textbook entitled "Good Boss? Bad Boss? Three Leadership Styles," which appears as Reading Selection 4-1. Notice that the actual outline has been given the same title as the selection itself.

Guidelines for Mapping

KEY TERM **mapping** Informal way of organizing main ideas and supporting details by using boxes, circles, lines, arrows, etc.

Another form of textbook note-taking is mapping. **Mapping** is an informal way of organizing main ideas and supporting details by using boxes, circles, lines, arrows, and the like. The idea is to show information in a way that clarifies relationships among ideas. Like outlining, mapping is done on a separate sheet of paper rather than in the textbook. With some maps, it works better to turn the page sideways.

One simple type of map consists of the topic in a circle or box in the middle of the sheet of paper, with main ideas written on lines radiating out from it, or with the main idea in the center with the supporting details radiating out. Another type has the main idea in a box at the top of the page, with the supporting ideas in smaller boxes below it and connected to it by arrows or leader lines. If the information is sequential (for instance, significant events in World War I), a map can take the form of a flowchart. Samples of these kinds of maps are shown below.

Three Examples of Mapping

We welcome you to *New Worlds*. We hope your journey through this textbook is an enjoyable and rewarding experience.

Joe Cortina Janet Elder

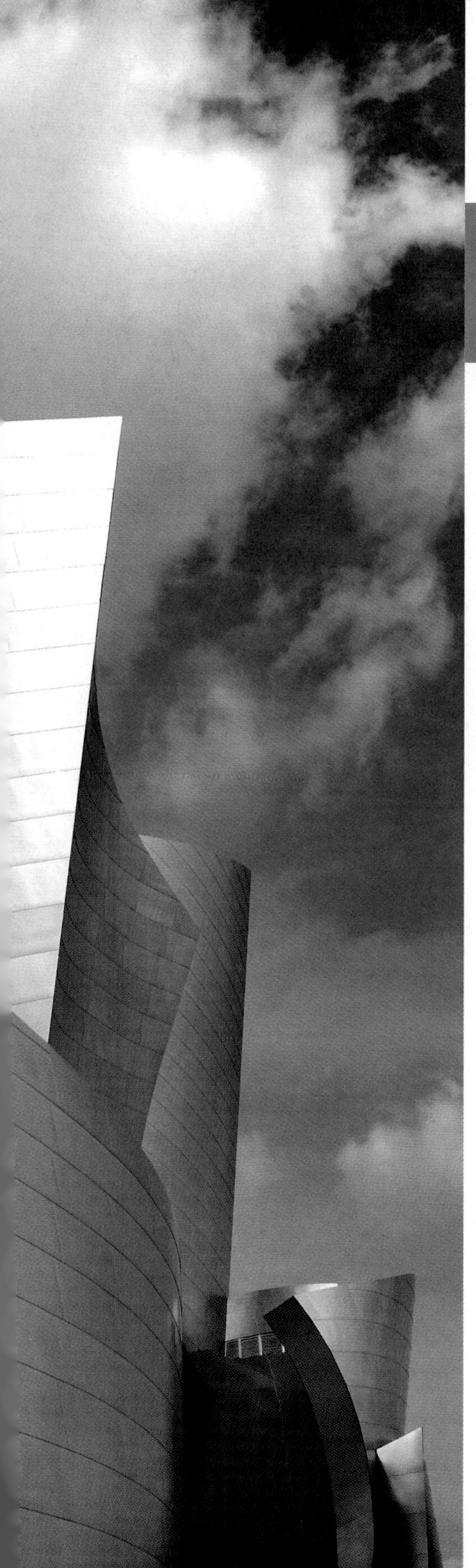

PART 1

A New World of Learning

Reading and Studying in College

CHAPTERS IN PART ONE

✓ **Related Resources**

See pages IG-6 to IG-8 of the *Annotated Instructor's Edition* for general suggestions related to the chapters in Part One.

CHAPTER 1

Introduction to Reading and Studying

Being Successful in College

CHAPTER OBJECTIVES

In this chapter you will learn the answers to these questions:

- What do I need to know about the process of reading and studying?
- What are the keys to studying textbooks?
- What is comprehension monitoring and why is it important?
- What is the SQ3R study system?
- How can I adjust my reading rate when I study?
- What do I need to do to be successful in college?
- Why is it important to set goals for myself?
- What are learning styles?

✓ **Timely Words**

"You find the key to success under the alarm clock."
(Benjamin Franklin)

"Never put off until tomorrow what you can do today."
(Thomas Jefferson)

"It's never too late to be what you might have been."
(George Eliot)

WHAT DO YOU NEED TO KNOW ABOUT THE READING AND STUDYING PROCESS?

KEY TERMS

prior knowledge

What you already know about a topic.

Prior knowledge is also known as *background knowledge.*

previewing

Examining material to determine its topic and organization before actually reading it.

predicting

Anticipating what is coming next as you read.

✓ **Teaching Tip**

The "It's Your Call" feature will remind students that a great deal of information about studying textbooks and preparing for tests appears in Chapters 10 and 11 of *New Worlds.*

Take time to preview Chapters 10 and 11 with students. They can use some of the information from the start of the semester, although it will make much more sense after they have completed the chapters that precede them. The main goal in doing this is for students to see "where they are going," how they will actually use—and benefit from—the important reading skills they learn in the "comprehension core" of *New Worlds* (Chapters 3–9). Highly motivated students in particular will appreciate these "It's Your Call" opportunities to preview these topics or examine them in more depth.

Knowing more about the reading process can make your reading and your studying more effective. Did you know, for instance, that reading is more than just moving your eyes in a certain way and decoding and pronouncing words? In reality, reading is a form of the *thinking* process, and the goal is to comprehend the author's message. To do this, you must "think along" with the author; that is, you must follow and understand his or her train of thought. Furthermore, you must make connections between what you are reading and what you already know about the topic. This background knowledge—what you already know about a topic—is called **prior knowledge.**

How can you activate your prior knowledge when you begin reading an assignment? One way is to preview the assignment. **Previewing** means examining material to determine its topic and organization before actually reading it. To see what it is about and how it is organized, look at the introduction, headings, illustrations, and chapter summary. Think about the information you are about to learn and try to recall anything you already know about the topic. In other words, activate and assess your prior knowledge. If the material is challenging and you do not know very much about the topic, you may want to learn a little bit more about it first. To accomplish this, you might look up a topic in an encyclopedia, a good dictionary, or go online to get additional information from the Internet. After you finish previewing, take a few minutes to reflect on this information. You may even take a few introductory notes about what you will be studying.

Good readers are active readers. They know that as they read they must constantly ask questions and think about how the material is organized. They use the skill of **predicting** to anticipate what is coming next. Predicting helps readers concentrate on what they are reading and helps them read actively and effectively.

Skillful readers prepare themselves to read by previewing and assessing their prior knowledge. Then they ask and answer questions as they read. Finally, they review material by rehearsing the answers to their questions. The reason good readers ask themselves questions as they read is to check their comprehension (understanding) of what they are reading. Whenever they realize they are not comprehending, they take specific steps to fix the problem.

You may be surprised to learn that even good readers have to reread certain things when they are studying. They are especially likely to reread when the material is complicated and when the topic is new or unfamiliar to them.

IT'S YOUR CALL

Want More Information Now about *Reading, Studying, and Memory*?

Information about the reading process and study techniques is presented here to help you get off to a good start. If you would like additional, in-depth information now, you are welcome to look ahead:

Rehearsal and Memory, pages 617–618

Following Directions, pages 626–627

In addition, Selection 1–2, "Yes, You *Can* Strengthen Your Memory Skills!" on pages 35–39, presents information on studying and memory.

It's Your Call: *If you want or need information about these skills, explore these sections now.*

Skillful readers also adjust their reading strategies and reading rate according to the *type* of material they are reading (such as a textbook, a newspaper, a book of poems, a comic strip) and their *purpose* for reading (to gain information to entertain themselves, to receive inspiration of comfort, and so forth). You will learn more about all of these strategies in *New Worlds.*

WHAT ARE THE KEYS TO STUDYING COLLEGE TEXTBOOKS?

It can take considerable time to read assignments and learn the material in your textbooks. Although experienced college students know this, new students sometimes do not. Beginning students often greatly underestimate the amount of time it will take to understand and learn information in their textbooks and to prepare for tests. In fact, they may be shocked to discover how much time studying actually requires. Or if they are spending a great deal of time studying, they may mistakenly imagine that they are the only ones who have to spend so much time.

Of course, successful studying requires a sufficient amount of time. However, simply spending large amounts of time studying does not by itself guarantee success: What you *do* during your study time is even more important.

Looking at the words in a book is not the same as reading and comprehending them, nor is sitting at a desk the same as studying. Some students who think they are "studying" are really sitting there daydreaming. Others read a chapter or section of a textbook without going back to mark or highlight anything or to make a single annotation. Still others highlight almost everything they read only to discover later that they do not understand or remember much of what they marked.

There are proven techniques that make studying more productive. This chapter and Chapters 10 and 11 describe specific techniques that will help you read and study your textbooks more efficiently and, therefore, *learn more as you study*. Often, what makes the difference between being a successful student and being a less successful one is *applying these study skills in a systematic way.*

You may already be familiar with some of these study techniques, or you may be learning them for the first time. In either case, using them can make you a more effective student. They will serve you well in all your courses, and they will help you in a variety of other learning situations as well: There will always be situations in college and in the workplace in which you must read, organize, learn, and remember information.

IT'S YOUR CALL

Want More Information Now about *Taking Notes from Textbooks and Preparing for Tests*?

This brief introduction to techniques for studying textbooks is presented here to get you off to a good start. If you would like additional, in-depth information now, you are welcome to look ahead:

Underlining, Highlighting, and Annotating Textbooks, pages 618–620

Outlining, Mapping, and Summarizing, pages 621–626

In addition, Selection 1-3, "Wise Up! The When and How of Preparing for Tests," on pages 47–51, presents information on studying for tests.

It's Your Call: *If you want or need information about these skills, explore these sections now.*

The keys to effective reading and studying are to:

- Monitor your comprehension.
- Be selective as you read and study.
- Organize the information as you read and study.
- Rehearse the information in order to remember it.

There is nothing magic about these study strategies. They are proven techniques that will be effective if you take the time and effort to learn how to do them and then apply them regularly. If you use them consistently, you will become a better and better student each semester.

WHAT IS COMPREHENSION MONITORING, AND WHY IS IT IMPORTANT?

KEY TERM
monitoring your comprehension

Evaluating your understanding as you read and correcting the problem whenever you realize that you are not comprehending.

Comprehension monitoring means evaluating your understanding as you read and correcting the problem whenever you realize that you are not comprehending. You should monitor your comprehension whenever you read and study.

As you are reading and studying a textbook passage or chapter, monitor your comprehension by asking yourself this question from time to time: "*Am I understanding what I am reading*?" If you do not understand what you are reading, try to pinpoint the problem by asking yourself, "*Why am I not understanding*?" If you can determine why you are not comprehending, you can take steps to correct the problem.

Listed below are some common reasons for comprehension problems and strategies for solving them.

Problem:

I am not understanding because the topic is completely new to me. Textbooks frequently introduce you to topics you have not learned about before. Sometimes even a single paragraph can contain a lot of information that is new to you.

Solutions:

- Read a bit further to see if the information that confuses you is explained or becomes clear to you.
- Look up the topic in an encyclopedia or another textbook.
- Stop and ask for a brief explanation from someone who is knowledgeable about the topic (the instructor, a tutor, or a classmate).
- Read simpler or supplemental materials on the same topic (usually available from a library).

Problem:

I am not understanding because there are words I do not know. College-level material is written at a high level. In addition, it often contains an abundance of new words and specialized or technical vocabulary that you must learn.

Solutions:

- Try to use the rest of the sentence or paragraph (the context) to figure out the meaning of an unfamiliar word.
- Look up unfamiliar words in a dictionary or in the glossary at the back of the textbook.

- Ask someone the meaning of the unfamiliar words.
- Write down the definitions of the new words you are learning.

Problem:

I am not understanding because distractors are interfering with my concentration. Distractors may be *physical* (such as noise or being hungry) or *psychological* (such as daydreaming or worrying about other things you have to do).

Solutions:

Identify any *physical* distractors that are interfering with your concentration and take steps to eliminate them. For example,

- Move to a quiet room or close the door.
- Do not sit facing a window.
- Turn off the television and background music.
- Do not answer the telephone.
- Take a short break and drink a glass of water or eat a light snack.
- Do not try to study lying down—you will fall asleep.

Identify any *psychological* distractors that are interfering with your concentration and take steps to eliminate them. For example,

- If you are worrying about things you need to do, jot the items down. Then, *after* studying, take care of the items on your "to do" list.
- If you are daydreaming or worrying about a personal problem, refocus your attention by making a deliberate decision to concentrate on what you are reading.

Monitoring your comprehension enables you to determine when you *are* understanding and when you are not. This, in turn, enables you to take steps to correct the situation when you are *not* understanding what you are reading.

Make comprehension monitoring a habit. After all, if you do not understand what you are reading, you are not really reading. You are just looking at the words.

How Can You Be Selective as You Read and Study?

KEY TERM
being selective as you read and study
Focusing on main ideas and major supporting details.

Too many students think that they can (and must) learn and remember *everything* in their textbooks, but this mistaken idea leads only to frustration. **Being selective as you read and study** means focusing on main ideas and major supporting details. If you are selective, you will be less likely to feel overwhelmed by the material, and you will be more likely to remember the most important points the author wants you to learn.

How Can You Organize as You Read and Study?

KEY TERM
organizing as you read and study
Arranging main ideas and supporting details in a meaningful way.

Organization is another key to learning and remembering what you read when you study. The reason is simple: Organized material is easier to learn, memorize, and recall than unorganized material. **Organizing as you read and study** means arranging main ideas and supporting details in a meaningful way. This is something that you should do on paper. Organizing material as you read and study is one way to transfer what you are learning to your long-term (permanent) memory.

How Can You Rehearse Information to Remember It?

KEY TERM
rehearsing to remember information

Saying or writing material to transfer it into long-term memory.

Rehearsing to remember information means saying or writing material to transfer it into long-term memory. Rehearsal is *not* merely rereading, nor is it a casual overview. Rehearsal is an active way to review. Ideally, it should involve *visual learning* (looking at the information you have organized into notes or review cards), *auditory learning* (saying information out loud several times so that you hear the information), and *tactile learning* (writing the information several times). Rehearsal is especially important when the material you are studying is complex.

It is important to understand that comprehending and remembering are two separate tasks. The fact that you comprehend textbook material does not mean you will automatically remember it, although material that you understand will be much easier to memorize. To *remember* material as well as understand it, you must take an additional step: you must rehearse it. Just as actors begin to memorize their lines long before a performance, you need to rehearse textbook material frequently, and you should start long before a test.

These four keys to studying college textbooks that we have just discussed are interrelated. That is, these techniques complement each other, so *all* of them should be used whenever you study. Monitoring your comprehension as you read helps you be selective as to what is important. Being selective helps you organize information efficiently. Organizing information makes it easier to rehearse it. Rehearsing information will help you remember the information.

WHAT IS THE SQ3R STUDY SYSTEM?

The SQ3R study system is a widely advocated textbook study system developed by Francis P. Robinson in 1946. The steps in the SQ3R method, **Survey, Question, Read, Recite, and Review,** offer a simple, systematic approach to studying textbook material. Using this method of asking and answering questions as you read and study a textbook chapter can enhance your reading comprehension and retention of what you read.

SQ3R STUDY SYSTEM

SURVEY	Get an overview before you begin reading the chapter. Look at headings and subheadings, charts, tables, photographs, and words in special print. Read the preface and chapter summary.
QUESTION	Ask questions based on your preview during the Survey step. Turn chapter headings into questions. Create at least one question for each subsection or section in the chapter. Read any questions the author includes in the chapter.
READ	Read each section with your question in mind. Read actively and search for answers to the questions you developed in the Question step. Reading with a purpose is essential to comprehension and retention.
RECITE	After reading each section, stop, recite your questions, and try to answer them aloud from memory. If you cannot answer a question, go back to the section and reread. Don't go on to the next section until you can recite the answer from memory.
REVIEW	After you have completed reading the chapter using the Question, Read, and Recite steps, review all your questions, answers, and other material from the chapter to transfer the information into your long-term memory.

IT'S YOUR CALL

Want More Information Now about *Methods for Studying a Textbook*?

Information about the SQ3R method is presented here to help you get off to a good start. If you would like additional, in-depth information now, you are welcome to look ahead:

Three-Step Process for Studying Textbooks, pages 559–563
Interpreting Visual and Graphic Aids, pages 572–589
Textbook Features, pages 564–571

It's Your Call: *If you want or need information about these skills, explore these sections now.*

There are many variations on Robinson's study reading system, such as SQ4R system (Survey, Question, Read, Recite, 'Rite [Write], and Review) and the PQ3R system (Preview, Question, Read, Recite, and Review). Chapter 10 of *New Worlds* (pages 559–563) presents a detailed explanation of a three-step study reading process for reading and studying college textbook material.

HOW CAN YOU ADJUST YOUR READING RATE WHEN YOU STUDY?

When you study textbook material you should preview it first, of course. Ask yourself about your specific purpose for reading it. Also, ask yourself how much you already know about it. If the topic is new to you, then you will need to read more slowly. If you are very familiar with the topic, you may be able to read at a faster rate. The point is to read *flexibly,* adjusting your rate as needed. Often, you must continue to adjust your rate *as* you are reading, slowing down when necessary and reading a bit faster when possible.

When to Slow Down

Here are some situations in which you should slow down when you are reading:

- You know very little about the topic or it is entirely new to you.
- A passage consists of complicated or technical material that you need to learn.
- A passage has details you need to remember.
- A passage contains new or difficult vocabulary.
- The material presents directions that you must follow.
- The material is accompanied by charts or graphs to which you must shift your attention as you read.
- The material requires you to visualize something in your mind (a section on the digestive system in a biology text would be an example).
- The writing is beautiful, artistic, descriptive, or poetic and invites you to linger and enjoy each word. (You may want to read such material aloud to yourself.)
- The material contains ideas you want to consider carefully (such as two sides of an argument) or "words to live by" (such as philosophical, religious, or inspirational writing).

When to Speed Up

Here are some situations in which you can speed up your reading:

- The whole passage is easy; there are no complicated sentences, no complex ideas, and no difficult terms.
- There is an easy passage within a longer, more difficult section.
- A passage gives an example of something you already understand or explains it in different words.
- You are already knowledgeable about the topic.
- You want only main ideas and are not concerned about details.
- The material is not related to your purpose for reading (for example, you might "speed" through a section of a magazine article that does not pertain to the topic you are researching).

How Can You Improve Your Reading Speed?

College students often remark that because they read slowly, they spend most of their study time just reading their textbook assignments. They often ask, "How can I learn to read faster?" The answer, of course, is to practice reading faster on material that is easy. Although you will never be able to read college textbooks as fast as simpler material, you can learn to read them at a faster rate than you presently do. The chart below shows various reading rates and their uses.

Here are tips for increasing your reading rate by practicing on easy material:

1. Practice regularly with easy, interesting material, including newspapers (such as *USA Today*), favorite magazines (such as *People* or *Reader's Digest*), short, easy novels (such as *The Old Man and the Sea* or *Animal Farm*), or other easy reading.

FLEXIBLE READING: INFORMATION-GATHERING TECHNIQUES AND READING RATES

Information-Gathering Techniques	Approximate Rate (Words per Minute)	Uses
Scanning	1,000 wpm (words per minute) or more	To find a particular piece of information (such as a name, date, or a number)
Skimming	800–1,000 wpm	To get an overview of material
Reading rates:		
Rapid reading	300–500 wpm	For fairly easy material; when you want only important facts or ideas; for leisure reading
Average reading	200–300 wpm	For textbooks, news magazines, journals, and literature
Study reading	50–200 wpm	For new vocabulary, complex concepts, technical material, and retaining details (such as material to be memorized, legal documents, and material of great interest or importance)

2. Read for 15 to 20 minutes each day, pushing yourself to read at a rate that is slightly too fast for you—in other words, a rate that is slightly uncomfortable. Once this rate becomes comfortable, push yourself to read a little faster. (Some students enjoy using a timer when they practice. Set a timer for 15 to 20 minutes and see how many pages you read before the timer goes off.) Keep track of the number of pages you read each day.
3. Strive to maintain concentration. If you are momentarily distracted, return immediately to your reading.

As you continue to practice, you will find that you are able to read more pages in the same amount of time. You will also find that you can usually understand the important points in a passage even though you are reading it at a faster rate. There is another bonus: As you read each day, you will be adding to the background knowledge. This will enable you to read related material even more efficiently in the future.

WHAT DO YOU NEED TO DO TO BE SUCCESSFUL IN COLLEGE?

You've entered the exciting new world of college reading and studying. It's a world in which you can be successful—if you do the right things. Most students want to be successful, of course, but not every college student knows what to do in order to succeed. One way is simply to examine what successful college students do and then make sure you do the same things yourself.

✓ **Related Resources**
See pages IG-6 to IG-7 of the *Annotated Instructor's Edition* for general suggestions related to Chapter 1.

What characterizes college students who are successful? According to a study in the *Journal of College Reading and Learning,* there seem to be at least six important factors. What is interesting about these factors is that they are so logical and obvious. Yes, these things require self-discipline, but so do most things in life that are worthwhile and lead to a feeling of accomplishment. These success behaviors and attitudes are within the reach of nearly all students. In fact, you may already do several of them. Keep doing them! However, there may be ones you can improve upon or do more consistently. They are all strategies you can begin using today, and if you use them consistently, semester by semester, you will become an even more effective and successful student. In short, anyone who wants to be a successful college student must do the things successful college students do.

The six characteristics are:

1. **Successful students are prepared for class.** In most college courses, preparing for class means much more than completing homework assignments. Successful students prepare for class by reading the textbook assignment carefully, underlining or highlighting main points in the text, and taking notes from the text. They also look over the information in their text and notes again before class so that they can understand what the instructor will be talking about and so that they can take better notes in class. Being prepared for class enables students to participate in class discussions and to ask questions that help them understand the material and keep their attention focused.
2. **Successful students attend every class and pay close attention.** Not only do they attend every class, but they arrive early. They sit where the instructor can see them and they can see the instructor. They turn off their cell phones, iPods, and PDAs. They focus on what the instructor is saying, and they take note. They participate in class discussions, even if their participation is limited at first to asking questions. They know that going to class gives them the opportunity to learn more about the important information in their homework assignments. They know that

identifying the material the instructor considers important is especially helpful when it is time to prepare for a test. These students do more than just attend class: They "attend" in the sense that they are "attentive." They pay attention and they participate. Successful students view attending class as an opportunity to learn—not as an occasion for socializing with friends.

3. **Successful students perceive instructors as experts.** Successful students know that their instructors are expert resources and that instructors want students to do well. Because successful students are always prepared for class and attend class regularly, they feel comfortable approaching the instructor when they need assistance. They do not wait until they need a favor or need help to establish rapport with the instructor. More important, they do not wait until failure is inevitable before they ask for help. Some students perceive asking for help as showing their ignorance. Successful students, however, view this action as a positive one. They realize most instructors are very pleased when a student is interested enough to seek help.
4. **Successful students follow an organized study routine.** Organized students regularly take time to think about (*a*) the things they need to do, (*b*) which things they need to start working on now, and, (*c*) what they can do later. They are aware of when they are using their time well and when they are wasting time. They routinely establish daily objectives that will help them fulfill both short- and long-term goals. (Goal setting is discussed later in this chapter.) Successful students often work ahead so that work does not pile up and so that tests and deadlines do not cause them undue stress.
5. **Successful students develop a set of study skills strategies.** Successful students constantly review what they are learning. To do this, they develop creative ways to reorganize course material. For example, they might put the information in the form of review cards, summary notes, charts, or diagrams. Depending on their learning style, some students find that making a digital recording is helpful. (Ways of organizing information are discussed in Chapter 11; learning styles are discussed later in this chapter.) Reorganizing information requires students to work actively with the information to make sense of it and then organize it in a way that helps them remember it. When preparing for exams, successful students isolate themselves from friends (other than study groups) and other distractions. They start early, review the material, and reread all the important points. They rewrite their notes. They ask for help on material they still do not understand.
6. **Successful students take responsibility for their own success.** Successful students are realistic about the amount of time they need to study. They pass up temptations to socialize or to entertain themselves instead of study because they place a higher priority on their schoolwork than on their social life. They are willing to make sacrifices in order to keep up their grades because they value the long-term rewards associated with completing a college education. They have a clear idea of why they want to earn a college degree (and it is not simply to make money), and they often know what they want to do once they have completed their college education. (If you are unclear about your major or career interest, talk with one of your college's advisors or career planning specialists.)

The *Journal of College Reading and Learning* article concludes: "Most students attain the maturity to balance their academic and social life. Those who do not know where to draw the line often drop out or fail out of college." The good news, though, as noted at the beginning of this chapter, is that the characteristics described here are ones that almost any student can acquire and use.

Source: Adapted from Robert Nelson, "Using a Student Performance Framework to Analyze Success and Failure," *Journal of College Reading and Learning* 29, no. 1, Fall 1998, pp. 82–89.

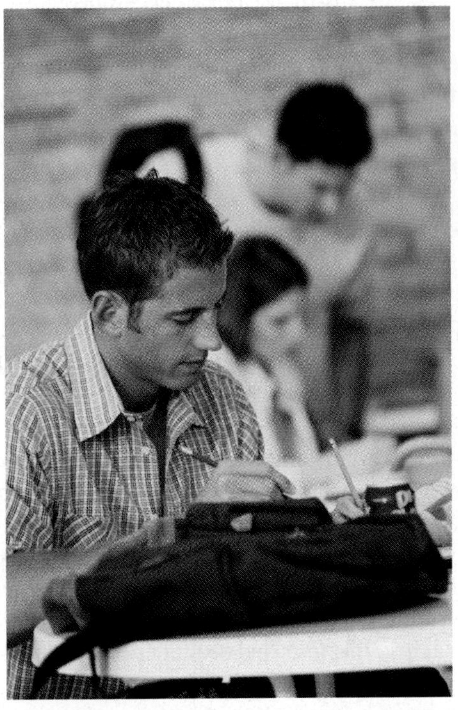

Becoming a successful student involves behaviors and attitudes that nearly all students can adopt.

WHY IS IT IMPORTANT TO SET GOALS?

As noted previously, successful students have a clear idea of why they want to earn a college degree and what they want to do once they finish college. In other words, they have specific goals they want to achieve. Setting goals is a habit that distinguishes not only successful students, but successful people as well.

Setting goals involves identifying things that you would like to accomplish, writing them down, and making a commitment to achieve them.

There are several benefits from setting goals:

- **Having goals keeps you motivated.** When you set goals, you identify future achievements that are important and meaningful to you.
- **Having goals enables you to make good decisions about how you use your time and energy.** At any given moment, you can ask yourself whether what you are doing is moving you toward achieving one of your goals or whether it is moving you away from it.
- **Having clear, written goals enables you to measure your progress toward achieving them.** It is satisfying to accomplish goals and to look back on ones you have achieved.

To be useful, goals must be specific and clear. They should also be realistic, that is, things that you can actually achieve (even though some may require considerable effort). An example of a clear, specific, and realistic goal is "I will complete all of my courses this semester and make at least a B average." (An example of a vague goal is "I'll do better this semester." An example of an unrealistic goal is "I'll work 40 hours a week, take six courses this semester, and make all As.")

It is also important to put your goals in writing. Goals that are not written down are not much better than wishes. Writing them down helps you make a commitment to them.

Keep a copy of them on your desk or some other place where you will see them often. Read them daily and visualize yourself achieving them. Be sure, too, that you review the goals themselves on a regular basis, perhaps at the beginning of each month. Update them as needed by modifying them, adding new ones, and removing ones you have attained.

You should designate your goals as short-term goals, intermediate goals, or long-term goals. These designations refer to the length of time you think it will take to accomplish the goals.

KEY TERMS

short-term goal

Goal you want to accomplish within three to six months.

intermediate goal

Goal you want to accomplish within the next three to five years.

long-term goal

Goal you want to accomplish during your lifetime.

- **Short-term goals** are goals that you want to accomplish within three to six months (or during a semester). Examples would be "to learn to use a word-processing program," "to find a part-time job," and "to save enough money to take a ski trip during the semester break."
- **Intermediate goals** are those you want to accomplish within the next three to five years. Examples are "to attain my undergraduate degree," "to obtain an entry-level job in my career field," and "to complete a marathon."
- **Long-term goals** are large, often more complex goals that you want to accomplish during your lifetime. Examples are "to establish and run my own software company," "to get married and have a family," and "to travel throughout Europe."

In addition to identifying a time frame for each goal, you may find it helpful to categorize your goals. Use categories such as personal, financial, health, educational, travel, career, spiritual, and so forth.

✓ **Teaching Tips**

- Emphasize to students that goals are personal and private and that you do not intend for them to share their goals with you or with their classmates. Allow them to write their goals on notebook paper or index cards instead of on this page.
- Of course, some goals may fall between half a year and three years. Even so, it's helpful for students to think of goals as being short-, intermediate-, or long-term.

PUTTING YOUR SHORT TERM, INTERMEDIATE, AND LONG-TERM GOALS IN WRITING

Take a few minutes to write out your goals. Write at least three goals for each category. These are personal and private, and they do not have to be shared with anyone.

What are my short-term goals?

On the lines below, write at least three things you want to accomplish this semester.

1. ______________________________

2. ______________________________

3. ______________________________

4. ______________________________

5. ______________________________

What are my intermediate goals?

On the lines below, write at least three things you want to accomplish within three to five years.

1. ______________________________

2. ______________________________

3. ______________________________

4. ______________________________

5. ______________________________

(continued on next page)

What are my long-term goals?

On the lines below, write at least three things you want to accomplish and achieve during your lifetime.

1. ______________________________
2. ______________________________
3. ______________________________
4. ______________________________
5. ______________________________

WHAT ARE LEARNING STYLES?

Being aware of your learning style, or how you learn best, can help you become a more successful student. To gain insight into your learning style, complete the learning styles inventory that follows. When you have completed the survey and totaled your responses, read the rest of this section.

IDENTIFYING YOUR LEARNING STYLE

✓ **Teaching Tip**
This survey makes a good in-class activity. Ask students to reveal their preferred learning style with a show of hands.

To gain insight into your learning style, answer the following questions. For each item, circle all the answers that describe you.

1. When I go someplace new, I usually
   a. trust my intuition about the right direction or route to take.
   b. ask someone for directions.
   c. look at a map or printed directions.
2. I like to go to places where
   a. there is a lot of space to move around.
   b. people are talking or there is music that matches my mood.
   c. there is good "people watching" or there is something interesting to watch.
3. If I have many things to do, I generally
   a. am fidgety until I get most of them done.
   b. repeat them over and over to myself so that I won't forget to do them.
   c. make a list of them or write them on a calendar or organizer.
4. When I have free time, I like to
   a. work on a hobby or do crafts, or do an activity such as play a sport or exercise.
   b. listen to music or talk on the phone.
   c. watch television, play a video game, go online, or see a movie.
5. When I am talking with other people, I usually
   a. move close to them so I can get a feel for what they are telling me.
   b. listen carefully so that I can hear what they are saying.
   c. watch them closely so that I can see what they are saying.

6. When I meet someone new, I usually pay most attention to
  a. the way the person walks or moves, or to the gestures the person makes.
  b. the way the person speaks and how his or her voice sounds.
  c. the way the person looks (appearance, clothes, etc.).

7. When I choose a book or article to read, I typically choose one that
  a. deals with sports or fitness, hobbies and crafts, or other activities.
  b. tells me about a topic of particular interest to me.
  c. includes a lot of photos, pictures, or illustrations.

8. Learning about something is easier for me when I can
  a. use a hands-on approach.
  b. have someone explain it to me.
  c. watch someone show me how to do it.

Total your As, Bs, and Cs:

_______ As _______ Bs _______ Cs

If your highest total is As, you are a *tactile* or *kinesthetic* learner.
If your highest total is Bs, you are an *auditory* learner.
If your highest total is Cs, you are a *visual* learner.

✓ **Teaching Tip**
The term *kinesthetic* is sometimes used in conjunction with *tactile*. Kinesthetic refers to sensing the movement of muscles, tendons, and joints. Kinesthetic learners benefit from incorporating movement when learning.

KEY TERMS

learning style
The modality through which an individual learns best.

visual learner
One who prefers to see or read information to be learned.

auditory learner
One who prefers to hear information to be learned.

tactile learner
One who prefers to write information to be learned or to manipulate materials physically.

The term **learning style** refers to the modality through which an individual learns best. The modalities are visual, auditory, and tactile. A person whose learning style is visual prefers reading or seeing, an auditory learner prefers hearing information. Tactile learners prefer a hands-on approach—touching or manipulating materials.

Most students are capable of learning in any of these ways. Even so, most people have a preferred style, that is, one that they prefer because it makes learning easier for them. For example, one student may prefer to look at a map, while another may prefer to listen to directions for reaching the same destination; still another might find it helpful to actually draw the map or trace the route with a fingertip. Some students might be comfortable with any of these ways or prefer a combination of them.

Students who are primarily **visual learners** learn best when they see or read material. They benefit from books, class notes, review cards, test review sheets, and the like. Students who are primarily **auditory learners** learn best when they hear the material one or more times. They benefit from classes that feature lectures and discussions. Auditory learners also benefit from reciting material or reading it aloud to themselves, making digital recordings, and participating in study groups. Students who are primarily **tactile learners** benefit from writing information down or manipulating materials physically. They learn best from laboratory work and other types of hands-on activities. The following chart summarizes this information on learning styles. Once you have identified your preferred learning style, you can choose course formats, classroom settings, and study techniques that let you use your style to full advantage.

As noted, most students have a learning style that they *prefer* to use. However, all students will find themselves in situations that require them to utilize the other learning styles. For this reason, it is important to develop and practice a variety of study and learning skills.

In addition to knowing your learning style, you should think about whether you prefer to work by yourself or with others. If you study more effectively alone, you may need to take steps to protect your study time and your study space. If you find it helpful to study with others, find a serious study partner or form a study group with other motivated students. And remember that being part of a study group is not a substitute for reading and studying on your own. To benefit fully from a study group, every member must prepare by reading and studying alone first.

THREE LEARNING STYLES

If This Is Your Learning Style . . .	Then These Are the Most Helpful to Your Learning
Visual Learner (prefers to read or see information)	Reading textbooks and seeing information in print Seeing information on a computer screen, video monitor, or large classroom screen Reviewing class notes and concept maps Reading your chapter review cards Studying test review sheets
Auditory Learner (prefers to hear information)	Listening to class lectures and discussions Reciting material (saying it out loud) Reading aloud to oneself Listening to audio tapes Participating in study groups
Tactile Learner (prefers to write material down or to manipulate materials physically)	Taking notes from lectures and from your textbooks Making concept maps Rewriting lecture notes after class Preparing study cards Doing laboratory work (computer labs, science labs, etc.) Going through steps or procedures in a process Taking hands-on classes (science, computer science, engineering, and other technical or vocational subjects)

CREATING CHAPTER REVIEW CARDS

Student Online Learning Center (OLC)
***Go to* Chapter 1.**
***Select* Chapter Test.**

Review cards or *summary cards* are a way to select, organize, and summarize the important information in a textbook chapter. Preparing review cards helps you organize the information so that you can learn and memorize it more easily. In other words, chapter review cards are effective study tools.

Preparing chapter review cards for each chapter of *New Worlds* will give you practice in creating these valuable study tools. Once you have learned how to make chapter review cards, you can use actual index cards to create them for textbook material in your other courses and use them when you study for tests.

Now complete the chapter review cards for Chapter 1 by answering the questions or following the directions on each card. The page numbers indicate the place in the chapter where the information can be found. Use the type of handwriting that is easiest for you to reread (printing or cursive) and write legibly. You will find it easier to complete the review cards if you remove these pages before filling them in.

✓ **Teaching Tip**
Remind students that the student OLC contains a 10-item **Chapter Test** for this chapter. After completing the chapter review cards below, students should complete the Chapter Test on the OLC.

✓ **Teaching Tip**
Page numbers for chapter review card items are provided in the student edition in Chapters 1–5 only.

The Reading Process
What is *reading*? (See pages 5–6.)
Reading is a form of the thinking process; the goal is to comprehend the author's message.
What is *prior knowledge*? (See page 5.)
What you already know about a topic
What is *previewing*? (See page 5.)
Examining material to determine its topic and organization before actually reading it.
What do readers do when they *predict*? (See page 5.)
They anticipate what is coming next.
Card 1 Chapter 1: Introduction to Reading and Studying

✓ **Teaching Tips**
1. Remind students to take advantage of the Key Term definitions (that appear in the margins) as they complete the review cards.
2. Students will find it more efficient to remove the review card pages prior to filling them in. It saves flipping pages back and forth.

✓ **Related Resources**
See pages IG-6 to IG-8 of the *Annotated Instructor's Edition* for general suggestions related to chapters in Part One.

Keys for Studying Textbook Material

What are *four keys* to studying textbook material? (See page 7.)

1. Monitor your comprehension.
2. Be selective as you read and study.
3. Organize the information as you read and study.
4. Rehearse the information in order to remember it.

Card 2 Chapter 1: Introduction to Reading and Studying

Comprehension Monitoring

Define *comprehension monitoring.* (See page 7.)

Comprehension monitoring means evaluating your understanding as you read and correcting the problem whenever you realize that you are not comprehending.

Why is it important to monitor your comprehension? (See pages 7–8.)

Monitoring your comprehension enables you to determine when you are understanding and when you are not.

Card 3 Chapter 1: Introduction to Reading and Studying

SQ3R Study System

Describe each of the five steps in the SQ3R study system. (See page 9.)

Survey: Get an overview before you begin reading. Look at headings, subheadings and words in special print. Read the preface and chapter summary.

Question: Ask questions based on your preview. Turn chapter headings into questions. Create at least one question for each subsection.

Read: Read each section with your question in mind. Read actively and search for answers you developed in the Question step.

Recite: After reading each section, stop, recite your questions, and try to answer them aloud from memory. Go back and reread if you cannot answer a question.

Review: After you have completed reading the chapter using the Question, Read and Recite steps, review all your questions and answers to transfer the information into your long-term memory.

Card 4 Chapter 1: Introduction to Reading and Studying

Flexible Reading Rates

1. List two reading rates appropriate to *information gathering*. Include the purpose and wpm for each. (See page 11.)
   - scanning (1,500 wpm or more); to search for a specific item
   - skimming (800–1,000 wpm); to get an overview
2. List three other reading rates, the number of words per minute (wpm), and the types of material each rate is appropriate for. (See page 11.)
   - rapid reading (300–500 wpm); for easy material
   - average reading (200–300 wpm); for texts
   - study reading (50–200 wpm); for complex material

Card 5 Chapter 1: Introduction to Reading and Studying

Doing What Successful Students Do

List the six characteristics of successful students. (See pages 12–13.)

1. Successful students are prepared for class.
2. Successful students attend every class and pay close attention.
3. Successful students perceive instructors as experts.
4. Successful students follow an organized study routine.
5. Successful students develop a set of study skills strategies.
6. Successful students take responsibility for their own success.

Card 6 Chapter 1: Introduction to Reading and Studying

Setting Goals

List three reasons it is useful to set goals. (See page 14.)

1. Having goals keeps you motivated.
2. Having goals enables you to make good decisions about how you use your time and energy.
3. Having clear written goals enables you to measure your progress toward achieving them.

Card 7 Chapter 1: Introduction to Reading and Studying

Three Types of Goals

Describe these three types of goals: (See page 15.)

Short-team goals: goals that you want to accomplish within three to six months (or during a semester)

Intermediate goals: goals that you want to accomplish with'n the next three to five years

Long-term goals: goals that you want to accomplish during your lifetime

Card 8 Chapter 1: Introduction to Reading and Studying

Three Learning Styles

Define the three learning styles and describe several helpful activities for learning for each style. (See pages 17–18.)

Visual learners: prefer to see or read the material to be learned

Most helpful activities for learning: books, computer screens, class notes, review cards, test review sheets, and the like

Auditory learners: prefer to hear the material one or more times

Most helpful activities for learning: classes that feature lectures and discussions, reciting material, or reading aloud to themselves

Tactile learners: prefer to write information down or manipulate materials

Most helpful activities for learning: taking notes and rewriting notes, laboratory work, and other types of hands-on activities

Card 9 Chapter 1: Introduction to Reading and Studying

SELECTION **1-1**

Nonfiction

A MOTHER'S ANSWER

From *The Big Picture: Getting Perspective on What's Really Important*
By Ben Carson with Gregg Lewis

Ben Carson is the director of pediatric neurosurgery at the Johns Hopkins Hospital in Baltimore, Maryland. At Hopkins, where he received his training in neurosurgery, this handsome, calm, soft-spoken man with the "gifted hands" was only 33 when he was appointed the director of his department, the youngest person in the United States to be appointed to such a position. He is internationally known for his success in the intricate, delicate surgeries for separating conjoined twins who are born joined at the head and for hemispherectomies, removing one side of the brain to treat those with extreme seizure disorders.

Carson also specializes in giving young people an inspirational boost. Despite his demanding schedule, he goes out of his way to address groups of schoolchildren. In 1994 Carson and his wife, who have three sons of their own, established the Carson Scholars Fund by earmarking half a million dollars of their own money for it. Their ultimate goal is to have a Carson Scholar in every state.

When Carson was a child, no one ever would have predicted that he would become a world-famous brain surgeon. He grew up in an inner city in extreme poverty, came from a broken home, and had a hot, hair-trigger temper. By the middle of fifth grade, he was failing every subject. What changed his life and started him on a path that eventually led to a scholarship to Yale University and then on to the University of Michigan School of Medicine?

Looking back at his childhood, Carson says, "My poor mother was mortified. Here she was with a third-grade education, working two or three jobs as a domestic, cleaning other people's houses, knowing that life didn't hold much for her, and seeing my brother and me going down the same road. She didn't know what to do, so she prayed and asked God to give her wisdom. What could she do to get her two young sons to understand the importance of education so that they could determine their own destiny?" In the selection below, Carson tells about the answer his mother found that helped him and his brother—and ultimately changed his life forever.

1 God gave her the wisdom—though my brother and I didn't think it was all that wise. It was to turn off the television. From that point on she would let us watch our choice of only two or three television programs during the week. With all that spare time, we were to read two books a week from the Detroit Public Library.

2 I was extraordinarily unhappy about this new arrangement. All my friends were outside, having a good time. I remember my mother's friends coming to her and saying, "You can't keep boys in the house reading. Boys are supposed to be outside playing and developing their muscles. When they grow up, they'll hate you. They will be sissies. You can't do that!"

3 Sometimes I would overhear this and I would say, "Listen to them, Mother." But she would never listen. We were going to have to read those books.

4 Sometimes, when I tell this story, people come up to me afterwards and ask, "How was your mother able to get you to read those books? I can't get my kids to read or even turn off the television or Nintendo."

5 I just have to chuckle and say, "Well, back in those days, the parents ran the house. They didn't have to get permission from

Prediction Exercises

Directions: Use the skill of predicting to anticipate what certain paragraphs will be about. At each of the points indicated below, answer the question "What do you predict will happen next?"

Prediction Exercise

What do you predict will happen next?

(Answers will vary.)

the kids." That seems to be a novel concept to a lot of people these days.

6 At any rate, I started reading. The nice thing was my mother did not dictate what we had to read. I loved animals, so I read every animal book in the Detroit Public Library. And when I finished those, I went on to plants. When I finished those, I went on to rocks because we lived in a dilapidated section of the city near the railroad tracks. And what is there along railroad tracks, but rocks? I would collect little boxes of rocks and take them home and get out my geology book. I would study until I could name virtually every rock, tell how it was formed, and identify where it came from.

✓ **Teaching Tip**
The focus of the Prediction Exercise is to introduce students to the skill of predicting; the correctness of their answers is less important.

7 Months passed. I was still in fifth grade. Still the dummy in the class. Nobody knew about my reading project.

8 One day the fifth grade science teacher walked in and held up a big, shiny black rock. He asked, "Can anybody tell me what this is?"

Prediction Exercise

What do you predict will happen next?
(Answers will vary.)

9 Keep in mind that I never raised my hand. I never answered questions. So I waited for some of the smart kids to raise their hands. None of them did. So I waited for some of the dumb kids to raise their hands. When none of them did, I thought, *This is my big chance*. So I raised my hand . . . and everyone turned around to look. Some of my classmates were poking each other and whispering, "Look, look, Carson's got his hand up. This is gonna be good!"

10 They couldn't wait to see what was going to happen. And the teacher was shocked. He said, "Benjamin?"

11 I said, "Mr. Jaeck, that's obsidian." And there was silence in the room because it sounded good, but no one knew whether it was right or wrong. So the other kids didn't know if they should laugh or be impressed.

✓ **Teaching Tip**
For articles with color photos of Ben Carson, see *People Magazine*, 6/21/99, and *Time*, 8/20/01, Vol. 158, No. 7.

12 Finally the teacher broke the silence and said, "That's right! This is obsidian."

13 I went on to explain, "Obsidian is formed after a volcanic eruption. Lava flows down and when it hits water there is a super-cooling process. The elements coalesce, air is forced out, the surface glazes over, and . . ."

14 I suddenly realized everyone was staring at me in amazement. They couldn't believe all this geological information spewing from the mouth of a dummy. But you know, I was perhaps the most amazed person in the room, because it dawned on me in that moment that I was no dummy.

Prediction Exercise

What do you predict will happen next?
(Answers will vary.)

15 I thought, *Carson, the reason you knew the answer is because you were reading those books. What if you read books about all your subjects—science, math, history, geography, social studies? Couldn't you then know more than all these students who tease you and call you a dummy?* I must admit the idea appealed to me—to the extent that no book was safe from my grasp. I read everything I could get my hands on. If I had five minutes, I had a book. If I was in the bathroom, I was reading a book. If I was waiting for the bus, I was reading a book.

16 Within a year and a half, I went from the bottom of the class to the top of the class—much to the consternation of all those students who used to tease me and call me Dummy. The same

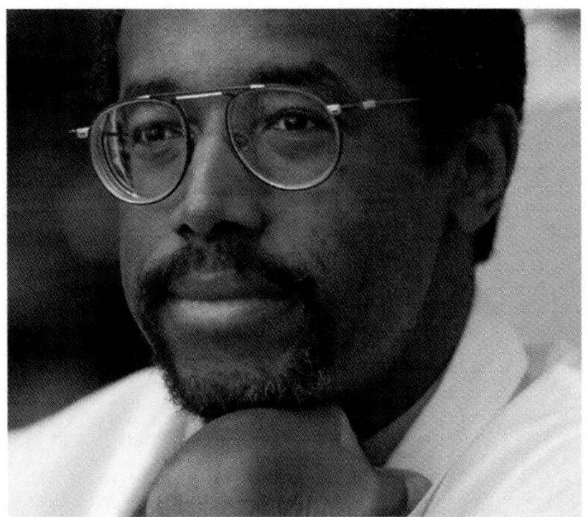

Dr. Benjamin Carson has been director of the division of pediatric neurosurgery at Johns Hopkins since 1984. He is a professor of neurosurgery, plastic surgery, oncology, and pediatrics. He is also the co-director of the Johns Hopkins Craniofacial Center. His practice includes traumatic brain injuries, brain and spinal cord tumors, achondroplasia, neurological and congenital disorders, craniosynostosis, epilepsy, and trigeminal neuralgia. This work includes active research programs.

Dr. Carson has written more than 100 neurosurgical publications. He has been awarded 40 honorary degrees and dozens of national citations of merit. He is the author of three best-selling books, *Gifted Hands, Think Big,* and *The Big Picture.* His newest book is *Take the Risk.*

On June 19, 2008, the White House awarded Dr. Carson the Presidential Medal of Freedom, the nation's highest civilian award. It was awarded for his groundbreaking contributions to medicine and his efforts to inspire and help young people achieve their dreams.

ones would come to me in seventh grade to ask, "Hey, Benny, how do you work this problem?" And I would say, "Sit at my feet, youngster, while I instruct you."

17 I was perhaps a little bit obnoxious. But after all those years it felt so good to say that to those who had tormented me.

18 The important point here is that I had the same brain when I was still at the bottom of the class as I had when I reached the top of the class.

19 The difference was this: In the fifth grade, I thought I was dumb so I acted like I was dumb, and I achieved like a dumb person. As a seventh grader I thought I was smart, so I acted and achieved accordingly. So what does that say about what a person thinks about his own abilities? What does this say about the importance of our self-image? What does it say about the incredible potential of the human brain our Creator has given us?

✓ **Teaching Tip**

In February 2009, TNT aired the program "Gifted Hands: The Ben Carson Story" Cuba Gooding, Jr., played the role of Ben Carson.

Carson's brother, Curtis, is a successful engineer. Their mother, Sonya, earned her GED and an associate degree. She was chosen by *Parade* magazine as "Mother of the Year."

There are currently Carson Scholars in 26 states. By the end of 2008, the Carson Scholars Fund had awarded 3,400 scholarships to four-year colleges and universities.

Source: Dr. Benjamin Carson with Gregg A. Lewis, *The Big Picture: Getting Perspective on What's Really Important* (Grand Rapids, MI: 1999), Zondervan Publishing House, pp. 48–50. Copyright © 1999 by Benjamin Carson. Used by permission of Zondervan.

SELECTION 1-1
Nonfiction
(continued)

Comprehension and Vocabulary Quiz

This quiz has four parts. Your instructor may assign some or all of them.

Comprehension

✓ **Teaching Tip**
You may find it convenient to have students transfer their answers to a 20-item Scantron Form 2020 machine-scorable answer sheet.

Directions: Items 1–5 test your comprehension (understanding) of the material in this selection. These questions are much like those that a content-area instructor would expect you to know after reading and studying this selection. For each comprehension question below, use information from the selection to determine the correct answer. Refer to the selection as you answer the questions. Write your answers in the spaces provided.

¶11 b **1.** The type of rock Ben identified was:
- *a.* lava.
- *b.* obsidian.
- *c.* opal.
- *d.* onyx.

¶10 c **2.** Mr. Jaeck's reaction to Ben raising his hand was:
- *a.* joy.
- *b.* anger.
- *c.* shock.
- *d.* disappointment.

(inference) d **3.** Before the event described in the passage, the reason Ben never raised his hand was:
- *a.* he didn't want to show off.
- *b.* he didn't want to embarrass those who didn't know the answer.
- *c.* he was waiting for his big chance.
- *d.* he didn't know the answer.

(inference) a **4.** As an adult, Ben Carson probably believes that:
- *a.* parents should set the rules.
- *b.* children should set the rules.
- *c.* parents and children should set the rules together.
- *d.* there should be no rules.

¶18 b **5.** Ben Carson says that he realized that he "had the same brain" when he was still at the bottom of the class as he had when he reached the top. He mentions this to show that:
- *a.* he did not expect his brain ever to change in any way.
- *b.* although he was intelligent, his perception of himself had caused him to act as if he were a "dummy."
- *c.* he did not have high enough expectations for himself when he was at the top of the class.
- *d.* more research needs to be done on the human brain.

Vocabulary in Context

Directions: Items 6–10 test your ability to determine the meaning of the word by using context clues. *Context clues* are words in a sentence that allow the reader to deduce (reason out) the meaning of an unfamiliar word in that sentence. Context clues also enable the reader to determine which meaning the author intends when a word has more than one meaning. For each vocabulary item below, a sentence from the selection containing an important word (*italicized, like this*) is quoted first. Next, there is an additional sentence using the word in the same sense and providing another context clue. Use the context clues from *both* sentences to deduce the meaning of the italicized word. *Be sure the answer you choose makes sense in both sentences.* If you need to use a dictionary to confirm your answer choice, remember that the meaning you select must still fit the context of *both* sentences. Write your answers in the spaces provided. **Note:** Chapter 2 presents the skill of using context clues.

Pronunciation Key: ă **pat** ā **pay** âr **care** ä **father** ĕ **pet** ē **be** ĭ **pit**
ī **tie** îr **pier** ŏ **pot** ō **toe** ô **paw** oi **noise** ou **out** ŏŏ **took** ōō **boot**
ŭ **cut** yōō **abuse** ûr **urge** th **thin** *th* **this** hw **which** zh **vision**
ə **about** *Stress mark:* ′

¶6 ___b___ **6.** The nice thing was my mother did not *dictate* what we had to read.

Our company's dress code prohibits nose rings, brow rings, and other facial "jewelry," but otherwise does not *dictate* what we may wear at work.

dictate (dĭk′ tāt) means:

a. like

b. say as an order or command

c. say aloud in order to be written down

d. understand

¶6 ___a___ **7.** When I finished those, I went on to rocks because we lived in a *dilapidated* section of the city near the railroad tracks.

The city refurbished the *dilapidated* Civil War mansion and turned it into a museum.

dilapidated (dĭ lăp′ ĭ dāt əd) means:

a. shabby; rundown

b. historic

c. fashionable; up-to-date

d. dangerous

¶13 ___d___ **8.** The elements *coalesce,* air is forced out, the surface glazes over, and . . .

Scientists believe that planets may form because great heat and pressure cause particles to *coalesce.*

coalesce (kō ə lĕs′) means:

a. disintegrate; dissolve

b. disappear

c. fly apart

d. fuse; unite

¶14 ___a___ **9.** They couldn't believe all this geological information *spewing* from the mouth of a dummy.

My car's radiator hose broke, *spewing* hot water everywhere.

spewing (spyōō′ ĭng) means:

a. gushing forth; streaming out

b. sending

c. trickling; dribbling

d. gathering

¶16 ___c___ **10.** Within a year and a half, I went from the bottom of the class to the top of the class—much to the *consternation* of all those students who used to tease me and call me Dummy.

My brother's tattoos caused my conservative parents great *consternation.*

consternation (kŏn stər nā′ shən) means:

a. joy; happiness

b. relief

c. dismay; upset

d. pride

Word Structure

Directions: Items 11–15 test your ability to use word-structure clues to help determine a word's meaning. *Word-structure clues* consist of roots, prefixes, and suffixes. In these exercises, you will learn the meaning of a word part (a root) and use it to determine the meaning of the several other words that have the same word part. If you need to use a dictionary to confirm an answer choice, do so. Write your answers in the spaces provided. **Note:** Chapter 2 presents the skill of using word-structure clues.

In paragraph 6 of the selection, you encountered the word **dictate.** This word contains the Latin root ***dict,*** which means "say" or "tell." The word *dictate* has several meanings, including "to *say* as an order or a command" and "to *say* aloud information that is to be written down." Use the meaning of ***dict*** and the list of prefixes on pages 68–69 to help you determine the meaning of each of the following words.

___c___ **11. Predictable** means:

a. able to explain what has happened.

b. preventable; avoidable.

c. able to say or tell ahead of time.

d. not able to know in advance.

___d___ **12.** When one person **contradicts** another, it means that person is:

a. speaking with anger.

b. saying something with impatience.

c. speaking in defense of the other person.

d. saying the opposite of what the other person has said.

a 13. Speech teachers help students with their **diction,** which means:
- *a.* the quality of their speaking.
- *b.* stuttering.
- *c.* proper breathing.
- *d.* the ability to carry on a conversation.

c 14. A **dictator** is one who:
- *a.* says the opposite of what others say.
- *b.* says what others want to hear.
- *c.* tells others what to do or say.
- *d.* tells interesting stories.

b 15. A religious **edict** is a:
- *a.* ceremony; ritual.
- *b.* document that tells or proclaims a new law.
- *c.* follower of a religion; believer.
- *d.* place of worship.

✓ **Teaching Tip**
Let students know that the skills included in this Reading Skills Application section have not been introduced yet. This section serves as a valuable preview of these skills, however. Students typically get several of the items correct, and they find this encouraging.

Reading Skills Application

Directions: Items 16–20 test your ability to *apply* certain reading skills to information in this selection. These types of questions provide valuable practice for all students, especially those who must take standardized reading tests and state-mandated basic skills tests. You have not studied all of the skills at this point, so these items will serve as a helpful preview. The comprehension and critical reading skills in this section are presented in Chapters 3 through 9 of *New Worlds;* vocabulary and figurative language skills are presented in Chapter 2. As you work through *New Worlds,* you will practice and develop these skills. Write your answers in the spaces provided.

author's purpose for writing (Chapter 8)

a 16. What is the authors' primary purpose for writing this selection?
- *a.* to prove that self-image affects whether a person uses his or her potential
- *b.* to explain the important role reading can play in a person's life
- *c.* to pay tribute to a mother's wisdom
- *d.* to show that students can be wrong about a classmate they view as a "dummy"

¶5 vocabulary in context (Chapter 2)

d 17. Which of the following is the meaning of the word *novel* as it is used in paragraph 5?
- *a.* frightening
- *b.* unpleasant
- *c.* familiar
- *d.* new

✓ **Teaching Tip**
We suggest that rather than include this Reading Skills Application section as part of the quiz grade, you use it to give students a helpful preview of upcoming skills. It makes an excellent collaborative activity. All students will find this practice helpful, especially those who must take course exit tests, standardized reading tests, or state-mandated basic skills tests.

¶15 authors' writing patterns (Chapter 7)

b 18. Which pattern has been used to organize the information in paragraph 15 of the selection?
- *a.* comparison-contrast
- *b.* cause and effect
- *c.* sequence
- *d.* list

✓ **Teaching Tip**
Signal words: *reason, because*
Cause: reading books Effect: knowing information about every subject. Cause: desire to learn about everything Effect: he read every free moment.

¶16 stated main idea (Chapter 4) ___a___ **19.** Which of the following statements best expresses the main idea of paragraph 16?

a. Within a year and a half, I went from the bottom of the class to the top of the class—much to the consternation of all the students who used to tease me and call me Dummy.

b. The same ones would come to me in the seventh grade to ask, "Hey, Benny, how do you work this problem?"

c. And I would say, "Sit at my feet, youngster, while I instruct you."

d. Other students teased Ben and called him Dummy.

author's point of view (Chapter 8) ___c___ **20.** Based on the information in the selection, the authors would most likely agree with which of the following statements?

a. Even slow learners can be successful.

b. Being a good reader is the one key to success.

c. Believing in yourself can be the key to success.

d. A person's mother is the key to his or her success.

SELECTION **1-1**

Nonfiction

(continued)

Writing and Collaborating to Enhance Your Understanding

Option for collaboration: Your instructor may direct you to work with other students or, in other words, to work *collaboratively.* In that case, you should form groups of three or four students as directed by your instructor and work together to complete the exercises. After your group discusses each item and agrees on the answer, have a group member record it. Every member of your group should be able to explain all of your group's answers.

Collaboration Option

1. Reacting to What You Have Read: Think of an experience in school—good or bad—that made you see yourself differently as a student. Describe the experience and explain how it changed the way you perceived yourself.

(Answers will vary.)

2. Comprehending the Selection Further: Even though she herself could not read, Ben Carson's mother required her young sons to read two books each week and write book reports. She pretended to read them and then put check marks on them. Based on her actions, what conclusions can you draw about the importance she placed on reading?

His mother considered it very important to have good reading and good writing skills.

His mother believed that reading a wide variety of books would help her sons gain useful information that would help them achieve later in life.

She believed that becoming better readers could help her sons start to achieve in school.

✓ **Teaching Tips**

From the start emphasize that the overall main idea must be written as a complete sentence.

Let students know that the main idea sentence can be worded more than one way *as long as the meaning is correct.*

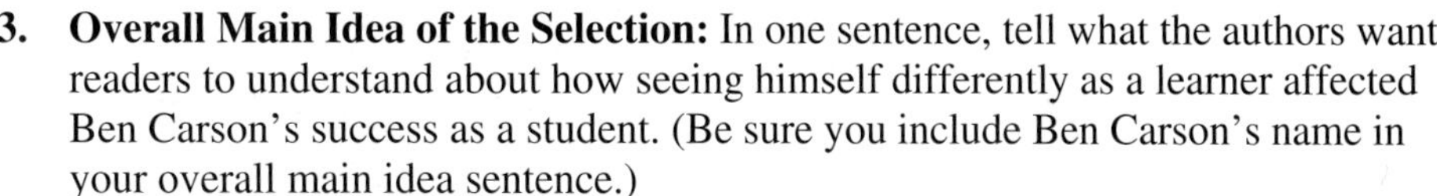

3. **Overall Main Idea of the Selection:** In one sentence, tell what the authors want readers to understand about how seeing himself differently as a learner affected Ben Carson's success as a student. (Be sure you include Ben Carson's name in your overall main idea sentence.)

Once Ben Carson began to view himself as smart, he performed that way in school.

OR

Ben Carson discovered that how we perceive ourselves influences how much we achieve.

Internet Resources

Read More about This Topic on the World Wide Web

Directions: For further information about the topic of the selection, visit these websites:

www.carsonscholars.org
This website includes color photos of Carson's book covers, information about him, and information about his foundation.

www.myhero.com
The My Hero website includes biographies and articles about extraordinary people. Type in "Ben Carson" in the Hero Search box.

www.amazon.com
This online bookstore features customer reviews of nonfiction books and novels. Type in the title of Dr. Carson's book *The Big Picture* to find readers' reviews and learn more about Dr. Carson.

You can also use your favorite search engine such as Google, Yahoo!, or AltaVista (www.google.com, www.yahoo.com, www.altavista.com) to discover more about this topic. To locate additional information, type in combinations of keywords such as:

Ben Carson

Keep in mind that whenever you go to *any* website, it is a good idea to evaluate the website and the information it contains. Ask yourself questions such as:

"Who sponsors this website?"
"Is the information contained in this website up-to-date?"
"What type of information is presented?"
"Is the information objective and complete?"
"How easy is it to use the features of this website?"

SELECTION **1-2**
Student Success

YES, YOU *CAN* STRENGTHEN YOUR MEMORY SKILLS!

From *Peak Performance: Success in College and Beyond*
By Sharon Ferrett

You may have heard people say, "I just don't have a good memory." Do you have a good memory? Do you think some people are simply born with better memories? In reality, memory is a process. As a complex process, memory is not an isolated activity that takes place in one part of the brain. It involves many factors that you can control. How well you remember depends on factors such as your attitude, interest, intent, awareness, mental alertness, observation skills, senses, distractions, memory devices, and willingness to practice. Most people with good memories say that the skill is mastered by learning the strategies for storing and recalling information.

The following selection may look lengthy, but it is clearly written and contains valuable information. It presents valuable strategies that can help you remember information. Keep in mind that the first step of remembering is consciously intending to remember. To remember information, you must be willing and interested in remembering it.

Memory Strategies

1 **1. Use all your senses.** Memory is sensory, so using all your senses (sight, hearing, touch, smell, and taste) will give your brain a better chance of retaining information. Assume that you are taking a medical terminology or vocabulary-building course. You may want to look at pictures and visualize in your mind images with the new terms or words. Actively listen in class, tape all lectures (ask for instructor's permission), and play them back later. Recite definitions and information aloud. Rewrite key words and definitions on note cards. Draw pictures and illustrations of these words whenever possible. Use the computer to write definitions or descriptions. Discuss the new terms with your study team. Try to use the new words in your own conversations. Listen for the new words and notice how others use them in conversation. Keep a log of new words, definitions, and uses of the word.

2 **2. Make learning visual.** Consider a student who is preparing for a test in a computer class. She is primarily a visual learner and feels most comfortable reading the manual, reading her textbook, and reviewing her notes. Visual learners recall information best when they see it. They like watching a video and looking at illustrations and pictures.

3 **3. Make learning auditory.** Another student in the computer class is an auditory learner. He remembers best when he hears instructions and responds more to spoken words. Auditory learners need to hear the message by listening to tapes and CDs, and talking aloud when they study.

4 **4. Make learning physical.** A third student in the computer class likes hands-on experience. He writes out commands and directions and gets actively involved. Whether you like

Prediction Exercises

Directions: Use the skill of predicting to anticipate what the upcoming paragraphs will be about.

Prediction Exercise

What do you predict the paragraphs in this section will be about?

Memory strategies

____

____

✓ Teaching Tip

Remind students that they identified their preferred learning style earlier in the chapter. See pages 16–18.

Successful students use a variety of strategies to strengthen their recall of important information.

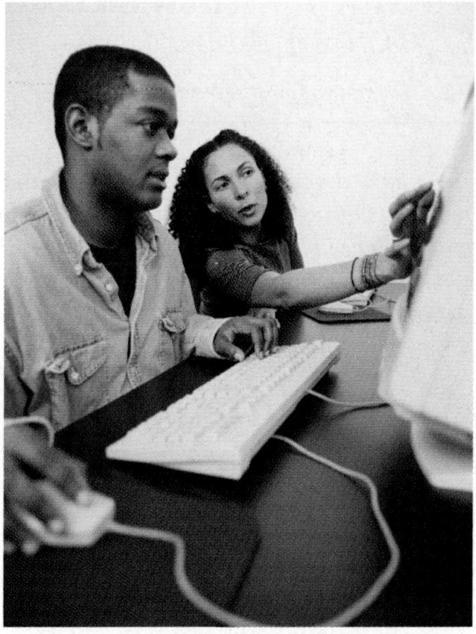

to learn by reading or listening, you will retain information better if you use all your senses and make learning physical. Read aloud, read while standing, jot down notes, lecture in front of the classroom to yourself or your study team, go on field trips, draw diagrams and models, and join a study group.

5 5. **Write down information.** Writing is physical and enhances learning. When you write down information, you are reinforcing learning by using your eyes, hand, fingers, and arm. Writing uses different parts of the brain than does speaking or listening.
   - Writing down a telephone number helps you remember it.
   - Taking notes in class prompts you to be logical and concise and fills in memory gaps.
   - Underlining important information and then copying it onto note cards reinforces information.
   - Writing a summary after reading a chapter will also reinforce information.
   - Summarizing in your own words helps to transfer information to long-term memory.

6 6. **Study in short sessions.** The brain retains information better in short study sessions. After about an hour, the brain needs a break to process information effectively. Break large goals into specific objectives and study in short sessions. For example, if you are taking a marketing course, preview a chapter in your textbook for 20 minutes and mind map the chapter on sales for 20 minutes. [Mapping is discussed in Chapter 11 of *New Worlds*.] Then, take a ten-minute break. Tips for this type of studying include:
   - Take regular, scheduled breaks.
   - Treat yourself to a small, healthy snack.
   - Return to complete your goal.

Even when you are working on something complex, such as completing a term paper or a major project, you are more effective when you take frequent breaks.

7 7. **Integrate your left brain and your right brain.** Think of both sides of your brain as members of a team that can cooperate, appreciate, and support each other. By using both sides of your brain, you can enhance your memory. For example, you may have a term paper assignment that constitutes 50 percent of your final grade. You want to turn in a well-researched, accurately written, neatly typed paper. The left side of your brain insists that it be error-free. Your preferred style of learning leans toward the right side, so your reaction to this assignment might be frustration, fear, and resistance.

8 By using a word processor, you can support both sides of the brain. You satisfy the structured side that wants a flawless paper while allowing your creative side to correct mistakes easily by using the spell check.

9 8. **Go from the general to the specific.** Many people learn best by looking at the big picture and then learning the details. Try to outline from the general (main topic) to the specific (subtopics). Previewing a chapter gives you an overview and makes the topic more meaningful. Your brain is more receptive to specific details when it has a general idea of the main topic.

10 9. **Associate and connect.** By associating and linking new material with old material, you make it meaningful. Suppose you are learning about the explorer Christopher Columbus's three ships. Think of three friends whose names start with the same first letter as the ships' names: Pinta, Santa Maria, and Nina (e.g., Paul, Sandy, and Nancy). Associate these names with the three ships, and you should be able to recall the ships' names.

11 10. **Recite.** When you say information aloud, you use your throat, voice, and lips, and you hear yourself recite. You may find this recitation technique helpful when you are dealing with difficult reading materials. Reading aloud and hearing the material will reinforce it for you and help move information from your short-term memory to your long-term memory. (See Figure on next page.) Reciting may also be helpful when preparing to give a speech. Try to practice in the actual place where you will be speaking. Visualize the audience, practice demonstrating your visual aids, write on the board, use gestures and pauses. Tape your speech and play it back. To remember names, recite the person's name when you meet and say it several times to yourself out loud.

12 11. **Use mnemonic devices.** Mnemonic (nee-MON-nik) devices are memory tricks that help you remember information. However, there are problems with memory tricks. It can take time to develop a memory trick, and it can be hard to remember the trick if you make it too complicated. Also, they don't help in understanding the information or develop skills

✓ **Teaching Tip**

With regard to item 7: Neuroscience now rejects the notion of "left brain learners" and "right brain learners" because both sides of the brain are involved in all learning. Even so, using multiple learning strategies does make learning stronger and more efficient. More than a decade ago, research indicated that the hemispheres interact to perform functions: "It is sometimes said that our brain consists of a left hemisphere that excels in intellectual, rational, verbal, and analytical thinking and a right hemisphere that excels in sensory discrimination and in emotional, nonverbal, and intuitive thinking. However, in the normal brain, with extensive commissural interconnections, the interaction of the two hemispheres is such that we cannot dissociate clearly their specialized functions." (Kandel, Schwartz, and Jessel, *Essentials of Neural Science and Behavior,* Appleton & Lange, 1995.)

"On the whole, I think it would be better for educationalists and therapists to forget about the hemispheres and concentrate on the skills themselves. The hemispheres are convenient pegs on which to hang our prejudices." (Michael Corballis, split-brain specialist and author of *The Lopsided Ape.*)

With regard to items 8–10: Remind students that on pages 5–7 (on the process for reading and studying textbooks), they were introduced to *previewing* in Step 1, Prepare to Read (a textbook assignment); to associating and connecting (*activating prior knowledge*); and to *reciting,* as part of Step 3, Review by Rehearsing the Answers to Your Questions.

Prediction Exercise

What do you predict paragraphs 12–19 will be about?

Mnemonic devices

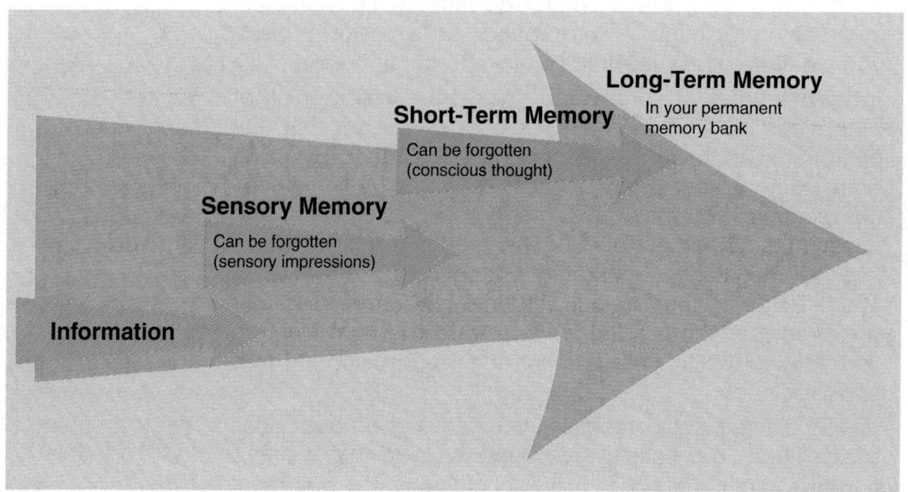

in critical thinking. Memory tricks are best used for sheer rote memorization. Some mnemonic devices include:

13 • *Rhythm and rhymes.* In elementary school, you might have learned the rhyme, "In 1492 Columbus sailed the ocean blue." It helped you to remember the date of Columbus' voyage. Rhythms can also be helpful. Many people have learned to spell the word *Mississippi* by accenting all the *i*'s and making the word rhythmic.

14 • *Acronyms.* Acronyms are words formed from the first letters of a series of other words, such as HOMES for the Great Lakes (Huron, Ontario, Michigan, Erie, and Superior) and EPCOT (Experimental Prototype Community of Tomorrow).

15 • *Grouping.* Grouping long lists of information or numbers can break up the task and make it easier for you. Most people can remember up to seven numbers in a row, so it is fortunate that phone numbers (without area codes) are no longer than that.

16 • *Association.* If your ATM identification number is 9072, you might remember it by creating associations with dates. Maybe 1990 is the year that you graduated from high school, and 1972 was the year you were born.

17 • *The method-of-place technique.* As far back as 500 B.C., the Greeks were using a method of imagery called *loci*—the method-of-place technique. This method is still effective today because it uses imagery and association to aid memory. Here's how it works:

18 Memorize a setting in detail and then place the item or information that you want to remember at certain places on your memory map. Some people like to use a familiar street, their home, or their car as a map on which to place their information. The concept is the same. You memorize certain places on your street,

✓ **Teaching Tip**
For ease in locating information, bullets are numbered as separate paragraphs.

in your home, or in your car. You memorize a specific order or path in which you visit each place. Once you have this map memorized, you can position various items to remember at different points.

19 These strategies are very effective in strengthening your memory skills. Certain strategies might work better for you than others, depending upon your personality and learning styles. Everyone has his or her personal strengths and abilities. You can master the use of memory strategies with effort, patience, and practice. As you build your memory skills, you will also enhance your study habits and become more disciplined and aware of your surroundings.

Review and Reflection

20 The sooner and the more often you review information, the easier it is to recall. Ideally, your first review should be within the first hour after hearing a lecture or reading an assignment. Carry note cards with you and review them again during that first day. Studies show that within 48 hours, you forget 85 percent of what you have learned. If you review right after you hear it and again within 24 hours, however, your recall soars to 90 percent. Discuss, write, summarize, and recite in your own words what you have just read or heard.

21 Practice information that you want to remember. For example, when you first start driver training, you learn the various steps involved in driving. At first, they may seem overwhelming. You may have to stop and think through each step. After you have driven a car for a while, however, you don't even think about all the steps required to start it and back out of the driveway. You check your mirror automatically before changing lanes, and driving safely has become a habit. The information is in your long-term memory. The more often you use information, the easier it is to recall. You could not become a good musician without hours of practice. Sports, public speaking, flying an airplane, and learning to drive all require skills that need to be repeated and practiced many times.

Prediction Exercise

What do you predict the paragraphs in this section will be about?

Review and reflection

✓ Teaching Tip

Remind students that Rehearse/Review is Step 3 of the Three-Step Process for Studying College Textbooks that is presented in Chapter 10.

Source: Adapted from Sharon Ferrett, *Peak Performance: Success in College and Beyond,* 5th ed., pp. 6-2, 6-7, 6-9, 6-11 to 6-13, 6-17.

SELECTION 1-2 Student Success *(continued)*

Comprehension and Vocabulary Quiz

This quiz has four parts. Your instructor may assign some or all of them.

Comprehension

Directions: Items 1–5 test your comprehension (understanding) of the material in this selection. These questions are much like those that a content-area instructor would expect you to know after reading and studying this selection. For each comprehension question below, use information from the selection to determine the correct answer. Refer to the selection as you answer the questions. Write your answers in the spaces provided.

¶s1–4 d **1.** Memorizing information is easier if you:

a. make learning visual.
b. make learning auditory.
c. make learning physical.
d. all of the above

¶3 b **2.** An auditory learner could memorize information more easily by:

a. writing key words and definitions on note cards.
b. talking aloud when studying.
c. going on field trips.
d. drawing diagrams and models.

¶6 a **3.** After about an hour of studying, the brain needs:

a. time to process information.
b. to be creative.
c. a healthy snack.
d. reinforcement from a study group.

¶14 a **4.** Using "ROY G. BIV" to represent the colors of the rainbow (red, orange, yellow, green, blue, indigo, violet) is an example of the mnemonic device known as:

a. an acronym.
b. grouping.
c. association.
d. imagery.

¶20 c **5.** If you do not review within 48 hours, you will forget what percent of what you have learned?

a. 24%
b. 80%
c. 85%
d. 90%

Vocabulary in Context

Directions: Items 6–10 test your ability to determine the meaning of the word by using context clues. *Context clues* are words in a sentence that allow the reader to deduce (reason out) the meaning of an unfamiliar word in that sentence. Context clues also enable the reader to determine which meaning the author intends when a word has more than one meaning. For each vocabulary item below, a sentence from the selection containing an important word (*italicized, like this*) is quoted first. Next, there is an additional sentence using the word in the same sense and providing another context clue. Use the context clues from *both* sentences to deduce the meaning of the italicized word. *Be sure the answer you choose makes sense in both sentences.* If you need to use a dictionary to confirm your answer choice, remember that the meaning you select must still fit the context of *both* sentences. Write your answers in the spaces provided.

Pronunciation Key: ă **pat** ā **pay** âr **care** ä **father** ĕ **pet** ē **be** ĭ **pit** ī **tie** îr **pier** ŏ **pot** ō **toe** ô **paw** oi **noise** ou **out** o͝o **took** o͞o **boot** ŭ **cut** yo͞o a**bu**se ûr **ur**ge th **thin** *th* **this** hw **wh**ich zh vision ə **a**bout *Stress mark:* ′

¶5, bullet 2 c

6. Taking notes in class *prompts* you to be logical and concise and fills in memory gaps.

A health scare usually *prompts* people to take better care of themselves.

prompts (prŏmpts) means:

a. prevents

b. hurries

c. moves to action

d. enables

¶5, bullet 2 b

7. Taking notes in class prompts you to be logical and *concise* and fills in memory gaps.

TV Guide gives *concise* thumbnail descriptions of shows and movies.

concise (kən sīs′) means:

a. informative

b. succinct

c. useful

d. attentive

¶7 a

8. For example, you may have a term paper assignment that *constitutes* 50 percent of your final grade.

In the United States, the Bill of Rights *constitutes* the basis of democracy.

constitutes (kŏn′ stĭ to͞ots) means:

a. amounts to; equals

b. replaces; substitutes for

c. decreases; reduces

d. is confused with

¶8 _____ **9.** You satisfy the structured side that wants a *flawless* paper while allowing your creative side to correct mistakes easily by using the spell check.

The ice skater's *flawless* performance earned her a 10 from each of the judges.

flawless (flô′ lĭs) means:

a. lengthy

b. thorough

c. simple

d. perfect; without error

¶12 _____ **10.** Memory tricks are best used for sheer *rote memorization.*

Because I did not understand the quadratic formula, I learned it by *rote memorization.*

rote memorization (rōt mĕm ə rə zā′ shən) means:

a. a memorizing process using physical movement.

b. a memorizing process using repetition, often without full comprehension

c. a memorizing process using rhymes and rhythms

d. a memorizing process using visual cues

Word Structure

Directions: Items 11–15 test your ability to use word-structure clues to help determine a word's meaning. *Word-structure clues* consist of roots, prefixes, and suffixes. In these exercises, you will learn the meaning of a word part (a root) and use it to determine the meaning of several other words that have the same word part. If you need to use a dictionary to confirm your answer choice, do so. Write your answers in the spaces provided.

In paragraph 2 of the selection, you encountered the word **visual.** This word contains the Latin root ***vis,*** which means "to see." The word *visual* describes something that can be seen by the eye or that pertains to the sense of sight. Use the meaning of ***vis*** and the list of prefixes on pages 68–69 to help you determine the meaning of each of the following words that contain the same root.

_____ **11.** If you **revise** a paper you are writing, you:

a. look for a different topic to write about.

b. look at it again to see if you need to make corrections or changes.

c. retype it.

d. start over on it.

_____ **12.** **Provisions** for a camping trip consist of:

a. things you see while camping.

b. food and other items you foresee that you will need.

c. the plans you make.

d. the route you plan to drive to get there.

d 13. In the business world, Bill Gates is considered **visionary** because he:
a. tells fantasy stories.
b. sees things all wrong.
c. prescribes glasses.
d. foresees what will be important in the future.

c 14. A **visionless** person:
a. has no imagination.
b. has no glasses.
c. is blind.
d. wears glasses.

b 15. An Olympic downhill skier who **visualizes** the course before competing:
a. skis the course first for practice.
b. sees the course in his or her mind.
c. looks at a picture of the course ahead of time.
d. looks at a map of the course.

✓ **Teaching Tip**
Let students know that the skills included in this Reading Skills Application section have not been introduced yet. This section serves as a valuable preview of these skills, however. Students typically get several of the items correct, and they find this encouraging.

Reading Skills Application

Directions: Items 16–20 test your ability to *apply* certain reading skills to information in this selection. These types of questions provide valuable practice for all students, especially those who must take standardized reading tests and statemandated basic skills tests. You have not studied all of the skills at this point, so these items will serve as a helpful preview. The comprehension and critical reading skills in this section are presented in Chapters 3 through 9 of *New Worlds;* vocabulary and figurative language skills are presented in Chapter 2. As you work through *New Worlds,* you will practice and develop these skills. Write your answers in the spaces provided.

title; numbered items; authors' writing patterns (Chapter 7)

c 16. The overall organization of the selection is a:
a. comparison.
b. sequence.
c. list.
d. contrast.

¶17 supporting details (Chapter 6)

b 17. According to information in the selection, the method-of-place technique:
a. uses recitation.
b. has been used for centuries.
c. is based on rhymes.
d. involves grouping.

¶15 conclusion (Chapter 9)

c 18. It can be concluded that a ZIP code is easier to remember than a driver's license number because:
a. the ZIP code can be made into an acronym.
b. you can use all of your senses to learn it.
c. a ZIP code has fewer than 7 digits.
d. you can apply the method-of-place technique to learn the ZIP code.

¶12 author's point of view (Chapter 8) ___c___ **19.** The author would be most likely to agree with which of the following statements?

a. Mnemonics should be used all of the time.

b. Mnemonics are foolproof.

c. Mnemonics are useful, but they have limitations.

d. Mnemonics are difficult to learn.

¶21 stated main idea (Chapter 4) ___a___ **20.** Which of the following sentences represents the main idea of paragraph 21?

a. Practice information that you want to remember.

b. For example, when you first start driver training, you learn the various steps involved in driving.

c. You may have to stop and think through each step.

d. Sports, public speaking, flying an airplane, and learning to drive all require skills that need to be repeated and practiced many times.

✓ **Teaching Tip**

We suggest that rather than include this section as part of the quiz grade, you use it to give students practice with the skills they have studied and as a helpful preview of upcoming skills. It makes an excellent collaborative activity. All students will find this practice helpful, especially those who must take course exit tests, standardized reading tests, or state-mandated basic skills tests.

SELECTION **1-2**

Student Success

(continued)

Collaboration Option

Writing and Collaborating to Enhance Your Understanding

Option for collaboration: Your instructor may direct you to work with other students or, in other words, to work *collaboratively.* In that case, you should form groups of three or four students as directed by your instructor and work together to complete the exercises. After your group discusses each item and agrees on the answer, have a group member record it. Every member of your group should be able to explain all of your group's answers.

1. **Reacting to What You Have Read:** Of the memory strategies mentioned in the selection, which ones do you already use? Describe the courses and/or ways in which you use them. (If you do not use any of the techniques mentioned in the selection, describe thc techniques that you use instead.)

(Answers will vary.)
____
____
____
____
____
____

2. **Comprehending the Selection Further:** Based on information in the selection about learning styles and memory techniques, check which techniques might work best for each style. For each strategy, place a check mark in the appropriate column. Some strategies may work for more than one type of learner.

	Visual Learners	Auditory Learners	Hands-on Learners
1. Recite definitions.		✓	
2. Draw pictures and illustrations.	✓		✓
3. Read the textbook silently.	✓		
4. Write out key terms and important information.	✓		✓
5. Listen to tapes of class lectures.		✓	
6. Participate in study groups.		✓	
7. Watch a video.	✓		
8. Actively listen in class.		✓	
9. Build a model.			✓
10. Read the textbook aloud.		✓	

3. **Overall Main Idea of the Selection:** In one sentence, tell what the author wants readers to understand about memory. (Be sure to include the word "memory" in your overall main idea sentence.)

You can strengthen your *memory* if you use certain memory strategies and techniques, review material soon after encountering it, and then practice the information.

Internet Resources

Read More about This Topic on the World Wide Web

Directions: For further information about the topic of the selection, visit these websites:

www.usu.edu/arc/idea_sheets/index.htm
This site is sponsored by the Utah Academic Resource Center. It presents "Idea Sheets" that contain information, strategies, self-assessment, and practice exercises. Check out the section on "Memory Improvement"; it includes idea sheets on concentration, forgetting, memory improvement, and mnemonic devices.

www.mindtools.com/pages/main/newMN_TIM.htm
This site provides a wealth of information about the principles behind the use of mnemonic devices, as well as an array of specific techniques.

You can also use your favorite search engine such as Google, Yahoo!, or AltaVista (www.google.com, www.yahoo.com, www.altavista.com) to discover more about this topic. To locate additional information, type in combinations of keywords such as:

memory strategies

or

mnemonics

Keep in mind that whenever you go to *any* website, it is a good idea to evaluate the website and the information it contains. Ask yourself questions such as:

"Who sponsors this website?"

"Is the information contained in this website up-to-date?"

"What type of information is presented?"

"Is the information objective and complete?"

"How easy is it to use the features of this website?"

SELECTION 1-3
Study Skills

WISE UP! THE WHEN AND HOW OF PREPARING FOR TESTS

From *P.O.W.E.R. Learning: Strategies for Success in College and Life*
By Robert S. Feldman

Do you feel uneasy whenever your instructor announces that there will be a test? Do you wait until the last minute to start preparing for tests? Are you usually surprised by the types of questions or type of material on tests? If you answered yes to any of these questions, then this selection is for you! The author, Dr. Robert Feldman, is a psychology professor who has extensive expertise in strategies for academic success.

As noted at the beginning of this chapter, you should start preparing for your final exams from the first day of the semester. In other words, you should learn as you go. In this selection, Dr. Feldman takes this a step further by giving specific strategies for preparing for various types of test questions and for dealing with test anxiety. This reading selection is presented in Chapter 1 of New Worlds *so that you can use the valuable techniques in it from the beginning of the semester. Chapter 11 presents strategies for organizing textbook information so that you can learn it for tests.*

Ready Your Test-Taking Skills

1 How much you reap the benefits of a test depends on a number of considerations: the kind of test it is, the subject matter involved, and above all how well you prepare for it. Preparation for tests requires a number of strategies. Among the most important are the following:

Remember Everything You Do in a Course Is Preparation for a Test

2 Completing a reading assignment. Writing a paper. Filling out a worksheet. Everything you do during a course helps to prepare you for a test. There is no surer way to get good grades on tests than to attend class faithfully and to complete all class assignments seriously and on time. Preparing for tests is a long-term proposition. It's not a matter of "giving your all" the night before the test. Instead, it's a matter of giving your all to every aspect of the course.

Know What You Are Preparing For

3 Determine as much as you can about the test before you begin to prepare for it. The more you know about the test, the better you'll be able to get ready. To find out about an upcoming test, ask these questions:

- Is the test called a "test," "exam," "quiz," or something else? As you can see in Table 1 on page 48, the names imply different things. For simplicity's sake, we'll use the term *test* throughout this selection, but know that these distinctions exist and they should affect the way you prepare.
- What material will the test cover?
- How many questions will be on it?
- How much time is it expected to take? A full class period? Only part of the period?

Prediction Exercises

Directions: Use the skill of predicting to anticipate what certain sections will be about. At each of the points indicated below, answer the question "What do you predict this section will be about?"

- What kinds of questions will be on the test?
- How will it be graded?
- Will sample questions be provided?
- Are tests from previous terms available?

Form a Study Group

4 Study groups are small, informal groups of students who work together to learn the course material and study for a test. Forming such a group can be an excellent way to prepare. Some study groups are formed for particular tests, while others meet consistently throughout the term.

5 The typical study group meets a week or two before a test and plans a strategy for studying. Members share their understanding of what will be on the test, based on their own perceptions of what an instructor has said in class about the upcoming test. Together, they develop a list of review questions to guide their individual study. The group breaks up and the members study on their own.

6 A few days before the test, members of the study group meet again. They discuss answers to the review questions, go over the material, and share any new information they may have about the upcoming test. They may also quiz one another about the material to identify any weaknesses or gaps in their knowledge.

7 Study groups can be extremely powerful tools because they help accomplish several things:

- They help members to organize and structure the material, which forces members to approach the material in a systematic and logical way.
- They aid in the sharing of different perspectives on the material.
- They help prevent students from overlooking any potentially important information.
- They force their members to rethink the course material, explaining it in words that they and the other group members will understand. This helps both understanding and recall of the information when it is needed on the test.
- They also help motivate members to do their best. When you're part of a study group, you're no longer working just for yourself; your studying also benefits the other study-group members. Not wanting to let down your classmates in a study group may sometimes give more of a push to your study habits than you get from working only for yourself.

8 There are some potential drawbacks to keep in mind. Study groups don't always work well for students with certain kinds of learning styles in which they prefer to work independently. In addition, "problem" members, who don't pull their weight, may result in difficulties for the group. In general, though, the advantages of study groups usually far outweigh their possible disadvantages.

TABLE 1
QUIZZES, TESTS, EXAMS . . . WHAT'S IN A NAME?

Although they may vary from one instructor to another, the following definitions are the ones most frequently used:

Quizzes. A **quiz** is a brief assessment, usually covering a relatively small amount of material. Some quizzes cover as little as one class's worth of reading. Although a single quiz usually doesn't count very much, instructors often add quiz scores together, and collectively they can become a significant part of your final course grade.

Tests. A **test** is a more extensive, more heavily weighted assessment than a quiz, covering more material. A test may come every few weeks of the term, often after each third or quarter of the term has passed, but this varies with the instructor and the course.

Exams. An **exam** is the most substantial kind of assessment. In many classes, just one exam is given—a *final exam* at the end of the term. Sometimes there are two exams, one at the midpoint of the term (called, of course, a midterm) and the other at the end. Exams are usually weighted quite heavily because they are meant to assess your knowledge of all the course material up to that point.

✓ **Teaching Tips**

Even though a student's ability to focus and work productively in a study group has a lot to do with his or her learning style, encourage students to try creating study groups for your course. Help them create a schedule of meeting times.

When you assign the first test in your course, go back and review this selection with them. They should be able to answer the questions in the section "Know What You Are Preparing For."

Match Test Preparation to Question Types

9 Test questions come in different types (see Table 1, page 48), and each requires a somewhat different style of preparation.

10 **Essay Questions** Essay questions are meant to see if you have a broad knowledge of the material being tested. You'll need to know not just a series of facts, but also the connections between them, and you will have to be able to discuss these ideas in an organized and logical way. Essay exams focus on the ways in which the various pieces of information on a topic fit together. The best approach to studying for an essay exam involves four steps:

- Carefully read your class notes and any notes you've made on assigned readings that will be covered on the upcoming exam. Also go through the readings themselves, reviewing underlined or highlighted material and marginal notes.
- Play professor: Think of likely exam questions. To do this, you can use the key words, phrases, concepts, and questions you've earlier created in your notes. In addition, your instructor may have given you a list of possible essay topics.
- Without looking at your notes or your readings, answer each potential essay question aloud. Don't feel embarrassed about doing this. Talking aloud is often more useful than answering the questions silently in your head. You can also write down the main points that any answer should cover. But you probably shouldn't write out complete and full answers to the questions, because your time is probably better spent learning the material you'll be tested on. The one exception: if your instructor tells you exactly what essay question is going to be on the exam. In that case, it pays to write out the answer.
- After you've answered the questions, check yourself by looking at the notes and readings once again. If you feel confident that you've answered particular questions adequately, check them off. You can go back later for a quick review. But if there are questions that you have trouble with, review that material immediately. Then repeat the third step above, answering the questions again.

Prediction Exercise

What do you predict this section (paragraphs 9–16) will be about?

(Answers will vary.)

✓ **Teaching Tips**

See Chapter 10, Step 3 (of the process for studying college textbooks), p. 562. See also Chapter 11, pp. 617–618, on rehearsal and memory.

Study groups, made up of a few students who study together for a test, not only help members organize material, but can also provide new perspectives and motivate members to do their best.

11 **Multiple-Choice, True-False, and Matching Questions** While the focus of review for essay questions should be on major issues and controversies, and on integration of the material—more of a "big picture" focus—studying for multiple-choice, true-false, and matching questions requires more attention to the details.

12 Almost anything is fair game for multiple-choice, true-false, and matching questions, and so you can't afford to overlook anything when studying. This means that your studying needs to be detail-oriented. And it means that you must put your memory into high gear and master a great many facts.

13 It's a particularly good idea to write down important facts on index cards like the samples below. Remember the advantages of these cards: They're portable and available all the time, and the act of creating them helps drive the material into your memory. Furthermore, you can shuffle them and test yourself repeatedly until you know you've mastered the material.

✓ **Teaching Tip**
Help students make the connection between these cards and the Chapter Review cards they are learning to make in *New Worlds*.

14 **Short-Answer and Fill-In Questions** Short-answer and fill-in questions are similar to essays in that they require you to recall key pieces of information; that is, you have to dredge the information up from your memory rather than, as is the case with multiple-choice, true-false, and matching questions, finding it on the page in front of you. However, short-answer and fill-in questions—unlike essay questions—typically don't demand that you integrate or compare different types of

Political reforms of progressive age:

-direct primaries: people vote for whom they want to run; not appointed
-initiative: people propose laws on their own
-referendum: gov. proposes; people say yes or no
-recall: people can remove politicians from office before they finish term

Endoplasmic reticulum (ER):

Smooth ER—makes fats (lipids)
Rough ER—has ribosomes which make proteins

Together, they make membranes for whole cell
(for plasma membrane, mitochondrion, etc.)
Also make more of themselves

information. Consequently, the focus of your study should be on the recall of specific, detailed information.

15 **Test Yourself** Once you feel you've mastered the material, test yourself on it. There are several ways to do this. One is to create a complete test for yourself in writing, making its form as close as possible to what you expect the actual test to be. For instance, if your instructor has told you the classroom test will be primarily made up of short-answer questions, your test should be too. One bonus: Constructing a test is actually an excellent way of studying the material and cementing it into memory.

16 You might also construct a test and administer it to a classmate or a member of your study group. In turn, you could take a test that someone else has constructed. The combined experience of making and taking a test on the same general subject matter is among the very best ways to prepare for the real thing.

✓ **Teaching Tip**

Chapter 11 presents information about marking and annotating textbooks, outlining, mapping, and summarizing—valuable test preparation techniques. (It also includes the section "How Are Rehearsal and Memory Related?" pp. 617–618.)

17 **Deal with Test Anxiety** What does the anticipation of a test do to you? Do you feel shaky? Frantic, like there's not enough time to get it all done? Do you feel as if there's a knot in your stomach? Do you grit your teeth? Fortunately, test anxiety is a temporary condition characterized by fears and concerns about test taking. Almost everyone experiences it to some degree, but if it is too great, it can make it harder for you to study and do your best on a test.

18 You'll never eliminate test anxiety completely, nor do you want to. A little bit of nervousness can energize you, making you more attentive and vigilant. Like any competitive event, testing can motivate you to do your best. So think of test anxiety as a desire to perform at your peak—an ally at test time.

19 On the other hand, for many, anxiety can spiral into the kind of paralyzing fear that makes your mind go blank. So you definitely want to keep it in its place. There are several ways to do this:

Prediction Exercise

What do you predict this section (paragraphs 17–19) will be about?

(Answers will vary.)

- *Prepare thoroughly.* The more you prepare, the less test anxiety you'll feel. Good preparation can give you a sense of control and mastery, and it will prevent test anxiety from overwhelming you.
- *Take a realistic view of the test.* Remember that no single test determines how you'll do for the rest of your life. Your future success does not hinge on your performance on any single exam.
- *Learn relaxation techniques.* You can learn to reduce or even eliminate the jittery physical symptoms of test anxiety by using relaxation techniques. The basic process is straightforward: You want to breathe evenly, gently inhaling and exhaling. Focus your mind on a pleasant, relaxing scene such as a beautiful forest or a peaceful spread of farmland, or on a sound such as ocean waves.
- *Visualize success.* Think of an image of your instructor handing back your test, on which you've received an A. Or imagine your instructor congratulating you on your fine performance the moment you walk into your classroom on the day after the test. Positive visualizations such as these, which highlight your potential success, can help replace negative images of failure that may be fueling your test anxiety.

✓ **Teaching Tip**

Point out that students sometimes say they "go blank" on tests when the reality is, they are blank to begin with—they just discover it when they take the tests. The solution: better test preparation. If they can't say or write information from memory before the test, they don't know it.

Source: Adapted from Robert S. Feldman, *P.O.W.E.R. Learning: Strategies for Success in College and Life,* pp. 142–148.

SELECTION 1-3
Study Skills
(continued)

Comprehension and Vocabulary Quiz

This quiz has four parts. Your instructor may assign some or all of them.

Comprehension

Directions: Items 1–5 test your comprehension (understanding) of the material in this selection. These questions are much like those that a content-area instructor would expect you to know after studying this selection. For each comprehension question below, use information from the selection to determine the correct answer. Refer to the selection as you answer the questions. Write your answers in the spaces provided.

All ¶s ___d___ **1.** A good strategy for preparing for a test is to:

a. find out as much as you can about the type of test, length, grading, etc.
b. match your test preparation to the type of questions that will be on the test.
c. form a small study group.
d. all of the above

¶13 ___a___ **2.** Preparing study cards is an effective way to prepare for multiple-choice test questions because:

a. the very act of creating them helps drive the material into your memory.
b. they allow you to discover different perspectives on the material.
c. they allow you to "play professor."
d. they help you "give your all" the night before the test.

¶15 ___c___ **3.** In order to prepare for any exam, you should:

a. memorize as many specific details as possible in the order that they were presented in class.
b. eliminate test anxiety completely.
c. test yourself on the material once you feel you've mastered it.
d. all of the above

¶14 ___d___ **4.** Essay questions are similar to short-answer and fill-in questions in that they both:

a. require you to integrate and compare different types of information.
b. require more attention to details when you are studying.
c. require you to put your memory in high gear and master a great many facts.
d. require you to recall key pieces of information.

¶7 ___d___ **5.** Most students benefit from participating in a study group because it:

a. helps prevent students from overlooking any potentially important information.
b. forces members to approach the material in a systematic and logical way.
c. helps motivate members to do their best.
d. all of the above

Vocabulary in Context

Directions: Items 6–10 test your ability to determine the meaning of the word by using context clues. *Context clues* are words in a sentence that allow the reader to deduce (reason out) the meaning of an unfamiliar word in that sentence. Context clues also enable the reader to determine which meaning the author intends when a word has more than one meaning. For each vocabulary item below, a sentence from the selection containing an important word (*italicized, like this*) is quoted first. Next, there is an additional sentence using the word in the same sense and providing another context clue. Use the context clues from *both* sentences to deduce the meaning of the italicized word. *Be sure the answer you choose makes sense in both sentences.* If you need to use a dictionary to confirm your answer choice, remember that the meaning you select must still fit the context of *both* sentences. Write your answers in the spaces provided.

Pronunciation Key: ă **pat** ā **pay** âr **care** ä **father** ĕ **pet** ē **be** ĭ **pit** ī **tie** îr **pier** ŏ **pot** ō **toe** ô **paw** oi **noise** ou **out** o͝o **took** o͞o **boot** ŭ **cut** yo͞o a**buse** ûr **urge** th **thin** *th* **this** hw **which** zh **vision** ə **about** *Stress mark:* ′

¶7 ___b___ **6.** Study groups help members to organize and structure the material, which forces members to approach the material in a *systematic* and logical way.

Using a *systematic* approach to managing your money can lead you to early financial freedom and security.

systematic (sĭs tə măt′ ĭk) means:

a. related to money

b. methodical in procedure or plan

c. determined by a group rather than an individual

d. difficult and unrewarding

¶8 ___b___ **7.** In general, though, the advantages of study groups usually far *outweigh* their possible disadvantages.

Our company president took early retirement because he felt the stress of the job had begun to *outweigh* the benefits.

outweigh (out wā′) means:

a. to cancel out

b. to have greater importance than

c. to weigh more than

d. to decrease

¶14 ___c___ **8.** Short-answer and fill-in questions are similar to essays in that they require you to recall key pieces of information; that is, you have to *dredge* the information up from your memory rather than, as is the case with multiple-choice, true-false, and matching questions, finding it on the page in front of you.

My grandmother is remarkable: It takes her a few minutes, but she is always able to *dredge* up birthdates of all 16 of her grandchildren.

dredge (drĕj) means:

a. to record in written form

b. to forget

c. to come up with by deep searching

d. to comment upon with insight

¶18 ___d___ **9.** A little bit of nervousness can energize you, making you more attentive and *vigilant.*

Vigilant parents would never allow their elementary-school-age children to go to the mall unsupervised or alone.

vigilant (vĭj′ ə lənt) means:

a. selfish and uncaring

b. extremely immature

c. highly emotional

d. alertly watchful

¶19 ___a___ **10.** Positive visualizations such as these, which highlight your potential success, can help replace negative images of failure that may be *fueling* your test anxiety.

The actor and his wife were seen having a loud argument in public, thus *fueling* rumors of a possible divorce.

fueling (fyo͞o ′ əl ĭng) means:

a. supporting; stimulating

b. diminishing; decreasing

c. ending; stopping

d. spreading

Word Structure

Directions: Items 11–15 test your ability to use word-structure clues to help determine a word's meaning. *Word-structure clues* consist of roots, prefixes, and suffixes. In these exercises, you will learn the meaning of a word part (a root) and use it to determine the meaning of the several other words that have the same word part. If you need to use a dictionary to confirm an answer choice, do so. Write your answers in the spaces provided.

In paragraph 13 of the selection, you encountered the word **portable.** This word contains the Latin root ***port,*** which means "to carry" or "to bear." The word *portable* describes something that can be carried or moved about. Use the meaning of ***port*** and the list of prefixes on pages 68–69 to help you determine the meaning of each of the following words that contain this same root.

___a___ **11.** If someone is arrested for **transporting** illegal goods across a state line, the person was trying to:

a. move illegal goods from one state to another.

b. sneak across the state line.

c. induce others to pursue a life of crime.
d. report a crime to the police.

b **12.** Newspaper and television **reporters** gather information and:
a. write it down.
b. bring it to the public.
c. disprove it.
d. speak it into a microphone.

c **13.** People who are in the **import-export** business:
a. sell items in a retail store.
b. inspect products brought into a country.
c. bring some products into a country and send out others.
d. produce items to be sold wholesale.

d **14.** If illegal immigrants are **deported** from a country, they are:
a. charged with a crime.
b. placed in jail.
c. given citizenship.
d. legally forced to leave the country.

c **15.** If there are large beams that **support** the roof of a structure, the beams:
a. angle toward the ceiling.
b. are curved.
c. bear the weight of the roof.
d. are made of wood.

✓ **Teaching Tip**
Let students know that the skills included in this Reading Skills Application section have not been introduced yet. This section serves as a valuable preview of these skills, however. Students typically get several of the items correct, and they find this encouraging.

Reading Skills Application

Directions: Items 16–20 test your ability to *apply* certain reading skills to information in this selection. These types of questions provide valuable practice for all students, especially those who must take standardized reading tests and state-mandated basic skills tests. You have not studied all of the skills at this point, so these items will serve as a helpful preview. The comprehension and critical reading skills in this section are presented in Chapters 3 through 9 of *New Worlds;* vocabulary and figurative language skills are presented in Chapter 2. As you work through *New Worlds,* you will practice and develop these skills. Write your answers in the spaces provided.

author's purpose for writing (Chapter 8)

b **16.** What is the author's primary purpose for writing this selection?
a. to prove that test preparation and test grades are highly correlated
b. to explain how to prepare for tests and deal with test anxiety
c. to explain the different types of tests
d. to prove that working with a study group can enhance test performance

¶10 vocabulary in context (Chapter 2)

d **17.** Which of the following is the meaning of *key* as it is used in the second bulleted item in paragraph 10?
a. familiar
b. confusing

c. foreign

d. important

¶7 author's writing patterns (Chapter 7) ___d___ **18.** Which pattern has been used to organize the information in paragraph 7 of the selection?

a. comparison and contrast

b. cause and effect

c. sequence

d. list

author's point of view (Chapter 8) ___a___ **19.** Based on the information in the selection, the author would most likely agree with which of the following statements?

a. If students know more about test preparation, they can improve their performance on tests.

b. Test anxiety is a fact of life and nothing can be done about it.

c. There are test-taking techniques that can make every student successful in college.

d. Study groups are the secret of success when preparing for tests in college.

✓ **Teaching Tip**
We suggest that rather than include this section as part of the quiz grade, you use it to give students practice with the skills they have studied and as a helpful preview of upcoming skills. It makes an excellent collaborative activity. All students will find this practice helpful, especially those who must take course exit tests, standardized reading tests, or state-mandated basic skills tests.

author's credibility (Chapter 9) ___c___ **20.** The author has credibility because he:

a. has had experience himself as a highly successful college student.

b. presents the results of interviews with successful students.

c. is an expert on learning and study skills.

d. has conducted extensive research projects on study skills.

✓ **Teaching Tip**
Explain that if an author has *credibility,* it means readers can *believe* or *trust* what the writer is telling them.

SELECTION **1-3**
Study Skills
(continued)

Writing and Collaborating to Enhance Your Understanding

Option for collaboration: Your instructor may direct you to work with other students or, in other words, to work *collaboratively.* In that case, you should form groups of three or four students as directed by your instructor and work together to complete the exercises. After your group discusses each item and agrees on the answer, have a group member record it. Every member of your group should be able to explain all of your group's answers.

Collaboration Option

1. Reacting to What You Have Read: "Know thyself," the old saying goes. Through experience, most college students discover techniques that prepare them to do well on tests. List at least three things that you have discovered that help *you* prepare effectively for tests.

(Answers will vary.)
___
___
___
___
___
___

2. **Comprehending the Selection Further:** List and explain the four ways to deal with test anxiety.

- *Prepare thoroughly.* (The more you prepare, the less test anxiety you'll feel. Good preparation can give you a sense of control and mastery.)
- *Take a realistic view of the test.* (Remind yourself that your future success does not hinge on your performance on any single exam.)
- *Learn relaxation techniques.* (Breathe evenly and gently. Focus your mind on a pleasant, relaxing scene.)
- *Visualize success.* (Imagine receiving an A on your test; imagine your instructor congratulating you on your fine performance on the test.)

✓ **Teaching Tip**
Continue to stress that the overall main idea must be expressed as a complete sentence.

3. **Overall Main Idea of the Selection:** In one sentence, tell what the author wants readers to understand about what you should do when preparing for tests. (Be sure to include the words "prepare," "test," and "test anxiety" in your overall main idea sentence.)

There are many things you can do to prepare successfully for a test and deal with test anxiety.

Internet Resources

Read More about This Topic on the World Wide Web

Directions: For further information about the topic of the selection, visit these websites:

www.aboutcollege.com
The About College website contains information pertinent to students, parents, and anyone else interested in learning about the adjustment to college life.

www.mhhe.com/power
This website presents additional information about Professor Feldman's textbook, *P.O.W.E.R. Learning: Strategies for Success in College and Life.*

You can also use your favorite search engine such as Google, Yahoo!, or AltaVista (www.google.com, www.yahoo.com, www.altavista.com) to discover more about this topic. To locate additional information, type in combinations of keywords such as:

test taking
or
test anxiety

Keep in mind that whenever you go to *any* website, it is a good idea to evaluate the website and the information it contains. Ask yourself questions such as:

"Who sponsors this website?"
"Is the information contained in this website up-to-date?"
"What type of information is presented?"
"Is the information objective and complete?"
"How easy is it to use the features of this website?"

CHAPTER 2

Developing a College-Level Vocabulary

A New World of Words

CHAPTER OBJECTIVES

In this chapter you will learn the answers to these questions:

- Why is it important for me to develop a college-level vocabulary?
- What are context clues, and how can I use them?
- What are word-structure clues, and how can I use them?
- How do I use a dictionary pronunciation key?
- What is figurative language?
- How do I interpret figures of speech?

✓ Timely Words

"Words are the soul's ambassadors who go abroad on her errands to and fro." (James Howell, writer)

"Genius without education is like silver in a mine." (Benjamin Franklin)

"An investment in knowledge always pays the best interest." (Benjamin Franklin)

CHAPTER CONTENTS

Why Is It Important to Develop a College-Level Vocabulary?

What Are Context Clues, and How Do You Use Them?

What Are Word-Structure Clues, and How Do You Use Them?

How Do You Use a Dictionary Pronunciation Key?

What Is Figurative Language, and How Do You Interpret Figures of Speech?

Other Things to Keep in Mind When Developing A College-Level Vocabulary

- Certain punctuation marks in a sentence can signal a definition.
- The most common and helpful roots, prefixes, and suffixes in English come from Latin and ancient Greek.
- A word's etymology (origin and history) indicates the word parts it was created from, including Latin or Greek ones.

CREATING CHAPTER REVIEW CARDS

TEST YOUR UNDERSTANDING

Context Clues

Word-Structure Clues

Figurative Language

READINGS

Selection 2-1 ***(Human Development)***
"Should Teenagers Work Part-Time?"
from *Human Development* by Diane Papalia and Sally Olds

Selection 2-2 ***(Business)***
"McDonaldization: The Sun Never Sets on the Golden Arches"
from *Understanding Business* by William Nickels, James McHugh, and Susan McHugh

Selection 2-3 ***(Health)***
"Rage on the Road: The Danger of Aggressive Driving"
from *Understanding Your Health* by Wayne Payne and Dale Hahn

WHY IS IT IMPORTANT TO DEVELOP A COLLEGE-LEVEL VOCABULARY?

The most important reason to develop a college-level vocabulary, of course, is so that you can understand your college textbooks. Increasing your vocabulary can make your college work easier in other ways besides reading. It will enable you to understand more of what others—especially professors—say. It will make your own speaking and writing more precise and more interesting. If all that is not enough, your increased vocabulary may result in an increased salary. Research tells us that the size of a person's vocabulary correlates with how much money the person earns: The larger your vocabulary, the larger your income is likely to be. Thinking of each word you learn as potential "money in the bank" may be an incentive for you to add new words to your vocabulary! Indeed, developing a powerful vocabulary is a process that takes time and effort, but it is an asset that will benefit you all your life.

How can you develop a strong vocabulary? Read. Every time you read, you have an opportunity to expand your vocabulary. The more you read, the better your vocabulary can become—*if* you develop an interest in words and their meanings.

When you read, there are four strategies you can use to expand your vocabulary. The strategies are:

1. **Use context clues.** Reason out the likely meaning of a word from clues provided by the surrounding words and sentences. The word might be completely unfamiliar to you, or it might be a common word that has another meaning you are unaware of. Ask yourself, "What would this word have to mean in order to make sense in this sentence?"
2. **Use word-structure clues.** Determine a word's meaning by examining any prefix, root, or suffix it contains.
3. **Use a dictionary.** Determine a word's pronunciation and the precise meaning as it is used in the passage you are reading.
4. **Know how to interpret figurative language.** Understand the nonliteral meaning of words and phrases when they are used in figures of speech.

In this chapter, we will take a close look at each of these skills. To give you ample practice applying them, there are extensive vocabulary exercises that accompany every reading selection in *New Worlds*.

WHAT ARE CONTEXT CLUES, AND HOW DO YOU USE THEM?

KEY TERM
context clues

Words in a sentence or paragraph that help the reader deduce (reason out) the meaning of an unfamiliar word.

Textbook authors want you to understand what they have written. When they use words that might be unfamiliar to the reader, they often help by providing context clues. **Context clues** are words in a sentence or paragraph that help the reader deduce (reason out) the meaning of an unfamiliar word. Such clues are called "context" clues because *context* refers to the setting in which something occurs. In this case, it refers to the rest of the sentence and the paragraph in which the unfamiliar word appears.

Context clues can help you figure out the meaning of an unfamiliar word, so think of them as gifts the writer gives you to make your job easier. How can you take advantage of these "gifts"? Simply read the sentence carefully and pay attention to the words and other sentences surrounding the unfamiliar word. If you encounter an unfamiliar word when you are reading, ask yourself, "What would this word have to mean in order for it to make sense in this sentence?" For example, suppose you read this sentence: "My four-year-old nephew Carlos loves cookies, cakes, candy, *churros*, and anything else that is sweet." You can deduce the meaning of the word *churros* from

Developing a strong vocabulary takes time and effort, but it is well worth it.

the context: It is some type of dessert or snack food. The context clues in this sentence are the examples of "cookies, cakes, candy" and the words "and anything else that is sweet." For the sentence to make sense, *churros* would have to refer to some type of sweet, sugary food. (You may already know that *churros* are sugar-coated, fried-dough snacks that are enjoyed throughout Latin America.)

✓ **Teaching Tip**
Starting each row of the context clue chart with the example gives students a chance to *reason out* each type of context clue. This enhances their understanding.

For words with more than one meaning, context clues can also help you determine which meaning the author intends. You may know one meaning of the word *consume* is "to eat," as in this sentence: "Americans consume millions of hot dogs every year." Suppose, however, you encounter this sentence: "On average, Americans consume almost 19 million barrels of oil a day." "Eat" makes no sense in a sentence about consuming barrels of oil. You can deduce, therefore, that in this sentence, the word consume means "use." This is the meaning the author intends.

In the chart on page 63 are six common types of context clues. The chart explains what to ask yourself and what to look for when you encounter each type of context clue. The chart then presents example sentences that illustrate each type of context clue. You also have the opportunity to learn the meaning of any unfamiliar words in the example sentences.

Using the context is the first strategy you should use when you encounter an unknown word. Remember, however, that context clues enable you to make an educated guess; they do not always allow you to determine the meaning of a word accurately. For example, you might read the sentence "He spent the entire weekend visiting used car dealerships, but in spite of his *exhaustive* search he was unable to find a suitable car in his price range." Although *exhaustive* might appear from the context to mean "exhausting" or "tiring," it actually means "thorough" or "complete." (For example, a scientist might do exhaustive research about a particular subject.) In this case, the context is not sufficient to reason out the meaning of the word.

USING CONTEXT CLUES TO DETERMINE THE MEANING OF UNFAMILIAR WORDS

Example	Type of Clue	What to Ask Yourself	What to Look For
A ***panic attack*** is *defined as* a mood disorder that is characterized by sudden, unexpected feelings of fear.	***Definition clue***	Are there *definition clues* and a definition?	Phrases that introduce a definition, such as: *is defined as, is called, is, is known as, that is, refers to, means, the term;* a term that is in bold print, italics, or color; certain punctuation marks that set off a definition or a term. (See pages 76–77.)
A ***puma,*** *or mountain lion,* has a large, powerful body.	***Synonym clue***	Is there a *synonym* for the unfamiliar word? That is, is the meaning explained by a word or phrase that has a *similar meaning*? The synonym may be set off by commas, parentheses, a colon, dashes, or brackets. (See pages 76–77.)	Phrases that introduce synonyms, such as: *in other words, or, that is to say, also known as, by this we mean, that is.*
Unlike his *talkative* older brother, Alvin is a ***taciturn*** person.	***Contrast clue***	Is there an *antonym* for the unfamiliar word? That is, is the unfamiliar word explained by a contrasting word or phrase with the *opposite meaning*?	Words and phrases that indicate opposites: *instead of, but, in contrast, on the other hand, however, unlike, although, even though.*
Because he prefers ***solitude,*** *he lives alone in an isolated mountain cabin with no telephone.*	***Experience clue***	Can you draw on your *experience and background knowledge* to help you deduce (reason out) the meaning of the unfamiliar word?	A sentence that includes a *familiar experience* (or information you already know) can help you figure out the meaning of the new word.
He enjoys many types of ***cuisine,*** *such as Mexican, Italian, Chinese, Thai, and Indian foods.*	***Example clue***	Are there *examples* that illustrate the meaning of the unfamiliar word?	Words that introduce examples of the meaning of the unfamiliar word: *for example, such as, to illustrate, like.*
Her taste in music is very ***eclectic.*** She likes *opera, rock, hip-hop, classical, and jazz.*	***Clue from another sentence***	Is there *another sentence* in the paragraph that explains the meaning of the unfamiliar word?	*Additional information in another sentence* that may help explain the unfamiliar word.

EXERCISE 1

Directions: The context clue exercises below present sentences from college textbooks. Each sentence contains an important word that is *italicized*. Next, there is an additional sentence that uses the word in the same sense. Read both sentences and ask yourself, "What would this word have to mean in order to make sense in *both* sentences?" Use the context from both sentences to *deduce* the meaning of the italicized word. The answer you choose must make sense in both sentences.

d

1. We often think that our *affairs,* great or small, must be tended to continuously and with great detail or our world will fall apart.

Balancing your checkbook, keeping an appointment calendar, and using efficient time management techniques enables you to keep your *affairs* in order.

affairs means:

a. romantic relationships
b. financial matters
c. weekly schedules
d. personal business

c

2. High levels of stress are *correlated* with health problems.

The number of years of education is *correlated* with the amount of income a person earns in a lifetime.

correlated means:

a. prevented by
b. caused by
c. related to
d. determined by

b

3. Although there is no cure for the common cold, there are medications that can *alleviate* its symptoms.

There are many ways to *alleviate* the stresses of everyday living.

alleviate means:

a. to remedy or cure
b. to lessen or make more bearable
c. to increase or enhance
d. to change the form of

WHAT ARE WORD-STRUCTURE CLUES, AND HOW DO YOU USE THEM?

KEY TERM
word-structure clues

Roots, prefixes, and suffixes that help you determine a word's meaning. Word-structure clues are also known as *word-part clues.*

Although context clues should be your first strategy in determining the meaning of unknown words, examining the structure of words can also be extremely helpful. **Word-structure clues,** or word-part clues, consist of roots, prefixes, and suffixes that help you determine a word's meaning. Prefixes and suffixes are called affixes because they are "fixed" (attached or joined) to a root word. Word-structure clues can often be used to confirm the meaning suggested by the context of the sentence.

Word-structure clues can help you in other ways as well. First, they can help you remember the meaning of a word. Second, they allow you to enlarge your vocabulary by learning families of related words that come from the same root (called *cognates*). Finally, knowing prefixes, roots, and suffixes can help you improve your spelling. For instance, if you know the prefix *mis* (meaning "bad" or "wrong"), then you will understand why the word *misspell* has two s's: One is in the prefix and one is in the root word: mis + spell.

The more prefixes, roots, and suffixes you know, the more you will be able to utilize this vocabulary-building strategy. This means that it is well worth your time to memorize common word parts. Of these, roots and prefixes are by far the most helpful. (Lists of common roots, prefixes, and suffixes appear on pages 66–70.)

As you can tell, there are three categories of word parts—prefixes, roots, and suffixes. Each will be discussed in this chapter. Here are their definitions:

Root: Base word that has a meaning of its own.

Prefix: Word part attached to the beginning of a root that adds its meaning to the root.

Suffix: Word part attached to the end of a root word.

To use word-structure clues, examine an unfamiliar word to see if it has a word part that you recognize that gives you a clue to its meaning. Think of roots and affixes as puzzle parts that can help you figure out the meaning of unfamiliar words. Keep in mind that, as noted above, you increase your chances of figuring out an unfamiliar word's meaning if you are able to use *both* context clues and word-structure clues together. Now, let's take a closer look at each of the three types of word parts.

KEY TERM
root

Base word that has a meaning of its own.

A **root** is a base word that has a meaning of its own. Roots are powerful vocabulary-building tools because entire families of words in English are based on the same root. For example, if you know that the root *aud* means "to hear," then you will understand the connection between *audience* (people who come to hear something or someone), *auditorium* (a place where people come to hear something), *auditory* (pertaining to hearing, as in *auditory nerve*), and *audiologist* (a person specially trained to evaluate hearing). Knowing the meaning of a word's root makes it easier to remember the meaning of the word.

KEY TERM
prefix

Word part attached to the beginning of a word that adds its meaning to that base word.

A **prefix** is a word part attached to the beginning of a word that adds its meaning to the meaning of the base word. For example, adding the prefix *tele* (meaning "distant" or "far") to the word *marketing* creates the word *telemarketing*, selling goods and services from a distance (in this case, over the telephone), rather than face-to-face. By adding the prefixes *pre* (meaning "before") and *re* (meaning "back" or "again") to the word *view,* you have the words *preview* (to view or see something ahead of time) and *review* (to see or look back at something again).

Remember, however, that just because a word begins with the same letters as a prefix, it does not necessarily contain that prefix. The prefix *mal* means "wrong" or "bad," as in *malnutrition* (bad nutrition). However, the words *mall* and *male* also begin with the letters *mal,* but they have no connection with the prefix *mal.* Nor does the word *rent,* for example, contain the prefix *re,* or the word *pressure* the prefix *pre.*

KEY TERM
suffix

Word part attached to the end of a root word.

A **suffix** is a word part attached to the end of a root word. Some suffixes add their meaning to a root, but most suffixes simply change a word's part of speech or inflection. Inflectional endings include, for example, adding *-s* to make a word plural or *-ed* to make a verb past tense. Consider these other forms of *predict* (a verb) that are created by adding suffixes: *prediction* (a noun), *predictable* (an adjective), and *predictably* (an adverb).

Suffixes are not as helpful as roots or prefixes in determining the meaning of unfamiliar words because many suffixes have similar or even the same meanings. Also, some suffixes cause roots to change their spelling before the suffix is added. For instance, when certain suffixes are added to words that end in *y*, the *y* becomes an *i*: *sleepy* becomes *sleepier, sleepiness,* and *sleepily*.

A word may consist of one or more of the word parts. For example, the word *graph* consists of a root only. The word *telegraph* consists of a prefix (*tele*) and a root (*graph*). The word *graphic* consists of a root (*graph*) and a suffix (*ic*). *Telegraphic* consists of a prefix, a root, and a suffix.

✓ **Teaching Tip**
See www.lexfiles.com for lists of common Latin and Greek roots.

It is unlikely that you or any other student will learn every Greek and Latin word part, but the more word parts you know, the easier it will be to use word-structure clues and, of course, the larger your vocabulary will become. A good place to begin is by familiarizing yourself with the common roots, prefixes, and suffixes on the lists that follow. (You probably already know many of the word parts on these lists.) Then watch for these word parts in new words you encounter. Use these word-structure clues to help you confirm the educated guess you made about a word's meaning based on the context.

COMMON ROOTS

Root	Meaning	Examples
1. anthro	man, humankind	anthropology, misanthrope
2. aud	hear	audience, auditorium
3. auto	self	autobiography, automatic
4. bene	good, well	beneficial, benediction
5. biblio	book	bibliography, bibliophile
6. bio	life	biology, biopsy
7. cede, ceed	go, move	precede, proceed
8. chron	time	chronology, chronic
9. cide	kill	homicide, suicide
10. clud, clus	close, shut	exclude, inclusive
11. corp, corpus	body	corporal, corps
12. cred	believe, belief	credible, credit
13. dic, dict	say, speak	predict, dictionary
14. duc, duct	lead	produce, conductor
15. fac	make, do	manufacture, factory
16. fid, fide	faith	fidelity, confidence
17. gam, gamy	marriage	bigamist, monogamy
18. gen	birth, race, origin	generation, genealogy
19. geo	earth	geology, geography
20. graph, gram	write	graphic, diagram, photograph
21. gress	go, move	progression, regress

Root	Meaning	Examples
22. ject	throw, hurl	reject, projection
23. man, manu	hand	manual, manipulate
24. mater, matri	mother	maternal, matricide
25. mem	memory	remember, commemorate
26. meter	measure	thermometer, metric
27. miss, mit	send, sent	mission, transmit
28. mor, mort	death	morgue, mortal, morbid
29. mot, mob	move, go	motion, promote, mobile
30. nov	new	novelty, innovation
31. nym, nom	name	synonym, nominate
32. pater, patri	father	paternal, patriotic
33. pel	push, drive, thrust	repel, compel
34. pend	hang	pendulum, dependent
35. phil, phile	love	philosophy, audiophile
36. phobia	fear	claustrophobia, phobic
37. phon	sound	phonics, telephone
38. photo	light	photograph, photosynthesis
39. pod, pedi	foot	podiatrist, pedestrian
40. port	carry	portable, import, export
41. pos	put, place	pose, position, deposit
42. psych, psycho	mind	psychic, psychology
43. rupt	break, burst	rupture, bankrupt, interrupt
44. scribe, script	write	inscribe, prescription
45. sol	one, alone, only	solo, solitude
46. spec	see, look	spectacle, inspect
47. ten	grasp, hold, stretch	attention, retention
48. therm	heat	thermometer, thermal
49. tempor	time, occasion	temporary, contemporary
50. tort	twist, bend	tortuous, contort
51. tract	drag, pull	tractor, contract, attract
52. ven, vene	come	convention, intervene
53. vers, vert	turn	reverse, convert
54. vid, vis	see	video, vision
55. viv, vive	live, living	vivid, survive
56. voc	voice, call, say	vocal, invocation

COMMON PREFIXES

Prefix	Meaning	Examples
Prefixes That Mean "No" or "Not":		
1. a-	not	atypical, asocial
2. an-	not	anarchy, anaerobic
3. in-, il-, im-, ir-	not	insecure, illegal, immoral, irresponsible
4. non-	not	nonviolent, nonpoisonous
5. un-	not	unhappy, unkind, uneducated
6. dis-	not, opposite of, undo	displease, disservice, disconnect
7. mis-	wrong, bad	mistreat, mistake, misplace
8. mal-	bad, evil	maladjusted, malevolent
9. ant-, anti-	against	antagonize, antivirus, antiwar
10. contra-	against	contradict, contrary, contrast
Prefixes That Relate to Time:		
11. ante-	before	antebellum, antecedent
12. ex-	former	ex-boss, ex-spouse
13. post-	after	posttest, posterior
14. pre-	before	predict, precede
15. re-	again	repeat, recycle
Prefixes That Show Placement:		
16. ab-	away, away from	absent, abnormal
17. circum-	around	circumference, circumlocution
18. co-, col-, com-	together or with	cooperate, colleague, comparison
19. de-	down from, away	descend, depart
20. dis-	away	displace, disappear
21. ex-	out	exit, export, exterior, exurbs
22. in-	in	inside, interior, inhale
23. inter-	between, among	interstate, interrupt, interfere
24. intra-	within, inside	intrastate, intramural, intravenous
25. pro-	forward, ahead	progress, promote
26. re-	back	return, revert, report
27. sub-, sup-	down	submarine, suppress, suburbs
28. tele-	far, distant	television, telepathy, telescope
29. trans-	across	transatlantic, transport
30. hetero-	different, other	heterosexual, heterogeneous

Prefix	Meaning	Examples
Other Prefixes:		
31. hom-, homo-	same	homophobia, homogeneous
32. syn-	same, similar, together	synthesize, synchronize
33. urb-	city	urban, urbanite
Prefixes That Indicate How Many or How Much:		
34. extra-	outside, beyond	exterior, extraordinary, extracurricular
35. hemi-	half	hemisphere, hemiplegic
36. hyper-	too much, excessive	hyperactive, hyperbole
37. hypo-	under, too little	hypothermia, hypodermic
38. macro-	large	macroeconomics, macrobiotic
39. micro-	small	microscope, microorganisms
40. omni-	all, every	omnipotent, omniscient
41. poly-	many	polygamy, polygon
42. pseudo-	false	pseudonym, pseudosophisticated
43. semi-	half	semiconscious, semiformal
44. super-	over, above	supervisor, superlative
Prefixes That Show Number or Quantity:		
45. uni-	one	united, unify, uniform, universal
46. mono-	one	monopoly, monocle
47. bi-	two	bicycle, bisect
48. du-	two	duet, dual, duel
49. tri-	three	triangle, triplet, tripod
50. quad-, quar	four	quadrant, quarter, quart
51. quint-	five	quintet, quintuple
52. penta-	five	Pentagon, pentathlon
53. sex-	six	sextuplet, sexagenarian
54. hex-	six	hexagon, hexagram
55. sept-	seven	septuplets, septuagenarian, septet
56. octo-, oct-	eight	octagon, octopus
57. nov-	nine	novena, November, nonagenarian
58. dec-, deci-	ten	decimal, decade, decimate
59. cent-	hundred	century, cent
60. mill-, kilo-	thousand	millennium, kilowatts, kilometer

✓ **Teaching Tips**

- The prefixes that show number or quantity are arranged in order of increasing quantity.
- Before the 12-month Gregorian calendar was introduced in 1582, there were only 10 months in a year. In the earlier calendar, known as the Julian calendar, *Sept*ember was the seventh month, *Oct*ober was the eighth month, *Nov*ember was the ninth month, and *Dec*ember was the tenth month. The names of the months still reflect the ancient 10-month year.
- *Millennium* is frequently misspelled. You may want to point out the two *l*'s in *mille* and the two *n*'s in the root *ennium*, meaning years.

COMMON SUFFIXES

Suffix	Meaning	Examples
Suffixes That Indicate a Person:		
1. -er, -or, -ist	one who (does what the root word indicates)	banker, inventor, scientist, pacifist, terrorist
Suffixes That Indicate a Noun:		
2. -ance, -ence, -tion, -sion, -ment, -ness, -ity, -ty, -tude, -hood, -age	state of, quality of, condition of, act of	tolerance, permanence, retention, vision, government, happiness, maturity, beauty, gratitude, statehood, marriage
3. -itis	inflammation of (whatever the root indicates)	sinusitis, tonsillitis
4. -ology	study or science of (whatever the root indicates)	psychology, microbiology, sociology
5. -ism	philosophy of or belief in	terrorism, Buddhism, pacifism
Suffixes That Indicate an Adjective:		
6. -al, -ic, -ish, -ical, -ive	pertaining to (whatever the root indicates)	normal, hormonal, psychic, pacific, selfish, magical, defective
7. -less	without, lacking (whatever the root indicates)	homeless, toothless
8. -ous, -ful	full of (whatever the root indicates)	harmonious, colorful
9. -able, -ible	able to do or be (whatever the root indicates)	comfortable, comprehensible, audible
Suffixes That Indicate a Verb:		
10. -ify, -ate, -ize, -en	to do (whatever the root indicates)	pacify, meditate, criticize, enlighten
Suffixes That Indicate an Adverb:		
11. -ly	in the manner (indicated by the root)	slowly, heavily, peacefully
12. -ward	in the direction of (whatever the root indicates)	eastward, homeward, backward

EXERCISE 2

Directions: The word-structure exercises below present sentences containing *italicized* words whose word parts give a clue to its meaning. Use the word part that is in **boldface** print to give you a clue to the word's meaning.

1. If you are making a ***spec****tacle* of yourself at a party, other people are likely to:
- *a.* report you to the police.
- *b.* applaud you.
- *c.* stop and watch you.
- *d.* wish they were you.

2. If protesters *dis****rupt*** a speech the president is giving, they:
- *a.* applaud and cheer enthusiastically.
- *b.* link arms and sway from side to side.
- *c.* say and do things that cause the president to temporarily stop speaking.
- *d.* turn their backs on him.

3. A prisoner who is placed in ***sol****itary* confinement is:
- *a.* assigned to a different prison.
- *b.* put on suicide watch.
- *c.* given restricted food rations.
- *d.* isolated from other prisoners.

HOW DO YOU USE A DICTIONARY PRONUNCIATION KEY?

Most college students know how to locate a word in the dictionary and how to determine which definition pertains to what they are reading. But like many students, you still may not be skilled or confident in using a dictionary pronunciation key. Being able to use a pronunciation key is important when you need to remember a word because one of the most helpful things you can do is learn its correct pronunciation and say it aloud. Checking and practicing a word's pronunciation takes only a moment or two.

Most dictionaries have an *abridged* (shortened) pronunciation key at or near the bottom of each page. An abridged key gives only vowel sounds and the less common consonant sounds, and usually looks similar to this one:

Pronunciation Key: ă **pat** ā **pay** âr **care** ä **father** ĕ **pet** ē **be** ĭ **pit**
ī **tie** îr **pier** ŏ **pot** ō **toe** ô **paw** oi **noise** ou **out** ŏŏ **took**
ōō **boot** ŭ **cut** yōō **abuse** ûr **urge** th **thin** *th* **this** hw **which**
zh **vision** ə **about** *Stress mark:* ′

A complete pronunciation key appears at the beginning of every dictionary. Typically, it looks similar to the example shown on page 72. Notice that the complete pronunciation key gives a familiar word that contains a particular sound, accompanied by the symbol that dictionary uses to represent that sound. For example, the first word, *pat*, contains the sound of short *a*. That sound is represented in this dictionary by the

DICTIONARY PRONUNCIATION KEY

A list of pronunciation symbols used in this dictionary is given below in the column headed **AHD** (*American Heritage Dictionary*). The column headed **Examples** contains words chosen to illustrate how the **AHD** symbols are pronounced. The letters that correspond in sound to the **AHD** symbols are shown in boldface. The third column, headed **IPA** (International Phonetic Alphabet), gives the equivalent transcription symbols most often used by scholars. Although similar, the **AHD** and **IPA** symbols are not precisely the same because they were conceived for different purposes.

Examples	AHD	IPA
p**a**t	ă	æ
p**ay**	ā	e
c**are**	âr	ɛr, er
f**a**ther	ä	ɑː, ɑ
bi**b**	b	b
chur**ch**	ch	tʃ
dee**d**, mill**ed**	d	d
p**e**t	ĕ	ɛ
b**ee**	ē	i
fi**f**e, **ph**ase, rou**gh**	f	f
ga**g**	g	g
hat	h	h
which	hw	hw (also ʍ)
p**i**t	ĭ	ɪ
p**ie**, b**y**	ī	aɪ
p**ier**	îr	ɪr, ir
ju**dge**	j	dʒ
ki**ck**, **c**at, pi**que**	k	k
lid, need**le***	l (nēd′l)	l, l̩ [′nidl̩]
mu**m**	m	m
no, sudd**en***	n (sŭd′n)	n, n̩ [′sʌdn̩]
thi**ng**	ng	ŋ
p**o**t	ŏ	ɑ
t**oe**	ō	o
c**augh**t, p**aw**	ô	ɔ
n**oi**se	oi	ɔɪ
t**oo**k	o͝o	ʊ
b**oo**t	o͞o	u
out	ou	aʊ
po**p**	p	p
roa**r**	r	ɹ
sau**c**e	s	s
ship, di**sh**	sh	ʃ
tigh**t,** stopp**ed**	t	t
thin	th	θ
this	*th*	ð
c**u**t	ŭ	ʌ
urge, t**er**m, f**ir**m, w**or**d, h**ear**d	ûr	ɝ, ɜr
val**v**e	v	v
with	w	w
yes	y	j
zebra, **x**ylem	z	z
vi**s**ion, plea**s**ure, gara**ge**	zh	ʒ
about, it**e**m, edi**b**le, gall**o**p, circ**u**s	ə	z
butt**er**	ər	ɚ

Foreign	AHD	IPA
French f**eu**		ø
German sch**ö**n	œ	
French **oeu**f		œ
German zw**ö**lf		
French t**u**	ü	y
German **ü**ber		
German i**ch**		ç
German a**ch**	KH	
Scottish lo**ch**		x
French bo**n****	N (bôN)	~ [bõ]

*In English the consonants *l* and *n* often constitute complete syllables by themselves.

**The IPA symbols show nasality with a diacritic mark over the vowel, whereas the dictionary uses N to reflect that the preceding vowel is nasalized. In French four nasalized vowels occur, as in the phrase *un bon vin blanc:* AHD (œn *bôn* văn blän), IPA (œ bō væ blä).

symbol ă. The pronunciation of words in the dictionary will be written using these phonetic symbols. For example, suppose you read the sentence "Marjorie is an *avid* football fan who hasn't missed a Dallas Cowboys home game in eight years." When you look up the word *avid*, you confirm what you suspect, that it means having a great interest and enthusiasm for something. You also see that the pronunciation for *avid* is written this way: ăv′ ĭd. To pronounce this word, you simply find the phonetic symbols for ă and ĭ in the pronunciation key and determine the way they sound in simple, familiar words. The ă and the ĭ are pronounced the same as the *a* in the word *pat* and the *i* in the word *pit*. When you substitute those sounds in place of the symbols in the pronunciation, you will know how to pronounce the word correctly.

As you work through *New Worlds,* you will have numerous opportunities to practice this skill because the pronunciation is given for each vocabulary term in the quizzes that accompany the reading selections. To help you interpret the symbols, the sample pronunciation key is repeated in each of these exercises. Your instructor can give you further guidance and practice in using a dictionary pronunciation key, if you need it.

WHAT IS FIGURATIVE LANGUAGE, AND HOW DO YOU INTERPRET FIGURES OF SPEECH?

KEY TERM
figurative language

Words that present unusual comparisons or create vivid pictures in the reader's mind. Figurative expressions are also called *figures of speech.*

Knowing how to interpret figurative language is yet another way to develop your understanding of words' meanings and interpret an author's message correctly. **Figurative language** refers to words that present unusual comparisons or create vivid pictures in the reader's mind. Figurative expressions are also called *figures of speech.* Because figures of speech do not literally mean what they say, your job as a reader is to *interpret* their meaning. If you take the words literally, you will misunderstand the author's meaning. When you encounter figurative language, think about what the author wants to convey by presenting a comparison or creating a vivid mental image.

You use figurative language every day, although you may not know it by this name. Whenever you say something such as "That homework assignment was a killer!" you really mean, "That was a tough assignment!" When you say, "I made such a good grade on my test they'll probably ask me to teach the course next semester!" you really mean "I made a very high grade on the test."

Because figurative language does not literally mean what the words say, the reader or listener must interpret the meaning. If you say, "I bombed my last math test," you expect your listener to understand that you did not do well on your math test.

There are four very common types of figurative language. These figures of speech are *metaphor, simile, hyperbole,* and *personification.* Let's look at each of them.

KEY TERM
metaphor

Figure of speech suggesting a comparison between two seemingly dissimilar things, usually by saying that one of them *is* the other.

A **metaphor** is a figure of speech suggesting a comparison between two seemingly dissimilar things, usually by saying that one of them *is* the other (rather than saying it is "like" something else). On the surface, the two things seem very different from each other, yet they are alike in some significant way. The reader must figure out the way in which they are similar.

The author assumes readers will not take a metaphor literally, but will understand that it is a figure of speech whose meaning must be interpreted. That is, the sentence is to be taken *figuratively*. For example, in the sentence "James *is a walking encyclopedia,*" the writer is making a comparison between James and an encyclopedia to suggest that James has a vast amount of knowledge. To interpret this metaphor correctly, the reader must compare James and an encyclopedia and think about the way in which they could be similar: Both have knowledge, a multitude of facts and information. The author, of course, does not mean that James is literally an encyclopedia.

KEY TERM
simile

Figure of speech presenting a comparison between two seemingly dissimilar things by saying that one of them is *like* the other.

A **simile** is a figure of speech presenting a comparison between two seemingly dissimilar things by saying that one of them is *like* the other. Whereas a metaphor makes comparisons using the words *is, are, was,* and *were,* a simile is usually introduced by the words *like* or *as.* An example of a simile is "James is *like* an encyclopedia." The meaning (interpretation) is the same as in the metaphor: James has a vast amount of knowledge.

Here are some examples of similes: "David felt *like a king* when the company chose him as its new president" and "Aisha's mind is as fast and accurate with numbers *as a computer.*" In the first sentence, David's feeling about being chosen president of the company is compared to the feeling of being a king. The author wants us to understand that being chosen as president made David feel as important (and perhaps even as powerful!) as if he were a real king. In the second simile, Aisha's mind is compared to a computer. In other words, Aisha's mind is extremely fast.

To repeat: A simile says that one thing is *like* another. (The word *sim*ile suggests a *sim*ilarity between two things.) When you encounter a simile, first determine which things are being compared. Then determine the important way in which the author considers them to be similar.

KEY TERM
hyperbole

Figure of speech using obvious exaggeration for emphasis and effect.

A third type of figurative language is **hyperbole,** in which obvious exaggeration is used for emphasis and effect. (The prefix *hyper,* meaning "too much" or "excessive," will help you remember that a hyperbole is an obvious exaggeration. Note, too, that the word *hyperbole* has four syllables and is pronounced: hī pûr′ bə lē.) "If I have to type one more paper this week, *my fingers will fall off!*" is an example of hyperbole. Of course, the student's fingers are not literally going to fall off. To interpret the hyperbole correctly, you must understand the point of the exaggeration: to convey that the student has already had to type several papers this week and is extremely tired of typing.

As noted, hyperboles are also used to achieve a particular effect, such as humor. For example, to achieve a comic effect, someone might write, "If I eat one more serving of fish on this diet, I'm going to grow fins!"

KEY TERM
personification

Figure of speech in which nonhuman or nonliving things are given human traits.

In **personification,** nonhuman or nonliving things are given human traits. (You can actually see the word *person* in *person*ification. Note, however, that the pronunciation is pər sŏn ə fĭ kā′ shən.) For example, consider the human characteristics or qualities used in this sentence about a vending machine: "The vending machine *swallowed* my money and then *refused* to give me my candy." Swallowing and refusing to do something are human behaviors. Vending machines, of course, cannot do these things intentionally or in the same sense that a person would. The author wants the reader to understand that the machine accepted the money but did not produce any candy in return. In this case, the interpretation is the machine is broken (it malfunctioned).

The box on page 75 summarizes metaphor, simile, hyperbole, and personification and gives additional examples of each.

FOUR TYPES OF FIGURATIVE LANGUAGE

Figures of Speech	Examples
Metaphor: Implied comparison between two seemingly dissimilar things using *is, are, was,* or *were.*	The old man's face was a *raisin.* Our apartment is a *disaster area.*
Simile: Stated comparison between two seemingly dissimilar things, usually introduced by the word *like* or *as.*	After being stranded in the airport for two days, she felt *as if her teeth had little sweaters on them.* After we had slept outside in tents for a week, the motel seemed *like a palace* to us.
Hyperbole: Obvious exaggeration for emphasis and effect.	It took *forever* to download the DVD file! The steak they served me at the restaurant *would have fed a dozen people!*
Personification: Giving human characteristics or qualities to nonhuman or nonliving things.	The letters *danced* on the page before my tired eyes. Poverty *stole* their childhood.

Skillful readers ask themselves, "Is the author using figurative language?" If the answer is yes, they ask these additional questions:

- "Are two things being compared and, if so, how are they alike?" (metaphor and simile)
- "Is there an obvious exaggeration?" (hyperbole)
- "Are human traits being given to nonliving or nonhuman things?" (personification)

Understanding figurative language helps you interpret an author's message correctly, and it also makes material more interesting and enjoyable to read.

EXERCISE 3

Directions: The sentence below contains a *figure of speech.* The figure of speech is *italicized.* Read the sentence and answer the questions below.

Miguel is the chef in a very popular restaurant where, on busy nights, keeping up with all the customers' orders is *like trying to drink out of a fire hose.*

c **1.** What two things are being compared?

a. Miguel and a popular restaurant
b. a chef and a restaurant
c. keeping up with customers' orders at a busy restaurant and trying to drink out of a fire hose
d. A chef in a popular restaurant and drinking out of a fire hose

d **2.** How are they alike?

a. Both are unusual.
b. Both are busy.
c. Both require training and skill.
d. Both are extremely challenging, but practically impossible.

d **3.** How should this figure of speech be interpreted?

a. Miguel is an excellent chef.
b. On busy nights, Miguel's job is extremely challenging.
c. Keeping up with customers' orders is a priority.
d. A chef's job is a lot like a firefighter's job.

OTHER THINGS TO KEEP IN MIND WHEN DEVELOPING A COLLEGE-LEVEL VOCABULARY

Here are three helpful things you should keep in mind with regard to developing a college-level vocabulary:

1. Certain punctuation marks in a sentence can signal a definition.

Commas, parentheses, brackets, dashes, and colons can be used to set off definitions in sentences. Each of the sample sentences below presents the statement "Ayurveda is older than Chinese medicine." However, because the author knows that many readers may not be familiar with the term *ayurveda,* he includes the definition in the sentence as well. Notice how the punctuation marks in each example signal that a definition is being given. The definition in each sentence appears in italics.

- *Commas* — Ayurveda, *traditional Indian medicine based on herbal remedies,* is older than Chinese medicine.

  or

  A form of medicine that is older than Chinese medicine is ayurveda, *traditional Indian medicine based on herbal remedies.*
- *Parentheses* — Ayurveda (*traditional Indian medicine based on herbal remedies*) is older than Chinese medicine.
- *Brackets* — Ayurveda [*traditional Indian medicine based on herbal remedies*] is older than Chinese medicine.
- *Dashes* — Ayurveda—*traditional Indian medicine based on herbal remedies*—is older than Chinese medicine.
- *Colon* — A form of medicine that is older than Chinese medicine is ayurveda: *traditional Indian medicine based on herbal remedies.*

As you can see, there are several ways an author can use punctuation marks to set off a definition. In Chapter 7, "Recognizing Authors' Writing Patterns," you will learn about the definition pattern, a pattern that appears often in textbooks.

2. The most common and helpful roots, prefixes, and suffixes in English come from Latin and ancient Greek.

Although English is a Germanic language, it has thousands of words derived from Latin and ancient Greek. Today, the English language contains a considerable number of technological, scientific, and medical terms that are derived from Latin and Greek. If you take college courses in any of these areas, you will benefit greatly from knowing common Latin and Greek word parts.

Incidentally, knowing common Latin word parts also makes it easier to learn Spanish, French, Italian, Portuguese, and Romanian. These languages are referred to as *romance languages,* not because they have anything to do with love, but because they all draw so heavily on Latin. Latin was the "Roman" language because it was spoken in ancient Rome. For that reason, languages derived from Latin came to be known as romance languages. Of course, many Spanish, French, and Italian words such as *rodeo, boutique,* and *galleria* have also become words in English.

(continued)

3. A word's etymology (origin and history) indicates the word parts it was created from, including Latin or Greek ones.

A word's etymology is its origin and history. Dictionaries usually give the etymology of a word in brackets [ ] before or after the definition. An etymology can be helpful because it tells the meaning of the original word parts from which the current word was derived. This can help you understand and remember the word's meaning more easily. For example, the prefix *re* means *back* and the root *ject* means to *throw.* The English word *reject* literally means "to throw back" (that is, not accept) something.

When you look up a word in the dictionary, make it a habit to examine the word's etymology. See if the word contains familiar word parts. Over time, you will expand not only your vocabulary, but also your knowledge of word parts. And the more word parts you know, the easier it will be to develop your vocabulary. Below are examples of interesting words that have come into English from other languages. Their etymologies are given in brackets after the definitions.

al•ge•bra (ăl′ jə brə) *n.* A generalization of arithmetic in which symbols represent members of a specified set of numbers and are related by operations that hold for all numbers in the set. [< Arabic: al - jabr, "the (science of) reuniting."] al • ge • bra • ic (ăl jə brā′ ĭc) adj.

bou•tique (bo͞o tēk′) *n.* A small retail shop that specializes in gifts, fashionable clothes, and accessories. [French: from Old French, *botique,* small shop, from Old Provençal *botica,* from Latin *apothēca,* storehouse.]

cor•ral (kĕ răl′) *n.* 1. An enclosure for confining livestock. 2. An enclosure formed by a circle of wagons for defense against attack during an encampment.—*v. -ralled, -ralling, -als.* 1. To drive into and hold in a corral. 2. To arrange (wagons) in a corral. 3. To take control or possession of. *Informal.* To seize; capture. [Spanish: from Vulgar Latin **currāle,* enclosure for carts, from Latin *currus,* cart, from *currere,* to run.]

gal•le•ri•a (găl′ ərē ə) *n.* A roofed passageway or indoor court usually containing a variety of shops or businesses. [Italian: from Old Italian.]

ro•de•o (rō′ dē ō, rō dā′ ō) *n., pl.* -os. 1. A cattle roundup. 2. A public exhibition of cowboy skills, including riding broncos, lassoing, etc. [Spanish: *rodear,* to surround.]

yen (yĕn) *n. Informal.* A yearning; a longing. [Cantonese: *yan.*]

CREATING CHAPTER REVIEW CARDS

Student Online Learning Center (OLC)
***Go to* Chapter 2.**
***Select* Chapter Test.**

✓ **Teaching Tip**
Remind students that the student OLC contains a 10-item **Chapter Test** for this chapter. After completing the chapter review cards below, students should complete the Chapter Test on the OLC.

Review cards or *summary cards* are a way to select, organize, and summarize the important information in a textbook chapter. Preparing review cards helps you organize the information so that you can learn and memorize it more easily. In other words, chapter review cards are effective study tools.

Preparing chapter review cards for each chapter of *New Worlds* will give you practice in creating these valuable study tools. Once you have learned how to make chapter review cards, you can use actual index cards to create them for textbook material in your other courses and use them when you study for tests.

Now complete the chapter review cards for Chapter 2 by answering the questions or following the directions on each card. The page numbers indicate the place in the chapter where the information can be found. Use the type of handwriting that is easiest for you to reread (printing or cursive) and write legibly. You will find it easier to complete the review cards if you remove these pages before filling them in.

✓ **Teaching Tip**
Page numbers for chapter review card items are provided in the student edition in Chapters 1–5 only.

Context Clues

What are *context clues*? (See page 61.)

Words in a sentence or paragraph that help the reader deduce (reason out) the meaning of an unfamiliar word.

Describe six types of context clues. (See the box on page 63.)

1. ***definition:*** a word's definition is included in the sentence
2. ***synonym:*** a word's meaning is explained by a word or a phrase that has a similar meaning
3. ***contrast:*** a word's meaning is explained by a contrasting word or phrase
4. ***experience:*** you draw on your experience or background knowledge to deduce a word's meaning
5. ***example:*** a word's meaning is illustrated by an example
6. ***clue from another sentence:*** a word's meaning is explained by another sentence in the paragraph

Card 1 Chapter 2: Developing a College-Level Vocabulary

Word-Structure Class

1. What are *word-structure clues*? (See page 64.)

Roots, prefixes, and suffixes that help you determine a word's meaning.

Word-structure clues are also called "word-part clues."

2. Define each of these terms. (See page 65.)

root: base word that has a meaning of its own

prefix: word part attached to the beginning of a word that adds meaning to that base word

suffix: word part that is attached to the end of a root word

Card 2 Chapter 2: Developing a College-Level Vocabulary

Figurative Language

1. What is *figurative language*? (See page 73.)

Words that create unusual comparisons or vivid pictures in the reader's mind.

Figurative expressions are also called "figures of speech."

2. Define each of these figures of speech. (See pages 73–75.)

metaphor: figure of speech suggesting a comparison between two seemingly dissimilar things, usually by saying that one of them "is" the other

simile: figure of speech presenting a comparison of two seemingly dissimilar things, saying that one of them is "like" the other

hyperbole: figure of speech using obvious exaggeration for emphasis or effect

personification: figure of speech in which nonhuman or nonliving things are given human traits

Card 3 Chapter 2: Developing a College-Level Vocabulary

TEST YOUR UNDERSTANDING
CONTEXT CLUES

✓ **Teaching Tips**

- From the beginning, get students in the habit of numbering the steps and marking keywords in sets of directions.
- Emphasize that the definition that students choose must make sense in *both* sentences.
- You may wish to have students transfer answers to a machine-scorable answer sheet.

REVIEW: **Context clues** are words in a sentence or paragraph that help the reader deduce (reason out) the meaning of an unfamiliar word. The types of context clues are:

- **Definition clue**—a definition for the word is given in the sentence.
- **Synonym clue**—a word is explained by a word or phrase that has a similar meaning.
- **Contrast clue**—a word is explained by a word or phrase that has an opposite meaning.
- **Experience clue**—the meaning can be understood based on your background knowledge or experience.
- **Example clue**—a word is explained by examples that illustrate its meaning.
- **Clue from another sentence**—another sentence in the paragraph explains the word.

DIRECTIONS: Items 1–20 present sentences primarily from college textbooks. Each contains an important word or term that is *italicized.* Next, there is an additional sentence that uses the word in the same sense. This sentence provides a second context clue. Read both sentences and ask yourself, "What would this word have to mean in order to make sense in *both* sentences?" Use the context clues from both sentences to *deduce* the meaning of the italicized word. Remember, the answer you choose must make sense in both sentences. Write your answer in the space provided.

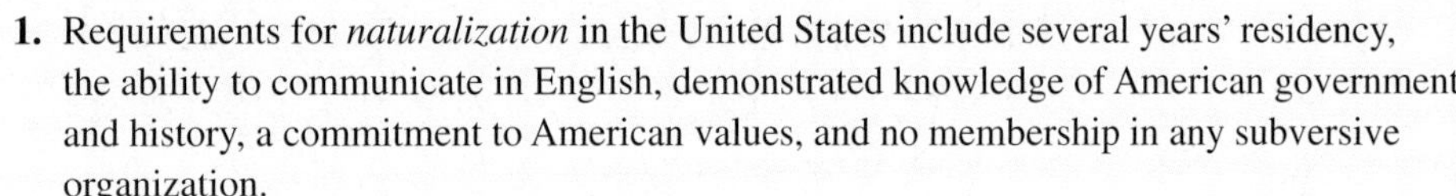

___c___ **1.** Requirements for *naturalization* in the United States include several years' residency, the ability to communicate in English, demonstrated knowledge of American government and history, a commitment to American values, and no membership in any subversive organization.

Through *naturalization,* millions of immigrants to the United States have become American citizens.

naturalization means:

a. process of becoming an immigrant
b. process of making something more natural
c. process by which a foreigner becomes a citizen of a different country
d. process of establishing residency in a country

✓ **Teaching Tip**
Have students identify the *type* of context clue in each sentence. This makes a good collaborative activity.

___b___ **2.** *Tsunamis,* or seismic sea waves, are often incorrectly called tidal waves.

Tsunamis are produced by underwater earthquakes.

tsunamis means:

a. underwater earthquakes
b. seismic sea waves
c. tidal waves
d. earthquakes

___a___ **3.** We harbor *stereotypes,* or prejudgments, of college professors, Asians, hairdressers, used car salespeople, the elderly, preachers, Southerners, Democrats, rap singers, and countless other groups of people.

Stereotypes originally referred to a metal printing plate or mold, but now refers to long-standing, oversimplified, exaggerated, inflexible prejudgments about groups of people.

stereotype means:

a. printing done with a metal plate
b. numerous groups of people
c. oversimplification
d. prejudgment about a group of people

a

4. The blurring of gender roles is clearly evident in many of today's *androgynous* styles and fashions, such as wearing earrings or having tattoos.

✓ **Teaching Tip**
andro- root meaning *man; gyn-* root meaning *woman; -ous* suffix meaning *full of*

Both the male and female employees protested their company's new uniforms of khaki slacks and blue shirts; they complained that the uniforms looked *androgynous.*

androgynous means:

a. not clearly masculine or feminine, as in dress, appearance, or behavior
b. wearing earrings or having long hair
c. wearing the styles and fashions of today
d. wearing a uniform

b

5. For a special promotion, many retail stores deliberately sell a product below its customary price, or even below cost, to attract attention to it. The purpose of this *loss-leader pricing* is not to sell more of that particular product but, rather, to attract customers in hopes that they will buy other products as well.

Mass merchandisers, such as Target, often sell DVDs at half their customary price because *loss-leader pricing* draws many customers to their stores.

loss-leader pricing means:

a. special promotions to sell videos
b. selling a product below its customary price, or even below cost, to attract customers in hopes that they will buy other products as well
c. retailing technique used by all mass merchandisers
d. attracting customers by selling things half price

c

6. *Blues* grew out of African American folk music, such as work songs, spirituals, and the field hollers of slaves.

It is uncertain exactly when *blues* originated, but by around the 1890s it was sung in rural areas in the South and was often performed with a guitar accompaniment.

blues means:

a. African American folk music that originated around the 1890s
b. work songs, spirituals, and field hollers of slaves
c. a form of vocal and instrumental music that grew out of African American folk music
d. music performed in the South

a **7.** A densely populated area containing two or more cities and their suburbs has become known as a *megalopolis.*

An example of a *megalopolis* is the 500-mile corridor that stretches from Boston south to Washington, D.C., and includes New York City, Philadelphia, and Baltimore—one-sixth of the total population of the United States!

megalopolis means:

a. densely populated area containing two or more cities and their suburbs

b. areas existing in the United States, Great Britain, Germany, Italy, Egypt, India, Japan, and China

c. the 500-mile corridor that stretches from Boston south to Washington, D.C.

d. areas that equal one-sixth of the total population of the United States

b **8.** Motorists are aware of an increasing sense of aggression on America's *congested* highways.

Malls can become so *congested* with Christmas shoppers that potential buyers give up and go home.

congested means:

a. flowing freely

b. overfilled or overcrowded

c. hostile

d. filled with pollution

d **9.** New mothers seem more *susceptible* to stress and fatigue because they are now primary caregivers as well as wives, homemakers, and often employees as well.

Not eating a balanced diet or getting enough sleep can make you more *susceptible* to colds and other infections.

susceptible means:

a. having an unknown effect

b. unaffected by

c. having no effect upon

d. easily affected by

a **10.** Listing your qualifications on your résumé gives a prospective employer *tangible* clues about the type of person you are.

Many people enjoy volunteer work immensely even though they receive no pay or other *tangible* rewards for their time and service.

tangible means:

a. pertaining to an actual object or something real

b. free; having no cost

c. pertaining to a legal matter

d. expensive; costly

11. Many states have now prohibited *capital punishment,* but some states still execute those who are convicted of first-degree murder.

Opponents of *capital punishment* cite numerous death-row inmates who have been cleared of crimes as a result of DNA testing that is now available.

capital punishment means:

a. severe punishment
b. the penalty of death for a crime
c. punishment decreed by the government
d. life imprisonment

12. The Mississippi River, the longest river in the United States, *meanders* from Minnesota to Louisiana before emptying into the Gulf of Mexico.

The writer described himself as a vagabond who *meanders* through life, open to every new adventure and experience.

meander means:

a. flows
b. stays
c. wanders
d. visits

13. The *façades* of art deco style buildings are characterized by the use of chrome, steel, glass and aluminum, geometric patterns, and a rich display of surface decoration.

Over time air pollution has eroded the *façade* of many ancient buildings in Venice, Italy.

façade means:

a. building
b. exterior
c. interior
d. windows

14. "Ice cold," "little baby," and "old antique" are examples of *redundant* phrases.

To use time effectively, employees should avoid *redundant* activities such as writing an e-mail message and leaving the same message on voice mail.

redundant means:

a. needlessly repetitive; unnecessary
b. useful; helpful
c. exact; precise
d. boring; uninteresting

b 15. Many art treasures exist today because rulers such as the Roman emperor Augustus and the Byzantine emperor Justinian chose to *glorify* themselves through art.

Throughout the ages cathedrals, hymns, and paintings have been created to *glorify* God.

glorify means:

a. to make larger

b. to give glory, honor, or praise

c. to hide weaknesses

d. to create a portrait of

c 16. In their autobiography, sisters Sarah and Elizabeth Delany, who both lived more than 100 years, attributed their *longevity* to doing what they felt was right for them and to helping others.

Careful eating, regular exercise, sufficient rest, and a positive attitude contribute to a person's *longevity.*

longevity means:

a. intelligence

b. wealth

c. long length of life

d. physical endurance

d 17. The *Middle Ages,* the period of European history between ancient times and modern times, began with the fall of Rome in the fifth century and ended with the Renaissance in the fourteenth century.

During the *Middle Ages,* life for peasants was difficult, harsh, and short.

Middle Ages means:

a. ancient times

b. the period of time when peasants lived

c. the period in a person's life between the ages of forty and sixty

d. the period of European history between ancient times and modern times

b 18. The white marble Taj Mahal, a magnificent tomb built in the mid-seventeenth century by a Mogul emperor for his beloved wife, is perhaps the most famous *mausoleum* in the world.

In England, the ancestors of distinguished families are often buried in a *mausoleum* on the grounds of the family's estate.

mausoleum means:

a. a simple, unmarked grave

b. a building designed as a burial vault

c. a building constructed of stone

d. a place where bodies are kept before burial

c **19.** By learning how to reduce conflict, managers and supervisors can help angry employees avoid an *altercation.*

To avoid danger to themselves, police officers receive training in how to break up violent *altercations.*

altercation means:

a. loud party
b. loud music
c. loud argument
d. loud celebration

b **20.** Strokes can result in paralysis which, in turn, can cause the unused muscles to *atrophy.*

When a broken arm or leg is placed in a cast, the muscles begin to *atrophy* from lack of movement.

atrophy means:

a. to grow stronger
b. to shrink
c. to stretch
d. to disappear

TEST YOUR UNDERSTANDING
WORD-STRUCTURE CLUES

✓ **Teaching Tip**
Complete item 1 together in class to be sure students understand what to do. Point out that answer choice *b* is also the only one that fits the context.

REVIEW: **Word-structure clues** are roots, prefixes, and suffixes that help you determine a word's meaning. The three categories of word parts are:

- **Roots**—base words that have meaning on their own.
- **Prefixes**—word parts attached to the beginnings of roots that add their meaning to the roots.
- **Suffixes**—word parts attached to the ends of root words.

DIRECTIONS: Items 1–20 present sentences containing *italicized* words whose word parts—roots, prefixes, or suffixes—give a clue to its meaning. Use the word part that is in **boldface** print to give you a clue to the word's meaning. (See the lists of roots, prefixes, and suffixes on pages 66–70.) Some words contain more than one word part; this will give you additional help in determining the meaning of the word. (When possible, use context clues to confirm your answer choice.) Write your answers in the spaces provided.

b ______ **1.** Harold is an ***a**typical* student because he started college when he was 16.
a. typical
b. not typical
c. normal
d. ordinary

b ______ **2.** It is easy to understand her on the telephone because of her ***dict**ion.*
a. pleasant way of saying things
b. clear, distinct pronunciation
c. use of complex words
d. use of the dictionary

c ______ **3.** The serial killer known as Jack the Ripper was a notorious *miso**gyn**ist* who slashed many women to death in London in the late nineteenth century.
a. someone who fails at marriage
b. someone who hates marriage
c. someone who hates women
d. someone who hates adolescents

a ______ **4.** The ***biblio**phile* owned more than a thousand volumes and was proud of his extensive book collection.
a. book lover
b. librarian
c. bookseller
d. rare book dealer

b 5. The Vietnam Memorial in Washington, D.C., is a black marble monument that is permanently *inscribed* with the names of all persons in the U.S. armed services who died in the Vietnam War.

a. illustrated
b. engraved
c. painted
d. decorated

a 6. Teenagers who drive recklessly must think they are *immortal.*

a. not able to die
b. above the law
c. impressive
d. susceptible to injury

d 7. Lisa tried to *convert* other members of her family to vegetarianism, but they refused to give up meat.

a. dissuade
b. discourage
c. turn aside
d. turn others to one's way of thinking or behaving

a 8. The lifeguard quickly pulled the child from the bottom of the swimming pool and *revived* him with CPR.

a. brought back to life or consciousness
b. expelled water from the lungs
c. made strong again
d. rescued

c 9. The historian *chronicled* the events leading up to the Iraq War.

a. disproved
b. discussed
c. presented in order
d. disapproved of

a 10. *Polygamy* is illegal in the United States.

a. being married to two or more people at the same time
b. being married to two women at the same time
c. being married to two men at the same time
d. being married to two or more people one at a time

a 11. My father has four sisters, and of all my *paternal* aunts, I like Aunt Jane best.

a. pertaining to the father
b. pertaining to the mother
c. pertaining to relatives
d. pertaining to brothers

a 12. Adriana is a ***vers****atile* artist who works in clay, stone, and metal.

a. able to do many different things
b. hardworking
c. beginning
d. outdoor

d 13. We refused to open the front door until the police officers showed us their ***cred****entials.*

a. weapon
b. police car
c. subpoena
d. identification or other evidence of authority

b 14. Professor Howe chose an office on the first floor because she has *acro****phobia.***

a. a fear of earthquakes
b. a fear of heights
c. a fear of work
d. a fear of thunderstorms

a 15. I tell my sister Mary everything; she has been my best friend and *con****fid****ant* all my life.

a. person you trust will keep your secrets
b. relative who is close in age
c. enjoyable companion
d. person who belongs to a religious order

a 16. The surgeon took a ***bio****psy* from the tumor and sent it to the laboratory for analysis.

a. sample of living tissue
b. fluid
c. x-ray
d. report

a 17. The body of the homeless person was sent to the city ***mor****gue* until an identification could be made.

a. place where dead bodies are kept temporarily
b. place where bodies are cremated
c. place where bodies are prepared for burial
d. place where bodies are maintained in crypts

c 18. Collectors who have ***soph****isticated* taste in art often have their paintings featured in art magazines.

a. too expensive for the average collector
b. unusual
c. knowledgeable and informed
d. modern or contemporary

a **19.** Although spanking used to be a common way to handle disciplinary problems, most school districts now prohibit ***corpor**al* punishment.

a. pertaining to the body
b. pertaining to the military
c. pertaining to schools
d. pertaining to young children

a **20.** The young millionaire was a generous ***phil**anthropist* who paid for a new wing of the children's hospital.

a. one who does things for love of humankind
b. one who has limited financial resources
c. one who has great interest in medical research
d. one who has had a serious illness

TEST YOUR UNDERSTANDING
FIGURATIVE LANGUAGE

REVIEW: **Figurative language** is the use of words that present unusual comparisons or create vivid pictures in the reader's mind. Four types of figurative language are:

- **Metaphor**—figure of speech suggesting a comparison between two seemingly dissimilar things, usually by saying that one of them *is* the other.
- **Simile**—figure of speech presenting a comparison between two seemingly dissimilar things by saying that one of them is *like* the other.
- **Hyperbole**—figure of speech using obvious exaggeration for emphasis and effect.
- **Personification**—figure of speech in which nonhuman or nonliving things are given human traits.

DIRECTIONS: Items 1–20 present sentences from college textbooks that contain *figures of speech.* Each figure of speech is *italicized.* Read each sentence. Answer the questions that follow each sentence. Remember that in order to answer the last question for each item correctly, you must *interpret* the meaning of the figurative language. Write your answer in the space provided.

When I saw the truck coming toward me in my lane, I felt fear wash over me *like a tidal wave.*

d _____ **1.** What two things are being compared?

a. a truck and a tidal wave
b. a truck and fear
c. the person and a truck
d. fear and a tidal wave

b _____ **2.** How are they alike?

a. Both are unusual.
b. Both are overwhelming.
c. Both are temporary.
d. Both pertain to water.

a _____ **3.** How should this simile be interpreted?

a. The driver felt terrified.
b. The driver felt irritated.
c. The driver felt relieved.
d. The driver felt wet.

My supervisor refused to let me have Saturday off to go to my family reunion. Her *heart is a stone!*

b _____ **4.** What two things are being compared?

a. a family reunion and the supervisor's heart
b. the supervisor's heart and a stone
c. a stone and a supervisor
d. the supervisor and the family

a 5. How are they alike?

a. Both are hard and unyielding.

b. Both are alive.

c. Both are broken.

d. Both are attending a reunion.

a 6. How should this metaphor be interpreted?

a. The supervisor is hard-hearted.

b. The family reunion is Saturday.

c. The supervisor dislikes family reunions.

d. The speaker is hard-hearted.

If I lived in Hawaii, I'd go to the beach and *spend 24 hours a day on my surfboard!*

b 7. What is the hyperbole (exaggeration)?

a. living in Hawaii

b. spending 24 hours a day on a surfboard

c. going to the beach

d. knowing how to surf

a 8. How should this hyperbole be interpreted?

a. The person loves to surf.

b. The person wants to live in Hawaii.

c. The person has a lot of free time.

d. The person wants to learn to surf.

The fax machine *went crazy and spit* paper all over the floor.

a 9. What is being given human traits?

a. fax machine

b. paper

c. floor

d. all of the above

d 10. How should this personification be interpreted?

a. The fax machine made strange noises.

b. The floor was covered with paper.

c. The fax machine stopped.

d. The fax machine malfunctioned.

Pat's cousin is as tall *as a telephone pole.*

b 11. What two things are being compared?

a. Pat and her cousin

b. Pat's cousin and a telephone pole

c. Pat and a telephone pole

d. all of the above

__a__ **12.** How are they alike?

a. Both are tall.
b. Both have excellent posture.
c. Both like to talk on the telephone.
d. Both work for the phone company.

__b__ **13.** How should this simile be interpreted?

a. Pat is very tall.
b. Pat's cousin is very tall.
c. A telephone pole is very tall.
d. A telephone pole is very straight.

The twin sisters are *as alike as mirror images.*

__b__ **14.** What is being compared?

a. twin sisters
b. a set of twin sisters and mirror images
c. twins and sisters
d. mirror images

__b__ **15.** How are they alike?

a. They have similar personalities.
b. They are identical in appearance.
c. They often behave in the same manner.
d. They have similar beliefs.

__a__ **16.** How should this metaphor be interpreted?

a. The twins are identical twins.
b. The sisters are looking in the mirror.
c. The sisters are twins.
d. Mirror images are identical.

After I received an "A" on my history test, I picked up my books and *danced all the way home!*

__c__ **17.** What is the hyperbole (exaggeration)?

a. receiving an "A" on my history test
b. picking up my books
c. dancing all the way home
d. all of the above

__c__ **18.** How should this hyperbole be interpreted?

a. The person is an excellent student.
b. The person likes history.
c. The person was very excited about the history test grade.
d. The person loves to dance.

Opportunity knocks **on everyone's door at least once.**

__a__ **19.** What is being given human traits?

a. opportunity
b. the door
c. everyone
d. all of the above

__d__ **20.** How should this personification be interpreted?

a. Some people never have a good opportunity in life.
b. There are only a few opportunities in each person's life.
c. No one deserves more than one opportunity in his or her lifetime.
d. Everybody receives at least one good opportunity during his or her life.

SELECTION **2-1**
Human Development

SHOULD TEENAGERS WORK PART-TIME?

From *Human Development*
By Diane Papalia and Sally Olds

Did you have a part-time job when you were in high school? If so, you are very typical: Eight out of every ten American teenagers have jobs at some point during their school years. Did you work because of necessity or simply to have some spending money? Was the work itself a valuable experience?

In 2005, the U.S. Department of Labor reported that two million teens work during the school year and three million during the summer. According to a report from the National Research Council and the Institute of Medicine, teens who work more than 20 hours per week after school are less likely to finish high school and more likely to use drugs. This was true, regardless of the teens' economic background. The report also noted that twice as many teens as adults are injured at work: Approximately 100,000 teens wind up in hospital emergency rooms each year with job-related injuries. Other experts point out, however, that having a job teaches punctuality, money management, and how to work effectively with others. Obviously, there is more than one side to this issue. The selection below, from a human development textbook, presents both positive and negative effects of part-time work on teenage students.

1 Many teenage students today hold part-time jobs. This trend conforms to the American belief of the moral benefits derived from working. However, some research challenges the value of part-time work for teenage students who do not have to work to help support their families. Let's look at both sides of the issue.

2 On the *positive* side, paid work is generally believed to teach young people to handle money responsibly. It helps them develop good work habits, such as promptness, reliability, and efficient management of time.

3 A good part-time job helps a teenager assume responsibility and work with people of different ages and backgrounds. It enables an adolescent to learn workplace skills, such as how to find a job and how to get along with employers, co-workers, and sometimes the public. By helping a young person learn more about a particular field of work, it may guide her or him in choosing a career. Furthermore, by showing adolescents how demanding and difficult the world of work is and how unprepared they are for it, part-time jobs, especially menial ones, sometimes motivate young people to continue their education.

4 On the *negative* side, research has questioned the benefits of part-time work and has identified serious costs. Most high school students who work part-time have low-level, repetitive jobs in which they do not learn skills useful later in life. Teenagers who work are no more independent in making financial decisions and are not likely to earn any more money as adults than those who do not hold jobs during high school.

Prediction Exercises

Directions: Use the skill of predicting to anticipate what the upcoming paragraphs will be about.

Prediction Exercise

What do you predict the next few paragraphs will be about?

(Answers will vary.)

✓ **Teaching Tip**

When you introduce this selection, ask for a show of hands by students who worked part-time in high school. Ask how many are working now and how many hours per week they work. Ideally, students should strike an appropriate balance between their school and work load.

5 Outside work seems to undermine performance in school, especially for teenagers who work more than 15 to 20 hours per week. Grades, involvement in school, and attendance decline. Students who work more than 15 hours a week are more likely to drop out of school and thus to be less prepared for careers and for life.

6 There are several drawbacks to working while you are a student. Young people who work long hours are less likely to eat breakfast, exercise, get enough sleep, or have enough leisure time. They spend less time with their families and may feel less close to them. They have little contact with adults on the job, and their jobs usually reinforce gender stereotypes. Some teenagers spend their earnings on alcohol or drugs, develop cynical attitudes toward work, and cheat or steal from their employers.

7 However, some of these undesirable effects may result, not from working itself, but from the factors that motivate some teenagers to take jobs. Some may want to work because they are already uninterested in school or feel alienated from their families or because they want money to buy whatever they want. Jobs may actually help keep such young people out of trouble by providing legal ways for them to earn money.

Prediction Exercise

What do you predict the next few paragraphs will be about?

(Answers will vary.)

Source: Adapted from Diane E. Papalia and Sally Olds, *Human Development,* 7th ed., p. 360.

SELECTION 2-1
Human Development
(continued)

Comprehension and Vocabulary Quiz

This quiz has four parts. Your instructor may assign some or all of them.

Comprehension

Directions: Items 1–5 test your comprehension (understanding) of the material in this selection. These questions are much like those that a content-area instructor (such as a human development professor) would expect you to know after reading and studying this selection. For each comprehension question below, use information from the selection to determine the correct answer. Refer to the selection as you answer the questions. Write your answers in the spaces provided.

¶3 ___c___ **1.** A good part-time job helps a teenager:

a. become independent from his or her parents.
b. spend more time with his or her family.
c. learn workplace skills such as how to get along with employers and co-workers.
d. decide whether or not to continue his or her education.

¶4 ___b___ **2.** A negative aspect of teenagers working part-time is that it:

a. interferes with their social life.
b. seems to hurt their academic performance.
c. causes them to sleep too much on weekends.
d. prohibits any participation in athletic events.

¶2 ___d___ **3.** Which of the following is a benefit of teenagers working?

a. may teach them how to handle money responsibly
b. encourages the development of good work habits
c. allows them to assume responsibility
d. all of the above

All¶ ___d___ **4.** Based on information in this selection, we can conclude that:

a. teenagers should not work part-time.
b. teenagers should work part-time.
c. a teenager's parents should decide whether their child should work part-time.
d. whether teenagers should work part-time when they don't have to is a complex issue.

¶5 ___a___ **5.** Teenagers who work more than 15 hours per week:

a. are more likely to drop out of school.
b. cause more discipline problems at school.
c. are more likely to save money for their college education.
d. tend to cheat their employers or steal from them.

Vocabulary in Context

Directions: Items 6–10 test your ability to determine the meaning of the word by using context clues. *Context clues* are words in a sentence that allow the reader to deduce (reason out) the meaning of an unfamiliar word in that sentence. Context clues also enable the reader to determine which meaning the author intends when a word has more than one meaning. For each vocabulary item below, a sentence from the selection containing an important word (*italicized, like this*) is quoted first. Next, there is an additional sentence using the word in the same sense and providing another context clue. Use the context clues from *both* sentences to deduce the meaning of the italicized word. *Be sure the answer you choose makes sense in both sentences.* If you need to use a dictionary to confirm your answer choice, remember that the meaning you select must still fit the context of *both* sentences. Write your answers in the spaces provided.

Pronunciation Key: ă **pat** ā **pay** âr **care** ä **father** ĕ **pet** ē **be** ĭ **pit**
ī **tie** îr **pier** ŏ **pot** ō **toe** ô **paw** oi **noise** ou **out** o͝o **took**
o͞o **boot** ŭ **cut** yo͞o ab**use** ûr **urge** th **thin** *th* **this** hw **which**
zh vision ə **a**bout *Stress mark:* ′

¶1 a **6.** This trend *conforms* to the American belief of the moral benefits derived from working.

Nicole *conforms* to her school's dress code, but she complains constantly about the uniform they must wear.

conforms (kən fôrmz′) means:

a. complies with

b. resents strongly

c. dislikes intensely

d. enjoys

¶1 c **7.** This trend conforms to the American belief of the moral benefits *derived* from working.

Residents at the nursing home *derived* great pleasure from visits by college-age volunteers.

derived (dĭ rīvd′) means:

a. prevented

b. suffered

c. obtained

d. avoided

¶3 b **8.** Furthermore, by showing adolescents how demanding and difficult the world of work is and how unprepared they are for it, part-time jobs, especially *menial* ones, sometimes motivate young people to continue their education.

Because Marcos was hired as a waiter, he resented having to do *menial* tasks such as sweeping the floor and refilling salt and pepper shakers.

menial (mē′ nē əl) means:

a. time-consuming

b. suitable for a servant

c. feminine

d. challenging

¶5 ___a___ **9.** Outside work seems to *undermine* performance in school, especially for teenagers who work more than 15 to 20 hours per week.

Not scheduling sufficient study time will *undermine* a college student's chance of success.

undermine (ŭn′ dər mīn) means:

a. weaken

b. ruin

c. defeat

d. enhance

¶6 ___d___ **10.** Some teenagers spend their earnings on alcohol or drugs, develop *cynical* attitudes toward work, and cheat or steal from their employers.

Adolescents whose parents have divorced sometimes become *cynical* about marriage.

cynical (sĭn′ ĭ kəl) means:

a. elated

b. curious

c. eager

d. scornful

Word Structure

Directions: Items 11–15 test your ability to use word-structure clues to help determine a word's meaning. *Word-structure clues* consist of roots, prefixes, and suffixes. In these exercises, you will learn the meaning of a word part (a root) and use it to determine the meaning of several other words that have the same word part. If you need to use a dictionary to confirm your answer choice, do so. Write your answers in the spaces provided.

In paragraph 7 of the selection, you encountered the word **factors.** This word contains the Latin root ***fac,*** which means "make" or "do." In this selection, *factor* means something that "*makes* an active contribution to an accomplishment, result, or process." Use the meaning of ***fac*** and the list of prefixes on pages 68–69 to help you determine the meaning of each of the following words that contain this same root.

d 11. A **factory** is a place where things are:

a. bought.

b. sold.

c. traded.

d. made.

a 12. To feel **satisfaction** means to feel:

a. content.

b. angry.

c. silly.

d. ill.

a 13. To **manufacture** items is to:

a. produce them.

b. recycle them.

c. collect them.

d. donate them.

b 14. In comic books and cartoons, **malefactors** are characters who:

a. are superheroes.

b. do criminal or evil things.

c. are able to change form.

d. are disguised as animals.

c 15. A **benefactor** is a person who:

a. inherits money.

b. reads widely.

c. does good by giving money.

d. grows abundant crops.

✓ **Teaching Tip**
Let students know that most of the skills included in this section have not been introduced yet. This section serves as a valuable preview of these skills, however. Students typically get several of the items correct, and they find this encouraging.

Reading Skills Application

Directions: Items 16–20 test your ability to *apply* certain reading skills to information in this selection. These types of questions provide valuable practice for all students, especially those who must take standardized reading tests and state-mandated basic skills tests. You have not studied all of the skills at this point, so some items will serve as a helpful preview. The comprehension and critical reading skills in this section are presented in Chapters 3 through 9 of *New Worlds;* vocabulary and figurative language skills are presented in Chapter 2. As you work through *New Worlds,* you will practice and develop these skills. Write your answers in the spaces provided.

¶6 stated main idea (Chapter 4)

a 16. Which of the following statements best expresses the main idea of paragraph 6 of the selection?

a. There are several drawbacks to working while you are a student.

b. Young people who work long hours are less likely to eat breakfast, exercise, get enough sleep, or have enough leisure time.

c. They spend less time with their families and may feel less close to them.
d. They have little contact with adults on the job, and their jobs usually reinforce gender stereotypes.

authors' writing patterns (Chapter 7) ___a___ **17.** The author has used which of these patterns to organize the information in the selection?

a. a contrast between the advantages and disadvantages of teenagers working part-time
b. the causes of teenagers working part-time
c. a sequence of reactions of teenagers to working part-time
d. a list of the ways teenagers benefit from working part-time

supporting details (Chapter 6) ___d___ **18.** Which of the following is *not* mentioned as a drawback to teenagers who work part-time?

a. spending less time with their families and feeling less close to them
b. being less likely to get enough sleep
c. developing cynical attitudes toward work
d. not being able to meet and make new friends

evaluating the author's argument (Chapter 9) ___c___ **19.** Which of the following statements represents an accurate assessment of the author's objectivity?

a. The author is biased in favor of teenagers working part-time.
b. The author is biased against teenagers working part-time.
c. The author presents both sides of the issue objectively.
d. It is not possible to evaluate the author's objectivity.

¶3 vocabulary in context (Chapter 2) ___a___ **20.** What is the meaning of *demanding* as it is used in paragraph 3 of the selection?

a. requiring much effort
b. highly interesting
c. frustrating
d. exhausting

✓ **Teaching Tip**
We suggest that rather than include this Reading Skills Application section as part of the quiz grade, you use it to give students a helpful preview of upcoming skills. It makes an excellent collaborative activity. All students will find this practice helpful, especially those who must take course exit tests, standardized reading tests, or state-mandated basic skills tests.

SELECTION 2-1
Human Development
(continued)

Collaboration Option

Writing and Collaborating to Enhance Your Understanding

Option for collaboration: Your instructor may direct you to work with other students or, in other words, to work *collaboratively*. In that case, you should form groups of three or four students as directed by your instructor and work together to complete the exercises. After your group discusses each item and agrees on the answer, have a group member record it. Every member of your group should be able to explain all of your group's answers.

1. **Reacting to What You Have Read:** In this selection the authors look at both sides of the issue of students working part-time when it is not a financial necessity.

Which side of the issue do you support? Give the reasons you think high school students should or should not work part-time.

(Answers will vary.)

2. **Comprehending the Selection Further:** Many college students work part-time (or even full-time!), but how much is *too* much? What, in your opinion, is the maximum number of hours per week a full-time college student should attempt to work? In your opinion, what are the worst kinds of jobs for college students? What are the best kinds of jobs for them? (Be sure to answer all of these questions.)

(Answers will vary.)

3. **Overall Main Idea of the Selection:** In one sentence, tell what the authors want readers to understand about teenagers working part-time. (Be sure to include the words "teenagers working part-time" in your overall main idea sentence.)

There are both advantages and disadvantages to teenagers working part-time.

Internet Resources

Read More about This Topic on the World Wide Web

Directions: For further information about the topic of the selection, visit these websites:

www.jobsearch.about.com/cs/justforstudents/a/parttimejob.htm
This website contains an article titled "Getting Your First Part-Time Job" by Jay Pipes, a writer for GrooveJob.com.

You can also use your favorite search engine such as Google, Yahoo!, or AltaVista (www.google.com, www.yahoo.com, www.altavista.com) to discover more about this topic. To locate additional information, type in combinations of keywords such as:

part-time jobs teens

or

teenagers jobs

Keep in mind that whenever you go to *any* website, it is a good idea to evaluate the website and the information it contains. Ask yourself questions such as:

"Who sponsors this website?"

"Is the information contained in this website up-to-date?"

"What type of information is presented?"

"Is the information objective and complete?"

"How easy is it to use the features of this website?"

SELECTION **2-2**
Business

McDONALDIZATION: THE SUN NEVER SETS ON THE GOLDEN ARCHES

From *Understanding Business*
By William Nickels, James McHugh, and Susan McHugh

Nearly everyone in America—certainly every child—recognizes McDonald's "golden arches." This business textbook selection explains why McDonald's is the premier example of a global franchiser: McDonald's has been supremely successful in tailoring its outlets to the values of the countries in which its franchised restaurants are located. (A franchiser is a company that sells people the right to offer its products or services in a given territory.) Also, it will help you to know that the word "abroad" means "in a foreign country" or "not of one's own country."

About the title: There was once a famous saying, "The sun never sets on the British Empire." The British Empire began in the 16th century, and at the height of its glory (around 1900), it included Australia, Canada, India, New Zealand, extensive portions of Africa, and many smaller territories throughout the world. In other words, the British Empire was so vast and extended to so many parts of the globe that it was always daytime somewhere in the empire. The authors of this selection have titled it "The Sun Never Sets on the Golden Arches" to suggest the global vastness of McDonald's "empire." McDonald's operates more than 31,000 restaurants in 119 countries and territories and employs more than 1.5 million people. It is estimated that 10 to 20 percent of U.S. workers have been employed by McDonald's at one time or another. Each day, McDonald's serves almost 50 million customers worldwide.

1 The tremendous expansion of franchising, led by the U.S. companies, has changed the landscape of the global market. Today small, midsize, and large franchises cover the globe, offering business opportunities in areas from exercise to education. Still, when the word *franchise* comes to mind, one name dominates all others: "McDonaldization" symbolizes the spread of franchising and the weaving of American pop culture into the world fabric. Whether in South Africa, Mexico, Germany, or Hong Kong, no one adapts better and blends the franchise values into the local culture better than McDonald's.

2 For example, after setting up its first franchises in Hong Kong in 1975, McDonald's altered the breakfast menu after realizing that customers there liked burgers for breakfast, then preferred chicken or fish for the rest of the day. The company also found that it was advisable to keep napkin dispensers away from the customers. It seems that older people in Hong Kong who went through hard times after World War II took huge wads of napkins from the holders and stuffed them in their pockets. Now it's one napkin per customer. McDonald's even spruced up the notoriously dirty toilet facilities that were a negative trademark of Hong Kong restaurants.

3 In Hong Kong, as in all markets in which it operates, the company continuously listens to customers and adapts to their preferences. For example, McDonald's quickly responded to Hong Kong customers' anxious appetite for promotions. To the delight of Hong Kong customers, McDonald's offered popular Japanese cat figures called Hello Kitty dolls as a follow-up to a

Prediction Exercises

Directions: Use the skill of predicting to anticipate what the upcoming paragraphs will be about.

Prediction Exercise

What do you predict the next paragraph will be about?

(Answers will vary.) __________

____

____

____

Competition today is global. This means that companies from all over the world can compete in the United States, just as American firms can seek new markets beyond our borders. This McDonald's restaurant, for example, is in Moscow. McDonald's actually sells more hamburgers and fries in other countries than it does in the United States. In 2007, 65 percent of its revenue came from abroad. Its European sales exceed U.S. sales.

very popular Snoopy doll promotion. Even executives at high-tech companies and leading financiers gladly waited in line for the Hello Kitty dolls coveted by their children. Hong Kong children also cannot wait to visit "Suk-Suk" McDonald (Uncle Ronald McDonald) on their birthdays, since the company began to tout such events on local television. The company also encourages college students in Hong Kong to use the local McDonald's as a place to socialize and study.

4 By using adaptive strategies in global markets, McDonald's reaps a large payoff. By 2002, the company derived more than half of its $72 billion in sales from abroad. Hong Kong actually boasts two of the world's busiest McDonald's, and about half of the city's 6.8 million people eat at a McDonald's restaurant every week. James L. Watson, a Harvard University anthropologist, perhaps said it best: "McDonald's has become a very important part of global culture. The company's efforts involving hygiene in its restrooms is just one example. Their efforts caused other restaurants to follow the lead. That's not bad diplomacy."

Prediction Exercise

What do you predict the next paragraph will be about?

(Answers will vary.)

✓ **Teaching Tips**

- Ask your students if they have worked at McDonald's, or have friends who have.
- McDonald's is the world's largest purchaser of beef, pork, potatoes, and apples.
- In 2006, McDonald's began a major redesign of its restaurants, with terra-cotta and a warmer gold replacing the bright red and yellow. Wood and brick will also soften the environment.

Source: Adapted from William G. Nickels, James M. McHugh, and Susan M. McHugh, *Understanding Business,* 6th ed., p. 69.

SELECTION **2-2**
Business
(continued)

Comprehension and Vocabulary Quiz

This quiz has four parts. Your instructor may assign some or all of them.

Comprehension

Directions: Items 1–5 test your comprehension (understanding) of the material in this selection. These questions are much like those that a content-area instructor (such as a business professor) would expect you to know after reading and studying this selection. For each comprehension question below, use information from the selection to determine the correct answer. Refer to the selection as you answer the questions. Write your answers in the spaces provided.

¶2 __b__ **1.** In 1975, McDonald's franchises in Hong Kong changed their breakfast menu because:

a. they discovered customers preferred chicken and fish instead of burgers.
b. they realized customers liked burgers for breakfast.
c. their prices were too high.
d. French fries and milkshakes did not fit the local culture.

¶3 __d__ **2.** A large part of McDonald's success as a global franchiser results from:

a. the appeal of low-priced fast food.
b. improving the hygiene in its restrooms.
c. the popularity of "McDonaldization."
d. adapting to customer preferences.

¶4 __c__ **3.** In 2002, how much of McDonald's total sales came from abroad?

a. $72 billion
b. $6.8 million
c. more than half of its total sales
d. a relatively small portion of its total sales

✓ **Teaching Tip**
By 2002, McDonald's *total* sales was $72 billion. Sales from abroad accounted for *more than half* of this amount.

¶3 __d__ **4.** McDonald's has become a tremendous success in Hong Kong because:

a. it has responded to Hong Kong customers' love of promotions like the Hello Kitty dolls and the Snoopy doll.
b. it knows how to blend American pop culture with the local culture.
c. it encourages college students to use the restaurants as a place to socialize and study.
d. all of the above

photo caption __a__ **5.** Today, McDonald's:

a. sells more burgers and fries internationally than it does in the United States.
b. has restaurants in virtually every country in the world.
c. changes its menus often in order to spread American pop culture.
d. is a leader in international diplomacy.

Vocabulary in Context

Directions: Items 6–10 test your ability to determine the meaning of the word by using context clues. *Context clues* are words in a sentence that allow the reader to deduce (reason out) the meaning of an unfamiliar word in that sentence. Context clues also enable the reader to determine which meaning the author intends when a word has more than one meaning. For each vocabulary item below, a sentence from the selection containing an important word (*italicized, like this*) is quoted first. Next, there is an additional sentence using the word in the same sense and providing another context clue. Use the context clues from *both* sentences to deduce the meaning of the italicized word. *Be sure the answer you choose makes sense in both sentences.* If you need to use a dictionary to confirm your answer choice, remember that the meaning you select must still fit the context of *both* sentences. Write your answers in the spaces provided.

Pronunciation Key: ă **pat** ā **pay** âr **care** ä **father** ĕ **pet** ē **be** ĭ **pit**
ī **tie** îr **pier** ŏ **pot** ō **toe** ô **paw** oi **noise** ou **out** o͝o **took**
o͞o **boot** ŭ **cut** yo͞o **abuse** ûr **urge** th **thin** *th* **this** hw **which**
zh **vision** ə **about** *Stress mark:* ′

¶1 ___d___ **6.** Whether in South Africa, Mexico, Germany, or Hong Kong, no one *adapts* better and blends the franchise values into the local culture better than McDonald's.

Philip is a popular speaker because he always *adapts* his presentation to the particular audience to whom he is speaking.

adapts (ə dăpts′) means:

a. reveals

b. stumbles through

c. explains carefully

d. adjusts according to circumstances

¶3 ___b___ **7.** Hong Kong children also cannot wait to visit "Suk-Suk" McDonald (Uncle Ronald McDonald) on their birthdays, since the company began to *tout* such events on local television.

The movie studio has planned a multimillion-dollar advertising campaign to *tout* its new science fiction thriller.

tout (tout) means:

a. to cancel without prior notice

b. to publicize loudly or extravagantly

c. to sponsor

d. to recall

¶4 ____c____ **8.** By using such adaptive strategies in global markets, McDonald's *reaps* a large payoff.

A person who lies invariably *reaps* the consequences.

reaps (rēps) means:

a. to avoid by using deception

b. to misunderstand

c. to obtain in return

d. to suffer

¶4 ____b____ **9.** By 2002, the company *derived* more than half of its $72 billion in sales from abroad.

The study confirmed that volunteers *derived* great satisfaction from doing charitable work.

derived (dĭ rīvd′) means:

a. to spend

b. to receive

c. to give up

d. to save

¶4 ____a____ **10.** James L. Watson, a Harvard University *anthropologist,* perhaps said it best: "McDonald's has become a very important part of global culture."

Because of her interests in various cultures of the world, Marie decided to become an *anthropologist.*

anthropologist (ăn thrə pŏl′ ə jĭst) means:

a. one who studies the development and behavior of humans and their cultures

b. one who studies the development of towns and cities

c. one who studies ancient manuscripts

d. one who studies the behavior of bees and ants

Word Structure

Directions: Items 11–15 test your ability to use word-structure clues to help determine a word's meaning. *Word-structure clues* consist of roots, prefixes, and suffixes. In these exercises, you will learn the meaning of a word part (a root) and use it to determine the meaning of several other words that have the same word part. If you need to use a dictionary to confirm your answer choice, do so. Write your answers in the spaces provided.

In paragraph 3 of the selection, you encountered the word **promotions.** This word contains the Latin root ***mot,*** which means "to move" or "motion." The word *promotions* refers to methods of "moving" merchandise (increasing sales of merchandise) through advertising, publicity, or discounting. Use the meaning of ***mot*** and the list of prefixes on pages 68–69 to help you determine the meaning of each of the following words that contain this same root.

b **11.** If a person in the military is **demoted,** he or she:

a. stays at the same rank for an unusually long period of time.
b. is moved to a lower rank.
c. is moved to a higher rank.
d. is forced to withdraw completely from the military.

c **12.** A **remote** control allows you to change TV channels:

a. by pressing buttons on the TV set.
b. through preprogramming the VCR.
c. without having to get up and move to the TV set itself.
d. after consulting the TV schedule.

b **13.** If there is a **commotion,** there is:

a. an all-night party going on.
b. agitated movement or a disturbance of some sort.
c. a loud, noisy celebration.
d. a bus or a train going by.

a **14. Emotion** refers to:

a. the moving or stirring up of feelings.
b. feelings that are dormant.
c. feelings that are not apparent or obvious.
d. the suppression or control of feelings.

d **15.** A **motive:**

a. prevents an action from occurring.
b. causes an action to stop.
c. slows down a process.
d. moves a person to do something.

✓ **Teaching Tip**
Let students know that most of the skills included in this Reading Skills Application section have not been introduced yet. This section serves as a valuable preview of these skills, however. Students typically get several of the items correct, and they find this encouraging.

Reading Skills Application

Directions: Items 16–20 test your ability to *apply* certain reading skills to information in this selection. These types of questions provide valuable practice for all students, especially those who must take standardized reading tests and state-mandated basic skills tests. You have not studied all of the skills at this point, so some items will serve as a helpful preview. The comprehension and critical reading skills in this section are presented in Chapters 3 through 9 of *New Worlds;* vocabulary and figurative language skills are presented in Chapter 2. As you work through *New Worlds,* you will practice and develop these skills. Write your answers in the spaces provided.

¶2 vocabulary in context (Chapter 2)

a **16.** In paragraph 2 of the selection, *spruced up* means:

a. neatened in appearance.
b. decorated with trees.
c. enlarged or expanded.
d. sealed up or closed.

conclusions (Chapter 9) ___d___

17. Based on the material presented in the selection, which of the following is a logical conclusion?

a. McDonald's is the most successful company in the world.

b. McDonald's franchises were more difficult to establish in Hong Kong than in other foreign cities.

c. Toy giveaways and other similar promotions are the key to McDonald's worldwide success.

d. Other companies who want to offer international franchises could benefit from emulating McDonald's adaptability.

¶4 authors' writing patterns (Chapter 7) ___b___

18. What pattern is used to organize the information in paragraph 4 of the selection?

a. comparison and contrast

b. cause and effect

c. sequence

d. list

✓ **Teaching Tip**
cause = adaptive strategies
effect = reaps a large payoff

¶4 stated main idea (Chapter 4) ___a___

19. Which of the following statements best expresses the main idea of paragraph 4?

a. By using adaptive strategies in global markets, McDonald's reaps a large payoff.

b. Hong Kong actually boasts two of the world's busiest McDonald's, and about half of the city's 6.8 million people eat at a McDonald's restaurant every week.

c. James L. Watson, a Harvard University anthropologist, perhaps said it best: "McDonald's has become a very important part of global culture."

d. The company's efforts involving hygiene in its restrooms are just one example.

distinguishing facts from opinion (Chapter 9) ___d___

20. Which of the following statements represents an opinion rather than a fact?

a. By 2002, the company derived more than half of its $72 billion in sales from abroad.

b. Hong Kong actually boasts two of the world's busiest McDonald's, and about half of the city's 6.8 million people eat at a McDonald's restaurant every week.

c. "Their efforts caused other restaurants to follow the lead."

d. "That's not bad diplomacy."

✓ **Teaching Tip**
Choices *a, b,* and *c* can be researched and confirmed, so they are facts.

✓ **Teaching Tip**
We suggest that rather than include this section as part of the quiz grade, you use it to give students practice with the skills they have studied and as a helpful preview of upcoming skills. It makes an excellent collaborative activity. All students will find this practice helpful, especially those who must take course exit tests, standardized reading tests, or state-mandated basic skills tests.

SELECTION 2-2

Business

(continued)

Writing and Collaborating to Enhance Your Understanding

Option for collaboration: Your instructor may direct you to work with other students or, in other words, to work *collaboratively.* In that case, you should form groups of three or four students as directed by your instructor and work together to complete the exercises. After your group discusses each item and agrees on the answer, have a group member record it. Every member of your group should be able to explain all of your group's answers.

Collaboration Option

1. **Reacting to What You Have Read:** Have you ever visited a McDonald's restaurant in some other city, state, or country? If so, there were probably some differences between that franchise and the one you frequent near your home or school. Describe some of the ways you observed that McDonald's franchisers adapted their menus and their restaurants to the local culture. If you have not visited McDonald's in other locations, describe the general types of adaptations you *think* franchisers could make.

   - the presence of playground equipment in areas with lots of children
   - spicier items on the menu in some areas or countries
   - opening or closing at times that suit an area best
   - saying things the "local" way—e.g., "take away" rather than "carry out" or "to go."

2. **Comprehending the Selection Further:** List some of the "lessons" McDonald's franchisers learned about attracting customers in Hong Kong.

   - Customers like burgers for breakfast but prefer chicken or fish during the rest of the day.
   - Older customers take too many napkins home, so it is advisable not to use self-serve napkin dispensers.
   - Customers appreciate the improved hygiene in restrooms.
   - Customers like promotions such as the Hello Kitty dolls and Snoopy dolls.
   - Children enjoy visiting Uncle Ronald McDonald on their birthdays.
   - College students are encouraged to use McDonald's as a place to socialize and study.

3. **Overall Main Idea of the Selection:** In one sentence, tell what the author wants readers to understand about the success of McDonald's international franchises. (Be sure to include the phrase "the success of McDonald's international franchises" in your overall main idea sentence.)

The tremendous *success of McDonald's international franchises* is due to its adaptive marketing strategies and its ability to blend franchise values into the local culture.

Internet Resources

Read More about This Topic on the World Wide Web

Directions: For further information about the topic of the selection, visit these websites:

www.mcdonalds.com
This is the official website for the McDonald's corporation. It includes links for podcasts, international market sites, and corporate information.

www.slowfood.com
This is the website for an international organization called SlowFood. Its aim is "to protect the pleasures of the table from the homogenization of modern fast food and life."

You can also use your favorite search engine such as Google, Yahoo!, or AltaVista (www.google.com, www.yahoo.com, www.altavista.com) to discover more about this topic. To locate additional information, type in combinations of keywords such as:

McDonald's

or

McDonald's worldwide locations

Keep in mind that whenever you go to *any* website, it is a good idea to evaluate the website and the information it contains. Ask yourself questions such as:

"Who sponsors this website?"

"Is the information contained in this website up-to-date?"

"What type of information is presented?"

"Is the information objective and complete?"

"How easy is it to use the features of this website?"

READING

SELECTION 2-3
Health

RAGE ON THE ROAD: THE DANGER OF AGGRESSIVE DRIVING

From *Understanding Your Health*
By Wayne Payne and Dale Hahn

Today there are more cars than ever on the road. The number of drivers and miles driven has increased dramatically during the last 35 years, with only 10 percent more roads built. Nationwide today, men spend an average of 84 minutes per day behind the wheel and women spend an average of 64 minutes. All of this can lead to some frustrating moments and aggression on the part of drivers. Moreover, half of all drivers confronted with aggression respond with aggression of their own (honking, shouting, making obscene gestures, cutting off other drivers).

Have you ever been the victim of an aggressive driver expressing "road rage"? If so, you may also have felt road rage. This selection from a health textbook addresses the increase in aggressive driving and explains what you can do to avoid feeling road rage yourself and provoking aggressive behavior in other drivers.

1 Motorists are aware of an increasing sense of aggression on America's congested highways. An unthinking act or no provocation at all can result in a deadly face-off with a complete stranger. Over the last six years, aggressive drivers have killed 218 people and injured another 12,610, at a frequency that increases about 7 percent each year. This is just the tip of the iceberg. For every incident serious enough to result in a police report or newspaper story, hundreds or thousands of other incidents take place that are never reported. The problem of road rage has become so bad that, according to a National Highway Safety Administration report, the public is more concerned about aggressive drivers (40%) than drunk drivers (33%).

Prediction Exercises

Directions: Use the skill of predicting to anticipate what the three subsections of this selection will be about. Use the subheadings to help you.

Characteristics of Aggressive Drivers

2 Although there is no profile *per se* of the typical aggressive driver, most aggressive drivers are men between the ages of 18 and 26. Many of these men are poorly educated, and some have criminal records or histories of violence and substance abuse, but hundreds of others are successful men and women, of all ages, with no such history.

3 Between the sexes, men are angered most by police presence and slow driving, whereas illegal behavior and traffic obstructions tend to frustrate women. When all factors are added in, though, men and women do not differ in total driving anger scores. Increasingly, women are acting on their anger. Only 4 percent of recorded aggressive driving incidents involved women drivers, but during the last 15 years the number of fatal accidents involving women drivers has increased dramatically while men's risks have dropped. Most of the increase for women has occurred because more women are on the road at riskier times, but women are also increasingly displaying the more aggressive driving tactics common among men.

4 Individually, people generally think of themselves as better-than-average drivers. This holds true even among younger

Prediction Exercise

You have read the first paragraph. What do you predict the next section will be about?

characteristics of aggressive drivers

(Answers may vary.)

✓ **Teaching Tips**

- The headings in this selection illustrate how much help authors often provide in letting readers know "where they're going."
- People who use cell phones while driving are more aggressive than those who do not talk on the cell phone while driving.

The stress of home, work, and commuting; the anonymity of driving; and other factors can add up to rage on the road.

people, who consider themselves to be good drivers but their peers to be the worst drivers of any age group. But perceptions and reality are not always identical. While some people are aware of their aggressive tendencies on the road, other people see themselves as innocent and the issue of aggressive driving as everyone else's problem. The truth is we're all human and can let our emotions run away from us.

Causes of Aggressive Driving

5 Violent traffic disputes result not from single incidents but from personal attitudes and accumulated stress in motorists' lives. Specifically, drug use; domestic arguments or violence; racism; the desire to evade or attack police; and the everyday stresses of home, work, and commuting can lead to aggressive driving. For the general population, the anonymity and physical excitement of driving, combined with a feeling of control and power and the ability to drive away, sow the seeds of aggression. Some people drive to "win" rather than to arrive safely at their destination. Adding to this climate are overpowered cars, driver's licenses that are easy to qualify for, and sporadically lax enforcement of traffic laws.

Prediction Exercise

What do you predict this subsection will be about?

causes of aggressive driving

(Answers will vary.)

Ways to Avoid Provoking Aggressive Drivers

6 The best way to stay out of driving conflicts is not to be an aggressive driver yourself. You can do a number of things to reduce your stress and thus reduce the tendency toward aggression. First, allow plenty of time for your trip. We tend to

overschedule our days and not allow enough time to get from one place to the next. Sure, under perfect conditions you could cover X number of miles in X amount of time, but weather, traffic, and road construction are facts of life. Not building extra travel time into our schedules causes us to run late when we encounter these variables and then get angry and possibly aggressive. Other ways to reduce stress are to listen to soothing music, improve the comfort of your vehicle, and probably, most of all, understand that you can't control the traffic—only your reaction to it.

Prediction Exercise

What do you predict this subsection will be about?

ways to avoid provoking aggressive drivers

(Answers will vary.)

7 To avoid provoking road rage, practice driving courtesy and keep the following points in mind:

- Do not make obscene gestures.
- Use your horn sparingly.
- Do not block the passing lane.
- Do not switch lanes without signaling.
- Do not block the right-hand turn lane.
- Do not take more than one parking space.
- If you are not disabled, do not park in a space reserved for disabled people.
- Do not allow your door to hit the car parked next to you.
- Do not tailgate.
- If you travel slowly, pull over and allow traffic to pass.
- Avoid unnecessary use of high-beam headlights.
- Do not let the car phone distract you.
- Do not stop in the road to talk to a pedestrian or another driver.
- Do not inflict loud music on neighboring cars.

8 Avoid engaging other drivers by following the limousine drivers' rule: Duty bound to protect their passengers, they do not make eye contact with other drivers. If another driver is following you, don't drive home. Instead, drive to a public place, ideally a police station. This or using your cell phone to call for help is usually enough to scare off the offending driver.

9 Of course, it's hard not to respond when challenged. It may help to look at the other driver's mistakes and actions objectively and not take them personally. Leave their poor behavior as their problem; don't make it yours. Remember how dangerous the situation can become.

10 It's not one driver's job to teach other drivers proper manners. In all certainty, you won't be successful. Instead, try being extra nice to a fellow driver. Courtesy can be as contagious as road rage.

Source: Wayne A. Payne and Dale B. Hahn, *Understanding Your Health,* 5th ed., pp. 604–07. Copyright © 1998 by The McGraw-Hill Companies, Inc. Reprinted by permission of The McGraw-Hill Companies, Inc.

SELECTION 2-3
Health
(continued)

Comprehension and Vocabulary Quiz

This quiz has four parts. Your instructor may assign some or all of them.

Comprehension

Directions: Items 1–5 test your comprehension (understanding) of the material in this selection. These questions are much like those that a content-area instructor (such as a health professor) would expect you to know after reading and studying this selection. For each comprehension question below, use information from the selection to determine the correct answer. Refer to the selection as you answer the questions. Write your answers in the spaces provided.

¶1 ___b___ **1.** Statistics show that aggressive driving is common, but the problem may be worse than we think because:

a. young drivers have less experience than in the past.
b. many aggressive driving incidents are never reported.
c. many drivers are killed every year.
d. aggressive drivers often go unnoticed.

¶2 ___c___ **2.** The typical aggressive driver is a:

a. man with a criminal record.
b. young man or woman between the ages of 16 and 18.
c. man between the ages of 18 and 26.
d. young man who is frustrated.

¶3 ___b___ **3.** Aggressive women drivers tend to become frustrated by:

a. slow driving and the presence of police.
b. illegal behavior and traffic obstructions.
c. speed limits and traffic rules.
d. the presence of children in the car.

¶6 ___b___ **4.** The best way to avoid driving conflicts is to:

a. observe all traffic rules and speed limits.
b. not be an aggressive driver yourself.
c. avoid tailgating and travel slowly and cautiously.
d. not inflict loud music on neighboring cars.

¶6 ___a___ **5.** One way to reduce your own chances of becoming an aggressive driver is to:

a. allow plenty of time for your trips.
b. maintain eye contact with other drivers.
c. report drivers who disregard traffic rules.
d. travel slowly and stay in the right-hand lane.

Vocabulary in Context

Directions: Items 6–10 test your ability to determine the meaning of the word by using context clues. *Context clues* are words in a sentence that allow the reader to deduce (reason out) the meaning of an unfamiliar word in that sentence. Context clues also enable the reader to determine which meaning the author intends when a word has more than one meaning. For each vocabulary item below, a sentence from the selection containing an important word (*italicized, like this*) is quoted first. Next, there is an additional sentence using the word in the same sense and providing another context clue. Use the context clues from *both* sentences to deduce the meaning of the italicized word. *Be sure the answer you choose makes sense in both sentences.* If you need to use a dictionary to confirm your answer choice, remember that the meaning you select must still fit the context of *both* sentences. Write your answers in the spaces provided.

Pronunciation Key: ă **pat** ā **pay** âr **care** ä **father** ĕ **pet** ē **be** ĭ **pit**
ī **tie** îr **pier** ŏ **pot** ō **toe** ô **paw** oi **noise** ou **out** o͝o **took**
o͞o **boot** ŭ **cut** yo͞o **abuse** ûr **urge** th **thin** *th* **this** hw **which**
zh **vision** ə **about** *Stress mark:* ′

¶12 ___b___ **6.** Although there is no profile *per se* of the typical aggressive driver, most aggressive drivers are men between the ages of 18 and 26.

With assembly-line jobs, it is not the work *per se* that is the problem; it is the constant pressure to work quickly and accurately at a repetitive task.

per se (per sā′) means:

a. by law

b. by itself

c. by chance

d. by choice

¶13 ___b___ **7.** Most of the increase for women has occurred because more women are on the road at riskier times, but women are also increasingly displaying the more aggressive driving *tactics* common among men.

George Patton's knowledge of military *tactics* made him one of the most effective U.S. generals of World War II.

tactics (tăk′ tĭks) means:

a. military strategies

b. set of actions designed to achieve a goal

c. tricks

d. unfair or illegal actions

¶5 c **8.** For the general population, the *anonymity* and physical excitement of driving, combined with a feeling of control and power and the ability to drive away, sow the seeds of aggression.

Hoping for *anonymity,* Princess Diana sometimes wore a disguise when she was in public.

anonymity (ăn ə nĭm′ ĭ tē) means:

a. invisibility

b. high level of danger

c. state of being unknown

d. avoidance of the press and other media

¶7 a **9.** Do not *inflict* loud music on neighboring cars.

The nurse gave inoculations in a way that did not *inflict* any unnecessary discomfort on patients.

inflict (ĭn flĭkt′) means:

a. impose

b. share

c. prevent

d. cause

¶8 a **10.** Avoid *engaging* other drivers by following the limousine driver's rule: Duty bound to protect their passengers, they do not make eye contact with other drivers.

Engaging troubled children in play therapy can help them communicate and work through problems they are experiencing.

engaging (ĕn gāj′ ēng) means:

a. attracting and holding the attention of

b. supporting

c. irritating and annoying

d. entertaining by amusing

Word Structure

Directions: Items 11–15 test your ability to use word-structure clues to help determine a word's meaning. *Word-structure clues* consist of roots, prefixes, and suffixes. In these exercises, you will learn the meaning of a word part (a root) and use it to determine the meaning of several other words that have the same word part. If you need to use a dictionary to confirm your answer choice, do so. Write your answers in the spaces provided.

In this selection you encountered the word **aggressive** several times. This word contains the Latin root ***gress,*** which means "go" or "step." "Aggressive" literally means "going against something or someone" in a hostile manner. Use the meaning of ***gress*** and the list of prefixes on pages 68–69 to help you determine the meaning of each of the following words that contain this same root.

b 11. If a young child **regresses** when a baby brother or sister is born, the child:

a. becomes more hostile.

b. goes back to less mature behavior.

c. improves in behavior.

d. remains consistent in behavior.

c 12. You are talking about one thing, *digress,* and then return to your original topic. To **digress** means to:

a. interrupt someone.

b. laugh loudly.

c. stray from your topic.

d. begin talking in a whisper.

a 13. If a person makes **progress,** it means that he or she:

a. goes forward or ahead.

b. steps to the side.

c. goes backward.

d. steps out of line.

b 14. A sign on a door that says "**Egress**" has the same meaning as a sign that says:

a. "Open."

b. "Exit."

c. "Push."

d. "Private."

d 15. If someone plays a **progression** of notes on the piano, the person plays:

a. a chord.

b. three notes.

c. a short song.

d. a sequence of notes.

✓ **Teaching Tip**

Let students know that most of the skills included in this Reading Skills Application section have not been introduced yet. This section serves as a valuable preview of these skills, however. Students typically get several of the items correct, and they find this encouraging.

Reading Skills Application

Directions: Items 16–20 test your ability to *apply* certain reading skills to information in this selection. These types of questions provide valuable practice for all students, especially those who must take standardized reading tests and state-mandated basic skills tests. You have not studied all of the skills at this point, so some items will serve as a helpful preview. The comprehension and critical reading skills in this section are presented in Chapters 3 through 9 of *New Worlds;* vocabulary and figurative language skills are presented in Chapter 2. As you work through *New Worlds,* you will practice and develop these skills. Write your answers in the spaces provided.

¶1 vocabulary in context (Chapter 2) ___d___

16. In paragraph 1 of the selection, the authors use *tip of the iceberg* to refer to:

a. the part of a floating ice mass that is above the surface of the ocean.

b. careless drivers who injure and kill others.

c. a disaster that cannot be avoided.

d. a relatively small but obvious problem that signals an even larger problem.

¶4 stated main idea (Chapter 4) ___a___

17. Which of the following statements best expresses the main idea of paragraph 4?

a. Individually, people generally think of themselves as better-than-average drivers, but perceptions and reality are not always identical.

b. We're all human and can let our emotions run away from us.

c. Young people consider themselves to be good drivers but their peers to be the worst drivers of any age group.

d. Some people are aware of their aggressive tendencies on the road.

author's intended audience (Chapter 8) ___d___

18. The authors most likely intend the audience of this selection to be:

a. aggressive drivers.

b. those who must deal with aggressive drivers.

c. teenage drivers.

d. all drivers.

supporting details (Chapter 6) ___d___

19. According to the selection, which of the following is an accurate statement about typical aggressive drivers?

a. They are usually men between the ages of 16 and 28.

b. They are women who are on the road at riskier times.

c. They are teenagers who have criminal records or histories of violence and substance abuse.

d. There is no profile *per se* of the typical aggressive driver, but most are men between the ages of 18 and 26.

conclusions (Chapter 9) ___b___

20. Based on information in the selection, which of the following is a logical conclusion?

a. The problem of road rage will gradually decrease over time.

b. Reducing sources of stress in motorists' lives could reduce the amount of road rage.

c. Requiring all drivers to take a course in driving courtesy could eliminate road rage.

d. Nothing can be done to deal with the problem of road rage.

✓ **Teaching Tip**

In item 16, point out that "tip of the iceberg" is figurative language. The sentence following the one in which the phrase appears provides the context clue.

✓ **Teaching Tip**

We suggest that rather than include this section as part of the quiz grade, you use it to give students practice with the skills they have studied and as a helpful preview of upcoming skills. It makes an excellent collaborative activity. All students will find this practice helpful, especially those who must take course exit tests, standardized reading tests, or state-mandated basic skills tests.

SELECTION **2-3**
Health
(continued)

Writing and Collaborating to Enhance Your Understanding

Option for collaboration: Your instructor may direct you to work with other students or, in other words, to work *collaboratively.* In that case, you should form groups of three or four students as directed by your instructor and work together to complete the exercises. After your group discusses each item and agrees on the answer, have a group member record it. Every member of your group should be able to explain all of your group's answers.

Collaboration Option

1. **Reacting to What You Have Read:** When you are in the car (either as a driver or a passenger), what do other drivers do that triggers your anger and frustration?

   (Answers will vary.)

2. **Comprehending the Selection Further:** Many drivers are angered when other drivers run red lights. Some cities are now installing video cameras at major intersections to videotape drivers who run the light. These drivers are then mailed tickets. Do you think this strategy will reduce this type of aggressive driving? Why or why not?

   (Answers will vary.)

3. **Overall Main Idea of the Selection:** In one sentence, tell what the authors want readers to understand about road rage. (Be sure to include the words "road rage" in your overall main idea sentence.)

   Because *road rage* has become a serious national problem, it is important to understand the causes and to know how to avoid provoking other drivers.

Internet Resources

Read More about This Topic on the World Wide Web

Directions: For further information about the topic of the selection, visit these websites:

www.awesomelibrary.org/road-rage.html
This website contains information about protecting yourself from the road rage of others.

www.webhome.idirect.com/~kehamilt/rage.htm
This website presents a humorous quiz to determine your potential for road rage.

You can also use your favorite search engine such as Google, Yahoo!, or AltaVista (www.google.com, www.yahoo.com, www.altavista.com) to discover more about this topic. To locate additional information, type in combinations of keywords such as:

aggressive drivers

or

road rage

Keep in mind that whenever you go to *any* website, it is a good idea to evaluate the website and the information it contains. Ask yourself questions such as:

"Who sponsors this website?"

"Is the information contained in this website up-to-date?"

"What type of information is presented?"

"Is the information objective and complete?"

"How easy is it to use the features of this website?"

PART 2

A New World of Understanding

Using Core Comprehension Skills When You Read College Textbooks

✓ **Teaching Tip**

Point out to students that Part Two is the "comprehension core" of the text. Mention that there are interrelationships among the skills presented in Chapters 3–7.

CHAPTERS IN PART TWO

✓ **Related Resources**

See pages IG-8 to IG-11 of the *Annotated Instructor's Edition* for general suggestions related to the chapters in Part Two.

CHAPTER 3

Determining the Topic

CHAPTER OBJECTIVES

In this chapter you will learn the answers to these questions:

- What is a topic of a paragraph?
- Why is it important to determine the topic of a paragraph?
- What are four clues for determining the topic of a paragraph?

✓ **Timely Words**

"If you don't know where you're going, you may end up somewhere else."
(Anonymous)

"Grasp the subject: the words will follow."
(Cato the Elder, Roman statesman, soldier, and writer)

WHAT IS THE TOPIC OF A PARAGRAPH, AND WHY IS IT IMPORTANT?

KEY TERM
topic

Word, name, or phrase that tells who or what the author is writing about.

The topic is also known as the *subject* or the *subject matter.*

Comprehension Monitoring Question for Topic

"Who or what is this paragraph about?"

Every paragraph is written about something. Whenever you write a paragraph, you have to decide who or what you want to write about. In other words, you have to select a topic. Every paragraph has a **topic:** a word, name, or phrase that tells who or what the author is writing about. All of the sentences in a paragraph relate in some way to the topic. The topic may be a name (such as *Oprah Winfrey* or *New York City* or *Napoleon*), a word (for instance, *cloning*), or a phrase (such as *good study habits* or *advantages of attending college*). In a writing course or an English course, your instructor may call the topic the *subject* or the *subject matter.*

Why is it important to determine the topic of paragraphs you read? It is important because determining the topic is the first step in comprehending a paragraph. (This will become clearer to you as you learn about main ideas in Chapters 4 and 5.) In addition, determining the topic helps you focus your attention on what you are reading.

After you have read a paragraph, determine its topic by asking yourself this comprehension monitoring question: "Who or what is this paragraph about?" When you answer this question correctly, you will have determined the topic. Of course, you must make sure you understand the meaning of the word or phrase that tells the topic. Fortunately, in college textbooks, the meaning of the topic is usually defined for you or explained in the context of the paragraph.

WHAT ARE THE CLUES FOR DETERMINING THE TOPIC OF A PARAGRAPH?

Student Online Learning Center (OLC) ***Go to* Chapter 3. *Select* Video.**

✓ **Teaching Tip**
Remind students that the student OLC contains an audio and video feature for Chapters 3 through 9 that present **Key Comprehension Terms** and **Comprehension Monitoring Questions.**

College textbook paragraphs typically contain clues to help you determine the topic. Take advantage of these clues:

- The topic appears as a *heading,* or *title.*
- The topic appears in *special type* such as **bold print,** *italic,* or **color.**
- The topic is *repeated* throughout the paragraph.
- The topic appears once at the beginning and is then referred to throughout the paragraph by *pronouns* (or other words). (Pronouns are words such as *he, she, it, they.*)

Typically, a paragraph does not have all of these clues, but all paragraphs have at least one of them. The following four examples are paragraphs from college textbooks. Each illustrates and explains one of the four clues that can help you determine the topic of a paragraph.

Clue 1: Look for a Heading or Title That Indicates the Topic

Pay attention to titles and headings because textbook authors often give the topic in them. This excerpt from a human development textbook illustrates this clue (as well as some others). Read this paragraph and notice that its heading indicates its topic.

Determining the topic is the important first step in comprehending a paragraph and also helps you focus your attention on what you are reading.

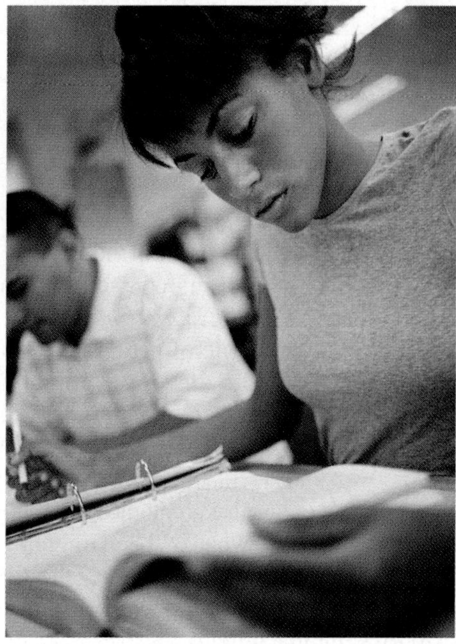

Marriage

Marriage customs vary widely, but the universality of some form of marriage throughout history and around the world suggests that it meets fundamental needs. In most societies, marriage is considered the best way to ensure the orderly raising of children. It allows for a division of labor within a consuming and working unit. Ideally, it offers intimacy, commitment, friendship, affection, sexual fulfillment, companionship, and an opportunity for emotional growth, as well as new sources of identity and self-esteem.

Source: Adapted from Diane E. Papalia, Sally Wendkos Olds, and Ruth Duskin Feldman, *Human Development,* 9th ed., p. 508. Copyright © 2004 by The McGraw-Hill Companies, Inc. Reprinted by permission of The McGraw-Hill Companies, Inc.

Stop and Annotate

Go back to the textbook excerpt. Underline or highlight the heading, which indicates the topic.

Notice that the heading of this paragraph tells its topic: *marriage*. The term *marriage* indicates the "what" that is discussed in the paragraph. The topic, marriage, is what all the sentences in this paragraph have in common. (Also notice that the word *marriage* appears three times in the paragraph.)

Although the heading of a textbook paragraph typically gives the topic, you should read the entire paragraph carefully to be sure that the heading gives the topic completely and accurately. For example, by itself, a general heading such as *The Crisis* is not complete enough to indicate what a paragraph is about. It could be about an earthquake, a stock market crash, a political scandal, or some other type of crisis. When the heading is inadequate, you must read the paragraph to determine the precise topic.

EXERCISE 1

This paragraph comes from a speech communications textbook.

Plagiarism

The term **plagiarism** comes from the Latin word *plagiarus*, or "kidnapper." To plagiarize means to present another person's language or ideas as your own. When you plagiarize, you give the impression that you have written or thought of something yourself when you have actually taken it from someone else.

Source: Adapted from Stephen E. Lucas, *The Art of Public Speaking,* 9th ed., p. 41. Copyright © 2007, The McGraw-Hill Companies, Inc. Reprinted by permission of the McGraw-Hill Companies, Inc.

Write a word, name, or phrase that tells the topic: plagiarism (or plagiarizing).

Clue(s) heading (also, what the sentences have in common.)

Clue 2: Look for a Word, Name, or Phrase in the Paragraph That Appears in Special Print

A second clue to the topic of a paragraph is the author's use of *italic* or **bold** print or **color** to emphasize a word, name, or phrase. The paragraph below is from a textbook on public speaking. Read this paragraph and notice that the term in bold print indicates its topic.

Search engines index Web pages and scan them to find what you want. Because each works a little differently and indexes different pages, the results of any search will vary depending on the engine you use. Taken together, the major search engines cover about 40 percent of the total number of Web pages, and no single search engine covers more than 15 or 20 percent. Depending on the topic of your speech and the information you're looking for, you may find exactly what you need right away. If not, don't despair—it may well show up on another search engine.

Source: Stephen Lucas, *The Art of Public Speaking,* 8th ed., p. 148. Copyright © 2004 by The McGraw-Hill Companies, Inc., Reprinted by permission of The McGraw-Hill Companies, Inc.

Stop and Annotate

Go back to the textbook excerpt. Underline or highlight the words in *bold print* that indicates the topic.

Notice how the words in bold print indicate the topic: *search engines*. (Notice also that the term *search engines* appears three more times in the paragraph and that the word *search* appears as well.) The entire paragraph discusses *search engines*, software programs that make it possible to scan and locate information on millions of websites.

As you can see, the topic of a paragraph sometimes consists of a combination of words, or a combination of names, or even phrases. Your task is to identify these important elements and put them together to form the complete topic. For example, a health textbook paragraph might have the words *bulimia* and *anorexia* in special print. Both of them together would comprise the topic: *bulimia and anorexia*. Or a paragraph might repeatedly mention the names of two U.S. presidents, George W. Bush and Barack Obama. The complete topic would be *George W. Bush and Barack Obama*.

Also, be aware that while italic often signals the topic of a paragraph, it is also used by authors merely to show emphasis. For example, an author may put the word "except" or "not" in italic, such as in this sentence: "In general, it is *not* a good idea for college students to work more than 20 hours a week."

EXERCISE 2

This paragraph comes from an information technology textbook.

How would you feel if someone obtained a driver's license and credit cards in your name? What if that person then assumed your identity to buy clothes, cars, and a house? It happens every day. It happens in every state. Every year, well over 100 million people are victimized in this way. The illegal assumption of someone's identity for the purposes of economic gain is called **identity theft**. It is one of the fastest-growing crimes in the country.

Source: Adapted from Timothy J. O'Leary and Linda I. O'Leary, *Computing Essentials*, p. 279. Copyright © 2008 by The McGraw-Hill Companies, Inc. Reprinted by permission of The McGraw-Hill Companies, Inc.

Write a word, name, or phrase that tells the topic: identity theft

Clue(s) special print (also, what the sentences have in common)

Clue 3: Look for a Word, Name, or Phrase That Is Repeated throughout the Paragraph

A third clue to the topic is the repetition of a word, name, or phrase in a paragraph. This clue is helpful when there is no heading and the paragraph does not contain any words in special print. (Even though the previous two examples illustrate other clues, they also illustrate this clue.) Read the paragraph below from a business management textbook. Notice the repeated words that indicate the topic.

Reference checks are attempts to obtain job-related information about job applicants from individuals who are knowledgeable about the applicants' qualifications. Reference checks can be obtained by mail, by telephone, and in person. Such checks are conducted to verify information on application blanks and résumés and, sometimes, to collect additional data that will facilitate the selection decision. One reason for the widespread use of reference checks is that, according to one estimate, between 20 and 25 percent of all candidate applications and résumés contain at least one major fabrication.

Source: Adapted from Kathryn M. Bartol and David C. Martin, *Management*, 3rd ed., pp. 328–29. Copyright © 1998 by The McGraw-Hill Companies, Inc. Reprinted by permission of The McGraw-Hill Companies, Inc.

Stop and Annotate

Go back to the textbook excerpt above. Underline or highlight the repeated words that indicate the topic.

Notice *reference checks* appears three times, indicating that it is the topic of the paragraph. In addition, when the authors mention "such checks" in the third sentence, they are still referring to *reference checks*.

Keep in mind that it is possible to express the same topic more than one way. For example, the topic of a paragraph on *reference checks* could also be expressed as *checking on references* or *checking a job applicant's references*.

EXERCISE 3

This paragraph comes from a psychology textbook.

At one time or another, almost all of us have difficulty sleeping—a condition known as insomnia. A case of insomnia could be due to a particular situation, such as the breakup of a relationship, concern about a test score, or the loss of a job. Some cases of insomnia, however, have no obvious cause. Some people are simply unable to fall asleep easily, or they go to sleep readily but wake up frequently during the night. Insomnia is a problem that afflicts as many as one-third of all people.

Source: Adapted from Robert S. Feldman, *Understanding Psychology,* 8th ed. pp.154–55. Copyright © 2008 by The McGraw-Hill Companies, Inc. Reprinted by permission of the McGraw-Hill Companies, Inc.

Write a word, name, or phrase that tells the topic: insomnia

Clue(s) repeated words (also, what the sentences have in common)

Clue 4: Look for a Word, Name, or Phrase Referred to throughout the Paragraph by Pronouns or Other Words

A fourth clue to the topic is a word, name, or phrase that appears at or near the beginning of the paragraph and is then referred to throughout the paragraph by a pronoun (such as *he, she, it, they, his, her, its,* etc.) or by other words. For example, the topic *smoking* might be referred to later in a paragraph as *this habit* or *this addiction.* Read this paragraph from a computer science textbook and notice how pronouns are used to refer to the topic:

Bill Gates taught himself programming at age 13. As a Seattle teenager, he and his friends would ride their bicycles to a local computer company to help them look for programming errors. In 1962 he took a leave from high school when TRW offered him a job at $20,000. In 1975 he formed Microsoft Corporation, which wrote system programs for Altair and Apple microcomputers and expanded BASIC for other computers. IBM asked him to write an operating system for its new PC machine. The result was MS-DOS, one of the widest-selling operating systems in the world. This creative genius also directed software development for the MacIntosh and Radio Shack Model 100 microcomputers. Microsoft kept producing winning software such as *Word, Works*, and *Flight Simulator*. In 1987 IBM chose Microsoft's *Windows* for the PS/2 computer. *Windows* has since become a new standard. It is no surprise that this gifted entrepreneur is the richest man in the world.

*Source:*Adapted from Timothy N. Trainor and Diane Krasnewich, *Computers!*, 5th ed. Copyright © 1996 by The McGraw-Hill Companies, Inc. Reprinted by permission of The McGraw-Hill Companies, Inc.

Stop and Annotate

Go back to the textbook excerpt above. Underline or highlight the topic, the pronouns, and other words that refer to the topic.

Notice that the name Bill Gates appears only in the first sentence, but it is obvious from the pronouns *he, his*, and *him* that the rest of the paragraph continues to discuss Bill Gates. When the authors say, "this creative genius" and "this gifted entrepreneur," they are still referring to Bill Gates. Therefore, *Bill Gates* is the topic of this paragraph.

EXERCISE 4

This paragraph comes from a science textbook.

On August 29, 2005, Hurricane Katrina came ashore on the U.S. Gulf coast between Mobile, Alabama, and New Orleans, Louisiana. It was an enormous hurricane, just one of the 26 named storms that hit the Americas in the worst Atlantic hurricane season in history. A few hours after the hurricane made landfall, the combination of the storm surge and the torrential rain falling inland overwhelmed levees that were supposed to protect New Orleans. The storm caused almost 80 percent of the city to flood. Close to 1,000 people died in Louisiana alone, with most of those deaths occurring in New Orleans. Mandatory evacuation orders were issued for New Orleans' 500,000 residents in the days that followed the storm.

Source: Adapted from Eldon D. Enger and Bradley F. Smith, *Environmental Science: A Study of Interrelationships*, 11th ed., p. 24. Copyright © 2008 by The McGraw-Hill Companies, Inc. Reprinted by permission of the McGraw-Hill Companies, Inc.

Write a word, name, or phrase that tells the topic: Hurricane Katrina

Clue(s) mentioned at the beginning and referred to throughout by other words (It, the hurricane, the storm)

One or more of the four clues described above will always help you determine the topic of a paragraph. However, if the topic is still not clear to you, you may find it helpful to reread the paragraph and ask yourself what all the sentences pertain to. Ask yourself the comprehension monitoring question, "Who or what is this paragraph about?"

Determining the topic is the essential first step in comprehending as you read. It is also a key to locating the stated main idea sentence of a paragraph, as you will see in Chapter 4.

EXERCISE 5

Could This Be a Topic?

The topic is a *word, name,* or *phrase* that tells who or what a paragraph is about. Here are some examples of things that could—or could not—be topics:

- Going to college for the first time (*Yes; this could be a topic because it's a phrase.*)
- Barack Obama (*Yes; it's a name.*)
- Happy (*No; this is an adjective, a word that describes, so it could not be a topic.*)
- Happiness (*Yes; this is a noun that tells what a passage is about, so it could be a topic.*)
- Why soccer is popular (*Yes; this is a phrase.*)
- Soccer is popular because it is a fast-moving game. (*No; this is a complete sentence.*)

Directions: Decide whether each item below could be used as a topic that describes who or what a paragraph is about. Write Y for *Yes.* If it does not, write N for *No.* (There are periods after all of them, although not all of them are sentences.)

Y **1.** Changes in the new tax law.

Y **2.** The 2008 Beijing Olympics.

(*continued*)

Y 3. How to text message.
Y 4. Benjamin Franklin.
Y 5. The war in Afganistan.
Y 6. Why business is a good choice as a college major.
N 7. Washing your hands often can prevent flu and colds.
Y 8. The benefits of exercise.
Y 9. The effects of sleep deprivation on college students.
Y 10. Why hybrid cars make sense.
Y 11. Ten tips for passing objective tests.
Y 12. Safety measures for airline passengers.
N 13. Yoga is a way to reduce stress.
N 14. Speed kills.
Y 15. Starting a new job.

OTHER THINGS TO KEEP IN MIND WHEN DETERMINING THE TOPIC

Here are three helpful things that you should keep in mind about determining the topic:

1. **You should use a *name, word,* or *phrase,* but never a sentence, to express the topic. This means you must know the difference between a phrase and a sentence.**

   As you know, the topic of a paragraph not only can be expressed as a word or a name, but can be expressed as a *phrase.* A phrase is a meaningful group of words (even a long group of words) that does *not* express a complete thought. A sentence, on the other hand, has a subject and a verb and *always* expresses a complete thought. Phrases can be used to express the topic, but sentences should *never* be used to express a topic.

   The left column below gives examples of phrases that could be used as topics. The right column contains sentences that include the topic. The items in the right column could not be used as topics because they are complete sentences.

Could Be Used as a Topic (because it is a phrase)	**Could *Not* Be Used as a Topic (because it is a complete sentence)**
my cell phone	My cell phone was stolen.
my new cell phone	My new cell phone was stolen.
my new cell phone with a two-inch screen	My new cell phone with a two-inch screen was stolen.
my new cell phone with a two-inch screen and video camera	My new cell phone with a two-inch screen and video camera was stolen.
traveling by plane	Traveling by plane is the fastest way to travel long distances to foreign countries.
fatality rates for passengers traveling by plane	Fatality rates of passengers traveling by plane are significantly lower than fatality rates for passengers traveling by car.
why traveling by plane is the best way to go	There are several reasons why traveling by plane is the best way to go.
how to overcome fear of traveling by plane	Psychologists have several methods to teach people how to overcome fear of traveling by plane.

(continued on next page)

2. You must know the difference between "general" and "specific."

It is important to be precise when you determine the topic. If you choose a word or phrase that is too general or too specific, you will not be expressing the topic accurately. A topic that is too general goes beyond what is discussed in the paragraph. In other words, it is too broad. On the other hand, a topic is *too specific* if it fails to describe all of the things discussed in the paragraph. In other words, it is too narrow.

Suppose, for instance, that the topic of a paragraph is *causes of voter apathy.* As the following chart shows, the words *voter* or *apathy,* or even the phrase *voter apathy,* would be too general to express this topic accurately. The phrase *lack of interest in candidates as a cause of voter apathy* would be too specific, even though "lack of interest in candidates" might be mentioned in the paragraph as one cause of voter apathy.

Too General (Too Broad)	Accurate Topic (Precise)	Too Specific (Too Narrow)
voters	causes of voter apathy	voter apathy due to lack of interest in the candidates
apathy		voter apathy due to lack of interest in the issues
voter apathy		voter apathy because one candidate has an overwhelming likelihood of winning

3. A longer passage has an overall topic.

Just as every paragraph has a topic, so do longer selections that consist of several paragraphs. In a writing course or an English course, your instructor may call the overall topic the *subject.*

How can you determine the overall topic of a longer selection? First, ask yourself the question "Who or what is this entire selection about?" Then use some of the clues presented in this chapter:

- Look at the title or heading for the entire selection or section.
- Look for a word, name, or phrase that appears in special print.
- Look for a word, name, or phrase that is repeated throughout the selection or section.

Once you have finished reading an entire selection or section of a textbook, it is a good idea to reflect on the topics of the paragraphs themselves to see who or what they all pertain to. This will also lead you to the overall topic. For example, five paragraphs of a section in a history book might have these topics: Thomas Jefferson's birth, Jefferson's boyhood, his education, his role in writing the Declaration of Independence, and his presidency. The overall topic of the selection would be *Thomas Jefferson's life.* This overall topic is a general topic that sums up the topics of the five individual paragraphs that comprise the selection.

CREATING CHAPTER REVIEW CARDS

Student Online Learning Center (OLC)
***Go to* Chapter 3.**
***Select* Chapter Test.**

Review cards or *summary cards* are a way to select, organize, and summarize the important information in a textbook chapter. Preparing review cards helps you organize the information so that you can learn and memorize it more easily. In other words, chapter review cards are effective study tools.

Preparing chapter review cards for each chapter of *New Worlds* will give you practice in creating these valuable study tools. Once you have learned how to make chapter review cards, you can use actual index cards to create them for textbook material in your other courses and use them when you study for tests.

Now complete the chapter review cards for Chapter 3 by answering the questions or following the directions on each card. The page numbers indicate the place in the chapter where the information can be found. Use the type of handwriting that is easiest for you to reread (printing or cursive) and write legibly. You will find it easier to complete the review cards if you remove these pages before filling them in.

✓ **Teaching Tips**

Remind students that the student OLC contains a 10-item **Chapter Test** for this chapter. After completing the chapter review cards below, students should complete the Chapter Test on the OLC.

Page numbers for chapter review card items are provided in the student edition in Chapters 1–5 only.

Determining the Topic

1. What is the definition of the *topic* of a paragraph? (See page 129.)

The topic of a paragraph is a word or a phrase that tells who or what the author is writing about.

2. List two reasons it is important to determine the topic of a paragraph. (See page 129.)

It is the first step in understanding a paragraph.

It helps you focus your attention on what you are reading.

3. What comprehension monitoring question should you ask yourself in order to determine the topic of a paragraph? (Be sure you write a *question*.) (See page 129.)

Who or what is this paragraph about?

Card 1 Chapter 3: Determining the Topic

✓ **Teaching Tip**

For item 3 on Card 1, point out the "Comprehension Monitoring Question for Topic" in the margin on page 129 and guide students to write their answer as a question (including a question mark). You may wish to have students complete the first card together in class.

Clues to Determining the Topic

List four clues textbook authors use to indicate the topic of a paragraph. (See pages 129–133.)

1. Look for a heading or title that indicates the topic.
2. Look for a word, name, or phrase in the paragraph that appears in special print.
3. Look for a word, name, or phrase that is repeated throughout the paragraph.
4. Look for a word, name, or phrase referred to throughout the paragraph by pronouns or other words.

Card 2 Chapter 3: Determining the Topic

When Determining the Topic, Keep in Mind . . .

What are the three other things you should keep in mind when you are determining the topic? (See pages 135–136.)

1. You should use a name, word, or a phrase, but never a sentence, to express a topic.
2. You must know the difference between "general" and "specific."
3. A longer passage has an overall topic.

Card 3 Chapter 3: Determining the Topic

TEST YOUR UNDERSTANDING DETERMINING THE TOPIC, PART ONE

REVIEW: The **topic** of a paragraph tells *who* or *what* the author is writing about. Topics are expressed as *words* or *phrases*, but never as sentences. Clues to a paragraph's topic are headings, special print, repeated words, or are mentioned at the beginning and referred to throughout by pronouns or other words.

EXAMPLE: Study the example paragraph in the box below to see how the information you learned in this chapter can be used to determine the topic of a paragraph. Read the explanation that is given for the correct answer. When you are sure you understand the explanation, complete the five exercises in Part One.

This paragraph comes from a speech textbook.

Ethnocentrism is the belief that our own group or culture—whatever it may be—is superior to all other groups or cultures. Because of ethnocentrism, we identify with our group or culture and see its values, beliefs, and customs as "right" or "natural." Moreover, we tend to think of the values, beliefs, and customs of other groups or cultures as "wrong" or "unnatural."

Source: Adapted from Stephen Lucas, *The Art of Public Speaking,* 6th ed., p. 25. Copyright © 1998 by The McGraw-Hill Companies, Inc. Reprinted by permission of The McGraw-Hill Companies.

__c__ What is the topic of this paragraph?

a. customs
b. groups or cultures
c. ethnocentrism
d. values, beliefs, and customs

The correct answer is c. There are several clues that suggest *ethnocentrism* is the topic: The word *ethnocentrism* appears in bold print in the first sentence. The word also appears in the second sentence. And all three sentences in the paragraph pertain to the topic *ethnocentrism.* (Topics are important. Be sure you understand the *meaning* of the topic.)

DIRECTIONS: To determine the topic of a paragraph, read the paragraph carefully and then ask yourself, "Who or what is this paragraph about?" To help you answer this question, use the four clues to the topic you learned in this chapter. Mark any clues in the paragraph that helped you determine its topic. Then select the answer choice that tells the topic and write the letter in the space provided.

1. This paragraph comes from a human development textbook.

In 1990, two psychologists, Peter Salovey and John Mayer, coined the term ***emotional intelligence*** (sometimes called EQ). It refers to the ability to understand and regulate emotions: to recognize and deal with one's own feelings and the feelings of others. Daniel Goleman, the psychologist and science writer who popularized the term, expanded it to include qualities such as optimism, conscientiousness, motivation, empathy, and social competence.

Source: Diane E. Papalia, Sally Wendkos Olds, and Ruth Duskin Feldman, *Human Development,* 9th ed., p. 477. Copyright © 2004 by The McGraw-Hill Companies, Inc. Reprinted by permission of The McGraw-Hill Companies.

b What is the topic of this paragraph?

a. psychologists

b. emotional intelligence

c. understanding and regulating emotions

d. Daniel Goleman

2. This paragraph comes from a psychology textbook.

Daydreams

Many features of directed and flowing consciousness and dreams are combined in the state of waking consciousness called daydreams. They are a period of thinking and feeling that is not bound by what is logical or likely to happen. Daydreams are not a sometime thing; most of us daydream many times each day.

Source: Benjamin B. Lahey, *Psychology,* 8th ed., p. 162. Copyright © 2004 by The McGraw-Hill Companies, Inc. Reprinted by permission of The McGraw-Hill Companies.

c What is the topic of this paragraph?

a. flowing consciousness and dreams

b. waking consciousness

c. daydreams

d. a period of thinking and feeling

3. This paragraph comes from a psychology textbook.

The hypothalamus is a small, but vitally important part of the brain. It lies underneath the thalamus, just in front of the midbrain. It is intimately involved in our motives and emotions. It also plays a key role in regulating body temperature, sleep, endocrine gland activity, and resistance to disease; controlling glandular secretions of the stomach and intestines; and maintaining the normal pace and rhythm of such body functions as blood pressure and heartbeat. It is the brain center most directly linked to the functions of the autonomic nervous system.

Source: Benjamin B. Lahey, *Essentials of Psychology,* 8th ed., p. 74. Copyright © 2004 by The McGraw-Hill Companies, Inc. Reprinted by permission of The McGraw-Hill Companies.

d What is the topic of this paragraph?

a. a small, but vitally important part of the brain

b. midbrain

c. the brain center

d. the hypothalamus

4. This paragraph comes from a human development textbook.

As adolescents begin to separate from their families and spend more time with peers, they have less time and less need for the emotional gratification they used to get from the sibling bond. Changes in sibling relationships may well precede similar changes in the relationship between adolescents and parents: more independence on the part of the younger person and less authority exerted by the older person. As children reach high school, their relationships with their siblings become progressively more equal. Older siblings exercise less power over younger ones, fight with them less, are not as close to them, and are less likely to look to them for companionship. Adolescents still show intimacy, affection, and admiration for their brothers and sisters, but they spend less time with them, and their relationships are less intense.

Source: Adapted from Diane E. Papalia, Sally Wendkos Olds, and Ruth Duskin Feldman, *Human Development,* 9th ed. Copyright © 2004 by The McGraw-Hill Companies, Inc. Reprinted by permission of The McGraw-Hill Companies.

a What is the topic of this paragraph?

a. changes in sibling relationships among adolescents

b. adolescents

c. lack of companionship among siblings

d. older siblings

5. This paragraph comes from a management textbook.

Distinguishing between Change and Innovation

In considering more closely the concepts of change and innovation, it is useful to distinguish between the two terms. **Change** is any alteration of the status quo, whereas innovation is a more specialized kind of change. **Innovation** is a new idea applied to initiating or improving a process, product, or service. As long as an idea for bringing about an improvement is perceived as new by the individuals involved, it is generally considered to be an innovation even though outside observers may view it as an imitation of something already existing elsewhere. All innovations imply change; but not all changes are innovations, since changes may not involve new ideas or lead to significant improvements.

Source: Kathryn M. Bartol and David C. Martin, *Management,* 2nd ed. Copyright © 1994 by The McGraw-Hill Companies, Inc. Reprinted by permission of The McGraw-Hill Companies, Inc.

c What is the topic of this paragraph?

a. change

b. innovation

c. change and innovation

d. the status quo

TEST YOUR UNDERSTANDING
DETERMINING THE TOPIC, PART TWO

REVIEW: The **topic** of a paragraph tells *who* or *what* the author is writing about. Topics are expressed as words or phrases, but never as sentences. Clues to a paragraph's topic are headings, special print, repeated words, or words that are mentioned at the beginning and then referred to throughout the paragraph by pronouns or other words.

EXAMPLE: Study the example paragraph in the box below to see how the information you learned in this chapter can be used to determine the topic of a paragraph. Read the explanation that is given for the correct answer. When you are sure you understand the explanation, complete the five exercises in Part Two.

This paragraph comes from a psychology textbook.

Pressure

Does the pressure of working for good grades ever get to you? If you have been employed, was it a high-pressure job? The term **pressure** is used to describe the stress that arises from threats of negative events. In school, there is always the possibility that you will not perform well and you will fail. Some jobs are loaded with possibilities for making a mess of things and getting fired. Some unhappy marriages are sources of pressure because one spouse always seems to displease the other, no matter how hard he or she tries to avoid it.

Source: Adapted from Benjamin B. Lahey, *Psychology,* 8th ed., p. 503. Copyright © 2004 by The McGraw-Hill Companies, Inc. Reprinted by permission of The McGraw-Hill Companies, Inc.

Write the topic: pressure

Clue(s) The word "pressure" appears in the heading and in bold print in the paragraph. It also appears several times in the paragraph.

Explanation: The topic of the paragraph, pressure, appears in the heading and in bold print. The word *pressure* also appears several times in the paragraph.

DIRECTIONS: To determine the topic of a paragraph, read the paragraph carefully and then ask yourself, "Who or what is this paragraph about?" To help you answer this question, use the four clues to the topic you learned in this chapter. Mark any clues in the paragraph that helped you determine its topic. Then in the space provided beneath each paragraph, write a word or a phrase that tells the topic.

✓ **Teaching Tip**
Remind students to mark clues in the paragraphs.

1. This paragraph comes from a computer science textbook.

Facsimile Machines

For many organizations the *facsimile machine,* or fax, has become an increasingly popular way to transmit ideas and important information. Just as a telephone transmits voice messages, a fax machine transmits images of printed material. The data can be a drawing, a photo, a handwritten document, or even your take-out lunch order.

Source: Timothy N. Trainor and Diane Krasnewich, *Computers!,* 5th ed. Copyright © 1996 by The McGraw-Hill Companies, Inc. Reprinted by permission of The McGraw-Hill Companies, Inc.

Write a word, name, or phrase that tells the topic: facsimile machines or fax machines

Clue(s) heading; special print; repetition

✓ **Teaching Tip**
Students must have "grandparents and great-grandparents" in order to have the complete, correct topic. "They" in the passage refers to both grandparents *and* great-grandparents.

2. This paragraph comes from a human development textbook.

Grandparents and great-grandparents are important to their families. They are sources of wisdom, companions in play, links to the past, and symbols of the continuity of family life. They are engaged in the ultimate generative function: expressing the human longing to transcend mortality by investing themselves in the lives of future generations.

Source: Diana E. Papalia and Sally Wendkos Olds, *Human Development,* 6th ed. Copyright © 1995 by The McGraw-Hill Companies, Inc. Reprinted by permission of The McGraw-Hill Companies, Inc.

Write a word, name, or phrase that tells the topic: grandparents and great-grandparents

Clue(s) mentioned at beginning and referred to throughout by other words (the pronoun "they")

3. This paragraph comes from a psychology textbook.

Who are the characters in your dreams—your friends and family? Are there strangers in your dreams? Are you a character in your dreams? Because you are always the "author" of your dreams, it is not surprising that you often play a leading role. The dreamer has an active role in nearly three-fourths of dreams, and you are absent from your own dreams only 10 percent of the time. About half of the other characters in your dreams are friends, acquaintances, or family members, but the other half are people you do not know or cannot recognize—or are animals 4 percent of the time. The characters in dreams are about an even mixture of men and women, with men being slightly more likely to dream about men than women are.

Source: Benjamin B. Lahey, *Psychology,* 8th ed., p. 171. Copyright © 2004 by The McGraw-Hill Companies, Inc. Reprinted by permission of The McGraw-Hill Companies.

Write a word, name, or phrase that tells the topic: characters in (your) dreams or who appears in dreams

Clue(s) repeated words (also, what all the sentences have in common)

4. This paragraph comes from a government textbook.

One area in which African-Americans have made progress since the 1960s is elective office. Although the percentage of black elected officials is still far below the proportion of African-Americans in the population, it has risen sharply over recent decades. As of 2004, there were more than 20 black members of Congress and 400 black mayors—including the mayors of some of this country's largest cities.

Source: Thomas E. Patterson, *We the People,* 6th ed., p. 158. Copyright © 2006 by The McGraw-Hill Companies, Inc. Reprinted by permission of the The McGraw-Hill Companies, Inc.

✓ **Teaching Tip**
"African-Americans" is too general.

Write a word, name, or phrase that tells the topic: African-Americans in public office or percentage of black elected officials

Clue(s) repeated words (also, what all the sentences have in common)

5. This paragraph comes from a human development textbook.

Sisters are especially vital in maintaining family relationships. Also, older people who are close to their sisters feel better about life and worry less about aging than those without sisters or without close ties to them. Another effect of being close to a sister is that it lifts the morale of older widows. Among a national sample of bereaved adults in the Netherlands, those coping with the death of a sister experienced more difficulty than those who had lost a spouse or a parent.

Source: Diana E. Papalia and Sally Wendkos Olds, *Human Development,* 6th ed. Copyright © 1995 by The McGraw-Hill Companies, Inc. Reprinted by permission of The McGraw-Hill Companies, Inc.

✓ **Teaching Tip**
Remind students that the topic may be expressed more than one way as long as the meaning is correct. For item 5, "sisters" is too general.

Write a word, name, or phrase that tells the topic: sisters and family relationships OR the effect of sisters on family relationships OR effects on family members of being close to a sister

Clue(s) repeated words (also, what all the sentences have in common)

SELECTION **3-1**

Human Development

IS THERE A BETTER WAY TO PARENT? A LOOK AT THREE PARENTING STYLES

From *Human Development*

By Diane Papalia and Sally Olds

What kind of parents did you have? What kind of a parent are you, or what kind of parent will you be? Psychologist Diana Baumrind has studied three different styles of parenting and found that one style of parenting enhances children's competence more than the others.

Baumrind: Three Parenting Styles

1 Why does Stacy hit and bite the nearest person when she cannot finish a jigsaw puzzle? What makes David sit and sulk when he cannot finish the puzzle, even though his teacher offers to help him? Why does Consuelo work on the puzzle for 20 minutes and then shrug and try another? Why are children so different in their responses to the same situation? Temperament is a major factor, of course; but some research suggests that *styles of parenting* may affect children's competence in dealing with their world.

2 In her pioneering research, Diana Baumrind studied 103 preschool children from 95 families. Through interviews, testing, and home studies, she measured how children were functioning, identified three parenting styles, and described typical behavior patterns of children raised according to each.

3 *Authoritarian parents* value control and unquestioning obedience. They try to make children conform to a set standard of conduct and punish them arbitrarily and forcefully for violating it. They are more detached and less warm than other parents. Their children tend to be more discontented, withdrawn, and distrustful.

4 *Permissive parents* value self-expression and self-regulation. They consider themselves resources, not models. They make few demands and allow children to monitor their own activities as much as possible. When they do have to make rules, they explain the reasons for them. They consult with children about policy decisions and rarely punish. They are warm, noncontrolling, and undemanding. Their preschool children tend to be immature—the least self-controlled and the least exploratory.

5 *Authoritative parents* respect a child's individuality but also stress social values. They have confidence in their ability to guide children, but they also respect children's independent decisions, interests, opinions, and personalities. They are loving, consistent, demanding, firm in maintaining standards, and willing to impose limited, judicious, punishment—even occasional, mild spanking when necessary, within the context of a warm, supportive relationship. They explain the reasoning behind their stands and encourage verbal give-and-take.

Annotation Practice Exercises

Directions: For each exercise below, write the topic of the paragraph on the lines beside the paragraph.

Practice Exercise

Topic of paragraph 2:

Baumrind's research on parenting styles

(clue: mentioned at the beginning and then discussed throughout)

Practice Exercise

Topic of paragraph 3:

authoritarian parents

(clue: special print)

Practice Exercise

Topic of paragraph 4:

permissive parents

(clue: special print)

Their children apparently feel secure in knowing both that they are loved and what is expected of them. These preschoolers tend to be the most self-reliant, self-controlled, self-assertive, exploratory, and content.

6 Why does authoritative parenting seem to enhance children's competence? It may well be because authoritative parents set reasonable expectations and realistic standards. In authoritarian homes, children are so strictly controlled that often they cannot make independent choices about their own behavior. In permissive homes, children receive so *little* guidance that they may become uncertain and anxious about whether they are doing the right thing. In authoritative homes, children know when they are meeting expectations and can decide whether it is worth risking parental displeasure or other unpleasant consequences to pursue a goal. These children are expected to perform well, fulfill commitments, and participate actively in family duties as well as family fun. They know the satisfaction of meeting responsibilities and achieving success.

Practice Exercise

Topic of paragraph 5:

authoritative parents

(clue: special print)

Practice Exercise

Topic of paragraph 6:

why authoritative parenting enhances children's competence

(clue: mentioned at the beginning and then discussed throughout)

✓ **Teaching Tips**

- The beginning of paragraph 6 gives the topic. The topic is never written as a question, however.
- Maccoby and Martin added a fourth style: uninvolved and neglectful.

SELECTION 3-1 Human Development (continued)

Comprehension and Vocabulary Quiz

This quiz has four parts. Your instructor may assign some or all of them.

Comprehension

Directions: Items 1–5 test your comprehension (understanding) of the material in this selection. These questions are much like those that a content-area instructor (such as a human development professor) would expect you to know after reading and studying this selection. For each comprehension question below, use information from the selection to determine the correct answer. Refer to the selection as you answer the questions. Write your answers in the spaces provided.

¶1 b **1.** Baumrind's research suggests that, in addition to temperament, children's competence in dealing with the world may be influenced by:
- *a.* the general level of the children's intelligence.
- *b.* the parenting style of their parents.
- *c.* the experiences that children have in school.
- *d.* the socioeconomic level of their family.

¶3 c **2.** Parents who value unquestioning obedience and control are referred to as:
- *a.* authoritative parents.
- *b.* permissive parents.
- *c.* authoritarian parents.
- *d.* noncontrolling parents.

¶4 b **3.** Compared with children who experience authoritarian or authoritative parenting styles, preschool children of permissive parents tend to be:
- *a.* more discontented, withdrawn, and distrustful.
- *b.* immature, less self-controlled, and less exploratory.
- *c.* more self-reliant and self-controlled.
- *d.* more content and secure.

¶5 c **4.** With regard to punishing their children, authoritative parents tend:
- *a.* never to spank their children.
- *b.* to spank their children often and forcefully.
- *c.* to use occasional, mild spanking when necessary.
- *d.* to use force to make children conform to strict standards.

¶6 d **5.** Authoritative parenting seems to enhance a child's competence because authoritative parents:
- *a.* allow children to express their unique personalities.
- *b.* make children conform to a set standard of conduct.
- *c.* allow children to monitor their own activities as much as possible.
- *d.* set reasonable expectations and realistic standards for their children.

Vocabulary in Context

Directions: Items 6–10 test your ability to determine the meaning of the word by using context clues. *Context clues* are words in a sentence that allow the reader to deduce (reason out) the meaning of an unfamiliar word in that sentence. Context clues also enable the reader to determine which meaning the author intends when a word has more than one meaning. For each vocabulary item below, a sentence from the selection containing an important word (*italicized, like this*) is quoted first. Next, there is an additional sentence using the word in the same sense and providing another context clue. Use the context clues from *both* sentences to deduce the meaning of the italicized word. *Be sure the answer you choose makes sense in both sentences.* If you need to use a dictionary to confirm your answer choice, remember that the meaning you select must still fit the context of *both* sentences. Write your answers in the spaces provided.

Pronunciation Key: ă **pat** ā **pay** âr **care** ä **father** ĕ **pet** ē **be** ĭ **pit**
ī **tie** îr **pier** ŏ **pot** ō **toe** ô **paw** oi **noise** ou **out** o͝o **took**
o͞o **boot** ŭ **cut** yo͞o **abuse** ûr **urge** th **thin** *th* **this** hw **which**
zh **vision** ə **about** *Stress mark:* ′

¶11 __a__ **6.** *Temperament* is a major factor, of course; but some research suggests that styles of parenting may affect children's competence in dealing with their world.

Some breeds of dogs, such as cocker spaniels and labrador retrievers, make good family pets because of their gentle, calm *temperament.*

temperament (tĕm′ prə mənt) means:

a. typical manner of reacting
b. hostility; anger
c. inability to get along with other people
d. impulsiveness

¶13 __a__ **7.** *Authoritarian* parents value control and unquestioning obedience.

Nobody likes the new soccer coach because he is as *authoritarian* as a dictator.

authoritarian (ə thôr ĭ târ′ ē ən) means:

a. expecting others to obey without question
b. skilled in leadership
c. pertaining to an author
d. demanding an unreasonable amount of hard work

¶14 __c__ **8.** *Permissive* parents value self-expression and self-regulation.

The substitute teacher was so *permissive* that she allowed the children to do whatever they wanted.

permissive (pər mĭs′ ĭv) means:

a. asking permission; seeking approval
b. gloomy; expecting the worst

c. lenient; likely to give permission

d. lazy; unmotivated

¶5 ___d___ **9.** *Authoritative* parents respect a child's individuality but also stress social values.

Because the principal was so *authoritative,* the students did not hesitate to follow her instructions during the fire drill.

authoritative (ə thôr′ ĭ tā tĭv) means:

a. proud

b. hysterical

c. deserving scorn or ridicule

d. arising from proper authority

¶1 ___a___ **10.** Temperament is a major factor, of course; but some research suggests that styles of parenting may affect children's *competence* in dealing with their world.

Because of our tour guide's extraordinary *competence,* we thoroughly enjoyed our sightseeing in Paris.

competence (kom′ pĭ təns) means:

a. ability; skill

b. improvement; progress

c. inadequacy; ineptitude

d. inability to achieve or produce

Word Structure

Directions: Items 11–15 test your ability to use word-structure clues to help determine a word's meaning. *Word-structure clues* consist of roots, prefixes, and suffixes. In these exercises, you will learn the meaning of a word part (a root) and use it to determine the meaning of several other words that have the same word part. If you need to use a dictionary to confirm your answer choice, do so. Write your answers in the spaces provided.

In paragraph 5 of the selection, you encountered the word **impose**. This word contains the Latin root **pos**, which means to "put" or "place." The word **impose** means to *place* or *put* one's own values, beliefs, etc., on another person. Use the meaning of **pos** and the list of prefixes on pages 68–69 to help you determine the meaning of each of the following words that contain this same root. Write your answers in the spaces provided.

___a___ **11.** If you take a picture off the wall and **reposition** it, you:

a. rehang it in a different place.

b. store it away.

c. put it in a closet.

d. clean it.

___b___ **12.** If you accidentally **transpose** the letters in a word when you are typing, you:

a. delete the letters.

b. put the letters in the wrong order.

c. capitalize the letters.
d. add extra letters.

a 13. To **compose** a tune means to:
a. place notes in an order that makes a melody.
b. alter the sequence of notes in an existing melody.
c. plagiarize someone else's melody.
d. record the tune you create.

b 14. If a businessperson **proposes** that his or her company develop a new product, the person:
a. builds a model of the product.
b. suggests or puts forth the idea for the product.
c. hires someone to design the product.
d. researches the potential market for the product.

d 15. Bank vaults and safety deposit boxes are *repositories* for extremely important or valuable items. A **repository** is a place in which items are:
a. stored until they can be sold.
b. left indefinitely.
c. auctioned off.
d. put for safekeeping.

✓ **Teaching Tip**
Let students know that not all of the skills included in this Reading Skills Application section have been introduced yet. This section serves as a valuable preview of these skills, however. Students typically get several of the items correct, and they find this encouraging.

Reading Skills Application

Directions: Items 16–20 test your ability to *apply* certain reading skills to information in this selection. These types of questions provide valuable practice for all students, especially those who must take standardized reading tests and state-mandated basic skills tests. You may not have studied all of the skills at this point, so these items will serve as a helpful preview. The comprehension and critical reading skills in this section are presented in Chapters 3 through 9 of *New Worlds;* vocabulary and figurative language skills are presented in Chapter 2. As you work through *New Worlds,* you will practice and develop these skills. Write your answers in the spaces provided.

author's purpose for writing (Chapter 8)

a 16. The authors' primary purpose for writing this selection is to:
a. describe three styles of parenting and their effects on children.
b. persuade parents to adopt an authoritarian parenting style.
c. explain how parents develop parenting styles.
d. instruct parents how to change their parenting style.

¶3 vocabulary in context (Chapter 2)

c 17. Which of the following is the meaning of *conform* as it is used in the third paragraph?
a. cherish
b. create
c. obey
d. ignore

conclusion (Chapter 9) c

18. Based on information in the selection, which of the following represents a logical conclusion about the effect of parenting style on children's competence?

a. An authoritarian parenting style is the best style.

b. A permissive parenting style is the best style.

c. An authoritative parenting style is the best style.

d. There is no one best parenting style.

¶6 formulated main idea (Chapter 5) b

19. Which of the following statements is the main idea of paragraph 6?

a. Children know the satisfaction of meeting responsibilities and achieving success.

b. Authoritative parenting seems to enhance children's competence because authoritative parents set reasonable limits and realistic expectations.

c. In authoritarian homes, children are so strictly controlled that they cannot make independent choices about their own behavior.

d. In permissive homes, children receive so little guidance that they may become uncertain and anxious about whether they are doing the right thing.

author's tone (Chapter 8) d

20. Which of the following best describes the authors' tone?

a. impassioned

b. humorous

c. sarcastic

d. factual

✓ **Teaching Tip**

We suggest that rather than include this section as part of the quiz grade, you use it to give students practice with the skills they have studied and as a helpful preview of upcoming skills. It makes an excellent collaborative activity. All students will find this practice helpful, especially those who must take course exit tests, standardized reading tests, or state-mandated basic skills tests.

SELECTION **3-1**
Human Development
(continued)

Collaboration Option

Writing and Collaborating to Enhance Your Understanding

Option for collaboration: Your instructor may direct you to work with other students or, in other words, to work *collaboratively.* In that case, you should form groups of three or four students as directed by your instructor and work together to complete the exercises. After your group discusses each item and agrees on the answer, have a group member record it. Every member of your group should be able to explain all of your group's answers.

1. Reacting to What You Have Read: Was the parenting style of your parents (or the person or persons who reared you) authoritarian, permissive, or authoritative? Describe some of their actions as parents and their attitudes toward children that cause you to view them this way.

(Answers will vary.)

2. **Comprehending the Selection Further:** Put a check mark below the style of parenting that corresponds with each parental action or attitude. (You may refer to the selection.)

Parental action or attitude:	**Authoritarian**	**Permissive**	**Authoritative**
• detached, less warm	✓		
• values control	✓		
• explains reasoning behind their stands			✓
• views themselves as resources		✓	
• makes few demands on children		✓	
• imposes limited, judicious punishment			✓
• punishes arbitrarily	✓	✓	
• values self-regulation			
• stresses social values			✓
• is undemanding		✓	

Put a check mark below the style of parenting that corresponds with each of the characteristics of children of these parents.

Children's behavior or attitude:	**Authoritarian**	**Permissive**	**Authoritative**
• have input on policy decisions		✓	
• tend to be more distrustful	✓		
• participate in verbal give-and-take			✓
• tend to be withdrawn	✓		
• feel secure and loved		✓	✓
• are less self-controlled			
• cannot make independent choices about their own behavior	✓		
• know when they are meeting expectations			✓

- are uncertain and anxious about whether they are doing the right thing ____ ✓ ____
- fulfill commitments ____ ____ ✓

3. **Overall Main Idea of the Selection:** In one sentence tell what the authors want readers to understand about parenting styles and children's competence in dealing with their world. (Be sure to include the words "parenting style" and "children's competence in dealing with their world" in your overall main idea sentence.)

According to Baumrind, children's competence in dealing with their world is enhanced when they are raised by parents who have an authoritative parenting style.

OR

Research by Baumrind indicates that an authoritative parenting style enhances children's competence to deal with their world more than an authoritarian or permissive parenting style.

Internet Resources

Read More about This Topic on the World Wide Web

Directions: For further information about the topic of the selection, visit these websites:

www.parenting.ivillage.com
This website on pregnancy and parenting is sponsored by *iVillage.*

www.about our kids.org/articles/parentingstyles.html
This website presents an article titled "Parenting Styles and Children's Temperaments: The Match" by Anita Gurian, Ph.D.

http://pediatrics.about.com/cs/quizzes/l/bl_prnt_style.htm
What kind of parent are you? Take the Parenting Style Quiz at about.com.

You can also use your favorite search engine such as Google, Yahoo!, or AltaVista (www.google.com, www.yahoo.com, www.altavista.com) to discover more about this topic. To locate additional information, type in combinations of keywords such as:

parenting styles
or
effective parenting

Keep in mind that whenever you go to *any* website, it is a good idea to evaluate the website and the information it contains. Ask yourself questions such as:

"Who sponsors this website?"
"Is the information contained in this website up-to-date?"
"What type of information is presented?"
"Is the information objective and complete?"
"How easy is it to use the features of this website?"

SELECTION **3-2** **Speech Communication**

GIVING A SPEECH? IF YOU'RE NERVOUS, YOU'RE NORMAL!

From *Public Speaking for College and Career*
By Hamilton Gregory

It has been said that dying is the only thing Americans fear more than having to give a speech! To rank the fear of these two things so closely together indicates the extent to which many adults dread public speaking. Not surprisingly, many college students feel a bit panicky at the thought of having to give an oral report or make a presentation in class. (Some find it difficult even to make a comment or to ask a question in class.) In this selection from a public speaking textbook, the author describes four causes of this nervousness and reassures readers that it is an entirely normal feeling.

If public speaking makes you unusually nervous, consider enrolling in a speech course or joining a group such as Toastmasters. You will be with a supportive group of people who share the same anxiety. You will gain valuable instruction, practice, and—most important—confidence. Being able to speak well in public is an asset that will serve you well in college, in organizations to which you belong, and in your career.

1 Movie star Leonardo DiCaprio vividly remembers his two worst bouts of stage fright. The first occurred when he was in the eighth grade and he went out on his first date. "She was a beautiful Spanish girl named Cessl," he recalls, "and when I saw her, I was petrified. I couldn't even look her in the eye or speak to her." The movie they attended was no problem, since conversation was unnecessary, but dinner afterwards was a disaster because DiCaprio was painfully shy and tongue-tied. He was "so mortified" by his behavior that he avoided her for the next year even though he was "madly in love."

2 The second scare happened when DiCaprio, at age 19, was attending the Academy Awards ceremony and was terrified by the realization that he might win an Oscar and have to give an acceptance speech to a live audience of 4,000 people and a TV audience of 35 million. "I was shaking in my seat," he says. "My palms were sweaty, and I had this gut-wrenching fear that if I had to speak, I would slip up and do something horrible." When another actor won the award, he was immensely relieved.

3 During the next few years, whenever he was asked to give speeches to various organizations, he declined because he was afraid to speak to "big audiences."

4 By the time he was 25, however, he had become a different man. At the Earth Day 2000 rally in Washington, D.C., he confidently delivered a smooth, polished speech to 500,000 people. Since then, he has given dozens of other successful speeches to large audiences throughout the world.

5 What happened to Leonardo DiCaprio to transform him from a petrified to a polished public speaker? He explains: "I realized that if I make a mistake, so what? It's no big deal. There's no point in putting all that pressure on myself."

6 If you experience nervousness as a public speaker, you are not alone. Most people—even performers like DiCaprio—suffer from stage fright when called upon to speak in public. In fact, when researchers ask Americans to name their greatest fears,

Annotation Practice Exercises

Directions: For each exercise below, write the topic of the paragraph on the lines beside the paragraph.

Prediction Exercise

Topic of paragraph 6:

What transformed Leonardo into a polished public speaker

Actor Leonardo DiCaprio gives a presentation about global warming to the National Resources Defense Council. Once terrified of public speaking, DiCaprio gives speeches to audiences of all sizes.

the fear of speaking to a group of strangers is listed more often than fear of snakes, insects, lightning, deep water, heights, or flying in airplanes. With training and practice, you will be able to control your nervousness and—like Leonardo DiCaprio—become a confident speaker.

Prediction Exercise

Topic of paragraph 7:
reasons for nervousness (when giving a speech)
(clue: heading)

Reasons for Nervousness

7 Is it foolish to be afraid to give a speech? Is this fear as groundless as a child's fear of monsters? I used to think so, back when I first began making speeches. I was a nervous wreck, and I would often chide myself by saying, "Come on, relax; it's just a little speech. There's no good reason to be scared." But I was wrong. There *is* good reason to be scared. In fact, there are *four* good reasons for nervousness when giving a speech.

Fear of Being Stared At

8 In the animal world, a stare is a hostile act. Dogs, baboons, and other animals sometimes defend their territory by staring. Their hostile gaze alone is enough to turn away an intruder. We human beings have similar reactions; it is a part of our biological makeup to be upset by stares. Imagine that you are riding in a crowded elevator with a group of strangers. Suddenly you realize that the other people are staring directly at you. Not just glancing. *Staring.* You probably would be unnerved and frightened because a stare can be as threatening as a clenched fist—especially if it comes from people you don't know. That is why public speaking can be so frightening. You have a pack of total strangers "attacking" you with unrelenting stares, while you are obliged to stand alone, exposed and vulnerable—a goldfish in a bowl, subject to a constant scrutiny.

Fear of Failure

9 "We're all afraid of looking stupid," says Jim Seymour, a columnist for *PC* magazine. "I give about 40 speeches a year. . . .

Yet every single time I get ready to walk out in front of an audience, I get that old, scary feeling: *What if I make a fool of myself?* That's as deeply embedded in our psyches as our DNA chains are embedded in our cells, I suspect; I don't know anyone who doesn't get the sweats at the prospect of looking dumb to someone else."

Fear of Rejection

10 What if we do our best, what if we deliver a polished speech, but the audience still does not like us? It would be quite a blow to our ego because we want to be liked and, yes, even loved. We want people to admire us, to consider us wise and intelligent, and to accept our ideas and opinions. We don't want people to dislike us or reject us.

Fear of the Unknown

11 Throughout our lives we are apprehensive about doing new things, such as going to school for the first time, riding a bus without our parents, or going out on our first date. We cannot put a finger on exactly what we are afraid of, because our fear is vague and diffused. What we really fear is the unknown; we worry that some unpredictable disaster will occur. When we stand up to give a speech, we are sometimes assailed by this same fear of the unknown because we cannot predict the outcome of our speech. Fortunately, this fear usually disappears, as we become experienced in giving speeches. We develop enough confidence to know that nothing terrible will befall us, just as our childhood fear of riding in a bus by ourselves vanished after two or three trips.

12 All four of these fears are as understandable as the fear of lightning. There is no reason to be ashamed of having them.

Source: Hamilton Gregory, *Public Speaking for College and Career*, 7th ed., pp. 28–30. Copyright © 2005 by The McGraw-Hill Companies, Inc. Reprinted by permission of The McGraw-Hill Companies, Inc.

SELECTION 3-2 Speech Communication

Comprehension and Vocabulary Quiz

This quiz has four parts. Your instructor may assign some or all of them.

Comprehension

Directions: Items 1–5 test your comprehension (understanding) of the material in this selection. These questions are much like those that a content-area instructor (such as a speech communication professor) would expect you to know after reading and studying this selection. For each comprehension question below, use information from the selection to determine the correct answer. Refer to the selection as you answer the questions. Write your answers in the spaces provided.

¶5 b **1.** Leonardo DiCaprio was able to become a successful public speaker once he realized:

a. he needed to pour his heart and soul into reaching his audiences.

b. mistakes were no big deal.

c. he must spend more time preparing for his speeches.

d. putting pressure on himself was actually helpful.

¶6 c **2.** Feeling nervous before giving a speech is:

a. caused by strangers in the audience "attacking" you with unrelenting stares.

b. less common than fear of snakes, insects, and lightning.

c. normal.

d. a blow to our ego.

¶11 d **3.** When speaking to a group, our fear of the unknown usually lessens as we:

a. learn to look directly at people in the audience.

b. learn to control our egos.

c. become less afraid of "looking stupid."

d. become more experienced in giving speeches.

¶10 a **4.** The fear of rejection contributes to our nervousness when speaking to a group because:

a. we have a strong need for people to admire us and accept our ideas and opinions.

b. we want to reject the idea of giving a speech.

c. we do not know who will reject us.

d. all of the above

¶s 9, 10, 11 c **5.** All of the following are good reasons to be nervous about speaking to a group of strangers *except:*

a. we are apprehensive about doing something new.

b. we are afraid of looking foolish.

c. we fear that we have not prepared and rehearsed our speech adequately.

d. we fear that people in the audience won't like us or accept our ideas.

Vocabulary in Context

Directions: Items 6–10 test your ability to determine the meaning of the word by using context clues. *Context clues* are words in a sentence that allow the reader to deduce (reason out) the meaning of an unfamiliar word in that sentence. Context clues also enable the reader to determine which meaning the author intends when a word has more than one meaning. For each vocabulary item below, a sentence from the selection containing an important word (*italicized, like this*) is quoted first. Next, there is an additional sentence using the word in the same sense and providing another context clue. Use the context clues from *both* sentences to deduce the meaning of the italicized word. *Be sure the answer you choose makes sense in both sentences.* If you need to use a dictionary to confirm your answer choice, remember that the meaning you select must still fit the context of *both* sentences. Write your answers in the spaces provided.

Pronunciation Key: ă **pat** ā **pay** âr **care** ä **father** ĕ **pet** ē **be** ĭ **pit**
ī **tie** îr **pier** ŏ **pot** ō **toe** ô **paw** oi **noise** ou **out** o͝o **took** o͞o **boot**
ŭ **cut** yo͞o ab**u**se ûr **urge** th **thin** *th* **this** hw **which** zh vision
ə **about** *Stress mark:* ′

¶1 ___a___ **6.** He was "so *mortified*" by his behavior that he avoided her for the next year even though he was "madly in love."

My grandmother was mortified when her detures fell into her soup at a dinner party.

mortified (môr′ tə fīd) means:

a. feeling shame or humiliation

b. feeling amused

c. feeling numb

d. feeling courageous or bold

¶7 ___c___ **7.** Is this fear as *groundless* as a child's fear of monsters?

The judge ruled that the charges against the defendent were *groundless* and dismissed the case.

groundless (ground′ lĭs) means:

a. severe

b. able to be disputed

c. without basis

d. upsetting

¶8 ___b___ **8.** You have a pack of total strangers "attacking" you with *unrelenting* stares, while you are obliged to stand alone, exposed and vulnerable—a goldfish in a bowl, subject to a constant scrutiny.

Once we entered the grocery store, my children were so *unrelenting* in their demands for candy that I finally gave in and bought them some.

unrelenting (ŭn rĭ lĕn′ tĭng) means:

a. loud; vocal

b. constant; persistent

c. unreasonable

d. hostile; hateful

¶11 ___d___ **9.** We cannot put a finger on exactly what we are afraid of, because our fear is vague and *diffused*.

The patient's anxiety was so *diffused* that the psychiatrist was unable to identify the specific source of it.

diffused (dĭ fyo͞ozd′) means:

a. intense; focused

b. overwhelming to the point of incapacitating

c. distinct; clear

d. not concentrated on any one thing

¶11 ___a___ **10.** When we stand up to give a speech, we are sometimes *assailed* by this same fear of the unknown because we cannot predict the outcome of our speech.

After the tornado struck the state, the governor was *assailed* with criticism for not responding quickly enough to help its victims.

assailed (ə sāld′) means:

a. attacked

b. frightened

c. praised

d. ignored

Word Structure

Directions: Items 11–15 test your ability to use word-structure clues to help determine a word's meaning. *Word-structure clues* consist of roots, prefixes, and suffixes. In these exercises, you will learn the meaning of a word part (a root) and use it to determine the meaning of several other words that have the same word part. If you need to use a dictionary to confirm your answer choice, do so. Write your answers in the spaces provided.

In paragraph 10 of the selection, you encountered the word **rejection.** This word contains the Latin root ***ject,*** which means "to throw." The word *rejection* literally means that someone or something is "*tossed* back" (not accepted). Use the meaning of ***ject*** and the list of prefixes on pages 68–69 to help you determine the meaning of each of the following words that contain this same root. Write your answers in the spaces provided.

a 11. If a referee or umpire **ejects** players from a game, he or she:

a. throws them out.
b. cautions them against making future violations.
c. calls a penalty on them.
d. signals to them.

d 12. If you are **dejected,** you are feeling:

a. angry.
b. cheerful.
c. optimistic.
d. downcast.

b 13. If you **interject** your opinion into a conversation your friends are having, you:

a. keep your opinion to yourself.
b. interrupt them by tossing in your opinion.
c. ask them if they would like to know your opinion.
d. decide your opinion is worthless.

a 14. A film **projector** is designed to:

a. throw images on a screen.
b. block images from the screen.
c. blur images.
d. capture images on film.

c 15. If you receive an **injection,** the substance is:

a. given as a pill.
b. dispensed as a cream.
c. pushed beneath the skin.
d. placed in an inhaler.

✓ **Teaching Tip**
Let students know that not all of the skills included in this Reading Skills Application section have been introduced yet. This section serves as a valuable preview of these skills, however. Students typically get several of the items correct, and they find this encouraging.

Reading Skills Application

Directions: Items 16–20 test your ability to *apply* certain reading skills to information in this selection. These types of questions provide valuable practice for all students, especially those who must take standardized reading tests and state-mandated basic skills tests. You may not have studied all of the skills at this point, so these items will serve as a helpful preview. The comprehension and critical reading skills in this section are presented in Chapters 3 through 9 of *New Worlds;* vocabulary and figurative language skills are presented in Chapter 2. As you work through *New Worlds,* you will practice and develop these skills. Write your answers in the spaces provided.

¶s 7–12 authors' writing patterns (Chapter 7)

d 16. The information in paragraphs 7–12 of the selection is organized according to which of the following patterns?

a. comparison-contrast
b. problem-solution
c. sequence
d. cause-effect

author's purpose for writing (Chapter 8) d

17. The author's primary purpose for writing this selection is to:
a. persuade readers to become more like Leonardo DiCaprio.
b. instruct readers how to overcome their nervousness.
c. persuade readers to get more practice making speeches.
d. inform readers as to why giving a speech can make a person nervous.

¶7 stated main idea (Chapter 4) a

18. Which of the following statements best expresses the main idea of paragraph 7?
a. There are four good reasons to be nervous when you give a speech.
b. It is foolish to be afraid to give a speech.
c. The fear of giving a speech is groundless.
d. You can calm yourself by saying, "Relax, it's just a little speech."

¶7 phrase in context (Chapter 2) c

19. In paragraph 1, the phrase *with the weight of the world on his shoulders* means:
a. feeling pain in the back.
b. feeling angry.
c. feeling great pressure.
d. feeling challenged.

logical inference (Chapter 9) c

20. Based on information in the selection, it can be inferred that:
a. the fear of rejection is stronger in people than the fear of failure.
b. throughout our lives we are apprehensive about doing new things.
c. it is reassuring to know that it is normal to feel nervous about speaking in public.
d. most people eventually adjust to being stared at.

SELECTION **3-2**
Speech Communication
(continued)

Collaboration Option

Writing and Collaborating to Enhance Your Understanding

Option for collaboration: Your instructor may direct you to work with other students or, in other words, to work *collaboratively*. In that case, you should form groups of three or four students as directed by your instructor and work together to complete the exercises. After your group discusses each item and agrees on the answer, have a group member record it. Every member of your group should be able to explain all of your group's answers.

1. **Reacting to What You Have Read:** Have you ever been a victim of "mike fright"? Freezing up when a microphone or camcorder is thrust in one's face is a common experience. Describe a situation when your nervousness or fear interfered with your speaking in the classroom or some other public setting.
(Answers will vary.)

2. **Comprehending the Selection Further:** List and explain the four common reasons for nervousness when we are giving a speech.

- Fear of being stared at. We view staring as a hostile act; we don't like being subjected to constant scrutiny.
- Fear of failure. We fear looking stupid or foolish; we don't want to appear dumb to someone else.
- Fear of rejection. We want to be liked and loved; we don't want people to dislike us or reject us.
- Fear of the unknown. We are apprehensive about doing new things; this fear is vague and diffused; we worry that some unpredictable disaster will occur.

3. **Overall Main Idea of the Selection:** In one sentence, tell what the author wants readers to understand about being nervous when giving a speech. (Be sure to use the words "nervous" and "giving a speech" in your overall main idea sentence.)

There are several reasons to be nervous about giving a speech, but these fears are a part of normal human behavior and there is no reason to be ashamed of them.

Internet Resources

Read More about This Topic on the World Wide Web

Directions: For further information about the topic of the selection, visit these websites:

www.toastmasters.org
This is the official website for Toastmasters International, an organization that promotes effective communication. This site contains useful information about giving speeches and presentations.

You can also use your favorite search engine such as Google, Yahoo!, or AltaVista (www.google.com, www.yahoo.com, www.altavista.com) to discover more about this topic. To locate additional information, type in combinations of keywords such as:

nervousness in public speaking
or
giving a speech
or
stage fright

Keep in mind that whenever you go to *any* website, it is a good idea to evaluate the website and the information it contains. Ask yourself questions such as:

"Who sponsors this website?"
"Is the information contained in this website up-to-date?"
"What type of information is presented?"
"Is the information objective and complete?"
"How easy is it to use the features of this website?"

SELECTION **3-3**
Business

BETTER SLEEP IS BIG BUSINESS, BUT ARE RESTLESS NIGHTS OR ADVERTISEMENTS FUELING THE NEED?

From *Sunday Gazette-Mail*
By Fawn Vrazo

Ads are everywhere. The typical person sees 3,000 ads a day, and by age 25 has seen 2 million ads. As a consumer, you need to be able to make good decisions, and you can—if you are informed. Unfortunately, people often base some of their decisions strictly on ads. The following newspaper article examines the dramatic surge in the advertising—and sales—of prescription sleep aids. Manufacturers blanket the public with ads for these products, but do consumers actually need them? Read the article and draw your own conclusions.

As you read, you will also learn interesting and helpful information about sleep and sleep disorders, including insomnia and apnea. It is estimated that 70 million people in the United States have sleep problems, and college students are certainly among those who are chronically short on sleep. One-third of young adults between the ages of 18 and 29 years say they suffer from significant daytime sleepiness. If young adults do seek out sleep aids, one-fourth turn to alcohol. Ironically, alcohol can actually disrupt sleep. Worse, a combination of sleeping pills and alcohol can be dangerous, even deadly.

Everyone knows that sleep deprivation makes people more accident-prone, putting both themselves and others at risk. Of course, sleep deprivation causes them to feel tired and irritable. Did you know that it also causes weight gain, and the loss of concentration, creativity, and the ability to reason logically? For students, the last three can be especially problematic.

---

1 Z-Z-Z-Z-Z-Z-Z-Z-Z-Z. Every body has to have it. And suddenly Americans seem desperate to get it. The search for deep, uninterrupted, refreshing sleep has become a national obsession. It's driving everything from the development of new prescription sleeping pills to extensive bed makeovers in hotel chains.

2 In just 10 years, certified sleep clinics in the United States have nearly tripled, from 297 in 1995 to 883 by 2006, with more on the way. Sleep medicine has recently become an approved specialty and the number of sleep doctors is soaring—doubling in the past decade to 3,000 today.

3 Sleep medicine ads are unavoidable (unless you are asleep). In 2004, the makers of top-selling prescription sleep aids spent $61 million marketing their insomnia pills, according to the media research firm TNS Media. In the first seven months of this year, they spent $120 million. The biggest outlay came from Sepracor Inc., buying $57 million worth of TV ads in hopes of winning blockbuster status for its new *Lunesta*—the first prescription sleep aid that doesn't advise only short-term use. Who hasn't seen that softly glowing *Lunesta* lunar moth?

4 Sleep experts say they've never before seen so much interest in sleep. There has always been fascination with this mysterious part of the daily human cycle, says Karl Doghramji, head of the sleep disorders clinic at Thomas Jefferson University Hospital in Philadelphia. "Everyone sleeps. It's a common experience: you basically fall asleep and seven hours later wake up. There's a natural curiosity about that period of time." But what is new is broadening medical knowledge about sleep patterns, sleep disorders, and the severe consequences of too little sleep.

Annotation Practice Exercises

Directions: For each exercise below, write the topic of the paragraph on the lines beside the paragraph.

Practice Exercise

Topic of paragraph 3:

the vast amount of advertising by sleep medicine manufacturers OR the vast amount drug companies spend to advertise prescription sleep aids

5 Research has grown from the discovery of REM (rapid-eye-movement) sleep in 1957 to a more sophisticated understanding of sleep phases and the brain cells that regulate them. In the 1980s, experiments with rats proved that weeks of total sleep deprivation led to death. Now we know that mere sleepiness is deadly, too: An estimated 100,000 auto accidents a year are caused by drivers asleep or drowsy at the wheel. "Sleep is just as important as exercise or what we eat to our overall health," says Carl Hunt, head of the National Center on Sleep Disorders Research.

6 The public has followed sleep discoveries avidly. "One generation ago the word 'apnea' was not even in the vocabulary of the average person," says Meir Kryger, a sleep specialist on the National Sleep foundation board. "Now everyone uses the word 'apnea' like they learned it in grade 5."

7 While there's no clear evidence that sleep disorders are growing, the numbers are high enough to support a robust sleep industry. An estimated 10 percent of American adults—22 million—suffer from chronic insomnia and 5 percent to 7 percent have sleep apnea.

8 Population changes could push those numbers even higher. Apnea, the repeated cessation of breathing during sleep, is often related to obesity, and obesity figures are rising. Insomnia worsens with age and the onset of menopause, and hordes of Baby Boomers are entering the danger zone.

9 Don Delson, a 54-year-old investment banker, wryly observes that younger people sleep more soundly because "in your 30s, you aren't mature enough to worry whether your kids will find the right mate, and your bladder doesn't get you up." His own fix for a sound sleep? For himself and his family, Delson has purchased four Duxiana beds (average price $4,500 each). Swedish-made DUXs, which offer "advanced technology in sleeping" for up to $9,000 a bed, are at the higher end of a growing super-bed industry promising Americans better trips to the land of nod.

10 Pills, though, are increasingly the sleep aid of choice. Americans spent $2.1 billion on the top prescription sleeping pills in 2004, according to the pharmaceutical information company IMS Health. And a recent survey by the mail and retail prescription drug supplier Medco Health Solutions Inc. found remarkable increases in sleep drug use: Between 2000 and 2004, the number of adults using sleep medications doubled. In children ages 10 to 19, sleeping pill use rose 85 percent.

11 The top sleeping-pill seller by far is Sanofi-Aventis' *Ambien* ($1.8 billion in sales in 2004). Sepracor's *Lunesta,* introduced earlier this year, hit second place with sales of $112 million between January and July. Nipping on *Lunesta*'s heels and rounding out the spectrum are the new extended-release *Ambien CR,* and the new *Rozerem,* from Japan's Takeda Pharmaceuticals, which claims to avoid the dangers of dependence and abuse. Next up, if approved by the FDA, may be Pfizer's *Indiplon.*

12 But while the newer sleeping pills are considered safer and less addictive than older sleeping aids such as *Valium* and *Halcion,* doctors and sleep experts worry that hyper marketing may encourage overuse. Most sleeping pills are labeled for short-term use of a week or so, and even longer-use *Lunesta* has been tracked in studies for just six months.

✓ **Teaching Tips**

Students might enjoy a brief discussion of the ubiquity of ads. Ask them where they see them, including unusual places. Advertisers place ads on the sides of buses, on T-shirts, on computer screens and movie screens, and even at the bottom of cup holes on golf courses—not to mention ones for callers who are placed on hold!

Some students may not recognize that the Zs at the beginning of the article represent sleep (from the sound of snoring, perhaps). The term "Zs" ("I need to catch some Zs") is slang for sleep.

Practice Exercise

Topic of paragraph 6:

public interest in sleep discoveries

Practice Exercise

Topic of paragraph 8:

population changes that could increase the number of sleep problems

Practice Exercise

Topic of paragraph 10:

the increasing popularity (use) of sleeping pills

13 But many sleepless Americans take the drugs for longer and then suffer "rebound insomnia" when they try to quit, says Allan Pack, head of the expanding sleep clinic network of the University of Pennsylvania Health System. "It can be quite severe. It can be a long time before your own sleep system kicks in again."

14 Other experts note that sleep disorders are complicated. Do you feel sleepy during the day because you have insomnia? Or because undetected bouts of apnea wake you up all night? Could your sleeping problem be caused by obesity, depression, heart disease or other problems, which require their own treatments before you get relief?

15 The intense national focus on sleep is welcomed by advocacy groups such as Philadelphia-based Awake in America, which works for greater public awareness of sleep apnea and other disorders. But there's a suspicion that sleeping-pill marketing is what is really driving the sleep obsession trend. The marketing is at least starting a discussion, says Awake in America cofounder and apnea sufferer Dave Jackson. "But a lot of the doctors are listening to the pharmaceutical reps wanting to push drugs for insomnia. They're getting their information about sleep disorders from the reps."

16 Before you pop a sleeping pill, say the experts, get a proper diagnosis.

✓ **Teaching Tip**

According to the *Los Angeles Times* (3/30/09) prescriptions for sleeping medications exceeded 56 million in 2008 (a record), up 54 percent from 2004. Moreover, some specialists were predicting another record year for sleeping pill use.

Practice Exercise

Topic of paragraph 14:

the complicated nature of sleep disorders

✓ **Teaching Tip**

When students have completed Chapter 9 on critical thinking, you may want to return to this newspaper article to have them apply those skills to it. It's a great example of how critical thinking can be applied to reading in everyday life.

Source: Adapted from Fawn Vrazo, "Better Sleep is Big Business, but are Restless Nights or Advertisements Fueling the Need?" *Sunday Gazette-Mail,* January 1, 2006. © McClatchy-Tribune Information Services. All Rights Reserved. Reprinted with permission.

SELECTION 3-3 **Business** *(continued)*

Comprehension and Vocabulary Quiz

This quiz has four parts. Your instructor may assign some or all of them.

Comprehension

Directions: Items 1–5 test your comprehension (understanding) of the material in this selection. These questions are much like those that a content-area instructor (such as a business professor) would expect you to know after reading and studying this selection. For each comprehension question below, use information from the selection to determine the correct answer. Refer to the selection as you answer the questions. Write your answers in the spaces provided.

¶5 ___c___ **1.** An estimated 100,000 auto accidents a year are caused by drivers who are:

a. taking sleeping pills.
b. addicted to sleeping pills.
c. asleep or drowsy at the wheel.
d. experiencing rebound insomnia.

¶4, 6 ___a___ **2.** With regard to information and discoveries about sleep, the public:

a. is very interested.
b. has no interest.
c. has a limited understanding.
d. has no knowledge of them.

¶7 ___a___ **3.** The number of Americans who suffer from chronic insomnia is approximately:

a. 10 percent.
b. 22 percent.
c. 57 percent.
d. 85 percent.

¶8 ___c___ **4.** Apnea is related to:

a. high blood pressure.
b. age.
c. obesity.
d. the use of sleeping pills.

¶14 ___d___ **5.** Sleep disorders can be caused by:

a. obesity.
b. depression.
c. heart disease.
d. all of the above

Vocabulary in Context

Directions: Items 6–10 test your ability to determine the meaning of the word by using context clues. *Context clues* are words in a sentence that allow the reader to deduce (reason out) the meaning of an unfamiliar word in that sentence. Context clues also enable the reader to determine which meaning the author intends when a word has more than one meaning. For each vocabulary item below, a sentence from the selection containing an important word (*italicized, like this*) is quoted first. Next, there is an additional sentence using the word in the same sense and providing another context clue. Use the context clues from *both* sentences to deduce the meaning of the italicized word. *Be sure the answer you choose makes sense in both sentences.* If you need to use a dictionary to confirm your answer choice, remember that the meaning you select must still fit the context of *both* sentences. Write your answers in the spaces provided.

Pronunciation Key: ă **pat** ā **pay** âr **care** ä **father** ĕ pet ē be ĭ pit
ī tie îr **pier** ŏ pot ō **toe** ô **paw** oi n**oi**se ou **out** o͝o **took**
o͞o b**oo**t ŭ **cut** yo͞o ab**u**se ûr **ur**ge th **th**in *th* **th**is hw **wh**ich
zh vision ə **a**bout *Stress mark:* ′

¶3 d **6.** Who hasn't seen that softly glowing Lunesta *lunar* moth?

A *lunar* month is the average time between successive new or full moons, equal to 29 days 12 hours 44 minutes.

lunar (lo͞o′ nər) means:

a. pertaining to sleep

b. pertaining to moths

c. pertaining to calendars

d. pertaining to the moon

¶7 c **7.** While there's no clear evidence that sleep disorders are growing, the numbers are high enough to support a *robust* sleep industry.

People who take excellent care of themselves usually enjoy *robust* health.

robust (rō bŭst′) means:

a. deteriorating, failing

b. illegal, unlawful

c. strong, vigorous

d. temporary

¶8 c **8.** Apnea, the repeated *cessation* of breathing during sleep, is often related to obesity, and obesity figures are rising.

Smoking *cessation* programs are designed to help those addicted to tobacco quit smoking.

cessation (sĕ să′ shən) means:

a. continuation
b. improvement
c. the stopping or ceasing of
d. relief

¶8 b **9.** Insomnia worsens with age and the onset of menopause, and *hordes* of Baby Boomers are entering the danger zone.

On the same day *hordes* of demonstrators, more than one hundred thousand in all, gathered in several different countries to protest the war.

hordes (hôrdz) means:

a. small groups of people
b. large numbers of people
c. groups of religious people
d. groups of angry people

¶14 a **10.** Do you feel sleepy during the day because you have insomnia? Or because undetected *bouts* of apnea wake you up all night?

The homeless man's *bouts* of drinking became more frequent, and eventually he died of alcohol poisoning.

bouts (boutz) means:

a. periods of time spent in a particular way
b. contests, matches
c. attacks
d. rituals

Word Structure

Directions: Items 11–15 test your ability to use word-structure clues to help determine a word's meaning. *Word-structure clues* consist of roots, prefixes, and suffixes. In these exercises, you will learn the meaning of a word part (a root) and use it to determine the meaning of several other words that have the same word part. If you need to use a dictionary to confirm your answer choice, do so. Write your answers in the spaces provided.

In paragraph 11 of the selection, you encountered the word **spectrum.** This word contains the Latin root ***spec***, which means "to look" or "to see." The word *spectrum* has many meanings, but in this passage, it refers to seeing the energy (light) from a radiant source (here, a light bulb) distributed and arranged in order of the wavelengths. ("Daylight spectrum" light is full-spectrum light that looks like natural daylight.) Use the meaning of ***spec*** and the list of prefixes on pages 68–69 to help you determine the meaning of each of the following words that contain this same root.

a 11. If you make a **spectacle** of yourself at a party, other people are likely to:
- *a.* stop and watch you.
- *b.* applaud you.
- *c.* wish they were you.
- *d.* report you to the police.

c 12. If a person wishes in **retrospect** that he or she had finished college, the person wishes this:
- *a.* in vain.
- *b.* as a joke.
- *c.* while looking back at the past.
- *d.* in great frustration and regret.

d 13. A **spectator** at a baseball game is a person who:
- *a.* plays in the game.
- *b.* umpires the game.
- *c.* sells food in the stands.
- *d.* watches the game.

b 14. A **prospector** is a person who:
- *a.* wants free land.
- *b.* looks for mineral deposits or oil.
- *c.* seeks adventure.
- *d.* leads people to new territories.

a 15. A **specimen** is a sample of tissue or other material that a doctor or scientist:
- *a.* looks at in order to study it.
- *b.* preserves in chemicals.
- *c.* stores in a laboratory.
- *d.* obtains from another researcher.

✓ **Teaching Tip**
Let students know that not all of the skills included in this Reading Skills Application section have been introduced yet. This section serves as a valuable preview of these skills, however. Students typically get several of the items correct, and they find this encouraging.

Reading Skills Application

Directions: Items 16–20 test your ability to *apply* certain reading skills to information in this selection. These types of questions provide valuable practice for all students, especially those who must take standardized reading tests and state-mandated basic skills tests. You may not have studied all of the skills at this point, so these items will serve as a helpful preview. The comprehension and critical reading skills in this section are presented in Chapters 3 through 9 of *New Worlds;* vocabulary and figurative language skills are presented in Chapter 2. As you work through *New Worlds,* you will practice and develop these skills. Write your answers in the spaces provided.

¶s 1–3 distinguishing facts from opinions (Chapter 9) a **16.** Which of the following statements from the first three paragraphs represents an opinion rather than a fact?

a. The search for deep, uninterrupted, refreshing sleep has become a national obsession.

b. In just 10 years, certified sleep clinics in the United States have nearly tripled, from 297 in 1995 to 883 by 2006, with more on the way.

c. Sleep medicine has recently become an approved specialty and the number of sleep doctors is soaring—doubling in the past decade to 3,000 today.

d. In 2004, the makers of top-selling prescription sleep aids spent $61 million marketing their insomnia pills, according to the media research firm TNS Media.

¶10 stated main idea (Chapter 4) a **17.** The main idea of paragraph 10 is represented by which of the following statements?

a. Pills, though, are increasingly the sleep aid of choice.

b. Americans spent $2.1 billion on the top prescription sleeping pills in 2004, according to the pharmaceutical information company IMS Health.

c. And a recent survey by the mail and retail prescription drug supplier Medco Health Solutions Inc. found remarkable increases in sleep drug use: Between 2000 and 2004, the number of adults using sleep medications doubled.

d. In children ages 10 to 19, sleeping pill use rose 85 percent.

¶s 10, 12 conclusion (Chapter 9) d **18.** Based on the information in the selection, it can be concluded that sales of sleeping pills are likely to:

a. decrease significantly.

b. decrease slightly.

c. remain stable.

d. continue to increase.

¶2 authors' writing patterns (Chapter 7) c **19.** The information in paragraph 2 is organized using which of the following patterns?

a. list

b. sequence

c. comparison-contrast

d. cause-effect

¶9 phrase in context (Chapter 2) d **20.** In paragraph 9, the author uses the phrase "land of nod" to mean:

a. agreement.

b. dreams.

c. drowsiness.

d. sleep.

✓ **Teaching Tip**

We suggest that rather than include this section as part of the quiz grade, you use it to give students practice with the skills they have studied and as a helpful preview of upcoming skills. It makes an excellent collaborative activity. All students will find this practice helpful, especially those who must take course exit tests, standardized reading tests, or state-mandated basic skills tests.

SELECTION 3-3
Business
(continued)

Writing and Collaborating to Enhance Your Understanding

Option for collaboration: Your instructor may direct you to work with other students or, in other words, to work *collaboratively*. In that case, you should form groups of three or four students as directed by your instructor and work together to complete the exercises. After your group discusses each item and agrees on the answer, have a group member record it. Every member of your group should be able to explain all of your group's answers.

Collaboration Option

1. **Reacting to What You Have Read:** If you are like many, if not most, college students, you do not get enough sleep. On average, how much sleep do you get each night? Do you consider yourself sleep-deprived? What effect do you think this has on you? What steps do you think you (or any sleep-deprived student) could take to improve the situation?

   (Answers will vary.)

2. **Comprehending the Selection Further:** Now that you have read the article, how would you answer the question posed in the title? Are "restless nights" driving the increasing sales of sleeping pills and other sleeping aids, or is it the result of massive advertising by drug companies? Explain your answer.

   (Answers will vary.)

✓ **Teaching Tip**
Americans are using an ever-increasing number of sleeping pills. Ask students what effects they think this might have on society as a whole. To what do they attribute this increase?

3. **Overall Main Idea of the Selection:** In one sentence, tell what the authors want readers to understand about sleep aids and sleep problems. (Be sure to include the words "sleep aids" and "sleep problems" in your overall main idea sentence.)

   Sales of *sleep aids*, especially highly advertised sleeping pills, have increased dramatically in the United States, but people who have *sleep problems* should get a proper diagnosis before resorting to sleeping pills.

Internet Resources

Read More about This Topic on the World Wide Web

Directions: For further information about the topic of the selection, visit these websites:

www.sleepfoundation.org
This is the website of the National Sleep Foundation, an independent nonprofit organization dedicated to improving public health and safety by achieving understanding of sleep and sleep disorders and by supporting sleep-related education, research, and advocacy. Check out the section on Teens and Sleep, as well as the Quizzes and Tools section. Try the "Sleep Myths Quiz," the "Sleep IQ Test," and "How Safe a Sleeper Are You?" Take the "Insomnia Assessment Test."

http://health.nih.gov
Website of the National Institutes of Health, U.S. Department of Health and Human Services. Type "Sleep" in the Search box to see a range of helpful topics on the subject.

http://medlineplus.gov
A service of the U.S. National Library of Medicine and the National Institutes of Health. Go to Health topics, and then type "Sleep" in the Search Box. Topics include such things as sleep disorders, sleep apnea, and snoring.

You can also use your favorite search engine such as Google, Yahoo!, or AltaVista (www.google.com, www.yahoo.com, www.altavista.com) to discover more about this topic. To locate additional information, type in combinations of keywords such as:

sleep
or
sleep disorders

Keep in mind that whenever you go to *any* website, it is a good idea to evaluate the website and the information it contains. Ask yourself questions such as:

"Who sponsors this website?"
"Is the information contained in this website up-to-date?"
"What type of information is presented?"
"Is the information objective and complete?"
"How easy is it to use the features of this website?"

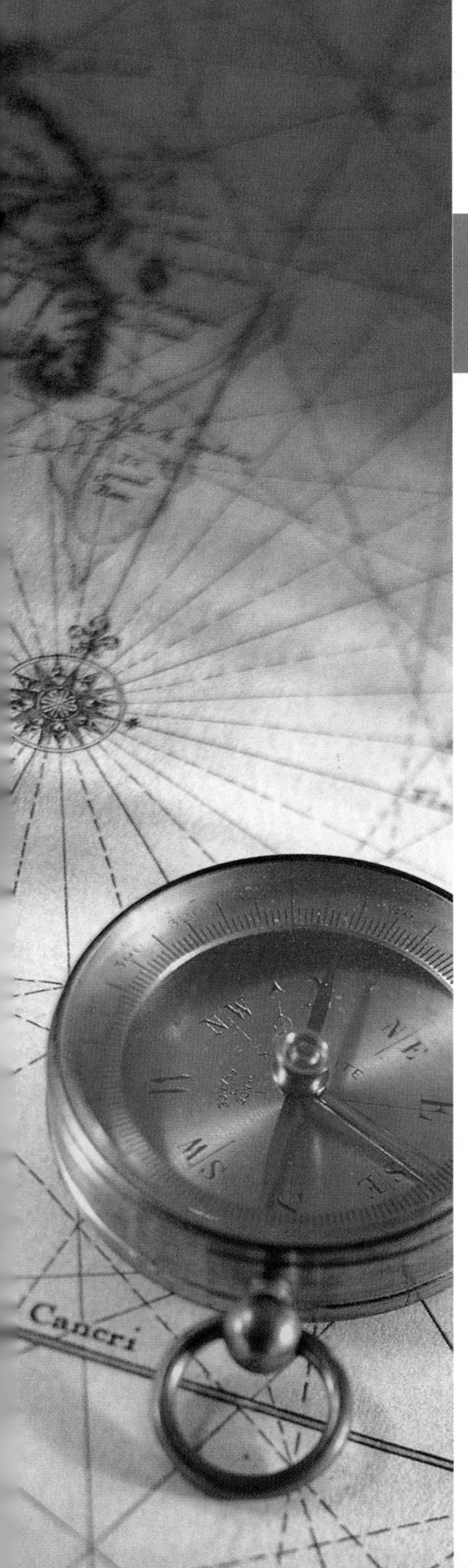

CHAPTER 4

Locating the Stated Main Idea

CHAPTER OBJECTIVES

In this chapter you will learn the answers to these questions:

- What is a stated main idea sentence?
- Why is the stated main idea sentence important?
- How can I locate the stated main idea sentence of a paragraph?
- Which sentence can be the stated main idea sentence in a paragraph?

✓ **Timely Words**

"Reading makes a full man, meditation a profound man, discourse a clear man." (Benjamin Franklin)

"I hear, I know.
I see, I remember.
I do, I understand."
(Confucius)

CHAPTER CONTENTS

WHAT IS A STATED MAIN IDEA SENTENCE, AND WHY IS IT IMPORTANT?

KEY TERM
stated main idea sentence

The sentence in a paragraph that contains both the topic and the author's single most important point about this topic.

A stated main idea sentence is also known as the *topic sentence.*

You already know that every paragraph has a topic. In addition, every paragraph has a main idea. It is the one idea about the topic the author considers most important for the reader to understand. Frequently, an author states the main idea directly as one of the sentences in the paragraph. A **stated main idea sentence** is the sentence in a paragraph that contains both the topic and the author's single most important point about this topic. A paragraph can have only one main—most important—idea.

In a writing or English course, your instructor may call the stated main idea sentence of a paragraph the *topic sentence.* Think about the name "topic sentence." It tells you a lot about a main idea: It must contain the *topic.* And, it tells you that the main idea must be a *sentence.* When locating a stated main idea, keep in mind that you are looking for the *author's* most important point, not what you think is most important or simply find interesting. (Sometimes the main idea is *not* directly stated by the author as one of the sentences in the paragraph. This is called an *implied* main idea, and you will learn about it in Chapter 5.)

Student Online Learning Center (OLC)
***Go to* Chapter 4.**
***Select* Video.**

Here are examples of topics and main idea sentences. In a paragraph whose topic is *Benjamin Franklin,* the author might write this stated main idea sentence: *A Founding Father of the United States, Benjamin Franklin was a genius who achieved remarkable success in a wide range of fields.* Or in a paragraph whose topic is *injuries caused by airbags,* the author might state as the main idea: *To avoid injuries caused by airbags, children under the age of 12 should be buckled in the backseat of a car.* Notice that the topic always appears in the main idea sentence.

Because stated main ideas are so important, authors sometimes draw attention to them by using certain phrases. Watch for phrases such as *The point is; It is obvious that; It is important to understand that; In short; therefore;* and *In conclusion.* These phrases often appear at the beginning of the main idea sentence, but they can appear within the sentence. For example, *Therefore, no person can serve more than two terms as president of the United States* and *No person, therefore, can serve more than two terms as president of the United States.*

✓ **Teaching Tip**
Remind students that the student OLC contains an audio and video feature for Chapters 3 through 9 that presents **Key Comprehension Terms** and **Comprehension Monitoring Questions.**

Why is it important to locate and understand stated main idea sentences? It is the sentence the author uses to present the single most important point he or she wants the reader to understand. Therefore, understanding main ideas is a key to identifying and learning the important material (in other words, material you will see on tests).

Understanding the main idea can help you:

- Comprehend more accurately and completely the material you are reading.
- Underline or highlight the most important material in your textbooks.
- Take better notes.
- Organize information into outlines and summaries.
- Locate and memorize more easily the important material for tests.
- Make higher test grades.

Skillful readers underline or highlight stated main ideas in their textbooks. You, too, will find it convenient and efficient to mark them since they are presented as single sentences. Remember to read the entire paragraph before deciding that you have located the stated main idea.

WHAT IS THE METHOD FOR IDENTIFYING THE STATED MAIN IDEA SENTENCE?

To identify the stated main idea sentence, look for a sentence that has the two necessary "ingredients": the *topic* and the author's *most important point* about the topic. This simple formula shows the two essential elements of all main idea sentences:

The *topic*	+	author's *most important point* about the topic	=	Main idea sentence

Comprehension Monitoring Question for Stated Main Idea

"What is the single most important point the author wants me to understand about the topic of this paragraph?"

You must begin, of course, by reading the paragraph and determining its topic. Then, locate the main idea by finding the sentence that answers the comprehension monitoring question, "What is the single most important point the author wants me to understand about the topic of this paragraph?" When you find a sentence that contains the topic *and* answers this question (tells the author's most important point about the topic), you have found the stated main idea sentence.

Next, make sure the sentence you are considering as the main idea makes complete sense because a stated main idea sentence must always make complete sense *by itself.* This means the sentence would make sense even if you were not allowed to see the rest of the paragraph. For example, the following sentence could be a stated main idea because it makes sense by itself: *Franklin Roosevelt is considered one of the greatest U.S. presidents of the 20th century.* In contrast, this could not be a stated main idea sentence because it does not make complete sense by itself: *He is considered one of the greatest U.S. presidents of the 20th century.* We are not told who *he* is. In other words, the sentence does not include the topic, a president's name (which president the author is referring to). Remember, a stated main idea sentence must contain the actual word, name, or phrase that is the topic *as well as* tell the author's single most important point about the topic.

Then, be sure the sentence you have chosen is a general sentence. The main idea sentence is often the most general sentence in a paragraph, that is, one that "sums up" the details but does not include them. Consider, for example, this main idea of a business textbook paragraph: *There are many important decisions to make when starting your own*

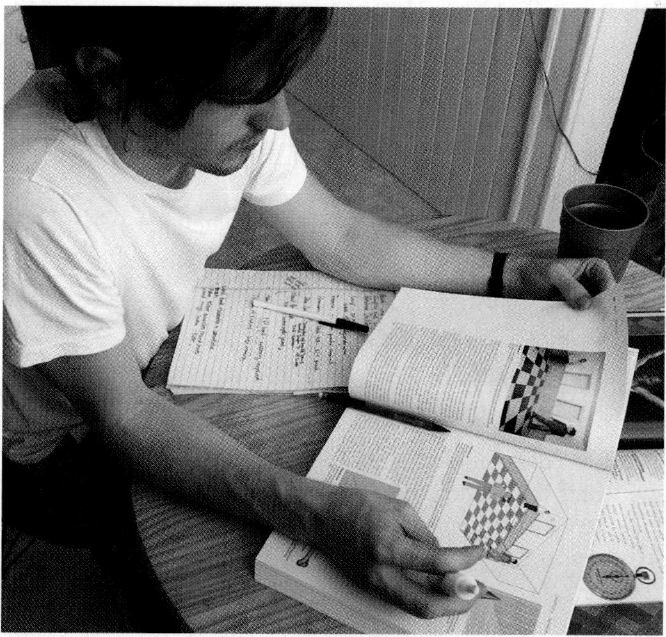

Skillful readers underline or highlight stated main ideas when they study.

company. The words *many important decisions* are very general; the rest of the paragraph (the supporting details in the other sentences) explain specifically what the "important decisions" are. (In Chapter 6 you will learn about identifying supporting details.)

Finally, see if the other sentences in the paragraph explain or tell more about the sentence you have chosen as the main idea sentence. If you have located the correct stated main idea sentence, the other sentences will be supporting details that explain, illustrate, or prove the general point expressed in the main idea sentence. For example, a main idea might be, *Sexually transmitted diseases present a particular threat to young adults.* The supporting details might give examples of specific diseases, such as HIV, hepatitis B, genital herpes, and gonorrhea, along with the threats posed by each.

Now let's see how the above technique is applied to a psychology textbook paragraph. Reread the paragraph below. (You read it earlier in the Chapter 3 Test Your Understanding exercises.) The topic is *hypothalamus.*

> The hypothalamus is a small, but vitally important part of the brain. It lies underneath the thalamus, just in front of the midbrain. It is intimately involved in our motives and emotions: eating, drinking, sexual motivation, pleasure, anger, and fear. It also plays a key role in regulating body temperature, sleep, endocrine gland activity, and resistance to disease. It controls glandular secretions of the stomach and intestines and it maintains the normal pace and rhythm of such body functions as blood pressure and heartbeat. It is the brain center most directly linked to the functions of the autonomic nervous system.
>
> *Source:* Benjamin B. Lahey, *Essentials of Psychology,* p. 45. Copyright © 2002 by The McGraw-Hill Companies, Inc. Reprinted by permission of The McGraw-Hill Companies, Inc.

The first sentence contains the topic *(hypothalamus)* and tells the author's most important point about the hypothalamus *(that it is a small, but vitally important part of the brain).* Did you notice, in fact, that the first sentence is the *only* sentence that contains the topic? The first sentence makes complete sense by itself and it is also very general. Finally, we can see that this general statement is explained by the details in the other sentences. (The supporting details describe functions of the hypothalamus that are "vitally important.") Therefore, it is clear that the first sentence is the stated main idea sentence.

WHICH SENTENCE IN A PARAGRAPH CAN BE THE STATED MAIN IDEA SENTENCE?

A stated main idea sentence often occurs at the beginning of a paragraph. The next most likely place is at the end of a paragraph. But the stated main idea sentence sometimes appears within a paragraph. Let's look at three sample paragraphs that illustrate these three placements of a stated main idea sentence.

First Sentence of the Paragraph

The first sentence of a paragraph is often the stated main idea sentence. Authors frequently begin with a stated main idea sentence because it can make the paragraph clearer and easier to understand. Also, putting the main point first draws attention to it. They know it is easier for readers to identify the supporting details when they already know the main idea.

The following biology textbook excerpt shows such a paragraph. Its topic is *cells.* Read the paragraph and ask yourself, "What is the most important point the author wants me to understand about *cells*?" The sentence that answers this question, the first sentence, is the stated main idea sentence.

Cells are quite small. A frog's egg, at about one millimeter in diameter, is large enough to be seen by the human eye. But most cells are far smaller than one millimeter; some are even as small as one micrometer—one thousandth of a millimeter. Cell inclusions and macromolecules are even smaller than a micrometer and are measured in terms of manometers.

Source: Sylvia S. Mader, *Biology,* 8th ed., p. 59. Copyright © 2004 by The McGraw-Hill Companies, Inc. Reprinted by permission of The McGraw-Hill Companies, Inc.

Stop and Annotate

Go back to the textbook excerpt above. Underline or highlight the stated main idea sentence, the first sentence of the paragraph.

In this excerpt, the first sentence is a general one that tells the most important point the author wants you to know: *Cells are quite small.* The other sentences support the main idea sentence by illustrating and explaining how tiny the cells and their parts are. In this paragraph, then, the first sentence states the main idea, and the rest of the sentences are supporting details that tell more about it.

EXERCISE 1

This paragraph comes from a psychology textbook.

Caffeine produces several reactions. One major behavioral effect is an increase in attentiveness. Another major behavioral effect is a decrease in reaction time. Caffeine can also bring about an improvement in mood, most likely by mimicking the effects of a natural brain chemical, adenosine. Too much caffeine, however, can result in nervousness and insomnia. People can build up a biological dependence on the drug. Regular users who suddenly stop drinking coffee may experience headache or depression. Many people who drink large amounts of coffee on weekdays have headaches on weekends because of the sudden drop in the amount of caffeine they are consuming.

Source: Adapted from Robert S. Feldman, *Understanding Psychology,* 8th ed., pp. 169–70. Copyright © 2008 by The McGraw-Hill Companies, Inc. Reprinted by permission of The McGraw-Hill Companies, Inc.

Write one word that tells the topic: caffeine

Now locate the stated main idea sentence of the paragraph and write it here:
Caffeine produces several reactions. (first sentence)

Last Sentence of the Paragraph

The stated main idea sentence is sometimes the last sentence of the paragraph. This is especially likely when readers need an explanation before they can understand the main idea, or when the author wants to lead up to an important general conclusion (the main idea). Putting the main idea sentence last is a way authors emphasize or draw attention to it.

Read the following excerpt from a health textbook. As the title suggests, the topic is *eating disorders.* As you read the paragraph, ask yourself, "What is the most important point the authors want me to understand about *eating disorders*?" The sentence that answers this question, the last sentence, is the stated main idea sentence.

Eating Disorders

Problems with body weight and weight control are not limited to excessive body fat. Anorexia nervosa is an eating disorder characterized by a refusal to maintain a minimally normal body weight. Bulimia nervosa is an eating disorder characterized by repeated episodes of binge eating followed by compensatory behaviors such as self-induced vomiting, the misuse of laxatives and diuretics, fasting, or excessive exercise. Binge-eating disorder is characterized by binge eating without regular use of compensatory behaviors. In summary, there are three major eating disorders: anorexia nervosa, bulimia nervosa, and binge-eating disorder.

Source: Adapted from Paul Insel and Walton Roth, *Core Concepts in Health,* Brief, 9th ed., p. 252. Copyright © 2002 by The McGraw-Hill Companies, Inc. Reprinted by permission of The McGraw-Hill Companies, Inc.

Stop and Annotate

Go back to the textbook excerpt. Underline or highlight the stated main idea sentence, the last sentence of the paragraph.

In this paragraph, the first sentence is an introductory sentence. The second sentence defines anorexia nervosa, an eating disorder. The third sentence defines bulimia nervosa, another eating disorder. The fourth sentence defines binge-eating disorder, a third type of eating disorder. Notice that the last sentence, the stated main idea, contains the topic and is a general statement that tells the authors' most important point about eating disorders. To draw attention to this important sentence, the authors begin it with *In summary.*

EXERCISE 2

This paragraph comes from a speech communications textbook.

Plagiarism and the Internet

When it comes to plagiarism no subject poses more confusion—or more temptation—than the Internet. Because it's so easy to copy information from the Web, many people are not aware of the need to cite sources (that is, to give credit to the author) when they use Internet materials in their research papers and speeches. To avoid plagiarism, you need to give credit to the authors of documents found on the Internet just as you need to give credit to the authors of print books and articles.

Source: Adapted from Stephen E. Lucas, *The Art of Public Speaking,* 9th ed., p. 46. Copyright © 2007 by The McGraw-Hill Companies, Inc. Reprinted by permission of The McGraw-Hill Companies, Inc.

Write one word that tells the topic: plagiarism and the Internet

Now locate the stated main idea sentence of the paragraph and write it here:

To avoid plagiarism, you need to give credit to the authors of documents found online just as you need to give credit to the authors of print books and articles. (last sentence)

A Sentence within the Paragraph

Sometimes the stated main idea sentence is not the first or the last sentence of a paragraph but, instead, is *within* the paragraph.

At times, authors prefer *not* to begin a paragraph with the stated main idea. Instead, they begin with an important question and then use the second sentence—the main idea sentence—to answer it. Or authors may begin with an introductory statement or with familiar or interesting examples. At other times, authors begin by stating a widely held misconception they wish to explain and disprove. Or they may begin with a surprising or controversial statement simply to get the reader's attention. Then they present their main idea sentence.

Here is a human development textbook paragraph in which the second sentence is the main idea sentence. The topic is *parents' influence on children's choice of peers.* (In this paragraph, *peers* means friends.) As you read this paragraph, ask yourself, "What is the most important point the author wants me to understand about parents' influence on children's choice of peers?"

Can parents really influence who their children choose as friends? Actually, parents have considerable indirect influence on their children's choice of peers. This influence is indirect because parents help shape prosocial or antisocial behavior, which leads children to gravitate toward particular crowds. In a study of 3,781 high school students, the extent to which parents monitored adolescents' behavior and schoolwork, encouraged achievement, and allowed joint decision making were related to academic achievement, drug use, and self-reliance. These behaviors, in turn, were linked with membership in such peer groups as "populars, jocks, brains, normals, druggies, and outcasts."

Source: Diane E. Papalia and Sally Olds, *Human Development,* 6th ed. Copyright © 1995 by The McGraw-Hill Companies, Inc. Reprinted by permission of The McGraw-Hill Companies, Inc.

Stop and Annotate

Go back to the textbook excerpt above. Underline or highlight the stated main idea sentence, the second sentence of the paragraph.

The second sentence contains the topic and tells the authors' most important point about this topic: *Actually, parents have considerable indirect influence on their children's choice of peers.* Notice that the paragraph opens with a question. The question is designed to lead the reader to the most important point, the *answer* to this question: the second sentence. Therefore, it is the stated main idea. (If you were tempted to select the question as the main idea, remember that a stated main idea *never* appears in the form of a question.) The third sentence explains why the parents' influence on their children's choice of friends is indirect. The last two sentences describe a research study that indicates that parents do, in fact, influence their children's choice of peers.

EXERCISE 3

This paragraph comes from a health textbook.

Would you like to have more variety in your workout routine? Consider joining a club! Health and fitness clubs offer members a wide variety of activities. Fitness clubs offer activities ranging from free weights to weight machines to step walking to general aerobics. Some health clubs have pools, saunas, and whirlpools and lots of frills. Others have course offerings that include wellness, smoking cessation, stress management, time management, dance, Pilates, and yoga.

Source: Adapted from Wayne A. Payne, Dale B. Hahn, and Ellen B. Lucas, *Understanding Your Health,* 10th ed., p. 153. Copyright ©2009 by The McGraw-Hill Companies, Inc. Reprinted by permission of The McGraw-Hill Companies, Inc.

Write a phrase that tells the topic: health and fitness clubs

Now locate the stated main idea sentence of the paragraph and write it here:

Health and fitness clubs offer members a wide variety of activities. (sentence from within the paragraph)

OTHER THINGS TO KEEP IN MIND WHEN LOCATING THE STATED MAIN IDEA SENTENCE

Here are four helpful things that you should remember about locating stated main idea sentences:

1. **All stated main idea sentences have certain characteristics in common.**
   - The main idea sentence must contain the topic of the paragraph.
   - The main idea sentence must tell the author's single most important point about that topic.
   - The main idea sentence makes complete sense by itself.
   - The main idea sentence is a general one that sums up the details in the paragraph.
   - The rest of the sentences in the paragraph explain or tell more about the main idea sentence.
2. **Avoid these three common mistakes when locating the stated main idea.**
   - It is a mistake to try to determine the main idea by looking only at the first and last sentences of a paragraph: You could miss a stated main idea sentence that appears within the paragraph. Read the entire paragraph *before* you try to determine the stated main idea sentence.
   - Avoid choosing a sentence as the main idea merely because it contains familiar or interesting information.
   - Do not select a question from a paragraph as the main idea. Stated main ideas are *never* written in the form of a question. However, the stated main idea is often a sentence that *answers* the question presented at the beginning of the paragraph.
3. **Signal words or phrases can help you locate a stated main idea and locate a stated main idea that is presented as a *conclusion.***

   Authors sometimes use a signal word or a phrase to make a stated main idea obvious. These signal words or phrases may appear in stated main ideas that are located at the beginning, middle, or end of a paragraph. Words and phrases that can signal a main idea include:

It is obvious . . .	Generally speaking . . .
To sum up . . .	The fact is . . .
The point is . . .	In summary . . .
Overall . . .	In reality . . .

   Sometimes an author emphasizes a stated main idea by presenting it as a *conclusion.* A stated conclusion is simply a main idea the author places at the end of a paragraph. And often the paragraph itself comes at the end of an entire selection. These signal words and phrases indicate that the conclusion is the main idea:

In conclusion . . .	As a result . . .
It is clear, then, . . .	As one can see . . .
Consequently . . .	So . . .
Therefore . . .	For these reasons . . .
Finally . . .	The point is this . . .
Thus . . .	Obviously, then, . . .

4. **A longer passage often has an overall main idea that is stated, too.**

   Authors sometimes include an *overall* stated main idea to present the general point of an entire selection. (A longer passage might consist of a section of a textbook chapter, a short reading selection, or an essay.) Often, the introductory or concluding sentence of a longer selection expresses the most important point or the overall message of the entire passage. An overall main idea sums up the main ideas of the individual paragraphs in the selection, just as the main idea of a paragraph sums up the details in the paragraph. Assume, for example, that a

(continued on next page)

passage consists of five paragraphs and begins with this overall main idea stated in an introductory paragraph: *There are several things students can do to make the most of their study time.* The main ideas of the other four paragraphs might be (1) making a study schedule can help students manage their time; (2) studying at the same time every day is also helpful; (3) using small amounts of free time to study is a useful technique; and (4) studying in the same place each day can also make study time more productive. As you can see, the overall main idea of this passage, *There are several things students can do to make the most of their study time,* is a general statement that sums up the four main ideas in the selection.

In a writing course or an English course, you may hear your instructor refer to the overall stated main idea of a selection as the *thesis sentence.* The thesis sentence usually appears at the beginning of a selection.

Student Online Learning Center (OLC) ***Go to*** **Chapter 4.** ***Select*** **Chapter Test.**

Review cards or *summary cards* are a way to select, organize, and summarize the important information in a textbook chapter. Preparing review cards helps you organize the information so that you can learn and memorize it more easily. In other words, chapter review cards are effective study tools.

Preparing chapter review cards for each chapter of *New Worlds* will give you practice in creating these valuable study tools. Once you have learned how to make chapter review cards, you can use actual index cards to create them for textbook material in your other courses and use them when you study for tests.

Now complete the chapter review cards for Chapter 4 by answering the questions or following the directions on each card. The page numbers indicate the place in the chapter the information can be found. Use the type of handwriting that is easiest for you to reread (printing or cursive) and write legibly.

✓ **Teaching Tips**

Remind students that the student OLC contains a 10-item **Chapter Test** for this chapter. After completing the chapter review cards below, students should complete the Chapter Test on the OLC.

Page numbers for chapter review card items are provided in the student edition in Chapters 1–5 only.

Stated Main Idea Sentences

1. What is the definition of the *stated main idea* of a paragraph? (See page 179.)

A stated main idea is the sentence in the paragraph that contains both the topic and tells the author's single most important point about this topic.

2. Why is it important to locate and understand the stated main idea of a paragraph? (See page 179.)

The stated main idea sentence is the sentence the author includes for the purpose of stating the single most important point he or she wants the reader to understand.

3. What question should you ask yourself in order to locate the stated main idea of a paragraph? Be sure you write a *question.* (See page 180.)

What is the single most important point the author wants me to understand about the topic of this paragraph?

Card 1 Chapter 4: Locating the Stated Main Idea

✓ **Teaching Tip**

For item 3 on Card 1, point out the "Comprehension Monitoring Question for Stated Main Idea" in the margin on page 180 and guide students to write their answer as a question (including a question mark).

The Importance of Understanding Main Ideas

List six ways understanding main ideas can help you when you are studying. (See page 179.) Understanding main ideas will enable you to:

1. Comprehend more accurately and completely the material you are reading.
2. Underline or highlight the most important material in textbooks.
3. Take better notes.
4. Organize information into outlines and summaries.
5. Locate and memorize more easily the important material for tests.
6. Make higher test grades.

Card 2 Chapter 4: Locating the Stated Main Idea

How to Locate the Stated Main Idea Sentence of a Paragraph

Draw boxes and write the formula that shows the two essential elements of a main idea sentence. (See page 180.)

The *topic* + author's *most important point* about the topic = Main idea sentence

List three places where the stated main idea sentence may occur in a paragraph. (See pages 181–184.)

1. at the beginning of a paragraph
2. at the end of a paragraph
3. within the paragraph

Card 3 Chapter 4: Locating the Stated Main Idea

When Locating the Stated Main Idea, Keep in Mind . . .

The five characteristics of a stated main idea sentence are: (See page 185.)

1. The main idea sentence must contain the topic of the paragraph.
2. The sentence must tell the author's single most important point about the topic.
3. The sentence must make complete sense by itself.
4. The sentence is a general one that sums up the details.
5. The rest of the sentences explain or tell more about the main idea.

List three common mistakes students make when locating the stated main idea sentence. (See page 185.)

1. It is a mistake to think that you can take a shortcut by looking only at the first and last sentences.
2. Avoid choosing a sentence merely because it is familiar.
3. Do not select a question; main ideas are always sentences.

Card 4 Chapter 4: Locating the Stated Main Idea

When Locating the Stated Main Idea, Keep in Mind . . .

1. List the signal words or phrases that can give you a clue to locating a stated main idea. (See page 185.)

It is obvious	Generally speaking
To sum up	The fact is
The point is	In summary
Overall	In reality

2. List the signal words or phrases that can give you a clue to locating a stated main idea that is presented as a *conclusion.* (See page 185.)

In conclusion	As a result
It is clear that	As one can see
Consequently	So
Therefore	For these reasons
Finally	The point is
Thus	Obviously then

Card 5 Chapter 4: Locating the Stated Main Idea

TEST YOUR UNDERSTANDING
LOCATING THE STATED MAIN IDEA, PART ONE

REVIEW: The **stated main idea** of a paragraph expresses the most important point the author wants to make about the topic. *Main ideas are always expressed as complete sentences.* As you learned in this chapter, stated main ideas can appear at the *beginning* of a paragraph, at the *end* of a paragraph, or *within* a paragraph.

EXAMPLE: Study the example paragraph below to see how the information you learned in this chapter can be used to locate the stated main idea of a paragraph. Read the explanation that is given for the correct answer. When you are sure you understand the explanation, complete the five exercises in Part One.

This excerpt comes from a speech textbook. It was used in Chapter 3 to illustrate strategies for determining the topic of a paragraph. As you can see, its topic is *ethnocentrism.* Reread the paragraph and ask yourself, "What is the single most important point the author wants me to understand about ethnocentrism?"

Ethnocentrism is the belief that our own group or culture—whatever it may be—is superior to all other groups or cultures. Because of ethnocentrism, we identify with our group or culture and see its values, beliefs, and customs as "right" or "natural." Moreover, we tend to think of the values, beliefs, and customs of other groups or cultures as "wrong" or "unnatural."

Source: Adapted from Stephen Lucas, *The Art of Public Speaking,* 8th ed., p. 25. Copyright © 2004 by The McGraw-Hill Companies, Inc. Reprinted by permission of The McGraw-Hill Companies, Inc.

The topic of this paragraph is *ethnocentrism.*

_______ What is the stated main idea of this paragraph?

a. Ethnocentrism is the belief that our own group or culture—whatever it may be—is superior to all other groups or cultures.

b. Because of ethnocentrism, we identify with our group or culture and see its values, beliefs, and customs as "right" or "natural."

c. We tend to think of the values, beliefs, and customs of other groups or cultures as "wrong" or "unnatural."

d. The belief called ethnocentrism.

The correct answer is a. The first sentence is the stated main idea sentence because it tells the single most important point the author wants you to know about ethnocentrism: what ethnocentrism is. The other sentences in the paragraph explains more about ethnocentrism by describing its effect on people.

DIRECTIONS: To determine the main idea, read the paragraph carefully and then ask yourself, "What is the single most important point the author wants me to understand about the topic of this paragraph?" (Notice that you are told the topic of each paragraph.) Then select the answer choice that expresses the main idea and write the letter in the space provided.

✓ **Teaching Tip**
Encourage students to see if their answer choice has all of the characteristics of the stated main idea sentences listed in #1 on page 185.

1. This paragraph comes from a human development textbook.

Exercise

Adults who exercise regularly obtain many benefits. Physical activity helps them maintain desirable body weight and builds muscles. Exercise also strengthens the heart and lungs. It lowers blood pressure, protects against heart attacks, stroke, diabetes, cancer, and osteoporosis (a thinning of the bones that tends to affect middle-aged and older women and causes fractures). It also relieves anxiety and depression and lengthens life.

Source: Diane E. Papalia and Sally Olds, *Human Development,* 6th ed. Copyright © 1995 by The McGraw-Hill Companies, Inc. Reprinted by permission of The McGraw-Hill Companies, Inc.

The topic of this paragraph is *exercise,* or *exercising regularly.*

a ______ What is the stated main idea of this paragraph?

a. Adults who exercise regularly obtain many benefits.

b. Physical activity helps them maintain desirable body weight and builds muscles.

c. Exercise also strengthens heart and lungs.

d. It also relieves anxiety and depression, and lengthens life.

2. This paragraph comes from a sociology textbook.

Health practitioners are still studying the various methods of transmitting the HIV virus. The reason for this is that there is still no vaccine or cure for AIDS (acquired immunodeficiency syndrome). While there are encouraging new therapies to treat people with HIV and AIDS, there is currently no way to eradicate AIDS medically. The point is, since there is no cure for AIDS, it is essential that people protect themselves by reducing the transmission of the HIV virus.

Source: Richard T. Schaefer and Robert Lamm, *Sociology,* 6th ed. Copyright © 1997 by The McGraw-Hill Companies, Inc. Reprinted by permission of The McGraw-Hill Companies, Inc.

The topic of this paragraph is *transmission of the HIV virus.*

d ______ What is the stated main idea of this paragraph?

a. Health practitioners are still studying the various methods of transmitting the HIV virus.

b. The reason for this is that there is still no vaccine or cure for AIDS (acquired immunodeficiency syndrome).

c. While there are encouraging new therapies to treat people with HIV and AIDS, there is currently no way to eradicate AIDS medically.

d. The point is, since there is no cure for AIDS, it is essential that people protect themselves by reducing the transmission of the HIV virus.

✓ **Teaching Tip**
Pork barrel projects refers to government projects that are unnecessary and are obtained by legislators simply to benefit their constituents.

3. This paragraph comes from a government textbook.

Members of Congress, once elected, are likely to be reelected. Members of Congress can use their office to publicize themselves. They pursue a "service strategy" of responding to the needs of individual constituents and secure pork barrel projects for their state or district. House members gain a greater advantage from these activities than do senators, whose larger constituencies make it harder for them to build close personal relations with voters and whose office is more likely to attract a strong challenger.

Source: Thomas E. Patterson, *We the People,* 2nd ed. Copyright © 1998 by The McGraw-Hill Companies, Inc. Reprinted by permission of The McGraw-Hill Companies, Inc.

The topic of this paragraph is *members of Congress.*

a What is the stated main idea of this paragraph?

a. Members of Congress, once elected, are likely to be reelected.

b. Members of Congress can use their office to publicize themselves.

c. They pursue a "service strategy" of responding to the needs of individual constituents and secure pork barrel projects for their state or district.

d. House members gain a greater advantage from these activities than do senators, whose larger constituencies make it harder for them to build close personal relations with voters and whose office is more likely to attract a strong challenger.

4. This paragraph comes from a biology textbook.

Human beings have always polluted their surroundings, but in the past it was easier for them to move on and live somewhere else. They knew that, given time, the environment would take care of pollution they left behind and they relied on the "out of sight, out of mind" philosophy. Today, an increasing human population, which uses an increasing amount of energy sources, no longer has the luxury to ignore pollution. The human population is approximately 7 billion. Our overall energy consumption has gone up by a hundredfold from 2,000 kcal/person/day to 230,000 kcal/person/day in modern industrial nations like the United States. This high energy consumption allows us to mass produce many useful and economically affordable organic products that pollute the atmosphere and groundwater, damage forests and lakes, cause global warming, and even deplete the ozone layer.

Source: Adapted from Sylvia S. Mader, *Biology,* 6th ed., p. 45. Copyright © 1998 by The McGraw-Hill Companies, Inc. Reprinted by permission of The McGraw-Hill Companies, Inc.

The topic of this paragraph is *human population and pollution.*

b What is the stated main idea of this paragraph?

a. Human beings have always polluted their surroundings, but in the past it was easier for them to move on and live somewhere else.

b. Today, an increasing human population, which uses an increasing amount of energy sources, no longer has the luxury to ignore pollution.

c. The human population is approximately 7 billion.

d. This high energy consumption allows us to mass produce many useful and economically affordable organic products that pollute the atmosphere and groundwater, damage forests and lakes, cause global warming, and even deplete the ozone layer.

5. This paragraph comes from a health textbook.

Volunteering

All major religions teach that it is more blessed to give than to receive. Of course, service benefits those in need, but volunteering is also good for the volunteer. It provides companionship, friendship, and fellowship in working toward a common goal. In our mobile society, volunteering allows us to meet people and thereby feel less isolated. Volunteering allows us to use skills and talents that we normally don't use at our daily jobs. In this way, volunteering encourages us to branch out, to learn new things, and become more well rounded.

Source: Wayne A. Payne and Dale B. Hahn, *Understanding Your Health,* 5th ed. Copyright © 1995 by The McGraw-Hill Companies, Inc. Reprinted by permission of The McGraw-Hill Companies, Inc.

The topic of this paragraph is *volunteering*.

b What is the stated main idea of this paragraph?

a. All major religions teach that it is more blessed to give than to receive.

b. Of course, service benefits those in need, but volunteering is also good for the volunteer.

c. Volunteering allows us to use skills and talents that we normally don't use at our daily jobs.

d. In this way, volunteering encourages us to branch out, to learn new things, and become more well rounded.

TEST YOUR UNDERSTANDING
LOCATING THE STATED MAIN IDEA, PART TWO

REVIEW: The **stated main idea** of a paragraph expresses the most important point the author wants to make about the topic. *Main ideas are always expressed as complete sentences.* As you learned in this chapter, stated main ideas can appear at the *beginning* of a paragraph, at the *end* of a paragraph, or *within* a paragraph.

EXAMPLE: Study the example paragraph below to see how the information you learned in this chapter can be used to locate the stated main idea of a paragraph. Read the explanation that is given for the correct answer. When you are sure you understand the explanation, complete the five exercises in Part Two.

This paragraph comes from a psychology textbook. It was used in Chapter 3 to illustrate strategies for determining the topic of a paragraph. As you can see, the topic is *pressure.* Reread the paragraph and ask yourself, "What is the single most important point the author wants me to understand about pressure?"

Pressure

Does the pressure of working for good grades ever get to you? If you have been employed, was it a high-pressure job? The term **pressure** is used to describe the stress that arises from threats of negative events. In school, there is always the possibility that you will not perform well and you will fail. Some jobs are loaded with possibilities for making a mess of things and getting fired. Some unhappy marriages are sources of pressure because one spouse always seems to displease the other, no matter how hard he or she tries to avoid it.

Source: Adapted from Benjamin B. Lahey, *Psychology,* 6th ed., p. 437. Copyright © 1998 by The McGraw-Hill Companies, Inc. Reprinted by permission of The McGraw-Hill Companies, Inc.

Write the topic: pressure

Underline or highlight the main idea sentence in the paragraph.

Explanation: The topic of this paragraph, *pressure,* appears in the heading and in bold print. The word *pressure* also appears several times in the paragraph. The third sentence has been underlined because it is the main idea sentence. It tells the author's most important point: the definition of *pressure* as it is used in psychology. The remaining sentences give examples of sources of pressure.

DIRECTIONS: Read each paragraph carefully and then determine the topic by asking yourself, "Who or what is this paragraph about?" Write the topic in the space provided beneath the exercise. *Remember that the topic is always expressed as a word, name, or a phrase. Do not write a sentence for the topic.* Then locate the stated main idea by asking yourself, "What is the single most important point the author wants me to understand about the topic of this paragraph?" Then, locate the stated main idea and *underline* or *highlight* the entire sentence.

✓ **Teaching Tip**
Encourage students to see if their answer choice has all of the characteristics of the stated main idea sentences listed in #1 on page 185.

1. This paragraph comes from a health and wellness textbook.

Perhaps you have heard of liposuction. In this procedure unwanted fat is sucked through a hollow tube after a surgical incision has been made. It was introduced in the United States several years ago. Now, about 100,000 Americans undergo liposuction every year. Not everyone agrees on its value: While liposuction may remove some unwanted fat, it does not cure obesity or deal with the underlying causes of weight problems. Liposuction has become one of the most popular and controversial forms of cosmetic surgery.

Source: Adapted from Marvin Levy, Mark Dignan, and Janet Shirreffs, *Targeting Wellness: The Core*, p. 68 (New York: McGraw-Hill, 1992).

Write one word that tells the topic: liposuction (clue: repeated word)

Now *underline* or *highlight* the stated main idea sentence in the paragraph.

2. This paragraph comes from a government textbook.

Political Apathy

Just as some people who did not grow up watching football would not attend the Super Bowl even if it were free and being played across the street, some people would not bother to vote even if a ballot were delivered to their door. A sense of political apathy—a general lack of interest in or concern with politics—is often the consequence of childhood socialization. This can occur when parents do not value voting and other forms of political participation. As a result, their children are likely to display a similar attitude when they reach voting age.

Source: Thomas E. Patterson, *We the People*, 2nd ed. Copyright © 1998 by The McGraw-Hill Companies, Inc. Reprinted by permission of The McGraw-Hill Companies, Inc.

Write a *two-word phrase* that tells the topic: political apathy

(clue: special print—italics)

Now *underline* or *highlight* the stated main idea sentence in the paragraph.

3. This paragraph comes from a biology textbook.

Beneficial Insects

Insects are necessary for the cross-fertilization of many crops. Bees pollinate almost $10 billion worth of food crops per year in the United States alone, and this value does not include pollination of forage crops for livestock or pollination by other insects. In addition, some insects produce useful materials: honey and beeswax from bees, silk from silkworms, and shellac from a wax secreted by the lac insects. Although most of us think of insects primarily as pests, humanity would have great difficulty in surviving if all of these beneficial insects were suddenly to disappear.

Source: Adapted from Cleveland P. Hickman, Jr., Larry S. Roberts, and Allan Larson, *Biology of Animals*, 7th ed. (Boston: WCB/McGraw-Hill 1998), p. 520.

Write a *two-word phrase* that tells the topic: beneficial insects

(clue: heading)

Now *underline* or *highlight* the stated main idea sentence in the paragraph.

4. This paragraph comes from a child development textbook.

Even children without histories of highly aggressive behavior can become more aggressive after watching television violence. This was dramatically demonstrated by research that compared children's behavior before and after TV was introduced in some isolated Canadian towns. Watching TV violence in childhood has been linked to aggressive behavior at age 18 and serious criminal behavior at age 30.

Source: Laurence Steinberg and Roberta Meyer, *Childhood.* Copyright © 1995 by The McGraw-Hill Companies, Inc. Reprinted by permission of The McGraw-Hill Companies, Inc.

Write a *phrase* that tells the topic: aggressive behavior and TV violence

or aggressive behavior in children who watch TV violence

(clue: mentioned at beginning, and then discussed throughout)

Now *underline* or *highlight* the stated main idea sentence in the paragraph.

5. This paragraph comes from a sociology textbook.

Xenocentrism is the belief that the products, styles, or ideas of one's society are inferior to those that originate elsewhere. In a sense, it is reverse ethnocentrism. For example, people in the United States often assume that French fashions or Japanese electronic devices are superior to our own. Are they, or are people unduly charmed by the lure of goods from exotic places? Such fascination with British china or Danish glassware can be damaging to competitors in the United States. Some companies have responded by creating products that *sound* European, such as Häagen-Dazs ice cream (made in New Jersey) or Nike shoes (produced in Oregon).

Source: Richard T. Schaefer and Robert P. Lamm, *Sociology,* 6th ed. Copyright © 1997 by The McGraw-Hill Companies, Inc. Reprinted by permission of The McGraw-Hill Companies, Inc.

Write *one word* that tells the topic: xenocentrism

(clue: special print—italics)

Now *underline* or *highlight* the stated main idea sentence in the paragraph.

SELECTION **4-1**

Business

GOOD BOSS? BAD BOSS? THREE LEADERSHIP STYLES

From *Understanding Business*

By William Nickels, James McHugh, and Susan McHugh

How would you describe your leadership style? Is there one "best" style of leadership? This selection from a business text addresses that question.

1 Nothing has challenged researchers in the area of management more than the search for the "best" leadership traits, behaviors, or styles. Thousands of studies have been made just to find leadership traits, that is, characteristics that make leaders different from other people. Intuitively, you would conclude about the same thing that researchers have found: leadership traits are hard to pin down. In fact, results of most studies on leadership have been neither statistically significant nor reliable. Some leaders are well groomed and tactful, while others are unkempt and abrasive—yet the latter may be just as effective as the former.

2 Just as there is no one set of traits that can describe a leader, there's also no one style of leadership that works best in all situations. Even so, we can look at a few of the most commonly recognized leadership styles and see how they may be effective.

3 **Autocratic leadership** involves making managerial decisions without consulting others. Such a style is effective in emergencies and when absolute followership is needed—for example, when fighting fires. Autocratic leadership is also effective sometimes with new, relatively unskilled workers who need clear direction and guidance.

4 Coach Phil Jackson used an autocratic leadership style to take the Los Angeles Lakers to three National Basketball Association championships. By following his leadership, a group of highly skilled *individuals* became a winning *team.*

5 **Participative (democratic) leadership** consists of managers and employees working together to make decisions. Research has found that employee participation in decisions may not always increase effectiveness, but it usually increases job satisfaction. Many progressive organizations are highly successful at using a democratic style of leadership that values traits such as flexibility, good listening skills, and empathy. John Chambers, CEO of Cisco Systems, is an example of a participative leader.

6 Organizations that have successfully used this style include Wal-Mart, FedEx, IBM, Cisco, AT&T, and most smaller firms. At meetings in such firms, employees discuss management issues and resolve those issues together in a democratic manner. That is, everyone has some opportunity to contribute to decisions. Many firms have placed meeting rooms throughout the company and allow all employees the right to request a meeting.

Annotation Practice Exercises

Directions: For each exercise below, write the topic of the paragraph on the lines beside the paragraph. Then, locate the stated main idea of the paragraph and underline or highlight it.

✓ **Teaching Tip**

See pages 622, 624, and 626 for an outline, study map, and summary of this selection.

Practice Exercise

Topic of paragraph 3:

autocratic leadership

Determine the *stated main idea* and underline or highlight it.

Practice Exercise

Topic of paragraph 5:

participative (democratic) leadership

Determine the *stated main idea* and underline or highlight it.

Coach Phil Jackson has been successful as an autocratic leader. That makes sense, since you don't want basketball players deciding whether or not to play as a team. On the other hand, can you see why it is not so good using autocratic leadership with doctors? What kind of leadership whould you expect in a nonprofit agency full of volunteers?

7 **Free rein leadership** involves managers setting objectives and employees being relatively free to do whatever it takes to accomplish those objectives. In certain organizations, where managers deal with doctors, engineers, or other professionals, often the most successful leadership style is free rein. The traits needed by managers in such organizations include warmth, friendliness, and understanding. More and more firms are adopting this style of leadership with at least some of their employees.

8 Individual leaders rarely fit neatly into just one of these categories. Researchers illustrate leadership as a continuum with varying amounts of employee participation, ranging from purely boss-centered leadership to subordinate-centered leadership (see Figure 1).

9 Which leadership style is best? Research tells us that successful leadership depends largely on what the goals and values of the firm are, and on who's being led and in what situations. It also supports the notion that any leadership style, ranging from autocratic to free rein, may be successful depending on the people and the situation. A manager may be autocratic but friendly with a new trainee; democratic with an experienced employee who has many good ideas that can only be fostered by a flexible manager who's a good listener; and free rein with a trusted, long-term supervisor who probably knows more about operations than the manager does.

Practice Exercise

Topic of paragraph 7:

free rein leadership

Determine the *stated main idea* and underline or highlight it.

✓ **Teaching Tip**

The term "free rein" comes from not pulling on a horse's rein, or in other words, letting it do what it wants without restraints.

FIGURE 1:
VARIOUS LEADERSHIP STYLES

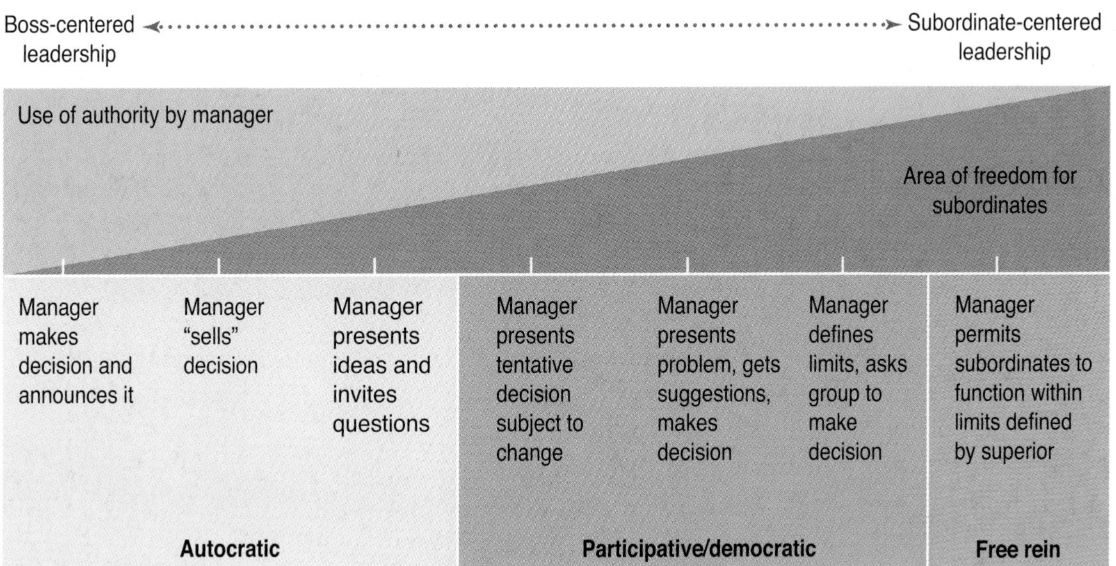

Source: Reprinted by permission of *Harvard Business Review*. From "How to Choose a Leadership Pattern" by Robert Tannenbaum and Warren Schmidt (May/June 1973). Copyright © 1973 by the Harvard Business School Publishing Corporation. All rights reserved.

10 There's no such thing as a leadership trait that is effective in all situations, or a leadership style that always works best. A truly successful leader has the ability to use the leadership style most appropriate to the situation and the employees involved.

Source: Adapted from William G. Nickels, James M. McHugh, and Susan McHugh, *Understanding Business,* 8th ed., pp. 194–96. Copyright © 2008 by The McGraw-Hill Companies, Inc. Reprinted by permission of The McGraw-Hill Companies, Inc.

SELECTION **4-1**
Business
(continued)

Comprehension and Vocabulary Quiz

This quiz has four parts. Your instructor may assign some or all of them.

Comprehension

Directions: Items 1–5 test your comprehension (understanding) of the material in this selection. These questions are much like those that a content-area instructor (such as a business professor) would expect you to know after reading and studying this selection. For each comprehension question below, use information from the selection to determine the correct answer. Refer to the selection as you answer the questions. Write your answers in the spaces provided.

¶5 __d__ **1.** A style of leadership that involves managers and employees working together to make decisions is called:
- *a.* cooperative leadership.
- *b.* autocratic leadership.
- *c.* free-rein leadership.
- *d.* democratic or participative leadership.

¶7 __c__ **2.** Managers who wish to adopt a free rein leadership style need traits such as:
- *a.* empathy, flexibility, and good listening skills.
- *b.* devotion and dedication.
- *c.* understanding, friendliness, and warmth.
- *d.* firmness and directness.

¶3 __b__ **3.** Autocratic leadership can be most effective:
- *a.* when employee participation is desired.
- *b.* in emergencies and when absolute followership is needed.
- *c.* for managers who deal with doctors, engineers, and other professionals.
- *d.* when the manager is a good listener.

¶5 __c__ **4.** Research has shown that when managers and employees work together to make decisions:
- *a.* it implies power over others.
- *b.* motivation to do a good job declines.
- *c.* it usually improves the way employees feel about their jobs.
- *d.* they both feel relatively free to do whatever it takes to get the job done.

¶10 __b__ **5.** A manager should:
- *a.* always set objectives and leave employees free to do whatever it takes to accomplish them.
- *b.* use the leadership style most appropriate to the situation and the employees involved.
- *c.* use a variety of leadership styles so employees will know that the manager is friendly and caring.
- *d.* select a leadership style that is comfortable and use it consistently.

Vocabulary in Context

Directions: Items 6–10 test your ability to determine the meaning of the word by using context clues. *Context clues* are words in a sentence that allow the reader to deduce (reason out) the meaning of an unfamiliar word in that sentence. Context clues also enable the reader to determine which meaning the author intends when a word has more than one meaning. For each vocabulary item below, a sentence from the selection containing an important word (*italicized, like this*) is quoted first. Next, there is an additional sentence using the word in the same sense and providing another context clue. Use the context clues from *both* sentences to deduce the meaning of the italicized word. *Be sure the answer you choose makes sense in both sentences.* If you need to use a dictionary to confirm your answer choice, remember that the meaning you select must still fit the context of *both* sentences. Write your answers in the spaces provided.

Pronunciation Key: ă **pat** ā **pay** âr **care** ä **father** ĕ **pet** ē **be** ĭ **pit**
ī **tie** îr **pier** ŏ **pot** ō **toe** ô **paw** oi **noise** ou **out** o͝o **took**
o͞o **boot** ŭ **cut** yo͞o **abuse** ûr **urge** th **thin** *th* **this** hw **which**
zh **vision** ə **about** *Stress mark:* ′

¶5 ___b___ **6.** Many *progressive* organizations are highly successful at using a democratic style of leadership that values traits such as flexibility, good listening skills, and empathy.

The college's foreign language department received national recognition because its *progressive* teaching methods enable students to speak a foreign language reasonably well after only two semesters of instruction.

progressive (prə grĕs′ ĭv) means:

a. increasing in severity
b. characterized by new ideas or progress
c. increasing steadily in difficulty
d. characterized by innovative teaching methods

¶5 ___c___ **7.** Many progressive organizations are highly successful at using a democratic style of leadership that values traits such as flexibility, good listening skills, and *empathy.*

My aunt has so much *empathy* that she laughs when the main character in a movie laughs and cries when the person cries.

empathy (ĕm′ pə thē) means:

a. feeling sympathy for someone
b. feeling hostile toward someone
c. feeling whatever another person is feeling
d. feeling sorry for someone

¶6 a **8.** At meetings in such firms, employees discuss management issues and *resolve* those issues together in a democratic manner.

Husbands and wives who are unable to *resolve* their marital problems often benefit from counseling or mediation.

resolve (rĭ zŏlv′) means:

a. deal with successfully; clear up

b. dissolve; melt

c. break into smaller components or parts

d. define; put into words

¶7 a **9.** More and more firms are *adopting* this style of leadership with at least some of their employees.

Our college's student organizations are formally *adopting* new guidelines that make membership open to everyone.

adopting (ə dŏpt′ ĭng) means:

a. agreeing to take and follow

b. assuming the role of parents

c. discontinuing

d. disregarding

¶9 d **10.** A manager may be autocratic but friendly with a new trainee; democratic with an experienced employee who has many good ideas that can only be *fostered* by a flexible manager who's a good listener; and free rein with a trusted, long-term supervisor who probably knows more about operations than the manager does.

The research study confirmed that participating in organized sports *fostered* teamwork and cooperation in elementary school age children.

fostered (fô′ stərd) means:

a. hindered the development of

b. changed the level of

c. ruined the possibility of

d. promoted the development of

Word Structure

Directions: Items 11–15 test your ability to use word-structure clues to help determine a word's meaning. *Word-structure clues* consist of roots, prefixes, and suffixes. In these exercises, you will learn the meaning of a word part (a root) and use it to determine the meaning of several other words that have the same word part. If you need to use a dictionary to confirm your answer choice, do so. Write your answers in the spaces provided.

In paragraph 3 of the selection, you encountered the word **autocratic.** This word contains the Greek root ***auto,*** which means "self." In this passage, the word *autocratic* describes a person who has all of the power to him*self* or her*self* (such as a dictator or a very controlling boss). Use the meaning of ***auto*** and the list of prefixes on pages 68–69 to help you determine the meaning of each of the following words that contain this same root.

b 11. If a hot iron shuts off **automatically** after 15 minutes of non-use, the iron shuts off:

a. when the person picks it up again.
b. by itself.
c. only if it is set on a low temperature.
d. when the person using it turns it off.

c 12. If an airplane is flying on **autopilot,** it is flying:

a. in circles.
b. in the wrong direction.
c. without the pilot controlling it directly.
d. at a high altitude.

a 13. Most teenagers like to think that they are **autonomous.** In other words, they like to think that they are:

a. independent and self-governing.
b. selfish and self-centered.
c. extremely mature.
d. smarter than their parents.

d 14. "Didactics" is the art of teaching or instruction. An **autodidact** is someone who is:

a. currently enrolled in school.
b. receiving tutoring.
c. uninterested in learning.
d. self-taught.

c 15. If you write an **autobiography** someday, you will be writing:

a. an adventure story.
b. a mystery.
c. the story of your life.
d. the story of someone else's life.

✓ **Teaching Tip**
Let students know that not all of the skills included in this Reading Skills Application section have been introduced yet. This section serves as a valuable preview of these skills, however. Students typically get several of the items correct, and they find this encouraging.

Reading Skills Application

Directions: Items 16–20 test your ability to *apply* certain reading skills to information in this selection. These types of questions provide valuable practice for all students, especially those who must take standardized reading tests and state-mandated basic skills tests. You may not have studied all of the skills at this point, so these items will serve as a helpful preview. The comprehension and critical reading skills in this section are presented in Chapters 3 through 9 of *New Worlds;* vocabulary and figurative language skills are presented in Chapter 2. As you work through *New Worlds,* you will practice and develop these skills. Write your answers in the spaces provided.

author's tone (Chapter 8) c

16. Which of the following best describes the authors' tone in this selection?

a. emotional

b. humorous

c. factual

d. sentimental

¶3 stated main idea (Chapter 4) a

17. The main idea of paragraph 3 is which of the following statements?

a. Autocratic leadership involves making managerial decisions without consulting others.

b. Motivation comes from threats, punishment, and intimidation of all kinds.

c. Such a style is effective in emergencies and when absolute followership is needed.

d. Some football, basketball, and soccer coaches have used this style.

¶9 authors' writing patterns (Chapter 7) b

18. The pattern of organization used in paragraph 9 of the selection is:

a. a list.

b. cause and effect.

c. a sequence.

d. a series.

✓ **Teaching Tip**
For item 18, the clue words to the pattern are "depends largely on."

author's purpose for writing (Chapter 8) b

19. The authors' purpose in writing this selection is to:

a. present the reasons people develop one of three leadership styles.

b. describe three leadership styles and explain when each is appropriate, and with whom.

c. explain why some leadership styles are more effective than others.

d. persuade managers to adopt a free rein leadership style.

¶8 phrase in context (Chapter 2) a

20. As used in paragraph 8 of the selection, the phrase *subordinate-centered leadership* refers to a leadership style in which:

a. employees below the top ranks are empowered.

b. all employees share the power equally.

c. the boss has all of the power.

d. the power shifts from group to group depending on the situation.

✓ **Teaching Tip**
We suggest that rather than include this section as part of the quiz grade, you use it to give students practice with the skills they have studied and as a helpful preview of upcoming skills. It makes an excellent collaborative activity. All students will find this practice helpful, especially those who must take course exit tests, standardized reading tests, or state-mandated basic skills tests.

SELECTION **4-1**
Business
(continued)

Writing and Collaborating to Enhance Your Understanding

Option for collaboration: Your instructor may direct you to work with other students or, in other words, to work *collaboratively.* In that case, you should form groups of three or four students as directed by your instructor and work together to complete the exercises. After your group discusses each item and agrees on the answer, have a group member record it. Every member of your group should be able to explain all of your group's answers.

Collaboration Option

1. **Reacting to What You Have Read:** Think of a boss or coach or teacher you have had. What leadership style did that person have? Did you like or dislike his or her style? Explain why.

(Answers will vary.)

2. **Comprehending the Selection Further:** Using the leadership terminology in this selection, describe your primary leadership style. Explain circumstances in which you have had a leadership role (at your job, in an organization you belong to, as a member of a team, etc.). Explain the behaviors you use that are characteristic of your primary style.

(Answers will vary.)

3. **Overall Main Idea of the Selection:** In one sentence, tell what the authors want readers to understand about leadership styles. (Be sure to include the words "leadership styles" in your overall main idea sentence.)

There are three common *leadership styles*, and managers use one or more of them depending on the situation and the employees involved.

Internet Resources

Read More about This Topic on the World Wide Web

Directions: For further information about the topic of the selection, visit these websites:

www.entrepreneur.com
This link is sponsored by *Entrepreneur Magazine.* In the search box, type "leadership style" for a list of articles.

www.motivation-tools.com/workplace/leadership_styles.htm
This website, sponsored by the Motivation Tool Chest, presents information on how leadership styles influence motivation.

You can also use your favorite search engine such as Google, Yahoo!, or AltaVista (www.google.com, www.yahoo.com, www.altavista.com) to discover more about this topic. To locate additional information, type in combinations of keywords such as:

business leadership styles

or

autocratic leadership

or

participative leadership

or

free rein leadership

Keep in mind that whenever you go to *any* website, it is a good idea to evaluate the website and the information it contains. Ask yourself questions such as:

"Who sponsors this website?"
"Is the information contained in this website up-to-date?"
"What type of information is presented?"
"Is the information objective and complete?"
"How easy is it to use the features of this website?"

SELECTION **4-2**
Human Development

ENGAGEMENT AND MARRIAGE: THE SAME—YET DIFFERENT—WORLDWIDE

From *Human Development*
By Diane Papalia, Sally Olds, and Ruth Feldman

You have certain concepts that come to mind when you hear the words "becoming engaged" and "being married." Perhaps "becoming engaged" conjures up images of a man—possibly on bended knee—asking the woman he loves to marry him and giving her a diamond engagement ring. "Being married" might bring to mind images of a couple living together in a place of their own, having and raising children, eventually becoming grandparents, and growing old together.

Virtually every culture includes customary ways couples become engaged, as well as holds views as to what constitutes "marriage." However, these vary considerably, and many are quite different from what the typical American thinks of. In this human development textbook selection, you will learn just how different these concepts can be for people who live in other countries and in other cultures.

Marriage

1 In Tibet, a man and his father have the same wife. In Zaire, it's just the opposite: a woman shares her husband with her mother. In many African societies, a woman—often one who is married to a man but is infertile—may take a "wife" to bear and care for her children. *Polygyny*—man's marriage to more than one woman at a time—is common in Islamic countries, African societies, and parts of Asia. In *polyandrous* societies, where women generally wield more economic power, a woman may take several husbands—in some Himalayan regions, a set of brothers. Marriage customs vary widely, but the universality of some form of marriage throughout history and around the world shows that it meets fundamental needs.

2 In most societies, marriage is considered the best way to ensure orderly raising of children. It allows for a division of labor within a consuming and working unit. Ideally, it offers intimacy, friendship, affection, sexual fulfillment, companionship, and an opportunity for emotional growth. In certain Eastern philosophical traditions, the harmonious union of a male and female is considered essential to spiritual fulfillment and the survival of the species. Clearly, society views marriage as providing many types of benefits.

3 Today some benefits of marriage, such as sex, intimacy, and economic security, are not confined to wedlock. Still, among a national sample of more than 2,000 adults ages 18 to 90, married people tended to be happier than unmarried people. Contrary to earlier studies, men and women were found to benefit equally from a marital attachment, but in different ways—women from economic support and men from emotional support.

Entering Matrimony

4 Historically and across cultures, the most common way of selecting a mate has been through arrangement, either by

Annotation Practice Exercises

Directions: For each exercise below, write the topic of the paragraph on the lines beside the paragraph. Then, locate the stated main idea of the paragraph and underline or highlight it.

Practice Exercise

Topic of paragraph 1:

marriage customs and the universality of marriage

Determine the *stated main idea* and underline or highlight it.

Practice Exercise

Topic of paragraph 2:

benefits of marriage

Determine the *stated main idea* and underline or highlight it.

the parents or by professional matchmakers. Among the chief considerations in arranged marriages are the wealth and social status of the families to be joined by the marriage. Sometimes betrothal takes place in childhood. The bride and groom may not even meet until their wedding day. Since the Renaissance, with the evolution of the nuclear family, free choice of mates on the basis of love has become the norm in the western world, but in Japan, 25 to 30 percent of marriages still are arranged.

5 The typical "marrying age" varies across cultures. In Eastern Europe, people tend to marry in or before their early 20s, as Ingrid Bergman did. But industrialized nations such as her native Sweden are seeing a trend toward later marriage as young adults take time to pursue educational and career goals or to explore relationships. In Canada, the average age of first marriage has risen from about 23 to 27 since 1961. In the United States, the median age of the first-time bridegrooms is nearly 27, and of first-time brides, 25—a rise of more than three years since 1975.

6 The transition of married life brings major changes in sexual functioning, living arrangements, rights and responsibilities, attachments, and loyalties. Among other things, marriage partners need to redefine the connection with their original families, balance intimacy with autonomy, and establish a fulfilling sexual relationship. To help newlyweds adjust, some traditional societies give them extra privacy; in other societies, their sexual and other activities are subject to prescribed rules and supervision. In some cultures, newlyweds set up their own household; in other cultures, they live with parents, temporarily or permanently. In some societies, such as the Rajputs of Khalapur, India, husband and wife live, eat, and sleep apart. In contrast to Anglo-American cultures, where the chief purpose of marriage is seen as love and companionship, the sole purpose of marriage in Rajput society is reproduction; emotional and social support come from same-sex relatives and friends.

Marriage is universal, though dress, celebratory customs, and even the number of partners vary. This Indian couple in Durban, South Africa, may have been introduced by a matchmaker—worldwide, the most common way of selecting a mate.

Practice Exercise

Topic of paragraph 5:

the typical marrying age

Determine the *stated main idea* and underline or highlight it.

✓ **Teaching Tip**

Point out that part of the section on "entering marriage" is referred to as "engagement" in the title.

Source: Adapted from Diane E. Papalia, Sally Wendkos Olds, and Ruth Duskin Feldman, *Human Development,* 8th ed., pp. 539–40.

SELECTION 4-2
Human Development
(continued)

Comprehension and Vocabulary Quiz

This quiz has four parts. Your instructor may assign some or all of them.

Comprehension

Directions: Items 1–5 test your comprehension (understanding) of the material in this selection. These questions are much like those that a content-area instructor (such as a human development professor) would expect you to know after reading and studying this selection. For each comprehension question below, use information from the selection to determine the correct answer. Refer to the selection as you answer the questions. Write your answers in the spaces provided.

¶3 ___a___ **1.** Most married people today:
- *a.* tend to be happier than unmarried people.
- *b.* are better off financially than unmarried people.
- *c.* waited until they were in their 30s before deciding to get married.
- *d.* require extra privacy and emotional support.

¶6 ___b___ **2.** In Anglo-American cultures, the chief purpose of marriage seems to be:
- *a.* sexual fulfillment.
- *b.* love and companionship.
- *c.* reproduction.
- *d.* setting up a household and redefining a connection to their original families.

¶1 ___c___ **3.** When a man is married to more than one woman at a time it is called:
- *a.* monogamy.
- *b.* polyandry.
- *c.* polygyny.
- *d.* an arranged marriage.

¶1 ___d___ **4.** In polyandrous societies:
- *a.* a man may take several wives.
- *b.* the majority of marriages are arranged.
- *c.* wives have more household duties and a greater responsibility for caring for children.
- *d.* women generally wield more economic power.

¶5 ___c___ **5.** Today, most first-time brides and bridegrooms in the United States:
- *a.* tend to marry soon after high school.
- *b.* live with parents temporarily or permanently.
- *c.* are following the trend toward later marriage.
- *d.* find marriage overwhelming and stressful.

Vocabulary in Context

Directions: Items 6–10 test your ability to determine the meaning of the word by using context clues. *Context clues* are words in a sentence that allow the reader to deduce (reason out) the meaning of an unfamiliar word in that sentence. Context clues also enable the reader to determine which meaning the author intends when a word has more than one meaning. For each vocabulary item below, a sentence from the selection containing an important word *(italicized, like this)* is quoted first. Next, there is an additional sentence using the word in the same sense and providing another context clue. Use the context clues from *both* sentences to deduce the meaning of the italicized word. *Be sure the answer you choose makes sense in both sentences.* If you need to use a dictionary to confirm your answer choice, remember that the meaning you select must still fit the context of *both* sentences. Write your answers in the spaces provided.

Pronunciation Key: ă **pat** ā **pay** âr **care** ä **father** ĕ **pet** ē **be** ĭ **pit**
ī **tie** îr **pier** ŏ **pot** ō **toe** ô **paw** oi **noise** ou **out** o͝o **took**
o͞o **boot** ŭ **cut** yo͞o ab**use** ûr **urge** th **thin** *th* **this** hw **which**
zh vision ə **about** *Stress mark:* ′

¶2 ___a___ **6.** In certain *Eastern* philosophical traditions, the harmonious union of a male and female is considered essential to spiritual fulfillment and the survival of the species.

Because my niece had traveled to several Asian countries and found them fascinating, she majored in *Eastern* religions in college.

Eastern (ē′ stərn) means:

a. pertaining to the eastern part of the earth, especially Asia and its neighboring islands

b. pertaining to island countries located in the southeastern part of the world

c. located on the east coast of countries

d. pertaining to ancient countries

¶3 ___a___ **7.** Still, among a national sample of more than 2,000 adults ages 18 to 90, married people *tended* to be happier than unmarried people.

In the 18th and 19th centuries, American families *tended* to be larger than families in the 20th century.

tended (tĕn′ dəd) means:

a. were inclined or likely

b. were opposed

c. were unable

d. were forced

¶4 ___c___ **8.** Historically and across cultures, the most common way of selecting a mate has been through arrangement, either by the parents or by professional *matchmakers.*

My immigrant grandparents told me that their marriage was arranged by a *matchmaker* and that this was a common practice in the old country.

matchmaker (măch′ mā kər) means:

a. person who manufactures safety matches

b. an older relative who chooses the husband or wife for a younger relative

c. person who is paid a fee by parents to locate a suitable marriage partner for their son or daughter

d. computer website on which people seeking spouses can register

¶4 ___c___ **9.** Sometimes *betrothal* takes place in childhood.

Yesterday's newspaper featured a lengthy article about the *betrothal* of the socially prominent bachelor and his aristocratic fiancée and announced their wedding next June.

betrothal (bĭ trō′ thəl) means:

a. wedding ceremony

b. premarital counseling entered into voluntarily

c. mutual promise for a future marriage

d. prenuptial agreement

¶4 ___b___ **10.** Since the Renaissance, with the evolution of the *nuclear family,* free choice of mates on the basis of love has become the norm in the western world, but in Japan, 25 to 30 percent of marriages still are arranged.

In the United States, the *nuclear family* is the norm, but in many countries a much larger group of relatives live together as a family.

nuclear family (no͞o′ klē ər făm′ ə lē) means:

a. a family group consisting of all living relatives

b. a family group that consists only of father, mother, and children

c. a family group that consists of parents, children, and maternal relatives

d. a family group that consists of parents, children, and all in-laws

Word Structure

Directions: Items 11–15 test your ability to use word-structure clues to help determine a word's meaning. *Word-structure clues* consist of roots, prefixes, and suffixes. In these exercises, you will learn the meaning of a word part (a root) and use it to determine the meaning of several other words that have the same word part. If you need to use a dictionary to confirm your answer choice, do so. Write your answers in the spaces provided.

In paragraph 6 of the selection, you encountered the word **prescribed.** This word contains the Latin root ***scrib,*** which means "to write" or "to record." The word *prescribed* literally means "put in *writing* before" (something else can occur). In the selection, the phrase "prescribed rules and supervision" means that the rules have been set down (*written*) by some authority (and, thus, must be obeyed). Use the meaning of ***scrib*** and the list of prefixes on pages 68–69 to help you determine the meaning of each of the following words that contain this same root. Write your answers in the spaces provided.

b 11. If a court reporter **transcribes** the proceedings recorded during a trial, the court reporter:

a. stores information on a computer disk.

b. writes out the information in complete form.

c. alters the information by shortening it.

d. checks the notes for errors in spelling and punctuation.

a 12. When you **subscribe** to a magazine, you:

a. sign an agreement to pay for a specific number of issues.

b. read it every month.

c. recycle the issue after you have read it.

d. remove your name from the mailing list.

c 13. In the Middle Ages, a **scribe's** job was to:

a. read documents and manuscripts to illiterate peasants.

b. translate documents written in other languages.

c. record information and make copies of documents and manuscripts.

d. memorize and recite important documents.

d 14. When children **scribble,** they:

a. draw pictures.

b. paint with finger paints.

c. cut out shapes from colored paper.

d. make meaningless marks or lines.

c 15. If the names of military heroes are **inscribed** on a marble monument, their names are:

a. printed in block letters.

b. written in gold.

c. chiseled in the stone.

d. crossed out.

✓ **Teaching Tip**
Let students know that not all of the skills included in this Reading Skills Application section have been introduced yet. This section serves as a valuable preview of these skills, however. Students typically get several of the items correct, and they find this encouraging.

Reading Skills Application

Directions: Items 16–20 test your ability to *apply* certain reading skills to information in this selection. These types of questions provide valuable practice for all students, especially those who must take standardized reading tests and state-mandated basic skills tests. You may not have studied all of the skills at this point, so these items will serve as a helpful preview. The comprehension and critical reading skills in this section are presented in Chapters 3 through 9 of *New Worlds;* vocabulary and figurative language skills are presented in Chapter 2. As you work through *New Worlds,* you will practice and develop these skills. Write your answers in the spaces provided.

¶3 authors' writing patterns (Chapter 7)

d 16. Which pattern is used to organize the information in paragraph 3?

a. list

b. sequence

c. cause-effect

d. comparison-contrast

¶4 supporting details (Chapter 6) ___c___

17. Based on information presented in the selection, parents in which country would be more likely to seek an arranged marriage for their children?

a. America
b. Zaire
c. Japan
d. Canada

¶1 vocabulary in context (Chapter 2) ___d___

18. In paragraph 1, *universality* is used to mean which of the following?

a. success
b. adoption
c. retreat from
d. condition of occurring everywhere

evaluating an author's argument (Chapter 9) ___c___

19. The authors of the selection present which of the following types of support?

a. case studies
b. expert testimony
c. research studies
d. personal experience

conclusion (Chapter 9) ___b___

20. Based on information in the selection, which of the following represents a logical conclusion?

a. Marriages based on love are more successful than arranged marriages.
b. Marriages of many types can be successful.
c. Marriages between Rajputs are empty and unfulfilling.
d. Throughout the world, various societies' concepts of marriage are becoming more similar.

SELECTION **4-2**
Human Development
(continued)

Collaboration Option

Writing and Collaborating to Enhance Your Understanding

Option for collaboration: Your instructor may direct you to work with other students or, in other words, to work *collaboratively.* In that case, you should form groups of three or four students as directed by your instructor and work together to complete the exercises. After your group discusses each item and agrees on the answer, have a group member record it. Every member of your group should be able to explain all of your group's answers.

1. Reacting to What You Have Read: What do you view as the primary purpose of marriage? What, in your opinion, is necessary for a marriage to be a successful marriage?

2. **Comprehending the Selection Further:** How do you think a person's age at the time of marriage is likely to affect the success of the marriage? In your opinion, what do you think is the minimum age a man should be before he marries? A woman? Explain your answer.

(Answers will vary.)

3. **Overall Main Idea of the Selection:** In one sentence, tell what the author wants readers to understand about engagement and marriage. (Be sure to include the phrase "engagement and marriage" in your overall main idea sentence.)

Engagement and marriage have existed throughout history and still exist around the world, although specific betrothal and marriage customs vary widely from culture to culture.

Internet Resources

Read More about This Topic on the World Wide Web

Directions: For further information about the topic of the selection, visit these websites:

www.lawrence.org/edlinks/wedding.htm
This website contains a list of other websites that describe wedding customs around the world.

www.weddingspecialistswny.com/info/info06/html
This website lists worldwide wedding customs by country.

You can also use your favorite search engine such as Google, Yahoo!, or AltaVista (www.google.com, www.yahoo.com, www.altavista.com) to discover more about this topic. To locate additional information, type in combinations of keywords such as:

marriage worldwide

or

engagement customs worldwide

or

betrothal customs worldwide

Keep in mind that whenever you go to *any* website, it is a good idea to evaluate the website and the information it contains. Ask yourself questions such as:

"Who sponsors this website?"
"Is the information contained in this website up-to-date?"
"What type of information is presented?"
"Is the information objective and complete?"
"How easy is it to use the features of this website?"

SELECTION **4-3** **Health**

SMOKERS VERSUS NONSMOKERS: A QUESTION OF RIGHTS

From *Understanding Your Health*
By Wayne Payne, Dale Hahn, and Ellen Mauer

In 2008 public health officials reported that for the first time on record, the smoking rate in the United States dropped below 20 percent of the total adult population. This drop was attributed to better medications that help people to quit, high cigarette taxes, and an increase in smoking bans in most public places. However, the "war" between nonsmokers and smokers continues.

Where do you stand? Have you ever asked someone not to smoke near you? Have you ever been asked not to smoke around someone? Do you think smoking should be prohibited in all public places? Do smoking regulations infringe on the individual freedoms of smokers? This selection from a health textbook presents information about both sides of the controversial issue of smokers' versus nonsmokers' rights.

1 A quiet battle is being waged in the United States over smoking, an activity that, in the past, was universally accepted. Within the last decade, new regulations restricting smoking have affected stores, restaurants, offices, colleges and universities, and many public buildings. It is difficult these days to find a place of business in the United States where smoking is totally unrestricted. Some of these restrictions are put in place by law or municipal ordinances; some are placed voluntarily by business management. It is clear that the voices of nonsmokers, long silent and largely ignored by society, are finally being heard and are behind the recent increase in restrictions on smoking.

Annotation Practice Exercises

Directions: For each exercise below, write the topic of the paragraph on the lines beside the paragraph. Then locate the stated main idea of the paragraph and underline or highlight it.

Practice Exercise

Topic of paragraph 1:

the voices of nonsmokers

(voices = political influence)

Determine the *stated main idea* and underline it or highlight it.

Changing Attitudes

2 For decades, people smoked whenever and wherever they wished. Smoking was glamorized in the movies, on television, and in print throughout most of the twentieth century. Famous athletes and movie stars were found in cigarette advertisements. Some ads even promoted the "health benefits" of smoking. Although a few people felt that smoking was dangerous, their voices had little effect on society's acceptance of tobacco use. Gradually, these attitudes began to change. As data from medical studies began to accumulate on the dangers of tobacco, antismoking advocates started to achieve some victories in society and in public policy.

✓ **Teaching Tip**

Show students where the answer to each comprehension question appears in the selection. You may prefer to have students work in pairs to identify where each answer appears.

Restrictions on Tobacco Use

3 In the 1980s, restrictions on smoking greatly increased. In 1987, smoking was banned on all domestic airplane flights of less than 2 hours. In 1990, this ban was increased to include all domestic flights of less than 6 hours. Now most international flights ban smoking as well. A growing number of state and local laws curtailing or banning smoking in places of business have been enacted. Many businesses that were not forced by law to

Practice Exercise

Topic of paragraph 3:

restrictions on smoking

Determine the *stated main idea* and underline it or highlight it.

restrict smoking did so anyway. Smoking is prohibited on over 80% of Amtrak trains, and 1400 company-owned McDonald's restaurants are now smoke-free. In fact, entire states have banned smoking in certain public buildings and facilities. Among others, Delaware, New York, Maine, Connecticut, and California now prohibit smoking inside restaurants and bars. Outside the United States, Ireland has banned smoking in pubs (public bars that also serve food) throughout the entire country.

✓ **Teaching Tip**

As of October 1, 2009, 17 states (and Puerto Rico) had passed strong comprehensive smokefree laws that include the workplace, restaurants, and bars. For the latest statistics, see www.no-smoke.org.

4 As a result of these restrictions, smoking areas in places of business are shrinking in size or are being eliminated. Congregations of smokers outside office buildings have become a common sight. Some smokers have taken the changes in stride. Others have cut back on smoking or have quit altogether. Many, however, are not happy about having to go outside in all kinds of weather to smoke. They feel ostracized and are speaking out against what they perceive as an outright attack on their personal freedoms.

The Prosmoker Defense

5 Smokers have started to become organized on a worldwide level and within individual communities and workplaces. They are clearly worried that this trend of restricting tobacco use will not stop until smoking is eliminated everywhere. They are also concerned that regulation over the manufacturing and sales of tobacco products will be brought under the control of the Food and Drug Administration, where restrictions on availability might be significantly greater than currently exists.

6 Groups such as the British-based Freedom Organization for the Right to Enjoy Smoking Tobacco (FOREST) have actively supported smokers' rights and have promoted the "benefits" of smoking. They cite controversial scientific studies demonstrating that smokers are less likely to develop Alzheimer's disease and Parkinson's disease.

7 Smokers are worried about how their smoking activities are perceived by employers and insurers. Companies are growing less tolerant of unhealthy activities by their employees, since they must pay increased insurance costs for coverage and treatment. Many fear that insurance companies will begin to refuse treatment to smokers who continue to smoke.

Practice Exercise

Topic of paragraph 7:

smokers' worries (regarding employers and insurers)

Determine the *stated main idea* and underline it or highlight it.

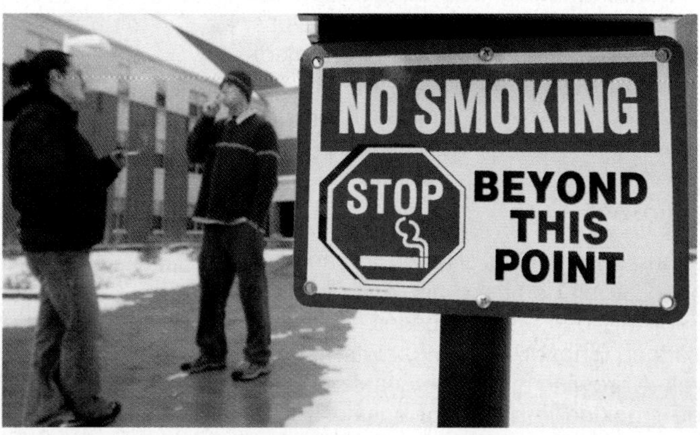

Since the 1980s, restrictions on smoking have increased steadily.

8 The worst-case scenario for smokers is that their smoking will even be restricted at home. A two-pack-a-day smoker worries, "Will we have to step outside of our own homes to smoke? I've also heard that we could have our kids taken away because we smoke at home." Another smoker asks, "What if the government starts keeping us from having kids because we smoke?" Some smokers who avoid smoking when they are at work worry that they will lose their jobs if their employers discover that they smoke when they are at home.

Fighting for Clean Air

9 Many nonsmokers are just as adamant about their position, saying that the restrictions are long overdue because smokers have been subjecting them to cancer-causing agents for decades. They are tired of having smoke blown in their faces in public. Antismoking activists find the "individual freedom" argument of smokers objectionable. "What about *my* right to breathe?" asks an office worker who is subjected to smoke from nearby cubicles. "The management, most of whom smoke, have decided that since we don't deal directly with the public in our office, smoking is okay," he complains.

10 Many nonsmoking activists feel that it is in the public's best interest to restrict exposure to tobacco smoke and cut back on all tobacco use. First, they are concerned not only because they have to be exposed to smoke, but also because a good portion of their insurance premiums is going toward health care costs resulting from smoking. Additionally, as the data accumulate on the hazards of smoking, many nonsmokers are worried about their exposure to secondhand smoke and its associated health risks. They are also worried about the addictive properties of nicotine and are concerned that their children may get hooked.

Practice Exercise

Topic of paragraph 10:

position of many nonsmoking activists

Determine the *stated main idea* and underline it or highlight it.

11 Although they have had much success in getting restrictions adopted, antismoking activists have also faced defeat in the legislatures. Municipalities in North Carolina can no longer pass local laws restricting smoking, thanks to a preemptive state law passed on July 15, 1993. As a result, the majority of workers in North Carolina have no legal protection at all from exposure to tobacco smoke.

12 Even without the health problems posed by tobacco smoke, many nonsmokers feel that smoking should be curtailed simply because of its unpleasant smell. Since smoking is not a self-contained activity, smoke diffuses far away from the smoker, often offending people many feet away. "What good does it do to seat a nonsmoker next to the smoking section in a restaurant?" notes an avid antismoking activist. "The smoke just drifts over anyway. It stinks, and not just during the meal. It gets into your clothes and hair and stays with you all day. Why must we tolerate smoke?"

Practice Exercise

Topic of paragraph 12:

position of many nonsmokers regarding the smell of tobacco smoke

Determine the *stated main idea* and underline it or highlight it.

What the Future May Hold

13 Such arguments may open the door to even more restrictions on smoking, a possibility that makes smokers' rights advocates furious. Many smokers are convinced that antismoking forces want nothing less than a total ban on tobacco use—or at

least want these bans to be enforced more aggressively. This might occur, according to smokers' rights advocates, by allowing the courts to use smoking as a factor in determining child custody cases or in defining parental smoking as a form of child endangerment.

14 Antismoking advocates do not see these regulations as restrictions on individual freedom. They view them as a means of liberation from decades of exposure to smoke with little or no form of legal recourse. Many nonsmokers feel that they should not be forced to breathe in smoke simply because someone wants to light up. Advocates for these regulations claim that tobacco-related illnesses increase health care costs for everyone. They also complain that their tax dollars are being used to subsidize the farming of tobacco and the tobacco industry as a whole. They feel, in effect, that they are paying to be exposed to the smoke of others.

15 Because smoking, by its very nature, is not a self-contained activity, conflicts between smokers and nonsmokers are inevitable. Perhaps some acceptable middle ground can be reached between smokers and nonsmokers, both in law and in society.

SELECTION 4-3
Health
(continued)

Comprehension and Vocabulary Quiz

This quiz has four parts. Your instructor may assign some or all of them.

Comprehension

Directions: Items 1–5 test your comprehension (understanding) of the material in this selection. These questions are much like those that a content-area instructor (such as a health professor) would expect you to know after reading and studying this selection. For each comprehension question below, use information from the selection to determine the correct answer. Refer to the selection as you answer the questions. Write your answers in the spaces provided.

¶3 ___b___ **1.** Restrictions on smoking:
a. began in the 1940s.
b. greatly increased in the 1980s.
c. declined in the 1990s.
d. are being eliminated in some public buildings and facilities.

¶3 ___b___ **2.** Smoking is prohibited inside all restaurants and bars in:
a. North Carolina and South Carolina.
b. several states.
c. England.
d. all of the above

¶7 ___d___ **3.** Companies are becoming less tolerant of employees who smoke because:
a. it is so difficult to quit smoking.
b. nonsmokers are better workers.
c. smokers are likely to perform poorly on the job.
d. they must pay increased insurance costs for health coverage and treatment.

¶8 ___a___ **4.** Some smokers are worried that:
a. their smoking will be restricted even in the privacy of their own homes.
b. the Food and Drug Administration will ban all tobacco products.
c. their individual freedoms will be taken away.
d. doctors will refuse treatment to smokers who continue to smoke.

¶10 ___a___ **5.** Nonsmoking activists feel that it is in the public's best interest to restrict exposure to tobacco smoke and cut back on all tobacco use because they are:
a. concerned that their children may become addicted to smoking.
b. worried about their exposure to secondhand smoke.
c. concerned that a portion of their insurance premiums is going toward health care costs resulting from smoking.
d. all of the above

Vocabulary in Context

Directions: Items 6–10 test your ability to determine the meaning of the word by using context clues. *Context clues* are words in a sentence that allow the reader to deduce (reason out) the meaning of an unfamiliar word in that sentence. Context clues also enable the reader to determine which meaning the author intends when a word has more than one meaning. For each vocabulary item below, a sentence from the selection containing an important word (*italicized, like this*) is quoted first. Next, there is an additional sentence using the word in the same sense and providing another context clue. Use the context clues from *both* sentences to deduce the meaning of the italicized word. *Be sure the answer you choose makes sense in both sentences.* If you need to use a dictionary to confirm your answer choice, remember that the meaning you select must still fit the context of *both* sentences. Write your answers in the spaces provided.

Pronunciation Key: ă **pat** ā **pay** âr **care** ä **father** ĕ **pet** ē **be** ĭ **pit**
ī **tie** îr **pier** ŏ **pot** ō **toe** ô **paw** oi **noise** ou **out** o͝o **took**
o͞o **boot** ŭ **cut** yo͞o ab**u**se ûr **ur**ge th **th**in *th* **th**is hw **wh**ich
zh vi**s**ion ə **a**bout *Stress mark:* ′

¶4 ___c___ **6.** *Congregations* of smokers outside office buildings have become a common sight.

On the same day, massive *congregations* of supporters turned out at peace rallies across the country.

congregations (kŏng grĭ gā′ shənz) means:

a. opponents
b. worshipers
c. gatherings
d. varieties

¶4 ___d___ **7.** They feel *ostracized* and are speaking out against what they perceive as an outright attack on their personal freedoms.

Immigrants often report that when they first settled in the United States they felt *ostracized* from their neighborhood and community activities.

ostracized (ŏs′ trə sīzd) means:

a. angered
b. attacked
c. welcomed
d. excluded

¶7 ____b____ **8.** Companies are growing less *tolerant* of unhealthy activities by their employees, since they must pay increased insurance costs for coverage and treatment.

The more Justine traveled to other states and countries, the more *tolerant* she became of other cultures and customs.

tolerant (tŏl′ ər ənt) means:

a. worried

b. respectful of the rights or practices of others

c. interested in a person's behavior and culture

d. able to help

¶9 ____a____ **9.** Many nonsmokers are just as *adamant* about their position, saying that the restrictions are long overdue because smokers have been subjecting them to cancer-causing agents for decades.

Despite Marco's pleading, his parents were *adamant* in their refusal to buy him a motorcycle.

adamant (ăd′ ə mənt) means:

a. inflexible; stubbornly unyielding

b. upset; angered

c. concerned about safety

d. overly strict

¶12 ____d____ **10.** Even without the health problems posed by tobacco smoke, many nonsmokers feel that smoking should be *curtailed* simply because of its unpleasant smell.

During our vacation, our sightseeing was somewhat *curtailed* because of heavy rain, strong winds, and cold temperatures.

curtailed (kər tāld′) means:

a. forbidden

b. encouraged

c. reconsidered

d. restricted

Word Structure

Directions: Items 11–15 test your ability to use word-structure clues to help determine a word's meaning. *Word-structure clues* consist of roots, prefixes, and suffixes. In these exercises, you will learn the meaning of a word part (a root) and use it to determine the meaning of several other words that have the same word part. If you need to use a dictionary to confirm your answer choice, do so. Write your answers in the spaces provided.

In paragraph 2 of the selection, you encountered the word **advocates.** This word contains the Latin root ***voc,*** which means "to say" or "to call." The word *advocates* describes people who speak out in order to argue or plead for a cause or people who support or defend a cause. Use the meaning of the root ***voc*** and the list of prefixes on pages 68–69 to help you determine the meaning of each of the following words that contain the same root.

__b__ **11.** If someone is described as a **vocal** person, he or she is:

a. difficult to understand.
b. outspoken; inclined to speak often and freely.
c. quiet and shy.
d. confused.

__c__ **12.** Your **vocabulary** consists of:

a. the words you can spell correctly.
b. a group of words borrowed from other languages.
c. words you understand and can use when you speak and write.
d. specialized definitions that you have memorized.

__a__ **13.** When you discover your **vocation,** you find:

a. your calling or occupation.
b. a solution.
c. a place to relax and renew yourself.
d. your family history or genealogy.

__c__ **14.** If a crowd makes a **vociferous** protest, they are:

a. serious; solemn.
b. joyful.
c. loud and noisy.
d. silent.

__d__ **15.** An **avocation,** such as coin collecting or stamp collecting, is:

a. a difficult assignment.
b. the search for something; a mystery.
c. an enormous project; a challenge.
d. a calling away from one's regular work; a hobby.

Reading Skills Application

Directions: Items 16–20 test your ability to *apply* certain reading skills to information in this selection. These types of questions provide valuable practice for all students, especially those who must take standardized reading tests and state-mandated basic skills tests. You may not have studied all of the skills at this point, so these items will serve as a helpful preview. The comprehension and critical reading skills in this section are presented in Chapters 3 through 9 of *New Worlds;* vocabulary and figurative language skills are presented in Chapter 2. As you work through *New Worlds,* you will practice and develop these skills. Write your answers in the spaces provided.

¶14 vocabulary in context (Chapter 2) b

16. Which of the following is the meaning of *subsidize* as it is used in paragraph 14?

a. to criticize
b. to support with money
c. to grow on a farm
d. to lessen

¶4 authors' writing patterns (Chapter 7) d

17. Which pattern is used to organize the information in paragraph 4?

a. list
b. sequence
c. comparison-contrast
d. cause-effect

author's purpose for writing (Chapter 8) c

18. The authors' primary purpose in writing this selection is to:

a. persuade readers to quit smoking.
b. instruct readers about smoking restrictions.
c. inform readers about both sides of the smoking issue.
d. convince readers that smoking is a serious problem in today's society.

¶2 implied main idea (Chapter 5) b

19. Which of the following represents the main idea of paragraph 2?

a. Smoking has been glamorized in the movies and on television for decades.
b. Although smoking was widely accepted in the past, there has been a gradual change in attitudes related to smoking.
c. Medical studies have proven the dangers of tobacco.
d. Antismoking advocates have had little effect on society's acceptance of tobacco use.

¶15 distinguishing facts from opinions (Chapter 9) a

20. Which of the following represents an opinion rather than a fact?

a. Perhaps some acceptable solution can be reached between smokers and nonsmokers.
b. Tobacco-related illnesses increase health care costs for everyone.
c. In the 1980s, restrictions on smoking increased.
d. Delaware, New York, Maine, Connecticut, and California now prohibit smoking inside restaurants and bars.

✓ **Teaching Tips**

Let students know that not all of the skills included in this Reading Skills Application section have been introduced yet. This section serves as a valuable preview of these skills, however. Students typically get several of the items correct, and they find this encouraging.

We suggest that rather than include this section as part of the quiz grade, you use it to give students practice with the skills they have studied and as a helpful preview of upcoming skills. It makes an excellent collaborative activity. All students will find this practice helpful, especially those who must take course exit tests, standardized reading tests, or state-mandated basic skills tests.

SELECTION **4-3**

Health

(continued)

Writing and Collaborating to Enhance Your Understanding

Option for collaboration: Your instructor may direct you to work with other students or, in other words, to work *collaboratively.* In that case, you should form groups of three or four students as directed by your instructor and work together to complete the exercises. After your group discusses each item and agrees on the answer, have a group member record it. Every member of your group should be able to explain all of your group's answers.

Collaboration Option

1. **Reacting to What You Have Read:** Should taxpayers be responsible for taking on the financial burden of those being treated for smoking-related diseases? Do you think employers and the government have the right to forbid people from smoking in their own home? Do you think that smoking at home around children is a form of child endangerment? Explain your answers to these questions.

   (Answers will vary.)

2. **Comprehending the Selection Further:** The authors of this selection discuss a variety of concerns that nonsmokers have about the use of tobacco. List those concerns here:

   1. Medical studies have proved the dangers of tobacco use.
   2. Smoking should be restricted or eliminated in all places of business.
   3. There are concerns about being exposed to secondhand smoke.
   4. Insurance costs are on the rise due to health care costs resulting from smoking.
   5. There are concerns that children may become addicted to smoking.
   6. To nonsmokers, the smell of smoke is unpleasant.
   7. There are concerns that children may be in danger if parents smoke at home.
   8. Tax dollars should not be used to subsidize the farming of tobacco.

3. **Overall Main Idea of the Selection:** In one sentence, tell what the authors want readers to understand about the rights of both nonsmokers and smokers. (Be sure to include the positions of "nonsmokers" and "smokers" in your overall main idea sentence.)

Nonsmokers are actively supporting the increase in restrictions on smoking and tobacco use in general, while smokers are increasingly concerned about their individual right to smoke.

Read More about This Topic on the World Wide Web

Internet Resources

Directions: For further information about the topic of the selection, visit these websites:

www.no-smoke.org
This site is sponsored by the American Nonsmokers' Rights Foundation (ANRF). ANRF promotes smoking prevention and education about smoking, passive smoke, and the economic effects of the tobacco industry.

www.smokersclubinc.com
The United Pro-Smokers' Rights newsletter, sponsored by The Smoker's Club, Inc., is featured on this website.

http://lungaction.org/reports/tobacco-control05.html
This site, sponsored by the American Lung Association, lists the tobacco control laws of each state.

You can also use your favorite search engine such as Google, Yahoo!, or AltaVista (www.google.com, www.yahoo.com, www.altavista.com) to discover more about this topic. To locate additional information, type in combinations of keywords such as:

smokers' rights
or
nonsmokers' rights

Keep in mind that whenever you go to *any* website, it is a good idea to evaluate the website and the information it contains. Ask yourself questions such as:

"Who sponsors this website?"
"Is the information contained in this website up-to-date?"
"What type of information is presented?"
"Is the information objective and complete?"
"How easy is it to use the features of this website?"

CHAPTER 5

Formulating an Implied Main Idea

CHAPTER OBJECTIVES

In this chapter you will learn the answers to these questions:

- What is an implied main idea sentence?
- Why is it important to be able to formulate a main idea?
- What are three formulas for using information in a paragraph to formulate the main idea?

✓ **Timely Words**

"Reading between the lines . . ." —a figurative phrase for "Understanding things that are implied rather than directly stated."

CHAPTER CONTENTS

WHAT IS AN IMPLIED MAIN IDEA, AND WHY IS IT IMPORTANT?

KEY TERMS
implied main idea

A sentence formulated by the reader that expresses the author's main point about the topic.

An implied main idea is also known as an *unstated main idea*, an *indirectly stated main idea*, and a *formulated main idea*.

Student Online Learning Center (OLC)
***Go to* Chapter 5.**
***Select* Video.**

✓ **Teaching Tip**
Explain that *imply* and *infer* are two halves of a complementary process. The sender of a message *implies* it (suggests or hints without stating it directly). The receiver *infers* the message (reasons it out) by picking up on the hints and piecing together the sender's point.

You already know that every paragraph has a main idea. Sometimes, authors *suggest* the most important point, rather than state it directly in a single sentence. In other words, the author *implies* the main point.

When authors do not state the main idea directly, it is the reader's job to infer it (reason it out) and write a sentence that expresses it. An **implied main idea** is a sentence formulated by the reader that expresses an author's main point about the topic. (In this book the terms *implied main idea sentence* and *formulated main idea sentence* are used interchangeably because they refer to the same thing.)

Why is it important for you to formulate an implied main idea sentence whenever the author does not state the main idea? There are several reasons: First, you limit your comprehension unless you can formulate main ideas that are implied. Also, when you formulate main ideas, it helps you remember material better. Finally, college instructors assume that you will read carefully enough to understand both stated and implied main ideas. Test items are just as likely to be based on implied main ideas as on stated main ideas.

In this chapter, you will learn three "formulas" that you can use to "formulate" an implied main idea. The formula you use will depend on the type of information the author gives you in the paragraph. Sometimes the only thing you need to do is add an essential word or a phrase to a sentence in the paragraph. In other cases, all you need to do is combine two or more sentences in the paragraph into one sentence. In still other cases, you will have to summarize ideas from several sentences or make a general inference based on the details. When a paragraph consists only of facts, descriptions, explanations, or examples that merely suggest the author's main point, it will be up to you to infer it and then formulate a general main idea sentence. Remember, the main idea sentence you formulate must always be *based on* what is presented in the paragraph.

To be an effective reader, then, you must be able to formulate the main idea sentence when the author implies it, just as you must be able to locate the main idea when the author states it directly.

When authors imply a main idea, it is the reader's job to infer the main point and formulate a sentence that expresses it.

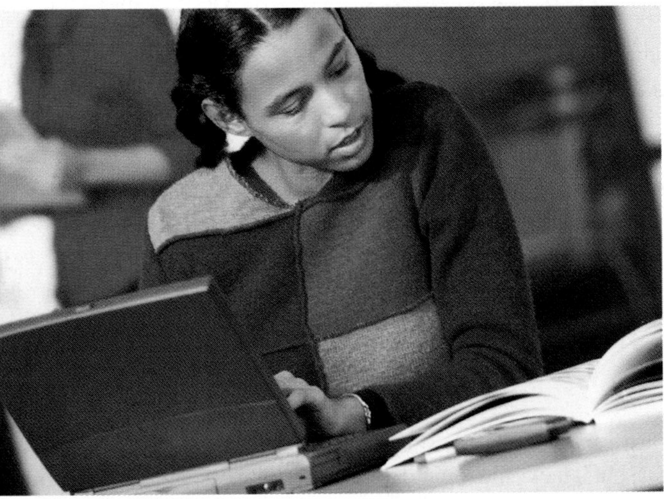

✓ **Teaching Tip**
Remind students that the student OLC contains an audio and video feature for Chapters 3 through 9 that presents **Key Comprehension Terms** and **Comprehension Monitoring Questions.**

THREE FORMULAS FOR USING INFORMATION IN A PARAGRAPH TO FORMULATE AN IMPLIED MAIN IDEA

Comprehension Monitoring Question for Implied Main Idea

"What is the single most important point the author wants me to *infer* about the topic of this paragraph?"

As always, you must begin by reading the paragraph and determining its topic. If you cannot locate a stated main idea sentence, ask yourself this comprehension monitoring question, "What is the single most important point the author wants me to *infer* about the topic of this paragraph?" Then use one of the three "formulas" to create the "formulated" main idea sentence. Here is an explanation of each formula, along with a simple example and one from an actual college textbook.

Formula 1: Add an Essential Word or Phrase to a Sentence in the Paragraph That Almost States the Main Idea

Sometimes, an author expresses *most* of the main idea in one sentence of the paragraph, yet that sentence lacks an essential piece of information. You must add that essential information to make the sentence express the *complete* main idea. Often, the sentence merely needs to have the topic (a word, name, or phrase) inserted to make it express the main idea completely.

When you read a paragraph that has a sentence that almost states the main idea yet lacks essential information, use **Formula 1** to create the complete main idea sentence:

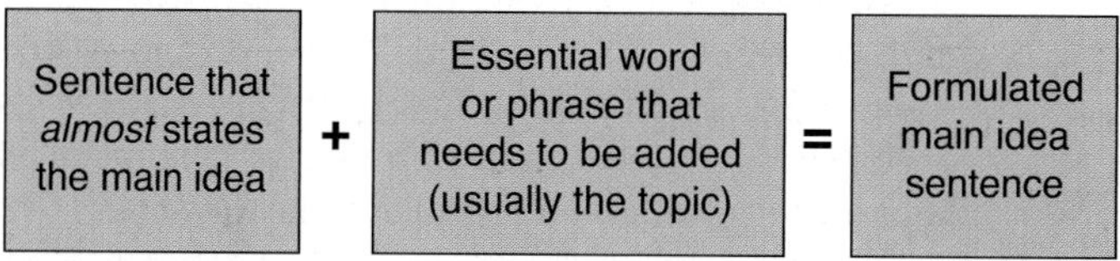
Sentence that *almost* states the main idea
+
Essential word or phrase that needs to be added (usually the topic)
=
Formulated main idea sentence

✓ **Teaching Tip**

To walk students through this process, have them identify the sentence that *almost* states the main idea and then underline or highlight it (the last sentence). Then have them mark out "He" and replace it with "Bob."

The simple paragraph below illustrates how this formula can be applied. Read the paragraph and determine the topic by asking yourself, "Who or what is this about?" Notice that there is a sentence that *almost* states the main idea, yet lacks an essential piece of information. Find that sentence.

> Bob is excellent with customers. He is knowledgeable about his company's products. Moreover, he is a hard worker who always exceeds his sales goals. He is the best salesperson in his company.

Here is Formula 1 with the appropriate information from the paragraph:

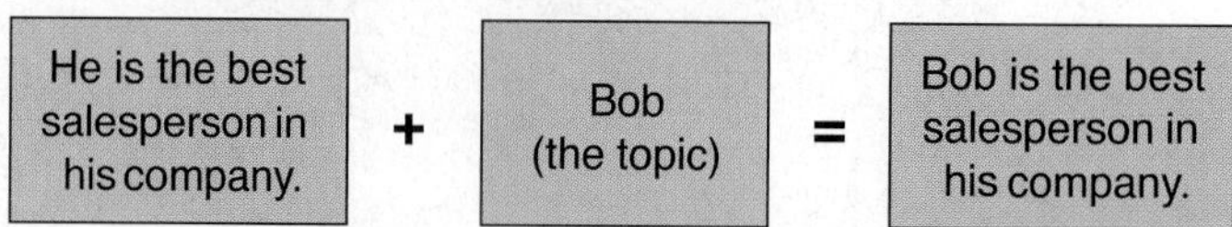
He is the best salesperson in his company.
+
Bob (the topic)
=
Bob is the best salesperson in his company.

The last sentence almost states the main idea ("He is the best salesperson in his company"), but it lacks the topic (Bob). When that essential information is added, you have the complete formulated main idea sentence: *Bob is the best salesperson in his company.*

When a paragraph contains a sentence that almost states the main idea, yet needs essential information added, it is the type of paragraph to which Formula 1 should be applied. Here is a paragraph from a management textbook where the main idea can be formulated using Formula 1. The topic of this paragraph is *McDonald's enviable success.*

What explains McDonald's enviable success? One major reason for it is the extent to which the company maintains strong controls over most aspects of its operations. These controls have helped McDonald's develop a competitive edge in the form of high product and service consistency. A Big Mac is likely to taste pretty much the same whether we are eating it in Boston or Bangkok. As noted economist Robert J. Samuelson reported in praising McDonald's, his Big Mac ordered at an outlet in Tokyo did not "merely taste like an American Big Mac"; it tasted "exactly the same."

Formulated Main Idea Sentence

One major reason for McDonald's enviable success is the extent to which the company maintains strong controls over most aspects of its operations.

Source: Adapted from Kathryn M. Bartol and David C. Martin, *Management,* 3rd ed., p. 510. Copyright © 1998 by The McGraw-Hill Companies, Inc. Reprinted by permission of The McGraw-Hill Companies, Inc.

Stop and Annotate

Go back to the textbook excerpt above. Write the formulated main idea sentence in the space provided by adding essential information to the sentence that almost states the main idea.

The second sentence of this paragraph *almost* states the authors' most important point, but it lacks an essential piece of information: the topic. A complete main idea sentence can be formulated by adding the topic, *McDonald's enviable success,* to the second sentence: *One major reason for McDonald's enviable success is the extent to which the company maintains strong controls over most aspects of its operations.*

EXERCISE 1

This paragraph comes from a psychology textbook.

What is meditation? It is a learned technique for refocusing attention that brings about an altered state of consciousness. Meditation typically consists of the repetition of a *mantra*—a sound, word, or syllable—over and over. In other forms of meditation, the focus is on a picture, flame, or specific part of the body. The procedure involves concentrating on something so thoroughly that the person who is meditating becomes unaware of any outside stimulation. He or she reaches a different state of consciousness.

Source: Adapted from Robert S, Feldman, *Understanding Psychology,* 8th ed., p.163. Copyright © 2008, by The McGraw-Hill Companies, Inc. Reprinted by permission of The McGraw-Hill Companies, Inc.

Write the topic: meditation

Formulate a main idea sentence: Meditation is a learned technique for refocusing attention that brings about an altered state of consciousness. (Formula 1; add topic to sentence 2.)

Formula 2: Combine Two Sentences from the Paragraph into a Single Sentence

✓ **Teaching Tip**
You may need to review sentence combining or refer students to a tutoring center or similar support service for help with this skill.

Sometimes a paragraph contains two sentences that each give *part* of the main idea. Each sentence contains important information, yet neither sentence by itself expresses the complete main idea. Therefore, you must *combine* these two sentences into *one* sentence that expresses the complete main idea. (You already know that any main idea must be written as a single sentence.) Often you will be able to use words such as *and, but,* or *however* to join the two sentences. The two sentences you combine may follow one another in the paragraph (for example, the first two sentences of the paragraph), or they may be separated (for example, the first sentence of the paragraph and the last sentence of the paragraph).

When you realize that two sentences in a paragraph each state *part* of the main idea, use **Formula 2** to create a complete main idea that is a single sentence:

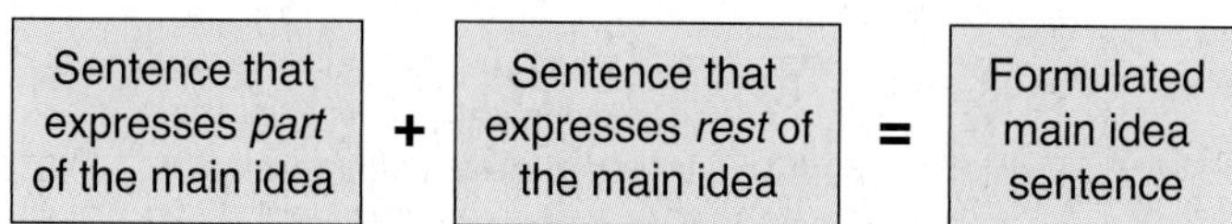

Here is a simple paragraph that shows how this formula can be applied. Read the paragraph and notice that there are two sentences that each give part of the main idea but that must be combined into a single sentence to formulate the complete main idea.

✓ **Teaching Tip**
Ask students to identify the two sentences that each give part of the main idea and underline or highlight them in two different colors. Then ask them to mark those sentences in the same two colors in the "main idea box" at the end of the formula.

> Maria is taking a full academic load this semester. She is taking history, psychology, computer science, math, and a writing course. She has classes five days a week. But she still finds time to do volunteer work. On Saturday mornings she is a volunteer at the library. On Sunday afternoons she does volunteer work at the hospital.

Here is Formula 2 with the appropriate information from the paragraph:

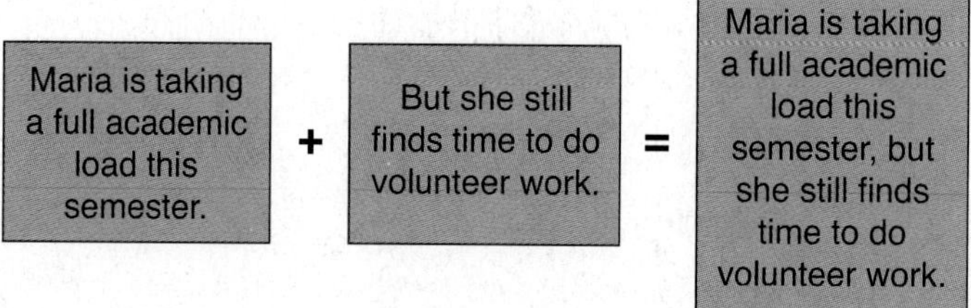

The first sentence and the fourth sentence express the important information, so they must be combined into one sentence. Therefore, the formulated main idea sentence is: *Maria is taking a full academic load this semester, but she still finds time to do volunteer work.*

Here is a psychology textbook paragraph whose main idea can be formulated using Formula 2. As the heading indicates, the topic of this paragraph is *the origins of sexual orientation.*

Origins of Sexual Orientation

It is not known why any person develops a particular sexual orientation. However, a good guess is that it develops through a complex interaction of biological and sociocultural factors. John Money has proposed a specific theory of sexual orientation that balances the roles of biological and sociocultural influences. He states that all sexual orientation has its origins in the womb when the nervous system is still developing. Money believes that the brain is shaped during fetal development by a complex interplay of genetics and hormones. The factors organize the brain in a way that predisposes the person toward either heterosexuality or homosexuality. Later, during sensitive periods of development in childhood or adolescence, sexual orientation is shaped by social and interpersonal experiences, but persons are more likely to develop a sexual orientation that is consistent with their biological predisposition.

Formulated Main Idea Sentence

It is not known why any person develops a particular sexual orientation; however, a good guess is that it develops through a complex interaction of biological and sociocultural factors.

Source: Benjamin B. Lahey, *Psychology,* 6th ed. Copyright © 1998 by The McGraw-Hill Companies, Inc. Reprinted by permission of The McGraw-Hill Companies, Inc.

Stop and Annotate

Go back to the textbook excerpt above. Write the formulated main idea sentence in the space provided by combining the two sentences in the paragraph that together express the complete main idea.

Because the first two sentences each tell half of the main idea, the main idea sentence is formulated by combining them into a single sentence. The first sentence explains that we are not exactly certain why a person develops a particular sexual orientation; the second sentence explains the probable reason a particular sexual orientation develops. When these two sentences are combined, you have a complete main idea sentence: *It is not known why a person develops a particular sexual orientation; however, a good guess is that it develops through a complex interaction of biological and sociocultural factors.*

Remember that there is more than one correct way to combine sentences to express an implied main idea. What is important is that the main idea is correct and complete. For example, the main idea of the excerpt could also be expressed: *It is not known why a person develops a particular sexual orientation, but a good guess is that it develops through a complex interaction of biological and sociocultural factors.*

EXERCISE 2

This paragraph comes from an information technology textbook.

How would you feel if someone obtained a driver's license and credit cards in your name? What if that person then assumed your identity to buy clothes, cars, and a house? It happens every day. It happens in every state. Every year, well over 100 million people are victimized in this way. The illegal assumption of someone's identity for the purposes of economic gain is called **identity theft.** It is one of the fastest-growing crimes in the country.

Source: Adapted from Timothy J. O'Leary and Linda I. O'Leary, *Computing Essentials,* p. 279. Copyright © 2008 by The McGraw-Hill Companies, Inc. Reprinted by permission of The McGraw-Hill Companies, Inc.

Write the topic: identity theft

Formulate a main idea sentence: The illegal assumption of someone's identity for the purposes of economic gain is called identity theft, and it is one of the fastest-growing crimes in the country.

(Formula 2; combine last two sentences.)

Formula 3: Summarize Important Ideas into One Sentence or Write One Sentence That Gives a General Inference Based on the Details

✓ **Teaching Tip**
Review with students the information in Chapter 3, page 136, on *general* versus *specific.*

With some paragraphs, you will either have to formulate a main idea sentence that *summarizes* the important information in the paragraph or formulate a sentence that gives a *general inference* based on the details. Which of these you do will depend upon the type of information you are given in the paragraph. When you create this kind of formulated main idea sentence, you will often have to use some of your own words along with certain important words from the paragraph.

When a paragraph has important ideas included in several sentences or the paragraph consists only of details, **Formula 3** should be used to formulate the main idea.

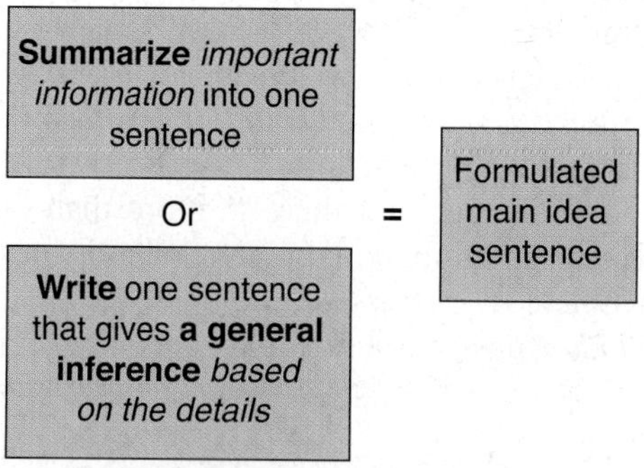

Summarize *important information* into one sentence

Or

Write one sentence that gives **a general inference** *based on the details*

=

Formulated main idea sentence

The simple paragraph on the following page shows how you can summarize important ideas to create the formulated main idea. Read the paragraph and notice which ideas have been summarized to create the formulated main idea.

> Johnny doesn't trust strangers. He does not trust his neighbors, nor does he trust his coworkers. He does, however, trust members of his family. And he trusts his best friend, Ramón.

Here is Formula 3 with the appropriate information from the paragraph.

Johnny – does not trust strangers – does not trust his neighbors – does not trust his coworkers – trusts members of his family – trusts his best friend, Ramón	=	Johnny does not trust many people, but he does trust family members and his best friend, Ramón.

A formulated main idea sentence that summarizes the important information into one sentence is *Johnny does not trust many people but he does trust family members and his best friend, Ramón.* Of course, this could also be expressed in shorter ways, *Johnny trusts only family members and his best friend,* or *Family members and his best friend are the only people Johnny trusts.*

A word of caution: Do not create one long sentence in which you merely restate all of the information, such as *Johnny doesn't trust strangers and he does not trust his neighbors and he does not trust his coworkers, but he does, however, trust members of his family and his best friend, Ramón.* Instead, summarize the information using some of your own words.

Now consider a paragraph that consists only of details. In this case, you must infer the general point the author wants to make. Then formulate a main idea sentence that expresses that point. Although none of the actual details appear in the main idea sentence, the main idea is *based* on them. For example,

> Tia likes to swim and water ski. She also enjoys snow skiing and ice skating. She has loved basketball since elementary school. She is captain of the tennis team this year. And she is very excited about her upcoming soccer season.

Here is Formula 3 with the appropriate information from the paragraph:

Tia likes
– swimming and water skiing
– snow skiing and ice skating
– basketball
– tennis
– soccer
=
Tia likes many sports.

The formulated main idea sentence gives a general inference *based* on the details: *Tia likes many sports*. Notice that although the word *sports* does not appear in the paragraph, it can be used as a general term to describe the activities mentioned in the details. Of course, the main idea sentence could also be expressed in any of these ways: *Tia loves several sports; Tia enjoys many sports;* or even *Tia participates in a variety of sports.*

Here is a study skills textbook paragraph whose implied main idea can be formulated using Formula 3. The topic is *being more successful on future tests.* The implied main idea can be formulated by writing a sentence that summarizes the important information into one sentence.

When you do poorly on a test, don't blame your teacher. And don't blame your textbook. Don't blame your job that kept you from studying. Analyze the situation. See what you can change to be more successful in the future.

Formulated Main Idea Sentence

When you do poorly on a test, analyze the situation to see what you can change to be more successful in the future.

Source: Adapted from Robert S. Feldman, *P.O.W.E.R. Learning: Strategies for Success in College and Life,* p. 14.

Stop and Annotate

Go back to the textbook excerpt above. Formulate a sentence that *summarizes* the important information from several sentences into a single sentence and write it in the space provided.

To create a main idea for this paragraph, examine the details, think about them, and ask yourself, "What is the important point the author wants me to *infer* about being more successful on future tests?" The formulated main idea is *When you do poorly on a test, analyze the situation to see what you can change to be more successful in the future.*

Here is another paragraph from the same study skills textbook that also has an implied main idea that can be formulated using Formula 3. The topic is *strategies for answering specific kinds of test questions.* The implied main idea can be formulated by writing a sentence that gives a general inference based on the details.

Are there specific strategies for answering various kinds of test questions? For essay questions, be sure to understand each question and each of its parts, interpret action words correctly, write concisely, organize the essay logically, and include examples. For multiple-choice questions, read the questions very carefully and then read all response choices. Educated guessing based on eliminating incorrect response choices is usually a reasonable strategy. For true-false and matching questions, quickly answer all the items that you are sure of and then go back to the remaining items. The best strategy for short-answer and fill-in questions is to be very sure what is being asked. Keep answers complete but brief.

Formulated Main Idea Sentence

There are specific strategies for answering various kinds of test questions.

Source: Adapted from Robert S. Feldman, *P.O.W.E.R., Learning: Strategies for Success in College and Life,* p. 141.

To create a main idea, examine the details, think about them, and ask yourself, "What is the single most general point the author wants me to *infer* about strategies for answering specific kinds of test questions?" A logical formulated main idea is *There are specific strategies for answering various kinds of test questions.*

Stop and Annotate

Go back to the previous textbook excerpt. Formulate a sentence by making a *general inference* based on the details and write it in the space provided.

EXERCISE 3

This paragraph comes from a health textbook.

Are fast food "meal deals" a good deal? Burger King's King Value Meal and Wendy's Classic Triple with Cheese plus Great Biggie Fries and a Biggie Cola supply more than an entire day's worth of calories and sodium and two days of saturated and trans fats. The Meat Lover's breakfast at Denny's, which comes with three pancakes, two eggs, two strips of bacon, and two sausage links, has 1,250 calories and 86 grams of fat, according to Denny's website. The Fabulous French Toast Platter—with three slices of French toast, two bacon strips, and two sausage links—contains 1,261 calories and 79 grams of fat. Hardee's has a Monster Thickburger, with 1,400 calories and 107 grams of fat.

Source: Adapted from Wayne A. Payne, Dale B. Hahn, and Ellen B. Lucas, *Understanding Your Health,* 10th ed., p. 154., Copyright © 2009 by The McGraw-Hili Companies, Inc. Reprinted by permission of The McGraw-Hill Companies, Inc.

Write the topic: fast food "meal deals"

Formulate a main idea sentence: Fast food "meal deals" contain far too many calories, sodium, and fats.

OR

Fast food "meal deals" are not a deal because they are unhealthy.

(Formula 3; general inference based on the details)

When you read a paragraph that does not have a stated main idea, use one of the formulas to create a sentence that tells the author's implied main idea. The chart on page 242 summarizes the three ways to formulate implied main idea sentences.

THREE WAYS TO FORMULATE IMPLIED MAIN IDEA SENTENCES

What the Author Presents in the Paragraph	What You Must Do with the Information in Order to Formulate the Implied Main Idea
A sentence that *almost* states the main idea, but lacks some essential piece of information (usually the topic)	*Use Formula 1.* *Add* the essential piece of information that is missing to that sentence. *How to apply the formula:* Use the sentence from the paragraph and simply add the essential piece of information to that sentence. *or* You can write the main idea in your own words as long as the meaning is the same.
Two sentences in the paragraph that each present *part* of the main idea	*Use Formula 2.* *Combine* them into one sentence (because the main idea must always be written as a single sentence). *How to apply the formula:* You will probably have to add a word or two in order to connect the two sentences (usually words such as *and, but, although,* etc.). *or* You can write the main idea in your own words, as long as the meaning is the same.
Important information in several sentences	*Use Formula 3.* Summarize important information into one sentence.
Details only	*Use Formula 3.* *Write* a *general sentence* that "sums up" the details or gives a general inference about the point the author is making. *How to apply the formula:* The sentence you write will contain several of your own words.

OTHER THINGS TO KEEP IN MIND WHEN FORMULATING AN IMPLIED MAIN IDEA SENTENCE

There are three helpful things you should know about when formulating main idea sentences that have been implied:

1. You must always use a sentence—not just a phrase—to express a formulated main idea. This means you must know the difference between a sentence and a phrase.

The main idea must be expressed as a complete sentence that has a subject and a verb and expresses a complete thought. A phrase, on the other hand, is a group of words that does not express a complete thought, even if it is a long group of words. Use sentences, not phrases, to express main ideas.

The left column (below) gives examples of phrases that could be used as topics. None of the items in this column could be used as main ideas because they are not complete sentences. The right column contains sentences that *could* be used to express main ideas because they are complete sentences. (Notice that in each case, the topic is part of the complete sentence.)

Could *Not* Be Used as a Formulated Main Idea (because it is a phrase)	**Could Be Used as a Formulated Main Idea (because it is a complete sentence)**
my cell phone	My cell phone was stolen.
my new cell phone	My new cell phone was stolen.
my new cell phone with a touch screen	My new cell phone with a touch screen was stolen.
my new cell phone with a touch screen and video camera	My new cell phone with a touch screen and video camera was stolen.
traveling by plane	Traveling by plane is the fastest way to travel long distances to foreign countries.
fatality rates for passengers traveling by plane	Fatality rates for passengers traveling by plane are lower than fatality rates for passengers traveling by car.
why traveling by plane is the best way to go	There are several reasons why traveling by plane is the best way to go.
how to overcome fear of traveling by plane	Psychologists have several methods to teach people how to overcome fear of traveling by plane.

2. All formulated (implied) main idea sentences have certain characteristics. A formulated main idea must:

- Be a *complete sentence* that includes the *topic* of the paragraph.
- Express the *author's most important general point about the topic.* (In other words, if the formulated main idea sentence were placed at the beginning of the paragraph, the other sentences would explain, prove, or tell more about it.)
- *Make complete sense by itself* without the reader having to read the rest of the paragraph.

Here is an example of a sentence that would not be meaningful by itself since the reader would not know who "her" refers to: *Most historians consistently rank her among the most effective leaders of the 20th century.* Therefore, this sentence could not be a correctly formulated main idea sentence. On the other hand,

(continued on next page)

this sentence could be a main idea sentence because it makes sense by itself: *Most historians consistently rank former British Prime Minister Margaret Thatcher among the most effective leaders of the 20th century.*

Remember also that an implied main idea sentence can be worded in various ways, as long as it meets the three requirements.

3. **A longer passage often has an implied overall main idea that you must formulate, too.**

Sometimes the reader must formulate an *overall* implied main idea that gives the general point of an entire selection. (A longer passage might consist of a section of a textbook chapter, a short reading selection, or an essay, for example.) The overall formulated main idea is a general statement or inference that is *based on* the main ideas of the selection. That is, the formulated overall main idea sentence summarizes or sums up the main ideas of the individual paragraphs in the selection, just as the main idea of each paragraph sums up the individual details in the paragraph. To be correct, a formulated overall main idea sentence must meet the same requirements as the formulated main idea of a paragraph.

EXERCISE 4

Could This Be a Formulated Main Idea Sentence?

The main idea must always be a *sentence;* it must also contain a *topic* and must make *complete sense* by itself. For example,

- There is no greater influence on children than their parents. *(Yes, this could be a stated main idea because the sentence makes complete sense by itself.)*
- There is no greater influence on children. *(No, this could not be a stated main idea sentence because we don't know what the influence is. The sentence does not make complete sense by itself.)*
- The greatest influence on children. *(No; this could not be a stated main idea because it isn't even a sentence.)*

Directions: For the items below, decide whether each could be a formulated main idea sentence. (All of them end with periods, although not all of them are sentences.) If an item contains a topic and makes complete sense by itself, write Y for Yes. If it does not, write N for No.

N **1.** The benefits of a healthy diet.
Y **2.** There are several reasons HIV has not yet been eradicated.
N **3.** It was the biggest scare New York City ever experienced.
N **4.** The importance of art and music in children's lives.
N **5.** It is the best treatment available for preventing a heart attack.
N **6.** There are three major types.
Y **7.** Cell phones can be dangerous if people use them while driving.
N **8.** They can be dangerous if people use them while driving.
N **9.** Most of them are sleep deprived.
N **10.** It was a crowning moment in Olympic history.
N **11.** Whether the new plan will work.
Y **12.** Using a study schedule has several benefits.
N **13.** The government should not adopt this policy.
N **14.** How working too many hours affects college students' academic success.
Y **15.** Working too many hours affects college students' academic success.
N **16.** He moved from Guatemala to the United States.
Y **17.** Gustavo moved from Guatemala to the United States.
N **18.** It was the turning point of his life.
N **19.** It was the turning point of Gustavo's life.
Y **20.** Gustavo's move from Guatemala was the turning point of his life.

Student Online Learning Center (OLC)
***Go to* Chapter 5.**
Select
Chapter Test.

Review cards or *summary cards* are a way to select, organize, and summarize the important information in a textbook chapter. Preparing review cards helps you organize the information so that you can learn and memorize it more easily. In other words, chapter review cards are effective study tools.

Preparing chapter review cards for each chapter of *New Worlds* will give you practice in creating these valuable study tools. Once you have learned how to make chapter review cards, you can use actual index cards to create them for textbook material in any of your other courses and use them when you study for tests.

Now complete the chapter review cards for Chapter 5 by answering the questions or following the directions on each card. The page numbers indicate the place in the chapter where the information can be found. Use the type of handwriting that is easiest for you to reread (printing or cursive) and write legibly.

✓ **Teaching Tip**

Remind students that the student OLC contains a 10-item **Chapter Test** for this chapter. After completing the chapter review cards below, students should complete the Chapter Test on the OLC.

Page numbers for chapter review card items are provided in the student edition in Chapters 1–5 only.

Implied Main Idea Sentences

1. What is the definition of an *implied main idea*? (See page 233.)

A sentence formulated by the reader that expresses the author's main point about the topic

2. List three reasons it is important to understand and formulate the implied main idea of a paragraph. (See page 233.)

- You limit your comprehension unless you are able to formulate main ideas that are implied.
- When you formulate main ideas, it helps you remember material better.
- College instructors assume that students will read carefully enough to understand both stated and implied main ideas.

3. What question should you ask yourself in order to formulate the implied main idea of a paragraph? Be sure you write a *question.* (See page 234.)

What is the single most important point the author wants me to infer about the topic of this paragraph?

Card 1 Chapter 5: Formulating an Implied Main Idea

✓ **Teaching Tip**

For item 3 on Card 1, point out the "Comprehension Monitoring Question for Implied Main Idea" in the margin on page 234 and guide students to write their answer as a question (including a question mark).

Three Ways to Formulate an Implied Main Idea Sentence

Write out the three formulas for creating implied main idea sentences. (See pages 234–238.)

Formula 1: Sentence that almost states the main idea + Essential word or phrase that needs to be added (usually the topic) = Formulated main idea sentence

Formula 2: Sentence that expresses *part* of the main idea + Sentence that expresses *rest* of the main idea = Formulated main idea sentence

Formula 3: Summarize *important information* into one sentence or Write one sentence that gives a general inference *based on the details* = Formulated main idea sentence

What determines the formula you will use? (See page 233.)

The formula you use will depend on what the author gives you to start with in the paragraph.

Card 2 Chapter 5: Formulating an Implied Main Idea

When Formulating the Implied Main Idea, Keep in Mind . . .

What are the three requirements for a correctly formulated implied main idea sentence? (See page 243.)

1. It must be a complete sentence that includes the topic of the paragraph.
2. It must express the author's most general point about the topic.
3. It must make complete sense by itself.

Card 3 Chapter 5: Formulating an Implied Main Idea

TEST YOUR UNDERSTANDING
FORMULATING IMPLIED MAIN IDEAS, PART ONE

REVIEW: An **implied main idea** is a sentence formulated by the reader that expresses the author's main point about the topic. *Formulated main ideas are always expressed as complete sentences.* As you learned in this chapter, there are three ways to formulate a main idea that has been implied:

- *Add an essential word or phrase to a sentence* in the paragraph that almost states the main idea.
- *Combine two sentences from the paragraph* into a single sentence.
- *Summarize important ideas into one sentence* or *write one sentence that gives a general inference based on the details.*

EXAMPLE: Study the example paragraph below to see how the information you learned in this chapter can be used to formulate the implied main idea of a paragraph. Read the explanation of the correct answer. When you are sure you understand the explanation, complete the five exercises in Part One.

This excerpt comes from a health textbook. Its topic is *single parents and child care.* To determine the implied main idea, read the paragraph and ask yourself, "What is the single most important point the author wants me to *infer* about single parents and child care?"

Child Care and Parenting

If single parents can find child care, it is often too costly and may not accommodate their work hours or class schedule. The expense of child care can consume 25% to 60% of the family income. If the parent moves into his or her parents' house to cut costs and have grandparents readily available for child care, there may be child-rearing conflicts. If the parent and grandparents set different rules, the children can become confused. Parental authority is weakened if the parent is viewed as a child again.

Source: From Wayne A. Payne, Dale B. Hahn, and Ellen Mauer, *Understanding Your Health,* 8th ed., p. 92. Copyright © 2005 by The McGraw-Hill Companies, Inc. Reprinted by permission of The McGraw-Hill Companies, Inc.

The topic of this paragraph is *single parents and child care.*

___b___ What is the implied main idea of this paragraph?

a. If single parents can find child care, it is often too costly.
b. Child care can present several difficulties for single parents.
c. If the parent moves into his or her parents' house, there may be child-rearing conflicts.
d. Parental authority is weakened if the parent is viewed as a child again.

The correct answer is b. This formulated main idea is a general sentence that expresses the most important point the author wants you to know about single parents and child care, that it can present several difficulties. Since it was necessary to write a sentence that gives a general inference based on the details in the paragraph, Formula 3 was applied. Choices *a, c,* and *d* are not correct because they express difficulties: the cost of child care, the possibility of child-rearing conflicts, and weakened parental authority. Also, choices *a* and *d* are stated in the paragraph, so neither can be the implied main idea.

DIRECTIONS: Read each paragraph carefully. Then determine the implied main idea by asking yourself, "What is the single most important point the author wants me to *infer* about the topic of this paragraph?" (Notice that you are told the topic of each paragraph.) Then select the answer choice that expresses the formulated main idea and write the letter in the space provided.

✓ **Teaching Tip**
The topic is given, but have students identify the clues to the topic that appear in each paragraph.

1. This paragraph comes from a biology textbook.

Fossils Tell a Story

Fossils are at least 10,000 years old. They include such items as pieces of bone and impressions of plants pressed into shale. Fossils also include insects trapped in tree resin (which we know as amber). They give a record of the history of life as recorded by remains from the past, and, over the last two centuries, paleontologists have studied them all over the world and have pieced together the story of past life.

Source: Adapted from Sylvia S. Mader, *Biology*, 8th ed., p. 292. Copyright © 2004 by The McGraw-Hill Companies, Inc. Reprinted by permission of The McGraw-Hill Companies, Inc.

The topic of this paragraph is *fossils.*

c ______ What is the implied main idea of this paragraph?

a. Fossils are at least 10,000 years old.

b. Fossils include such items as pieces of bone, impressions of plants pressed into shale, and insects trapped in tree resin.

c. Fossils give a record of the history of life as recorded by remains from the past, and, over the last two centuries, paleontologists have studied them all over the world and have pieced together the story of past life.

d. Fossils are at least 10,000 years old, and they include insects trapped in tree resin (amber).

✓ **Teaching Tip**
The topic ("Fossils") has been added in place of "They" (Formula 1).

2. This paragraph comes from an information technology textbook.

The World Wide Web, or just the Web, is only a few years old, but is growing at an astounding rate. Tens of thousands of computers are now connected so you can use your computer mouse to point and click your way around the world. On a trip through the Web, you can visit colleges, companies, museums, government departments, and other individuals like yourself. As you move through the Web, you can read data on almost every imaginable topic. You can visit stores to buy things or transfer movies, pictures, games, and other software to your computer, much of it free.

Source: Dennis P. Curtin, Kim Foley, Kunal Sen, and Cathleen Morin, *Information Technology: The Breaking Wave.* Boston: Irwin/McGraw-Hill, 1998. Reprinted by permission of the authors.

The topic of this paragraph is *the World Wide Web.*

a ______ What is the implied main idea of this paragraph?

a. The fast-growing World Wide Web can be used for a wide variety of purposes.

b. The World Wide Web, or just the Web, is only a few years old, but is growing at an astounding rate.

c. You can use it to buy things and to transfer movies, pictures, games, and other software to your computer, much of it free.

d. Tens of thousands of computers allow you to access data on almost every imaginable topic.

✓ **Teaching Tip**
Write a general sentence that sums up the details (Formula 3).

3. This paragraph comes from a communications textbook.

Receiving criticism can be tougher than giving it. When people are faced with criticism, the two most common responses are "fight" and "flight." Fighters react by counterattacking. "It's not my fault," they might protest. Another fighting response is to blame the others: "I'm not the only one who's at fault here." Those who prefer flight often avoid those who have criticized them by steering clear of them or not returning their phone calls. However, neither fighting nor fleeing is a very satisfactory way of dealing with the problem.

Source: Ronald Adler and Jeanne Elmhorst, *Communicating at Work,* 5th ed. Copyright © 1996 by The McGraw-Hill Companies, Inc. Reprinted by permission of The McGraw-Hill Companies, Inc.

The topic of this paragraph is *criticism.*

b What is the implied main idea of this paragraph?

a. Fighters react to criticism by blaming others and avoiding those who have criticized them.

b. When people are faced with criticism, the two most common responses are "fight" and "flight"; however, neither fighting nor fleeing is a very satisfactory way of dealing with the problem.

c. Receiving criticism can be tougher than giving it.

d. No one likes to receive criticism.

✓ **Teaching Tip** Combine the two sentences that each give part of the main idea (Formula 2).

4. This paragraph comes from a computer science textbook.

Modems

Compatibility between the digital signals of computers and the analog signals used by telephones requires special devices for encoding and decoding data. These devices are known as *modems* (from the terms *mod*ulation and *dem*odulation). When microcomputers exchange data by modems, the sending modem modulates digital data into analog form for transmission over standard telephone lines. The modem at the receiving end demodulates the analog signals back into digital form for input to the receiving computer.

Source: Timothy N. Trainor and Diane Krasnewich, *Computers!,* 5th ed. Copyright © 1996 by The McGraw-Hill Companies, Inc. Reprinted by permission of The McGraw-Hill Companies, Inc.

The topic of this paragraph is *modems.*

a What is the implied main idea of this paragraph?

a. Compatibility between the digital signals of computers and the analog signals used by telephones requires modems, special devices for encoding and decoding data.

b. When two computers exchange data, there must be a modem to modulate digital data.

c. The modem at the receiving end demodulates the signals and sends them to the receiving computer.

d. All computers use modems.

✓ **Teaching Tip** Insert topic in first sentence (Formula 1) *or* combine the first two sentences (Formula 2).

5. This paragraph comes from a human development textbook.

Culture and Children's Prosocial Behavior

Why are children in some cultures more prosocial than others? It may be because they experience more love and less rejection. For example, among the Papago Indians in Arizona, parents are warm, supportive, and nurturing. In contrast, Alores parents in Java are hostile and neglectful. This, among other differences, may account for the cooperative, peaceful personality typical of Papago children, as compared with the hostile, distrustful, and aggressive behavior of Alores children.

Source: Adapted from Diane E. Papalia and Sally Olds, *Human Development,* 6th ed. Copyright © 1995 by The McGraw-Hill Companies, Inc. Reprinted by permission of The McGraw-Hill Companies, Inc.

✓ **Teaching Tip** *Prosocial behavior* refers to voluntary activity intended to benefit another.

The topic of this paragraph is *culture and children's prosocial behavior.*

d What is the implied main idea of this paragraph?

a. Why are children in some cultures more prosocial than others?

b. Papago children are cooperative and have peaceful personalities as compared with the hostile, distrustful, and aggressive behavior of Alores children.

c. There are many differences between Papago children and Alores children.

d. The reason children in some cultures are more prosocial than others may be because they experience more love and less rejection.

✓ **Teaching Tip**

Insert topic in second sentence (Formula 1). Point out that the second sentence answers the important question posed by the authors. Authors expect readers to be able to answer that question after reading the paragraph.

TEST YOUR UNDERSTANDING
FORMULATING IMPLIED MAIN IDEAS, PART TWO

REVIEW: An **implied main idea** is a sentence formulated by the reader that expresses the author's main point about the topic. *Formulated main ideas are always expressed as complete sentences.* As you learned in this chapter, there are three ways to formulate a main idea that has been implied:

- *Add an essential word or phrase to a sentence* in the paragraph that almost states the main idea.
- *Combine two sentences from the paragraph* into a single sentence.
- *Summarize important ideas into one sentence* or *write one sentence that gives a general inference based on the details.*

EXAMPLE: Study the example paragraph below to see how the information you learned in this chapter can be used to formulate the implied main idea of a paragraph. Read the explanation that is given for the correct answer. When you are sure you understand the explanation, complete the five exercises in Part Two.

This excerpt comes from a communications textbook. As you will see, its topic is *the meaning of a word.* To determine the implied main idea, read the paragraph and ask yourself, "What is the single most important point the author wants me to *infer* about the meaning of a word?"

A common problem encountered in our use of language involves the belief that every word has only one meaning. This, of course, is not true. Surprisingly, the two thousand most frequently used words have approximately fourteen thousand meanings. In your vocabulary, you have these and probably countless words with multiple meanings and uses. The word *cat,* for example, can refer to a domestic animal, a type of tractor, a type of fish, a type of boat, a jazz musician, or a whip. In a similar fashion, the word *lap* can represent the distance around a track, a portion of one's anatomy, the drinking method of a cat or dog, or the sound of water washing gently against the side of a boat.

Source: Larry Samovar and Jack Mills, *Oral Communication: Speaking across Cultures,* 10th ed. Boston: McGraw-Hill, 1998, p. 256. Reprinted by permission of Oxford University Press, Inc.

Write the topic: the meaning of a word

Formulate a main idea sentence: A common problem encountered in our use of language involves the belief that every word has only one meaning, but this, of course, is not true.

Explanation: The topic, *the meaning of a word,* appears in the first sentence. In the first sentence, the authors explain a common belief that many people have. In the second sentence, they state that this belief is not true. The main idea of this paragraph can be formulated by using Formula 2 and combining these two sentences into a single sentence.

DIRECTIONS: Read each paragraph carefully and then determine the topic by asking yourself, "Who or what is this paragraph about?" Write the topic in the space provided below the paragraph. Remember that *the topic is always expressed as a word, name, or a phrase below. Do not write a sentence for the topic.* Then determine the paragraph's implied main idea by asking yourself, "What is the single most important point the author wants me to *infer* about the topic of this paragraph?" Then write a main idea sentence by using one of the three formulas you learned in this chapter. Write your formulated main idea sentence in the spaces provided. Remember that all of these paragraphs have implied main ideas. In other words, you cannot select a single sentence from the paragraph as your answer for the main idea. Your formulated main idea sentence must:

- be a complete sentence that includes the topic of the paragraph.
- express the author's most important point about the topic.
- make complete sense by itself without the reader's having to read the rest of the paragraph.

1. This paragraph comes from a health textbook.

✓ **Teaching Tip**
Clues to the topics are identified for you.

Bias and Hate Crimes

One sad aspect of any society is how some segments of the majority treat certain people in the minority. Nowhere is this more violently pronounced than in bias and hate crimes. These crimes are directed at individuals or groups of people solely because of a racial, religious, ethnic, sexual orientation, or other difference attributed to the victims. Victims are often verbally abused, their property is damaged or destroyed, and too frequently they are physically attacked.

Source: Wayne A. Payne, Dale B. Hahn, and Ellen Mauer, *Understanding Your Health,* 8th ed., p. 624. Copyright © 2005 by The McGraw-Hill Companies, Inc. Reprinted by permission of The McGraw-Hill Companies, Inc.

Write the topic: bias and hate crimes

Formulate a main idea sentence: Bias and hate crimes are directed at individuals and groups of people solely because of a racial, religious, ethnic, sexual orientation, or other difference attributed to the victims. (Formula 1; add topic to sentence 3)

2. This paragraph comes from a communications textbook.

✓ **Teaching Tip**
Students often identify the topic as "constructive criticism." Point out that it is not about constructive (helpful) criticism, but, rather, dealing *constructively* with criticism of any sort (that is, reacting to it in a way so that something good can come from it).

How can you deal constructively with criticism? There are at least two constructive ways. One way is to seek more information. This shows that you are taking the criticism seriously, but, at the same time, you are not accepting blame for the problem. (Example: "You've said that I'm not demonstrating a good attitude. Can you describe exactly what I'm doing?") A second way is to agree with the facts of the criticism if they are accurate ("You're right. I've been late three times this week.") or to agree with the person's perception ("I can understand why it might seem as if I didn't care about finishing this project on time. I did promise you that it would be done by Friday afternoon, and I missed the deadline. I'd be mad too if I were you.").

Source: Ronald Adler and Jeanne Elmhorst, *Communicating at Work,* 5th ed. Copyright © 1996 by The McGraw-Hill Companies, Inc. Reprinted by permission of The McGraw-Hill Companies, Inc.

Write the topic: dealing constructively with criticism

Formulate a main idea sentence: Two constructive ways to deal with criticism are to seek more information and to agree with all the facts if they are accurate. (Formula 1; add information to sentence 2)

✓ **Teaching Tip**
Topic clue: the words *category* and *hurricane* are repeated throughout the paragraph.

3. This paragraph comes from a geography textbook.

A category 1 hurricane has winds of 74–95 mph (miles per hour). Category 2 hurricane winds increase to 96–110 mph. At the category 3 level, the winds reach 111–130 mph. The next higher category hurricanes attain wind speeds of 131–155 mph. Finally, the strongest hurricanes, those in category 5, have wind speeds above 155 mph.

Source: Adapted from Arthur Getis, Judith Getis, and Jerome D. Fellmann, *Introduction to Geography,* 10th ed., p. 104. Copyright © 2006 by The McGraw-Hill Companies, Inc. Reprinted by permission of The McGraw-Hill Companies, Inc.

Write the topic: categories of hurricanes

Formulate a main idea sentence: Based on their wind speeds, hurricanes are placed in one of five categories.

OR

There are five categories of hurricanes.

(Formula 3; general inference based on the details)

4. This paragraph comes from a psychology textbook.

Narcolepsy

Narcolepsy is a rare sleep disorder, occurring in less than one-half of 1 percent of the general population. However, its impact can be quite serious. The narcoleptic often falls unexpectedly into a deep slumber in the middle of work or even conversations with others, especially when upset or stressed. Often the individual experiences loss of muscle tone and shows a lack of body movement, as if she or he has suddenly fallen into dream sleep, but laboratory studies show that narcoleptic sleep is not REM sleep. Narcolepsy is not just intense sleepiness, because it occurs in individuals who get adequate sleep. Narcolepsy often causes serious difficulties with the use of dangerous machines and other job-related activities.

Source: Benjamin B. Lahey, *Psychology: An Introduction,* 8th ed., pp. 424–25. Copyright © 2004 by The McGraw-Hill Companies, Inc. Reprinted by permission of The McGraw-Hill Companies, Inc.

Write the topic: narcolepsy

Formulate a main idea sentence: Narcolepsy is a rare sleep disorder, but its impact can be quite serious. (Formula 2; combine sentences 1 and 2)

✓ **Teaching Tip**
Ask students what a *myth* is and whether myths are true. Most of them know that myths are stories that are handed down and that are not factual. (You may also have to remind students to base their answer on information in the passage rather than their own beliefs.)

5. This paragraph comes from a psychology textbook.

Myths about Gays and Lesbians

It is a commonly believed myth that homosexual persons take on the gender roles of the other sex—that gay men act feminine and lesbian women are masculine. In fact, homosexual persons, like heterosexuals, exhibit a wide range of gender roles. Another myth is that gays and lesbians try to seduce heterosexuals into becoming homosexual. Again, there is no scientific evidence that supports this belief.

Source: Adapted from Benjamin B. Lahey, *Psychology: An Introduction,* 8th ed., pp. 424–25. Copyright © 2004 by The McGraw-Hill Companies, Inc. Reprinted by permission of The McGraw-Hill Companies, Inc.

Write the topic: myths about gays and lesbians

Formulate a main idea sentence: There are two commonly believed myths about gays and lesbians. (Formula 3; general inference based on the details. The details consist of the two myths described in the paragraph.)

SELECTION **5-1**
Art Appreciation

TWO ARTISTIC TRIBUTES: THE VIETNAM MEMORIAL AND THE AIDS QUILT

From *Living with Art*
By Rita Gilbert

This selection from an art appreciation textbook explains why the Vietnam Memorial and the AIDS Quilt, despite their obvious differences, are two works of art that share a great deal in common. The Vietnam Memorial has three million visitors a year and is ranked number 10 on the American Institute of Architects' "List of America's Favorite Architecture." The AIDS Quilt was first displayed in Washington, D.C., in 1987 and then displayed there again in 1992. Because of its ever-increasing size, the last full display of the quilt was in Washington, D.C., in 1996. Since then, sections of it continue to be lent to schools, libraries, and museums throughout the world to raise public awareness of AIDS and its impact on millions of lives.

1 There are two particular works of art that have much in common. Both commemorate death on a hideously large scale. Both are memorials to *unexpected* death—not the anticipated rest after a long life, but death coming prematurely, striking mostly the young. And both are meant to personalize each death among the many, to celebrate the individual life that was amid a mass tragedy.

2 The Vietnam Memorial in Washington, D.C., is the most-visited spot in the nation's capital. Completed in 1982, the memorial was designed by Maya Ying Lin, who was just twenty-two years old when her entry was selected from more than 1,400 submitted for this government commission.

3 When it was first unveiled to the public, its design was highly controversial. It is, after all, nothing more than two long walls of polished black granite, set into the earth so as to form a V. Many viewers felt "the Wall," as it has come to be called, flouted tradition, that it was not sufficiently respectful of those who fought the bloody Vietnam War. Many thought a statue of a heroic soldier marching off to battle would be more appropriate.

4 But public opinion changes. In time the American public came to accept this memorial—with its 58,000 names carved into the stark granite walls—as the most fitting tribute to those who died. Visitors who had no connection with the war, even young people who cannot remember the war, stand quietly before the roster of names—names on a mass tombstone. Many come to find a particular name, the name of a dead relative chiseled forever into the rock and not to be forgotten. They leave flowers and poems, teddy bears and ribbons, photographs and letters, reminders of the past. Mostly the relatives touch the Wall, running fingers over the carved letters as though to touch once again the life that is gone.

Annotation Practice Exercises

Directions: For each exercise below, write the topic of the paragraph on the lines beside the paragraph. Then formulate a main idea sentence for the paragraph and write it on the lines provided. (Remember that you cannot use any sentence exactly as it appears in the paragraph: the annotation exercise paragraphs do not have stated main ideas.)

Practice Exercise

Topic of paragraph 3:

the design of "the Wall"

Formulate the *implied main idea* of this paragraph and write your sentence here:

When the Wall was first unveiled to the public, its design was highly controversial.

OR

When it was first unveiled to the public, the Wall's design was highly controversial.

(Formula 1; add topic to sentence 1.)

Maya Ying Lin, Vietnam Memorial, Washington, D.C., 1982. Black granite, length 492′.

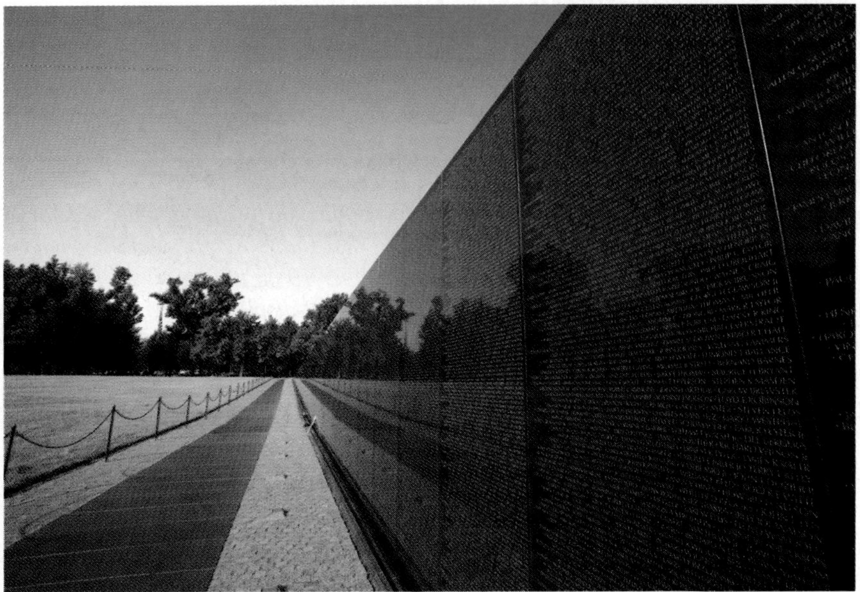

5 The Vietnam War is long over; no more names will be added to the Wall. But another wave of unexpected death has swept the nation and the world, also striking primarily the young, and it will not pass soon. In the United States, San Francisco has been especially hard-hit by the epidemic, and it was there that the Names Project began. The purpose of the Names Project is simple: to memorialize as *individuals* those who have died from AIDS, to remember that each was a unique human being, though all are bound together by a common death. No better means could have been chosen than the AIDS Quilt.

6 The AIDS Quilt consists of hand-sewn panels. Each commemorates one person who has died from AIDS. Some of the 3 by 6 feet panels have a name and a photograph, others just initials or forms symbolizing that person's interests, abilities, and achievements. Each panel tells a story, a story ended too soon, therefore all the more precious in the telling.

7 The choice of a quilt format is especially meaningful. Historically, quilts have often told lifetime stories, incorporating bits of fabric from important life events. Quilts make us think of warmth and protection and nurturing. And quilting has traditionally been a community activity, so it is natural that a community should form among those grieving death from common illness.

8 Unlike the Vietnam Memorial, the AIDS Quilt cannot possibly remember all who have died. Only those whose friends or families chose to be involved in the Names Project are represented. Tragically, that number has already created work of horrific scope. The illustration here shows the quilt spread out in Washington, D.C., in October of 1996. By that time the quilt had grown to more than 37,000 panels and spread out on the Mall for nearly a mile from the U.S. Capitol to the Washington Monument.

Practice Exercise

Topic of paragraph 6:

the AIDS Quilt

Formulate the *implied main idea* of this paragraph and write your sentence here:

The AIDS Quilt consists of hand-sewn panels, and each commemorates one person who has died from AIDS.

(Formula 2; combine sentences 1 and 2.)

The Names Project, Atlanta. *AIDS Memorial Quilt.* Displayed on the Mall; Washington, D.C., October 1996.

9 As a work of art, the AIDS Quilt presents many contradictions. Few of its panels, individually, might be considered great art, yet the whole makes a powerful artistic statement. In its entirety, as we watch it grow, the work is incomparably sad, yet each panel is the celebration of a single life. Inevitably, the quilt is a work in progress; it cannot be finished until the plague has been stopped. It is art for the dead—trying to make life bearable for the living.

✓ **Teaching Tip**

These were the statistics about the quilt as of 2007. Of course, they continue to increase yearly.

- Number of visitors to view the quilt: 15,200,000
- Number of panels in the quilt: 47,000
- Number of names on the quilt: more than 90,000
- Miles of fabric: 52.25
- Total weight: More than 54 tons
- Countries contributing to the quilt: More than 43
- The Quilt is warehoused in Atlanta, Georgia, when not on display.

Source: Adapted from Rita Gilbert, *Living with Art,* 5th ed., pp. 79–81. Copyright © 1998 by The McGraw-Hill Companies, Inc. Reprinted by permission of The McGraw-Hill Companies, Inc.

SELECTION 5-1
Art Appreciation
(continued)

Comprehension and Vocabulary Quiz

This quiz has four parts. Your instructor may assign some or all of them.

Comprehension

Directions: Items 1–5 test your comprehension (understanding) of the material in this selection. These questions are much like those that a content-area instructor (such as a human development professor) would expect you to know after reading and studying this selection. For each comprehension question below, use information from the selection to determine the correct answer. Refer to the selection as you answer the questions. Write your answers in the spaces provided.

¶9 b **1.** The most significant difference between the Vietnam Memorial and the AIDS Quilt is that:

a. one is stationary and the other can be moved.
b. one memorial is complete and the other is not.
c. one is black and the other is in color.
d. an individual person designed one memorial and thousands of people designed the other.

¶s 2, 4 c **2.** The Vietnam Memorial was:

a. completed in 1982 and has 1,400 names carved into its walls.
b. originally a statue of a heroic soldier marching off to battle.
c. completed in 1982 and has 58,000 names carved on its granite walls.
d. constructed in 1996 and includes 37,000 panels.

¶6 a **3.** Each panel of the AIDS Quilt:

a. represents one person who has died from AIDS.
b. contains a name and a photograph.
c. gives the initials and achievements of a person who died from AIDS.
d. can be considered great art.

¶7 c **4.** The choice of a quilt format for the Names Project is especially meaningful because quilts:

a. remind us of death.
b. are like the stark granite walls of a memorial.
c. make us think of warmth, protection, and nurturing.
d. are powerful artistic statements that make life bearable.

¶1 a **5.** Both the AIDS Quilt and the Vietnam Memorial are meant to:

a. memorialize the lives of individuals.
b. record the names of everyone who died in the Vietnam War or who died from AIDS.
c. grow as the names of those who have died are added.
d. memorialize a tragic war and a terrible disease.

Vocabulary in Context

Directions: Items 6–10 test your ability to determine the meaning of the word by using context clues. *Context clues* are words in a sentence that allow the reader to deduce (reason out) the meaning of an unfamiliar word in that sentence. Context clues also enable the reader to determine which meaning the author intends when a word has more than one meaning. For each vocabulary item below, a sentence from the selection containing an important word (*italicized, like this*) is quoted first. Next, there is an additional sentence using the word in the same sense and providing another context clue. Use the context clues from *both* sentences to deduce the meaning of the italicized word. *Be sure the answer you choose makes sense in both sentences.* If you need to use a dictionary to confirm your answer choice, remember that the meaning you select must still fit the context of *both* sentences. Write your answers in the spaces provided.

Pronunciation Key:
ă **pat** ā **pay** **âr care** ä **father** ĕ **pet** ē **be** ĭ **pit**
ī **tie** **îr pier** ŏ **pot** ō **toe** ô **paw** oi **noise** ou **out** ŏŏ **took**
ōō **boot** ŭ **cut** yōō ab**use** **ûr urge** th **thin** *th* **this** hw **which**
zh vision ə **about** *Stress mark:* ′

¶1 ___a___ **6.** Both works of art *commemorate* death on a hideously large scale.

On Veterans Day, our city holds a ceremony to *commemorate* the sacrifices of those in the armed services who gave their lives for their country.

commemorate (kə mĕm′ ə rāt) means:

a. to serve as a remembrance of
b. to celebrate the victory of
c. to comment negatively upon
d. to announce prematurely

¶3 ___b___ **7.** Many viewers felt "the Wall," as it has come to be called, *flouted* tradition, that it was not sufficiently respectful of those who fought the bloody Vietnam War.

The man refused to put out his cigarette and was asked to leave because he *flouted* the restaurant's no-smoking rule.

flouted (flou′ təd) means:

a. established; created
b. showed disrespect; had contempt for
c. improved upon; made better
d. followed; abided by

✓ **Teaching Tip**
Many students confuse *flout* with *flaunt* (to show off or display in a showy, ostentatious manner). Point out the difference.

¶4 c **8.** In time the American public came to accept this memorial—with its 58,000 names carved into the *stark* granite walls—as the most fitting tribute to those who had died.

✓ **Teaching Tip**
Granite is a very common, hard, coarse-grained rock that is often used for monuments and buildings. It is usually light-colored, so in this respect the Vietnam Memorial is unusual.

The prison cell was *stark* and uncomfortable; the only furniture in it was a metal cot.

stark (stärk) means:

a. elaborate; ornate
b. colorful; cheerful
c. bare; plain
d. lonely

¶4 a **9.** In time the American public came to accept this memorial—with its 58,000 names carved into the stark granite walls—as the most *fitting* tribute to those who had died.

It is only *fitting* that those who work the hardest receive the greatest rewards.

fitting (fĭt′ ĭng) means:

a. proper; right
b. adjusted correctly
c. logical; reasonable
d. pertaining to luck

¶9 c **10.** In its entirety, as we watch it grow, the work is *incomparably* sad, yet each panel of the AIDS Quilt is the celebration of a single life.

✓ **Teaching Tip**
Students often mispronounce *incomparably* (and *incomparable*) by accenting the wrong syllable. (They have the same problem with *pref′erable* and *pref′erably.*)

Monet produced *incomparably* beautiful impressionistic paintings; no other painter can equal his handling of light.

incomparably (ĭn kŏm′ pər ə blē) means:

a. confusingly
b. incompletely
c. immeasurably
d. slightly

Word Structure

Directions: Items 11–15 test your ability to use word-structure clues to help determine a word's meaning. *Word-structure clues* consist of roots, prefixes, and suffixes. In these exercises, you will learn the meaning of a word part (a root) and use it to determine the meaning of several other words that have the same word part. If you need to use a dictionary to confirm your answer choice, do so. Write your answers in the spaces provided.

In this selection, you encountered the words **commemorate, memorial,** and **memorialize.** These words all contain the Latin root ***mem,*** meaning "memory." In paragraph 1 *commemorate* means "to honor the memory (of someone or something)." In paragraph 4, *memorial* refers to "a monument that honors the memory of a person or an event." *Memorialize,* in paragraph 5, means "to provide a memorial for" or "to commemorate." Use the meaning of ***mem*** and the list of prefixes on pages 68–69 to help you determine the meaning of each of the following words that contain this same root. Write your answers in the spaces provided.

c **11.** Which of these would be a likely **remembrance** of a date you had with someone special?

a. a shoe

b. an embrace

c. a concert ticket stub

d. a book

a **12.** To **memorize** a poem means:

a. to commit it to memory.

b. to write it several times.

c. to say it aloud.

d. to interpret it correctly.

c **13.** If your boss sends you a **memorandum,** he or she sends you:

a. a certificate of achievement.

b. a financial report.

c. a written reminder.

d. computer software.

d **14.** If a former U.S. president writes his **memoir,** he writes:

a. a set of recommendations for the current president.

b. the history of the country.

c. an article on his political views.

d. recollections of his personal experiences.

d **15.** If your trip to Paris was **memorable,** it was:

a. taken within the last five years; recent.

b. highly unpleasant in some significant way.

c. won as a prize in a contest.

d. worth being remembered; remarkable.

✓ **Teaching Tip**
Let students know that not all of the skills included in this Reading Skills Application section have been introduced yet. This section serves as a valuable preview of these skills, however. Students typically get several of the items correct, and they find this encouraging.

Reading Skills Application

Directions: Items 16–20 test your ability to *apply* certain reading skills to the information in this selection. These types of questions provide valuable practice for all students, especially those who must take standardized reading tests and state-mandated basic skills tests. You may not have studied all of the skills at this point, so these items will serve as a helpful preview. The comprehension and critical reading skills in this section are presented in Chapters 3 through 9 of *New Worlds;* vocabulary and figurative language skills are presented in Chapter 2. As you work through *New Worlds,* you will practice and develop these skills. Write your answers in the spaces provided.

supporting details (Chapter 6)

a **16.** According to information in the selection, "the Wall":

a. will have no more names added to it.

b. is a memorial to a single life.

c. includes both names and photographs.

d. cannot be touched by visitors.

authors' writing patterns (Chapter 7) — d

17. The organization of the overall selection is a:

a. list.

b. cause-effect.

c. sequence.

d. comparison-contrast.

distinguishing opinion from fact (Chapter 9) — d

18. Which of the following represents an opinion rather than a fact?

a. The AIDS Quilt consists of hand-sewn panels.

b. Each panel commemorates one person who has died from AIDS.

c. Some of the 3 by 6 feet panels have a name and a photograph, others just initials or forms symbolizing that person's interests, abilities, and achievements.

d. Each panel tells a story, a story of a life ended too soon, and therefore all the more precious in the telling.

vocabulary in context (Chapter 2) — b

19. What is the meaning of *bound* as it is used in paragraph 5?

a. tied with a rope

b. linked

c. stitched together

d. forced

¶7 — a

20. Which of the following is the main idea of paragraph 7?

a. The choice of a quilt format is especially meaningful.

b. Historically, quilts have often told lifetime stories, incorporating bits of fabric from lifetime events.

c. Quilts make us think of warmth and protection and nurturing.

d. And quilting has traditionally been a community activity, so it is natural that a community should form among those grieving death from common illness.

✓ **Teaching Tip**
Choices *b, c,* and *d* are all details that explain or tell more about the stated main idea; choice *a* is the main idea of the paragraph.

✓ **Teaching Tip**
We suggest that rather than include this section as part of the quiz grade, you use it to give students practice with the skills they have studied and as a helpful preview of upcoming skills. It makes an excellent collaborative activity. All students will find this practice helpful, but especially those who must take course exit tests, standardized reading tests, or state-mandated basic skills tests.

SELECTION **5-1**
Art Appreciation
(continued)

Writing and Collaborating to Enhance Your Understanding

Option for collaboration: Your instructor may direct you to work with other students or, in other words, to work *collaboratively.* In that case, you should form groups of three or four students as directed by your instructor and work together to complete the exercises. After your group discusses each item and agrees on the answer, have a group member record it. Every member of your group should be able to explain all of your group's answers.

Collaboration Option

1. **Reacting to What You Have Read:** Have you or someone you know ever visited the Vietnam Memorial or seen panels of the AIDS Quilt displayed? Perhaps you have seen one or both on TV. Describe your reactions or those of the person you know who has seen either of these memorials. If you have not seen either in person, what is your reaction to the photos of them in the selection?

(Answers will vary.)
____
____

2. **Comprehending the Selection Further:** Of the two memorials you read about, which of them produces a stronger emotional response in you? Explain why.

(Answers will vary.)

3. **Overall Main Idea of the Selection:** In one sentence, tell what the author wants readers to understand about the Vietnam Memorial and the AIDS Quilt. (Be sure to include the words "Vietnam Memorial" and "the AIDS Quilt" in your overall main idea sentence.)

The *Vietnam Memorial* and *the AIDS Quilt* are works of art that have much in common, yet there is one significant difference.

OR

The *Vietnam Memorial* and *the AIDS Quilt* are both large-scale works of art that commemorate individual lives that ended too soon, but only *the AIDS Quilt* will continue to have names added to it.

Internet Resources

Read More about This Topic on the World Wide Web

Directions: For further information about the topic of the selection, visit these websites:

http://the virtualwall.org
This site is sponsored by the Vietnam Veterans Memorial Fund and includes a "Virtual Wall" honoring those who lost their lives in the Vietnam War.

http://the wall-usa.com
This website is dedicated to those who died in the Vietnam War and is maintained by Vietnam Veterans.

www.aidsquilt.org
This website is sponsored by The Names Project Foundation, caretakers of the AIDS Memorial Quilt. Visitors to this site can view the quilt and search for names of those memorialized on the quilt.

You can also use your favorite search engine such as Google, Yahoo!, or AltaVista (www.google.com, www.yahoo.com, www.altavista.com) to discover more about this topic. To locate additional information, type in combinations of keywords such as:

Vietnam Memorial

or

AIDS Quilt

or

Names Project

Keep in mind that whenever you go to *any* website, it is a good idea to evaluate the website and the information it contains. Ask yourself questions such as:

"Who sponsors this website?"

"Is the information contained in this website up-to-date?"

"What type of information is presented?"

"Is the information objective and complete?"

"How easy is it to use the features of this website?"

SELECTION 5-2 Biology

AVIAN FLU: A COMING PANDEMIC

From *Biology*
By Sylvia Mader

"Avian" means "pertaining to birds." "Flu" is short for "influenza," an acute contagious viral infection that causes inflammation of the respiratory tract, fever, chills, muscular pain, weakness, exhaustion, and even collapse. "Avian flu" is another name for "bird flu."

According to the National Library of Medicine, "Birds, just like people, get the flu. Bird flu viruses infect birds, including chickens, other poultry, and wild birds such as ducks. Most bird flu viruses can only infect other birds. However, bird flu can pose health risks to people. Human infection is still relatively rare, but the virus that causes the infection in birds might change, or mutate, to more easily infect humans. This could lead to a pandemic, or a worldwide outbreak of the illness. During an outbreak of bird flu, people who have contact with infected birds can become sick. It may also be possible to catch bird flu by eating poultry that is not well cooked or through contact with a person who has the virus. Bird flu can make people very sick and even cause death. There is currently no vaccine" (www.nlm.nih.gov/medlineplus/birdflu.html, accessed 27 April 2008).

The Centers for Disease Control and Prevention (CDC) reports that humans have little preexisting natural immunity to H5N1 virus infection (avian flu): "If H5N1 viruses gain the ability for efficient and sustained transmission among humans, an influenza pandemic could result, with potentially high rates of illness and death worldwide." The CDC reports further that although two antiviral medications commonly used for influenza have proved unsuccessful against the virus, there are two other drugs that should still be effective against currently circulating strains of H5N1 viruses. At present, the United States bans importing birds and bird products from H5N1-affected countries (www.cdc.gov/flu/avian, accessed 27 April 2008).

The World Health Organization (WHO) says that the world may be on the brink of an influenza pandemic, and that all countries will have inadequate medical supplies to deal with it when it begins and for many months after it starts. Many developing countries will have no access to medicines throughout a pandemic. Because of air travel, the WHO estimates the virus could hit every continent within three months and that millions of people would become sick and die (www.who.int/csr/disease/influenza/pandemic10things/en, accessed 27 April 2008). The following selection explains more about this global threat.

1 Imagine waking up one morning wlth a sore throat, slight fever, and achy muscles. After going to the doctor, you are diagnosed with a case of the flu. As you sit at home resting, you notice the latest news about the avian bird flu and you begin to worry, thinking it might be avian flu.

Jumping the Species Barrier

2 Birds can become infected by coming into contact with the saliva, feces, or mucus of another infected bird. Many forms of avian flu will cause mild or no symptoms in infected birds. However, some strains are producing a highly contagious and rapidly fatal disease.

3 Since 1997, a deadly strain of avian flu (H5N1) has been showing up in Asia. Vietnam, Cambodia, China, and several other Asian countries have experienced serious outbreaks of avian flu among their domesticated poultry (chicken, geese, and ducks).

4 The ability of a virus to "jump the species" and infect humans is what concerns the scientific community. In Hong Kong, in 1997, the virus was discovered in several people who had

Annotation Practice Exercises

Directions: For each exercise below, write the topic of the paragraph on the lines beside the paragraph. Then formulate a main idea sentence for the paragraph and write it on the lines provided. (Remember that you cannot use any sentence exactly as it appears in the paragraph: the annotation exercise paragraphs do not have stated main ideas.)

Practice Exercise

Topic of paragraph 2:

avian flu

___

___

been in close contact with infected birds. Six of the infected people died. In early February 2006, the confirmed death toll as a result of avian flu was 103 people. The lethal strain of bird flu has killed approximately one-third of the people that have been infected.

Possibility of a Pandemic

5 There is a growing concern among the scientific community that the bird flu could merge with a human flu virus to create a new hybrid virus. This new virus could be highly infectious, fatal, and easily transmitted from person to person. Rapid travel between countries would enable people to spread the flu virus across the globe at an unprecedented rate, triggering a global pandemic (a disease that occurs worldwlde).

6 There are two possibilities for the avian flu virus and human flu virus to merge and become a hybrid virus. The first possibility is when a human is infected with the human flu and then comes into contact with the avian flu. The two viruses could meet in the person's body and swap genes with each other. If the new hybrid virus has the avian flu gene for lethality and the human flu genes that allow it to be passed from person to person, a pandemic could be the result. The second possibility is if the two viruses infect a different host species and swap their genes in that host species. Pigs are seen as the potential alternate host species because they are susceptible to both the avian and human flu virus. If a new hybrid virus forms in the pigs, it could easily be passed back to human farmers who come in contact with infected pigs.

7 In January 2005, the first case of human-to-human transmission of avian flu was recorded. The woman

✓ Teaching Tip

H5N1, avian flu, should not be confused with H1N1, swine flu. H1N1 cases first appeared in the U.S. in spring 2009. The virus usually found in pigs, but occasionally mutates and becomes infectious in humans. Because humans have little or no immunity to it, it can spread quickly. Most people recover without medical care, but there have been deaths from it. H1N1 cannot be contracted from eating pork.

H1N1 preventive measures include:

- Covering your nose and mouth with a tissue when you cough or sneeze, and throwing the tissue away after using it.
- Washing your hands often with soap and water, especially after you cough or sneeze. You may also use alcohol-based hand cleaners.
- Avoiding touching your eyes, nose, or mouth, to avoid getting infected by germs.
- Avoiding close contact with sick people.

If you get flu or any sort, consider staying home from work or school so that you do not infect others or worsen your condition.

Source: https://www.google.com/health/ref/H1N1+(swine)+influenza; accessed 09/12/2009

Formulate the *implied main idea* of paragraph 2 and write your sentence here:

Many forms of avian flu will cause mild or no symptoms in infected birds; however, some strains are producing a highly contagious and rapidly fatal disease. (Formula 2: Combine the second and third sentences.)

Practice Exercise

Topic of paragraph 3:

avian flu *or* avian flu in Asia

Formulate the *implied main idea* of this paragraph and write your sentence here:

Since 1997 a deadly strain of avian flu (H5N1) has been showing up in Asia among domesticated poultry. (Formula 1: Add the important information "among domesticated poultry" to the first sentence.)

Practice Exercise

Topic of paragraph 7:

avian flu virus *or* avian flu virus and a hybrid virus

Formulate the *implied main idea* of this paragraph and write your sentence here:

Every time the avian flu virus jumps from a bird to a person, the risk of a hybrid virus increases. (Formula 1: insert the words "avian flu virus" in place of "it" in the first sentence.)

contracted the virus from her sick daughter, and both women died from the avian flu. Every time it jumps from a bird to a person, the risk of a hybrid virus increases.

Actions Taken

8 Currently, there are no known vaccinations that work against the bird flu. Several drugs are being trialed and have produced mixed results. Scientists are racing to find a potential vaccination. However, they face the challenge of dealing with a virus that is constantly evolving.

9 In countries that have been affected by the avian flu, governments have begun programs to remove the infected and potentially infected birds. In Asia, millions of domesticated birds have been killed in an attempt to control the spread of the virus. It is hoped that eliminating the birds will contain the virus and decrease the potential of spreading. The containment efforts by the infected Asian countries have been somewhat successful at keeping the virus from spreading among domesticated livestock.

10 Preventing the spread of the avian flu virus among wild waterfowl as they migrate across the globe is a major problem. As of February 2006, confirmations of the deadly strain of avian flu in waterfowl have been reported in Asia, Africa, the Middle East, and Europe. It is only a matter of time before it reaches the United States and Central and South America.

Practice Exercise

Topic of paragraph 8:

vaccinations against bird flu

Formulate the *implied main idea* of this paragraph and write your sentence here:

Currently, there are no known vaccinations that work against the bird flu, but scientists are racing to find a potential vaccination against this constantly evolving virus. (Formula 3: Combine information from several sentences.) Also acceptable: Scientists are racing to find a potential vaccination against bird flu; however, they face the challenge of dealing with a virus that is constantly evolving. (Formula 3: Combine information from several sentences.)

Practice Exercise

Topic of paragraph 10:

wild waterfowl and the spread of the avian flu virus

Formulate the *implied main idea* of this paragraph and write your sentence here:

Preventing the spread of the avian flu virus among wild waterfowl as they migrate across the globe is a major problem; therefore, it is only a matter of time before the virus reaches the United States and Central and South America. (Formula 2: Combine two sentences. Use connectors such as *therefore, consequently,* or *for this reason* to show the relationship of the two important ideas.)

✓ **Teaching Tip**

¶3: In the first sentence of the paragraph, ask students to find the context clue for *domesticated poultry,* the examples given in parentheses. Based on the examples have students reason out that *poultry* refers to domesticated fowls raised for meat or eggs.

- Have students locate Vietnam, Cambodia, and China on the world map in Appendix 3.

✓ **Teaching Tip**

¶8: *Trialed* is a term that refers to putting a potential drug through clinical trials to test its safety and effectiveness before it is approved for general use.

✓ **Teaching Tip**

¶10: Have students locate Asia, Africa, the Middle East, Europe, Central America, and South America on the world map in Appendix 3. To get a better sense of the virus's spread and potential spread, they may want to use a highlighter to shade these continents.

- Have students create a timeline of the events in the selection.

Source: Adapted from Sylvia Mader, *Human Biology*, 10th ed., p. 125. Copyright © 2008 by The McGraw-Hill Companies, Inc. Reprinted by permission of The McGraw-Hill Companies, Inc.

SELECTION 5-2
Biology
(continued)

Comprehension and Vocabulary Quiz

This quiz has four parts. Your instructor may assign some or all of them.

Comprehension

Directions: Items 1–5 test your comprehension (understanding) of the material in this selection. These questions are much like those that a content-area instructor (such as a health professor) would expect you to know after reading and studying this selection. For each comprehension question below, use information from the selection to determine the correct answer. Refer to the selection as you answer the questions. Write your answers in the spaces provided.

¶3 __b__ **1.** Since1997, birds infected with avian flu have been showing up in:
- *a.* the United States.
- *b.* Asia.
- *c.* Europe.
- *d.* South and Central America.

¶10 __b__ **2.** Infected migratory waterfowl pose a special problem in the spread of avian flu because:
- *a.* humans often consume them for food and become infected.
- *b.* they migrate across the globe.
- *c.* other animals can eat them for food and become infected.
- *d.* all of the above.

¶8 __d__ **3.** One reason scientists are finding it difficult to develop a vaccine against avian flu is:
- *a.* governments of some countries refuse to participate.
- *b.* there is no way to track where the cases are likely to occur.
- *c.* the avian flu virus has a hybrid nature.
- *d.* the virus keeps changing.

¶6 __a__ **4.** Pigs are a potential host species for a hybrid virus because:
- *a.* they can contract both avian flu virus and the human flu virus.
- *b.* H5N1 is a fatal virus.
- *c.* other animals could eat infected pigs.
- *d.* farmers often come in contact with pigs.

¶7 __d__ **5.** Human-to-human transmission of the avian virus:
- *a.* is predicted not to occur.
- *b.* has not yet occurred.
- *c.* has not yet occurred, but it is only a matter of time until it occurs.
- *d.* has already occurred.

Vocabulary in Context

Directions: Items 6–10 test your ability to determine the meaning of the word by using context clues. *Context clues* are words in a sentence that allow the reader to deduce (reason out) the meaning of an unfamiliar word in that sentence. Context clues also enable the reader to determine which meaning the author intends when a word has more than one meaning. For each vocabulary item below, a sentence from the selection containing an important word (*italicized, like this*) is quoted first. Next, there is an additional sentence using the word in the same sense and providing another context clue. Use the context clues from *both* sentences to deduce the meaning of the italicized word. *Be sure the answer you choose makes sense in both sentences.* If you need to use a dictionary to confirm your answer choice, remember that the meaning you select must still fit the context of *both* sentences. Write your answers in the spaces provided.

Pronunciation Key: ă **pat** ā **pay** âr **care** ä **father** ĕ **pet** ē **be** ĭ **pit**
ī **tie** îr **pier** ŏ **pot** ō **toe** ô **paw** oi **noise** ou **out** ŏŏ **took**
ōō **boot** ŭ **cut** yōō **abuse** ûr **urge** th **thin** *th* **this** hw **which**
zh **vision** ə **about** *Stress mark:* ′

¶4 c **6.** The ability of a virus to "jump the *species*" and infect humans is what concerns the scientific community.

Zoologists believe they may have discovered a new *species* of lizards that is similar to one that disappeared a few years ago.

species (spē′ shēz) means:

a. a group of organisms that has become extinct

b. a high barrier or obstruction

c. a group of organisms that resemble each other and are capable of breeding with each other

d. a group of organisms capable of moving from one group to another

¶4 d **7.** The *lethal* strain of bird flu has killed approximately one-third of the people that have been infected.

Because many household cleaning products contain *lethal* chemicals, parents should keep them away from young children.

lethal (lē′ thəl) means:

a. unusual

b. colorful

c. tempting

d. deadly

¶4 b **8.** The lethal *strain* of bird flu has killed approximately one-third of the people that have been infected

The scientists announced that they had developed a superior *strain* of corn that resists insects and disease.

strain (strān) means:

a. a physical injury resulting from excessive tension, effort, or use

b. organisms of the same species that have distinctive characteristics but are not considered a separate variety

c. extreme effort or work

d. the act of pulling or stretching tight

¶5 a **9.** Rapid travel between countries would enable people to spread the flu virus across the globe at an *unprecedented* rate, triggering a global pandemic (a disease that occurs worldwide).

The hospital was delighted with the *unprecedented* donation; it has never before received such a large donation.

unprecedented (ŭn prĕs′ ĭ dĕn tĭd) means:

a. having no earlier equivalent; unmatched

b. unacceptable; undesirable

c. gradually increasing

d. not capable of being understood; confusing

¶9 a **10.** It is hoped that eliminating the birds will *contain* the virus and decrease the potential of spreading.

In order to *contain* the measles outbreak, the elementary school canceled classes for a week.

contain (kən tān′) means:

a. to halt the spread or development of

b. to enclose within a larger object

c. to increase the scope of

d. to monitor by observing closely

(Point out the clue "control" in the preceding sentence in the paragraph.)

Word Structure

Directions: Items 11–15 below test your ability to use word-structure clues to help determine a word's meaning. *Word-structure clues* consist of roots, prefixes, and suffixes. In these exercises, you will learn the meaning of a word part (a root) and use it to determine the meaning of several other words that have the same word part. If you need to use a dictionary to confirm your answer choice, do so. Write your answers in the spaces provided.

In paragraph 8 of the selection, you encountered the word ***evolving.*** This word contains the Latin root ***volvere,*** which means "to roll, turn, twist." The word *evolving* literally means "unrolling." It is used to describe something that is changing or developing over time. Use the meaning of the root ***volvere*** and the list of prefixes on pages 68–69 to help you determine the meaning of each of the following words that contain the same root. Write your answers in the spaces provided.

b **11.** The Earth **revolves** around the sun. In other words, the Earth:

a. turns on its axis.

b. rolls around the sun.

c. moves uncontrollably.

d. rolls at an increasingly fast rate.

c 12. If the role of president **devolves** to the vice president:

a. those two people argue over who will be president.

b. those two people share the power equally.

c. the duty or responsibility shifts to the vice president.

d. the president refuses to give the vice president any power.

a 13. If you **involve** yourself in an argument between two of your friends, you:

a. roll yourself up in it as a participant.

b. refuse to take sides.

c. tell them both to apologize to each other.

d. stay away from both of them.

c 14. A **convoluted** rope is:

a. stretched out straight.

b. strong.

c. twisted into a coil.

d. coming apart.

d 15. To **revolt** against a government means to:

a. refuse to vote for it.

b. feel disgusted with it.

c. write negative articles about it.

d. turn against it and rebel.

Reading Skills Application

Directions: Items 16–20 test your ability to *apply* certain reading skills to information in this selection. These types of questions provide valuable practice for all students, especially those who must take standardized reading tests and state-mandated basic skills tests. You may not have studied all of the skills at this point, so these items will serve as a helpful preview. The comprehension and critical reading skills in this section are presented in Chapters 3 through 9 of *New Worlds;* vocabulary and figurative language skills are presented in Chapter 2. As you work through *New Worlds,* you will practice and develop these skills. Write your answers in the spaces provided.

¶5 vocabulary in context (Chapter 2)

b 16. Which of the following is the meaning of *triggering* as it is used in paragraph 5?

a. preventing

b. causing

c. slowing

d. stopping

✓ **Teaching Tips**

Let students know that not all of the skills included in this Reading Skills Application section have been introduced yet. This section serves as a valuable preview of these skills, however. Students typically get several of the items correct, and they find this encouraging.

¶6 author's writing pattern (Chapter 7) ___a___ **17.** Which pattern is used to organize the information in paragraph 6?

a. list
b. sequence
c. definition
d. cause-effect

• We suggest that rather than include this section as part of the quiz grade, you use it to give students practice with the skills they have studied and as a helpful preview of upcoming skills. It makes an excellent collaborative activity. All students will find this practice helpful, especially those who must take course exit tests, standardized reading tests, or state-mandated basic skills tests.

¶6 author's purpose for writing (Chapter 8) ___c___ **18.** The author's primary purpose in writing this selection is to:

a. persuade readers to pressure the government to deal with avian flu.
b. instruct readers how they can avoid getting avian flu.
c. inform readers about avian flu and the threat it poses.
d. convince readers that avian flu is a serious problem in the United States today.

¶6 stated main idea (Chapter 4) ___a___ **19.** Which of the following represents the main idea of paragraph 6?

a. There are two possibilities for the avian flu virus and human flu virus to merge and become a hybrid virus.
b. The two viruses could meet in the person's body and swap genes with each other.
c. The second possibility is if the two viruses infect a different host species and swap their genes in that host species.
d. Pigs are seen as the potential alternate host species because they are susceptible to both the avian and human flu virus.

¶9 distinguishing facts from opinions (Chapter 9) ___d___ **20.** Which of the following represents an opinion rather than a fact?

a. In countries that have been affected by the avian flu, governments have begun programs to remove the infected and potentially infected birds.
b. In Asia, millions of domesticated birds have been killed in an attempt to control the spread of the virus.
c. It is hoped that eliminating the birds will contain the virus and decrease the potential of spreading.
d. The containment efforts by the infected Asian countries have been somewhat successful at keeping the virus from spreading among domesticated livestock.

✓ **Teaching Tip**
#20: Choice d because of "somewhat." Choice b is not an opinion because it could be tested to see if this is the hope.

SELECTION 5-2
Biology
(continued)

Writing and Collaborating to Enhance Your Understanding

Option for collaboration: Your instructor may direct you to work with other students or, in other words, to work *collaboratively.* In that case, you should form groups of three or four students as directed by your instructor and work together to complete the exercises. After your group discusses each item and agrees on the answer, have a group member record it. Every member of your group should be able to explain all of your group's answers.

Collaboration Option

1. **Reacting to What You Have Read:** How much did you know about the avian flu before reading this selection? What steps do you think the government should take to deal with the threat of avian flu in this country?

   (Answers will vary.)

2. **Comprehending the Selection Further:** The author notes several reasons avian flu presents an unusually dangerous, worldwide threat. List at least five reasons this disease is so potentially devastating.

   - The disease can be fatal.
   - It is highly contagious.
   - It has already jumped the species from birds to humans.
   - It could merge with the human flu virus directly or through a host (such as pigs) and cause a pandemic.
   - Rapid travel between countries can cause it to spread across the globe quickly.
   - There are no known vaccines.
   - The virus is constantly evolving, which makes it harder to create a vaccine.
   - Containment efforts (killing infected birds) in infected Asian countries has been only "somewhat" effective.
   - It will be very difficult to prevent the spread because waterfowl migrate across the globe.

3. **Overall Main Idea of the Selection:** In one sentence, tell what the authors want readers to understand about the avian flu. (Be sure to include "avian flu" in your overall main idea sentence.)

Because avian flu, a potentially deadly disease that began in Asia, is difficult to treat and to contain, it will eventually spread to the United States and has the possibility of becoming a pandemic.

Internet Resources

Read More about This Topic on the World Wide Web

Directions: For further information about the topic of the selection, visit these websites:

www.nlm.nih.gov/medlineplus/birdflu.html
This government website is hosted by the National Library of Medicine and the National Institutes of Health. It includes, among many other things, an excellent, easily understandable multimedia tutorial on all aspects of bird flu. The tutorial is available in both English and Spanish.

www.mayoclinic.com/print/disaster-planning/FU00011/METHOD=print
Hosted by the Mayo Foundation for Medical Education and Research, this web page presents ten simple things you can do to stay healthy and minimize the risk of contracting bird flu.

www.cdc.gov/flu/avian
The government's Centers for Disease Control and Prevention website. Key facts, infections in humans, the current situation, as well as information about the virus, its spread, prevention, and the CDC's Influenza Pandemic Operation Plan.

www.who.int/csr/disease/influenza/pandemic10things/en
This World Health Organization (WHO) sponsored web page describes "Ten Things You Need to Know about Pandemic Influenza." When an influenza virus such as bird flu adapts into a strain that is contagious among humans, it has the potential to become pandemic. Influenza pandemics are rare, but they have killed millions of people around the world. They will continue to recur and will affect every country.

You can also use your favorite search engine such as Google, Yahoo!, or AltaVista (www.google.com, www.yahoo.com, www.altavista.com) to discover more about this topic. To locate additional information, type in combinations of keywords such as:

avian flu

or

bird flu

Keep in mind that whenever you go to *any* website, it is a good idea to evaluate the website and the information it contains. Ask yourself questions such as:

"Who sponsors this website?"

"Is the information contained in this website up-to-date?"

"What type of information is presented?"

"Is the information objective and complete?"

"How easy is it to use the features of this website?"

✓ **Teaching Tip**

Help students organize these key events related to avian flu:

1997: 1. Avian flu virus (H5N1) shows up in Asia killing domesticated poultry.

2. Avian virus discovered in several people in close contact with infected birds; six people die.

2005: First recorded (and fatal) cases of human-to-human transmission of avian flu occur.

2006: 1. The number of confirmed deaths from avian flu reaches 103.

2. By this year, there is confirmation of the deadly strain of avian flu in waterfowl in Asia, Africa, the Middle East, and Europe.

SELECTION 5-3 **Psychology**

WHY RELATIONSHIPS DEVELOP AND WHAT MAKES THEM LAST

From *Essentials of Psychology*
By Benjamin Lahey

What attracts people to each other? Are men and women attracted by the same things? What is involved in maintaining relationships? Why do people stay in them? Why do people break them off? In this psychology textbook selection, you will learn the answers to these questions.

Interpersonal Attraction

1 Throughout the complicated process of person perception (the process of forming perceptions of others), a unique impression of each person is formed. But, although person perception is a highly personal process, some *general* factors influence whether one person will be attracted to another. These include proximity, similar and complementary characteristics, competence, physical attractiveness, and mutual liking.

Proximity

2 An important, but not very romantic, cause of attraction is proximity, or geographical closeness. It's difficult to fall in love with someone you hardly ever spend time with. Physical closeness and the resulting interpersonal contact are essential to the development of attraction. You are more friendly with people who live next door to you than with people who live farther away. Why does this happen? Physical proximity increases interactions, and repeated exposure to people tends to increase liking. Perhaps you can remember a song you didn't like at first but learned to like after hearing it played on the radio many times—it's the same with people.

Similar and Complementary Characteristics

3 In terms of interpersonal attraction, do "birds of a feather flock together" or do "opposites attract"? Are you more likely to be attracted to someone as a friend or lover who is similar to you in many ways or quite different from you? The answer is *both,* in different ways.

4 It's enjoyable to have a friend who jogs with you, who pats you on the back for the healthy way you eat, and who shares long, delicious philosophical discussions with you. In general, similarity is highly important in attractiveness. We tend to be most attracted to those people who have similar values, interests, and attitudes.

5 Opposites can also attract, however. Sometimes the attractiveness of persons unlike us is purely erotic. But opposites also attract when the opposite characteristic *complements,* or advantageously "fits" with, one of our own characteristics. A woman might also be attracted to the fellow at the party tonight in part because he has an outgoing personality, whereas she is more reserved. She may feel that she is a good listener who gets

Annotation Practice Exercises

Directions: For each exercise below, write the topic of the paragraph on the lines beside the paragraph. Then formulate a main idea sentence for the paragraph and write it on the lines provided. (Remember that you cannot use a sentence exactly as it appears in the paragraph as your main idea sentence.)

along better with talkative people than with those who are quiet like herself. And she may feel that, when she is with an outgoing person at social gatherings, he makes it easier for her to interact with other couples than a quiet man does. Similarly, a dominant person might prefer a submissive person, and a person who likes to "take care of" others might prefer someone who likes to be taken care of.

6 Opposites can attract when people who are different from each other *like* each other. It's often more flattering and attractive to be liked by someone who holds opposite values and opinions than by someone who holds similar ones. But opposites usually do not attract; instead, opposites usually repel in personal relationships. A person who intensely advocates liberal causes probably would not like a person who vocally supports conservative causes. And a highly religious person probably would not find a disdain for religion attractive in another person.

Practice Exercise

Topic of paragraph 6:

attraction of opposites

Formulate the *implied main idea* of this paragraph and write your sentence here:

Opposites can attract when people who are different from each other *like* each other, but opposites usually do not attract; instead, opposites usually repel in personal relationships. (Formula 2; combine sentences 1 and 3.)

OR

Opposites can attract, but usually they repel in personal relationships.

Competence

7 We tend to be more attracted to competent than to incompetent people. Intelligence, strength, social skill, education, and athletic prowess are generally thought of as attractive qualities. But people who are seen as *too* competent may suffer a loss in attractiveness, perhaps because it makes us uncomfortable to compare ourselves unfavorably with them.

Physical Attractiveness

8 Other things equal, people tend to be more attracted to physically beautiful people. In the absence of other information, we tend to like beautiful people more and think of them as nicer, better adjusted, more sexual, and more intelligent. Not only is physical attractiveness important, but it also seems to be the *most* important factor in early stages of attraction.

9 But don't despair; there is hope for the rest of us! We might all prefer to be dating someone who looks like a movie star. People actually tend to choose dates and mates who closely match themselves in degree of physical attractiveness. What is more, physical beauty is a highly subjective quality. Thus, even if you do not think your next-door neighbor is much to look at, chances are that someone else will come along who thinks he or she is beautiful.

Practice Exercise

Topic of paragraph 9:

choosing dates and mates

Formulate the *implied main idea* of this paragraph and write your sentence here:

Although we might all prefer to date attractive people, we tend to choose dates and mates similar to ourselves in physical attractiveness. (Formula 2; combine sentences 2 and 3.)

10 Perhaps the nicest thing about physical attractiveness and liking, though, is that the relationship goes both ways. Not only is it true that we tend to like people better when we think they are beautiful, but, as we get to like people better, we begin to think they are more beautiful. Thus, to a certain extent, love *is* blind and beauty *is* in the eye of the beholder—and nothing could be nicer.

Mutual Liking

11 Let's end this discussion of factors involved in interpersonal attractiveness on an upbeat note. Liking often leads to liking in return. If Vicky likes Neal, she has made herself more attractive to Neal simply by liking him. Neal, if he is like almost everyone else, will be more attracted to people who like him than to people who do not like him. Liking someone will not turn you into an irresistible beauty, but it will help.

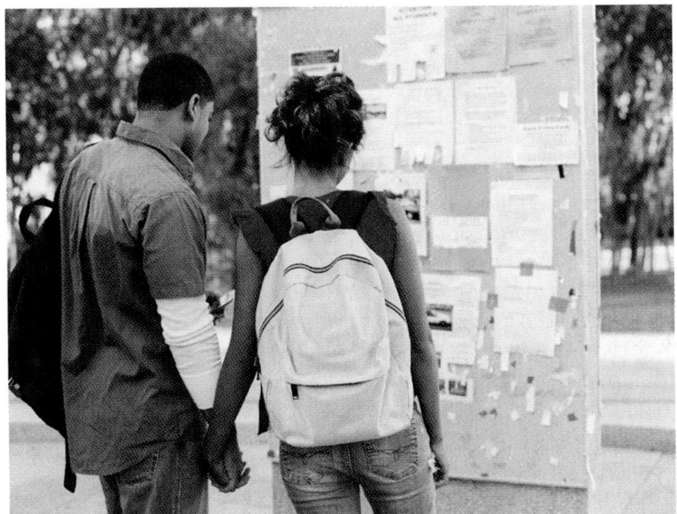

Physical attractiveness seems to be the most important factor in the early stages of attraction between people.

12 One reason this seems to be so is that liking someone actually makes you seem more *physically* attractive, especially if a little lust is thrown in. You have heard people say that a person is more beautiful when in love, and it's true. Your eyes are more attractive when you are in love. Your pupils tend to be more dilated (opened) when you look at someone you find sexually attractive, and others find large pupils more attractive sexually. And your posture and movements are often more attractive and seductive. In subtle ways, you are most physically alluring when you are attracted to another person.

13 Another reason that liking tends to lead to liking is that you are nicer to the people whom you like, and being nicer makes you more attractive to them. A number of studies show, for example, that we tend to like people more when they praise us or when they have done favors for us. Favors and praise feel nice, and we like the giver better for having given them to us. Thus, send him flowers or give her a compact disc—it might just tip the balance of love in your favor. As you might expect, there are limits on the impact of praise and favors. If they are excessive, and especially if the other person thinks you are insincere and have selfish motives for giving them, praise and gifts will not lead to increased liking and may even lessen the liking.

Gender Differences in Interpersonal Attraction

14 It's a commonly held belief in our culture that men are not very interested in romantic love but, rather, enter into long-term relationships for the sex and the domestic help (cooking, cleaning, and mending). Women, in contrast, are viewed in our society as approaching relationships in a more emotional, romantic way. The results of surveys conducted during the 1960s, however, suggested that this popular stereotype not only was incorrect but had reality reversed. Men rated falling in love as being a more important reason for beginning a relationship than did women.

Women saw other qualities of the relationship, such as respect and support, as being more important. In one survey, two-thirds of male unmarried college students said they would not marry unless they felt romantic love for their prospective wife, whereas less than one-fourth of college women felt that romantic love was a prerequisite for marriage.

15 However, more recent surveys suggest that things have changed in the United States concerning gender differences in valuing romantic love. Today, the great majority of both women and men feel that being in love is necessary for marriage. Perhaps, as women have come to feel less dependent on marriage for financial support, they have felt able to enter into marriage only when they are in love with their future partner.

16 This does not mean that men and women fall in love for all the same reasons, however. The evidence is clear that women place more emphasis on their romantic partner's intelligence, character, education, occupational stages, ambition, and income than do men. These qualities are not unimportant to men, but they are comparatively more important to women. In contrast, there are no gender differences in how much sense of humor and a pleasant personality are valued in romantic relationships, but men place greater emphasis on physical attractiveness than do women. Again, it is not that physical attractiveness does not play a role in romantic attraction for women (it does), but women place considerably less emphasis on physical attractiveness than do men. Interestingly, these same results have been found in different generations in the United States and across a number of cultures.

17 It is important to keep in mind, however, that there are large differences among the members of both genders. Perhaps the most striking thing about the cognitive algebra of person perception is that different people often seem to be using different equations! Whether a characteristic is considered positive or negative and how much weight it will carry in person perception differ markedly from individual to individual. Because different people evaluate the same characteristics in different ways, some people are going to love you, some are going to dislike you, and the rest will find you so-so.

Maintaining Relationships

18 We have talked about some of the factors that determine whether you will be attracted to another person. But how about the factors that are involved in maintaining relationships? Assuming that one of the people whom you are attracted to becomes your friend, lover, or spouse, what things determine whether you and your partner will stay in the relationship? So many relationships that begin in joy end in a long cry. Why? Two of the major factors are (1) the difference between what you expect to find in a relationship and what you actually find and (2) the degree to which the relationship is fairly balanced or equitable.

Expectations versus Reality in Relationships

19 When you begin a relationship with someone you do not know very well, part of what you fall in love with is what you *expect* the person to be like. Some expectations may be based on

good evidence. One of his friends has told you that he is an especially nice and fair person, so it's reasonable to expect him to be fair and nice to you. You know that he is in the same profession as you, so you can expect to be able to share your workday experiences easily with him. Other expectations are based on less evidence. He has behaved in a strong, self-assured way so far, so you assume that he will always be this way, even though the biggest challenge you have seen him handle is the waiter's mistake of bringing tomato soup instead of minestrone. You *know* that he is a wonderful lover, even though he has only just kissed you goodnight once. He dressed like an outdoorsman, so you expect him to love backpacking as much as you do. And he is well educated, so you feel sure he will share your love of serious literature.

20 The point is that, even when your expectations are fairly well grounded, some of them will turn out to be incorrect. He will not be exactly as you expect him to be before the relationship begins. This is one primary reason relationships end. If the other person turns out to be significantly different from the person you expected, you may be unwilling to stay in the relationship. This disappointment may not lead directly to an end of the relationship; it may affect the relationship indirectly. Disappointment can lead you to be an unenthusiastic or irritable partner, which can lead to discord and unhappy ending of the relationship.

21 Even when you know a person well before beginning a serious relationship, differences between expectations and reality can be a problem. One common source of unfulfilled expectations is the predictable shift from **passionate love** to greater **companionate love.** When two people fall in love, they often feel intense passions that are a heady and magnificent mixture of romantic, sexual, and other feelings. Even in the most healthy and enduring relationships, however, passionate love gradually becomes companionate love—a less intense but wonderful blend of friendship, intimacy, commitment, and security. Although romantic and sexual emotions often continue to be an important part of companionate love, these feelings almost inevitably become less intense over time.

22 If one or both partners does not expect passionate love to change, or if the change takes place before expected, the reality of passionate love's blending into companionate love can be difficult. On the other hand, if both partners truly want a long-term relationship (many people stay in relationships only as long as the passionate love remains, then leave feeling unfulfilled or hurt), and if the disappointment that often surrounds the lessening of romantic love is handled with compassion on both sides, the transition usually can be managed.

23 Finally, expectations about a love relationship can fail to match its reality because partners change over time. Sometimes, the outdoor person becomes a happy couch potato, and the party animal becomes a health-conscious, jogging vegetarian. If children arrive, and if promotions are received (or not received), these and other changes can alter the reality of the relationship as well. If these changes in one's partner are not welcome, the reality of the changed relationship can be upsetting. Sometimes, however, a change in a partner can make a good relationship even better.

Equity in Relationships

24 What do we know about whether relationships will last? They are more likely to endure when there is equity. In other words, they tend to last when the good things that we give to our partner are about equal to what our partner gives us. These good "things" that partners give to one another are many and varied. They include compliments, back rubs, help with homework, a day off without the kids, flowers, jokes, love making, a willingness to listen about a bad day, interesting meals, kisses, and interesting conversations. They also include things like physical attractiveness (a nice-looking person is enjoyable to look at), honesty, faithfulness, and integrity.

25 If either member of a relationship perceives the relationship to be inequitable, that partner will either take steps to restore equity or will leave the relationship. Interestingly, we become uncomfortable in relationships either when we feel that we receive too little compared with what we give or when we receive too much compared with what we give. In either case, we will be motivated to restore equity by giving more or less or by asking (or in some other way inducing) the other person to give more or less.

Practice Exercise

Topic of paragraph 24:

whether relationships will last–OR–

equity in relationships

Formulate the *implied main idea* of this paragraph and write your sentence here:

Relationships are more likely to last when there is equity. (Formula 1; add topic to sentence 2.)

Source: Adapted from Benjamin B. Lahey, *Essentials of Psychology*, pp. 462–66.

SELECTION 5-3 Psychology *(continued)*

Comprehension and Vocabulary Quiz

This quiz has four parts. Your instructor may assign some or all of them.

Comprehension

Directions: Items 1–5 test your comprehension (understanding) of the material in this selection. These questions are much like those that a content-area instructor (such as a psychology professor) would expect you to know after reading and studying this selection. For each comprehension question below, use information from the selection to determine the correct answer. Refer to the selection as you answer the questions. Write your answers in the spaces provided.

¶s 5, 6 d **1.** In relationships, opposites can attract when:

a. an opposite characteristic of a person complements one of our own characteristics.

b. someone who is different from you *likes* you.

c. the attractiveness of persons unlike us is purely erotic.

d. all of the above

¶2 c **2.** One reason a relationship might develop is:

a. expectations versus reality.

b. competition.

c. proximity.

d. all of the above

¶25 c **3.** If either member of a relationship perceives the relationship to be inequitable,

a. the partner or person who is giving less should give more.

b. the partner who is giving more should give less.

c. that partner will either leave the relationship or take steps to restore equity.

d. both partners should give more.

¶s 23, 21, 20 d **4.** Expectations about a love relationship can fail to match its reality because:

a. partners change over time.

b. there is often a shift from a passionate love to greater companionate love.

c. at least some of our expectations will turn out to be incorrect.

d. all of the above

¶8 a **5.** The most important factor in the early stages of attraction seems to be:

a. physical attractiveness.

b. equity.

c. competence.

d. complementary characteristics.

✓ **Teaching Tip**
Remind students that the OLC contains a 20-item **Reading Selection Quiz** that is similar to the one that appears here. You may assign this OLC activity before, after, or in place of this quiz. Many students benefit from the repetition and time-on-task this activity provides.

Vocabulary in Context

Directions: Items 6–10 test your ability to determine the meaning of the word by using context clues. *Context clues* are words in a sentence that allow the reader to deduce (reason out) the meaning of an unfamiliar word in that sentence. Context clues also enable the reader to determine which meaning the author intends when a word has more than one meaning. For each vocabulary item below, a sentence from the selection containing an important word *(italicized, like this)* is quoted first. Next, there is an additional sentence using the word in the same sense and providing another context clue. Use the context clues from *both* sentences to deduce the meaning of the italicized word. *Be sure the answer you choose makes sense in both sentences.* If you need to use a dictionary to confirm your answer choice, remember that the meaning you select must still fit the context of *both* sentences. Write your answers in the spaces provided.

Pronunciation Key: ă **pat** ā **pay** âr **care** ä **father** ĕ **pet** ē **be** ĭ **pit** ī **tie** îr **pier** ŏ **pot** ō **toe** ô **paw** oi **noise** ou **out** ŏŏ **took** ōō **boot** ŭ **cut** yōō **abuse** ûr **urge** th **thin** *th* **this** hw **which** zh **vision** ə **about** *Stress mark:* ′

¶5 ___a___ **6.** Sometimes the attractiveness of persons unlike us is purely *erotic.*

The movie was deemed unsuitable for children under the age of 18 because of the *erotic* scenes between the lovers.

erotic (ĭ rŏt′ ĭc) means:

a. pertaining to sexual love or desire
b. pertaining to physical violence
c. characterized by vulgar or offensive language
d. dramatically untrue

¶5 ___c___ **7.** A woman might also be attracted to the fellow at the party tonight in part because he has an outgoing personality, whereas she is more *reserved.*

My sister is normally very quiet and *reserved,* so her classmates were surprised on prom night when she jumped up on the stage and started to sing with the band.

reserved (rĭ zûrvd′) means:

a. lacking in feeling
b. showing contempt for others
c. restrained in words and actions
d. vain; arrogant

¶6 ___b___ **8.** But take note that opposites usually do not attract; instead, opposites usually *repel* in personal relationships.

I won't go to horror shows or war movies because violent, gory scenes *repel* me.

repel (rĭ pĕl′) means:

a. inspire to imitation
b. disgust; cause to avoid

c. attract; draw
d. influence positively

¶6 ___b___ **9.** And a highly religious person probably would not find a *disdain* for religion attractive in another person.

Society has *disdain* for those who neglect or abuse children.

disdain (dĭs dān′) means:

a. compassion
b. contempt
c. tolerance
d. lack of understanding

¶7 ___d___ **10.** Intelligence, strength, social skill, education, and athletic *prowess* are generally thought of as attractive qualities.

The physical *prowess* of Olympic athletes far exceeds that of the general population.

prowess (prou′ ĭs) means:

a. awards and medals
b. challenges
c. training
d. extraordinary ability

Word Structure

Directions: Items 11–15 test your ability to use word-structure clues to help determine a word's meaning. *Word-structure clues* consist of roots, prefixes, and suffixes. In these exercises, you will learn the meaning of a word part (a root) and use it to determine the meaning of several other words that have the same word part. If you need to use a dictionary to confirm your answer choice, do so. Write your answers in the spaces provided.

In paragraph 6 of the selection, you encountered the word **repel.** This word contains the Latin root ***pel,*** which means "to drive," "to push," or "to thrust." *Repel* literally means "to drive (away) someone or something." Use the meaning of ***pel*** and the list of prefixes on pages 68–69 to help you determine the meaning of each of the following words that contain this same root. Write your answers in the spaces provided.

___b___ **11.** A **propeller** is a device that:

a. thrusts a vehicle backward.
b. thrusts airplanes and boats forward.
c. brings an airplane or boat to a gradual halt.
d. pushes a vehicle faster and faster.

a 12. If the wind **dispels** the clouds, it:

a. drives them away.

b. causes them to form unusual shapes.

c. makes them look fluffy.

d. gives them a pink tinge.

d 13. If you are **compelled** to seek shelter from a hailstorm, you are:

a. too late to seek shelter.

b. reluctant to seek shelter.

c. considering seeking shelter.

d. forced to seek shelter.

b 14. If a student is **expelled** from school, he or she is:

a. asked to wait outside.

b. driven out or forced to leave.

c. given a serious warning.

d. recognized for excellence.

d 15. If your conscience **impels** you to tell the truth, it:

a. prevents you from being truthful.

b. makes you unable to distinguish the truth.

c. blurs the truth.

d. drives you to tell the truth.

✓ **Teaching Tip**
Let students know that not all of the skills included in this Reading Skills Application section have been introduced yet. This section serves as a valuable preview of these skills, however. Students typically get several of the items correct, and they find this encouraging.

Reading Skills Application

Directions: Items 16–20 test your ability to *apply* certain reading skills to information in this selection. These types of questions provide valuable practice for all students, especially those who must take standardized reading tests and state-mandated basic skills tests. You may not have studied all of the skills at this point, so these items will serve as a helpful preview. The comprehension and critical reading skills in this section are presented in Chapters 3 through 9 of *New Worlds;* vocabulary and figurative language skills are presented in Chapter 2. As you work through *New Worlds,* you will practice and develop these skills. Write your answers in the spaces provided.

distinguishing facts from opinion is (Chapter 9)

d 16. Which of the following statements from the selection represents an opinion rather than a fact?

a. Other things equal, people tend to be more attracted to physically beautiful people.

b. In the absence of other information, we tend to like beautiful people more and think of them as nicer, better adjusted, more sexual, and more intelligent.

c. Not only is it true that we tend to like people better when we think they are beautiful, but, as we get to like people better, we begin to think they are more beautiful.

d. Thus, to a certain extent, love is blind and beauty is in the eye of the beholder—and nothing could be nicer.

✓ **Teaching Tip**
The information in choices *a, b,* and *c* could be confirmed by research, so they do not represent opinions. In choice *d,* "nothing could be nicer" makes it an opinion.

¶9 author's tone (Chapter 8)

c **17.** Which of the following best describes the author's tone in paragraph 9?

a. hostile

b. sentimental

c. reassuring

d. nostalgic

¶14 authors' writing patterns (Chapter 7)

a **18.** The pattern that is used to organize the information in paragraph 14 is:

a. comparison-contrast.

b. problem-solution.

c. a list.

d. a sequence.

author's purpose for writing (Chapter 8)

b **19.** Which of the following best describes the author's primary purpose for writing this selection?

a. to explain why some long-term relationships ultimately fail

b. to explain factors that attract people to each other and that influence whether they stay in a relationship

c. to explain how to maintain a relationship

d. to explain gender differences in attraction and in the maintenance of relationships

¶24 formulated main idea (Chapter 5)

a **20.** Which of the following represents the main idea of paragraph 24?

a. Relationships tend to last when the good things that we give to our partner are about equal to what our partner gives us.

b. These good "things" that partners give to one another are many and varied.

c. They include compliments, back rubs, help with homework, a day off without the kids, flowers, jokes, love making, a willingness to listen about a bad day, interesting meals, kisses, and interesting conversations.

d. They also include things like physical attractiveness (a nice-looking person is enjoyable to look at), honesty, faithfulness, and integrity.

✓ **Teaching Tip**

We suggest that rather than include this section as part of the quiz grade, you use it to give students practice with the skills they have studied and as a helpful preview of upcoming skills. It makes an excellent collaborative activity. All students will find this practice helpful, but especially those who must take course exit tests, standardized reading tests, or state-mandated basic skills tests.

SELECTION 5-3
Psychology
(continued)

Writing and Collaborating to Enhance Your Understanding

Collaboration Option

Option for collaboration: Your instructor may direct you to work with other students or, in other words, to work *collaboratively.* In that case, you should form groups of three or four students as directed by your instructor and work together to complete the exercises. After your group discusses each item and agrees on the answer, have a group member record it. Every member of your group should be able to explain all of your group's answers.

1. **Reacting to What You Have Read:** Think of a past or current best friend, boyfriend, girlfriend, or, if you are married, your spouse. Describe the role each of these factors played or plays in your attraction to that person:

✓ **Teaching Tip**
Have students rank the importance of these five factors and then compare the rankings they have assigned with those of the class as a whole.

proximity (Answers will vary.) ______________________

____

similar and complementary characteristics ______________________

____

competence ______________________

____

physical attractiveness ______________________

____

mutual liking ______________________

____

2. **Comprehending the Selection Further:** Explain why each of these marriage relationships might or might not be long lasting.

- A relationship in which both people are deeply committed to each other

should last longer because there is an equal level of commitment

____

✓ **Teaching Tip**
Ask students to rank these three marriage relationships 1, 2, 3, with 1 being the longest lasting and 3 being the shortest.

- A relationship in which one person cares deeply about the other, but the other does not reciprocate

probably will not last because there is an inequality in caring

____

- A relationship in which neither partner has an especially deep commitment to the other

May or may not last. The level of commitment is equal, but low. It depends on whether both partners are comfortable with the low level.

3. **Overall Main Idea of the Selection:** In one sentence, tell what the author wants readers to understand about interpersonal attraction and maintaining relationships. (Be sure to mention how one person will be attracted to another and how people maintain a relationship when you formulate your overall main idea sentence.)

There are general factors that influence whether one person will be attracted to another, and there are also factors that determine whether people maintain a relationship.

Internet Resources

Read More about This Topic on the World Wide Web

Directions: For further information about the topic of the selection, visit this website:

www.bbc.co.uk/relationships/couples/love_secrets.shtml
This link, sponsored by the British Broadcasting Corporation, lists the seven essential elements for a successful relationship.

You can also use your favorite search engine such as Google, Yahoo!, or AltaVista (www.google.com, www.yahoo.com, www.altavista.com) to discover more about this topic. To locate additional information, type in combinations of keywords such as:

relationships that last

or

successful relationships

Keep in mind that whenever you go to *any* website, it is a good idea to evaluate the website and the information it contains. Ask yourself questions such as:

"Who sponsors this website?"
"Is the information contained in this website up-to-date?"
"What type of information is presented?"
"Is the information objective and complete?"
"How easy is it to use the features of this website?"

CHAPTER 6

Identifying Supporting Details

CHAPTER OBJECTIVES

In this chapter you will learn the answers to these questions:

- What are supporting details, and why is it important to be able to identify them?
- What is the method for identifying supporting details?
- What is the difference between major and minor details?

✓ **Timely Words**

"Beware of the man who won't be bothered with details."
(William Feather, Sr.)

WHAT ARE SUPPORTING DETAILS, AND WHY ARE THEY IMPORTANT?

KEY TERM
supporting details

Additional information in the paragraph that helps you understand the main idea completely.

Supporting details are also known simply as *support* or *details.*

A paragraph consists of a topic, a main idea, and supporting details. The topic and the main idea are essential to understanding the paragraph, of course, but it is the ***supporting details*** that provide the additional information that helps you understand the main idea *completely.*

Do not confuse a paragraph's supporting details with its main idea. Supporting details are *related* to the main idea, but they are not the same thing. The supporting details provide *specific* information (such as examples, descriptions, and explanations), while the main idea expresses the most important *general* point the author is making. Types of supporting details are names, dates, places, statistics, results of research studies, and other information that explains the main idea further or illustrates it by giving examples.

Student Online Learning Center (OLC) ***Go to*** **Chapter 6.** ***Select*** **Video.**

As noted above, every detail in a paragraph supports the main idea. However, some details are more important than others. These details are sometimes referred to as "primary details" because they relate *directly* to (support or explain) the main idea. Details that explain other details or that merely give examples are less important. These less important details are referred to as "minor details" or "secondary details." Consider the details in the following paragraph whose main idea is the first sentence. The three primary details are italicized. The other details are secondary details that explain these more important details.

✓ **Teaching Tip**
Ask students to number the three primary supporting details in this paragraph. Also, ask students to underline or highlight the signal words *also* and *finally.*

> Older workers and younger workers tend to have very different attitudes toward their jobs. ① *Older workers are more committed to their jobs than younger workers.* For example, older workers will more often go beyond the job requirements when a situation requires it. They will stay later or carry out extra responsibilities. *Older workers also tend to exhibit less job turnover than younger workers.* It is not unusual to find older workers who have had the same job all of their adult lives. ② *Finally, older workers report a higher degree of job satisfaction than younger workers.* This may be due to the fact that they are more experienced and, hence, competent; that they have the respect that goes with seniority; and are paid better wages than younger employees who are just starting out.

✓ **Teaching Tip**
Remind students that the student OLC contains an audio and video feature for Chapters 3 through 9 that presents **Key Comprehension Terms** and **Comprehension Monitoring Questions.**

Why is it important to identify supporting details? There are three reasons. First, the *details* explain or tell more about the main idea. When a paragraph has an implied main idea, the details help you formulate the main idea because the main idea is *based on* supporting details.

Second, listing the details after you read a textbook assignment can help you study more efficiently. Consequently, there will be many instances when you will want to list details in order to learn and remember them. This is why you should include important details on the chapter review cards you prepare. Instructors often base test questions on supporting details—names, dates, places, and other pertinent information. Noting the details that explain, illustrate, or support the main idea of the paragraph makes it easier for you to:

- Mark your textbooks effectively.
- Make study notes or create review cards.
- Remember the material.

Identifying supporting details that explain, illustrate, or support the main idea of a paragraph makes it easier for you to mark your textbooks effectively, take notes as you read, and remember the material you are studying.

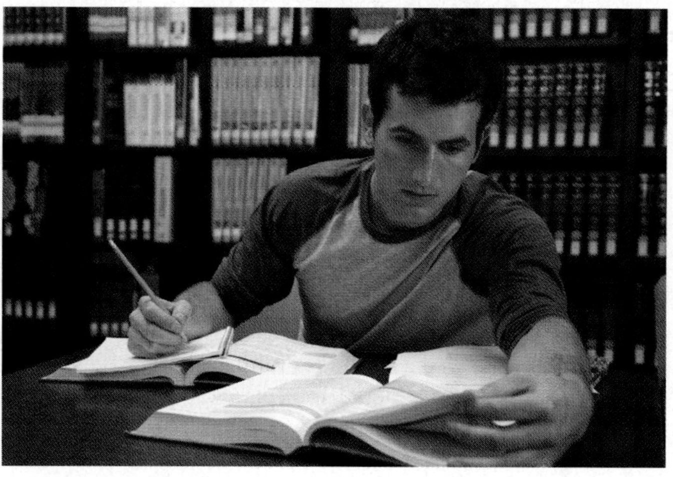

And third, identifying the details helps you grasp the pattern of organization of a paragraph. For example, authors may organize details as simple lists, as steps in a process (a sequence), as similarities and differences (comparisons and contrasts), or as reasons and results (causes and effects). (These patterns of organization will be discussed in Chapter 7.)

Along with determining the topic and the main idea, then, identifying supporting details will help you become a more successful reader and student.

WHAT IS THE METHOD FOR IDENTIFYING SUPPORTING DETAILS?

Comprehension Monitoring Question for Identifying Supporting Details

"What additional information does the author provide to help me understand the main idea completely?"

Once you have determined the stated main idea of a paragraph, you have also identified the supporting details: all the rest of the sentences in the paragraph. You can also ask yourself this comprehension monitoring question, "What additional information does the author provide to help me understand the main idea completely?" To determine what additional information you need to know, turn the main idea sentence into a question by using the words *who, what, where, when, why,* or *how.* For example, suppose the main idea is *In any club or organization, the treasurer has several important responsibilities.* You could change this sentence into the question "*What are* the important responsibilities of the treasurer?" This question would lead you to the details that describe those responsibilities and, therefore, help you understand the main idea completely.

From time to time, you may need to turn a main idea sentence into a two-part question. For example, suppose you read a paragraph with the main idea "Spreadsheets can serve small-business owners many ways." This could be changed into the two-part question: "What are spreadsheets, and how can they serve small business owners?"

Sometimes when you are reading a paragraph, it will become obvious that a list of details is about to be presented. For example, you would know to expect a list of details after phrases such as *There are many types of . . . , There are five reasons that . . . , Two kinds of . . . , There are several ways . . . ,* or *Some symptoms include . . . .*

Details are often introduced by signal words such as *for example, first, second, next, and, also, in addition,* and *moreover.* Authors also use clues such as numbers (1, 2, 3), letters *(a, b, c)*, and bullets (• • •) when they present details in the form of a list. Be aware, however, that not every detail is introduced by a signal word or other clue.

Here is an excerpt from a health textbook. Its topic is *date rape and post-traumatic stress syndrome.* The first sentence is the main idea: *Nearly all survivors of date rape seem to suffer from the effects of post-traumatic stress syndrome.* This main idea can be turned into the question "*What* are the effects of post-traumatic stress syndrome that date rape survivors suffer?" Now read the paragraph to identify the details that answer this question.

Nearly all survivors of date rape seem to suffer from post-traumatic stress syndrome. They can have ① anxiety, ② sleeplessness, ③ eating disorders, and ④ nightmares. Moreover, they can experience ⑤ guilt concerning their own behavior, ⑥ poor self-esteem, and the ⑦ negative judgment of others. In addition, ⑧ some individuals may require professional counseling.

Source: Adapted from Wayne A. Payne, Dale B. Hahn, and Ellen Mauer, *Understanding Your Health,* 8th ed. Copyright © 2005 by The McGraw-Hill Companies, Inc. Reprinted by permission of The McGraw-Hill Companies, Inc.

There are eight details that answer the question "What are the effects of post-traumatic stress syndrome that date-rape survivors suffer?" Notice that the details help you understand more about the main idea by explaining what the effects are. You can also see from examining the second and third sentences that a single sentence can contain more than one supporting detail. Here is a list of the effects of post-traumatic stress syndrome, the eight details in this paragraph:

- anxiety
- sleeplessness
- eating disorders
- nightmares
- guilt
- poor self-esteem
- negative judgment of others
- may require professional counseling

Stop and Annotate

Go back to the previous textbook excerpt. Locate the eight supporting details and number them with a small ①,②, ③, ④. etc.

Underline or highlight the signal words *and, Moreover,* and *In addition.*

Notice how clearly the details stand out when they are listed on separate lines and identified with bullets. Since you are responsible for understanding the details in textbooks, you may find it helpful to list them this way in your notes and review cards.

Or you may prefer, after you have read a paragraph, to go back and insert a number next to each detail. Numbering the details is helpful for at least three reasons. First, it helps you locate all the details. Second, it helps you remember how many details there were. Third, it prevents you from overmarking the paragraph by underlining or highlighting too much.

Here is another example. It is from a speech textbook. Its topic is *a person's religion.* The first sentence states the main idea: *A person's religion can influence his or her thinking on a number of matters.* To identify the details, turn this main idea sentence into the question "*How* does a person's religion influence his or her thinking on a number of matters?" Now read the paragraph to find the answer to this question.

> A person's religion can influence his or her thinking on a number of matters. We are all more than our religion, but, all things considered, you can expect ① Quakers to oppose all types of violent activity and be in favor of human rights. Someone who is ② Catholic is likely to oppose abortion and most types of birth control. ③ Jews, for thousands of years, have historically valued education, and are more inclined than others to support a tax increase if the money is earmarked for colleges and universities. ④ Mormons have a strong commitment to self-help and to viewing the church as being part of the family. They believe these two institutions, church and family, not the government, should take care of individuals who have financial problems. Therefore, they are not strong supporters of the current welfare system. And ⑤ Hindus, with their strong belief in reincarnation, are most likely not to feel rushed in making a decision.
>
> *Source:* Larry Samovar and Jack Mills, *Oral Communication: Speaking across Cultures,* 10th ed. Boston: McGraw-Hill, 1998, p. 256. Reprinted by permission of Oxford University Press, Inc.

Stop and Annotate

Go back to the textbook excerpt. Locate the five supporting details and number them with a small ①, ②, ③, ④, and ⑤.

Underline or highlight the signal word *And* that helped you identify the last detail.

The details of this paragraph are examples that answer the question "How does a person's religion influence his or her thinking on a number of matters?" Notice that even though there are five details in this paragraph, only one signal word is used (the word *And* is used to introduce this last detail). Here is a list of the five details (the examples) in this paragraph:

- Quakers—oppose all types of violent activity and favor human rights
- Catholics—likely to oppose abortion and most types of birth control
- Jews—value education and are willing to support it with taxes
- Mormons—strong commitment to self-help and to viewing church as part of family
- Hindus—due to their belief in reincarnation, not likely to feel rushed in making a decision

KEY TERM
paraphrasing

Restating an author's material in your own words.

In the list above, the details are not written exactly as they appear in the paragraph. When you are listing details, it is not necessary to use the exact words of the paragraph, nor is it necessary to use complete sentences. Rather, you will want to restate them briefly in your own words. Restating someone else's material in your own words is called **paraphrasing.** For example, you could paraphrase the items above in this even briefer way and list them on a study card with a question like this:

How can religion influence a person's thinking?
Quakers—against all violence; for human rights
Catholics—oppose abortion and birth control
Jews—value education and support taxes for it
Mormons—committed to self-help; church is part of family
Hindus—because of belief in reincarnation, don't rush to make a decision

EXERCISE 1

This paragraph comes from a science textbook.

The primary goal of a sustainable community is to protect and enhance the environment. Sustainable communities achieve this by using energy, water, and other natural resources efficiently and with care. Sustainable communities also minimize waste, then reuse or recover it through recycling, composting, or energy production. Another characteristic of a sustainable community is that it limits pollution to levels that do not damage natural systems. A sustainable community values and protects the diversity of nature.

Source: Adapted from Eldon D. Enger and Bradley F. Smith, *Environmental Science: A Study of Interrelationships,* 11th ed., p. 283. Copyright © 2008 by The McGraw-Hill Companies, Inc. Reprinted by permission of The McGraw-Hill Companies, Inc.

List the four supporting details about sustainable communities. Use a bullet for each detail and start each detail on a new line.

- Sustainable communities use energy, water, and other natural resources efficiently and with care.
- Sustainable communities minimize waste, then reuse or recover it through recycling, composting, or energy production.
- Sustainable communities limit pollution to levels that do not damage natural systems.
- Sustainable communities value and protect the diversity of nature.

There are other ways besides merely listing to organize details you must learn. Sometimes it is more helpful to organize details as numbered steps in a process (a sequence), in a table or chart that shows similarities and differences (comparisons and contrasts) or reasons and results (causes and effects). These patterns of organization are presented in Chapter 7. Also, you may discover that in some cases you prefer to include details in your study notes in the form of an outline or a study map. These techniques are presented in Chapter 11.

MAJOR AND MINOR DETAILS

KEY TERM
major details

Details that directly support the main idea.

Major details are also known as *primary details.*

All the details in a paragraph ultimately support the main idea by explaining, illustrating, or proving it. In each example presented earlier, all the details *directly* supported (explained) the main idea. Details that directly support the main idea are called **major details** (these are also known as *primary details*). However, there are also paragraphs in which some details support or explain *other details.* These are called **minor details** (they are also known as *secondary details*).

The following diagram shows the relationship between the main idea, major details, and minor details.

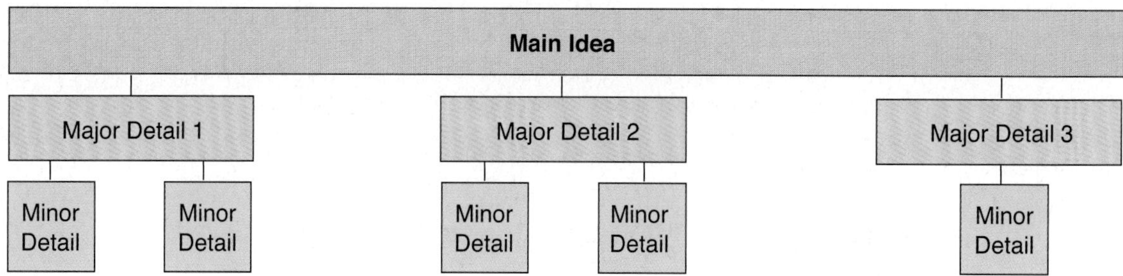

KEY TERM
minor details

Details that support other details.

Minor details are also known as *secondary details.*

The simple paragraph below illustrates major and minor details. Its topic is *uses of pepper.* Its stated main idea is the first sentence, *Throughout history, pepper has been used many different ways besides as a way to season food.* There are three major details that explain important uses of pepper. The other sentences are minor details that explain the major details.

> Throughout history, pepper has had many other uses besides as a way to season food. Pepper was also ① one of the first ways of preserving meat. During the Crusades pepper was used to preserve sausages. Pepper is still used to preserve meat today. Pepper has ② also been used as a medicine. In medieval times peppercorns were prescribed to cure aches and pains. Native Americans today use pepper to cure toothaches. Today, pepper is ③ also used to control insects. For example, the French and Dutch use pepper to kill moths and to repel other insects.

The following diagram shows the relationship between the main idea and the major and minor details for this paragraph.

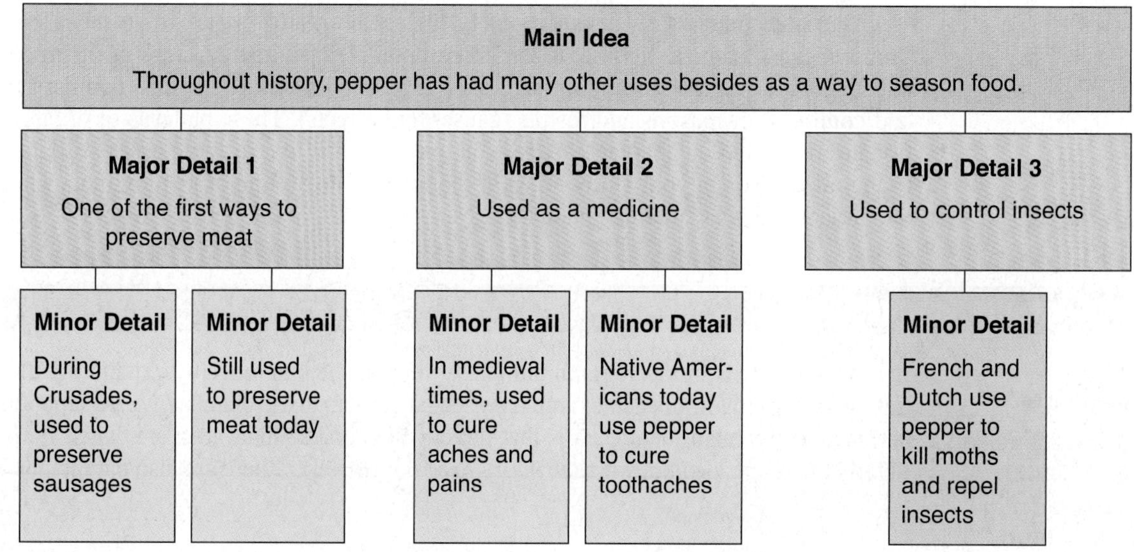

Again, notice that only three details directly answer the main idea question, "How has pepper been used in different ways throughout history besides as a way to season food?" Therefore, those three are major details. The passage would make sense with only the main idea and those details. However, the author explains even more fully by giving examples of the three ways pepper is used. Therefore, those details, which explain other details, are minor details.

Stop and Annotate

Go back to excerpt on page 298. Locate the three major details and number them with a serial ①, ②, and ③.

Remember, to identify the supporting details of a paragraph, ask yourself, "What *additional information* does the author provide to help me understand the main idea completely?" Change the main idea into a question; then look for the major details that answer the question. Be aware that the author might also include minor details. Don't spend too much time worrying about whether a detail is major or minor. The important thing is simply that you distinguish between the main idea and the details.

EXERCISE 2

This paragraph comes from a psychology textbook.

Parenting Styles and Social Development. Parents' child-rearing practices are critical in shaping their children's social competence, and—according to classic research by developmental psychologist Diana Baumrind—four main categories describe different parenting styles. Rigid and punitive, **authoritarian parents** value unquestioning obedience from their children. They have strict standards and discourage expressions of disagreement. **Permissive parents** give their children relaxed or inconsistent direction and, although warm, require little of them. In contrast, **authoritative parents** are firm, setting limits for their children. As the children get older, these parents try to reason and explain things to them. They also give clear goals and encourage their children's independence. Finally, **uninvolved parents** show little interest in their children. Emotionally detached, they view parenting as nothing more than providing food, clothing, and shelter for children. At their most extreme, uninvolved parents are guilty of neglect, a form of child abuse.

Source: Adapted from Robert S. Feldman, *Understanding Psychology*, 8th ed., pp. 419–20. Copyright © 2008 by The McGraw-Hill Companies, Inc. Reprinted by permission of The McGraw-Hill Companies, Inc.

Describe each of the four *major* supporting details.

- authoritarian parents: value unquestioning obedience; have strict standards; discourage disagreement: are rigid and punitive
- permissive parents: give children relaxed or inconsistent direction; require little from their children
- authoritative parents: are firm; set limits for their children; try to reason and explain things to children; give clear goals and encourage independence
- uninvolved parents: show little interest in their children; are emotionally detached; view parenting as nothing more than providing food, clothing, and shelter for children; are sometimes guilty of neglect

EXERCISE 3

This paragraph comes from an information technology textbook.

Microcomputers

Microcomputers are the most widely used and fastest-growing type of computer. There are several kinds of microcomputers. **Desktop computers** are small enough to fit on top of or alongside a desk yet are too big to carry around. An Apple iMac® is a popular example of a desktop computer. **Notebook computers,** also known as *laptop computers,* are portable, lightweight, and fit into most briefcases. The Dell Inspiron™ and Sony Vaio™ are examples of notebook computers. A **tablet PC** is a type of notebook that accepts your hardwriting. This input is digitized and converted to standardized text that can be further processed by programs such as word processors. An HP Pavillion™ is a widely used tablet PC. **Handheld computers** are the smallest kind of microcomputer and are designed to fit into the palm of one hand. Also known as *palm computers* or *personal digital assistants (PDAs),* these systems typically combine pen input, writing recognition, personal organizational tools, and communications abilities in a very small package. The Dell Axim™ and the HP iPAQ™ are examples of handheld computers.

List the four *major* supporting details. Use a bullet for each *major* detail. Below each major detail, list one or two *minor* details that give examples of each major detail. Use a separate line for each major and minor detail.

- desktop computers
  - Apple iMac®
- notebook computers (also known as laptop computers)
  - Dell Inspiron™ and Sony Vaio™
- tablet PCs
  - HP Pavillion™
- handheld computers (also known as palm computers or personal digital assistants)
  - Dell Axim™ and the HP iPAQ™

OTHER THINGS TO KEEP IN MIND WHEN IDENTIFYING SUPPORTING DETAILS

Here are three other helpful things you should know about identifying supporting details:

1. **Watch for clues that indicate a list of details. These include:**
   - Clue phrases such as *There are many types of . . . , Five reasons that . . . , Two kinds of . . . , There are several ways . . . ,* and *Some symptoms include . . . .*
   - Signal words such as *for example, first, second, next, and, also, in addition,* and *moreover.*
   - Items identified with numbers (1, 2, 3) and letters *(a, b, c).*
   - Lists with items identified with bullets (• • •).

   Remember, though, that not every detail will be introduced by signal words or other clues.
2. **Avoid overmarking your textbook by numbering the supporting details in a paragraph rather than highlighting or underlining them.**

   When you study, there will be many times when numbering the details will make it easier for you to locate and recall them. Of course, when the details are already presented as bulleted or numbered lists, you will not need to do anything more.
3. **Listing the details on separate lines in your study notes or on review cards can help you learn the information more efficiently.**

   Writing down the details in your study notes on review cards is one way to rehearse the material and transfer it into your long-term memory. It is especially helpful to write each detail *on a separate line.* That way, each detail stands out, making it easy to see how many there are. Listing paraphrased details below a question is an ideal format for study cards.

CREATING CHAPTER REVIEW CARDS

Student Online Learning Center (OLC) ***Go to*** **Chapter 6.** ***Select*** **Chapter Test.**

✓ **Teaching Tip**
Remind students that the student OLC contains and a 10-item **Chapter Test** for this chapter. After completing the chapter review cards below, students should complete the Chapter Test on the OLC.

Review cards or *summary cards* are a way to select, organize, and summarize the important information in a textbook chapter. Preparing review cards helps you organize the information so that you can learn and memorize it more easily. In other words, chapter review cards are effective study tools.

Preparing chapter review cards for each chapter of *New Worlds* will give you practice in creating these valuable study tools. Once you have learned how to make chapter review cards, you can use actual index cards to create them for textbook material in your other courses and use them when you study for tests.

Now complete the chapter review cards for Chapter 6 by answering the questions or following the directions on each card. Use the type of handwriting that is easiest for you to reread (printing or cursive) and write legibly.

✓ **Teaching Tip**
Point out to students that beginning with this chapter, page numbers are now omitted on the review cards. (They are provided in the AIE only.)

Supporting Details

1. What is the definition of *supporting details*? (See page 293.)

Supporting details are the additional information in the paragraph that helps you understand the main idea completely.

2. List three reasons why it is important to identify supporting details. (See pages 293–294.)

- Supporting details explain or tell more about the main idea.
- Listing supporting details after you read a textbook assignment helps you study more efficiently.
- Identifying supporting details will help you grasp the organization of a paragraph.

3. What question should you ask yourself to identify supporting details? Be sure you write a *question.* (See page 294.)

What additional information does the author provide in order to help me understand the main idea completely?

Card 1 Chapter 6: Identifying Supporting Details

✓ **Teaching Tip**
For item 3 on Card 1, point out the "Comprehension Monitoring Question for Identifying Supporting Details" in the margin on page 294 and guide students to write their answer as a question (including a question mark).

The Method for Identifying Supporting Details

1. What can be done to a main idea sentence of a paragraph to help you identify details that support it? (See page 294.)

Turn the main idea sentence into a question by using the words *who, what, when, where, why,* or *how.*

2. List some signal words and other clues an author may provide to help you identify a list of supporting details. (See pages 294–295.)

for example, also, letters (*a, b, c*), second, moreover,
first, in addition, numbers (1, 2, 3), next, bullets (• • •),
Phrases such as "there are many types of . . .",

3. What is the difference between major and minor details? (See page 297.)

Major details support the main idea and minor details support the major details.

Card 2 Chapter 6: Identifying Supporting Details

When Identifying Supporting Details, Keep in Mind . . .

Write the three things you should remember about identifying supporting details. (See page 301.)

1. Watch for clues that indicate a list of details.
2. Avoid overmarking your textbook by numbering the supporting details rather than highlighting them.
3. Listing supporting details in your study notes or on review cards can help you learn the information more efficiently.

Card 3 Chapter 6: Identifying Supporting Details

TEST YOUR UNDERSTANDING
IDENTIFYING SUPPORTING DETAILS, PART ONE

REVIEW: **Supporting details** provide additional information in the paragraph that helps you understand the main idea completely. As you learned in this chapter, *supporting details explain, illustrate, or prove the main idea of a paragraph.* Supporting details can be expressed in short phrases or complete sentences.

EXAMPLE: Study the example paragraph below to see how the information you learned in this chapter can be used to identify the supporting details of a paragraph. Read the explanation that is given for the correct answer. When you are sure you understand the explanation, complete the five exercises in Part One.

This excerpt comes from a communications textbook. Its topic is *barriers to listening.* Read the paragraph; then determine the main idea by asking yourself, "What is the most important point the authors want me to understand about barriers to listening?" To identify supporting details, ask yourself, "What additional information do the authors provide in order to help me understand more about barriers to listening?"

Mental distractions are perhaps the most common of all the barriers to listening and the most difficult to overcome. Mental distractions occur when we talk silently to our favorite companion—ourselves. It is a very natural tendency to make ourselves the central character in our daydreams and fantasies. However, when we "visit" with ourselves, we often forget about the speaker. How many times a day, when you are supposed to be listening, do you instead find yourself thinking about your next meal, planning tomorrow's activities, or evaluating what you did yesterday?

Source: Larry Samovar and Jack Mills, *Oral Communication: Speaking across Cultures,* 10th ed. Boston: McGraw-Hill, 1998, p. 256. Reprinted by permission of Oxford University Press, Inc.

The topic of this paragraph is *barriers to listening.*

___b___ What is the main idea of this paragraph?

a. How many times a day, when you are supposed to be listening, do you instead find yourself thinking about your next meal, planning tomorrow's activities, or evaluating what you did yesterday?
b. Mental distractions are perhaps the most common of all the barriers to listening and the most difficult to overcome.
c. Mental distractions occur when we visit with ourselves.
d. However, when we "visit" with ourselves, we often forget the speaker.

The correct answer is b. The first sentence of the paragraph is the stated main idea because it tells the single most important point the authors want you to know about mental distractions: they are perhaps the most common of all barriers to listening and are the most difficult to overcome. Answer choice *a* is a question, and the main idea is always a sentence and never a question.

___c___ Which of the following is a supporting detail?

a. Mental distractions are barriers to listening.
b. Mental distractions are perhaps the most common of all the barriers to listening and the most difficult to overcome.
c. Thinking about your next meal.
d. Avoiding mental distractors.

The correct answer is c. Thinking about your next meal is an example of a common mental distraction. Answer choice *a* gives the topic of the paragraph. Choice *b* is the stated main idea.

DIRECTIONS: Read each paragraph carefully and determine its main idea by asking yourself, "What is the single most important point the author wants me to *understand* about the topic of this paragraph?" (Notice that you are given the topic of each paragraph.) Select the answer choice that expresses the main idea and write the letter in the space provided. Then identify the supporting details by asking yourself, "What additional information does the author provide to help me understand the main idea completely?" Remember that main ideas are *general* and supporting detail are *specific.*

1. This paragraph comes from a human development textbook.

There are several drawbacks to working while you are a student. Young people who work long hours are less likely to eat breakfast, exercise, get enough sleep, or have enough leisure time. They spend less time with their families and may feel less close to them. They have little contact with adults on the job, and their jobs usually reinforce gender stereotypes. Some teenagers spend their earnings on alcohol or drugs, develop cynical attitudes toward work, and cheat or steal from their employers.

Source: Diane E. Papalia and Sally Olds, *Human Development,* 6th ed. Copyright © 1995 by The McGraw-Hill Companies, Inc. Reprinted by permission of The McGraw-Hill Companies, Inc.

The topic of this paragraph is *working while you are a student.*

c ____ What is the main idea of this paragraph?

a. Being a student has several drawbacks.

b. Students who work spend less time with their families and feel less close to them.

c. There are several drawbacks to working while you are a student.

d. Some teenagers spend their earnings on alcohol or drugs.

a ____ Which of the following is a supporting detail?

a. Students who work are less likely to get enough sleep.

b. Working while you are a student can have many negative effects.

c. Some teenagers work while they are in school.

d. Many students work to save money for college.

2. This paragraph comes from a communications textbook.

Cultures differ in the degree to which they tolerate ambiguity. That is to say, people from cultures such as the Greek, Japanese, French, and Portuguese do not like the unknown. They function much more efficiently when the uncertainties they face are reduced. However, some cultures have a very high tolerance for the ambiguous nature of life. People from the United States, Denmark, Sweden, Ireland, and Great Britain are quite different. They do not suffer great feelings of stress when some issues are left unresolved.

Source: Larry Samovar and Jack Mills, *Oral Communication: Speaking across Cultures,* 10th ed. Boston: McGraw-Hill, 1998, p. 256. Reprinted by permission of Oxford University Press, Inc.

The topic of this paragraph is *tolerating ambiguity, or dealing with the unknown.*

b ____ What is the main idea of this paragraph?

a. People from cultures such as the Greek, Japanese, French, and Portuguese do not like the unknown.

b. Cultures differ in the degree to which they tolerate ambiguity.

c. People from the United States suffer great feelings of stress when some issues are left unresolved.

d. People from the United States, Denmark, Sweden, Ireland, and Great Britain are quite different.

a Which of the following is a supporting detail?

a. People from the United States, Denmark, Sweden, Ireland, and Great Britain do not suffer great feelings of stress when some issues are left unresolved.

b. Most people like the unknown.

c. Cultures differ in the degree to which they tolerate ambiguity.

d. Tolerating ambiguity.

3. This paragraph comes from a management textbook.

Nonverbal communication is communication by means of elements and behaviors that are not coded into words. Studies estimate that nonverbal aspects account for between 65 and 93 percent of what is communicated. It is quite difficult to engage in verbal communication without some accompanying form of nonverbal communication. Important categories of nonverbal communication include kinesic behavior (body movements), proxemics (the influence of space on communication), paralanguage (vocal aspects of communication), and object language (the communicative use of material things such as clothing or cosmetics).

Source: Kathryn M. Bartol and David C. Martin, *Management,* 2nd ed. Copyright © 1994 by The McGraw-Hill Companies, Inc. Reprinted by permission of The McGraw-Hill Companies, Inc.

c The topic of this paragraph is *nonverbal communication.*

What is the main idea of this paragraph?

a. Kinesic behavior is an important category of nonverbal communication.

b. Studies estimate that nonverbal aspects account for between 65 and 93 percent of what is communicated.

c. Nonverbal communication is communication by means of elements and behaviors that are not coded into words, and verbal communication is almost always accompanied by nonverbal communication.

d. The importance of nonverbal communication.

b Which of the following is a supporting detail?

a. Nonverbal communication is communication by means of elements and behaviors that are not coded into words.

b. One type of nonverbal communication is kinesic behavior (body movement).

c. Nonverbal communication is effective.

d. It is quite difficult to engage in verbal communication.

4. This paragraph comes from a health textbook.

A Realistic Perspective on Stress and Life

Although we would like our lives to be stress-free, reality dictates otherwise. Therefore it is desirable that we approach life with a tough-minded optimism that provides a sense of hope and anticipation, as well as an understanding that life will never be without stress. The following suggestions can help you cope with today's fast-paced demanding lifestyle:

- *Do not be surprised by trouble.* Anticipate problems and see yourself as a problem solver.
- *Search for solutions.* Act on a partial solution, even when a complete solution seems distant.
- *Take control of your own future.* Do not view yourself as a victim.
- *Be cognizant of self-fulfilling prophecies.* Do not extend or generalize difficulties from one area into another.
- *Visualize success.* The very act of "imaging," in which a person sees himself or herself performing skillfully, has proven beneficial in a variety of performance-oriented activities.

- *Accept the unchangeable.* Cope as effectively as possible with those events over which you have no direct control; beyond a certain point, however, you must let go of those things over which you have little control.
- *Live each day well.* Combine activity, contemplation, and a sense of cheerfulness with the many things that must be done each day. Remember that our lives are far more heavily influenced by day-to-day events than they are by the occasional milestones in life.
- *Act on your capacity for growth.* Undertake new experiences and then extract from them new information about your own interests and capacities.
- *Allow for renewal.* Make time for yourself. Foster growth in each of the multiple dimensions of health—physical, emotional, social, intellectual, spiritual, occupational, and environmental.
- *Accept mistakes.* Mistakes, carefully evaluated, can serve as the basis for even greater control and more likely success in those activities you have undertaken.

Source: Abridged from Wayne A. Payne, Dale B. Hahn, and Ellen Mauer, *Understanding Your Health,* 8th ed., pp. 87–88. Copyright © 2005 by The McGraw-Hill Companies, Inc. Reprinted by permission of The McGraw-Hill Companies, Inc.

The topic of this paragraph is *coping with stress.*

c What is the main idea of this paragraph?

a. To cope with stress, anticipate problems and see yourself as a problem solver.

b. A tough-minded optimism can provide a sense of hope and anticipation.

c. Our lives will never be without stress, but there are things that can help you cope with today's fast-paced lifestyle.

d. Everyone has to deal with stress in their lives.

c Which of the following is a supporting detail?

a. Although we would like our lives to be stress-free, reality dictates otherwise.

b. There are things you can do to cope with stress.

c. Take control of your own future by not viewing yourself as a victim.

d. It is difficult to cope with stress.

5. This passage comes from a geography textbook.

The amount of damage an area sustains during an earthquake is governed in part by factors over which people have no control. These include the type of soil and rock underlying the areas that are struck. Also the depth of the quake and the way the seismic waves travel are factors. Finally, the quake's impact on ground movement affects the amount of damage that occurs.

Source: Arthur Getis, Judith Getis, and Jerome D. Fellmann, *Introduction to Geography,* 6th ed., p. 60. Copyright © 1998 by The McGraw-Hill Companies, Inc. Reprinted by permission of The McGraw-Hill Companies, Inc.

The topic of this paragraph is *the amount of damage caused by an earthquake.*

b What is the main idea of this paragraph?

a. There is usually serious damage caused by earthquakes' seismic waves.

b. The amount of damage an area sustains during an earthquake is governed in part by factors over which people have no control.

c. An earthquake's impact on ground movement affects the amount of damage that occurs.

d. Earthquakes can cause tremendous damage over a wide area.

b ______ Which of the following is a supporting detail?

a. People have only slight control over how much damage an area will have during a disaster.

b. The damage from an earthquake depends on the type of soil and rock underlying the areas that are struck.

c. The amount of damage an area sustains during an earthquake is governed in part by factors over which people have no control.

d. Predicting earthquakes is a difficult task.

TEST YOUR UNDERSTANDING
IDENTIFYING SUPPORTING DETAILS, PART TWO

REVIEW: **Supporting details** provide additional information in the paragraph that helps you understand the main idea completely. As you learned in this chapter, *supporting details explain, illustrate, or prove the main idea of a paragraph.* Supporting details can be expressed in short phrases or complete sentences.

EXAMPLE: Study the example paragraph below to see how the information you learned in this chapter can be used to identify the supporting details of a paragraph. Read the explanations that are given for the correct answers. When you are sure you understand the explanation, complete the five exercises in Part Two.

This excerpt comes from a biology textbook. Its topic is *animal research.* Read the paragraph; then determine the main idea by asking yourself, "What is the most important point the authors want me to understand about animal research?" To identify supporting details, ask yourself, "What additional information do the authors provide in order to help me understand more about animal research?"

Medical and veterinary progress depend on animal research. Every drug and every vaccine developed to improve the human condition has first been tested on an animal. Animal research has enabled medical science to eliminate smallpox and polio. It has provided immunization against previously common and often deadly diseases, such as diphtheria, mumps, and rubella. Animal research has helped create treatments for cancer, diabetes, and heart disease. It has also helped in the development of surgical procedures such as heart surgery, blood transfusions, and cataract removal. AIDS research is wholly dependent on animal studies largely because of the similarity of simian AIDS. Recent work indicates that cats, too, may prove to be useful models for the development of an AIDS vaccine.

Source: Adapted from Cleveland P. Hickman, Jr., Larry S. Roberts, and Allan Larson, *Biology of Animals,* 7th ed., p.14. (Boston: WCB/McGraw-Hill, 1998).

The topic of this paragraph is *animal research.*

Write the main idea sentence *Medical and veterinary progress depend on animal research.*

List the supporting details:

- *every drug and every vaccine developed to improve the human condition has first been tested on an animal*
- *enabled medical science to eliminate smallpox and polio*
- *provided immunization against previously common and deadly diseases*
- *helped in the development of surgical procedures*
- *helped in AIDS research*

Explanation: The main idea of this paragraph is stated (the first sentence). The rest of the paragraph presents details that explain the many ways that animal research has helped medical and veterinary progress.

DIRECTIONS: Read each paragraph carefully. (Notice that you are told the topic of each paragraph.) Determine the main idea by asking yourself, "What is the single most important point the author wants me to *understand* about the topic of this paragraph?" If the main idea is stated, write the entire stated main idea sentence in the spaces provided. If the main idea has been implied, formulate a main idea sentence and write the sentence in the spaces provided. Last, identify the supporting details by asking yourself, "What additional information does the author provide to help me understand the main idea completely?" *List each supporting detail on a separate line in the spaces provided.* You may find it helpful to number the details in the paragraph first or mark clue words that signal the details. To identify a writing pattern, ask yourself, "What pattern did the author use to organize the main idea and the supporting details?"

1. This paragraph comes from a communications textbook.

Types of Interviews

There are several different types of interviews, and each has a particular purpose. (1) *Survey interviews* gather information from a number of people. They are used to provide information from which to draw conclusions, make interpretations, and determine future action. Manufacturers and advertisers use them to assess market needs and learn consumer reactions to new products. Employers use them to gather employees' ideas about how space should be allotted in a new location or how much a new benefits program might be needed. (2) Diagnostic interviews allow health care professionals, attorneys, counselors, and other business and professional workers to gather information that helps them to respond to the needs of their clientele. (3) *Research interviews* provide information upon which to base future decisions. An entrepreneur who is thinking about opening a chain of restaurants might interview others with related experience when developing the concept and question people familiar with the target area to collect ideas about locations and clientele. On a more personal level, an employee thinking about a career change might interview several people who work in the field she is considering to seek advice about how to proceed. (4) *Investigative interviews* gather information to determine the causes of an event, usually a problem. Finally, (5) *exit interviews* help to determine why an employee is leaving an organization.

Source: Ronald Adler and Jeanne Elmhorst, *Communicating at Work*, 5th ed. Copyright © 1996 by The McGraw-Hill Companies, Inc. Reprinted by permission of The McGraw-Hill Companies, Inc.

✓ **Teaching Tips**

- Have students identify any clues (numbers, bullets, clue words) that indicate the details in a paragraph and insert a small number by each if is not already numbered. Emphasize that they are then to write the details *on separate lines.* This prepares them for note taking (Chapter 11).
- Tell students they can paraphrase the details if they like. (They are written out in full in the AIE, however.)

The topic of this paragraph is *types of interviews.*

Write the main idea sentence:

There are several types of interviews and each has a particular purpose.

(stated; first sentence)

List and number on separate lines the five supporting details, the types of interviews and their descriptions:

1. Survey interviews: gather information from a number of sources.
2. Diagnostic interviews: allow people in certain professions to gather information that helps them serve their clientele.
3. Research interviews: provide information upon which to base future decisions.
4. Investigative interviews: gather information to determine the causes of an event, usually a problem.
5. Exit interviews: help determine why an employee is leaving an organization.

✓ **Teaching Tip**
Ask students to number each detail in each paragraph. You may also ask them to identify clues that signal details (numbers, bullets, etc.

2. This selection comes from a communications textbook.

Wearing appropriate clothes when you are interviewed by a potential employer is vitally important. In one survey, recruiters ranked ① clothing as the leading factor in shaping their initial impressions of applicants (ahead of physical attractiveness and résumé). Furthermore, ② 79 percent of the recruiters stated that their initial impressions influenced the rest of the interview. While the best attire to wear will depend on the job you are seeking, ③ it is always safest to dress on the conservative side if you have any doubts.

Source: Ronald Adler and Jeanne Elmhorst, *Communicating at Work,* 5th ed. Copyright © 1996 by The McGraw-Hill Companies, Inc. Reprinted by permission of The McGraw-Hill Companies, Inc.

The topic of this paragraph is *wearing appropriate clothes to an interview.*

Write the main idea sentence:

Wearing appropriate clothes when you are interviewed by a potential employer is vitally important. (stated; first sentence)

List the three supporting details. Use a bullet for each detail and start each detail on a new line.

- Recruiters ranked clothing as the leading factor in shaping their initial impressions of applicants.
- 79 percent of the recruiters stated that their initial impressions influenced the rest of the interview.
- While the best attire to wear will depend on the job you are seeking, it is always safest to dress on the conservative side if you have any doubts.

✓ **Teaching Tip**
There are only three major details. In discussing this passage, show the minor (secondary) details and the major details they explain, or have students do this as a collaborative exercise.

3. This selection comes from an oceanography textbook.

Color

Some sea animals, like jellyfish, are transparent and blend with their background. ① Some fish conceal themselves with bright color bands and blotches. These colors disrupt ② the outline of the fish and may draw the predator's attention away from a vital area to a less important region. For example, a black stripe may hide the eye while a false eye spot appears on a tail or fin. Color is also used to send a warning. ③ Organisms that sting, taste foul, bear sharp spines, or have poisonous flesh are often striped and splashed with color, for example, sea slugs and some poisonous shellfish. Dark colors on backs and light ones on undersides are also common among fish that swim near the surface in well-lighted ④ water (for example, salmon, rockfish, herring, and tuna). This color pattern allows the fish to blend with the bottom when seen from above and with the surface when seen from below. It is obvious that color plays an important role in protecting fish and sea animals.

Source: Adapted from Alison B. Duxbury and Alyn C. Duxbury, *Fundamentals of Oceanography* (Boston: WCB/McGraw-Hill, 1996), p. 231.

The topic of this paragraph is *color in fish and sea animals.*

Write the main idea sentence:

It is obvious that color plays an important role in protecting fish and sea animals. (stated; last sentence)

List the four *major* (primary) supporting details. Use a bullet for each major detail and start each detail on a new line.

- Some sea animals are transparent and blend with their background.
- Some fish conceal themselves with bright color bands and blotches.
- Color is also used to send a warning.
- Dark colors on backs and light ones on undersides allow the fish to blend with the bottom when seen from above and with the surface when seen from below.

4. This selection comes from a communications textbook.

Minority Students

Although enrollment patterns at colleges and universities vary, the overall number of minority students is increasing. Today, according to the most recent figures available, about one in five college students is a minority student. African-Americans, Hispanic-Americans, Asian-Americans, and Native Americans represent the largest groups of minority students.

Source: Ronald Adler and Jeanne Elmhorst, *Communicating at Work,* 5th ed. Copyright © 1996 by The McGraw-Hill Companies, Inc. Reprinted by permission of The McGraw-Hill Companies, Inc.

The topic of this paragraph is *minority students in colleges and universities.*

Write the main idea sentence:

Although enrollment patterns at colleges and universities vary, the overall number of minority students is increasing. (stated; first sentence)

✓ **Teaching Tip**
Students tend to list the 4 minority groups as 4 separate details and to leave out the first detail altogether. Remind them to read the directions (which indicate the *number* of details).

List the two supporting details. Use a bullet for each detail and start each detail on a new line.

- Today about one of five college students is a minority student.
- African-Americans, Hispanic-Americans, Asian-Americans, and Native Americans represent the largest groups of minority students.

✓ **Teaching Tip**
Students often choose the first sentence as the stated main idea. Point out that the passage focuses only on *younger children,* so the second sentence tells half of the main idea.

5. This selection comes from a childhood development textbook.

All children of divorce are affected in some way. But younger children show the greatest signs of stress. There are two reasons for this. First, young children have few ① relationships outside the family to which they can turn for emotional support. Second, ② grasping the reasons for divorce is particularly hard for young children because they are emotionally and cognitively immature. Since they tend to view the world from their own perspective and are limited in their ability to reason logically, they tend to blame themselves for their parents' breakup.

Source: Laurence Steinberg and Roberta Meyer, *Childhood.* Copyright © 1995 by The McGraw-Hill Companies, Inc. Reprinted by permission of The McGraw-Hill Companies, Inc.

The topic of this paragraph is *the effect of divorce on children.*

Write the main idea sentence:

All children of divorce are affected in some way, but younger children show the greatest signs of stress. (implied; Formula 2: combine sentence 1 and sentence 2)

List the two *major* supporting details. Use a number for each detail and start each detail on a new line.

1. Young children have few relationships outside the family to which they can turn for emotional support.
2. Grasping reasons for divorce is particularly hard for young children because they are emotionally and cognitively immature.

SELECTION **6-1**

Environmental Science

"HOLD IT! YOU CAN RECYCLE THAT!" RECYCLING: A TWENTY-FIRST CENTURY NECESSITY

From *Environmental Science: A Study of Interrelationships*

By Eldon D. Enger and Bradley F. Smith

Plastic water bottles, glass containers, plastic milk bottles, newspapers, magazines, aluminum drink cans, plastic soft-drink bottles, cardboard boxes, steel cans—even tires and automobile batteries! All these items can be re-processed and therefore conserve resources, if they are recycled.

Are you a recycler? For many reasons, all of us should get into the habit of recycling, as this passage from an environmental science textbook explains. The selection contains many examples and presents statistics about recycling. Recycling is a great way to "go green" and is rapidly becoming a global necessity today.

1 **Recycling** has many benefits and is one of the best environmental success stories of the late twentieth century. (See Figure 1.) In the United States, recycling diverted about 30 percent of the solid waste stream from landfills and incinerators in 2005, up from about 16 percent in 1990. Some benefits of recycling are resource conservation, pollutant reduction, energy savings, job creation, and reduced need for landfills and incinerators. However, incentives are needed to encourage people to participate in recycling programs.

2 Several types of recycling programs have contributed to the increase in the recycling rate. *Container laws* provide an economic incentive to recycle. In October 1972, Oregon became the first state to enact a "bottle bill." The law required a deposit of two to five cents on all beverage bottles and cans. One of the primary goals of the law was to reduce the amount of litter, and it worked. Within two years of when it went into effect, beverage-container litter decreased by about 49 percent. *Mandatory recycling laws* provide a government regulated incentive to recycle. Many states and cities have passed mandatory recycling laws. Some of these laws simply require that residents separate their recyclables from other trash. Other laws are aimed at particular products such as beverage containers and require that they be recycled. Some are aimed at businesses and require them to recycle certain kinds of materials such as cardboard or batteries. Finally, some laws forbid the disposal of certain kinds of materials in landfills and these materials must be recycled or dealt with in some other way. For example, some states have banned yard waste from landfills. States with mandatory recycling laws understandably have high recycling rates. *Curbside recycling* provides a convenient way for people to recycle. In 1990, a thousand U.S. cities had curbside recycling programs. By 2005, the number had grown to about 10,000 cities. Some large cities—such as Portland (Oregon), San Jose and Los Angeles (California), and Minneapolis (Minnesota)—have achieved recycling rates of 50 percent or more. In general, these cities have curbside recycling and accept a wide variety of materials, including junk mail and cereal boxes. By contrast, cities that do not provide curbside recycling, such as El Paso, Texas, and Detroit, Michigan, have recycling rates of less than 10 percent.

Annotation Practice Exercises

Directions: For each exercise below, write the topic and the main idea on the lines beside the paragraph. (You may need to formulate the main idea.) Then identify the supporting details and list them *separately* on the lines provided.

Annotation Exercise

Topic of paragraph 1:

recycling

Main idea sentence of paragraph 1:

Recycling has many benefits and is one of the best environmental success stories of the late twentieth century, but incentives are needed to encourage people to participate in recycling programs. (Implied; Formula 2, first and last sentences.)

List the *supporting details* on separate lines:

- resource conservation
- pollutant reduction
- energy savings
- job creation
- reduced need for landfills and incinerators

Recycling Concerns

3 Although recycling programs have successfully reduced the amount of material that needs to be trucked to a landfill or incinerated, there are many technical and economic problems associated with recycling. Technical questions are of particular concern when recycling plastics. While the plastics used in packaging are recyclable, the recycling technology differs from plastic to plastic. There are many different kinds of plastic polymers. A milk container, an egg container, and a soft-drink bottle are each made from different types of plastics. Since each type has its own chemical makeup, different plastics cannot be recycled together. Until new technology is developed, separation of different plastics before recycling will be necessary.

4 The economics of recycling are also of primary concern. The stepped-up commitment to recycling in many developed nations has produced a glut of certain materials in some recycling markets. Warehouses and processing plants for collected materials fill up just like landfills. Unless the demand for recycled products keeps pace with the growing supply, recycling programs will face an uncertain future.

5 The long-term success of recycling programs is also tied to other economic incentives, such as taxing issues and the development of and demand for products manufactured from recycled materials. Additional government policies are needed to encourage recycling efforts internationally. On an individual level, we can have an impact by purchasing products made from recycled materials. The demand for recycled products must grow if recycling is to succeed on a global scale.

Beverage Container Waste

6 In 2002, consumers in the U.S. failed to recycle an estimated 140 billion aluminum, glass, and plastic beverage containers. This is 33 percent more beverage containers than were disposed of a decade ago. Disposal of beverage container waste continues to be a huge problem for several reasons. First, glass,

Annotation Exercise

Topic of paragraph 2:

types of recycling programs

Main idea sentence of paragraph 2:

Several types of recycling programs have contributed to the increase in the recycling rate. (Stated: first sentence)

List the *supporting details* on separate lines:

- container laws
- mandatory recycling laws
- curbside recycling

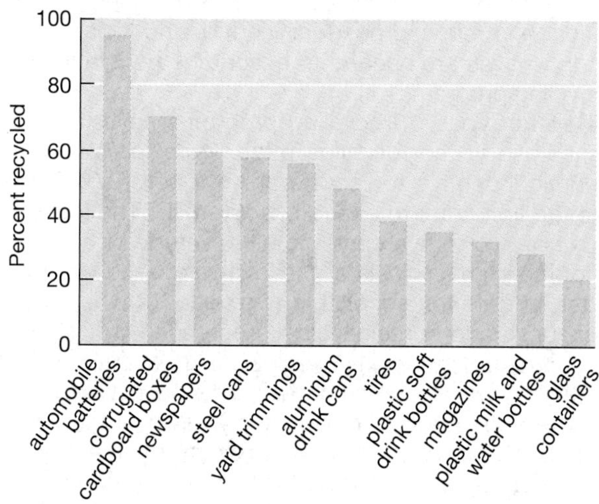

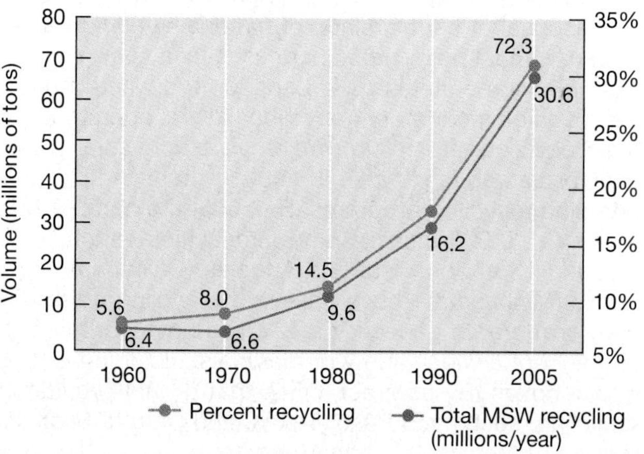

Figure 1 Recycling Rates for Various Materials (2005) and Recycling Rates from 1960–2005. Recycling rates for materials that have high value such as automobile batteries are extremely high. Other materials are more difficult to market. But recycling rates today are much higher than in the past as technology and markets have found uses for materials that once were considered valueless.

Source: Data from the U.S. Environmental Protection Agency. *Characterization of Municipal Solid Waste in the United States, 2005.*

aluminum, and plastic containers disposed of in landfills and incinerators represent a loss of valuable resources. Second, containers disposed of in this manner reduce employment opportunities in the domestic recycling industry. Third, disposal of these containers leads to increased greenhouse gas emissions and other forms of pollution when replacement containers are manufactured. Finally, beverage containers account for 40 percent of the total volume of litter on our roads and highways.

Paper or Plastic or Plastax?

7 Before 2002, Ireland's 3.9 million people were using 1.2 million plastic bags per year. These bags were generally nonrecyclable, took 20 to 1,000 years to break down in the environment, were littering the countryside and clogging storm drains, and were adding to the burden on the country's landfill sites.

8 The idea of the "plastax," or tax on plastic bags, was first announced in 1999 in Ireland and in 2002 the country's environment minister launched the program, one of the first of its kind in the world. For every bag used at the checkout counter of the supermarket a 15 Euro cents (about 19 U.S. cents) surcharge was added. The revenue raised from this tax would be put toward a "green fund" for environmental projects such as recycling refrigerators and other large appliances.

9 The results of this innovative program were immediate. Within the first three months of the program the use of plastic bags went down 90 percent, some 277 million fewer bags. It is estimated that by 2005 the program also raised some 3 million Euros (about 3.9 million U.S. dollars) for the Irish "green fund."

What You Can Do to Reduce Waste and Save Money

10 You can make a difference. While this statement is sometimes overused, it does speak the truth when it comes to your ability to lessen the stream of solid waste being generated every day. Here are a few ideas that are easy to follow, will save you money, and will help reduce waste: Buy things that last, keep them as long as possible, and have them repaired, if possible. Buy things that are reusable or recyclable, and be sure to reuse and recycle them. Buy beverages in refillable glass containers instead of cans or throwaway bottles. Use plastic or metal lunch boxes and metal or plastic garbage containers without throwaway plastic liners. Use rechargeable batteries. Skip the bag when you buy only a quart of milk, a loaf of bread, or anything you can carry with your hands. Recycle all newspaper, glass, and aluminum, and any other items accepted for recycling in your community.

Annotation Exercise

Topic of paragraph 6:

disposal of beverage container waste

Main idea sentence of paragraph 6:

Disposal of beverage container waste continues to be a huge problem for several reasons.

(Stated; first sentence)

List the *supporting details* on separate lines:

- Disposed plastic containers are a loss of valuable resources.
- Disposal plastic containers reduce employment opportunities in recycling.
- Disposal of these containers leads to increased greenhouse gas emissions and other forms of pollution when replacement containers are manufactured.
- Beverage containers account for 40 percent of the total volume of litter on our roads and highways.

✓ **Teaching Tip**

Plastic bottle recovery is down from a high of 65 percent in 1995 to less than 20 percent in 2005.

Source: Adapted from Eldon D. Enger and Bradley F. Smith, *Environmental Science: A Study of Interrelationships,* 11th ed., pp. 405–9 including Fig. 1. Copyright © 2008 by The McGraw-Hill Companies, Inc. Reprinted by permission of The McGraw-Hill Companies, Inc.

SELECTION **6-1**

Environmental Science

(continued)

Comprehension and Vocabulary Quiz

This quiz has four parts. Your instructor may assign some or all of them.

Comprehension

Directions: Items 1–5 test your comprehension (understanding) of the material in this selection. These questions are much like those that a content-area instructor (such as an environmental science or biology professor) would expect you to know after reading and studying this selection. For each comprehension question below, use information from the selection to determine the correct answer. Refer to the selection as you answer the questions. Write your answers in the spaces provided.

¶1 and graph ___a___ **1.** In 1990 the recycling rate for solid waste in the United States was about 16 percent, but by 2005 our nation's recycling rate had increased to about:

a. 30 percent.
b. 49 percent.
c. 50 percent.
d. 90 percent.

¶2 ___b___ **2.** Some large cities such as Portland, Oregon, and San Jose, California, have achieved recycling rates of 50 percent or more as a result of their:

a. mandatory recycling law.
b. curbside recycling program.
c. "plastax."
d. all of the above

¶2 ___c___ **3.** By 2005, the number of municipal curbside recycling programs in the United States increased to approximately:

a. 750.
b. 1,500.
c. 10,000.
d. 25,000.

¶8 ___c___ **4.** Ireland's "plastax" is a:

a. surcharge paid by citizens for plastic recycling.
b. deposit of two to five cents on all beverage bottles.
c. tax on plastic bags.
d. government regulation prohibiting the use of plastic bags.

¶3 ___b___ **5.** According to information presented in the selection, there are technical and economic problems associated with recycling plastics because:

a. not all plastics can be recycled.
b. different plastics cannot be recycled together and must be separated before re-processing.
c. plastics are becoming too expensive to recycle.
d. there is already an oversupply of recycled plastics.

✓ **Teaching Tip**

When going over the answers, show students where the answer to each comprehension question appears in the selection. Or you may prefer to have students work in pairs to identify where each answer appears.

Vocabulary in Context

Directions: Items 6–10 test your ability to determine the meaning of the word by using context clues. *Context clues* are words in a sentence that allow the reader to deduce (reason out) the meaning of an unfamiliar word in that sentence. Context clues also enable the reader to determine which meaning the author intends when a word has more than one meaning. For each vocabulary item below, a sentence from the selection containing an important word (*italicized, like this*) is quoted first. Next, there is an additional sentence using the word in the same sense and providing another context clue. Use the context clues from *both* sentences to deduce the meaning of the italicized word. *Be sure the answer you choose makes sense in both sentences.* If you need to use a dictionary to confirm your answer choice, remember that the meaning you select must still fit the context of *both* sentences. Write your answers in the spaces provided.

Pronunciation Key: ă **pat** ā **pay** âr **care** ä **fa**ther ĕ pet ē **be** ĭ **pit** ī **tie** îr **pier** ŏ **pot** ō **toe** ô **paw** oi **noi**se ou **out** o͝o **took** o͞o **boot** ŭ **cut** yo͞o ab**u**se ûr **ur**ge th **thin** *th* **this** hw **wh**ich zh vi**s**ion ə **a**bout *Stress mark:* ′

¶9 ______ **6.** The results of this *innovative* program were immediate.

Support for our new mayor increased dramatically due to her *innovative* ideas about how to stimulate business in our city.

innovative (ĭn′ ə vā tĭv) means:

a. controversial; disputable
b. popular; appealing
c. challenging; demanding
d. new; introductory

¶11 ______ **7.** However, *incentives* are needed to encourage people to participate in recycling programs.

The prospect of an exciting and interesting job, a good salary, and opportunities for career advancement are all *incentives* for earning a college degree.

incentives (ĭn sĕn′ tĭvs) means:

a. government regulations
b. specific results
c. rewards that produce action
d. requirements for success

¶2 ___d___ **8.** *Mandatory* recycling laws provide a government regulated incentive to recycle.

For international travel, possession of a valid passport is *mandatory.*

mandatory (măn′ də tôr ē) means:

a. complimentary
b. optional
c. recommended
d. required

¶2 ___b___ **9.** For example, some states have *banned* yard waste from landfills.

The use of cell phones while driving has been *banned* in many countries.

banned (bănd) means:

a. removed
b. prohibited
c. allowed
d. discouraged

¶4 ___c___ **10.** The stepped-up commitment to recycling in many developed nations has produced a *glut* of certain materials in some recycling markets.

The *glut* of new college graduates with majors in psychology made it extremely difficult for them to find jobs in their field.

glut (glŭt) means:

a. number
b. shortage
c. oversupply
d. problem

Word Structure

Directions: Items 11–15 below test your ability to use word-structure clues to help determine a word's meaning. *Word-structure clues* consist of roots, prefixes, and suffixes. In these exercises, you will learn the meaning of a word part (a root) and use it to determine the meaning of several other words that have the same word part. If you need to use a dictionary to confirm your answer choice, do so. Write your answers in the spaces provided.

In paragraph 9 of the selection, you encountered the word **innovative.** This word contains the Latin root ***nov,*** which means "new." The adjective *innovative* means "new" or "introductory." Use the meaning of the root ***nov*** and the list of prefixes on pages 68–69 to help you determine the meaning of each of the following words that contain the same root. Write your answers in the spaces provided.

b 11. If you are a **novice** at skiing, you are:

a. learning very quickly.
b. a beginner.
c. not interested in the sport.
d. looking for an outdoor sport.

c 12. At the beginning of the twentieth century, the automobile was still a **novel** invention. In other words, it was still:

a. extremely expensive.
b. inefficient and unreliable.
c. strikingly new or different.
d. unsafe to the point of dangerous.

d 13. If you **renovate** your kitchen, you:

a. make it larger.
b. repair it.
c. replace the appliances.
d. make it "like new" again.

c 14. Once the **novelty** of a toy wears off, children tend to:

a. put it in a safe place to save it for later.
b. play with it often because they have grown very fond of it.
c. become bored with it because it no longer seems new.
d. break it because they are frustrated with it.

b 15. A **nova** is a variable star that suddenly increases to several times its original brightness, but eventually returns to its original appearance. Astronomers call this a **nova** because:

a. it is a phenomenon that does not occur very often.
b. it temporarily looks like a new or different star.
c. it breaks into several different stars.
d. they do not know why this phenomenon happens.

✓ **Teaching Tip**
We suggest that rather than include this section as part of the quiz grade, you use it to give students practice with the skills they have studied and as a helpful preview of upcoming skills. It makes an excellent collaborative activity. All students will find this practice helpful, but especially those who must take course exit tests, standardized reading tests, or state-mandated basic skills tests.

Reading Skills Application

Directions: Items 16–20 test your ability to *apply* certain reading skills to information in this selection. These types of questions provide valuable practice for all students, especially those who must take standardized reading tests and state-mandated basic skills tests. You may not have studied all of the skills at this point, so these items will serve as a helpful preview. The comprehension and critical reading skills in this section are presented in Chapters 3 through 9 of *New Worlds;* vocabulary and figurative language skills are presented in Chapter 2. As you work through *New Worlds,* you will practice and develop these skills. Write your answers in the spaces provided.

¶2 supporting details (Chapter 6) — a

16. According to information in this selection, one of the primary goals of Oregon's "bottle bill" was to:

a. reduce the amount of litter in the state.

b. discourage consumers from buying glass containers.

c. raise money for resource conservation.

d. encourage soft-drink manufacturers to use plastic bottles that could be recycled.

Figure 1 interpreting graphic material (Chapter 10) — c

17. According to Figure 1, the graph of recycling rates for various materials, which materials have a higher recycling rate than plastic soft-drink bottles?

a. glass containers

b. magazines

c. aluminum drink cans

d. plastic milk and water bottles

¶9 authors' writing patterns (Chapter 7) — b

18. The information in paragraph 9 of the selection is organized by which of the following patterns?

a. list

b. cause-effect

c. comparison-contrast

d. sequence

all¶s authors' purpose (Chapter 8) — c

19. Which of the following describes the authors' primary purpose for writing this selection?

a. to explain why people do not participate in recycling programs

b. to show that there are many technical and economic difficulties associated with recycling

c. to persuade everyone to participate in recycling programs regularly and to convince readers that recycling is a global necessity today

d. to convince consumers to buy products made from recycled materials

¶10 formulated main idea (Chapter 5) — c

20. Which of the following is the main idea of paragraph 10 of this selection?

a. Recycle all newspaper, glass, aluminum, plastic, and all other items accepted for recycling in your community.

b. You can make a difference by purchasing only products made from recycled materials.

c. There are many things you can do to reduce waste and save money.

d. Individuals must be responsible for reducing the solid waste they generate each day.

✓ **Teaching Tip**

Let students know that not all of the skills included in this Reading Skills Application section have been introduced yet. This section serves as a valuable preview of these skills, however. Students typically get several of the items correct, and they find this encouraging.

SELECTION 6-1
Environmental Science
(continued)

Writing and Collaborating to Enhance Your Understanding

Option for collaboration: Your instructor may direct you to work with other students or, in other words, to work *collaboratively*. In that case, you should form groups of three or four students as directed by your instructor and work together to complete the exercises. After your group discusses each item and agrees on the answer, have a group member record it. Every member of your group should be able to explain all of your group's answers.

Collaboration Option

✓ **Teaching Tip**
When going over the answers, show students where the answer to each comprehension question appears in the selection. Or you may want to have students work in pairs to identify where each answer appears.

1. **Reacting to What You Have Read:** Do you think your community would support a "plastax" on plastic bags like the program launched in Ireland? Who would be opposed to such a program? How would a complete ban on plastic bags alter your lifestyle?

   (Answers will vary.)

2. **Comprehending the Selection Further:** At the end of the selection the authors include a section titled "What You Can Do to Reduce Waste and Save Money." List the ideas the authors suggest for reducing waste and promoting recycling. *Include at least three of your own suggestions in addition to those given in this section.*

   - Buy items that last, keep them as long as possible, and have them repaired, if possible.
   - Buy things that are reusable or recyclable; be sure to reuse or recycle them.
   - Buy beverages in refillable glass containers instead of cans or throwaway bottles.
   - Use plastic or metal lunch boxes.
   - Use metal or plastic garbage bags without throwaway plastic liners.
   - Use rechargeable batteries.
   - Skip the bag when you buy anything that you can carry with your hands.
   - Recycle all newspaper, glass, and aluminum, and other items accepted in your community.
   - Additional suggestion: Recycle cell phones, empty printer cartridges, and computer monitors.
   - Additional suggestion: Use reusable cloth shopping bags.
   - Additional suggestion: Recycle automobile and bicycle tires.

3. **Overall Main Idea of the Selection:** In one sentence, tell what the authors want readers to understand about recycling in the United States. (Be sure to include the words "recycling programs," "benefits," and "incentives" in your overall main idea sentence.)

Recycling programs have many benefits and are a twenty-first century necessity, but incentives are needed in order for them to be successful.

OR

Recycling programs have many benefits and have been one of the best environmental success stories of the twentieth century, but incentives are needed in order to encourage people to participate in recycling programs.

Read More about This Topic on the World Wide Web

Internet Resources

Directions: For further information about the topic of the selection, visit these websites:

http://en.wikipedia.org/wiki/America_Recycles_Day
This Wikipedia entry discusses recycling in the United States. It presents information about government involvement in recycling, the financial implications of recycling, and recycling education.

www.kab.org/site/PageServer?pagename=index
This is the site for Keep America Beautiful, Inc. The largest community improvement organization in the United States, this environmental organization was founded in 1953.

www.reusablebags.com/facts.php?id=20
This site is sponsored by *reusablebags.com*, a company that produces and sells all types of reusable bags. This link tells about Ireland's "plastax" program and includes a "ticker" that shows the number of plastic bags used so far this year worldwide.

You can also use your favorite search engine such as Google, Yahoo!, or AltaVista (www.google.com, www.yahoo.com, www.altavista.com) to discover more about this topic. To locate additional information, type in combinations of keywords such as:

U.S. recycling

or

reusable products

or

plastax

Keep in mind that whenever you go to *any* website, it is a good idea to evaluate the website and the information it contains. Ask yourself questions such as:

"Who sponsors this website?"

"Is the information contained in this website up-to-date?"

"What type of information is presented?"

"Is the information objective and complete?"

"How easy is it to use the features of this website?"

SELECTION 6-2 **History**

THE LIFE OF BUDDHA: THE PATH TO NIRVANA

From *The 100: A Ranking of the Most Influential Persons in History*
By Michael Hart

Gautama Buddha lived approximately 2,500 years ago (563 to 483 B.C.E.). He founded Buddhism, a worldwide religion that has influenced millions of people. Historian Michael Hart ranks Buddha among the top five most influential persons in the history of the world. In this selection he tells about Buddha's 80-year life and his beliefs, and he explains why he considers Buddha so influential.

Seated Buddha (Siddhartha Gautama).

1 Gautama Buddha, whose original name was Prince Siddhartha, was the founder of Buddhism, one of the world's great religions. Siddhartha was the son of a king ruling in Kapilavastu, a city in northeast India, near the borders of Nepal. Siddhartha himself (of the clan of Gautama and the tribe of Sakya) was purportedly born in 563 B.C., in Lumbini, within the present borders of Nepal. He was married at sixteen to a cousin of the same age. Brought up in the luxurious royal palace, Prince Siddhartha did not want for material comforts.

2 Nevertheless, Siddhartha was profoundly dissatisfied. He observed that most human beings were poor and continually suffered from want. Even those who were wealthy were frequently frustrated and unhappy, and all humans were subject to disease and ultimately succumbed to death. Surely, Siddhartha thought, there must be more to life than transitory pleasures, which were all too soon obliterated by suffering and death.

Annotation Practice Exercises

Directions: For each exercise below, write the topic and the main idea of the paragraph on the lines beside the paragraph. Then identify the supporting details and list them *separately* on the lines provided.

Practice Exercise

Topic of paragraph 1:

the early life of Gautama Buddha

Main idea sentence:

Gautama Buddha, whose original name was Prince Siddhartha, was the founder of Buddhism, one of the world's great religions. (stated; first sentence)

List the *supporting details* on separate lines:

- He was the son of an Indian King.
- He was born in 563 B.C. in Lumbini.
- He was married at 16 to a cousin.
- He was brought up in a luxurious royal palace.

3 When he was twenty-nine, just after the birth of his first son, Gautama decided that he must abandon the life he was living and devote himself wholeheartedly to the search for truth. He departed from the palace, leaving behind his wife, his infant son, and all his worldly possessions, and became a penniless wanderer. For a while he studied with some of the famed holy men of the day, but after mastering their teachings, he found their solutions to the problems of the human situation unsatisfactory. It was widely believed that extreme asceticism was the pathway to true wisdom. Gautama therefore attempted to become an ascetic by engaging in extreme fasts and self-mortification for several years. Eventually, however, he realized that tormenting his body only clouded his brain, without leading him any closer to true wisdom. He therefore resumed eating normally and abandoned asceticism.

4 In solitude, he grappled with the problems of human existence. Finally, one evening, as he sat beneath a giant fig tree, all the pieces of the puzzle seemed to fall into place. Siddhartha spent the whole night in deep reflection, and when the morning came, he was convinced that he had found the solution and that he was now a Buddha, an "enlightened one."

5 At this time, he was thirty-five years old. For the remaining forty-five years of his life, he traveled throughout northern India, preaching his new philosophy to all who were willing to listen. By the time he died, in 483 B.C., he had made thousands of converts. Though his words had not been written down, his disciples had memorized many of his teachings, and they were passed to succeeding generations by word of mouth.

6 The principal teachings of the Buddha can be summarized in what Buddhists call the "Four Noble Truths." These are first, that human life is intrinsically unhappy; second, that the cause of this unhappiness is human selfishness and desire; third, that individual selfishness and desire can be brought to an end—the resulting state, when all desire and cravings have been eliminated, is termed *nirvana* (literally "blowing out" or "extinction"); fourth, that the method of escape from selfishness and desire is what is called the "Eightfold Path": right views, right thought, right speech, right action, right livelihood, right effort, right mindfulness, and right meditation.

7 Buddha, as the founder of one of the world's major religions, clearly deserves a place among the most influential people in history. Since there are only about 200 million Buddhists in the world, compared with over 800 million Moslems and about one billion Christians, it would seem evident that Buddha has influenced fewer people than either Muhammad or Jesus. However, the difference in numbers can be misleading. One reason that Buddhism died out in India is that Hinduism absorbed many of its ideas and principles. In China, too, large numbers of persons who do not call themselves Buddhists have been strongly influenced by Buddhist philosophy.

8 Buddhism, far more than Christianity or Islam, has a very strong pacifist element. This orientation toward nonviolence has played a significant role in the political history of Buddhist countries.

Practice Exercise

Topic of paragraph 6:

the "Four Noble Truths"

Main idea sentence:

The principal teachings of the Buddha can be summarized in what Buddhists call the "Four Noble Truths." (stated; first sentence)

List the *supporting details* on separate lines:

- Human life is intrinsically unhappy.
- The cause of this unhappiness is human selfishness.
- Individuals' selfishness and desire can be brought to an end, resulting in Nirvana.
- The method of escape from selfishness and desire is what is called the "Eightfold Path."

✓ **Teaching Tips**

- Gautama Buddha is pronounced gô´ tə mə bōō´ də.
- Point out that the eight elements of the "Eightfold Path" in paragraph 6 are *minor* details.
- Point out how unusually long Buddha's life was compared with most people of that time.
- Remind students that their task is to comprehend the *author's* point of view about Buddha's influence, regardless of whether they agree or disagree (which they are free to do, of course).
- The selection's overall main point is given at the beginning of ¶7 (it is also the paragraph's main idea).

Source: Adapted from Michael Hart, *The 100: A Ranking of the Most Influential Persons in History.*

SELECTION **6-2**
History
(continued)

Comprehension and Vocabulary Quiz

This quiz has four parts. Your instructor may assign some or all of them.

Comprehension

Directions: Items 1–5 test your comprehension (understanding) of the material in this selection. These questions are much like those that a content-area instructor (such as a history professor) would expect you to know after reading and studying this selection. For each comprehension question below, use information from the selection to determine the correct answer. Refer to the selection as you answer the questions. Write your answers in the spaces provided.

¶1 ___b___ **1.** Gautama Buddha spent the first 29 years of his life:

a. as a penniless wanderer.
b. as a prince in a royal palace.
c. training to become a holy man.
d. as an ascetic.

¶4 ___a___ **2.** The term "Buddha" means:

a. enlightened one.
b. royal prince.
c. ascetic.
d. one whose teachings are passed to succeeding generations.

¶5 ___b___ **3.** The teachings of Buddha were memorized by his disciples and then:

a. written down in a holy book called *The Four Noble Truths.*
b. passed on by word of mouth.
c. developed into the "Eightfold Path."
d. adopted by Hinduism and Christianity.

¶6 ___b___ **4.** One of the four principal teachings of the Buddha is that:

a. Buddhism is open to all.
b. individual selfishness and desire can be brought to an end.
c. happiness is the natural state of human life.
d. human life is intrinsically happy.

¶8 ___a___ **5.** Buddhism has a strong orientation toward:

a. peace and nonviolence.
b. other religions such as Hinduism and Islam.
c. the teachings of Muhammad and Jesus.
d. asceticism and self-mortification.

Vocabulary in Context

Directions: Items 6–10 test your ability to determine the meaning of the word by using context clues. *Context clues* are words in a sentence that allow the reader to deduce (reason out) the meaning of an unfamiliar word in that sentence. Context clues also enable the reader to determine which meaning the author intends when a word has more than one meaning. For each vocabulary item below, a sentence from the selection containing an important word (*italicized, like this*) is quoted first. Next, there is an additional sentence using the word in the same sense and providing another context clue. Use the context clues from *both* sentences to deduce the meaning of the italicized word. *Be sure the answer you choose makes sense in both sentences.* If you need to use a dictionary to confirm your answer choice, remember that the meaning you select must still fit the context of *both* sentences. Write your answers in the spaces provided.

Pronunciation Key: ă **pat** ā **pay** âr **care** ä **father** ĕ **pet** ē **be** ĭ **pit** ī **tie** îr **pier** ŏ **pot** ō **toe** ô **paw** oi **noise** ou **out** o͝o **took** o͞o **boot** ŭ **cut** yo͞o **abuse** ûr **urge** th **thin** *th* **this** hw **which** zh **vision** ə **about** *Stress mark:* ′

¶1 ____c____ **6.** Brought up in the luxurious royal palace, Prince Siddhartha did not want for *material* comforts.

Many people complain that American society places too much emphasis on clothes, cars, electronic devices, and other *material* goods.

material (mə tĭr′ ē əl) means:

a. pertaining to cloth

b. pertaining to a humble lifestyle

c. pertaining to physical well-being

d. pertaining to things that are inexpensive

¶3 ____b____ **7.** Gautama therefore attempted to become an *ascetic,* for several years engaging in extreme fasts and self-mortification.

Because Jake is an *ascetic,* he chooses to live alone in a small mountain cabin with no electricity, no running water, and no telephone.

✓ **Teaching Tip**
Take a moment to demonstrate the pronunciation of this unusual word.

ascetic (ə sĕt′ ĭk) means:

a. extremely religious person

b. person who leads a life of self-discipline and without comforts

c. person who plans things in a careful, detailed manner

d. extremely unfriendly

¶4 c **8.** Siddhartha spent the whole night in deep reflection, and when the morning came, he was convinced that he had found the solution and that he was now a Buddha, an "*enlightened* one."

We all suddenly felt *enlightened* after hearing our math professor explain the difficult concepts in a way we could understand.

enlightened (ĕn līt′ nd) means:

a. made lighter
b. relieved; free from worry
c. having spiritual or intellectual insight
d. confused and frustrated

¶6

a **9.** The principal teachings of the Buddha can be summarized in what Buddhists call the "Four Noble Truths": first, that human life is *intrinsically* unhappy.

Because the judge is *intrinsically* fair, she is effective and highly respected.

intrinsically (ĭn trĭn′ zĭk lē) means:

a. inherently or naturally
b. from time to time
c. partially or incompletely
d. never

¶8

a **10.** Buddhism, far more than Christianity or Islam, has a very strong *pacifist* element.

Last week, antiwar demonstrators and other *pacifist* groups held protests in the nation's capital.

pacifist (păs′ ə fĭst) means:

a. opposed to war or violence as a means of settling disputes
b. from the Pacific coast region
c. well-organized politically
d. pertaining to religion

✓ **Teaching Tip**
Mention other words that include the root *pac* (peace, calm): *pac*ify, *pac*ifier, *Pac*ific Ocean.

Word Structure

Directions: Items 11–15 test your ability to use word-structure clues to help determine a word's meaning. *Word-structure clues* consist of roots, prefixes, and suffixes. In these exercises, you will learn the meaning of a word part (a root) and use it to determine the meaning of several other words that have the same word part. If you need to use a dictionary to confirm your answer choice, do so. Write your answers in the spaces provided.

In paragraph 3 of the selection, you encountered the word **self-mortification.** This word contains the Latin root ***mort,*** which means "death." The word *mortification* means "to discipline (one's body and physical appetites) by self-denial or self-inflicted privation." You can see the connection with the meaning of the root because if one "disciplined" and "denied" one's body to an extreme, it would result in death. (*Mortify* also has come to mean "to humiliate" and "to feel shame or wounded pride.") Use the meaning of ***mort*** and the list of prefixes on pages 68–69 to help you determine the meaning of each of the following words that contain this same root. Write your answers in the spaces provided.

__a__ **11.** A **mortuary** is a:

a. funeral home.
b. sacred shrine.
c. public area.
d. type of wreath.

__c__ **12.** An autopsy, or **post mortem** examination, is conducted:

a. on weekdays only.
b. only after employees complete their routine duties.
c. on the body after a person has died.
d. by a person involved in criminal investigation.

__d__ **13.** A **mortician** is a person who:

a. knows emergency procedures.
b. counsels families.
c. presides at a religious service.
d. is a funeral director or undertaker.

__b__ **14.** If a hospital patient is **moribund,** the person is:

a. ill.
b. dying.
c. in intensive care.
d. on a heart monitor.

__d__ **15.** If a solider receives a **mortal** wound, it is:

a. a serious injury.
b. a head wound.
c. an injury that causes extensive blood loss.
d. a fatal wound.

✓ **Teaching Tip**
Let students know that not all of the skills included in this Reading Skills Application section have been introduced yet. This section serves as a valuable preview of these skills, however. Students typically get several of the items correct, and they find this encouraging.

Reading Skills Application

Directions: Items 16–20 test your ability to *apply* certain reading skills to information in this selection. These types of questions provide valuable practice for all students, especially those who must take standardized reading tests and state-mandated basic skills tests. You may not have studied all of the skills at this point, so these items will serve as a helpful preview. The comprehension and critical reading skills in this section are presented in Chapters 3 through 9 of *New Worlds;* vocabulary and figurative language skills are presented in Chapter 2. As you work through *New Worlds,* you will practice and develop these skills. Write your answers in the spaces provided.

logical inference (Chapter 9) ___b___

16. Based on information in the selection, which of the following represents a logical inference about Buddha and his "search for truth"?

a. Buddha regretted his decision to leave his home and family to "search for truth."

b. If Buddha had grown up in poverty, he might never have begun a "search for truth."

c. Buddha's family and friends thought his decision to "search for truth" was foolish.

d. Buddha failed in his "search for truth" and died bitter and frustrated.

distinguishing facts from opinions (Chapter 9) ___d___

17. Which of the following represents an opinion about Buddha rather than a fact?

a. He was married at 16 to a cousin the same age.

b. He therefore resumed eating normally and abandoned asceticism.

c. By the time he died, in 483 B.C., he had made thousands of converts.

d. Buddha, as the founder of one of the world's major religions, clearly deserves a place among the most influential people in history.

¶3 vocabulary in context (Chapter 2) ___c___

18. Which of the following is the meaning of *clouded* as it is used in paragraph 3?

a. refreshed

b. strengthened

c. confused

d. destroyed

¶4 author's intended meaning (Chapter 9) ___a___

19. In paragraph 4 the author says "all the pieces of the puzzle seemed to fall into place" for Siddhartha, to mean that Siddhartha:

a. finally achieved the insight into human existence that he had sought for so long.

b. gave up because none of the solutions he found had worked.

c. continued to be puzzled and perplexed about the human condition.

d. became puzzled by the challenges that seemed to befall him.

¶s 1–6 authors' writing patterns (Chapter 7) ___a___

20. The pattern of organization in paragraphs 1–6 can best be described as a:

a. list.

b. sequence.

c. cause and an effect.

d. comparison.

✓ **Teaching Tip**

We suggest that rather than include this section as part of the quiz grade, you use it to give students practice with the skills they have studied and as a helpful preview of upcoming skills. It makes an excellent collaborative activity. All students will find this practice helpful, but especially those who must take course exit tests, standardized reading tests, or state-mandated basic skills tests.

SELECTION **6-2**

History *(continued)*

Writing and Collaborating to Enhance Your Understanding

Option for collaboration: Your instructor may direct you to work with other students or, in other words, to work *collaboratively.* In that case, you should form groups of three or four students as directed by your instructor and work together to complete the exercises. After your group discusses each item and agrees on the answer, have a group member record it. Every member of your group should be able to explain all of your group's answers.

Collaboration Option

1. Reacting to What You Have Read: Many people today buy more things than they can afford and, although they have more possessions, they complain that they are still not truly happy. Why do you think this is so?

(Answers will vary.)

2. **Comprehending the Selection Further:** Do you agree with Buddha's first "Noble Truth" that human life is intrinsically unhappy? Explain why you agree or disagree.

(Answers will vary.)

3. **Overall Main Idea of the Selection:** In one sentence tell what the author wants readers to understand about Buddha. (Be sure to include the name "Buddha" in your overall main idea sentence.)

Buddha, as the founder of one of the world's major religions, clearly deserves a place among the most influential people in history. (stated; first sentence of paragraph 7)

Internet Resources

Read More about This Topic on the World Wide Web

Directions: For further information about the topic of the selection, visit these websites:

www.buddhanet.net
This is the official website of the Buddha Dharma Education Association, sponsors of the Buddhist Information and Education Network.

www.fwbo.org/buddhism.html
This site, sponsored by the Friends of Western Buddhist Order, presents information on Buddhism and meditation.

You can also use your favorite search engine such as Goggle, Yahoo!, or AltaVista (www.google.com, www.yahoo.com, www.altavista.com) to discover more about this topic. To locate additional information, type in combinations of keywords such as:

Buddhism

or

Gautama Buddha

Keep in mind that whenever you go to *any* website, it is a good idea to evaluate the website and the information it contains. Ask yourself questions such as:

"Who sponsors this website?"
"Is the information contained in this website up-to-date?"
"What type of information is presented?"
"Is the information objective and complete?"
"How easy is it to use the features of this website?"

SELECTION **6-3**
History

THE NEW IMMIGRANTS: ASIAN AMERICANS AND LATINOS

From *Nation of Nations: A Narrative History of the American Republic*
By James Davidson et al.

Between 1990 and 2005, immigration to the United States changed dramatically. Never before had our nation experienced such ethnic and racial diversity among our immigrant newcomers. The U.S. Census Bureau projects that in 2050 the nation's population will be 46 percent Anglo, 30 percent Latino, 15 percent African American, and 9 percent Asian. This U.S. history textbook selection explains the background and nature of this dramatic shift.

1 The Immigration Act of 1965 altered the face of American life. The lawmakers who passed the act did not expect such far-reaching consequences, because they assumed that Europeans would continue to predominate among newcomers. Yet this reform of the old quota system opened the way for a wave of immigrants unequaled since the beginning of the century.

Economic and Political Causes of Immigration

2 Turmoil abroad pushed many immigrants toward the United States, beginning in the 1960s with Fidel Castro's revolution in Cuba and unrest in the Dominican Republic. The war in Vietnam and its aftermath produced more than 500,000 refugees in the 15 years after 1975. Revolutionary conflicts in Central America during the 1980s launched new streams. Yet economic factors played as great a role as the terrors of war. Although some Filipinos fled the repressive regime of Ferdinand Marcos, many more came to the United States in a more straightforward search for economic prosperity. When Mexico suffered an economic downturn in the 1980s, emigration there rose sharply.

3 In all, about 13 million immigrants arrived in the United States between 1990 and 2005. The nation's foreign-born population rose to 11.7 percent, the highest proportion since World War II. In the 1990s, the Latino population increased by over 35 percent to about 30.3 million. The Asian American population grew at an even faster rate, to about 10.8 million. Through the decade a steadily expanding economy made immigrants a welcome source of new labor. Prosperity, in turn, reduced—though it did not eliminate—conflict among long-standing residents, new immigrants, and people on the margin of the labor market.

THE NEW LOOK OF AMERICA—ASIAN AMERICANS

4 In 1970, 96 percent of Asian Americans were Japanese, Chinese, or Filipino. By the year 2000, those same three groups constituted only about half of all Asian Americans. As the diversity of Asian immigration increased, Asian Indians, Koreans, and Vietnamese came to outnumber Japanese Americans. The newcomers also varied dramatically in economic background, crowding both ends of the economic spectrum.

Annotation Practice Exercises

Directions: For each exercise below, write the topic and the main idea on the lines beside the paragraph. (You may need to formulate the main idea.) Then identify the supporting details and list them *separately* on the lines provided.

Annotation Exercise

Topic of paragraph 2:

reasons immigrants came to the United States

Main idea sentence of paragraph 2:

Turmoil and economic factors caused many immigrants to come to the United States. (Implied: Formula 3, combine important information)

List the *supporting details* on separate lines:

- Fidel Castro's revolution in Cuba
- unrest in the Dominican Republic
- war in Vietnam
- revolutionary conflicts in Central America
- Filipinos in search of economic prosperity
- Mexicans fleeing economic downturn

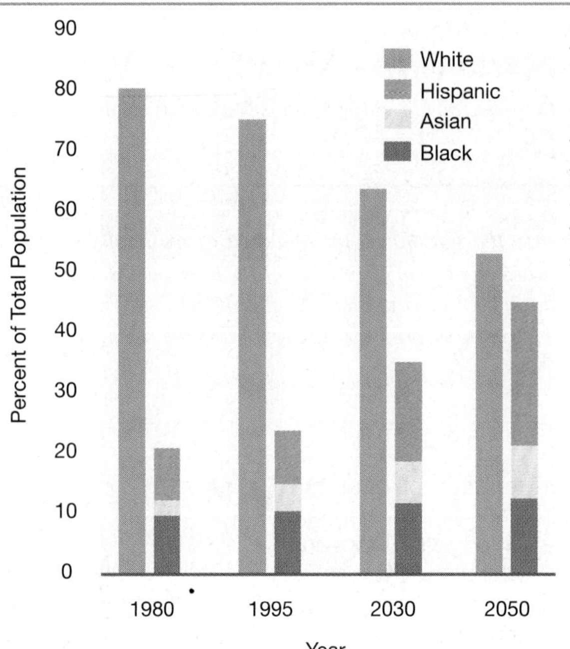

Projected Population Shifts, 1980–2050
The 6.5 million immigrants who arrived between 1990 and 1998 accounted for 32 percent of the increase in the total U.S. population. Census figures project an increasing racial and ethnic diversity. White population is projected to drop from 80 percent in 1980 to about 53 percent in 2050, with the nation's Latino population rising most sharply.

Prosperous Newcomers

5 The higher end included many Chinese students who, beginning in the 1960s, sought out the United States for a college education, then found a job and stayed, eventually bringing in their families. "My brother-in-law left his wife in Taiwan and came here as a student to get his Ph.D. in engineering," explained Subi Lin Felipe. "After he received his degree, he got a job in San Jose. Then he brought in a sister and his wife, who brought over one of her brothers and me. And my brother's wife then came."

6 Asian Indians were even more acculturated upon arrival because about two-thirds entered the United States already speaking English and with college degrees already in hand. Indian engineers played a vital role in the computer and software industries. Similarly, Korean and Filipino professionals took skilled jobs, particularly in medical fields.

Blue-Collar Asians

7 Yet Asian immigrants also included those on the lower rungs of the economic ladder. Among the new wave of Chinese immigrants, many blue-collar workers settled in the nation's Chinatowns, where they worked in restaurants or sewed in sweatshops. Without education and language skills, often in debt to labor contractors, most remained trapped in Chinatown's ethnic economy. Refugees from war and revolution in Southeast Asia often made harrowing journeys. Vietnamese families crowded into barely seaworthy boats, sometimes only to be terrorized by pirates, other times nearly drowned in storms before reaching poorly equipped Thai refugee camps. By 1990 almost a million war refugees had arrived in the United States, three-quarters of them from Vietnam, most of the others from Laos or Cambodia.

8 Thus the profile of Asian immigration resembled an hourglass, with the most newcomers either relatively affluent or extremely poor. Even so, such statistics could be misleading. More than half of all Asian American families lived in just five metropolitan areas—Honolulu, Los Angeles, San Francisco, Chicago, and New York—where the cost of living ranked among the nation's highest. High prices meant real earnings were lower. With professions like dentistry, nursing, and health technology where Asians found work, they often held lower-paying positions. Those Asians who worked in sales were more often retail clerks than insurance agents of stockbrokers.

Asian Downward Mobility

9 Asian American immigrants experienced two forms of downward mobility. First, highly educated Asian immigrants often found it difficult or impossible to land jobs in their professions. To American observers, Korean shopkeepers seemed examples of success, when in fact such owners often enough had been former professionals in their native countries. Here they were forced into the risky small-business world. Second, schools reported significant numbers of Asian American students who were failing. This "lost generation" were most often the children of families who entered the United States with little education and few job skills.

Annotation Exercise

Topic of paragraph 9:

Asian Americans and downward mobility

Main idea sentence of paragraph 9:

Asian American immigrants experienced two forms of downward mobility. (Stated; first sentence)

List the *supporting details* on separate lines:

- Highly educated Asians often found it difficult or impossible to land jobs in their professions.
- Schools reported significant numbers of Asian American students who were failing.

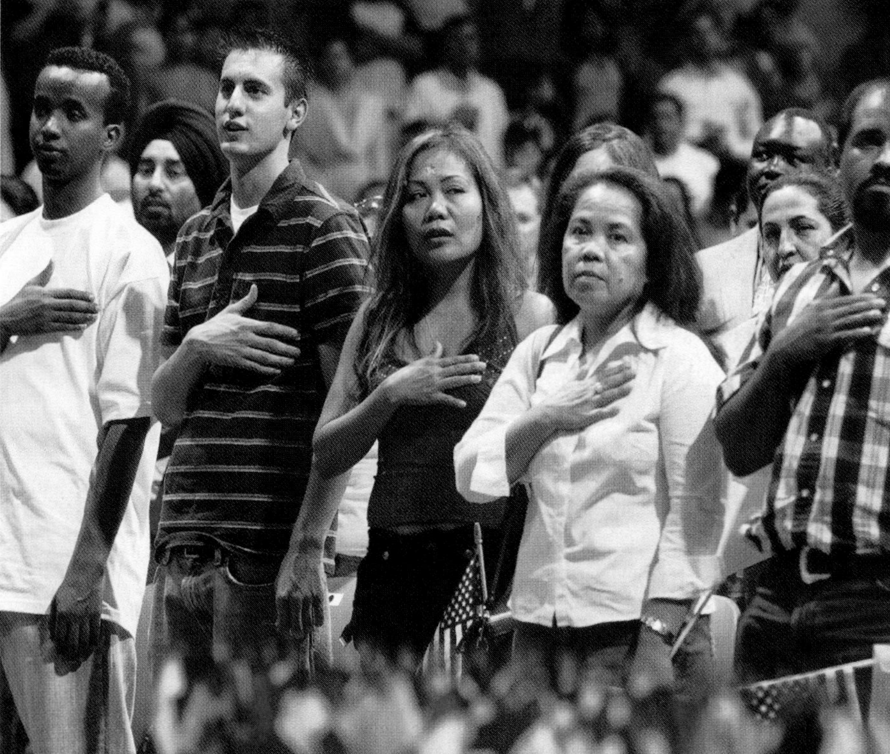

Today's immigrants represent a broad range of nationalities and cultures.

THE NEW LOOK OF AMERICA—LATINOS

10 Like Asian Americans, Latinos in the United States constituted a diverse group, reflecting dozens of immigrant streams. Although the groups shared a language, they usually settled in distinct urban and suburban barrios across the United States. Such enclave communities provided support to newcomers and an economic foothold for newly established businesses. Money circulated within a community; the workers and owners of an ethnic grocery, for example, spent their wages at neighboring stores, whose profits fueled other immigrant businesses in a chain reaction.

11 Washington Heights, at the northern tip of New York City, followed that path as nearly a quarter of a million Dominicans settled there during the 1970s and 1980s. A hundred blocks to the south, Manhattan's skyscrapers seemed distant; shopkeepers' stereos along the major thoroughfares boomed music of trumpets and congas, while peddlers pushed heavily loaded shopping carts through busy streets, crying "*¡A peso! ¡A peso!*" ("*For a dollar!*"). In addition, Dominican social clubs planned dances or hosted political discussions. Sports clubs competed actively. Similarly, in Miami and elsewhere in South Florida, Cuban Americans created their own self-sustaining enclaves. A large professional class and strong community leadership brought them prosperity and political influence.

12 Along the West Coast, Los Angeles was the urban magnet for many Latino (and Asian) immigrants. Mexican immigrants had long flocked to East Los Angeles, which in the 1990s continued to allow access to the jobs in factories, warehouses, and railroad yards across the river. Many Mexican Americans now owned their own businesses and homes. But beginning in the mid-1980s and 1990s the Los Angeles neighborhood of MacArthur Park became the focal point for the newest immigrants from Mexico and Central America. MacArthur Park was less developed as a community, and many of its residents were transient, passing quickly to other neighborhoods or jobs.

13 More factories and service industries became decentralized locating themselves beyond urban downtowns; the barrios followed as well. Las Americas near Houston was one example; but suburban barrios could be found dotted all across the nation, from Rockville, Maryland, to Pacoima, California, near Burbank. Pacoima's well-kept bungalows housed working-class Mexican Americans who had lived in California for decades. But the front lawns of many houses were often paved over to hold the cars of additional workers or families, and the garages were converted to dormitories with a sink and toilet, where four or five newcomers from Central America could rent a spot to lay a bedroll on the cement floor.

Changes in the Patterns of Global Immigration

14 By the end of the twentieth century, immigration patterns had changed in important ways. Although cities remained the mecca of most immigrants, many newcomers of the 1980s and 1990s settled in suburban areas, particularly in the West and Southwest. Industrial factories provided the lion's share in the 1890s, but a century later the service industries—grocery stores,

fast-food chains, janitorial companies—absorbed many more of the new arrivals. Even the faces had changed, as European immigrants found themselves outnumbered by Latinos and Asians, not to mention increasing numbers of Arabs from the Middle East and Africans.

15 This broad geographic range reflected perhaps the most important shift in immigration today: its truly global character.

Annotation Exercise

Topic of paragraph 14:

immigration patterns at the end of the twentieth century

Main idea sentence of paragraph 14:

By the end of the twentieth century, immigration patterns had changed in important ways.

(Stated; first sentence)

List the *supporting details* on separate lines:

- increase in immigrants settling in suburban areas
- shift from factory employment to employment in the service areas
- fewer Europeans: more Latinos and Asians
- increased immigration by Arabs and Africans

Source: Adapted from James Davidson et al., *Nation of Nations: A Narrative History of the American Republic,* 6th ed., pp. 958–61. Copyright © 2008 by The McGraw-Hill Companies, Inc. Reprinted by permission of The McGraw-Hill Companies, Inc.

SELECTION 6-3 History (continued)

Comprehension and Vocabulary Quiz

This quiz has four parts. Your instructor may assign some or all of them.

Comprehension

Directions: Items 1–5 test your comprehension (understanding) of the material in this selection. These questions are much like those that a content area instructor (such as a health professor) would expect you to know after reading and studying this selection. For each comprehension question below, use information from the selection to determine the correct answer. Refer to the selection as you answer the questions. Write your answers in the spaces provided.

¶2 c **1.** Immigration from Mexico rose sharply in the 1980s due to:
- *a.* political unrest.
- *b.* revolutionary conflicts in neighboring countries.
- *c.* downturn in the Mexican economy.
- *d.* all of the above.

bar graph and caption a **2.** The population group in the United States that is projected to have the sharpest increase during the next 50 years is:
- *a.* Hispanics.
- *b.* Asians.
- *c.* Blacks.
- *d.* Whites.

¶7 c **3.** By 1990, almost three-quarters of a million war refugees had arrived in the United States from:
- *a.* China.
- *b.* Thailand.
- *c.* Vietnam.
- *d.* Cambodia.

¶14 d **4.** By the end of the twentieth century, more immigrants:
- *a.* had settled in suburban areas.
- *b.* had found work in the service industries.
- *c.* were non-Europeans.
- *d.* all of the above.

bar graph and caption c **5.** The population group in the United States that is projected to remain about the same size during the next 50 years is:
- *a.* Hispanic.
- *b.* Asian.
- *c.* Black.
- *d.* White.

✓ **Teaching Tip**

Show students where the answer to each comprehension question appears in the selection or have students work in pairs to identify where each answer appears.

Vocabulary in Context

Directions: Items 6–10 test your ability to determine the meaning of the word by using context clues. *Context clues* are words in a sentence that allow the reader to deduce (reason out) the meaning of an unfamiliar word in that sentence. Context clues also enable the reader to determine which meaning the author intends when a word has more than one meaning. For each vocabulary item below, a sentence from the selection containing an important word (*italicized, like this*) is quoted first. Next, there is an additional sentence using the word in the same sense and providing another context clue. Use the context clues from *both* sentences to deduce the meaning of the italicized word. *Be sure the answer you choose makes sense in both sentences.* If you need to use a dictionary to confirm your answer choice, remember that the meaning you select must still fit the context of *both* sentences. Write your answers in the spaces provided.

Pronunciation Key: ă **pat** ā **pay** âr **care** ä **father** ĕ **pet** ē **be** ĭ **pit** ī **tie** îr **pier** ŏ **pot** ō **toe** ô **paw** oi **noise** ou **out** o͝o **took** o͞o **boot** ŭ **cut** yo͞o ab**use** ûr **urge** th **thin** *th* **this** hw **which** zh vi**sion** ə **about** *Stress mark:* ′

¶2 

6. *Turmoil* abroad pushed many immigrants toward the United States, beginning in the 1960s with Fidel Castro's revolution in Cuba and unrest in the Dominican Republic.

European countries have often experienced *turmoil* due to massive labor strikes.

turmoil (tûr′ moil) means:

a. arguments

b. agitation; disturbance

c. economic problems

d. revolution

¶2 ______

7. When Mexico suffered an economic downturn in the 1980s, *emigration* there rose sharply.

After the Nazis came to power, there was a large *emigration* of scientists from Germany to the United States.

emigration (ĕm ĭ grā′ shən) means:

a. problems caused by a poor economy

b. change in a population

c. entering or settling in a country or a region

d. leaving a country or region to settle in another

¶8 c **8.** Thus the profile of Asian immigration resembled an *hourglass,* with the most newcomers relatively affluent or extremely poor.

The children liked the *hourglass* on display at the museum; they were fascinated that sand trickling through it was once a way to tell time.

hourglass (our′ glăs) means:

a. a large, fragile clock

b. a piece of children's play equipment that consisted of loops and twists

c. an instrument for measuring time, consisting of two glass chambers connected by a narrow neck

d. an instrument of lenses and mirrors that functions as a small telescope

¶8 d **9.** More than half of all Asian American families lived in five *metropolitan* areas—Honolulu, Los Angeles, San Francisco, Chicago, and New York—where the cost of living ranked among the nation's highest.

The New York Times and *The Washington Post* are two of the best-known *metropolitan* newspapers.

metropolitan (mĕt rə pŏl′ ĭ tən) means:

a. highly interesting; intriguing

b. extremely competitive

c. related to the coast of the United States

d. related to a major city or urbanized area

¶12 b **10.** MacArthur Park was less developed as a community, and many of its residents were *transient,* passing quickly to other neighborhoods or jobs.

At harvest time, *transient* farm laborers go from farm to farm to pick crops.

transient (trăn′ zē ənt) means:

a. coming from another country

b. remaining in a place only a brief time

c. new to an area

d homeless

Word Structure

Directions: Items 11–15 below test your ability to use word-structure clues to help determine a word's meaning. *Word-structure clues* consist of roots, prefixes, and suffixes. In these exercises, you will learn the meaning of a word part (a root) and use it to determine the meaning of several other words that have the same word part. If you need to use a dictionary to confirm your answer choice, do so. Write your answers in the spaces provided.

In paragraph 9 of the selection, you encountered the word ***generation.*** This word contains the Latin root ***gen,*** which means "birth" or "origin." The word *generation* describes the children, grandchildren, and great-grandchildren of people, the offspring of a family through time. Use the meaning of the root ***gen*** and the list of prefixes on pages 68–69 to help you determine the meaning of each of the following words that contain the same root.

a 11. The science of **genetics** refers to:
a. the origins of inherited characteristics; heredity.
b. disease and illness.
c. the science of life; biology.
d. nutrition and exercise.

c 12. When a family records their **genealogy**, they:
a. maintain a health record.
b. write a family history.
c. document their descent from their ancestors and their origins.
d. collect heirlooms and memorabilia from relatives.

b 13. To **generate** ideas means:
a. to explain them to others.
b. to produce or give birth to them.
c. to examine or inspect them.
d. to accept them.

d 14. If a person is **ingenious**, he or she:
a. is unskilled.
b. has many relatives.
c. cannot learn new things quickly.
d. has inborn talent.

c 15. Your **progeny** are your:
a. ancestors.
b. enemies.
c. offspring or descendants.
d. friends and neighbors.

✓ **Teaching Tip**
Let students know that not all of the skills included in this "Reading Skills Application" section have been introduced yet. This section serves as a valuable preview of these skills, however. Students typically get several of the items correct, and they find this encouraging.

Reading Skills Application

Directions: Items 16–20 test your ability to *apply* certain reading skills to information in this selection. These types of questions provide valuable practice for all students, especially those who must take standardized reading tests and state-mandated basic skills tests. You may not have studied all of the skills at this point, so these items will serve as a helpful preview. The comprehension and critical reading skills in this section are presented in Chapters 3 through 9 of *New Worlds;* vocabulary and figurative language skills are presented in Chapter 2. As you work through *New Worlds,* you will practice and develop these skills. Write your answers in the spaces provided.

¶4 phrase in context (Chapter 2)

b 16. Which of the following is the meaning of the term *economic spectrum* as it is used in paragraph 4?
a. variety of backgrounds
b. range of incomes
c. economic specialties
d. wealthy newcomers

¶14 stated main idea (Chapter 4) ___c___

17. Which of the following statements best expresses the main idea of paragraph 14?

a. Although cities remained the mecca of most immigrants, many newcomers of the 1980s and 1990s settled in suburban areas, particularly in the West and Southwest.

b. Industrial factories provided the lion's share of work for immigrants in the 1890s, but a century later the service industries absorbed more of the new arrivals.

c. By the end of the twentieth century, immigration patterns had changed in important ways.

d. European immigrants found themselves outnumbered by Latinos and Asians.

¶2 author's writing patterns (Chapter 7) ___d___

18. Which of the following patterns was used to organize the information in paragraph 2?

a. list

b. sequence

c. comparison-contrast

d. cause-effect

chart and caption interpreting graphic material (Chapter 10) ___d___

19. According to data from the graph in the selection, which population group is projected to drop by 2050?

a. Hispanic

b. Asian

c. Black

d. White

authors' purpose for writing (Chapter 8) ___c___

20. Which of the following describes the authors' purpose for writing this selection?

a. to entertain readers with stories of how people who are just like they are came to the United States

b. to persuade readers to accept the new immigrants who have come to live in the United States

c. to inform readers about the significant changes in immigration that took place at the end of the twentieth century

d. to teach readers about the immigration process

✓ **Teaching Tip**

We suggest that rather than include this section as part of the quiz grade, you use it to give students practice with the skills they have studied and as a helpful preview of upcoming skills. It makes an excellent collaborative activity. All students will find this practice helpful, but especially those who must take course exit tests, standardized reading tests, or state-mandated basic skills tests.

SELECTION 6-3
History
(continued)

Writing and Collaborating to Enhance Your Understanding

Option for collaboration: Your instructor may direct you to work with other students or, in other words, to work *collaboratively.* In that case, you should form groups of three or four students as directed by your instructor and work together to complete the exercises. After your group discusses each item and agrees on the answer, have a group member record it. Every member of your group should be able to explain all of your group's answers.

Collaboration Option

1. **Reacting to What You Have Read:** Most U.S. states and cities have experienced notable immigration trends during the last 20 years. Name the immigrant groups that have settled recently in your city or region of the country. Have any population groups grown? Have any population groups declined?

   (Answers will vary.)

2. **Comprehending the Selection Further:** The authors of this selection discuss how immigration has become truly global, with immigrants coming to the United States from every part of the world. In what ways do immigrants who settle in the United States enrich our culture and economy?

   1. They are a welcome source of new labor.
   2. Many complete their college education in the United States and then join our professional workforce.
   3. Many know how to speak English and already have college degrees.
   4. Many start their own businesses and become homeowners.
   5. They bring fresh energy and talent.
   6. They bring their knowledge of other languages, cultures, and traditions.
   7. Many bring an enthusiasm and appreciation for their new country that reminds others of its benefits.

3. **Overall Main Idea of the Selection:** In one sentence, tell what the authors want readers to understand about the recent changes in immigration to the United States. (Be sure to include the words "immigration," "Asian Americans," and "Latino" in your overall main idea sentence.)

Between 1990 and 2005, immigration to the United States became more diverse than ever before, and there were significant increases in the number of Asian American and Latino immigrants.

Internet Resources

Read More about This Topic on the World Wide Web

Directions: For further information about the topic of the selection, visit these websites:

www.fordham.edu/HALSALL/MOD/modsbook28.html
This site is sponsored by the Internet Modern History Sourcebook Project. This web page contains information about Asian, Latin American, and European immigrants.

www.usimmigrationsupport.org
This is the United States Government Immigration Support site. It contains information about obtaining U.S. citizenship, green cards, and U.S. visas.

You can also use your favorite search engine such as Google, Yahoo!, or AltaVista (www.google.com, www.yahoo.com, www.altavista.com) to discover more about this topic. To locate additional information, type in combinations of keywords such as:

U.S. immigration

or

Asian American Immigration

or

Latin American Immigration

Keep in mind that whenever you go to *any* website, it is a good idea to evaluate the website and the information it contains. Ask yourself questions such as:

"Who sponsors this website?"
"Is the information contained in this website up-to-date?"
"What type of information is presented?"
"Is the information objective and complete?"
"How easy is it to use the features of this website?"

CHAPTER 7

Recognizing Authors' Writing Patterns

CHAPTER OBJECTIVES

In this chapter you will learn the answers to these questions:

- What are authors' writing patterns, and why are they important?
- How are transition words used to indicate the relationship of ideas within and between sentences?
- What is the method for recognizing authors' writing patterns?

✓ **Timely Words**

"A man only learns in two ways, one by reading, and the other by associating with smarter people." (Will Rogers)

"Wear the old coat and buy the new book." (Austin Phelps)

CHAPTER CONTENTS

WHAT ARE AUTHORS' WRITING PATTERNS, AND WHY ARE THEY IMPORTANT?

In the first part of this chapter, you will learn how authors use transition words to show the relationship of ideas within sentences and the relationship of ideas between sentences.

Next, you will be introduced to five common writing patterns textbook authors frequently use to organize paragraphs and longer selections they write:

- Definition pattern
- List pattern
- Sequence pattern
- Comparison-contrast pattern
- Cause-effect pattern

Finally, you will be introduced to other patterns you are likely to encounter in college textbooks and other materials:

- Definition and example pattern
- Generalization and example pattern
- Location or spatial order pattern
- Summary pattern
- Classification pattern
- Addition pattern
- Statement and clarification pattern

KEY TERM
writing patterns

Ways authors organize the information they present.

Writing patterns are also known as *organizational patterns, patterns of development,* and *thinking patterns.*

Writing patterns are ways authors organize the information they present. You may hear writing patterns referred to as *patterns of organization, patterns of development,* or *thinking patterns.* These are all names for the same thing.

We all use patterns to organize our thoughts in ways that seem logical to us. The patterns authors use are the same thinking patterns that you use every day. If you can identify the pattern an author is using and "think along" with the author as you read, you will find it easier to comprehend what he or she is saying.

The specific transition words or pattern an author uses depends on the important relationship among the ideas, the relationship he or she wants to emphasize. The author chooses the most logical pattern that will accomplish this.

Just as textbook authors use patterns to organize their thoughts, so do you and all college students. Here are everyday examples of how college students use patterns to organize their thoughts. Notice how the content of their comments matches the pattern of organization being used.

Student Online Learning Center (OLC)
***Go to* Chapter 7.**
***Select* Video.**

"My art professor asked me to prepare a portfolio, a representative collection of my work." *(definition)*

"I'm taking four courses this semester: history, psychology, reading, and math." *(list pattern)*

"I have my history class first, then psychology class. On alternate days, I have my reading class first, then my math class." *(sequence pattern)*

"I have weekly quizzes in history and math, but not in reading or psychology." *(comparison-contrast pattern)*

"If I maintain at least a B average this semester, my scholarship will be renewed." *(cause-effect pattern)*

✓ **Teaching Tip**
Remind students that the student OLC contains an audio and video feature for Chapters 3 through 9 that presents **Key Comprehension Terms** and **Comprehension Monitoring Questions.**

Although you use patterns when you speak or write, you may not be in the habit of recognizing them when you read and study your textbooks. This chapter will show you how to recognize the patterns when you are reading.

Why is it important to be able to recognize authors' writing patterns? There are four advantages to recognizing authors' writing patterns when you read and study:

- *Your comprehension will improve.* You will comprehend more because you will be able to follow and understand the writers' ideas more accurately and more efficiently.
- *You will be able to predict what is coming next.* As soon as you identify the pattern, you can make predictions about what is likely to come next in a paragraph. As you learned in Chapter 1, effective readers are active readers who make logical predictions as they read.
- *It will be easier to memorize information when you study.* You can memorize information more efficiently when you understand the way it is organized. Consequently, you will also be able to recall it more effectively.
- *Your writing will improve.* Using these patterns when you write will enable you to write paragraphs that are clearer and better organized. This also means you can write better answers on essay tests simply by using appropriate patterns to organize information.

TRANSITION WORDS THAT SIGNAL THE RELATIONSHIP OF IDEAS WITHIN SENTENCES AND BETWEEN SENTENCES

Did you realize that within each sample sentence on page 351 there was a relationship among the ideas it contained? These relationships are so common that we barely notice them when we read them or use them when we speak or write. We understand them and their importance, however. For example, you would have one expectation if your sister begins a sentence, "I was hoping my boyfriend would propose, *and* . . ." and another if she said, "I was hoping my boyfriend would propose, *but*. . . . " The words *and* and *but* suggest two very different endings to the sentence—and outcomes!

KEY TERM
transition words
Words and phrases that show relationships among ideas in sentences, paragraphs, and longer selections.

Like everyone else, authors use certain words to show the relationship of ideas within sentences and between sentences. Words and phrases that show relationships among ideas in sentences, paragraphs, and longer selections are called **transition words.** (You will learn later in the chapter that they use these same words to signal the organization of paragraphs and longer selections, as well.) You can improve your comprehension of college textbooks if you pay attention to transition words. Now read about the types of relationships below and the transition words that signal them. In the examples, the transition words are italicized.

✓ **Teaching Tip**
Although this section will be of help to all students, it will be particularly relevant to students who take the state-mandated test in Florida.

Addition The transition words signal the author is giving additional information. The order of the information or facts is not important. Transition words that signal addition include *moreover, another, in addition, also, first, second, next,* and so forth.

- *Within-sentence examples:* "In the 2008 Olympics, Michael Phelps won gold medals in all eight swimming events he entered; *moreover,* he set world records in seven of them" or "Michael Phelps set seven world records at the 2008 Olympics, and he swam in eight events."

- *Between-sentences example:* "At the opening ceremonies of the Olympics, the Olympic torch is ignited. *Another* tradition is the releasing of doves. *In addition,* each country's athletes parade around the stadium track."

Sequence The transition words signal the author is presenting things in the order in which they happened or will happen. Watch for words that indicate time, such as *first, then, later, previous, before, earlier, during, next, last,* and *finally*. Some of the same words used for the addition relationship can also indicate a time relationship if the order matters.

- *Within-sentence example:* "In December 1787, the *first* state to enter the United States was Delaware, *followed by* Pennsylvania, and *then* New Jersey."
- *Between-sentences example:* "*During* 1959, the final two states joined the Union. In August, Hawaii became the *last* state to join. Alaska joined eight months *earlier,* in January."

✓ **Teaching Tips**

- The Hale-Bopp comet will appear again in the year 4397.
- Paralympics should not be confused with the Special Olympics, which is open to all children and adults with intellectual disabilities, regardless of their levels of athletic ability. Paralympics = "other Olympics."
- Julius Caesar was honored because he reformed the calendar. Caesar Augustus was his grandnephew. The adjective *august* (au-GUST) means "grand" or "majestic."

Contrast The transition words signal the author is presenting a difference, an opposing view, or an exception. These words include *in contrast, but, on the other hand, on the contrary, unlike,* and *although.*

- *Within-sentence examples:* "*Although* presidential conventions used to be lively events, today they are duller, made-for-television affairs" and "There is still no cure for AIDS, *but* there are effective drugs."
- *Between-sentences examples:* "Crossword puzzles have always been popular. *However,* sudoku math puzzles are gaining widespread popularity" and "Halley's comet appears every 75 years. *In contrast,* the Hale-Bopp comet appears every 2,400 years."

Comparison The transition words signal the author is presenting one or more ways that things are alike (makes a comparison). Transition words such as *similarly, like, likewise, in the same way, along the same lines, in the same manner,* and *both* indicate that a comparison is being made.

- *Within-sentence example*: "The Olympics is a competition among the world's best athletes; *similarly,* the Paralympics is a world competition among people with physical disabilities who have top-level athletic ability."
- *Between-sentences example:* "Sending and receiving text messages is a high-frequency use of cell phones. *Along the same lines,* taking still pictures is a popular use."

Cause-Effect The transition words signal the author is presenting causes (reasons things happen) or effects (results or outcomes). Watch for transitions such as *resulted in, as a result, led to, caused, due to, because, caused by, so, consequently, therefore,* and *thus.*

- *Within-sentence example:* "*Because* the Senate of ancient Rome wanted to honor Julius Caesar, it named the month of July in his honor." (*cause:* Senate wanted to honor Julius Caesar; *effect/result:* it named the month of July after him.)
- *Between-sentences example:* "The Roman Senate also wanted to honor Emperor Augustus Caesar. *Consequently,* it named the month of August after him." (*cause:* Senate wanted to honor Emperor Augustus Caesar; *effect/result:* it named the month of August after him.)

Example The transition words signal the author is presenting an example that will help clarify or explain something. Transition words that announce examples are *to illustrate, such as, for instance,* and *for example.*

- *Within-sentence example:* "Florida boasts some unique national parks, *such as* the Everglades."
- *Between-sentences example:* "California has many famous national parks. *Examples* include Yosemite National Park, Redwood National Park, and Sequoia National Park."

Conclusion The transition words signal the author is presenting a conclusion, an outcome based on facts that preceded it. Signal words include *in conclusion, thus, therefore,* and *consequently.*

- *Within-sentence example:* "The chairman of the board was accused of wrongdoing, and *thus* he was forced to resign."
- *Between-sentences example:* "Bogus U.S. paper currency has become a massive problem. *Consequently,* the government is introducing paper currency that is much more difficult to counterfeit."

Summary The transition words signal the author is presenting a summary, a restatement of the most important point or points. Signal words include *to summarize, in summary, in brief,* and *in short.*

- *Within-sentence example:* "*In short,* world population increase and environmental damage go hand in hand."
- *Between-sentences example:* "Behavioral, genetic, hormonal, environmental, and cultural factors contribute to obesity. It can be said, *in summary,* that there are multiple causes of obesity."

Authors do not always use transition words to signal the relationship of ideas within sentences and between sentences. Even when there are no transition words, you still need to figure out the relationship among the ideas. Go back through the material and think about how it is organized. Seeing the relationship among ideas will help you understand and remember the material. And, as writing and English instructors will tell you, the correct use of transition words will make your own writing clearer and more effective.

Here is a short selection with the transition words italicized. Notice how they guide you through the material from one thought to the next:

> A cup of coffee is harmless, right? Perhaps, but people who drink too much coffee can experience undesirable changes in their heart rate, breathing rate, and blood pressure. *Moreover,* those who are allergic to caffeine can experience severe reactions, *such as* excruciating migraine headaches. Even those who do not have severe reactions may still experience irritation to their stomach lining when they drink coffee on an empty stomach. *And,* of course, everyone knows that coffee can make you jumpy and jittery. *On the other hand,* for those who are about to exercise, a small amount of caffeine can actually improve athletic performance. *The point is,* you must know your own body and respect its tolerance for coffee.

Here is the same passage, but explanations of the transitions have been inserted [*in italics, in brackets, and highlighted, like this*]. Notice how the author used the transitions to steer or guide readers through the ideas.

A cup of coffee is harmless, right? [*Introductory question designed to get the reader's attention.*] Perhaps, but people who drink too much coffee can experience undesirable changes in their heart rate, breathing rate, and blood pressure. [*Answers the introductory question by listing some possible negative effects.*] *Moreover,* [*the explanation of undesirable effects is going to be continued*] those who are allergic to caffeine can experience severe reactions, *such as* [*an example is being introduced*] excruciating migraine headaches. Even those who do not have severe reactions may still experience irritation to their stomach lining when they drink coffee on an empty stomach. *And,* [*more negative effects will be presented*] of course, everyone knows that coffee can make you jumpy and jittery. *On the other hand,* [*a change; something positive about coffee will be presented*] for those who are about to exercise, a small amount of caffeine can actually improve athletic performance. *The point is,* [*announces the main idea*] you must know your own body and respect its tolerance for coffee.

As you read, be alert for transition words that show the relationship of ideas within and between sentences. They also provide clues to the author's pattern of organization. Recognizing the pattern or "big picture" is a skill that will make you a more effective, efficient reader.

EXERCISE 1

Relationships of Ideas within and between Sentences

Directions: Read the following paragraph. Decide which transition word belongs in each sentence and write it in the blank.

later	and	as a result of	consequently	because	however

Mount Rushmore is South Dakota's most famous attraction. Sculptor Gutzon Borglum created it __because__ he wished to commemorate four great American presidents. In 1927, he began carving 60-foot-tall faces of Washington, Jefferson, Lincoln, __and__ Theodore Roosevelt on the side of the mountain. He died in 1941, __however__. __Consequently__, his son, Lincoln, completed the project __later__ that year. __As a result of__ Borglum's vision, dedication, and artistry, America gained a unique landmark.

Directions: Read the sentences of the following paragraph. Then circle the letter that answers each question about the relationships of ideas within and between sentences. The sentences in the paragraph are numbered for convenience.

(1) Thomas Edison is one of the most brilliant, hardworking, and prolific inventors in American history. (2) However, he had only three months of formal schooling. (3) Edison's teacher thought he was "addled," so Nancy Edison home-schooled her son. (4) Besides having limited formal education, young Edison developed hearing problems that worsened throughout his life.

(*continued on next page*)

(5) Despite these challenges, he ultimately held more than 1,300 U.S. and foreign patents for inventions he developed. (6) In short, Edison was remarkable both as a person and as an inventor.

1. What is the relationship between sentence 1 and sentence 2?
- (a.) contrast [*However;* contrasts achievement with limited formal education]
- *b.* conclusion
- *c.* example
- *d.* cause-effect

2. What is the relationship of the ideas within sentence 3?
- *a.* addition
- *b.* example
- *c.* summary
- (d.) cause-effect [*so,* home-schooled because Edison's teacher thought he was addled]

3. What is the relationship between the two ideas in sentence 4?
- (a.) addition [*Besides;* adds challenge of hearing problem to that of limited formal schooling]
- *b.* contrast
- *c.* summary
- *d.* cause-effect

4. What is the relationship between the two ideas in sentence 5?
- *a.* addition
- (b.) contrast [*Despite;* success contrasted with challenges]
- *c.* summary
- *d.* cause-effect

5. How does sentence 6 relate to the previous sentences?
- *a.* Sentence 6 adds information to the previous sentences.
- *b.* Sentence 6 presents a comparison with the previous sentences.
- *c.* Sentence 6 presents a cause-effect relationship with the previous sentences.
- (d.) Sentence 6 summarizes information from Sentence 2. [*In short;* sums up paragraph]

FIVE COMMON WRITING PATTERNS

Comprehension Monitoring Question for Recognizing Authors' Writing Patterns

"What pattern did the author use to organize the main idea and the supporting details?"

Five common writing patterns are described in this section, along with textbook excerpts that illustrate each pattern. You will be pleased to learn that every pattern has certain words and phrases that serve as signals or clues to the pattern that is being used. These signal words for a pattern will be the same regardless of what the material is about. For example, the words *In contrast* will still signal a contrast, or difference, regardless of whether the topic is types of trees or parenting styles. Keep in mind that the pattern will be determined by the organization of the ideas in the entire paragraph or selection, not by the presence of a single signal word or clue. In other words, seeing a word that can be used as a signal for a pattern does not automatically mean that the entire paragraph has that pattern. For example, a paragraph might contain the word *because* in one of its sentences, yet the entire paragraph could be a comparison and contrast pattern, not a cause-effect pattern.

After you read a textbook paragraph, ask yourself the comprehension monitoring question, "What pattern did the author use to organize the main idea and supporting details?"

Definition Pattern

Every college textbook contains important terms that will be new to students. To help you understand these key terms, authors typically define them. The sentence that gives the definition is usually the stated main idea. The rest of the paragraph will consist of additional information about the meaning of the term. When authors present the meaning of an important term that is discussed throughout the passage, they are using the **definition pattern.** Key terms and their definitions are important. Learn them, and learn to spell them. Expect to be asked them on tests.

KEY TERM
definition pattern

Pattern presenting the meaning of an important term discussed throughout the paragraph.

The definition can occur anywhere in a paragraph. Signal words that announce definitions are *this term, means, is known as, is called, refers to,* and *is defined as*. In addition, the key term may appear in **bold,** *italics,* or **color.** Sometimes the definition follows a colon (:) or a comma (,), is set off in parentheses ( ), or in brackets [], or appears after a dash (—) or between dashes. (See "Other Things to Keep in Mind When Developing a College-Level Vocabulary," page 380, for examples of definitions set off with punctuation.) The author may use a synonym (word or phrase with a similar meaning) to define the term. Synonyms are introduced by words such as *or, in other words,* and *that is*. A definition pattern paragraph is typically organized like this:

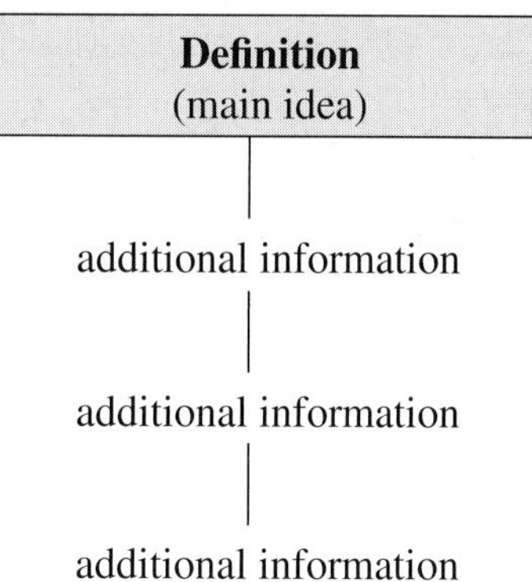

Here is a sample definition pattern paragraph from a business textbook. The topic is *productivity*. The first sentence presents the definition. Notice that it is also the main idea and that the other sentence is a detail that supplies additional information.

> **Productivity** refers to the amount of output you generate given the amount of input. The more you can produce in any given period of time, the more money you are worth to companies.
>
> *Source:* Adapted from William Nichols, James McHugh, and Susan McHugh, *Understanding Business*, 8th ed., p 13. Copyright © 2008 by The McGraw-Hill Companies, Inc. Reprinted by permission of The McGraw-Hill Companies, Inc.

Stop and Annotate

Go back to the textbook excerpt. Underline or highlight the signal words *refers to* that announce the definition.

The phrase *refers to* introduces the definition: "the amount of output you generate given the amount of input."

EXERCISE 2

Directions: In each sentence, underline the clues and signal words that indicate a definition, and then highlight the definition.

Example: *Inductive reasoning* is defined as the process of arriving at a general conclusion based on specific facts or instances. [clues: term in italics, "is defined as"]

1. Sociologists use the term **exogamy** to describe the custom of marrying outside the tribe, family, clan, or other social unit. ["the term"; term in bold]
2. A compassionate person who unselfishly helps others is often referred to as a "good Samaritan." ["referred to as"; term in quotation marks]
3. Some infomercials sell nostrums—quack medicines that contain "secret" ingredients and whose effectiveness is unproved. [definition follows a dash]
4. Writer Samuel Clements used "Mark Twain" as his pseudonym, or pen name. [definition after the word "or"]
5. When authors write under a ***pseudonym,*** it means they write under a fictitious rather than their own name [term in color, bold, italics; "means"]

EXERCISE 3

This paragraph comes from a science textbook.

The concept of an **ecological footprint** has been developed to help people measure their environmental impact on the earth. One's ecological footprint is defined as "the area of Earth's productive land and water required to supply the resources that an individual demands, as well as to absorb the wastes that the individual produces." Questionnaires posted on websites exist that allow you to estimate your ecological footprint and compare it to the footprint of others by answering a few questions about your lifestyle. Completing one of these questionnaires is a good way to gain a sense of personal responsibility for your own impact on our environment.

Source: Adapted from Eldon D. Enger and Bradley F. Smith, *Environmental Science: A Study of Interrelationships,* 11th ed., p. 30.

Which writing pattern did the author use to organize the main idea and the supporting details?

definition

Write the clues that caused you to choose this pattern.

the phrases "the concept of" and "is defined as"; terms in bold

EXERCISE 4

This paragraph comes from a psychology textbook.

The scientific study of behavior and mental processes is known as **psychology.** The phrase *behavior and mental processes* in the definition of psychology must be understood to mean many things: It encompasses not just people's actions, but also their thoughts, emotions, perceptions, reasoning processes, memories, and even the biological activities that maintain bodily functioning.

Source: Adapted from Robert S. Feldman, *Understanding Psychology*, 8th ed., p. 5. Copyright © 2008 by The McGraw-Hill Companies, Inc. Reprinted by permission of The McGraw-Hill Companies, Inc.

Which writing pattern did the author use to organize the main idea and the supporting details?

definition

Write the clues that caused you to choose this pattern.

the phrases "is known as" and "the definition of"; the term in bold

List Pattern

KEY TERM
list pattern

A group of items presented in no specific order since the order is unimportant.

The list pattern is also known as *listing pattern.*

As its name indicates, the **list pattern** presents a list of items that are *not in any specific order.* If the items were rearranged, the meaning would be the same. When you recognize that a list pattern is being used, it is important that you locate every item that is being listed.

If there is a stated main idea sentence, it will often explain what the list consists of (for example, *the symptoms of an illness* or *types of cell phones*). The details in the paragraph typically present the items in the list.

To emphasize or set off separate items in a list, authors often use:

- Words such as *and, also, another, in addition,* and *moreover*
- Numbers (1, 2, 3), even when the order of the items is not important (Numbering items in a list is referred to as *enumeration.*)
- Letters (*a, b, c*)
- Bullets (• • •)
- Asterisks (* * *)
- Certain punctuation marks, such as the colon (:)
- Phrases in the main idea sentence that suggest that the details will be presented as a list of items (*There are four types of . . . , Five ways to . . . , Several kinds of . . .*). Authors use these phrases not only to alert readers that a list is coming, but also to indicate how many items to expect. (Sometimes words such as *first, second,* and *third* are used to identify items on a list, even though the order is not important.)

Paragraphs with the list pattern are typically structured like this:

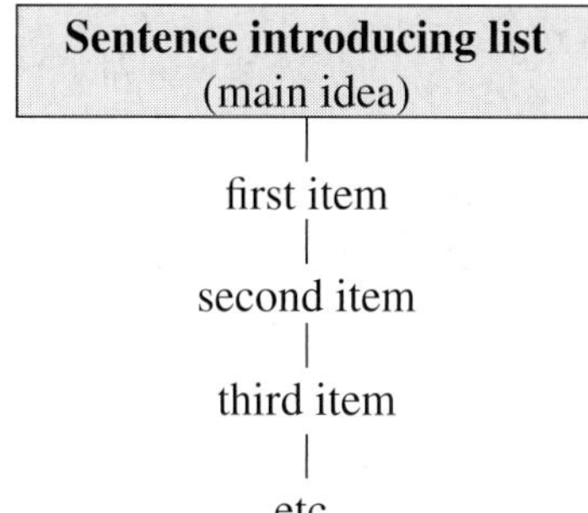

Here is a sample paragraph from a public speaking textbook. The topic is *handling audiences who know little or nothing about the topic of your speech.* The main idea (which is stated) is *There are five strategies for handling audiences that know little or nothing about the topic of your speech.* The author includes a list of details to explain what those strategies are. Notice that the details are not in any special order and are numbered so that each strategy is easy to identify. As you read the paragraph, ask yourself, "What are the strategies for handling audiences who know little or nothing about the topic of your speech?"

> What do your listeners already know about the topic? A lot? A moderate amount? Nothing at all? There are five strategies for handling audiences that know little or nothing about the topic of your speech. (1) To begin with, carefully limit the number of new ideas you discuss. People cannot absorb large amounts of new information in a short period of time. If you overwhelm them with too many concepts, they will lose interest and tune you out. (2) Whenever possible, use visual aids to help the listeners grasp the more complicated concepts. (3) Use down-to-earth language; avoid technical jargon. If you feel that you must use a specialized word, be sure to explain it. (4) Repeat key ideas, using different language each time. (5) Give vivid examples.
>
> *Source:* Adapted from Hamilton Gregory, *Public Speaking for College and Career,* 7th ed., p. 81. Copyright © 2005 by The McGraw-Hill Companies, Inc. Reprinted by permission of The McGraw-Hill Companies, Inc.

Stop and Annotate

Go back to the textbook excerpt. Underline or highlight the signal words *five strategies.* Then highlight the numbers that announce each strategy.

The author uses the phrase "There are five strategies" to alert readers to expect a list. The order in which the details (the suggestions) are presented is not important. What is important is that there are five strategies and what they are. This paragraph includes numbers, but not every paragraph does.

As you learned in Chapter 6, you should number (rather than underline or highlight) the details when you are marking your textbook. Writing a small number beside each detail helps you avoid overmarking. Also, you can see at a glance how many items there are in the list. This is important because every item in a list may not have a signal word or other clue to introduce it.

The next excerpt is from a computer science textbook. It illustrates the list pattern in a very obvious way: Each of the items in the list is bulleted. The topic of the paragraph is *the components of a computer system,* and its formulated main idea is *Five components are integral to every computer system.*

> Computers come in many sizes—from computers that occupy entire rooms, to notebook-sized computers, to computers as small as your fingernail. Although computer hardware is the most visible part of a computer, it is merely one part of a *computer system.* (A system is a collection of elements that work together to solve a specific problem.) Regardless of size, every computer needs the other components of the system to produce results. The components of a computer system are:
>
> ① • People
> ② • Data
> ③ • Procedures
> ④ • Hardware
> ⑤ • Software
>
> These components are integral to every computer system. Every time you use a computer to generate information, you become one of the five system components.
>
> *Source:* Timothy N. Trainor and Diane Krasnewich, *Computers!,* 5th ed. Copyright © 1996 by The McGraw-Hill Companies, Inc. Reprinted by permission of The McGraw-Hill Companies, Inc.

Stop and Annotate

Go back to the textbook excerpt. Underline or highlight the word *components* and the colon that signals a list. Then write a small ①, ②, ③, ④, and ⑤ beside the five items on the list.

The five details (the components in a computer system) are in no specific order and are in a list that is set off from the rest of the paragraph. It is announced by the phrase "The components of a computer system are" and also by a colon (:). Each of the five items is bulleted so that it stands out clearly. Writing small numbers beside each item will help you see (and remember) that there are five components. The word *components* also alerts readers to expect a list.

EXERCISE 5

Directions: In each sentence, underline or highlight the clues and signal words that indicate a list.

Example: Clouds are generally divided into two categories: convective and layered.

1. Be sure to see these tourist attractions in Philadelphia's Independence National Historical Park: Congress Hall, Independence Hall, and the Liberty Bell Pavilion. [colon]
2. Primary colors that can be combined to create a range of other colors are
   - red
   - blue
   - yellow
3. The governor will be at the fundraiser. In addition, both state senators, as well as four representatives, will be there.
4. Clouds are categorized according to their height above the earth. High clouds include (1) cirrus clouds, (2) cirrocumulus clouds, and (3) cirrostratus clouds.
5. In the Four Corners area of the southwestern United States, the corners of Colorado, New Mexico, Arizona, and Utah come together at right angles. [accept "Four Corners" as well]

EXERCISE 6

This pragraph comes from a health textbook.

The Millennial Generation

"Millennial generation" is the name given to today's young adults, 18 to 28 years old. Persons born between 1982 and 2000 are referred to collectively by sociologists as "millennials." Studies have found that millennials are more inclined to drop out of college for a period of time, and take longer to finish college even if they have not dropped out. Also, millennials are more likely to change colleges, and to change residences while attending the same college. In addition, they are more likely to share a residence with friends from college than to live alone or to return to home. Individuals within this generation are more likely to fill leisure time with technology-based media. Another characteristic of millennials is that they are more likely to have a diverse group of friends, in terms of both gender and race. Millennials are more likely to return home to live after completing college—the "boomerang" phenomenon.

Source: Adapted from Wayne A. Payne, Dale B. Hahn, and Ellen B. Lucas. *Understanding Your Health,* 10th ed., p. 2. Copyright © 2009 by The McGraw-Hill Companies, Inc. Reprinted by permission of The McGraw-Hill Companies, Inc.

Which writing pattern did the author use to organize the main idea and the supporting details?

list

Write the clues that caused you to choose this pattern.

the words and phrases "also," "and," "in addition," and "another"

KEY TERM
sequence pattern

A list of items presented in a specific order because the order is important.

The sequence pattern is also known as *time order, chronological order, a process,* or *a series.*

Sequence Pattern

In the **sequence pattern** a list of items is presented *in a specific order* because the order is important. A sequence is a type of list, but it differs from a list because the order of the items matters. A common type of sequence is a series of events presented in the order in which they happened. For this reason, the sequence pattern is sometimes called *time order, chronological order, a process,* or *a series.* Sets of directions (such as recipes, instructions for changing a tire or for loading a software program on a computer) are sequences you encounter daily. Examples of processes include life cycles described in a biology textbook or a description in a government textbook about how legislation is created.

To emphasize or set off separate items in a sequence pattern, authors often use:

- Words such as *first, second, third, then, next, finally*
- Words and phrases that refer to time, such as dates, days of the week, names of months or phrases such as *during the 20th century* or *in the previous decade*
- Enumeration (*1, 2, 3,* etc.)
- Letters (*a, b, c,* etc.)
- Signal words such as *steps, stages, phases, progression, process, series,* and even the word *sequence* (These often occur in the main idea sentence.)

Paragraphs with the sequence pattern are typically structured like this:

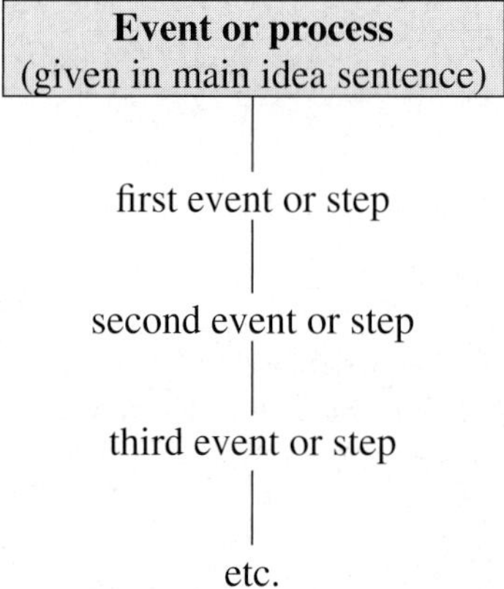

An excerpt from a music appreciation textbook appears on the following page. In it, the author uses a sequence pattern to show the order in which certain events occurred. The topic of this paragraph is *African-American musicians in the twentieth century.* The formulated main idea of this paragraph is *For many years, African-American musicians were barred as performers and conductors in established opera companies and symphony orchestras, but this began to change by the middle of the 20th century.* Read the paragraph and notice the dates that indicate that the events are being presented in chronological order.

African-American Musicians in the Twentieth Century

For many years, African-American musicians were admitted as students in music schools but were barred as performers and conductors in established opera companies and symphony orchestras. Color barriers in major American opera companies were not broken until ① the baritone Todd Duncan performed at the New York City Opera in 1945 and ② the contralto Marian Anderson sang at the Metropolitan Opera in 1955. ③ During the 1950s and 1960s black conductors like Dean Dixon and Everett Lee had to go to Europe to find permanent positions, but ④ starting in the 1970s, important conducting posts were occupied by such musicians as Henry Lewis, who directed the New Jersey Symphony, and James DePreist, who led the Quebec Symphony.

Source: Roger Kamien, *Music: An Appreciation,* 7th ed. p. 451. Copyright © 2000 by The McGraw-Hill Comapnies, Inc. Reprinted by permission of The McGraw-Hill Companies, Inc.

Stop and Annotate

Go back to the textbook excerpt. Underline or highlight the dates and the references to different decades that signal a sequence. Then write a ① beside *baritone Todd Duncan . . .* , a ② beside *contralto Marian Anderson . . .* , a ③ beside the phrase *During the 1950s and 1960s . . .* , and a ④ beside the phrase *starting in the 1970s . . . .*

The four supporting details in this sequence are identified by specific dates (1945 and 1955) and references to different decades of the 20th century (the 1950s, the 1960s, and the 1970s). Important events from these different decades are presented in order. In this paragraph, the order of the information is important because the sequence shows the progressive acceptance of African-American musicians.

EXERCISE 7

Directions: For each sentence, write on the line provided the event that happened first. Remember that you need to identify the event that came first in reality, which may or may not be the event mentioned first in the sentence. Underline the signal word or words in each sentence.

	Event That Happens or Happened First
Example: Paul addressed the postcard and then mailed it.	Paul addressed the postcard
1. A tadpole uses its front legs to crawl onto land after it reaches a certain stage of development.	it [tadpole] reaches a certain stage of development
2. It took until 5 o'clock to finish the project, even though we started at noon.	we started at noon
3. Information must enter short-term memory before it can move into long-term memory.	information must enter short-term memory
4. She did remember me, although I had to tell her my name first.	I had to tell her my name
5. We went to the aquarium and later we went to the zoo.	we went to the aquarium

EXERCISE 8

This paragraph comes from a psychology textbook.

The SQ3R Method

The SQ3R method has five steps, designated by the initials S-Q-R-R-R. The first step is to *survey* the material by reading the headings, figure captions, recaps, providing yourself with an overview of the major points of the chapter. The next step—the "Q" in SQ3R—is to *question*. Formulate questions about the material—either aloud or in writing—prior to actually reading a section of text. The next three steps in the SQ3R method ask you to *read, recite,* and *review* the material. *Read* carefully and, even more importantly, read actively and critically. While you are reading, answer the questions that you have asked yourself. The *recite* step involves describing and explaining to yourself the material you have just read and answering the questions you have posed earlier. Recite aloud; the recitation process helps to identify your degree of understanding of the material you have just read. Finally, *review* the material, looking it over, re-reading any summaries, and answering any review questions that are included at the end of a section.

Source: Adapted from Robert S. Feldman, *Understanding Psychology,* 8th ed., pp. xii–xiii.

Which writing pattern did the author use to organize the main idea and the supporting details?
sequence

Write the clues that caused you to choose this pattern.
the phrases and words "five steps," "first step," "next step," "next three steps," and "finally"

EXERCISE 9

This paragraph comes from a government textbook.

Early Colonization

American colonization began as a commercial enterprise. The first permanent British colony in North America was Jamestown, founded in 1607 by the Virginia Company of London for the purpose of developing trade and mining gold. By 1619, colonists realized that there was no gold, and harsh conditions coupled with conflicts with native populations hampered trade. The Crown took control of the failing colony in 1624, replacing the president with a royal governor.

Source: Adapted from Joseph Losco and Ralph Baker, *AM GOV,* pp. 17–18

Which writing pattern did the author use to organize the main idea and the supporting details?
chronological order (or sequence)

Write the clues that caused you to choose this pattern.
the words "began" and "first"; also, the dates "1607," "1619," and "1624"

Comparison-Contrast Pattern

KEY TERM
comparison-contrast pattern

Similarities (comparisons) between two or more things are presented, differences (contrasts) between two or more things are presented, or both similarities and differences are presented.

The comparison-contrast pattern is also known as *ideas in opposition.*

Often writers want to emphasize comparisons and contrasts. A *comparison* shows how two or more things are similar (alike). A *contrast* points out the differences between them. In the **comparison-contrast pattern** similarities (comparisons) between two or more things are presented, differences (contrasts) between two or more things are presented, or both similarities and differences are presented.

To signal comparisons, authors use words such as *similarly, likewise, both, same,* and *also.* To signal contrasts, authors use clues such as *on the other hand, in contrast, however, while, whereas, although, nevertheless, different, unlike,* and *some . . . others.* Contrasts are also signaled by words in a paragraph that have opposite meanings, such as *liberals and conservatives, Internet users and non-Internet users,* and *people who attended college and people who never attended college.*

Paragraphs organized to show comparisons and/or contrasts are typically structured like this:

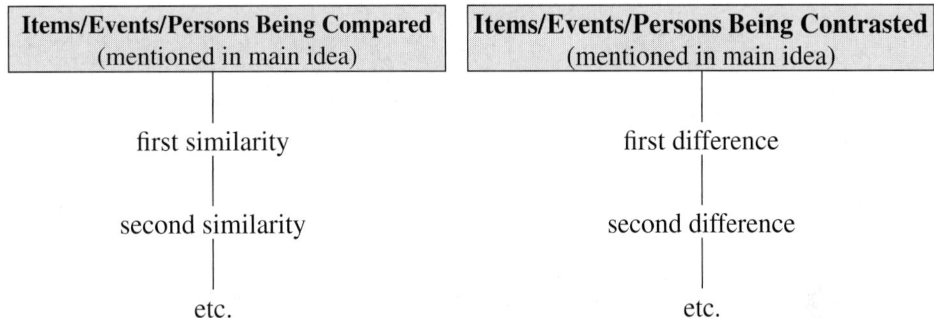

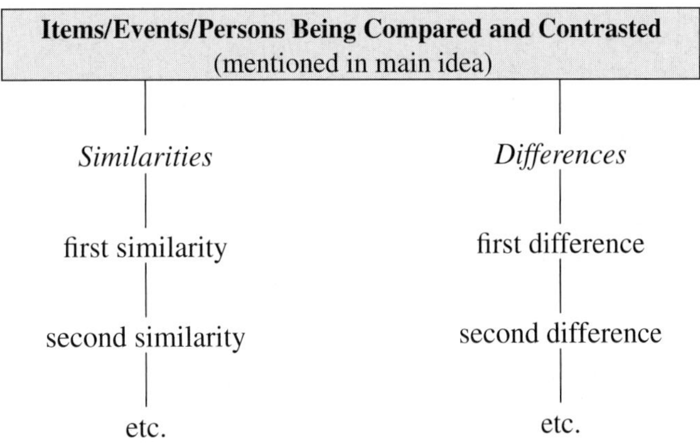

As the heading suggests, the following excerpt from an art appreciation textbook has as its topic, *the mall,* or more specifically, *how the mall is similar to the old-time village green and the medieval cathedral.* (A *green* was a grassy area in the center of a town that was set aside for use by the community as a whole.) The stated main idea is the first sentence, *The mall has become the equivalent of the old-time village green, a gathering place as comprehensive as the medieval cathedral.* As you read the paragraph, ask yourself, "In what way has the mall become the equivalent of the old-time village green and the medieval cathedral?"

The Mall

The mall has become the equivalent of the old-time village green, a gathering place as comprehensive as the medieval cathedral. In those days, the cathedral played a vital role in people's daily lives. Today, that role has largely been assumed by the mall. Like village greens and cathedrals, malls provide nearly all the social activities one could want. This gathering place provides opportunities for sports and entertainment, music and dramatic performances, socializing with friends, having a meal or a snack, and of course, buying or simply admiring an endless array of consumer goods. The people of medieval Europe walked, so their obvious gathering place was the cathedral in the center of town. The people of suburban North America drive cars and their obvious gathering place is the mall.

Source: From Rita Gilbert, *Living with Art,* 5th ed.

Stop and Annotate

Go back to the textbook excerpt. Underline or highlight the clues that signal a comparison-contrast pattern: *equivalent, old-time, In those days, Today, Like, The people of medieval Europe,* and *The people of suburban North America.*

The words *equivalent, old-time, In those days, Today, Like, The people of medieval Europe,* and *The people of suburban North America* are clues or signals that the author is presenting a comparison. The village green, the cathedral, and the mall are being compared since all have the similar function of being gathering places for people during different periods in history. The word *equivalent* in the main idea sentence and the word *like* in the fourth sentence signal this comparison.

EXERCISE 10

Directions: Decide whether each sentence presents a comparison or a contrast. On the line provided, write the items that are being compared or contrasted. Underline the signal word or words in each sentence that help you distinguish whether a comparison is being made or a contrast is being presented.

	Comparison or Contrast	Items Compared or Contrasted
Example: Bob likes baseball, although he likes football even more.	contrast	baseball, football (how much Bob likes each)
1. June is hot, but July is hotter.	contrast	June, July (how hot)
2. Both Juan and Maria serve as Red Cross volunteers.	comparison	Juan and Maria
3. We thought the test items would be multiple-choice; however, they consisted of only three essay questions.	contrast	type of test items
4. Beth is very easygoing, and her sister has a similar temperament. [also accept "and"]	comparison	temperament of Beth and her sister
5. Some students choose liberal arts majors; others choose majors in science or technical fields. [opposites: liberal arts, science/technical]	contrast	majors students choose

EXERCISE 11

This paragraph comes from a psychology textbook.

How to appropriately and effectively teach the increasing number of children who do not speak English is not always clear. Many educators maintain that *bilingual education* is best. With a bilingual approach, students learn some subjects in their native language while simultaneously learning English. Proponents of bilingualism believe that students must develop a sound footing in basic subject areas and that, initially at least, teaching those subjects in their native language is the only way to provide them with that foundation. In contrast, other educators insist that all instruction ought to be in English from the moment students, including those who speak no English at all, enroll in school. In *immersion programs,* students are immediately plunged into English instruction in all subjects. The reasoning is that teaching students in a language other than English simply hinders nonnative English speakers' integration into society and ultimately does them a disservice.

Source: Adapted from Robert S. Feldman, *Understanding Psychology,* 8th ed. pp 281–82. Copyright © 2008 by The McGraw-Hill Companies, Inc. Reprinted by permission of The McGraw-Hill Companies, Inc.

Which writing pattern did the author use to organize the main idea and the supporting details?

comparison-contrast

Write the clues that caused you to choose this pattern.

the phrase "In contrast"

KEY TERM
cause-effect pattern

Reasons (causes) and results (effects) of events or conditions are presented.

Cause-Effect Pattern

The **cause-effect pattern** presents reasons (causes) of events or conditions and results (effects) of events or conditions. Authors often use these words to indicate a cause: *because, the reasons, causes, is due to,* and *is caused by.* These words are often used to indicate an effect: *therefore, consequently, thus, as a consequence, led to, the result, as a result, the effect was,* and *this resulted in.*

In reality, causes always precede effects, and authors typically present causes first and then their effects. However, authors sometimes present an effect and *then* state its cause. Read these two sentences: *The extreme changes in the weather are due to global warming* and *Global warming has caused extreme changes in the weather.* Both sentences have the same message. And, in both cases, *global warming* is the cause and *the extreme changes in weather* is the effect. The order that the cause and effect are presented *in the sentence* does not change which one is the cause and which one is the effect. Do not assume that whatever is mentioned first *in a sentence* is always the cause! You must determine which event occurred first *in reality.*

Paragraphs organized to show causes and/or effects are typically structured in one of the following ways:

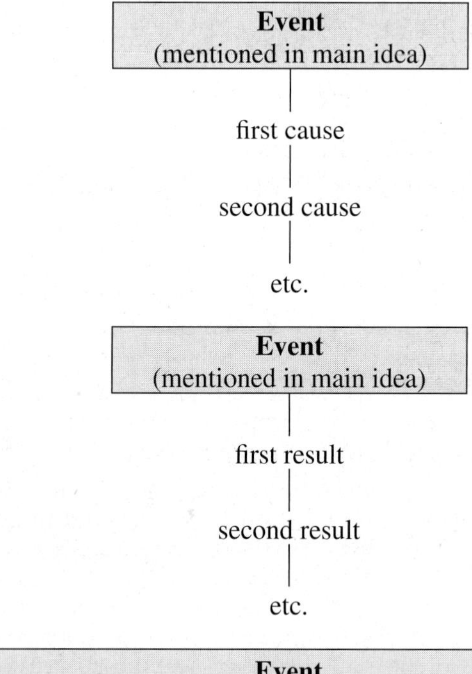

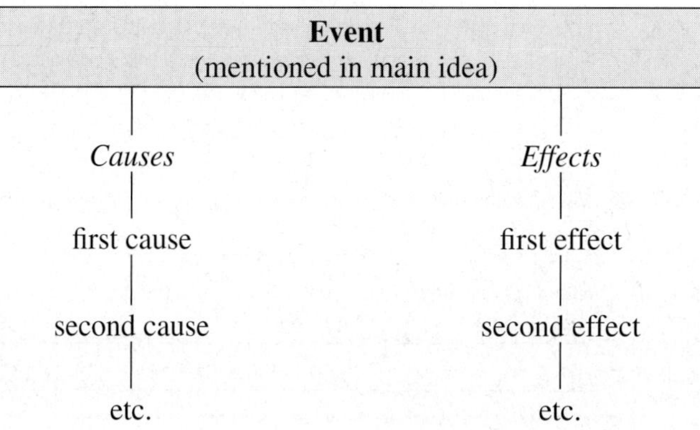

The following excerpt from a business textbook uses the cause-effect pattern. Its topic is *two-income families.* The stated main idea is the first sentence, *Several factors have caused a dramatic growth in two-income families.* As you read the paragraph, ask yourself, "What has caused the dramatic growth in two-income families?"

Two-Income Families

Several factors have led to a dramatic growth in two-income families in the United States. The high costs of housing and of maintaining a comfortable lifestyle, the high level of taxes, and the cultural emphasis on "having it all" have made it difficult if not impossible for many households to live on just one income. Furthermore, many women today simply want a career outside the home.

Source: William G. Nickels, James M. McHugh, and Susan M. McHugh, *Understanding Business,* 8th ed., p. 18. Copyright © 2008 by The McGraw-Hill Companies, Inc. Reprinted by permission of The McGraw-Hill Companies, Inc.

Stop and Annotate

Go back to the textbook excerpt. Underline or highlight the clue words that signal a cause-effect pattern: *led to.*

The words *led to* signal a cause-effect pattern. They are the only clue words in the paragraph. The effect or result is expressed at the end of the stated main idea: *the dramatic growth in two-income families.* The authors then present five other causes that contribute to the increase in the number of two-income families. The five reasons (causes) are presented in the details: the high cost of housing, the high cost of maintaining a comfortable lifestyle, the high level of taxes, the cultural emphasis on "having it all," and the fact that many women today want a career outside the home.

EXERCISE 12

Directions: On the lines provided, write the cause and the effect presented in each sentence. Underline the signal word or words in each sentence that helped you distinguish the cause from the effect.

	Cause	Effect
Example: He came in second; thus, he won the silver medal.	he came in second	he won the silver medal
1. Because of the rainstorm, the streets were flooded.	rainstorm	streets flooded
2. Banks are closed today due to the national holiday.	national holiday	banks closed
3. Carla's medication resulted in a weight gain.	medication	weight gain
4. The reason he left was that he was mad.	he was mad	he left
5. The cause of the accident was faulty brakes.	faulty brakes	accident

EXERCISE 13

This paragraph comes from a psychology textbook.

Caffeine produces several reactions. One major behavioral effect is an increase in attentiveness. Another major behavioral effect is a decrease in reaction time. Caffeine can also bring about an improvement in mood, most likely by mimicking the effects of a natural brain chemical, adenosine. Too much caffeine, however, can result in nervousness and insomnia. People can build up a biological dependence on the drug. Regular users who suddenly stop drinking coffee may experience headache or depression. Many people who drink large amounts of coffee on weekdays have headaches on weekends because of the sudden drop in the amount of caffeine they are consuming.

Source: Adapted from Robert S. Feldman, *Understanding Psychology*, 8th ed., pp. 169–70.

Which writing pattern did the author use to organize the main idea and the supporting details?

cause-effect

Write the clues that caused you to choose this pattern.

the words "reactions," "effect," "result," and "because"; the phrases "bring about" and "build up"

You have now met five common writing patterns that authors often use. You may have noticed the main idea sentence itself often contains important clues about which pattern is being used. Focus on the primary relationship between the main idea and the details that support it by asking yourself, "What pattern did the author use to organize the main idea and supporting details?"

SUMMARY OF FIVE COMMON PARAGRAPH PATTERN SIGNALS AND CLUE WORDS

1. Definition Pattern

words in bold
words in italics
words in color
means
the term
is, is known as
in other words
that is (also abbreviated *i.e,* for *id est,* Latin for "that is")
is defined as
refers to, is referred to as
is called
by this we mean
punctuation that sets off a definition or synonym , : ( ) [ ] —

2. List Pattern

and
also
another
moreover
in addition
first, second, third
finally
1, 2, 3 . . .
a, b, c . . .
bullets (•)
asterisks (*)
words that announce lists
(such as *categories, kinds, types, ways, classes, groups, parts, elements, characteristics, features,* etc.)

(continued on next page)

3. Sequence Pattern

first, second, third
now, then, next, finally
dates
1, 2, 3 . . .
a, b, c . . .
steps
phases
progression
words that refer to time
series
stages
when
before, during, after
at last
process, spectrum, continuum
hierarchy
instructions and directions

4. Comparison-Contrast Pattern

Comparisons:
similarly
likewise
both
same
also
resembles
parallels
in the same manner
in the same way
words that compare
(adjectives that describe comparisons, such as *safer, slower, lighter, more valuable, less toxic,* etc.)

Contrasts:
in contrast
however
on the other hand
whereas
while
although
nevertheless
instead (of)
different
unlike
conversely
rather than
as opposed to
some . . . others
opposite words

5. Cause-Effect Pattern

Causes:
the reason(s)
the causes(s)
because
is due to (cause)
was caused by (cause)
(cause) *led to*
resulted from (cause)
since

Effects:
the result(s)
the effect(s)
the outcome
the final product
therefore
thus
consequently
as a consequence
hence
on that account
resulted in, results in (effect)
(effect) *was caused by*
(effect) *is due to*
led to (effect)
(effect) *resulted from*

EXERCISE 14

Directions: Read each paragraph. Underline the signal and transition words. Then circle the letter of the pattern the author has used to organize the information in the paragraph.

1. Why is stress so damaging to the immune system? One reason is that stress may overstimulate the immune system, causing it to attack the body itself and damage healthy tissue instead of fighting invading bacteria, viruses, and other foreign invaders. When that happens, it can lead to disorders such as arthritis and an allergic reaction.

Source: Adapted from Robert S. Feldman, *Understanding Psychology*, 8th ed., p. 493. Copyright © 2008 by The McGraw-Hill Companies, Inc. Reprinted by permission of The McGraw-Hill Companies, Inc.

a. list pattern
b. sequence pattern
c. comparison-contrast pattern
d. cause-effect pattern

2. For male members of the Awa tribe in New Guinea, the transition from childhood to adulthood is a painful process. First come whippings with sticks and prickly branches, both for the boys' own past misdeeds and in honor of those tribesmen who were killed in warfare. In the next phase of the ritual, adults jab sharpened sticks into the boys' nostrils. Then they force a five-foot length of vine into the boys' throats, until they gag and vomit. Finally, tribesmen cut the boys' genitals, causing severe bleeding.

Source: Adapted from Robert S. Feldman, *Understanding Psychology*, 8th ed., p. 437. Copyright © 2008 by The McGraw-Hill Companies, Inc. Reprinted by permission of The McGraw-Hill Companies, Inc.

a. list pattern
b. sequence pattern
c. comparison-contrast pattern
d. cause-effect pattern

3. Smoking has both psychological and biological components, and few habits are as difficult to break. Long-term successful treatment typically occurs in just 15 percent of those who try to stop smoking, and once smoking becomes a habit, it is as hard to stop as an addiction to cocaine or heroin. In fact, some of the biochemical reactions to nicotine are similar to those to cocaine, amphetamines, and morphine.

Source: Adapted from Robert S. Feldman, *Understanding Psychology*, 8th ed., p. 504. Copyright © 2008 by The McGraw-Hill Companies, Inc. Reprinted by permission of The McGraw-Hill Companies, Inc.

a. list pattern
b. sequence pattern
c. comparison-contrast pattern
d. cause-effect pattern

4. There are several things patients can do to improve communication with doctors and other health care providers. Here are some tips provided by one physician:

1. Make a list of health-related concerns before you visit a health care provider.
2. Before a visit, write down the names and dosages of every drug you are currently taking.
3. Determine if your provider will communicate with you via e-mail and has your correct e-mail address.
4. If you find yourself intimidated, take along an advocate—friend or relative—who can help you communicate more effectively.
5. Take notes during the visit.

Source: Adapted from Robert S. Feldman, *Understanding Psychology*, 8th ed., p. 509. Copyright © 2008 by The McGraw-Hill Companies, Inc. Reprinted by permission of The McGraw-Hill Companies, Inc.

a. list pattern
b. sequence pattern
c. comparison-contrast pattern
d. cause-effect pattern (also acceptable)

5. A *transcript* is an official record of a student's courses and grades at a college or university. You can obtain one from the registrar's office (and perhaps online). If you transfer to a different school, you will be asked for a copy of your transcript. Many employers often ask job applicants for a transcript.

a. list pattern
b. sequence pattern
c. definition pattern
d. cause-effect pattern

ADDITIONAL PARAGRAPH PATTERNS

In this chapter so far, you have already learned about five very common patterns: definition, list, sequence (time order), cause-effect, and comparison-contrast. Besides these, there are additional patterns you will encounter in college textbooks and other material you read.

✓ **Teaching Tips**

- Although this section will be of help to all students, it will be particularly relevant to Florida students who will be taking the state-mandated test.
- After you introduce a pattern, have students go back and underline the signal words in each sample paragraph.

Definition and Example Pattern

Along with a definition, authors often include one or more examples. The main idea sentence usually states the definition. The examples (details) in the paragraph help explain or illustrate that definition. For that reason, the pattern is also known as the "definition and example" pattern. A definition and example paragraph is typically organized like this:

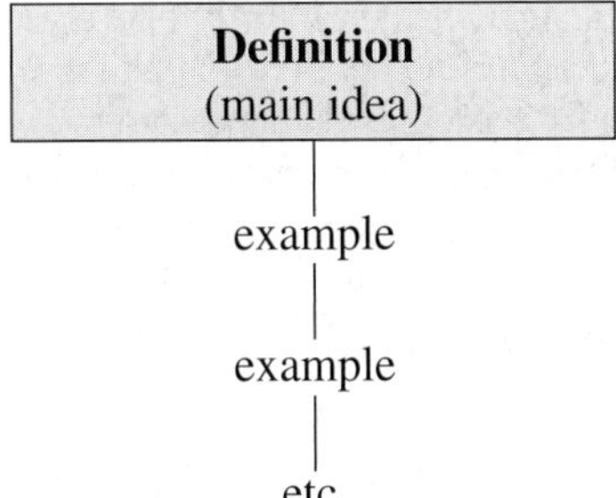

- Watch for signal words such as *this term, means, is known as, is called, refers to, is defined as,* and so forth, for the definition. In addition, the key term may appear in bold, italics, or color. Watch for *such as, to illustrate*, and *for example* to introduce the examples.
- *Example:* A biology text paragraph presents a definition in the first sentence (the main idea) along with examples (supporting details):

> An **organ** is a group of tissues that perform a specific function or set of functions. There are several organs in the human body, such as the brain, eyes, heart, and lungs. Other examples are the stomach, liver, kidneys, and bone.The largest organ is the skin.

Generalization and Example Pattern

This pattern is similar to the definition-and-example pattern, but instead of a definition and examples of a key term, the author presents an important general concept, rule, or principle, followed by examples. (You learned the difference between general and specific when you learned about topic. *A generalization* is a statement, idea, or principle that applies broadly; that is, it applies to many people or things, or in many circumstances.) The structure of a generalization and example paragraph is typically like this:

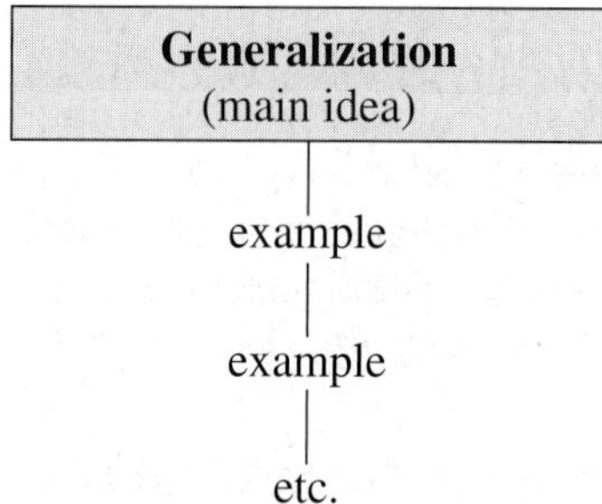

- Watch for signal words that introduce examples, such as *to illustrate, for example, for instance,* and *that is.*
- *Example:* A biology text paragraph opens with a generalization, followed by one or more specific examples:

> Life comes only from life; every living thing reproduces. For example, at the simplest level, even one-cell organisms multiply by dividing in two. In more complex organisms, such as human beings, reproduction occurs by a sperm fertilizing an egg, followed by innumerable cell divisions and differentiations.

Location or Spatial Order Pattern

This pattern is similar to time order, but it describes objects' *position* or *location* in space rather than events' place in time. (An art history textbook author might describe the floor plan of medieval cathedrals; an astronomy textbook author might describe the way the planets are arranged in the solar system.) A location or spatial order paragraph is usually organized this way:

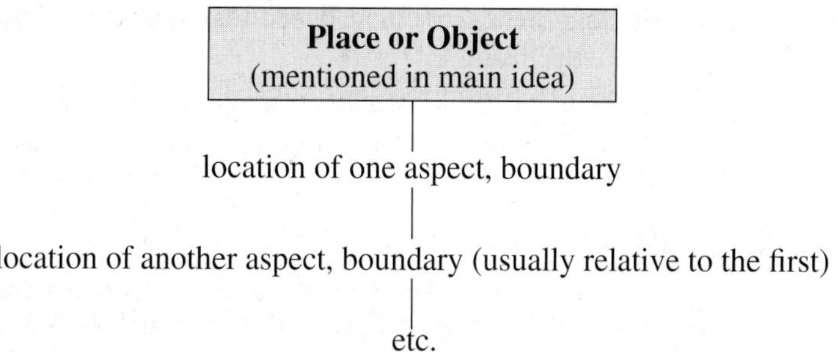

- Watch for signal words such as *above, below, behind, beside, near, farther from, within, facing, opposite, north/south/east/west of, to the left/right, outside of,* and other words that indicate the position of one object relative to another.
- *Example:* A sociology textbook presents a paragraph such as this one:

> According to the concentric zone theory of urban growth, cities develop outward in expanding rings or zones. At the center is the central business district. Expanding outward from it are the manufacturing district, low-class, middle-class, and high-class residential areas. Even farther out are the heavy manufacturing and outlying business district. The most distant zones are the residential suburb, industrial suburb, and the commuters' zone.

Summary Pattern

At the end of a section, an author may present a concluding paragraph that summarizes the section. (You were introduced to this concept in Chapter 4 on stated main ideas. Chapter 11 presents summarizing in depth.) The structure of a summary paragraph is typically like this:

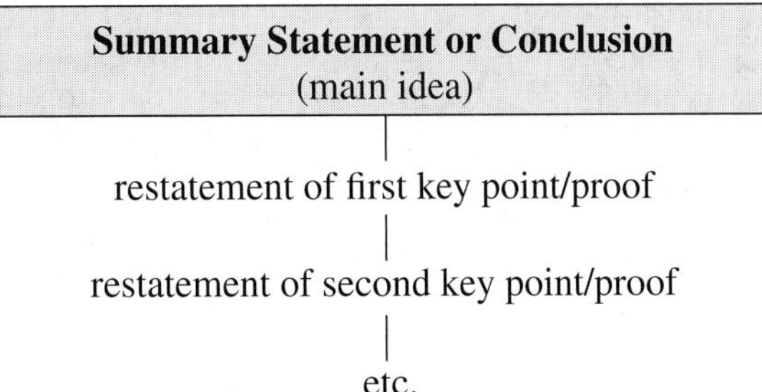

- Watch for signal words such as *In summary, In short, To sum up, In a nutshell, In brief, The point is, Thus, Therefore,* and so forth.
- *Example:* An author ends a section in a political science textbook with this paragraph:

> The point is, computer technology has made it increasingly easier for any business, government agency, or individual to retrieve information about individual citizens. Inappropriate access to personal information violates privacy rights. An important public policy issue today is how much the government should restrict access to electronic information.

Classification Pattern

This is simply a variation of the list pattern, but the items that are listed are put into groups or categories. The structure of a classification paragraph is typically like this:

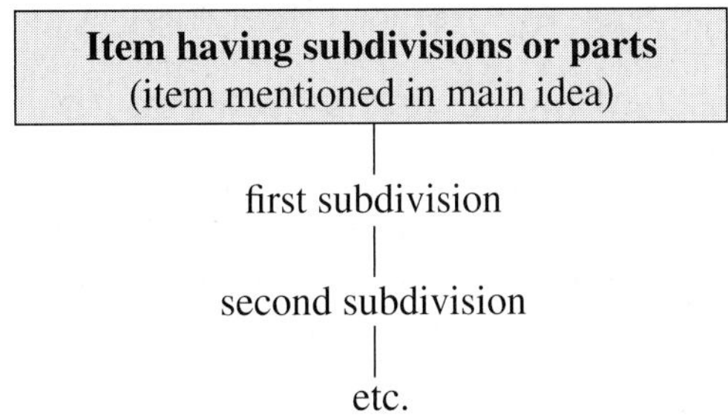

- Watch for signal words such as *groups, categories, ways, types, elements, factors,* and *classes.*
- *Example:* A biology text paragraph discusses the two layers of the skin:

> Skin has two layers: the epidermis and the dermis. The outer layer is the *epidermis*. It consists of epithelial cells. New cells come from basal cells that flatten and harden as they push to the surface. The *dermis,* the other layer, is a region of fibrous connective tissue beneath the epidermis. The dermis contains collagen and elastic fibers, as well as blood vessels that feed the skin.

Addition Pattern

The author simply adds information. It could mean adding items to a list, or it could be that the author is adding causes, effects, similarities, differences, categories, or examples. It is sometimes called the *elaboration* pattern since information is presented in greater detail. The structure of an addition paragraph is typically like this:

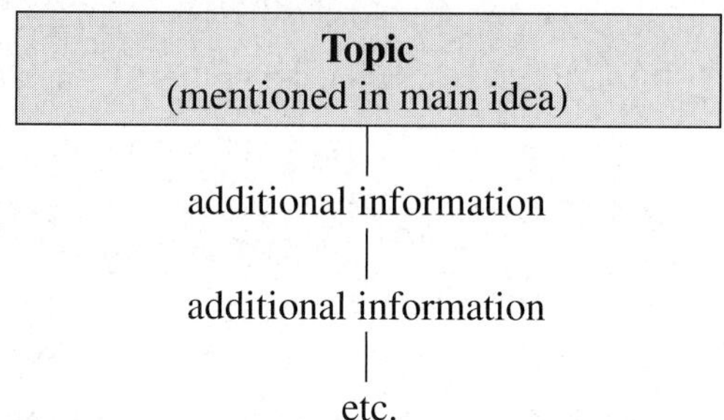

- Watch for signal words such as *also, besides, in addition, furthermore, and, further,* and *moreover.*
- *Example:* A music text tells facts about woodwind instruments:

> Most woodwind instruments produce vibrations of air within a tube made of wood, although modern flutes and piccolos are made of metal. In addition, woodwind instruments have holes that can be opened and closed when players place their fingers over them or press on mechanisms that control pads that cover the holes. Furthermore, some woodwind instruments, such as clarinets and oboes, have reeds that vibrate when the player blows into the mouthpiece.

Statement and Clarification Pattern

The passage consists of a general statement followed by additional information that clarifies the information in the general statement. (An education textbook might say that home-schooled children do not have as many opportunities to interact with others their same age during the school day. The rest of the paragraph might explain ways parents can compensate for this.) The structure of a statement and clarification paragraph is typically like this:

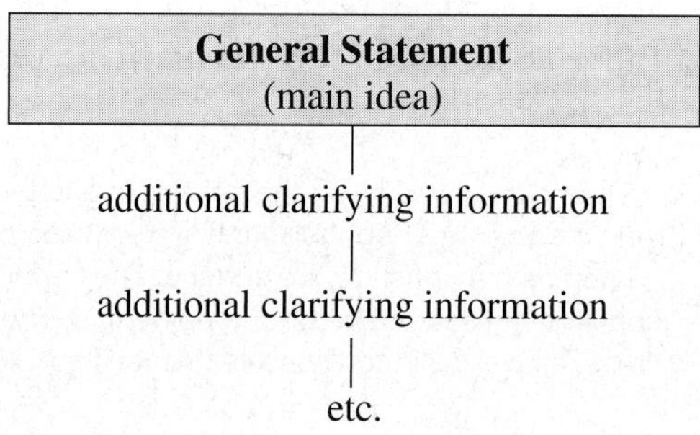

- Watch for signal words such as *in other words, in fact, obviously, as a matter of fact, evidently, clearly,* and *of course*.
- *Example:* An art history text paragraph opens with a general statement about "certain types of ancient vessels," clarifies what "ancient" means, and tells more about those "certain types" of vessels.

✓ **Teaching Tip**
C.E stands for Christian Era, the period beginning with the birth of Jesus.

Certain types of ancient ceramic jars and bowls are known today as Mimbres vessels. They are considered ancient artifacts because they date from the 3rd to the 12th centuries C.E. and most were recovered from ancient graves in what is now New Mexico. Evidently, these pottery vessels were used for household purposes. Painted with black-on-white designs, they are decorated with stylized animal or human figures or with geometric designs.

SUMMARY OF ADDITIONAL PARAGRAPH PATTERN CLUES AND SIGNAL WORDS

1. Definition and Example Pattern

Definition:		Examples:	
this term is called	*is referred to as*	*for example*	*for instance*
means	*refers to*	*to illustrate*	*such as*
is known as	*is defined as*		

2. Generalization and Example Pattern

General concept, rule, or principle, followed by examples introduced by

for example *for instance* *to illustrate* *such as*

3. Location or Spatial Order Pattern

above	*north/south/east/west of*
below	*facing*
behind	*opposite to*
beside	*to the left/right of*
near	*outside*
farther	*adjacent to*
from	*close by*
within	*inside*

4. Summary Pattern

In summary	*The point is*
In short	*On the whole*
To sum up	*Thus*
In a nutshell	*Therefore*
In brief	*In conclusion*
To summarize	

(continued on next page)

(continued from previous page)

5. Classification Pattern

groups	*elements*
categories	*factors*
ways	*classes*
types	*kinds*

6. Addition Pattern

also	*and*
besides	*moreover*
in addition	*further*
furthermore	*equally important*

7. Statement and Clarification Pattern

clearly	*in other words*
in fact	*as a matter of fact*
of course	*obviously*
evidently	

EXERCISE 15

Directions: Circle the answer choice of the letter that tells the pattern used in each paragraph.

1. In short, expect to see many changes in the banking system in coming years. Banks will increase their range of services: you will be able to buy insurance, real estate, stocks, and other securities through them. You will be able to get foreign currency, tickets to events, and music downloads from ATMs. Increasing use of online banking and electronic funds transfer may also change banking dramatically.

a. spatial pattern
b. definition and example pattern
c. summary pattern
d. classification pattern

2. *Caffeine* is a stimulant, a drug that affects the central nervous system by causing a rise in heart rate, blood pressure, and muscular tension. Coffee is the best-known example of a beverage that contains caffeine. Other examples of caffeine-containing foods and beverages are tea, soft drinks, energy drinks, and chocolate. Some maximun strength nonprescription drugs, such as Excedrin, Anacin, NoDoz tablets, and Dexatrim, also contain caffeine.

a. spatial pattern
b. definition and example pattern
c. summary pattern
d. classification pattern

3. The gastrocnemius, the largest muscle in the calf, is located on the backside of the leg. The heel raise is a good exercise for strengthening it. The correct position for this simple exercise is to stand with your feet pointed forward, shoulder-width apart. Rest the bar on the back of the shoulders, holding it in place with hands facing forward. Press down with your toes as you move your heels away from the floor. Return to the starting position.

a. spatial pattern
b. generalization and example pattern
c. addition pattern
d. classification pattern

4. Muscles, bones, connective tissues, and organ tissues are categorized as *fat-free mass.* The second type of body mass is *body fat.* There are two kinds of body fat: essential and nonessential.

a. spatial pattern
b. definition and example pattern
c. summary pattern
d. classification pattern

5. Spot reducing, trying to lose body fat in specific parts of the body by doing exercises for that part, is not effective. As a matter of fact, spot-reducing exercises aid fat loss only to the extent they burn calories. In other words, reducing fat in any specific area can be accomplished only by burning up more calories through metabolism and exercise than are consumed through food.

a. spatial pattern
b. statement and clarification pattern
c. summary pattern
d. classification pattern

6. Bustling New York City is located at the mouth of the Hudson River on the Eastern Atlantic coast of the United States. It's also the nation's largest city, with the 2000 census showing more than eight million inhabitants. In addition, it boasts the Statue of Liberty, Empire State Building, Central Park, Brooklyn Bridge, and Times Square. Known as "The Big Apple," the city is comprised of the five boroughs: Brooklyn, Queens, Manhattan, Staten Island, and the Bronx.

a. spatial pattern
b. statement and clarification pattern
c. addition pattern
d. classification pattern

7. The rule for planning weekly study time is to allot two hours of studying for every one hour you spend in class. To illustrate, if you take four three-hour courses, you spend 12 hours a week in class. That means you should allow twice that many hours—24 hours—of study time in your weekly schedule (since $2 \times 12 = 24$). [Point out that most "rules" are generalizations.]

a. spatial pattern
b. generalization and example pattern
c. addition pattern
d. classification pattern

OTHER THINGS TO KEEP IN MIND WHEN RECOGNIZING AUTHORS' WRITING PATTERNS

Here are four helpful things to keep in mind about authors' writing patterns:

1. **Lists and sequences differ in an important way.**
   Items in a list appear in no specific order; however, items in a sequence are presented in a specific order because the order is important. On a shopping list, for example, it makes no difference what order the items are in: "eggs, bread, milk" is the same as "milk, bread, eggs." In a recipe, though, the steps occur in a specific order because the sequence is important: "Add eggs and milk to the mixture, stir well, and then bake" is obviously not the same as "Bake, stir well, and then add eggs and milk to the mixture."
2. **Avoid identifying every paragraph as having a list pattern.**
   At first, it may seem as if every paragraph uses a list pattern. Whenever you encounter what appears to be a list, be cautious and ask yourself this additional question, "a list of *what*?" Your answer should help you recognize when the author is using one of the other patterns instead. For instance, if your answer is "a list of *events in a particular order,*" then the paragraph has a sequence pattern. If your answer is "a list of *similarities or differences,*" the paragraph has a comparison-contrast pattern. If your answer is "a list of *causes, reasons, or results,*" then the paragraph has a cause-effect pattern. View a paragraph as having a list pattern only when you are certain that no other pattern can be used to describe the way the ideas are organized.

   Sometimes the same clue words may be used in more than one pattern. For example, words such as *first, second,* and *third* are used for items in a sequence, but they can also be used to indicate items in a list (even though the order is not important).
3. **Authors often mix patterns in the same paragraph.**
   Each of the textbook excerpts in this chapter was used to illustrate a single pattern. However, authors often use a combination of two or more patterns in the same paragraph. This is called a *mixed pattern.* For example, a paragraph might present a series of events (sequence pattern) that led to a certain result (cause-effect pattern). Or an author could present causes and effects (cause-effect pattern), but describe some effects that were positive and other effects that were negative (comparison-contrast pattern). Remember, authors use the patterns or a combination of patterns that they believe organizes and presents their material in the most logical way.
4. **A longer selection may contain several patterns and have an overall pattern as well.**
   In addition to individual paragraphs, longer selections are often organized by an overall pattern. An entire selection may be organized as a list, a sequence, a comparison-contrast, or a cause-effect pattern. For example, you already know that a biography, the story of a person's life, usually follows a sequence pattern. Science textbooks often present information as steps in a process (sequence) and history textbooks often present information as causes and effects. Other subjects frequently use the comparison-contrast pattern to organize the information being presented.

   Remember, a longer textbook selection can consist of paragraphs with different patterns and have an overall pattern as well. For example, a section in a history textbook might discuss several events (causes) leading up to World War II, yet have a sequence as the overall pattern.

CREATING CHAPTER REVIEW CARDS

Student Online Learning Center (OLC) ***Go to*** **Chapter 7.** ***Select*** **Chapter Test.**

Review cards or *summary cards* are a way to select, organize, and summarize the important information in a textbook chapter. Preparing review cards helps you organize the information so that you can learn and memorize it more easily. In other words, chapter review cards are effective study tools.

Preparing chapter review cards for each chapter of *New Worlds* will give you practice in creating these valuable study tools. Once you have learned how to make chapter review cards, you can use actual index cards to create them for textbook material in any of your other courses and use them when you study for tests.

Now complete the chapter review cards for Chapter 7 by answering the questions or following the directions on each card. Use the type of handwriting that is easiest for you to reread (printing or cursive) and write legibly.

✓ **Teaching Tip**

Remind students that the student OLC contains a 10-item **Chapter Test** for this chapter. After completing the chapter review cards below, students should complete the Chapter Test on the OLC.

Authors' Writing Patterns

1. What is the definition of a *writing pattern*? (See page 351.)

Ways authors organize information they present

2. What are five common writing patterns textbook authors use? (See page 351.)

- definition
- list
- sequence
- comparison-contrast
- cause-effect

3. What are four advantages to recognizing authors' writing patterns? (See page 352.)

- Your comprehension will improve.
- You will be able to predict what is coming next.
- It will be easier to memorize information when you study.
- Your writing will improve.

4. What comprehension monitoring question should you ask yourself in order to recognize an author's writing pattern?

(See page 356.)

What pattern did the author use to organize the main idea and the supporting details?

Card 1 Chapter 7: Recognizing Authors' Writing Patterns

✓ **Teaching Tip**

For item 4 on Card 1, point out the "Comprehension Monitoring Question for Authors' Writing Patterns" in the margin on page 356 and guide students to write their answer as a question (including a question mark).

Transition Words That Signal the Relationship of Ideas within Sentences and between Sentences

1. What is the definition of *transition words*? (See page 352.)

   Transition words are words and phrases that show relationships among ideas in sentences, paragraphs, and longer selections.

2. Why is the *addition* relationship, and what are some transition words that signal it? (See page 352.)

   The transition words signal the author is giving additional information: *moreover, another, in addition also, first, second, next.*

3. What is the *sequence* relationship, and what are some transition words that signal it? (See page 353.)

   The transition words signal the author is presenting things in the order in which they happened or will happen: *first, next, then, later, previous, before, during, last, finally.*

Card 2 Chapter 7: Recognizing Authors' Writing Patterns

Transition Words That Signal the Relationship of Ideas within Sentences and between Sentences (*Continued*)

1. What is the *contrast* relationship, and what are some transition words that signal it? (See page 353.)

   The transition words signal the author is presenting a difference, opposing view, or an exception: *in contrast, but, on the other hand, on the contrary, unlike, although.*

2. What is the *comparison* relationship, and what are some transition words that signal it? (See page 353.)

   The transition words signal the author is presenting one or more ways things are similar: *similarly, like, likewise, in the same way, along the same lines, in the same manner, both.*

3. What is the *cause-effect* relationship, and what are some transition words that signal it? (See page 353.)

   The transition words signal the author is presenting causes (reasons things happen) or effects (results of outcomes): *moreover another, in addition, also, first, second, next.*

Card 3 Chapter 7: Recognizing Authors' Writing Patterns

Transition Words That Signal the Relationship of Ideas within Sentences and between Sentences *(Continued)*

1. What is the *example* relationship, and what are some transition words that signal it? (See page 354.)

The transition words signal an example that will help clarify or explain something: *to illustrate, such as, for instance, for example.*

2. What is the *conclusion* relationship, and what are some transition words that signal it? (See page 354.)

The transition words signal the author is presenting an outcome based on facts that preceded it: *moreover, another, in addition, also, first, second, next.*

3. What is the *summary* relationship, and what are some transition words that signal it? (See page 354.)

The transition words signal the author is presenting a restatement of the most important point or points: *to summarize, in summary, in brief, in short.*

Card 4 Chapter 7: Recognizing Authors' Writing Patterns

Authors' Writing Patterns

Define these five writing patterns commonly used by textbook authors. (See pages 357–370.)

Definition: Presents the meaning of an important term that is discussed throughout the passage

List: A group of items presented in no specific order since the order is not important

Sequence: A list of items presented in a specific order because the order is important

Comparison-Contrast: Similarities and differences between two or more things are presented.

Cause-Effect: Reasons and results of events or conditions are presented.

Card 5 Chapter 7: Recognizing Authors' Writing Patterns

Signal Words and Other Clues to Authors' Writing Patterns

Write the signal words and other clues that identify each of the five writing patterns.

Definition: (See page 357.)

key term in bold, italics, or color; may be set off by punctuation marks; *this term, means, is known as, is called, refers to, is defined as*

List: (See page 359.)

and, also, another, in addition, moreover, bullets, numbers, letters, asterisks, etc.

Sequence: (See page 362.)

first, second, next, then, finally, enumeration, letters, stages, phases, steps

Comparison-Contrast: (See page 365.)

comparisons: similarly, likewise, both, same, also

contrasts: on the other hand, in contrast, however, while, whereas, although, nevertheless

Cause-Effect: (See pages 368.)

causes: because, the reasons, the causes, is due to, is caused by

effects: therefore, consequently, thus, the effect, led to, resulted in

Card 6 Chapter 7: Recognizing Authors' Writing Patterns

Additional Paragraph Patterns

Tell the purpose of each pattern, and then list some transition words that signal it.

1. Definition and Example pattern (See page 373.)

definition with examples: *means is defined as the term: to illustrate, such as, for instance, for example*

2. Generalization and Example pattern (See pages 373–374.)

important concept rule or principle, followed by examples: *to illustrate, for example, such as, for instance*

3. Location or Spatial Order pattern (See page 374.)

describes objects' position or location in space: *below, behind, near facing within, to the left/right of*

4. Summary pattern (See page 375.)

a concluding paragraph that summarizes the section: *in summary, to sum up, in short, therefore, the point is*

Card 7 Chapter 7: Recognizing Authors' Writing Patterns

Additional Paragraph Patterns *(continued)*

Tell the purpose of each pattern, and then list some transition words that signal it.

1. Classification pattern (See page 375.)

   items that are listed are put into groups or categories: *groups, categories, ways, types, factors, classes, examples*

2. Addition pattern (See page 376.)

   author simply adds information: *also, besides, in addition, furthermore, and, further, moreover*

3. Statement and Clarification pattern (See pages 376–377.)

   general statement followed by additional information that clarifies the information in the general statement: *in other words, in fact, obviously, of course, as a matter of fact, evidently, clearly*

Card 8 Chapter 7: Recognizing Authors' Writing Patterns

As You Recognize Authors' Writing Patterns, Keep in Mind . . .

1. What is the difference between the list pattern and the sequence pattern? (See page 380.)

   Lists are in no specific order. Sequences are always in a specific order.

2. What additional question should you ask yourself to avoid identifying every paragraph as having a list pattern? (See page 380.)

   Ask yourself, "A list of *what?*"

3. What is a mixed pattern? (See page 380.)

   A combination of two or more patterns in a single paragraph

4. What is an overall pattern? (See page 380.)

   An overall pattern is the pattern of an entire section, selection, or article.

Card 9 Chapter 7: Recognizing Authors' Writing Patterns

TEST YOUR UNDERSTANDING
RECOGNIZING AUTHORS' WRITING PATTERNS, PART ONE

REVIEW: **Writing patterns** are ways that authors organize the information they present. Five writing patterns commonly used by textbook authors are:

- **definition**—presents the meaning of an important term discussed throughout the paragraph
- **list**—a group of items presented in no specific order since the order is not important
- **sequence**—a list of items presented in a certain order because the order is important
- **comparison-contrast**—similarities and differences between two or more things are presented
- **cause-effect**—reasons and results of events and conditions are presented

EXAMPLE: Study the example paragraph below to see how the information you learned in this chapter can be used to recognize authors' writing patterns. Read the explanations that are given for the correct answers. When you are sure you understand the explanations, complete the five exercises in Part One.

✓ **Teaching Tip**
Have students mark any *clues* in the paragraph that indicate the pattern.

This excerpt comes from a speech communication textbook.

You should use the Internet to supplement, not replace, library research because the Internet lacks important features of regular libraries. First, the Internet has no central information desk, no librarians, no catalogue, and no reference section. A second reason is that it does not have a person or department in charge of choosing new materials to make sure they are of high quality.

Source: Adapted from Stephen Lucas, *The Art of Public Speaking,* 8th ed., p. 147. Copyright © 2004 by The McGraw-Hill Companies, Inc. Reprinted by permission of The McGraw-Hill Companies, Inc.

The topic of this paragraph is *the Internet.*

___a___ What is the main idea of this paragraph?

a. You should use the Internet merely to supplement, not replace, library research because the Internet lacks important features of regular libraries.

b. First, the Internet has no central information desk, no librarians, no catalogue, and no reference section.

c. A second reason is that it does not have a person or department in charge of choosing new materials to make sure they are of high quality.

d. Today, using the Internet is important.

Explanation: The correct answer is a. The first sentence is the stated main idea. The other two sentences are details that explain more about it.

___c___ Which writing pattern did the authors use to organize the supporting details?

a. sequence

b. comparison-contrast

c. cause-effect

d. list

Explanation: The correct answer is c. The words *because* in the main idea sentence and *reason* in the third sentence indicate the cause-effect pattern. The effect is *you should use the Internet merely to supplement library research.* The cause is that *the Internet lacks important features of regular libraries.*

DIRECTIONS: Read each paragraph carefully and determine its main idea by asking yourself, "What is the single most important point the author wants me to *understand* about the topic of this paragraph?" (Notice that you are given the topic of each paragraph.) Select the answer choice that expresses the main idea of the paragraph and write the letter in the space provided. Then determine the writing pattern the author used to organize the information in the paragraph by asking yourself, "What pattern did the author use to organize the main idea and the supporting details?" Remember that the main idea sentence will often give you an additional clue to the pattern used by the author. Refer to the list of signals and clue words on pages 370–371 as you complete these exercises.

1. This paragraph comes from a management textbook.

Hierarchy of Needs Theory

One of the most widely known theories of motivation is the **hierarchy of needs theory,** developed by psychologist Abraham Maslow and popularized during the early 1960s, which argues that individual needs form a five-level hierarchy. According to this hierarchy, our first need is for survival, so we concentrate on the basic **physiological needs,** such as food, water, and shelter, until we feel fairly sure that these needs are covered. Next, we concern ourselves with **safety needs,** which pertain to the desire to feel safe and secure, and free from threats to our existence. Once we feel reasonably safe and secure, we turn our attention to relationships with others to fulfill our **belongingness needs,** which involve the desire to affiliate with and be accepted by others. With support from loved ones, we focus on **esteem needs,** which are related to the two-pronged desire to have a positive self-image and to have our contributions valued and appreciated by others. Finally, we reach the highest level, **self-actualization needs,** which pertain to developing our capabilities and reaching our full potential. At this level, we concern ourselves with such matters as testing our creativity, seeing our innovative ideas translated into reality, pursuing new knowledge, and developing our talents in uncharted directions.

The topic of this paragraph is *Maslow's hierarchy of needs theory.*

a What is the main idea of this paragraph?

a. Maslow's hierarchy of needs theory states that people have five levels of needs that range from basic survival needs to higher-level needs.

b. The hierarchy of needs theory is one of the most widely known theories of motivation.

c. Maslow created a widely known theory.

d. Finally, we reach the highest level, self-actualization needs, which pertain to developing our capabilities and reaching our full potential.

c Which writing pattern did the authors use to organize the supporting details?

a. cause-effect

b. list

c. sequence

d. comparison-contrast

2. This paragraph comes from a government textbook.

Conservatives are defined as individuals who emphasize the marketplace as the means of distributing economic benefits but look to government to uphold traditional social values. In contrast, **liberals** favor activist government as an instrument of economic redistribution but reject the notion that government should favor a particular set of social values. True liberals and conservatives could be expected to differ, for instance, on the issues of homosexual rights (a social values question) and government-guaranteed health care (an economic distribution question). Liberals would view homosexuality as a private issue and believe that government should see to it that everyone has access to adequate medical care. Conservatives would oppose government-mandated access to health care and favor government policies that discourage homosexual lifestyles.

Source: Thomas E. Patterson, *We the People,* 2nd ed. Copyright © 1998 by The McGraw-Hill Companies, Inc. Reprinted by permission of The McGraw-Hill Companies, Inc.

The topic of this paragraph is *conservatives and liberals.*

_____ What is the main idea of this paragraph?

a. Conservatives are defined as individuals who emphasize the marketplace as the means of distributing economic benefits but look to government to uphold traditional social values.

b. Conservatives and liberals both believe that government should uphold traditional social values.

c. Conservatives and liberals have opposite viewpoints on economic issues and social values.

d. Conservatives and liberals each blame the other for the nation's problems.

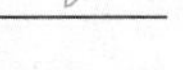

Which writing pattern did the author use to organize the supporting details?

a. cause-effect

b. comparison-contrast

c. sequence

d. list

3. This paragraph comes from a business textbook.

The Increase in the Number of Older Americans

By 2030, the baby boomers will be senior citizens. People ages 45 to 54 are currently the richest group in U.S. society. They have a median income of $55,917. They spend more than others on everything except health care and thus represent a lucrative market for restaurants, transportation, entertainment, education, and so on. What do such demographic changes mean for you and for businesses in the future? Think of the products the middle-aged and elderly will need—travel, medicine, nursing homes, assisted-living facilities, adult day care, home health care, recreation, and the like—and you'll see opportunities for successful businesses of the 21st century. Consequently, businesses that cater to them will have the opportunity for exceptional growth in the near future.

Source: William G. Nickels, James M. McHugh, and Susan M. McHugh, *Understanding Business,* 7th ed., pp. 22–23. Copyright © 2005 by The McGraw-Hill Companies, Inc. Reprinted by permission of The McGraw-Hill Companies, Inc.

The topic of this paragraph is *older Americans and their effect on business.*

_____ What is the main idea of this paragraph?

a. People ages 45 to 54 are currently the richest group in U.S. society.

b. Businesses that cater to older Americans will have exceptional growth opportunities in the near future.

c. Those with money will demand more and better health care, more recreation and travel, and new and different products and services of all kinds.

d. By 2030, the baby boomers will be senior citizens.

a Which writing pattern did the authors use to organize the supporting details?

a. cause-effect

b. sequence

c. comparison-contrast

d. definition

4. This paragraph comes from a psychology textbook.

✓ **Teaching Tip**
Point out the opposite words *attractive* and *unattractive, wealthy* and *poor,* and the contrasting terms *African-Americans* and *whites.*

Who Is More Likely to Be Acquitted?

Although we would like to believe that all of us would be treated equally in court, it is not always the case. Your chance of being acquitted in a criminal trial in the United States is better if you are physically attractive, wealthy, and white. In contrast, poor people are more likely to be convicted than affluent ones when charged with similar assault and larceny charges. Physically attractive defendants are less likely to be convicted than unattractive ones, unless the attractiveness seemed to play a part in the crime (as in a swindle). And racially prejudiced white jury members are more likely to vote to convict African-Americans than whites.

Source: Benjamin B. Lahey, *Psychology: An Introduction,* 8th ed., p. 699. Copyright © 2004 by The McGraw-Hill Companies, Inc. Reprinted by permission of The McGraw-Hill Companies, Inc.

The topic of this paragraph is *who is more likely to be acquitted.*

a What is the main idea of this paragraph?

a. Your chance of being acquitted in a criminal trial in the United States is better if you are physically attractive, wealthy, and white.

b. We should all be treated equally in court.

c. When charged with similar assault and larceny charges, poor people are more likely to be convicted than affluent ones.

d. Jury members should be screened more carefully.

b Which writing pattern did the author use to organize the supporting details?

a. list

b. comparison-contrast

c. sequence

d. cause-effect

5. This paragraph comes from a speech communications textbook.

Characteristics of an Emotionally Well Person

The characteristics most people associate with being emotionally well (and very likely psychologically well also) are listed below. Emotionally well people:

- Feel comfortable about themselves.
- Are capable of experiencing the full range of human emotions.
- Are not overwhelmed by their emotions (either positive or negative emotions).
- Accept life's disappointments.
- Feel comfortable with others.
- Receive and give love easily.
- Feel concern for others when appropriate.
- Establish goals, both short term and long term.
- Function autonomously where and when appropriate.
- Generally trust others.

Source: Ronald Adler and Jeanne Elmhorst, *Communicating at Work,* 5th ed. Copyright © 1996 by The McGraw-Hill Companies, Inc. Reprinted by permission of The McGraw-Hill Companies, Inc.

The topic of this paragraph is *the characteristics of an emotionally well person.*

b ______ What is the main idea of this paragraph?

a. Emotionally well people always feel comfortable about themselves.

b. There are certain characteristics that are associated with being an emotionally well person.

c. To be an emotionally well person, you must feel comfortable with others and trust them.

d. Emotionally well people receive and give love easily.

a ______ Which writing pattern did the authors use to organize the supporting details?

a. list

b. comparison-contrast

c. definition

d. sequence

TEST YOUR UNDERSTANDING
RECOGNIZING AUTHORS' WRITING PATTERNS, PART TWO

REVIEW: **Writing patterns** are ways that authors organize the information they present. Five writing patterns commonly used by textbook authors are:

- **definition**—presents the meaning of an important term discussed throughout the paragraph
- **list**—a group of items presented in no specific order since the order is not important
- **sequence**—a list of items presented in a certain order because the order is important
- **comparison-contrast**—similarities and differences between two or more things are presented
- **cause-effect**—reasons and results of events and conditions are presented

EXAMPLE: Study the example paragraph below to see how the information you learned in this chapter can be used to recognize authors' writing patterns. Read the explanations that are given for the correct answers. When you are sure you understand the explanation, complete the five exercises in Part Two.

This excerpt comes from a government textbook. Its topic is *the death penalty.* Read the paragraph; then determine the main idea by asking yourself, "What is the most important point the author wants me to understand about the death penalty?" Then ask yourself, "What pattern did the authors use to organize the supporting details?"

The Death Penalty

State laws vary greatly in the application of the death penalty: some states prohibit it, but others apply it liberally. Texas, Florida, and Virginia are far and away the leaders in its application. Roughly a third of all executions in the past quarter-century have taken place in Texas alone. States that prohibit capital punishment have certain factors in common. States without the death penalty are concentrated in the North. Most of these states are relatively affluent, rank high on indicators of educational attainment, and have a small minority-group population.

Source: Thomas E. Patterson, *We the People: A Concise Introduction to American Politics,* 7th ed., p. 140. Copyright © 1998 by The McGraw-Hill Companies, Inc, Reprinted by permission of The McGraw-Hill Companies, Inc.

The topic of this paragraph is *the death penalty.*

Write the main idea sentence: State laws vary greatly in the application of the death penalty: some states prohibit it, but others apply it liberally.

Which writing pattern did the author use to organize the supporting details?

Comparison-contrast

Write the clue(s) that caused you to choose this pattern.

"vary," "some," "others," "factors in common"

Explanation: The stated main idea is the first sentence of the paragraph. The words *vary greatly, some* and *others* suggest a contrast. The phrase *factors in common* indicates a comparison.

DIRECTIONS: Read each paragraph carefully and determine its main idea by asking yourself, "What is the single most important point the author wants me to *understand* about the topic of this paragraph?" (Notice that you are given the topic of each paragraph.) If the main idea of the paragraph is stated, write the entire stated main idea sentence in the spaces provided. If the main idea of the paragraph has been implied, formulate a main idea sentence and write the sentence in the spaces provided. Next, determine the writing pattern the author used to organize the information in the paragraph by asking yourself, "What pattern did the author use to organize the main idea and the supporting details?" Write the name of the pattern the author used in the spaces provided. Finally, list the clue words or signals that indicated the pattern that was used by the author. (Refer to the list of signals and clue words on pages 370–371 as you complete these exercises.)

1. This paragraph comes from a speech communications textbook.

The Résumé

Whether you type your résumé yourself or have it done for you, the final product should reflect the professional image you want to create. It should meet these criteria:

- Be neat and error-free.
- Contain plenty of white space to avoid crowding.
- Be printed on heavyweight paper, either white or a light neutral color.
- Be reproduced clearly on a high-quality printer or copy machine.

Source: Ronald Adler and Jeanne Elmhorst, *Communicating at Work,* 5th ed. Copyright © 1996 by The McGraw-Hill Companies, Inc. Reprinted by permission of The McGraw-Hill Companies, Inc.

The topic of this paragraph is *the résumé.*

Write the main idea sentence:

There are certain criteria your typed résumé must meet if you want to create a professional image.

Which writing pattern did the authors use to organize the supporting details?

list

Write the clue(s) that caused you to choose this pattern.

The phrase "these criteria:"; list of bulleted items in no particular order that follow a colon.

2. This paragraph comes from an accounting textbook.

Because accounting and bookkeeping both are concerned with financial information and records, some people mistakenly think they are the same thing. In fact, accounting involves much more than bookkeeping. Although bookkeeping is critical to developing useful accounting information, it is only the clerical part of accounting. That is, bookkeeping is the part of accounting that records transactions and other events, either manually or with computers. In contrast, accounting involves analyzing transactions and events, deciding how to report them in financial statements, and interpreting the results. Accounting also involves designing and implementing systems to produce useful reports and to control the operations of the organization. Accounting involves more professional expertise and judgment than bookkeeping because accountants must analyze complex and unusual events.

Source: Kermit D. Larson and Barbara Chiapetta, *Fundamental Accounting Principles,* 14th ed. (Chicago: Irwin, 1996).

The topic of this paragraph is *accounting and bookkeeping.*

Write the main idea sentence:

Although accounting and bookkeeping both are concerned with financial information and records, they are not the same thing. —OR—

Accounting involves much more than bookkeeping. —OR—

First sentence (stated)

Which writing pattern did the authors use to organize the supporting details?

comparison-contrast

Write the clue(s) that caused you to choose this pattern.

The phrases "both are," "much more than," "Although bookkeeping," and "In contrast."

3. This paragraph comes from a speech communications textbook.

Having a Sense of Humor

Recognizing the humor in daily situations and occasionally being able to laugh at yourself will make you feel better not only about others but also, more importantly, about yourself. Additional benefits are that others will enjoy being associated with you, and your ability to perform physically and to recover from injuries and illnesses will probably be enhanced. For example, any student-athlete who has experienced a career-threatening injury can attest that sense of humor was a key ingredient in relation to the speed and extent of recovery.

Source: Adapted from Ronald Adler and Jeanne Elmhorst, *Communicating at Work,* 5th ed. Copyright © 1996 by The McGraw-Hill Companies, Inc. Reprinted by permission of The McGraw-Hill Companies, Inc.

✓ **Teaching Tip**
Students mistakenly select the first sentence as the main idea. Since the paragraph discusses other benefits of having a sense of humor ("Additional benefits . . ."), the main idea must be formulated.

The topic of this paragraph is *having a sense of humor.*

Write the main idea sentence:

Having a sense of humor benefits you in many ways.

OR

There are many benefits of having a sense of humor.

Which writing pattern did the authors use to organize the supporting details?

cause-effect

Write the clue(s) that caused you to choose this pattern.

The phrase "will make you" indicates a result. Also, the "benefits" are the result of having a sense of humor.

4. This paragraph comes from a health textbook.

Time Management

Although there is no single best approach to managing your time, most experts suggest that it is helpful to follow certain general steps.

- Keep a log of how you use your time for one week. Check about each half hour to see what you are doing at that time.
- Analyze these records, and eliminate those activities that take too much time relative to their importance.
- Once you have made these eliminations, divide your time into blocks so that related activities can be scheduled together. There should be a block for each major area of responsibility. Examples might include academics, employment, recreation, and socializing.
- Finally, schedule specific activities within each block of time. Attempt to complete each activity you start.

Reassess your activities occasionally and make adjustments when necessary.

Source: Wayne A. Payne and Dale B. Hahn, *Understanding Your Health*, 5th ed. Copyright © 1998 by The McGraw-Hill Companies, Inc. Reprinted by permission of The McGraw-Hill Companies, Inc.

The topic of this paragraph is *time management.*

Write the main idea sentence:

Although there is no single best approach to managing your time, most experts suggest that it is helpful to follow certain general steps. (stated; first sentence)

Which writing pattern did the authors use to organize the supporting details?

sequence

Write the clue(s) that caused you to choose this pattern.

The phrases "certain general steps," "for one week," "once you have," and the word "finally." Also, the items in the sequence are bulleted.

✓ **Teaching Tip**
In addition to the primary contrast between mergers and acquisitions, there are also the minor comparisons of a merger to a marriage and an acquisition to buying a house.

5. This paragraph comes from a business textbook.

What's the difference between mergers and acquisitions? A **merger** is the result of two firms forming one company. It is similar to a marriage joining two individuals as one. An **acquisition** is one company buying the property and obligations of another company. It is more like buying a house than entering a marriage.

Source: William G. Nickels, James M. McHugh, and Susan M. McHugh, *Understanding Business*, 7th ed., p. 156. Copyright © 2005 by The McGraw-Hill Companies, Inc. Reprinted by permission of The McGraw-Hill Companies, Inc.

The topic of this paragraph is *mergers and acquisitions.*

Write the main idea sentence:

A merger and an acquisition are different.

OR

A merger is the result of two firms forming one company, while an acquisition is one company buying the property and obligations of another company.

Which writing pattern did the authors use to organize the supporting details?

comparison-contrast

Write the clue(s) that caused you to choose this pattern.

The words "difference", "similar (to)", "more like . . . than"

SELECTION 7-1
Health

ACHOOOO! YOU'VE CAUGHT ANOTHER COLD!

From *Understanding Your Health*
By Wayne Payne and Dale Hahn

People often joke (or complain!) that scientists can put an astronaut on the moon but they can't find a cure for the common cold. Although there isn't a cure for this nuisance, there are things that you can do to relieve your symptoms, and even, perhaps, protect yourself from catching a cold in the first place.

1 The common cold, an acute upper-respiratory-tract infection, must reign as humankind's supreme infectious disease. Also known as **acute rhinitis,** this highly contagious viral infection can be caused by any of the nearly 200 known rhinoviruses. Colds are particularly common when people spend time in crowded indoor environments, such as classrooms.

2 The signs and symptoms of a cold are fairly predictable. Runny nose, watery eyes, general aches and pains, a listless feeling, and a slight fever all may accompany a cold in its early stages. Eventually the nasal passages swell, and the inflammation may spread to the throat. Stuffy nose, sore throat, and coughing may follow. The senses of taste and smell are blocked, and appetite declines.

3 When you notice the onset of symptoms, you should begin managing the cold promptly. After a few days, most of the cold's symptoms subside. In the meantime, you should isolate yourself from others, drink plenty of fluids, eat moderately, and rest. Antibiotics are effective only against bacterial infections—not viral infections like colds.

4 Some of the many OTC (over-the-counter or nonprescription) cold remedies can help you manage a cold. These remedies will not cure your cold but may lessen the discomfort associated with it. Nasal decongestants, expectorants, cough syrups, and aspirin or acetaminophen can give some temporary relief. Using some of these products for more than a few days is not recommended, however, because this may produce a rebound effect.

Annotation Practice Exercises

Directions: For each exercise below, write the topic and the main idea of the paragraph on the lines beside the paragraph. Then identify the writing pattern the authors used to organize the supporting details.

Practice Exercise

Topic of paragraph 2:

signs and symptoms of a cold

Main idea sentence:

The signs and symptoms of a cold are fairly predictable. (stated; first sentence)

Writing pattern:

sequence (clues: "early stages", "eventually")

✓ **Teaching Tip**

Have students identify and mark any pattern clues in the paragraphs used in the Practice Exercises.

5 Sometimes a cold persists. There may be prolonged chills, fever above 103 degrees Fahrenheit, chest heaviness, or aches, shortness of breath, coughing up rust-colored mucus, or persistent sore throat or hoarseness. If this happens, you should contact a physician.

6 Unfortunately, preventing colds appears to be nearly impossible. Because we now consider colds to be transmitted most readily by hand contact, you should wash your hands frequently.

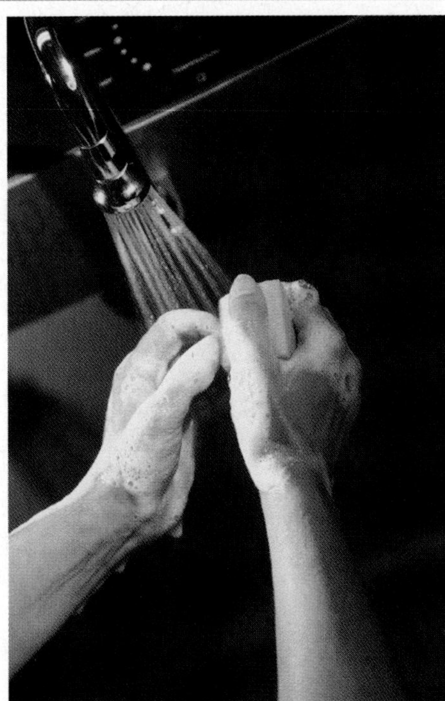

Washing your hands often is the best way to prevent the common cold.

Practice Exercise

Topic of paragraph 5:

when a cold persists

Main idea sentence:

If a cold persists, you should contact a physician.
(formulated; combine first sentence and last sentence)

Writing pattern:

cause-effect

Practice Exercise

Topic of paragraph 6:

preventing colds

Main idea sentence:

Preventing colds is almost impossible, but washing your hands frequently can help.
(formulated; combine important information)

Writing pattern:

cause-effect (clue word: "Because")

SELECTION 7-1
Health
(continued)

Comprehension and Vocabulary Quiz

This quiz has four parts. Your instructor may assign some or all of them.

Comprehension

Directions: Items 1–5 test your comprehension (understanding) of the material in this selection. These questions are much like those that a content-area instructor (such as a business professor) would expect you to know after reading and studying this selection. For each comprehension question below, use information from the selection to determine the correct answer. Refer to the selection as you answer the questions. Write your answers in the spaces provided.

¶1 b **1.** The common cold, also known as acute rhinitis, is caused by:
a. bacterial infections.
b. rhinoviruses.
c. cold, damp weather.
d. drafts and chills.

¶1 b **2.** Colds are particularly common among people who:
a. spend time outdoors.
b. spend time in crowded indoor environments.
c. have swollen nasal passages.
d. are overtired and stressed.

¶3 a **3.** Which of the following will *not* help you manage your cold?
a. taking antibiotics
b. drinking plenty of fluids
c. getting plenty of sleep
d. eating in moderation

¶4 c **4.** Decongestants, expectorants, cough syrups, and aspirin:
a. can cause shortness of breath and persistent sore throat.
b. will cure your cold.
c. can cause a rebound effect.
d. will not give you any relief from a cold.

¶6 b **5.** Colds are easily transmitted by:
a. washing your hands.
b. shaking hands with someone.
c. bacteria floating in the air.
d. talking to someone who has a cold.

Vocabulary in Context

Directions: Items 6–10 test your ability to determine the meaning of the word by using context clues. *Context clues* are words in a sentence that allow the reader to deduce (reason out) the meaning of an unfamiliar word in that sentence. Context clues also enable the reader to determine which meaning the author intends when a word has more than one meaning. For each vocabulary item below, a sentence from the selection containing an important word (*italicized, like this*) is quoted first. Next, there is an additional sentence using the word in the same sense and providing another context clue. Use the context clues from *both* sentences to deduce the meaning of the italicized word. *Be sure the answer you choose makes sense in both sentences.* If you need to use a dictionary to confirm your answer choice, remember that the meaning you select must still fit the context of *both* sentences. Write your answers in the spaces provided.

Pronunciation Key: ă **pat** ā **pay** âr **care** ä **father** ĕ **pet** ē **be** ĭ **pit**
ī **tie** îr **pier** ŏ **pot** ō **toe** ô **paw** oi **noise** ou **out** o͝o **took**
o͞o b**oo**t ŭ **cut** yo͞o ab**u**se ûr **urge** th **thin** *th* **this** hw **which**
zh vision ə **about** *Stress mark:* ′

¶1 ___a___ **6.** The common cold, an *acute* upper-respiratory-tract infection, must reign as humankind's supreme infectious disease.

Migraines are a type of headache that causes *acute* pain.

acute (ə kyo͞ot′) means:

a. severe; intense

b. widespread; epidemic

c. unbearable

d. of extremely short duration

¶2 ___c___ **7.** Runny nose, watery eyes, general aches and pains, a *listless* feeling, and slight fever all may accompany a cold in its early stages.

We ate such a large Thanksgiving dinner that we felt *listless* the rest of the day.

listless (lĭst′ lĭs) means:

a. renewed; refreshed

b. well-rested

c. having no energy

d. bored

¶3 ___a___ **8.** When you notice the *onset* of symptoms, you should begin managing the cold promptly.

The steadily decreasing hours of daylight signal the *onset* of winter.

onset (ŏn′ sĕt) means:

a. beginning

b. change; difference

c. mildness; gentleness

d. severity; seriousness

¶3 ___b___ **9.** After a few days, most of the cold's symptoms should *subside.*

I felt nervous when I first walked onto the stage, but once I began my speech, my anxiety began to *subside.*

subside (səb sīd′) means:

a. to feel normal

b. to decrease or lessen

c. to respond to treatment

d. to increase gradually

¶5 ___c___ **10.** If a cold persists, as evidenced by *prolonged* chills, fever above 103 degrees Fahrenheit, chest heaviness, or aches, shortness of breath, coughing up rust-colored mucus, or persistent sore throat or hoarseness, you should consult a physician.

Prolonged exposure to secondhand smoke can cause respiratory problems in children.

prolonged (pro lôngd′) means:

a. caused by a virus

b. pertaining to physical or emotional well-being

c. lengthy; lasting a long time

d. painful

Word Structure

Directions: Items 11–15 test your ability to use word-structure clues to help determine a word's meaning. *Word-structure clues* consist of roots, prefixes, and suffixes. In these exercises, you will learn the meaning of a word part (a root) and use it to determine the meaning of several other words that have the same word part. If you need to use a dictionary to confirm your answer choice, do so. Write your answers in the spaces provided.

In paragraph 4 of the selection, you encountered the word **temporary.** This word contains the Latin root ***tempor,*** which means "time." The word temporary means "lasting for a limited time." Use the meaning of ***tempor*** and the list of prefixes on pages 68–69 to help you determine the meaning of each of the following words that contain this same root. Write your answers in the spaces provided.

___c___ **11.** If you give an **extemporaneous** toast at a friend's wedding reception, you:

a. are very fond of your friend.

b. have had too much to drink.

c. speak without taking time to prepare formal remarks.

d. are a member of the wedding party.

___a___ **12.** My grandfather likes to spend time with his *contemporaries* at the senior citizens' center. **Contemporaries** means people who:

a. are about the same age.

b. get along well.

c. enjoy social activities.

d. like to play card games.

d 13. If a **temporal** childhood fantasy is to become a superhero, the fantasy:

a. endures into adolescence.

b. disappears as soon as it occurs.

c. lasts a lifetime.

d. lasts for only a limited time.

b 14. The *tempo* of life is slower in Latin American countries than in European countries. **Tempo** means:

a. enjoyment or pleasure.

b. pace.

c. length or duration.

d. destruction or extinction.

d 15. A museum of **contemporary** art is a museum that:

a. contains primarily art works that have been donated to it.

b. displays only sculptures and large-scale works of art.

c. focuses on paintings from other countries.

d. features modern art or art from the present time.

Reading Skills Application

Directions: Items 16–20 test your ability to *apply* certain reading skills to information in this selection. These types of questions provide valuable practice for all students, especially those who must take standardized reading tests and state-mandated basic skills tests. You may not have studied all of the skills at this point, so these items will serve as a helpful preview. The comprehension and critical reading skills in this section are presented in Chapters 3 through 9 of *New Worlds;* vocabulary and figurative language skills are presented in Chapter 2. As you work through *New Worlds,* you will practice and develop these skills. Write your answers in the spaces provided.

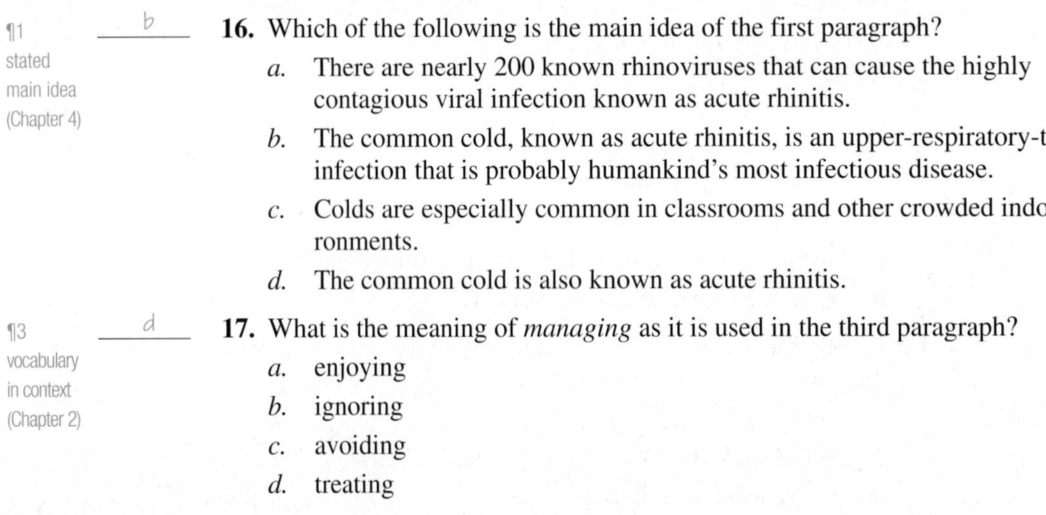

¶1 stated main idea (Chapter 4)

b 16. Which of the following is the main idea of the first paragraph?

a. There are nearly 200 known rhinoviruses that can cause the highly contagious viral infection known as acute rhinitis.

b. The common cold, known as acute rhinitis, is an upper-respiratory-tract infection that is probably humankind's most infectious disease.

c. Colds are especially common in classrooms and other crowded indoor environments.

d. The common cold is also known as acute rhinitis.

¶3 vocabulary in context (Chapter 2)

d 17. What is the meaning of *managing* as it is used in the third paragraph?

a. enjoying

b. ignoring

c. avoiding

d. treating

supporting details (Chapter 6) b

18. According to information in the selection:

a. OTC cold remedies can cure colds.

b. OTC cold remedies may lessen the discomfort associated with colds.

c. nasal decongestants and cough syrups always produce rebound effects.

d. OTC cold remedies can be used for as long as cold symptoms last.

author's purpose for writing (Chapter 8) a

19. The primary purpose the authors wrote this selection is to:

a. inform readers what colds are, how to treat them, and how to prevent them.

b. persuade readers to avoid others who have colds.

c. illustrate the range of symptoms that can accompany these highly contagious upper-respiratory-tract infections.

d. instruct readers about steps they can take to avoid catching colds.

¶1 authors' writing patterns (Chapter 7) b

20. The pattern of organization in paragraph 1 is which of the following?

a. list

b. definition

c. sequence

d. contrast

✓ **Teaching Tip**

We suggest that rather than include this section as part of the quiz grade, you use it to give students practice with the skills they have studied and as a helpful preview of upcoming skills. It makes an excellent collaborative activity. All students will find this practice helpful, but especially those who must take course exit tests, standardized reading tests, or state-mandated basic skills tests.

SELECTION **7-1**
Health
(continued)

Writing and Collaborating to Enhance Your Understanding

Option for collaboration: Your instructor may direct you to work with other students or, in other words, to work *collaboratively.* In that case, you should form groups of three or four students as directed by your instructor and work together to complete the exercises. After your group discusses each item and agrees on the answer, have a group member record it. Every member of your group should be able to explain all of your group's answers.

Collaboration Option

1. **Reacting to What You Have Read:** Did your mother, grandmother, or any other member of your family have any special ways to treat a cold? Did they have any special ways to *prevent* a cold? List or describe them. (If they did not have any, describe any folk remedies you have heard about.)

(Answers will vary.)

2. **Comprehending the Selection Further:** Because colds are transmitted most frequently by hand contact, washing your hands is the best way to prevent infection. What are other sources of infection (such as using public telephones) that hand washing afterward might prevent? What sources of infection are typical on college campuses?

(Answers will vary, but on college campuses, sources of infection include door handles, faucets, computer keyboards, shared pens and pencils, buttons and knobs on water fountains, vending machines, ATM machines, etc.)

3. **Overall Main Idea of the Selection:** In one sentence, tell what the authors want readers to understand about the common cold. (Be sure to use the words "common colds" in your overall main idea sentence.)

Common colds are highly contagious viral infections in which symptoms follow a predictable pattern; colds cannot be cured, but their symptoms can be managed, and washing one's hands is the best way to prevent them.

Internet Resources

Read More about This Topic on the World Wide Web

Directions: For further information about the topic of the selection, visit these websites:

www.commoncold.org
This website provides a comprehensive source of information on the common cold, including "Common Cold Myths."

www.niaid.nih.gov/factsheets/cold.htm
This National Institutes of Health fact sheet contains information about the causes, symptoms, transmission, and treatment of the common cold.

You can also use your favorite search engine such as Google, Yahoo!, or AltaVista (www.google.com, www.yahoo.com, www.altavista.com) to discover more about this topic. To locate additional information, type in combinations of keywords such as:

common cold

or

common cold cures

Keep in mind that whenever you go to *any* website, it is a good idea to evaluate the website and the information it contains. Ask yourself questions such as:

"Who sponsors this website?"
"Is the information contained in this website up-to-date?"
"What type of information is presented?"
"Is the information objective and complete?"
"How easy is it to use the features of this website?"

SELECTION **7-2**
Government

THE RIGHT TO VOTE: VALUED BUT UNDER UTILIZED

From *We the People: A Concise Introduction to American Politics*
By Thomas E. Patterson

Historically, young adults have been much less likely to vote than middle-aged and senior citizens. The 2008 election, however, was historic in that between 22 and 24 million Americans aged 18–29 voted. This means an estimated 49.3 to 54.5 percent of eligible young adults voted, an increase of 1 to 6 percentage points over the estimated youth turnout in 2004. (The only election in which turnout was higher in this group was in 1972, the first presidential election in which 18-year-olds could vote.) Because 66 percent of young adult voters voted for one candidate, Barack Obama, they made a crucial difference in the outcome of the election. Declare Yourself is a nonpartisan initiative dedicated to youth voters. In a survey it conducted, 61 percent of young adult voters said they will be more active in politics in the future, while only 2 percent said they would be less active; 37 percent said they will participate the same amount.

Along with age, economic class and education affect voter turnout. Americans at the bottom of the economic ladder are much less likely to vote than those at the top. In presidential elections, for example, the turnout rate of low-income citizens is only about half that of high-income citizens. Persons with a college education are about 40 percent more likely to vote than persons with a grade school education. Education, in fact, is the single best predictor of voter turnout.

If you were qualified to vote in the last presidential election, did you vote? Most Americans recognize that voting is a form of political participation, a way they can exert influence on public policy and leadership. In light of that, do you think that the majority of Americans vote in most elections? Do Americans who do not vote still value their right to vote? How does voter turnout in this country compare with voter turnout in other democracies? These questions and many more are answered in this excerpt from a government textbook.

Voter Participation

1 At the nation's founding, **suffrage**—the right to vote—was restricted to property-owning males. Tom Paine ridiculed this policy in *Common Sense.* Noting that a man whose only item of property was a jackass would lose his right to vote if the jackass died, Paine asked, "Now tell me, which was the voter, the man or the jackass?" It was not until 1840 that all states extended suffrage to propertyless white males, a change made possible by their insistence on the vote and by the realization on the part of the wealthy that the nation's abundant opportunities offered a natural defense against attacks on property rights by the voting poor.

2 Women did not secure the vote until 1920, with the ratification of the Nineteenth Amendment. By then, men had run out of excuses for denying women the vote. Senator Wendell Phillips expressed the prosuffrage view: "One of two things is true: either woman is like man—and if she is, then a ballot based on brains belongs to her as well as to him. Or she is different, and then man does not know how to vote for her as she herself does."

3 African Americans had to wait nearly fifty years longer than women to be granted full suffrage. They seemed to have won the right to vote with passage of the Fifteenth Amendment after the Civil War, but they were effectively disenfranchised in the South by a number of electoral tricks, including poll taxes, literacy tests, and whites-only primary elections. The poll tax was a fee

Annotation Practice Exercises

Directions: For each exercise that follows, write the topic and the main idea of the paragraph on the lines beside the paragraph. Then identify the writing pattern the author used to organize the supporting details.

After a hard-fought, decades-long campaign, American women finally won the right to vote in 1920.

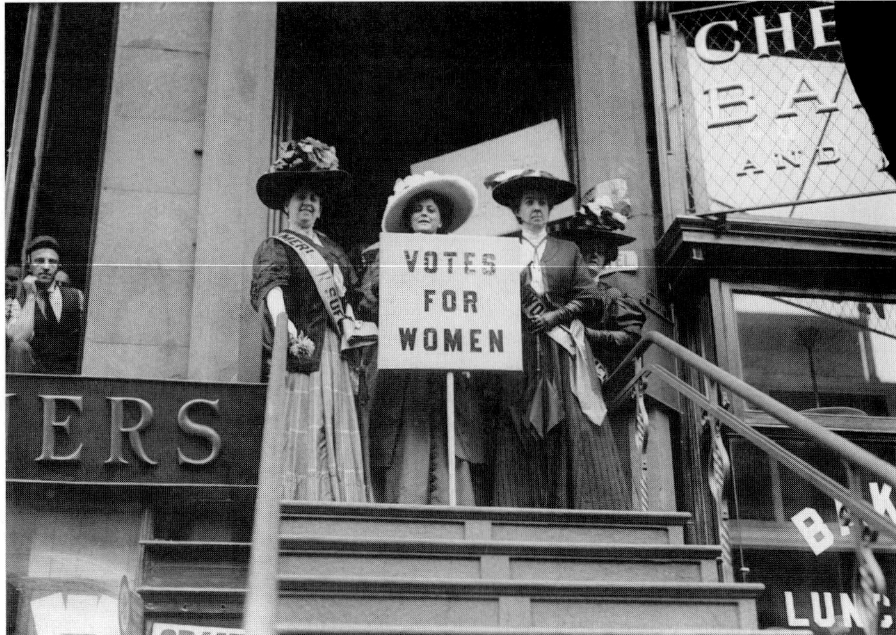

of several dollars that had to be paid before one could register to vote. Since most blacks in the South were too poor to pay it, the poll tax barred them from voting. Not until the ratification of the Twenty-fourth Amendment in 1964 was the poll tax outlawed in national elections. Supreme Court decisions and the Voting Rights Act of 1965 swept away other legal barriers to fuller participation of African Americans.

4 In 1971, the Twenty-sixth Amendment extended voting rights to include those eighteen years of age or older. Previously, nearly all states had restricted voting to those twenty-one years of age or older.

5 Today virtually any adult American—rich or poor, man or woman, black or white—who is determined to vote can legally and actually do so. Americans attach great importance to the power of their votes. They claim that voting is important. They view it as the greatest source of influence over political leadership and their strongest protection against an uncaring or corrupt government. They also rank voting as one of the most essential obligations of citizenship (see Table). In view of this attitude and the historical struggle of various groups to gain voting rights, however, the surprising fact is that Americans are not active voters. Millions of them choose not to vote regularly, a tendency that sets them apart from citizens of most other Western democracies.

Factors in Voter Turnout: The United States in Comparative Perspective

6 **Voter turnout** is the proportion of persons of voting age who actually vote in a given election. Since the 1960s the turnout level in presidential elections has not reached 60 percent

Practice Exercise

Topic of paragraph 5:

Americans and voting

Main idea sentence:

Although virtually all adult Americans can vote and claim that it is important, millions of them choose not to vote regularly, in sharp contrast to citizens in most Western democracies. (formulated; combine important information)

Writing pattern:

comparison-contrast

(clues: however, sets them apart from)

TABLE
OPINIONS ON OBLIGATIONS OF CITIZENS
Americans rank voting as one of the essential obligations of citizenship.

	Essential Obligation	Very Important Obligation	Somewhat Important	Personal Preference
Treating all people equally regardless of race or ethnic background	57%	33%	6%	4%
Voting in elections	53	29	9	9
Working to reduce inequality and injustice	41	42	12	6
Being civil to others with whom we may disagree	35	45	14	6
Keeping fully informed about the news and other public issues	30	42	19	10
Donating blood or organs to help with medical needs	20	37	18	26
Volunteering time to community service	16	42	26	16

Source: Thomas E. Patterson, *The American Democracy,* 4th ed. Copyright © 1999 by The McGraw-Hill Companies, Inc. Reprinted by permission of The McGraw-Hill Companies, Inc.

(see Graph on next page). In 2000, only about half of all adults cast a vote for president.

7 Voter turnout is even lower in the midterm congressional elections that take place between presidential elections. Midterm election turnout has not reached 50 percent since 1920, nor made it past the 40 percent mark since 1970. After a recent midterm election, the cartoonist Rigby showed an election clerk eagerly asking a stray cat that had wandered into a polling place, "Are you registered?"

8 Nonvoting is far more prevalent in the United States than in nearly all other democracies. In recent decades, turnout in major national elections has averaged less than 60 percent in the United States, compared with more than 90 percent in Belgium, and more than 80 percent in France, Germany, and Denmark. The disparity in turnout between the United States and other nations is not so great as these official voting rates indicate, however. Some nations calculate turnout solely on the basis of eligible adults, while the United States bases its figures on all adults, including noncitizens and other ineligible groups. Nevertheless, even when such statistical disparities are accounted for, turnout in U.S. elections is relatively low.

✓ **Teaching Tip**
Remind students that "Western" refers to the non-Communist countries of Europe and America.

Practice Exercise

Topic of paragraph 7:

voter turnout

Main idea sentence:

Voter turnout is even lower in the midterm congressional elections that take place between presidential elections.

(stated; first sentence)

Writing pattern:

comparison-contrast

(clue: "even lower")

✓ **Teaching Tip**
Have students identify any clues they use to help them answer the pattern question in the Practice Exercises.

Voter Turnout in Presidential Elections, 1960–2004
Voter turnout has declined substantially since the 1960s, but increased among the young in 2008.
Source: U.S. Bureau of the Census.

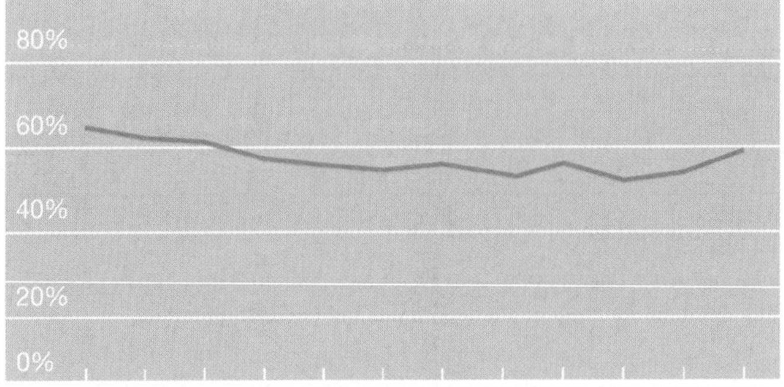

9 Why don't more Americans vote? Voting does not require vast amounts of time. It takes most people longer to go to a mall and buy a pair of shoes than it takes them to go to the neighborhood polling place and cast a ballot. Thus the relatively low voter turnout rate of Americans must be attributable to other causes: registration requirements, the frequency of elections, and the lack of clear-cut differences between the political parties.

Practice Exercise

Topic of paragraph 9:

Why more Americans don't vote

OR

causes of low voter turnout rate

Main idea sentence:

Thus, the relatively low voter turnout rate of Americans must be attributable to causes other than the amount of time it takes.

OR

Low voter turnout among Americans is attributable to causes other than the amount of time it requires.

Writing pattern:

cause-effect

(clues: "why," "thus," and "other causes")

Source: Adapted from Thomas E. Patterson, *We the People: A Concise Introduction to American Politics,* 6th ed., pp. 228–33.

SELECTION 7-2
Government
(continued)

Comprehension and Vocabulary Quiz

This quiz has four parts. Your instructor may assign some or all of them.

Comprehension

Directions: Items 1–5 test your comprehension (understanding) of the material in this selection. These questions are much like those that a content-area instructor (such as a government professor) would expect you to know after reading and studying this selection. For each comprehension question below, use information from the selection to determine the correct answer. Refer to the selection as you answer the questions. Write your answers in the spaces provided.

¶2 ___b___ **1.** Suffrage for women in the United States was attained with the ratification of the:

a. Fifteenth Amendment after the Civil War.
b. Nineteenth Amendment in 1920.
c. Twenty-fourth Amendment in 1964.
d. Twenty-sixth Amendment in 1971.

¶5 ___b___ **2.** Americans tend to rank voting:

a. as only somewhat important.
b. as one of the essential obligations of citizenship.
c. higher than most other Western democracies.
d. higher during midterm congressional elections.

Figure ___b___ **3.** During the 2000 presidential election, voter turnout was slightly above:

a. 40 percent.
b. 50 percent.
c. 62 percent.
d. 80 percent.

¶9 ___d___ **4.** The low voter turnout rate of Americans must be attributable to:

a. the lack of clear-cut differences between the political parties.
b. the frequency of elections.
c. registration requirements.
d. all of the above

¶4 ___c___ **5.** Voting rights were extended to include those 18 years of age or older in:

a. 1920.
b. 1964.
c. 1971.
d. 2000.

Vocabulary in Context

Directions: Items 6–10 test your ability to determine the meaning of the word by using context clues. *Context clues* are words in a sentence that allow the reader to deduce (reason out) the meaning of an unfamiliar word in that sentence. Context clues also enable the reader to determine which meaning the author intends when a word has more than one meaning. For each vocabulary item below, a sentence from the selection containing an important word (*italicized, like this*) is quoted first. Next, there is an additional sentence using the word in the same sense and providing another context clue. Use the context clues from *both* sentences to deduce the meaning of the italicized word. *Be sure the answer you choose makes sense in both sentences.* If you need to use a dictionary to confirm your answer choice, remember that the meaning you select must still fit the context of *both* sentences. Write your answers in the spaces provided.

Pronunciation Key: ă **pat** ā **pay** âr **care** ä **father** ĕ **pet** ē **be** ĭ **pit**
ī **tie** îr **pier** ŏ **pot** ō **toe** ô **paw** oi **noise** ou **out** o͝o **took**
o͞o **boot** ŭ **cut** yo͞o **abuse** ûr **urge** th **thin** *th* **this** hw **which**
zh **vision** ə **about** *Stress mark:* ′

¶2 ___d___ **6.** Women did not secure the vote until 1920, with the *ratification* of the Nineteenth Amendment.

Officials from both countries met last week for a ceremony celebrating the *ratification* of their new trade agreement.

ratification (răt ə fĭ cā′ shən) means:

a. open discussion

b. complete dissolution

c. quick reversal

d. formal approval

¶3 ___b___ **7.** They seemed to have won the right to vote with passage of the Fifteenth Amendment after the Civil War, but they were effectively *disenfranchised* in the South by a number of electoral tricks, including poll taxes, literacy tests, and whites-only primary elections.

Many women continue to feel *disenfranchised* because in certain jobs they are still not paid the same wages that men are for doing the same work.

disenfranchised (dĭs ĕn frăn′ chīzd) means:

a. hostile; angry

b. deprived of a legal right

c. offended

d. unwilling to cooperate

¶3 ___a___ **8.** Since most blacks in the South were too poor to pay it, the poll tax *barred* them from voting.

Olympic athletes who test positive for steroids or other banned performance-enhancing drugs are *barred* from competition.

barred (bärd) means:

a. excluded

b. listed

c. encouraged

d. convinced

¶8 ___d___ **9.** Nonvoting is far more *prevalent* in the United States than in nearly all other democracies.

Asthma and other chronic respiratory problems are more *prevalent* in densely populated urban areas than in rural areas.

prevalent (prĕv′ ə lənt) means:

a. important

b. irritating

c. damaging

d. widespread

¶8 ___c___ **10.** The *disparity* in turnout between the United States and other nations is not so great as these official voting rates indicate, however.

The *disparity* in the two bank tellers' accounts of the missing money made the bank president suspicious.

disparity (dĭ spăr′ ĭ tē) means:

a. increase

b. change

c. difference

d. decrease

Word Structure

Directions: Items 11–15 test your ability to use word-structure clues to help determine a word's meaning. *Word-structure clues* consist of roots, prefixes, and suffixes. In these exercises, you will learn the meaning of a word part (a root) and use it to determine the meaning of several other words that have the same word part. If you need to use a dictionary to confirm your answer choice, do so. Write your answers in the spaces provided.

In paragraph 4 of the selection, you encountered the word **include.** This word contains the Latin root ***clude,*** which means "to close," or "to shut." *Include* literally means "to close in," or "to contain (something) within as part of the whole." Use the meaning of ***clude*** and the list of prefixes on pages 68–69 to help you determine the meaning of each of the following words that contain this same root. Write your answers in the spaces provided.

___b___ **11.** If a sign at an amusement park says, "Children under age 5 are **excluded** from this ride," it means these children:

a. must be accompanied by a parent or adult.

b. are not permitted to ride. (shut out)

c. are required to have a ticket.

d. are restricted in the number of times they can ride.

b **12.** If a person's coronary artery is **occluded,** the artery is:

a. torn through.
b. blocked. (closed off)
c. weak.
d. punctured.

a **13.** If you seek a **secluded** spot for a picnic, you are looking for a place that is:

a. far enough away to shut out other people and noise.
b. green and grassy.
c. situated in an open area.
d. in a field or meadow.

c **14.** If a broken arm **precludes** you from participating in a tennis tournament, your broken arm:

a. limits your participation.
b. increases your participation.
c. prevents your participation. (shuts you off before you can begin)
d. delays your participation.

c **15.** If diplomats **conclude** negotiations between their countries, they:

a. begin or enter into them.
b. continue or maintain them.
c. close out or finish them.
d. break off or terminate.

Reading Skills Application

Directions: Items 16–20 test your ability to *apply* certain reading skills to information in this selection. These types of questions provide valuable practice for all students, especially those who must take standardized reading tests and state-mandated basic skills tests. You may not have studied all of the skills at this point, so these items will serve as a helpful preview. The comprehension and critical reading skills in this section are presented in Chapters 3 through 9 of *New Worlds;* vocabulary and figurative language skills are presented in Chapter 2. As you work through *New Worlds,* you will practice and develop these skills. Write your answers in the spaces provided.

logical inference (Chapter 9)

d **16.** Based on information from the selection, it can be inferred that:

a. during the 21st century voter turnout in the United States is likely to exceed that of other countries.
b. there is virtually no difference between voter turnout in midterm congressional elections and presidential elections.
c. women did not secure the vote until 1920.
d. throughout most of this nation's history, there was a general belief that those under the age of 21 could not be intelligent voters.

✓ **Teaching Tip**
Point out that information *given* in the selection (i.e., answer choice *c*) cannot be inferred.

authors' writing patterns (Chapter 7) c

17. According to the selection, which of the following represents the order in which these three groups were able to exercise their right to vote?

a. African Americans, women, 18-year-olds
b. women, 18-year-olds, African Americans
c. women, African Americans, 18-year-olds
d. 18-year-olds, African Americans, women

interpreting graphic material (Chapter 10) c

18. According to the graph in this selection, voter turnout increased in which of these years?

a. 1976
b. 1980
c. 1984
d. 1988

¶2 vocabulary in context (Chapter 2) a

19. What is the meaning of *secure* in paragraph 2 of the selection?

a. acquire
b. fasten
c. protect
d. buy

¶8 authors' writing patterns (Chapter 7) b

20. Which of the following patterns was used to organize the information in paragraph 8 in the selection?

a. list
b. comparison-contrast
c. cause-effect
d. sequence

✓ **Teaching Tip**

We suggest that rather than include this section as part of the quiz grade, you use it to give students practice with the skills they have studied and as a helpful preview of upcoming skills. It makes an excellent collaborative activity. All students will find this practice helpful, but especially those who must take course exit tests, standardized reading tests, or state-mandated basic skills tests.

SELECTION **7-2**
Government
(continued)

Writing and Collaborating to Enhance Your Understanding

Option for collaboration: Your instructor may direct you to work with other students or, in other words, to work *collaboratively.* In that case, you should form groups of three or four students as directed by your instructor and work together to complete the exercises. After your group discusses each item and agrees on the answer, have a group member record it. Every member of your group should be able to explain all of your group's answers.

Collaboration Option

1. **Reacting to What You Have Read:** If you are qualified to vote, do you? Why or why not? If you are not yet qualified to vote, do you think you will exercise this right when you are? Why or why not?

(Answers will vary.)

2. **Comprehending the Selection Further:** List at least three reasons (according to the selection) that U.S. citizens *do not* vote and three reasons why they *should* vote.

Reasons U.S. citizens do not vote:

- registration requirements
- the frequency of elections
- lack of clear-cut differences between the political parties

Reasons why U.S. citizens should vote:

- Virtually any adult American citizen determined to vote can legally do so.
- It is an essential obligation of citizenship.
- Voting does not require vast amounts of time.
- Many groups have had to struggle to gain voting rights.
- It is the greatest source of influence over political leadership.
- It is the strongest protection against an uncaring or corrupt government.

3. **Overall Main Idea of the Selection:** In one sentence, tell what the author wants readers to understand about our right to vote. (Be sure to include the phrase "right to vote" in your overall main idea sentence.)

Since the nation's founding, the *right to vote* has been extended to virtually every adult American, yet U.S. voter turnout is lower than voter turnout in nearly all other democracies.

Internet Resources

Read More about This Topic on the World Wide Web

Directions: For further information about the topic of the selection, visit these websites:

www.infoplease.com/ipa/A0781450.htm
This fact sheet shows U.S. presidential election results from 1789 to 2004.

www.lwv.org
This is the official website for the League of Women Voters. It contains information about voter registration, voter turnout, candidates, and national, state, and local elections.

You can also use your favorite search engine such as Google, Yahoo!, or AltaVista (www.google.com, www.yahoo.com, www.altavista.com) to discover more about this topic. To locate additional information, type in combinations of keywords such as:

U.S. voter participation

Keep in mind that whenever you go to *any* website, it is a good idea to evaluate the website and the information it contains. Ask yourself questions such as:

"Who sponsors this website?"
"Is the information contained in this website up-to-date?"
"What type of information is presented?"
"Is the information objective and complete?"
"How easy is it to use the features of this website?"

SELECTION 7-3 **Health**

WOULD YOU EAT "FRANKENFOOD"?

From *Understanding Your Health*
By Wayne Payne, Dale Hahn, and Ellen Mauer

Chances are you've had it for breakfast. And lunch. And dinner. It is now virtually impossible for Americans to avoid eating genetically modified, or GM, foods. British tabloid newspapers have given this new kind of food a nickname, "Frankenfood," *after the literary character Frankenstein, the creature assembled from parts of dead bodies and brought to life. This passage from a health textbook presents both the risks and the advantages of GM foods and explains why many people avoid them.*

1 In Britain and throughout Europe, public fears about **genetically modified** (GM) foods are running high and have even provoked a trade war with the United States. Britain's Prince Charles has said that he would never eat the stuff and won't stand for it being grown on his land. Americans, however, appear only dimly aware of GM foods. Many Americans are quite surprised to learn that GM foods are sold in most supermarkets.

2 In September of 2000 Kraft Foods recalled millions of taco-shells because they contained GM corn. This didn't prove to be the tide-turning disaster that some GM critics had hoped for. The taco shells contained traces of corn meal from StarLink, a genetically engineered variety of corn that hadn't been approved for human consumption in the United States. No one suffered any harm from eating the shells, but the episode caused many Americans to think about what would happen if allergens or other harmful substances, added to food by design or by accident, could have found their way into our stomachs.

Bioengineered Food

3 Since the mid-1990s, armed with new knowledge about genetic "code" material called DNA, scientists have been able to manipulate the genetic code of organisms that are food sources for humans. They have created new strains of plants and animals capable of growing larger in less time on less suitable soil or in less suitable conditions. Some of the new plant strains can do this while also resisting insect pests.

4 Farmers have long engaged in traditional genetics, using seeds from plants with the most desirable characteristics or crossbreeding closely related species of animals. Scientists have also tried to speed up the growth of plants by exposing them to chemicals and radiation. These ongoing experiments produce hundreds of mutations among genes, some of which may be useful.

5 Unlike traditional genetics, **genetic engineering** is very specific. It allows scientists to select a single gene for a single characteristic and insert that segment of DNA into another organism. Genetic engineers can also select a segment of DNA from one species and insert it into another species.

Annotation Practice Exercises

Directions: For each exercise below, write the topic of the main idea of the paragraph on the lines beside the paragraph. Then identify the writing pattern the authors used to organize the supporting details.

Practice Exercise

Topic of paragraph 1:

awareness of genetically modified foods

Main idea sentence of paragraph 1:

In Britain and Europe, public fears about genetically modified foods are widespread; however, Americans are less aware of genetically modified foods. (formulated)

Writing pattern of paragraph 1:

comparison-contrast (clue: "however")

6 The ability to alter diverse forms of plant life through genetic engineering has had a profound effect on U.S. agriculture and on the food we purchase in the grocery store. An example is the Flavr-Savr tomato, developed by Calgene to soften more slowly, meaning it can stay on the vine longer and develop a fuller taste. Because it ripens more slowly, it has a longer shelf life at the grocery store, reducing waste.

7 The use of genetically modified seed is now estimated to approach 40 to 60 percent of all U.S. planting. The seeds are modified either to make the crops resistant to weedkillers or to produce their own pesticides. Bioengineered corn and soybeans in particular are used as ingredients in a wide range of processed food, from soft drinks and beer to chips and breakfast cereal. Genetically modified organisms are fed to farm animals. Even health-food products like tofu and canola oil often contain genetically modified ingredients.

8 Genetically modified crops hold down food production costs and reduce the need for pesticides and herbicides. Modified foods being developed now are yielding more productive grains and more drought-resistant crops. Some are being developed to be more nutritious and flavorful. Caffeine-free coffee beans and even plants that produce drugs and vaccines have been developed.

What Are the Potential Health Risks?

9 While the potential benefits of higher-yielding GM food seem appealing, many people cite a number of serious health concerns about foods altered in this way. First, biotechnology foes warn that we do not know enough about the way genes operate and interact to be sure of the outcome of any genetic modification. In addition, they worry that alterations could accidentally lead to substances that are poisonous or that trigger allergies. Critics also fear that the use of DNA from plant viruses and bacteria in the modification of crops may also somehow trigger disease. Finally, they also argue that antibiotic-resistant genes could be passed to the microorganisms that make us sick, creating "superviruses" and other "superbugs" that we might not have the drugs to fight.

10 Environmental concerns are also an issue. Environmentalists are worried about genes that make crops resistant to herbicides and insects. They believe some of these genes could somehow "escape" and be transferred to other crops, resulting in the emergence of "superweeds." They fear this leakage could cause the disappearance of familiar species of insects and birds as food chains are damaged.

How Do Bioengineers Counter These Objections?

11 The biotechnology industry claims that there is no evidence of any GM food causing serious ill effects. They note that while genetic modification may result in the emergence of new allergens, so too may conventional plant breeding. Further, they claim that genetic modifications allow us to improve the flavor, texture, nutritional value, and the shelf life of food. It could boost the vitamin content

Practice Exercise

Topic of paragraph 6:

altering plant life through genetic engineering

Main idea sentence of paragraph 6:

The ability to alter diverse forms of plant life through genetic engineering has had a profound effect on U.S. agriculture and on the food we purchase in the grocery store. (stated, first sentence)

Writing pattern of paragraph 6:

cause-effect (clue: "effect")

Practice Exercise

Topic of paragraph 9:

health concerns about GM food

Main idea sentence of paragraph 9:

While the potential benefits of GM food seem appealing, many people cite a number of serious health concerns about foods altered in this way. (stated, first sentence)

Writing pattern of paragraph 9:

list (clues: "a number of," "First," "In addition," "also," "Finally") of fruits and vegetables, incorporate anti-cancer substances, and reduce our exposure to less healthy fats and oils. A recent example of genetically engineered food is "miracle" rice that contains higher levels of vitamin A. This crop was developed with the hope that rice with boosted nutritional value will stave off illness in developing countries.

Can You Avoid GM Food?

12 As more and more Americans learn about bioengineered foods, they are beginning to ask, "Should I be avoiding GM foods?" As a result, some companies are bowing to perceived customer pressure by shying away from genetically modified ingredients. Baby food manufacturers Gerber and Heinz have removed themselves from the debate by saying no to genetically modified corn and soybeans, at least for now. Frito-Lay stopped using engineered corn in its chips. McDonald's has asked suppliers to stop shipping genetically altered potatoes, as has McCain Foods, the world's largest producer of french fries.

13 Britain, Japan, Australia, Italy, and a dozen other nations currently require labels on foods containing genetically altered ingredients. U.S. regulators so far have rejected pressure for similar labeling requirements, saying GM foods are no different from those grown in conventional ways.

14 The Food and Drug Administration is expected to issue volunteer labeling guidelines for U.S. companies that wish to say a food does or does not contain GM ingredients. Critics, however, say that consumers need a clear choice at the grocery store. In response, the environmental organization Greenpeace has issued a "shopping list" that includes thousands of brand-name cereals,

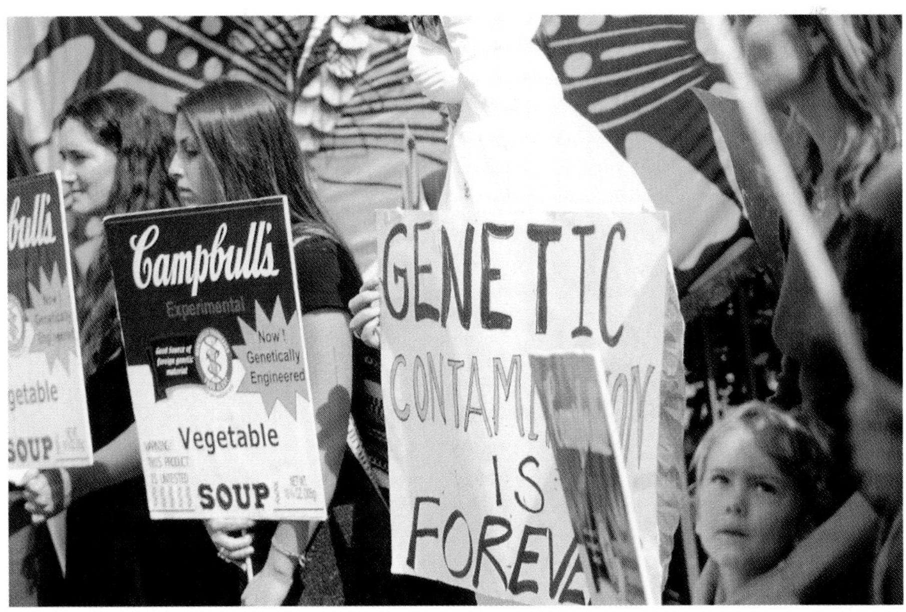

Many consumers take steps to avoid genetically modified foods.

snacks, frozen dinners, and other foods that contain genetically altered corn, soybeans, and other ingredients in an effort to help consumers avoid foods with GM ingredients. The True Food Network, a free service for consumers who want to end the use of genetically engineered ingredients in our foods, has posted a "True Food Shopping List" on the Internet (www.truefoodnow.org) to help American consumers avoid genetically engineered food.

Source: Adapted from Wayne A. Payne, Dale B. Hahn, and Ellen B. Mauer, *Understanding Your Health,* 8th ed., pp. 169–70.

SELECTION 7-3
Health
(continued)

Comprehension and Vocabulary Quiz

This quiz has four parts. Your instructor may assign some or all of them.

Comprehension

Directions: Items 1–5 test your comprehension (understanding) of the material in this selection. These questions are much like those that a content-area instructor (such as a health professor) would expect you to know after reading and studying this selection. For each comprehension question below, use information from the selection to determine the correct answer. Refer to the selection as you answer the questions. Write your answers in the spaces provided.

¶1 __b__ **1.** Genetically modified (GM) foods:

a. are banned in Britain and throughout Europe.

b. are sold in most supermarkets throughout the United States.

c. have been available since the 1940s.

d. are more expensive and time consuming to produce.

¶7 __c__ **2.** To what extent is genetically modified seed used for crop planting in the United States?

a. less than 5 percent

b. approximately 10 to 15 percent

c. approximately 40 to 60 percent

d. more than 90 percent

¶14 __a__ **3.** Consumers who want to avoid GM foods often find this difficult because:

a. the Food and Drug Administration does not require U.S. companies to label food products indicating that they do or do not contain GM ingredients.

b. GM ingredients are used in almost all brand-name food products available in supermarkets today.

c. even health-food products contain GM ingredients.

d. foods produced without GM ingredients are more expensive than food produced with GM ingredients.

¶4 __c__ **4.** An example of traditional genetics is:

a. selecting a single gene for a single characteristic and inserting that segment of DNA into another organism.

b. "miracle" rice that contains higher levels of vitamin A.

c. using seeds from plants with the most desirable characteristics.

d. all of the above

¶13 c **5.** Labels indicating whether or not food products contain genetically altered ingredients are currently required in:

a. all health-food stores.

b. the United States.

c. Britain.

d. some fast-food establishments.

Vocabulary in Context

Directions: Items 6–10 test your ability to determine the meaning of the word by using context clues. *Context clues* are words in a sentence that allow the reader to deduce (reason out) the meaning of an unfamiliar word in that sentence. Context clues also enable the reader to determine which meaning the author intends when a word has more than one meaning. For each vocabulary item below, a sentence from the selection containing an important word (*italicized, like this*) is quoted first. Next, there is an additional sentence using the word in the same sense and providing another context clue. Use the context clues from *both* sentences to deduce the meaning of the italicized word. *Be sure the answer you choose makes sense in both sentences.* If you need to use a dictionary to confirm your answer choice, remember that the meaning you select must still fit the context of *both* sentences. Write your answers in the spaces provided.

Pronunciation Key: ă **pat** ā **pay** âr **care** ä **father** ĕ **pet** ē **be** ĭ **pit**
ī **tie** îr **pier** ŏ **pot** ō **toe** ô **paw** oi **noise** ou **out** ŏŏ **took**
ōō **boot** ŭ **cut** yōō **abuse** ûr **urge** th **thin** *th* **this** hw **which**
zh **vision** ə **about** *Stress mark:* ′

¶2 a **6.** The taco shells contained traces of corn meal from StarLink, a genetically engineered variety of corn that hadn't been approved for human *consumption* in the United States.

It is likely alcohol *consumption* would decline if taxes were raised on all liquor, beer, and wine.

consumption (kŏn sŭmp′ shən) means:

a. eating or drinking; ingesting

b. abuse

c. modification; change

d. enjoyment

¶8 c **7.** Modified foods being developed now are *yielding* more productive grains and more drought-resistant crops.

Now that our vegetable garden is properly irrigated, it is *yielding* an abundance of tomatoes, beans, and peppers.

yielding (yēld′ ĭng) means:

a. developing

b. spending

c. producing; bearing

d. coming up with; inventing

¶9 ______ **8.** Biotechnology *foes* warn that we do not know enough about the way genes operate and interact to be sure of the outcome of any genetic modification.

Members of the animal rights organization People for the Ethical Treatment of Animals (PETA) view people who buy and wear fur coats as their *foes.*

foes (fōz) means:

a. scientists

b. opponents; adversaries

c. supporters; proponents

d. consumers

¶13 ______ **9.** U.S. regulators so far have rejected pressure for similar labeling requirements, saying GM foods are no different from those grown in *conventional* ways.

To please their parents, grandparents, and great-grandparents, Michelle and William agreed to have a *conventional* church wedding.

conventional (kən vĕn′ shə nəl) means:

a. experimental

b. inexpensive

c. out of the ordinary; unusual

d. done in accordance with established practice; traditional

¶14 ______ **10.** In response, the environmental organization Greenpeace has issued a "shopping list" that includes thousands of brand-name cereals, snacks, frozen dinners, and other foods that contain genetically *altered* corn, soybeans, and other ingredients in an effort to help consumers avoid foods with GM ingredients.

Cary *altered* his study schedule in order to spend more time on the subjects that were challenging for him.

altered (ôl′ tərd) means:

a. substituted; replaced

b. modified; changed

c. shortened; reduced

d. lengthened; increased

Word Structure

Directions: Items 11–15 test your ability to use word-structure clues to help determine a word's meaning. *Word-structure clues* consist of roots, prefixes, and suffixes. In these exercises, you will learn the meaning of a word part (a root) and use it to determine the meaning of several other words that have the same word part. If you need to use a dictionary to confirm your answer choice, do so. Write your answers in the spaces provided.

In paragraph 3 of the selection, you encountered the word **manipulate.** This word contains the Latin root ***man*** (also spelled *manu*) which means "hand." The word *manipulate* means to arrange, operate, or control by the skilled use of the hands. Use the meaning of ***man*** and the list of prefixes on pages 68–69 to help you determine the meaning of each of the following words that contain the same root.

b **11.** **Manual** labor is:

a. performed by men only.
b. done by hand.
c. performed by machines.
d. completed quickly.

c **12.** Ancient **manuscripts** were:

a. written in code.
b. rare.
c. written by hand.
d. difficult to read.

d **13.** When you **manage** your budget, you:

a. check it.
b. copy it by hand.
c. change it.
d. control it or take it in hand.

d **14.** A prisoner in **manacles** is wearing:

a. a striped prison uniform.
b. a number.
c. prison-issued shoes.
d. thick metal hand restraints.

c **15.** When you **maneuver** your car in traffic, you:

a. proceed as fast as possible.
b. stop immediately.
c. maintain control as you handle your way through.
d. discover a shorter route to your destination.

Reading Skills Application

Directions: Items 16–20 test your ability to *apply* certain reading skills to information in this selection. These types of questions provide valuable practice for all students, especially those who must take standardized reading tests and state-mandated basic skills tests. You may not have studied all of the skills at this point, so these items will serve as a helpful preview. The comprehension and critical reading skills in this section are presented in Chapters 3 through 9 of *New Worlds;* vocabulary and figurative language skills are presented in Chapter 2. As you work through *New Worlds,* you will practice and develop these skills. Write your answers in the spaces provided.

¶1 implied main idea (Chapter 5) d

16. The main idea of paragraph 1 is best expressed by which of the following sentences?

a. Americans are aware that GM foods are now sold in most supermarkets.

b. Britain's Prince Charles has said that he would never eat the stuff and won't stand for it being grown on his land.

c. GM foods are responsible for a trade war between Britain and the United States.

d. In Britain and Europe, fears about genetically modified foods are widespread; however, Americans are less aware of genetically modified foods.

¶s 3, 7, 8 supporting details (Chapter 6) d

17. According to information in the selection, genetically modified crops can:

a. grow larger in less time.

b. produce their own pesticides.

c. hold down food production costs.

d. all of the above

¶4 phrase in context (Chapter 2) a

18. Which of the following is the meaning of the phrase *engaged in* as it is used in paragraph 4 of the selection?

a. to have been involved with

b. to have had ownership of

c. to have manufactured

d. to have made a promise

¶2 authors' writing patterns (Chapter 7) d

19. Which of the following patterns was used to organize the information in paragraph 2?

a. list

b. sequence

c. comparison-contrast

d. cause-effect

author's purpose for writing (Chapter 8) b

20. Which of the following describes the authors' primary purpose for writing this selection?

a. to persuade consumers to avoid buying any foods with genetically modified ingredients

b. to explain both the advantages and the perceived dangers of GM foods

c. to convince consumers GM foods are safe

d. to entertain readers with the story of "Frankenfood"

✓ **Teaching Tip**

We suggest that rather than include this section as part of the quiz grade, you use it to give students practice with the skills they have studied and as a helpful preview of upcoming skills. It makes an excellent collaborative activity. All students will find this practice helpful, but especially those who must take course exit tests, standardized reading tests, or state-mandated basic skills tests.

SELECTION 7-3
Health
(continued)

Writing and Collaborating to Enhance Your Understanding

Option for collaboration: Your instructor may direct you to work with other students or, in other words, to work *collaboratively.* In that case, you should form groups of three or four students as directed by your instructor and work together to complete the exercises. After your group discusses each item and agrees on the answer, have a group member record it. Every member of your group should be able to explain all of your group's answers.

Collaboration Option

1. **Reacting to What You Have Read:** What is your position on GM food? Explain why you support the use of genetically modified food or oppose using food that has been altered in this way.

   (Answers will vary.)

2. **Comprehending the Selection Further:** The authors of this selection discuss a variety of concerns that people have about genetically modified food. List those concerns.

   1. We may not know enough about the way genes operate and interact.
   2. Genetic alterations could accidentally lead to substances that are poisonous or that trigger allergies.
   3. Use of plant viruses and bacteria in the modification of crops may somehow trigger disease.
   4. Altered genes could create drug-resistant "superviruses" and "superbugs."
   5. Altered genes could result in the emergence of "superweeds," leading to the disappearance of species of insects and birds as food chains are damaged.

3. **Overall Main Idea of the Selection:** In one sentence, tell what the authors want readers to understand about the safety of genetically modified foods. (Be sure to include the phrase "genetically modified crops" or "genetically modified food" in your overall main idea sentence.)

Although many food producers are convinced that *genetically modified crops* and ingredients are safe, an increasing number of Americans are concerned about the safety of foods altered in this way.

OR

While the potential benefits of *genetically modified food* seem appealing, many people have concerns about food altered in this way.

Internet Resources

Read More about This Topic on the World Wide Web

Directions: For further information about the topic of the selection, visit these websites:

www.truefoodnow.org
This is the official site for the True Food Network, a free service for consumers who want to end the use of genetically engineered ingredients in our foods. The True Food Network has posted a "True Food Shopping List" on its site to help American consumers avoid genetically engineered food.

www.innerself.com/Health/frankenfood.htm
This site contains an article titled "Are You Eating Frankenfood?" that has been excerpted from *Genetically Engineered Food,* © 2001, by Martin Teitel and Kimberly Wilson.

You can also use your favorite search engine such as Google, Yahoo!, or AltaVista (www.google.com, www.yahoo.com, www.altavista.com) to discover more about this topic. To locate additional information, type in combinations of keywords such as:

genetically modified foods

or

genetically engineered foods

or

Frankenfood

Keep in mind that whenever you go to *any* website, it is a good idea to evaluate the website and the information it contains. Ask yourself questions such as:

"Who sponsors this website?"
"Is the information contained in this website up-to-date?"
"What type of information is presented?"
"Is the information objective and complete?"
"How easy is it to use the features of this website?"

PART 3

A New World of Reading and Thinking Critically

CHAPTERS IN PART THREE

✓ **Related Resources**
See page IG-11 of the *Annotated Instructor's Edition* for general suggestions related to the chapters in Part Three.

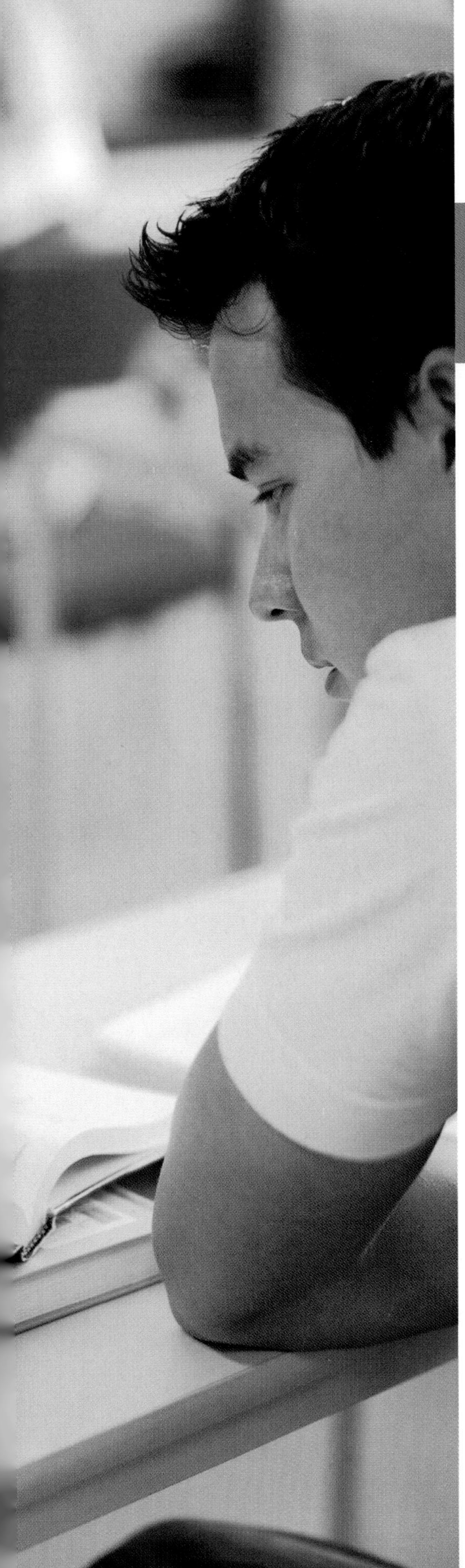

CHAPTER 8

Reading Critically

CHAPTER OBJECTIVES

In this chapter you will learn the answers to these questions:

- What is critical reading, and why is it important?
- How can I determine an author's point of view?
- How can I determine an author's purpose?
- How can I determine an author's intended audience?
- How can I determine an author's tone?

✓ **Timely Words**

"What we see depends mainly on what we look for."
(John Lubbock)

"A man is but a product of his thoughts. What he thinks, he becomes."
(Mohandas Gandhi)

CHAPTER CONTENTS

WHAT IS CRITICAL READING, AND WHY IS IT IMPORTANT?

KEY TERM
critical reading

Gaining additional insights and understanding that go beyond comprehending the topic, main idea, and supporting details.

Critical reading is also referred to as *critical reasoning* or *critical thinking.*

Student Online Learning Center (OLC)
***Go to* Chapter 8.**
***Select* Video.**

✓ **Teaching Tip**

Remind students that the student OLC contains an audio and video feature for Chapters 3 through 9 that presents **Key Comprehension Terms** and **Comprehension Monitoring Questions.**

When you read, you should always identify the basic information of topic, main idea, and supporting details. You should also note the author's organizational pattern, especially if you are reading a textbook. However, you often need to understand more than these basic elements and read critically. **Critical reading** means going *beyond* comprehending the topic, main idea, and supporting details to gain additional insights and understanding.

To understand an author's message accurately and completely, you must often read critically. Your professors expect you to be able to do this.

In this chapter, you will be introduced to these critical reading skills:

- Determining an author's point of view (the author's position on an issue)
- Determining an author's purpose (the author's reason for writing)
- Determining an author's intended audience (whom the author had in mind as his or her readers)
- Determining an author's tone (a way the author reveals his or her attitude toward the topic)

Reading critically involves asking certain comprehension monitoring questions after you read a passage. Once you have asked yourself these questions, you must take time to reread and reconsider the author's message in depth. This enables you to make more intelligent judgments about what you are reading and to gain additional insights and greater understanding.

Let's take a closer look at the four critical reading skills listed above and the comprehension monitoring questions that will guide you toward reading critically.

WHAT IS AUTHOR'S POINT OF VIEW, AND HOW CAN YOU DETERMINE IT?

KEY TERM
point of view

An author's position (opinion) on an issue.

Point of view is also known as the *author's argument* or the *author's bias.*

There is always more than one side to any issue. An author may be in *favor* of an issue (support it) or he or she may be *opposed* to it (is against it). For example, one author might have this point of view on state lotteries: "State lotteries encourage gambling and should be prohibited." Another author may have the opposite point of view: "State lotteries are harmless entertainment and should be allowed." **Point of view** refers to an author's position on an issue. The author's position is his or her opinion on an issue. Point of view is also known as the *author's argument* (the overall main idea the author is "arguing" for) and the *author's bias* (the side of an issue the author favors). If you do not determine an author's point of view correctly, you will not understand which side of an issue the author supports.

Comprehension Monitoring Question for Determining an Author's Point of View

"What is the author's position on this issue?"

To determine the author's point of view, critical readers ask themselves this comprehension monitoring question: "What is the author's position on this issue?" To answer this question, look for words that reveal the author's support of or opposition to something. Here are examples of wording that reflect a point of view in *favor* of having a state lottery:

- *Supporting* state lotteries is *essential* because . . .
- The proposed lottery will *benefit* all the citizens of our state because . . .

Here are examples of wording that reflect a point of view in *opposition* to the same issue:

- It is *not in the best interest of* the state to have a lottery because . . .
- Voters should *oppose* the creation of a state lottery because . . .
- Concerned citizens should *speak out against* the proposed lottery because . . .

Now read the following health textbook excerpt. Its title, *Smoking,* indicates the topic. The stated main idea is *Since the damage from smoking can be reversed, people who smoke should consider quitting, regardless of how long they have smoked.* To determine the authors' point of view, ask yourself, "What is the authors' position on the issue of smoking?"

Smoking

For years it was commonly believed that if you had smoked for many years, it was pointless to try to quit; the damage to one's health could never be reversed. However, the American Heart Association now indicates that by quitting smoking, regardless of how long or how much you have smoked, your risk of heart disease declines rapidly. For people who have smoked a pack or less of cigarettes per day, within three years after quitting smoking their heart disease risk is virtually the same as those who never smoked. Since the damage from smoking can be reversed, people who smoke should consider quitting, regardless of how long they have smoked. Of course, if you have just started to smoke, the healthy approach would be to quit now before the nicotine controls your life and damages your heart.

What is the authors' point of view?

The authors oppose smoking and want smokers to quit.

Source: Wayne A. Payne and Dale B. Hahn, *Understanding Your Health,* 5th ed. Copyright © 1998 by The McGraw-Hill Companies, Inc. Reprinted by permission of The McGraw-Hill Companies, Inc.

Stop and Annotate

Go back to the textbook excerpt above. Write the authors' point of view in the space provided.

In this excerpt the authors give their point of view (their position) on smoking: They oppose smoking and want smokers to quit. Then they explain why smokers should quit: they believe smokers should stop smoking, and explain why. No matter how long a person has smoked, stopping smoking reverses the damage. To convey how strongly they oppose smoking, they urge readers to "*quit now* before nicotine *controls* your life and *damages* your heart." The authors have a strong bias against smoking.

Here is another excerpt from the same health textbook. Its topic is *regular physical activity.* The formulated main idea is *Regular physical activity can help you have a lifetime of cardiovascular health.* Read this passage; then determine the authors' point of view by asking yourself, "What is the authors' position on the issue of regular physical activity?"

With all the benefits that come with physical activity, it amazes health professionals that so many Americans refuse to participate in regular exercise. Perhaps people feel that they do not have enough time or that they must work out strenuously. However, only twenty to sixty minutes of moderate aerobic activity three to five times each week is recommended. This is not a large price to pay for a lifetime of cardiovascular health. Find a partner and get started!.

What is the authors' point of view?

The authors are in favor of regular physical activity, and they want people to exercise on a regular basis.

Source: Wayne A. Payne and Dale B. Hahn, *Understanding Your Health,* 5th ed. Copyright © 1998 by The McGraw-Hill Companies, Inc. Reprinted by permission of The McGraw-Hill Companies, Inc.

In this excerpt the authors' point of view (their position) on regular physical activity is: They favor regular physical activity, and they want people to exercise regularly. They believe people should engage in moderate aerobic exercise at least three times a week, and they explain why they hold this position: because it promotes cardiovascular health. To convey how strongly they support regular exercise, they remind readers that only 20 to 60 minutes of moderate activity three to five times a week is recommended and urge readers to "get started!"

Stop and Annotate

Go back to the textbook excerpt above. Write the authors' point of view in the space provided.

EXERCISE 1

This paragraph comes from a personal finance textbook. Read the paragraph and determine the authors' point of view by asking yourself. "What is the authors' position on this issue?"

Should You Cosign a Loan?

Suppose a relative or friend asks you to cosign a loan. It may not sound like much to ask, but they are asking you to guarantee that *you* will pay their debt if they are unable to. Even if they have every intention of repaying the loan, all kinds of things can go wrong. Could you afford to pay off their debt if you had to? Even if you could afford it, do you really want to accept that responsibility? Some studies of certain types of lenders show that *as many as three of four cosigners are asked to wholly or partially repay the loan.* That statistic should not surprise you. After all, you are being asked to take a risk that a professional lender will not take. Think about it for a minute: the lender would not require a consigner if the borrower met the lender's criteria for making a loan. An even more frightening fact is that in most states, if your relative or friend misses a payment, *the lender can collect the entire debt from you immediately without first pursuing the borrower.* Moreover, the creditor can sue you or garnish your wages to collect. If you can't pay immediately, you could be charged penalties and late fees in addition to the amount of the debt. If the matter goes to court, you could get stuck with legal fees, and if the lender wins, it may be able to take your wages and property. If you default on the loan, it may become part of your credit record and damage your credit rating or your ability to get a loan. And if these potential problems aren't enough to dissuade you, agreeing to cosign a loan can permanently ruin a relationship if the borrower defaults. You'd better think twice before signing on the dotted line! The potential trouble that can result from cosigning a loan should make you reluctant to be a cosigner—ever.

Source: Based on Jack Kapoor, Les Dlabay, and Robert Hughes, *Personal Finance,* 8th ed., pp. 181–82. Copyright © 2007 by The McGraw-Hill Companies, Inc. Reprinted by permission of The McGraw-Hill Companies, Inc.

What is the *authors' point of view* about cosigning a loan? The potential trouble that can result from cosigning a loan should make you reluctant to be cosigner—ever.

WHAT IS AUTHOR'S PURPOSE, AND HOW CAN YOU DETERMINE IT?

KEY TERM
purpose

An author's reason for writing.

Comprehension Monitoring Question for Determining an Author's Purpose

"Why did the author write this?"

A second critical reading skill is determining the author's purpose. Whenever authors write, they write for specific purposes. For that matter, so do you. An author's **purpose** is simply his or her reason for writing. The author's purpose may be *to inform, to instruct, to entertain,* or *to persuade* the reader to believe something or to take a certain action.

Most textbook authors write for the purpose of informing (giving information or explaining something) or instructing (teaching the reader how to do something). However, some authors, such as scientists, historians, newspaper editors, political writers, movie critics, and other experts in their fields, write to give their opinion or to persuade. Finally, other writers, such as humorists or certain newspaper columnists, write for the purpose of entertaining. They may write humorous stories or enjoyable descriptions. It is important to understand an author's purpose for writing. If you are aware of his or her motive for writing, you will have greater insight as to what is important in the message.

To determine an author's purpose, critical readers ask themselves this comprehension monitoring question: "Why did the author write this?" Fortunately, authors often state their purpose directly. For example, the author of a biology textbook might write, "The purpose of this section is to define and explain the types of root systems in plants" (to inform). Or the author of a newspaper editorial may state, "The citizens of our city should vote 'yes' on funding a new municipal sports arena" (to persuade). Sometimes, authors do not directly state their purposes for writing because they feel the purpose is clear, and they assume the reader can infer it.

To determine an author's purpose, notice the words the author uses and the way the information is presented:

- When the author's purpose is *to inform (give information,* or *explain),* he or she will use phrases such as *It is interesting to know that . . .* or *There are different types of. . . .*
- When the author's purpose is *to instruct,* he or she will typically give a set of directions *(instructions)* or a sequence of steps to follow.
- When the author's purpose is *to persuade,* he or she will use emotional language or choose words that are designed to influence your thinking and convince you to respond a certain way. *Any reasonable person will agree that . . . , Only an uninformed student would believe that . . . ,* and *The only intelligent choice, then, is . . .* are examples of such language.
- When the author's purpose is *to entertain,* he or she may tell a funny story, use wild exaggeration (hyperbole), or simply describe a pleasant event or place. For example, writers might begin, *A funny thing happened to me on the way to . . .* or *Vermont is perhaps the loveliest place to be in autumn.*

✓ **Teaching Tip**
Students are fascinated by the information in this paragraph about the land bridge that existed between the two continents. Point out the Bering Strait on a map. You may also want to mention that there are physical similarities among Asians, Eskimos, and Native Americans.

Here is an excerpt from a U.S. history textbook. Its topic is *the first people to come to America.* The formulated main idea is *The first people probably came from Asia to America by walking across a land bridge that existed thousands of years ago.* Read this passage; then determine the authors' purpose by asking yourself, "Why did the authors write this?"

People probably first came from Asia to America during a prehistoric glacial period—either before 35,000 B.C. or about 10,000 years later—when huge amounts of the world's water froze into sheets of ice. Sea levels dropped so drastically that the Bering Strait became a broad, grassy plain. Across that land bridge between the two continents both humans and animals escaped icebound Siberia for ice-free Alaska. Whenever the first migration took place, the movement of Asians to America continued, even after 8000 B.C. when world temperatures rose again and the water from melting glaciers flooded back into the ocean, submerging the Bering Strait.

What is the authors' purpose?

to inform readers of the way people probably first came from Asia to America

Source: Adapted from James Davidson, William Geinapp, Christine Heyrman, Mark Lytle, and Michael Stoff, *Nation of Nations: A Narrative History of the American Republic,* 5th ed. Copyright © 2005 by The McGraw-Hill Companies, Inc. Reprinted by permission of The McGraw-Hill Companies, Inc.

Stop and Annotate

Go back to the textbook excerpt above. Write the authors' purpose in the space provided.

The authors' purpose for writing this passage is *to inform* the reader about a particular event: the way people probably first came from Asia to America. The passage consists of historical information the authors want you to know. (People from Asia came on foot to America over a land bridge that existed thousands of years ago.) Notice that the authors are not trying to instruct the reader how to do anything, nor trying to persuade you to accept their ideas, nor trying to entertain you.

Here is a passage from a health textbook. Its topic is given in the heading: *dealing with a stalker.* The formulated main idea is *There are steps you can take if you are being stalked.* Now read the passage and determine the authors' purpose by asking yourself, "Why did the authors write this?"

Dealing with a Stalker

Nearly every state has passed a law making stalking a crime in and of itself. But what can *you* do if you are being stalked? If someone bothers or intimidates you with phone calls, written notes or letters, or unwanted gifts, take the following steps:

- Contact your local police immediately and fill out a report.
- Report the harassment to the telephone company and ask that they install call-tracing devices and tape recorders to gather evidence against the stalker.
- Keep a detailed record, with dates, times, and exact wording of all incidents or threats, including the number of telephone calls, letters, or other harassments.
- Save all letters, answering machine tapes, and other evidence.

What is the authors' purpose?

to instruct the reader what to do when dealing with a stalker

(continued on next page)

- Contact the local prosecutor and seek a court order prohibiting the stalker from any further contact. If the stalker violates the court order, press the prosecutor to take action, such as indicting the stalker.
- Keep the pressure on police to take the appropriate action.
- Law-enforcement officials urge against any contact with the stalker. Let the police, telephone company, postal investigators, and prosecutors handle the problem.

Source: Wayne A. Payne and Dale B. Hahn, *Understanding Your Health,* 5th ed. Copyright © 1998 by The McGraw-Hill Companies, Inc. Reprinted by permission of The McGraw-Hill Companies, Inc.

Stop and Annotate

Go back to the textbook excerpt above. Write the authors' purpose in the space provided.

The authors' purpose for writing this passage is *to instruct* the reader what to do when dealing with a stalker. They say "take the following steps"; then they list the things you should do if you suspect or know that you are being stalked. Notice that the authors are doing more than merely presenting information. Their primary purpose is to instruct you about the appropriate actions to take. They are not writing primarily to persuade you to accept their suggestions (although they undoubtedly hope you will follow their suggestions if you ever need them). And they certainly did not write this passage to entertain you.

The next excerpt comes from a business textbook. As the heading indicates, the topic is *the Internet.* The main idea is *Because the Internet will only become more important as a resource, college students should learn how to use it.* Now read the passage and determine the authors' purpose by asking yourself, "Why did the authors write this?"

The Internet

Never before have students had access to information as easily as they do now. What makes information gathering so easy now is the Internet. In fact, you will find more material than you could use in a lifetime. On the Internet you can search through library catalogs all over the world, find articles from leading business journals, view paintings from leading museums, and more—much more. This resource will become even more important in the future. Information changes rapidly, and it is up to you to stay current. If you don't already know how to use the Internet, learn to do so now!

What is the authors' purpose?

to persuade college students that the Internet is such an important resource, they should learn how to use it

Source: William G. Nickels, James M. McHugh, and Susan M. McHugh, *Understanding Business,* 7th ed. Copyright © 2005 by The McGraw-Hill Companies, Inc. Reprinted by permission of The McGraw-Hill Companies, Inc.

Stop and Annotate

Go back to the textbook excerpt above. Write the authors' purpose in the space provided.

The author's purpose for writing this passage is *to persuade* college students to learn to use an extremely important resource, the Internet. The passage explains the reasons they believe students need to do this—the Internet makes it easy to access information—and gives specific examples of the vast range and amount of information the Internet makes accessible. To convince readers further, the authors state that the Internet will become increasingly important. Notice the exclamation points (!) at the end of the final sentence of the paragraph. It is the authors' way of urging students to learn how to use the Internet. Notice that the authors are doing more than merely presenting information. Their purpose is to convince you to accept their advice. They do not, however, instruct you as to how to use the Internet, nor did they write this passage merely to entertain.

EXERCISE 2

This paragraph about cosigning a loan appeared earlier in this chapter. Reread the paragraph and determine the authors' purpose by asking yourself, "Why did the authors write this?"

Should You Cosign a Loan?

Suppose a relative or friend asks you to cosign a loan. It may not sound like much to ask, but they are asking you to guarantee that *you* will pay their debt if they are unable to. Even if they have every intention of repaying the loan, all kinds of things can go wrong. Could you afford to pay off their debt if you had to? Even if you could afford it, do you really want to accept that responsibility? Some studies of certain types of lenders show that *as many as three of four cosigners are asked to wholly or partially repay the loan.* That statistic should not surprise you. After all, you are being asked to take a risk that a professional lender will not take. Think about it for a minute: the lender would not require a consigner if the borrower met the lender's criteria for making a loan. An even more frightening fact is that in most states, if your relative or friend misses a payment, *the lender can collect the entire debt from you immediately without first pursuing the borrower.* Moreover, the creditor can sue you or garnish your wages to collect. If you can't pay immediately, you could be charged penalties and late fees in addition to the amount of the debt. If the matter goes to court, you could get stuck with legal fees, and if the lender wins, it may be able to take your wages and property. If you default on the loan, it may become part of your credit record and damage your credit rating or your ability to get a loan. And if these potential problems aren't enough to dissuade you, agreeing to cosign a loan can permanently ruin a relationship if the borrower defaults. You'd better think twice before signing on the dotted line! The potential trouble that can result from cosigning a loan should make you reluctant to be a cosigner—ever.

Source: Based on Jack Kapoor, Les Dlabay, and Robert Hughes, *Personal Finance,* 8th ed., pp. 181–82. Copyright © 2007 by The McGraw-Hill Companies, Inc. Reprinted by permission of the McGraw-Hill Companies, Inc.

What is the *authors' purpose* in writing this selection? to persuade readers not to cosign another person's loan

____

WHAT IS AUTHOR'S INTENDED AUDIENCE, AND HOW CAN YOU DETERMINE IT?

When speakers make a presentation, they have an audience, and they adjust their presentation to the type of people in the audience. Suppose a doctor is asked to give a presentation on alcoholism. If her audience is other doctors, her speech will probably be very technical and contain specialized medical terms. If, however, her audience is students in a high school biology class, then her presentation will be quite different.

KEY TERM
Intended audience
People an author has in mind as his or her readers.

When authors write, they also have specific "audiences" in mind. Their audiences, of course, are the people they anticipate will be reading what they have written. An author's **intended audience** is the people the author has in mind as his or her readers. For instance, a computer scientist may write an introductory-level textbook for students who have no knowledge of computer programming. Having this particular audience in mind will influence the material the computer scientist includes, how he or she presents it, and how simple or sophisticated an approach he or she chooses. However, if that same computer scientist were writing an article for other computer scientists, the level of the material and how it is presented would be very different.

Why is it important to determine an author's audience? There are several reasons. First, if you are not among those in the intended audience (people knowledgeable about computer programming, for example), you may need to do extra work in order to understand the material. Second, if you are doing research, you can decide whether material on the topic is written for the audience you are part of (for example, those who know little or nothing about computer programming). Third, knowing who the audience is gives you insight into the author's purpose, his or her reason for writing. This, in turn, allows you to evaluate whether or not that purpose was accomplished. Perhaps the most important reason for becoming aware of audience is that it can make you a better writer: Writing instructors can help you learn to shape your message to your intended audience, and this will enable you to communicate your message more effectively.

Comprehension Monitoring Question for Determining an Author's Intended Audience

"Who did the author intend to read this?"

Critical readers ask themselves the comprehension monitoring question "Who did the author intend to read this?" Sometimes an author will state who the intended audience is, but if the author does not, you can determine the audience by considering these three things:

- *the topic* (Is it a common topic? Or is it an unusual or specialized one?)
- *the level of language used* (Is it simple? Sophisticated? Specialized?)
- *the author's purpose for writing* (Is it to inform? To instruct? To persuade?)

Here is the excerpt on smoking that you read earlier. Reread it and then determine the authors' audience by asking yourself, "Who did the authors intend to read this?"

Smoking

For years it was commonly believed that if you had smoked for many years, it was pointless to try to quit; the damage to one's health could never be reversed. However, the American Heart Association now indicates that by quitting smoking, regardless of how long or how much you have smoked, your risk of heart disease declines rapidly. For people who have smoked a pack or less of cigarettes per day, within three years after quitting smoking their heart disease risk is virtually the same as those who never smoked. Since the damage from smoking can be reversed, people who smoke should consider quitting, regardless of how long they have smoked. Of course, if you have just started to smoke, the healthy approach would be to quit now before the nicotine controls your life and damages your heart.

Who is the authors' intended audience?

everyone who smokes, including those who have just started to smoke

Source: Wayne A. Payne and Dale B. Hahn, *Understanding Your Health*, 5th ed. Copyright © 1998 by The McGraw-Hill Companies, Inc. Reprinted by permission of The McGraw-Hill Companies, Inc.

Stop and Annotate

Go back to the textbook excerpt. Write the authors' intended audience in the space provided.

The authors' intended audience is *everyone who smokes, including those who have just started to smoke.* In the last sentence of the paragraph, the authors use the word "you" and refer to "your life" and "your heart" because they are speaking directly to readers who smoke.

Here is the passage you read earlier about the *Internet*. Now reread it and then determine the authors' intended audience. Ask yourself, "Who did the authors intend to read this?"

The Internet

Never before have students had access to information as easily as they do now. What makes information gathering so easy now is the Internet. In fact, you will find more material than you could use in a lifetime. On the Internet you can search through library catalogs all over the world, find articles from leading business journals, view paintings from leading museums, and more—much more. This resource will become even more important in the future. Information changes rapidly, and it is up to you to stay current. If you don't already know how to use the Internet, learn to do so now!

Source: William G. Nickels, James M. McHugh, and Susan M. McHugh, *Understanding Business,* 7th ed., p. 15. Copyright © 2005 by The McGraw-Hill Companies, Inc. Reprinted by permission of The McGraw-Hill Companies, Inc.

Who is the authors' intended audience?

students who want to be successful in college

Stop and Annotate

Go back to the textbook excerpt. Write the authors' intended audience in the space provided.

The authors indicate their intended audience at the beginning of the paragraph: *students.* The authors explain why students should learn to use the Internet. Even when the authors use "you," they are referring to college students who are reading their textbook.

EXERCISE 3

Determine the authors' intended audience for this paragraph by asking yourself, "Who did the authors intend to read this?"

Should You Cosign a Loan?

Suppose a relative or friend asks you to cosign a loan. It may not sound like much to ask, but they are asking you to guarantee that *you* will pay their debt if they are unable to. Even if they have every intention of repaying the loan, all kinds of things can go wrong. Could you afford to pay off their debt if you had to? Even if you could afford it, do you really want to accept that responsibility? Some studies of certain types of lenders show that *as many as three of four cosigners are asked to wholly or partially repay the loan.* That statistic should not surprise you. After all, you are being asked to take a risk that a professional lender will not take. Think about it for a minute: the lender would not require a consigner if the borrower met the lender's criteria for making a loan. An even more frightening fact is that in most states, if your relative or friend misses a payment, *the lender can collect the entire debt from you immediately without first pursuing the borrower.* Moreover, the creditor can sue you or garnish your wages to collect. If you can't pay immediately, you could be charged penalties and late fees in addition to the amount of the debt. If the matter goes to court, you could get stuck with legal fees, and if the lender wins, it may be able to take your wages and property. If you default on the loan, it may become part of your credit record and damage your credit rating or your ability to get a loan. And if these potential problems aren't enough to dissuade you, agreeing to cosign a loan can permanently ruin a relationship if the borrower defaults. You'd better think twice before signing on the dotted line! The potential trouble that can result from cosigning a loan should make you reluctant to be a cosigner—ever.

Source: Based on Jack Kapoor, Les Dlabay, and Robert Hughes, *Personal Finance,* 8th ed., pp. 181–82. Copyright © 2007 by The McGraw-Hill Companies, Inc. Reprinted by permission of The McGraw-Hill Companies, Inc.

Who is the *authors' intended audience*? general public

WHAT IS AUTHOR'S TONE, AND HOW CAN YOU DETERMINE IT?

When people speak, their tone of voice often reveals their attitude toward whatever they are speaking about. To convey a tone, speakers rely on pitch, volume, and inflection, along with their choice of words. You can usually tell by people's tone, for example, if they are serious, joking, happy, upset, or angry. If a friend said, "I made a C on my history test!" you would know by his or her tone whether your friend was thrilled, relieved, or disappointed.

KEY TERM
tone

Manner of writing (choice of words and writing style) that reveals an author's attitude toward a topic.

Comprehension Monitoring Question for Determining an Author's Tone

"What do the author's choice of words and style of writing reveal about his or her attitude toward the topic?"

Authors use tone just as speakers do. An author's **tone** is a manner of writing that reveals the author's attitude toward a topic. Authors' tone helps convey their point of view and purpose. Authors might, for example, use tones that are factual, humorous, urgent, encouraging, angry, or sarcastic. You can determine an author's tone by examining his or her word choice and writing style. It may also help you to think about what the author's tone of voice would sound like if he or she were saying the material to you rather than writing it.

It is important to determine an author's tone because if you misunderstand the tone, you may misinterpret the message. To illustrate, you might think the author was being sincere when he was actually joking or being sarcastic. To determine an author's tone, ask yourself, "What do the author's choice of words and style of writing reveal about his or her attitude toward the topic?"

As noted above, *word choice* is one way authors reveal their tone. For example, when describing an angry athlete's behavior, one sports writer might use "temper tantrum" to convey a disapproving tone. Another sportswriter, who thinks the athlete's behavior was justified, might describe it with the milder words "outburst" or "incident" to convey a more sympathetic tone.

Now consider how an author's *writing style* can be used to convey tone. Each of these sentences contains the same message, but the writing style makes their tone quite different:

- The most successful college graduates of tomorrow will be those who can use a wide range of computer applications effectively.
- Unless you want to flip burgers all your life, you'd better learn how to use that laptop!

Both sentences suggest that it is important to educate yourself about the use of computers, but the first sentence has a formal, serious tone. It is the type of sentence you might find in a business or computer science textbook. The second sentence, however, has a much more informal tone. The phrase *unless you want to flip burgers all your life* reveals this tone. This sentence might appear in a flyer advertising computer training, but it would not be appropriate for a college textbook.

There are many words that can describe an author's tone, but 48 common ones are listed and defined in the chart that follows. You should familiarize yourself with any of these words that are new to you.

WORDS THAT DESCRIBE TONE

There are many words that can be used to describe tone, and you already know lots of them, such as *happy, sad,* and *angry.* There are many others, however, that you may not be familiar with. Here is a list of several. (They are also valuable words to have in your own vocabulary.) To make it easier for you to learn the words, they are grouped into general categories.

Words That Describe a *Neutral* Tone

(typically used in textbooks, reference material, sets of directions, instructional manuals, most newspaper and magazine articles, and other factual, objective material that is presented in a straightforward manner)

unemotional involving little or no emotion or feeling
dispassionate devoid of or unaffected by passion, emotion, or bias
indifferent appearing to have no preference or concern

Words That Describe a *Serious* Tone

(typically used in important formal announcements and obituaries, for example)

solemn deeply earnest, serious, and sober
serious grave, earnest, not trifling or jesting; deeply interested or involved
reserved marked by self-restraint and reticence

Words That Describe an *Emotional* Tone

(typically found in personal articles, political writing, and some persuasive writing, such as editorials)

compassionate showing kindness, mercy, or compassion; sympathetic
concerned caring deeply about a person or issue
impassioned characterized by passion or zeal
nostalgic feeling bittersweet longing for things, persons, or situations in the past
sentimental based on emotion rather than reason
remorseful feeling regret
self-pitying feeling sorry for oneself
urgent calling for immediate attention; instantly important
defiant intentionally contemptuous; resisting authority or force

Words That Describe a *Critical, Disapproving* Tone

(typically found in movie and book reviews, editorials, some magazine articles)

critical inclined to criticize or find fault
disapproving passing unfavorable judgment upon; condemning
pessimistic expecting the worst; having a negative attitude or gloomy outlook
intolerant not allowing a difference of opinion or sentiment
indignant angered by something unjust, mean, or unworthy; irate

(continued on next page)

Words That Describe a *Humorous, Sarcastic, Ironic,* or *Satiric* Tone

(can appear in writing of many sorts, including literature and social criticism and some newspaper and magazine columns and articles)

lighthearted	not being burdened by trouble, worry, or care; happy and carefree
irreverent	disrespectful; critical of what is generally accepted or respected; showing a lack of reverence
cynical	scornful of the motives, virtue, or integrity of others; expressing scorn and bitter mockery
scornful	treating someone or something as despicable or unworthy; showing utter contempt
contemptuous	showing open disrespect or haughty disdain
mocking	treating with scorn or contempt
malicious	intended to cause harm or suffering; having wicked or mischievous intentions or motives
ironic	humorously sarcastic or mocking
sarcastic	characterized by the desire to show scorn or contempt
bitter	characterized by sharpness, severity, or cruelty
skeptical	reluctant to believe; doubting or questioning everything
disbelieving	not believing; refusing to believe

Words That Describe a *Supportive* Tone

(found in writing of many types, such as certain textbooks, inspirational writing, some magazine articles, and personal correspondence)

encouraging	showing support
supportive	showing support or assistance
enthusiastic	showing excitement
optimistic	expecting the best; having a positive outlook
approving	expressing approval or agreement
positive	being in favor of; supportive; optimistic
sympathetic	inclined to sympathy; showing pity
tolerant	showing respect for the rights or opinions or practices of others

Some *Other* Words That Can Describe Tone

authoritative	speaking in a definite and confident manner
ambivalent	having opposite feelings or attitudes at the same time
conciliatory	willing to give in on some matters
cautious	careful; not wanting to take chances; wary
arrogant	giving oneself an undue degree of importance; haughty
grim	gloomy; dismal; forbidding
humble	marked by meekness or modesty; not arrogant or prideful
apologetic	self-deprecating; humble; offering or expressing an apology or excuse

Here is the passage about dealing with a stalker that you read earlier in this chapter. To determine the tone the authors use, reread this passage and then ask yourself, "What do the authors' choice of words and style of writing reveal about their attitude toward dealing with a stalker?"

Dealing with a Stalker

Nearly every state has passed a law making stalking a crime in and of itself. But what can *you* do if you are being stalked? If someone bothers or intimidates you with phone calls, written notes or letters, or unwanted gifts, take the following steps:

- Contact your local police immediately and fill out a report.
- Report the harassment to the telephone company and ask that they install call-tracing devices and tape recorders to gather evidence against the stalker.
- Keep a detailed record, with dates, times, and exact wording of all incidents or threats, including the number of telephone calls, letters, or other harassments.
- Save all letters, answering machine tapes, and other evidence.
- Contact the local prosecutor and seek a court order prohibiting the stalker from any further contact. If the stalker violates the court order, press the prosecutor to take action, such as indicting the stalker.
- Keep the pressure on police to take the appropriate action.
- Law-enforcement officials urge against any contact with the stalker. Let the police, telephone company, postal investigators, and prosecutors handle the problem.

What is authors' tone?

serious and unemotional

Source: Wayne A. Payne and Dale B. Hahn, *Understanding Your Health,* 5th ed. Copyright © 1998 by The McGraw-Hill Companies, Inc. Reprinted by permission of The McGraw-Hill Companies, Inc.

Stop and Annotate

Go back to the previous textbook excerpt above. Write the authors' tone in the space provided.

The authors' tone is *serious* and *unemotional.* Even though stalking can be an emotional issue, the authors do not use an emotional tone. Their tone is not upset or alarmed. They use the words "bothers" and "intimidates" instead of stronger, more emotional words such as "harasses," "torments," "terrifies," or "threatens." They then calmly suggest some "steps" you can take to deal with the problem.

Here is one more passage that you read earlier in the chapter. It is about the *benefits of regular aerobic activity*. To determine the tone the authors use in writing about the need for regular physical activity and the benefits it brings, reread the passage and ask yourself, "What do the authors' choice of words and style of writing reveal about their attitude toward the benefits of regular aerobic activity?"

With all the benefits that come with physical activity, it amazes health professionals that so many Americans refuse to participate in regular exercise. Perhaps people feel that they do not have enough time or that they must work out strenuously. However, only twenty to sixty minutes of moderate aerobic activity three to five times each week is recommended. This is not a large price to pay for a lifetime of cardiovascular health. Find a partner and get started!

What is authors' tone?

enthusiastic

encouraging

urgent

Source: Wayne A. Payne and Dale B. Hahn, *Understanding Your Health,* 5th ed. Copyright © 1998 by The McGraw-Hill Companies, Inc. Reprinted by permission of The McGraw-Hill Companies, Inc.

Stop and Annotate

Go back to the textbook excerpt above. Write the authors' tone in the space provided.

The authors' tone is *enthusiastic, encouraging,* and perhaps even *urgent.* Readers are admonished to "Find a partner and get started!" The authors use an exclamation point for added emphasis.

EXERCISE 4

Determine the authors' tone for this paragraph by asking yourself, "What do the authors' choice of words and style of writing reveal about their attitude toward the topic?"

Should You Cosign a Loan?

Suppose a relative or friend asks you to cosign a loan. It may not sound like much to ask, but they are asking you to guarantee that *you* will pay their debt if they are unable to. Even if they have every intention of repaying the loan, all kinds of things can go wrong. Could you afford to pay off their debt if you had to? Even if you could afford it, do you really want to accept that responsibility? Some studies of certain types of lenders show that *as many as three of four cosigners are asked to wholly or partially repay the loan.* That statistic should not surprise you. After all, you are being asked to take a risk that a professional lender will not take. Think about it for a minute: the lender would not require a consigner if the borrower met the lender's criteria for making a loan. An even more frightening fact is that in most states, if your relative or friend misses a payment, *the lender can collect the entire debt from you immediately without first pursuing the borrower.* Moreover, the creditor can sue you or garnish your wages to collect. If you can't pay immediately, you could be charged penalties and late fees in additions to the amount of the debt. If the matter goes to court, you could get stuck with legal fees, and if the lender wins, it may be able to take your wages and property. If you default on the loan, it my become part of your credit record and damage your credit rating or your ability to get a loan. And if these potential problems aren't enough to dissuade you, agreeing to cosign a loan can permanently ruin a relationship if the borrower defaults. You'd better think twice before signing on the dotted line! The potential trouble that can result from cosigning a loan should make you reluctant to be a cosigner—ever.

Source: Based on Jack Kapoor, Les Dlabay, and Robert Hughes, *Personal Finance,* 8th ed., pp. 181–82. Copyright © 2007 by The McGraw-Hill Companies, Inc. Reprinted by permission of The McGraw-Hill Companies, Inc.

What is the *authors' tone* in this selection? concerned (suggested by italics: "think twice," exclamation point)

As you may have noticed, author's purpose, tone, point of view, and intended audience are related to each other. The chart below shows *interrelationship* among author's purpose, tone, point of view, and intended audience.

HOW THE CRITICAL READING SKILLS ARE INTERRELATED

The author's purpose causes him or her to use a certain tone to convey a point of view to an intended audience.

- The author decides on a ***purpose*** (reason) for writing:
  to inform to instruct to persuade to entertain
- To accomplish his or her purpose, the author uses an appropriate ***tone,*** such as:

serious	formal	sincere	enthusiastic
disapproving	sympathetic	informal	humorous
ironic	lighthearted	ambivalent	encouraging

- To convey his or her main idea or ***point of view*** (position on an issue):
  expresses *support* for an issue or ***opposition*** to an issue.
- To an ***intended audience:***
  the general public a specific group a particular person

The chart below illustrates the application of critical reading skills to a piece of writing, a music critic's review of an imaginary CD. It is also designed to show that critical reading skills are often part of everyday reading.

EXAMPLE OF CRITICAL READING APPLIED TO A MUSIC CRITIC'S REVIEW OF A NEW CD

The controversial group The Gate Crashers has just released its first CD, *The Gate Crashers—Live!* Is it a good CD? That depends: Do you like vulgar lyrics that glorify violence? Do you mind listening to painfully bad hip-hop musicians? Do you have any problem sitting through twelve tracks (65 excruciating minutes!) of mind-numbing noise? If not, then you'll surely want to add *The Gate Crashers—Live!* to your collection.

Questions	**Answers**
What is the author's purpose?	To persuade readers not to buy this new CD
Who is the author's intended audience?	People who buy CDs
What is the author's point of view?	*The Gate Crashers—Live!* CD is awful.*
What is the author's tone?	Sarcastic

*Notice that this is also the author's main idea, or "argument."

OTHER THINGS TO KEEP IN MIND WHEN READING CRITICALLY

Here are five helpful things you should keep in mind about critical reading:

1. **You should avoid seeing the purpose of everything you read as *to inform*.**

   When you are determining the author's purpose, use *inform* as a last choice. Instead of really thinking about the author's purpose, you may be tempted to label the purpose of every passage as "to inform." If the author is explaining how to do something, then the purpose is to *instruct*. If the author is trying to convince readers of something, then the purpose is *to persuade*. If the author is presenting material that is simply amusing or pleasant to read, then the purpose is *to entertain*. Only when the author is just providing information is the purpose to inform.

2. **If the author's purpose is to persuade you to adopt his or her point of view, you should determine which side of an issue he or she favors.**

   One way you can determine which side of an issue an author favors is by examining whether or not the author presents both sides of an issue, or whether the author presents good things about only one side (the side he or she favors). You can check to see if the author has left out important information that might weaken his or her position. Or perhaps the author presents only negative things about the side or position he opposes.

   There are times, of course, when an author does present both sides of an issue and, rather than taking a position, allows readers to make up their own minds. If the author presents both sides fairly, we say that he is *objective* or *unbiased*. When an author favors one side of an issue, we say he is *biased*.

3. **Understanding the author's tone will enable you to grasp the true or intended meaning, even when the author's words may appear to be saying something different.**

   Although an author's tone is often obvious, there may be times when the tone is less clear and requires careful thought on your part. If you misunderstand an author's tone, you may misinterpret the message. You may think she is saying something different from what she really means. For example, if you read a short story and you miss the author's ironic tone, you will mistakenly think her meaning is the opposite of what it actually is. Or if you overlook irony, you may think authors are being serious when they are actually joking; you may think that they are calm when, in fact, they are angry, or that they are in favor of something when, in reality, they oppose it.

4. **There are two forms of irony: irony in tone and irony in situations.**

   When authors are being ironic, they create a deliberate contrast between their apparent meaning and their intended meaning; they say one thing but mean the opposite. That is, the words are intended to express something different from their literal meaning. You use irony every day in conversation. For example, you might say, "Well, that test was a breeze!" but your ironic tone makes it clear how difficult the test actually was.

   Another form of irony occurs when there is incongruity or difference between what is expected and what actually occurs. For example, it would be ironic if you made a surprise visit to a friend in another city, and your friend was not there because he was making a trip to pay a surprise visit to you in your city!

5. **Sarcasm and irony are not the same thing.**

   Students sometimes confuse sarcasm with irony. *Sarcasm* is a cutting, often ironic remark that is intended to convey contempt or ridicule. Sarcasm is always meant to hurt; irony is not. An example of a hurtful, sarcastic remark is "That college must have bought its band uniforms at a thrift shop sale!" An example of an ironic remark is "This winter makes last winter seem like a day at the beach" (meaning this winter is much colder than last winter).

CREATING CHAPTER REVIEW CARDS

Student Online Learning Center (OLC)
***Go to* Chapter 8.**
***Select* Chapter Test.**

Review cards or *summary cards* are a way to select, organize, and summarize the important information in a textbook chapter. Preparing review cards helps you organize the information so that you can learn and memorize it more easily. In other words, chapter review cards are effective study tools.

Preparing chapter review cards for each chapter of *New Worlds* will give you practice in creating these valuable study tools. Once you have learned how to make chapter review cards, you can use actual index cards to create them for textbook material in your other courses and use them when you study for tests.

Now complete the chapter review cards for Chapter 8 by answering the questions or following the directions on each card. Use the type of handwriting that is easiest for you to reread (printing or cursive) and write legibly.

✓ **Teaching Tip**
Remind students that the student OLC contains a 10-item **Chapter Test** for this chapter. After completing the chapter review cards below, students should complete the Chapter Test on the OLC.

Reading Critically

1. Define *critical reading*. (See page 435.)

   Going beyond comprehending the topic, main idea, and supporting details to gain additional insights and understanding

2. Why is it important to be able to read critically? (See page 435.)

   So that you can understand an author's message accurately and completely

Card 1 Chapter 8: Reading Critically

Author's Point of View

1. What is meant by *author's point of view*? (See page 435.)

An author's position on an issue

2. Why is it important to determine an author's point of view? (See page 435.)

So you will know which side of an issue an author favors

3. What comprehension monitoring question should you ask yourself in order to determine an author's point of view?

(See page 435.)

What is the author's position on this issue?

Card 2 Chapter 8: Reading Critically

Author's Purpose

1. Define *author's purpose*. (See page 438.)

An author's reason for writing

2. List four common purposes that authors have: (See page 438.)

1) to inform (explain)

2) to instruct (teach)

3) to persuade (convince)

4) to entertain (humor)

3. What comprehension monitoring question should you ask yourself in order to determine an author's purpose?

(See page 438.)

Why did the author write this?

Card 3 Chapter 8: Reading Critically

Author's Intended Audience

1. Define *author's intended audience.* (See page 441.)

The people the author had in mind as his or her readers

2. List three factors that can help you determine the author's intended audience: (See page 442.)

1) the topic

2) the level of language used

3) the author's purpose for writing

3. What comprehension monitoring question should you ask yourself in order to determine an author's audience?

(See page 442.)

Who did the author intend to read this?

Card 4 Chapter 8: Reading Critically

Author's Tone

1. Define *author's tone.* (See page 444.)

Manner of writing that reveals the author's attitude toward a topic

2. List two factors that can help you determine the author's tone: (See page 444.)

1) word choice

2) writing style

3. What comprehension monitoring question should you ask yourself in order to determine an author's tone? (See page 444.)

What does the author's word choice or writing style reveal about his or her attitude toward the topic?

Card 5 Chapter 8: Reading Critically

TEST YOUR UNDERSTANDING
CRITICAL READING, PART ONE

REVIEW: **Critical reading** involves gaining insights and going beyond comprehending the topic, main idea, and supporting details. Reading critically requires you to ask certain questions after you read a passage and to think carefully about what you have read. The four critical reading skills presented in this chapter are *interrelated.* An author's *purpose* causes him or her to present certain facts and opinions, and to use a certain *tone* to convey a *point of view* to an *intended audience.*

- **Author's point of view**—an author's *position* (opinion) on an issue. To identify an author's point of view, ask yourself, "What is the author's position on this issue?"
- **Author's purpose**—an author's *reason* for writing. To identify an author's purpose, ask yourself, "Why did the author write this?"
- **Author's intended audience**—people an author has in mind as his or her *readers*. To identify an author's intended audience, ask yourself, "Who did the author intend to read this?"
- **Author's tone**—manner of writing that reveals an author's *attitude* toward a topic. To identify an author's tone, ask yourself, "What do the author's choice of words and style of writing reveal about his or her attitude toward the topic?"

EXAMPLE: Study the example paragraph below to see how the information you learned in this chapter can be used to read critically. Read the explanations that are given for the correct answers. When you are sure you understand the explanations, complete the five exercises in Part One.

This passage comes from a health textbook. Its topic is *sexual victimization*. Read the paragraph; notice that the paragraph's main idea is given below it. Then determine the authors' purpose and tone by asking yourself these comprehension monitoring questions: "Why did the authors write this?" and "What do the authors' choice of words and style reveal about their attitude?"

Sexual Victimization

Ideally, sexual intimacy is a mutual, enjoyable form of communication between two people. Far too often, however, relationships are approached in an aggressive, hostile manner. These sexual aggressors always have a victim—someone who is physically or psychologically traumatized. Sexual victimization occurs in many forms and in a variety of settings. Sexual victimization includes rape and sexual assault, sexual abuse of children, sexual harassment, and the commercialization of sex.

Source: Wayne A. Payne, Dale B. Hahn, and Ellen B. Mauer, *Understanding Your Health,* 8th ed., p. 626. Copyright © 2005 by The McGraw-Hill Companies, Inc. Reprinted by permission of The McGraw-Hill Companies, Inc.

Main idea: *Sexual victimization occurs in many forms and in a variety of settings.*

__a__ What is the authors' purpose?

a. to inform
b. to instruct
c. to persuade
d. to entertain

__b__ What is the authors' tone?

a. disapproving and bitter
b. unemotional and straightforward

(continued on next page)

c. nostalgic

d. indifferent

Explanation: The correct answer to the first question is a. The author's purpose is *to inform* readers about sexual victimization. *The correct answer to the second question is b.* Although this topic could be a highly emotional one, it is presented in an unemotional tone.

DIRECTIONS: Read each paragraph carefully. (Notice that you are given the main idea of each paragraph.) Answer the questions about the author's point of view, purpose, intended audience, or tone and write your answers in the spaces provided.

1. This paragraph comes from a sociology textbook.

Segregation

Segregation refers to the physical separation of two groups of people in terms of residence, workplace, and social functions. Generally, it is imposed by a dominant group on a minority group. However, segregation is rarely complete; intergroup contact inevitably occurs even in the most segregated societies.

Source: Richard T. Schaefer and Robert P. Lamm, *Sociology,* 6th ed. Copyright © 1997 by The McGraw-Hill Companies, Inc. Reprinted by permission of The McGraw-Hill Companies, Inc.

Main idea: *Segregation refers to the physical separation of two groups of people in terms of residence, workplace, and social functions; however, segregation is rarely complete.*

a What is the authors' purpose?

a. to inform readers of the definition of segregation

b. to instruct readers in how to avoid segregation

c. to persuade readers to accept segregation

d. to persuade readers to reject segregation

d What is the authors' tone?

a. compassionate; sympathetic

b. skeptical; disbelieving

c. humorous; teasing

d. unemotional; neutral

2. This paragraph comes from a communications textbook.

To truly live comfortably with yourself, make an honest commitment to learn to accept yourself on the basis of what you discover through self-examination. Recognition of both strengths and limitations can be difficult, but it is necessary as a basis for your emotional health. To grow toward *real* maturity, however, you must learn to reach beyond mere acceptance of your qualities and begin to learn how to be yourself. Once accomplished, you will be living on the basis of your authentic self.

Source: Ronald Adler and Jeanne Elmhorst, *Communicating at Work,* 5th ed. Copyright © 1996 by The McGraw-Hill Companies, Inc. Reprinted by permission of The McGraw-Hill Companies, Inc.

Main idea: *Examine and accept your strengths and limitations so that you can learn to live on the basis of your authentic self.*

c What is the authors' purpose?

a. to persuade readers to live comfortably

b. to instruct readers in how to accept their limitations

c. to persuade readers to take steps that will enable them to live as their authentic selves
d. to instruct readers in how to make an honest commitment

b What is the authors' point of view?

a. One should always grow toward real maturity.
b. Honest self-examination, self-acceptance, and learning how to be yourself are the basis for living authentically.
c. One should recognize one's strengths even though it might be difficult to do so.
d. People should always act in a mature way.

3. This paragraph comes from a health textbook.

Stalking

✓ **Teaching Tip** Students tend to confuse the authors' likely attitude toward stalking (disapproval) with the tone of their writing.

In recent years the crime of **stalking** has received considerable attention. Stalking refers to an assailant's planned efforts to pursue an intended victim. Most stalkers are male. Many of these stalkers are excessively possessive or jealous and pursue people with whom they formerly had a relationship. Some stalkers pursue people with whom they have had only an imaginary relationship.

Source: Wayne A. Payne, Dale B. Hahn, and Ellen B. Mauer, *Understanding Your Health,* 8th ed. Copyright © 2005 by The McGraw-Hill Companies, Inc. Reprinted by permission of The McGraw-Hill Companies, Inc.

Main idea: *Stalking refers to an assailant's planned efforts to pursue an intended victim.*

a What is the authors' purpose?

a. to inform readers about stalking
b. to instruct readers in how to recognize stalkers
c. to persuade readers to avoid stalkers
d. to inform readers about the possessive, jealous nature of stalkers

d What is the authors' tone?

a. hostile
b. tolerant
c. scornful
d. neutral

4. This paragraph comes from a multimedia literacy textbook.

Internet Addiction Disorder

The Internet can be addicting, so much so that **Internet Addiction Disorder (IAD)** has entered the medical lexicon. University of Pittsburgh researcher Kimberly Young maintains that IAD is as real as alcoholism, characterized by loss of control, cravings and withdrawal symptoms, social isolation, marital discord, academic failure, excessive financial debt, and job termination. Certain kinds of people may prefer cyberlife to real life. If you feel yourself becoming addicted, set a time limit for how long you spend on the Internet each day, and try to stay focused on the task at hand. Many Web pages contain enticing ads intended to draw you away from your original purpose. You can reduce the amount of time you spend online if you stay focused on accomplishing your intent instead of surfing off in other directions.

Source: Fred Hofstetter, *Multimedia Literacy.* Copyright © 1995 by The McGraw-Hill Companies, Inc. Reprinted by permission of The McGraw-Hill Companies, Inc.

Main idea: *Internet Addiction Disorder (IAD) is as real a problem as alcoholism, but there are steps you can take to deal with the problem.*

__c__ Who is the author's intended audience?

a. people who cannot stay focused on the task at hand

b. people who are alcoholic

c. people who use the Internet

d. people who spend more than an hour a day using computers

__d__ What is the author's point of view?

a. People who are alcoholic should be very careful about using the Internet.

b. If you are addicted to the Internet, you should join a support group.

c. If you suffer from IAD, you should seek medical help.

d. If you sense you are becoming addicted to the Internet, you can take certain actions to prevent it.

5. This paragraph comes from a psychology textbook.

Prior to 1968, individuals who had strong objections to the death penalty were routinely barred from serving on juries in cases involving a possible death penalty. In a landmark ruling in 1968, however, an appeals judge commuted a death penalty to life imprisonment in the case of *Witherspoon v. Illinois* on the grounds that the jury was composed only of persons who favored the death penalty and was not, therefore, a fair and "representative" jury. In making this ruling, the judge cited a Gallup poll conducted at that time that found that only about 55 percent of the people surveyed favored the death penalty. The judge ruled that prospective jurors could be excluded only when they were so opposed to the death penalty that they would vote against it regardless of the evidence.

Source: Benjamin B. Lahey, *Psychology: An Introduction,* 8th ed., p. 670. Copyright © 2004 by The McGraw-Hill Companies, Inc. Reprinted by permission of The McGraw-Hill Companies, Inc.

Main idea: *Due to the landmark* Witherspoon v. Illinois *ruling in 1968, prospective jurors can be excluded only when they are so opposed to the death penalty that they would vote against it regardless of the evidence.*

__a__ What is the author's purpose?

a. to inform readers of the effect of *Witherspoon v. Illinois* on jury selection

b. to instruct readers in how to avoid jury duty

c. to persuade readers to oppose the death penalty

d. to inform readers about the history of the jury selection process

__c__ What is the author's tone?

a. sarcastic

b. sentimental

c. unemotional

d. urgent

TEST YOUR UNDERSTANDING
CRITICAL READING, PART TWO

REVIEW: **Critical reading** involves gaining insights and going beyond comprehending the topic, main idea, and supporting details. Reading critically requires you to ask certain questions after you read a passage and to think carefully about what you have read. The four critical reading skills presented in this chapter are *interrelated.* An author's *purpose* causes him or her to present certain facts and opinions, and to use a certain *tone* to convey a *point of view* to an *intended audience.*

- **Author's point of view**—an author's *position* (opinion) on an issue. To identify an author's point of view, ask yourself, "What is the author's position on this issue?"
- **Author's purpose**—an author's *reason* for writing. To identify an author's purpose, ask yourself, "Why did the author write this?"
- **Author's intended audience**—people an author has in mind as his or her *readers.* To identify an author's intended audience, ask yourself, "Who did the author intend to read this?"
- **Author's tone**—manner of writing that reveals an author's *attitude* toward a topic. To identify an author's tone, ask yourself, "What do the author's choice of words and style of writing reveal about his or her attitude toward the topic?"

EXAMPLE: Study the example paragraph below to see how the information you learned in this chapter can be used to read critically. Read the explanations that are given for the correct answers. When you are sure you understand the explanations, complete the five exercises in Part Two.

This excerpt comes from a speech communications textbook. Its topic is *choosing an approach for your résumé.* Read the paragraph; notice that the paragraph's main idea is given below it. Then determine the authors' purpose and tone by asking yourself these comprehension monitoring questions: "Why did the author write this?" and "Whom did the author intend to read this?"

✓ **Teaching Tip**
Some students put "readers" whenever they are asked who the intended audience is. Tell them to be more specific (e.g., people with allergies, parents of twins, etc.).

Although you want to make yourself stand out from the crowd, when you apply for a job, you should be cautious about using unusual kinds of paper or typefaces on your résumé. A novel approach may capture the fancy of a prospective boss, but it may be a turn-off. The more you know about the field and the organization itself, the better your decision will be about the best approach. Be sure that the approach you choose is compatible with the nature of the organization.

Source: From Ronald Adler and Jeanne Elmhorst, *Communicating at Work,* 5th ed. Copyright © 1996 by The McGraw-Hill Companies, Inc. Reprinted by permission of The McGraw-Hill Companies, Inc.

Main idea: *Be sure that the approach you choose for your résumé is compatible with the nature of the organization with which you are seeking employment.*

What is the authors' purpose?

to instruct

Explanation: The authors' purpose is to *instruct* readers about the correct approach for a résumé. The authors explain why it is important to choose an appropriate paper and typeface for a résumé, and advise readers to learn more about the field and the organization.

(continued on next page)

Who is the authors' intended audience?

those who will be submitting résumés when applying for jobs

Explanation: It is clear from the first sentence that the authors' intended audience is those persons who will be creating and submitting résumés when applying for jobs.

DIRECTIONS: Read each paragraph carefully and determine its main idea by asking yourself, "What is the single most important point the author wants me to *understand* about the topic of this paragraph?" If the main idea of the paragraph is stated, write the entire stated main idea sentence in the spaces provided. If the main idea of the paragraph has been implied, formulate a main idea sentence and write the sentence in the spaces provided. Finally, read critically to answer the questions about the author's point of view, purpose, intended audience, or tone and write your answers in the spaces provided.

- For author's point of view, *write a sentence that gives the author's position or opinion.*
- For author's purpose, *determine if the author wants to inform, instruct, persuade,* or *entertain.*
- For author's intended audience, *tell who the author had in mind to read the paragraph.*
- For author's tone, *select tone words that tell the author's attitude toward the topic.*

1. This paragraph comes from a health textbook.

Risk Factors That Can Be Changed

Six cardiovascular risk factors are influenced, in large part, by our lifestyle choices. These risk factors are tobacco smoke, physical inactivity, high blood cholesterol level, high blood pressure, diabetes mellitus, and overweight. Healthful behavior changes you make concerning these "big six" risk factors can help you protect and strengthen your cardiovascular system.

Source: Wayne A. Payne, Dale B. Hahn, and Ellen B. Mauer, *Understanding Your Health,* 8th ed., p. 337. Copyright © 2005 by The McGraw-Hill Companies, Inc. Reprinted by permission of The McGraw-Hill Companies, Inc.

Write the main idea sentence:

Six cardiovascular risk factors are influenced, in large part, by our lifestyle choices.

(stated; first sentence)

Who is the authors' intended audience?

anyone who is at risk of cardiovascular disease —OR— general public

What is the authors' point of view?

You should make choices that will enhance your cardiovascular health.

What is the authors' purpose?

to instruct (readers in how to reduce their cardiovascular risk)

2. This paragraph comes from a communications textbook.

The Importance of a Sense of Humor

Recognizing the humor in daily situations and occasionally being able to laugh at yourself will make you feel better not only about others but also, more importantly, about yourself. Others will enjoy being associated with you, and your ability to perform physically and to recover from injuries and illnesses will probably be enhanced. For example, any student-athlete who has experienced a career-threatening injury can attest that a positive outlook and a sense of humor were key ingredients in relation to the speed and extent of recovery. Develop your sense of humor. Learn to laugh at yourself. It's good for you!

Source: Adapted from Ronald Adler and Jeanne Elmhorst, *Communicating at Work,* 5th ed. Copyright © 1996 by The McGraw-Hill Companies, Inc. Reprinted by permission of The McGraw-Hill Companies, Inc.

✓ **Teaching Tip**
Students usually select the first sentence as the main idea, but it is a detail that explains *one* of the many benefits of having a sense of humor.

Write the main idea sentence:

Having a sense of humor can benefit you in many ways. (implied; Formula 3)

What is the authors' purpose?

to persuade (readers of the benefits of having a sense of humor)

What is the authors' tone?

encouraging

What is the authors' point of view?

You should develop your sense of humor.

3. This paragraph comes from the introduction to a computer science textbook.

It is obvious that computers are part of everyone's life. Your future success requires a basic level of knowledge about computers and skill in using them. This book is designed to help you attain these goals. As you read and complete the assignments in this text, you will learn to involve computers in your critical thinking. As a student in the 21st century, you should understand how computers affect your life and how they are used to solve everyday problems. You should be able to talk intelligently about computers. Equally important, you should be prepared for the changes computers will bring in your life.

Source: Timothy N. Trainor and Diane Krasnewich, *Computers!,* 5th ed. Copyright © 1996 by The McGraw-Hill Companies, Inc. Reprinted by permission of The McGraw-Hill Companies, Inc.

Write the main idea sentence:

Your future success requires a basic level of knowledge about computers and skill in using them, and this book is designed to help you attain these goals. (Implied, Formula 2)

Who is the authors' intended audience?

students who want a successful future

What is the authors' point of view?

Students should educate themselves about computers.

4. This paragraph comes from a health textbook.

Avoiding Date Rape

✓ **Teaching Tip**
Be sure students understand that the entire paragraph explains the *first* step in avoiding date rape. Also, students tend to choose, incorrectly, one of the last two sentences in the paragraph as the stated main idea of the paragraph, but neither contains the topic.

One key to avoiding date rape is to consider your partner's behaviors. Many, but not all, date rapists show one or more of the following behaviors: a disrespectful attitude toward you and others, lack of concern for your feelings, violence and hostility, obsessive jealousy, extreme competitiveness, a desire to dominate, and unnecessary physical roughness. Consider these behaviors as warning signs for possible problems in the future. Reevaluate your participation in the relationship.

Source: Wayne A. Payne, Dale B. Hahn, and Ellen B. Mauer. *Understanding Your Health,* 8th ed., p. 628. Copyright © 2005 by The McGraw-Hill Companies, Inc. Reprinted by permission of The McGraw-Hill Companies, Inc.

Write the main idea sentence:

One key to avoiding date rape is to consider your partner's behaviors.

(stated; first sentence)

What is the authors' purpose?

to instruct

What is the authors' tone?

serious; unemotional

5. This paragraph comes from a child development textbook.

Homelessness

For children who have no homes, the consequences of poverty are especially severe. Sadly, families are the fastest growing segment of the homeless population, about 2.5 million people, one-third of whom are single mothers and young children. Compared to most poor children, the majority of homeless children living in emergency shelters are developmentally delayed and suffer from anxiety, depression, and learning difficulties. Young girls are the most affected. While the large majority of poor children attend Head Start or other preschool education programs, only 15 percent of homeless children are enrolled. Many never get to such programs, and tragically, others are so disturbed that they are rejected even by Head Start.

Source: Adapted from Laurence Steinberg and Roberta Meyer, *Childhood.* Copyright © 1995 by The McGraw-Hill Companies, Inc. Reprinted by permission of The McGraw-Hill Companies, Inc.

Write the main idea sentence:

For children who have no homes, the consequences of poverty are especially severe.

(stated; first sentence)

What is the authors' purpose?

to inform (readers about the plight of homeless children)

What is the authors' tone?

sympathetic; compassionate; concerned ("sadly," "tragically")

SELECTION **8-1**

Fiction

FROM *FOR ONE MORE DAY*

By Mitch Albom

Mitch Albom, a former sportswriter, first gained public acclaim in 1997 for his book Tuesdays with Morrie. *The book, which chronicles the days he spent with a beloved, dying college professor of his, stayed on the* New York Times *bestseller list for four straight years. Albom's novels* The Five People You Meet in Heaven *and* For One More Day *have also become bestsellers, and all three have been made into successful TV movies.*

On his website, Albom explains, "For One More Day *is a story about a former baseball player named Charley 'Chick' Benetto who receives the gift—or is it a hallucination—of spending 'one more day' with his mother, Posey, who has been deceased for several years. In* For One More Day, *the love between a mother and her child is shown to be strong enough to save that child, now a grown man, from the clutches of death. By spending 'one more day' with his mother, Charley learns that even a life replete with errors is worth living. 'Never give up' is the message that Posey gives her son Charley as she returns him to the world of the living." Albom continues, "The inspiration for* For One More Day *came, again, from a real person, my mother, who stood up for me all my life, even when I didn't always stand up for her. I have imagined what life will be like when she is no longer here, and I know I will want another day with her" (www.albom.com). In this selection, Chick tells about the day his mother took him to college for the first time.*

1 I would guess the day I went to college was one of the happiest of my mother's life. At least it started out that way. The university had offered to pay half my tuition with a baseball scholarship, although, when my mother told her friends, she just said "scholarship," her love of that word eclipsing any possibility that I was admitted to hit the ball, not the books.

2 I remember the morning we drove up for my freshman year. She'd been awake before sunrise, and there was a full breakfast waiting for me when I stumbled down the stairs: pancakes, bacon, eggs—six people couldn't have finished that much food. My sister Roberta had wanted to come with us, but I said no way—what I meant was, it was bad enough that I had to go with my mother—so she consoled herself with a plateful of syrup-covered French toast. We dropped her at a neighbor's house and began our four-hour trek.

3 Because, to my mother, this was a big occasion, she wore one of her "outfits"—a purple pantsuit, a scarf, high heels, and sunglasses, and she insisted that I wear a white shirt and a necktie. "You're starting college, not going fishing," she said. Together we would have stood out badly enough in Pepperville Beach, but remember, this was college in the mid-60s, where the less correctly you were dressed, the more you were dressed correctly. So when we finally got to campus and stepped out of our Chevy station wagon, we were surrounded by young women in sandals and peasant skirts, and young men in tank tops and shorts, their hair worn long over their ears. And there we were, a necktie and a purple pantsuit, and I felt, once more, that my mother was shining a ridiculous light on me.

4 She wanted to know where the library was, and she found someone to give us directions. "Charley, look at all the books," she marveled as we walked around the ground floor. "You could stay in here all four years and never make a dent."

Annotation Practice Exercises

Directions: After you have read the selection, answer the critical reading questions below. This will help you gain additional insights about what you have read.

Practice Exercise

Who is the *author's intended audience*?

general public

Practice Exercise

What is the *author's purpose* in writing this?

To inform readers about the day Chick goes to college for the first time. (Also accept "entertain," since it's a novel.)

5 Everywhere we went she kept pointing. "Look! That cubicle—you could study there." And, "Look, that cafeteria table, you could eat there." I tolerated it because I knew she would be leaving soon. But as we walked across the lawn, a good looking girl—gum-chewing, white lipstick, bangs on her forehead—caught my eye and I caught hers and I flexed my arm muscles and I thought, my first college girl, who knows? And at that very moment my mother said, "Did we pack your toiletry kit?"

6 How do you answer that? A yes? A no? A "Gee, Mom!" It's all bad. The girl continued past us and she sort of guffawed, or maybe I just imagined that. Anyhow, we didn't exist in her universe. I watched her sashay over to two bearded guys sprawled under a tree. She kissed one on the lips and she fell in alongside them, and here I was with my mother asking about my toiletry kit.

7 An hour later, I hoisted my trunk to the stairwell of my dorm. My mother was carrying my two "lucky" baseball bats with which I had led the Pepperville County Conference in home runs.

8 "Here," I said, holding out my hand, "I'll take the bats."

9 "I'll go up with you."

10 "No, it's all right."

11 "But I want to see your room."

12 "Mom."

13 "What?"

14 "Come on."

15 "You know. Come on."

16 I couldn't think of anything else that wouldn't hurt her feelings, so I just pushed my hand out farther. Her face sank. I was six inches taller than her now. She handed me the bats. I balanced them atop the trunk.

17 "Charley," she said. Her voice was softer now, and it sounded different. "Give your mother a kiss."

18 I put the trunk down with a small thud. I leaned toward her. Just then two older students came bounding down the stairs, feet thumping, voices loud and laughing. I instinctively jerked away from my mother.

19 "Scuse please," one of them said as they maneuvered around us.

20 Once they were gone, I leaned forward, only intending a peck on the cheek, but she threw her arms around my neck and she drew me close. I could smell her perfume, her hair spray, her skin moisturizer; all the assorted potions and lotions she had doused herself with for this special day.

21 I pulled away, lifted the trunk, and began my climb, leaving my mother in the stairwell of a dormitory, as close as she would ever get to a college education.

Practice Exercise

This fictional story is told by Chick, the main character. Rather than the *author's tone* in this selection, what is the tone of Chick, the narrator?

frustrated, annoyed, ashamed

embarrassed (by his mother).

Practice Exercise

Rather than the *author's point of view,* what is Charley's point of view regarding his mother's taking him to college?

He wishes she weren't there because

he is embarrassed by her. Her presence

makes him feel that he's still a child.

SELECTION 8-1
Fiction
(continued)

Comprehension and Vocabulary Quiz

This quiz has four parts. Your instructor may assign some or all of them.

Comprehension

✓ **Teaching Tips**
Show students where the answer to each comprehension question appears in the selection. (You may want to have students work in pairs to identify where each answer appears.)

Directions: Items 1–5 test your comprehension (understanding) of the material in this selection. These questions are much like those that a content-area instructor (such as an English professor) would expect you to know after reading and studying this selection. For each comprehension question below, use information from the selection to determine the correct answer. Refer to the selection as you answer the questions. Write your answers in the spaces provided.

¶21 ___b___ **1.** Regarding a college education, Charley's mother:

a. believes a college education should be only for those who have scholarships.
b. respects a college education, but never had an opportunity for one herself.
c. sees a college education as a way to meet people who can help you later in life.
d. feels a true college education comes from reading the books in the college's library.

¶s8–19 (implied) ___b___ **2.** Charley doesn't want his mother to come up to his dorm room because:

a. it is up several flights of stairs.
b. it would be embarrassing to have her accompany him.
c. she would try to arrange and decorate it.
d. women are not allowed in dorm rooms.

¶s2–3 ___d___ **3.** It is clear that taking Charley to college is important to his mother because she:

a. awoke before sunrise that day.
b. fixed him an unusually large breakfast.
c. wore one of her special outfits.
d. all of the above. [also ¶20: doused herself with perfume and other "potions and lotions"]

¶1 ___b___ **4.** The university gave Charley:

a. an academic scholarship.
b. a baseball scholarship.
c. a combined academic and baseball scholarship.
d. no scholarship money.

¶2 ___a___ **5.** The university is located:

a. several hours from Charley's home.
b. in the next state.
c. in Charley's hometown.
d. Pepperville.

Vocabulary in Context

Directions: Items 6–10 test your ability to determine the meaning of the word by using context clues. *Context clues* are words in a sentence that allow the reader to deduce (reason out) the meaning of an unfamiliar word in that sentence. Context clues also enable the reader to determine which meaning the author intends when a word has more than one meaning. For each vocabulary item below, a sentence from the selection containing an important word (*italicized, like this*) is quoted first. Next, there is an additional sentence using the word in the same sense and providing another context clue. Use the context clues from *both* sentences to deduce the meaning of the italicized word. *Be sure the answer you choose makes sense in both sentences.* If you need to use a dictionary to confirm your answer choice, remember that the meaning you select must still fit the context of *both* sentences. Write your answers in the spaces provided.

Pronunciation Key: ă **pat** ā **pay** âr **care** ä **father** ĕ **pet** ē **be** ĭ **pit**
ī **tie** îr **pier** ŏ **pot** ō **toe** ô **paw** oi **noise** ou **out** o͝o **took**
o͞o **boot** ŭ **cut** yo͞o **abuse** ûr **urge** th **thin** *th* **this** hw **which**
zh **vision** ə **about** *Stress mark:* ′

¶1 b **6.** The university had offered to pay half my tuition with a baseball scholarship, although, when my mother told her friends, she just said "scholarship," her love of that word *eclipsing* any possibility that I was admitted to hit the ball, not the books.

The actress complained that in important scenes, the presence of a child actor kept *eclipsing* her own role.

eclipsing (ē klĭp′ sĭng) means:

a. circling
b. diminishing in importance
c. causing disgrace or humiliation
d. removing from sight

¶6 b **7.** The girl continued past us and she sort of *guffawed,* or maybe I just imagined that.

The children squealed, clapped, and *guffawed* whenever they watched cartoons.

guffawed (gə fôd′) means:

a. acted in an unkind manner
b. laughed loudly
c. paid no attention
d. rolled the eyes upward

¶6 b **8.** I watched her *sashay* over to two bearded guys sprawled under a tree.

At parties, she likes to *sashay* around so that everyone will see her trendy clothes and jewelry.

sashay (să shā′) means:

a. move quickly and directly
b. strut in a showy, self-important manner

c. wait for others to approach

d. twirl, spin

¶7 ___a___ **9.** An hour later, I *hoisted* my trunk to the stairwell of my dorm.

The divers hooked cables to the sunken ship and *hoisted* it from the bottom of the sea.

hoisted (hoist′ əd) means:

a. lifted; hauled up

b. did not disturb; left in place

c. tilted; angled

d. returned

¶20 ___c___ **10.** I could smell her perfume, her hair spray, her skin moisturizer; all the assorted potions and lotions she had *doused* herself with for this special day.

The arsonist *doused* the car with gasoline and then set it on fire.

doused (dousd) means:

a. cleaned

b. refreshed

c. wet thoroughly; drenched

d. decorated; adorned

Word Structure

Directions: Items 11–15 below test your ability to use word-structure clues to help determine a word's meaning. *Word-structure clues* consist of roots, prefixes, and suffixes. In these exercises, you will learn the meaning of a word part (a root) and use it to determine the meaning of several other words that have the same word part. If you need to use a dictionary to confirm your answer choice, do so. Write your answers in the spaces provided.

In paragraph 20 of the selection, you encountered the word **intending.** This word contains the Latin root ***ten,*** which means "to stretch" or "to hold or grasp." The word *intending* literally means "stretching toward something," or, in other words, having a specific purpose or plan in mind. Use the meaning of the root ***ten*** and the list of prefixes on pages 68–69 to help you determine the meaning of each of the following words that contain the same root.

___d___ **11.** If a professor **extends** the deadline for turning in an assignment, it means that:

a. the assignment is due immediately.

b. students can decide the point at which they turn in the assignment.

c. the deadline has been canceled, so there is no deadline.

d. the time until it is due has been lengthened or stretched out.

___c___ **12.** If you are a **tenacious** person, it means you:

a. like to shake hands with other people.

b. have a birthday on the tenth day of the month.

c. hang on and do not give up.

d. are a kind, gentle person.

b 13. If a scientific theory turns out to be **untenable,** the theory:
a. is unpopular with the general public.
b. does not hold up when tested or examined logically.
c. cannot be understood by anyone other than scientists.
d. does not conflict with other theories.

c 14. If a dog eats tainted food that **distends** its stomach, the dog's stomach is:
a. upset.
b. empty.
c. swollen.
d. ruptured.

a 15. When you pay **attention** to something you:
a. concentrate or hold your focus on it.
b. display it proudly.
c. disregard it.
d. try to make sense of it.

✓ **Teaching Tip**
Let students know that not all of the skills included in this Reading Skills Application section have been introduced yet. This section serves as a valuable preview of these skills, however. Students typically get several of the items correct, and they find this encouraging.

Reading Skills Application

Directions: Items 16–20 test your ability to *apply* certain reading skills to information in this selection. These types of questions provide valuable practice for all students, especially those who must take standardized reading tests and state-mandated basic skills tests. You may not have studied all of the skills at this point, so these items will serve as a helpful preview. The comprehension and critical reading skills in this section are presented in Chapters 3 through 9 of *New Worlds;* vocabulary and figurative language skills are presented in Chapter 2. As you work through *New Worlds,* you will practice and develop these skills. Write your answers in the spaces provided.

¶3 vocabulary in context (Chapter 2)

a 16. Which of the following is the meaning of *"shining a ridiculous light on me"* as it is used in paragraph 3?
a. making me look foolish
b. pointing a funny-looking light at me
c. showing me how to do something
d. making me appear clever

¶18 author's writing pattern (Chapter 7)

c 17. Which pattern is used to organize the information in paragraph 18?
a. list
b. sequence
c. cause-effect
d. comparison-contrast

¶3 implied main idea (Chapter 5)

a 18. Which of the following represents the main idea of paragraph 3?
a. Charley was embarrassed by the way he and his mother were dressed.
b. Charley was much better dressed than the other students.
c. Clothing styles in the mid-60s were very casual.
d. Charley's mother had poor taste in clothes.

¶16 logical inference (Chapter 9) ___b___ **19.** Based on the selection, it can be inferred that Charley:

a. was angry with his mother and didn't care if he hurt her feelings.

b. did care about his mother and did not want to hurt her feelings any more than necessary.

c. was very pleased that his mother was so interested in him and his first day of college.

d. wished he had decided not to attend college.

¶3 supporting details (Chapter 6) ___d___ **20.** In paragraph 3, the details about the other students' dress and appearance are used to illustrate:

a. how badly college students dress.

b. the styles that were popular among college students during the mid-60s.

c. the need for a campus dress code for students.

d. what was popular and how different it was from what Charley and his mother were wearing.

SELECTION **8-1**
Fiction
(continued)

Writing and Collaborating to Enhance Your Understanding

Option for collaboration: Your instructor may direct you to work with other students or, in other words, to work *collaboratively*. In that case, you should form groups of three or four students as directed by your instructor and work together to complete the exercises. After your group discusses each item and agrees on the answer, have a group member record it. Every member of your group should be able to explain all of your group's answers.

Collaboration Option

1. **Reacting to What You Have Read:** What was your first day of college like? Did you come by yourself? If not, who came with you? Did you feel that you fit in with the other students? Explain your answers to these questions.

(Answers will vary.)

2. **Comprehending the Selection Further:** The author provides ample evidence that Charley's mother loves him. List at least three bits of evidence from the selection that show this.

1. She told all of her friends about Charley's scholarship.
2. She fixed Charley a special breakfast his last morning at home.
3. She drove for four hours to take him to the campus.
4. She wore an outfit that she considers special.
5. She worried that he has everything he needs (e.g., that he might have forgotten his toiletries).
6. She wanted to go with him to see his dorm room.

7. She asked him for a kiss.

8. She accepted his refusal to let her go with him to his dorm room, although she'd wanted to see it.

3. **Overall Main Idea of the Selection:** In one sentence, tell what the author wants readers to understand about Charley's first day of college. (Be sure to include "Charley" and the phrase "first day of college" in your overall main idea sentence.)

Charley was embarrassed by his mother's taking him to college the first day and he put his feelings above his mother's.

Read More about This Topic on the World Wide Web

Directions: For further information about the topic of the selection, visit these websites:

www.albom.com
This site is the official online resource for information about Mitch Albom and his work.

www.authorsontheweb.com/features/authormonth/0309albom/albom-mitch.asp
Mitch Albom is featured on this website as a previous author of the month.

You can also use your favorite search engine such as Google, Yahoo!, or AltaVista (www.google.com, www.yahoo.com, www.altavista.com) to discover more about this topic. To locate additional information, type in combinations of keywords such as:

Mitch Albom

or

"For One More Day" + novel

Keep in mind that whenever you go to *any* website, it is a good idea to evaluate the website and the information it contains. Ask yourself questions such as:

"Who sponsors this website?"
"Is the information contained in this website up-to-date?"
"What type of information is presented?"
"Is the information objective and complete?"
"How easy is it to use the features of this website?"

SELECTION **8-2**
Memoir

I NEVER MADE IT TO THE NFL

From *The Last Lecture*
By Randy Pausch with Jeffrey Zaslow

Professors are sometimes asked what they would say in a "last lecture." In other words, what wisdom and important life lessons would they share, if they knew it was their last chance? When Carnegie-Mellon computer science professor Randy Pausch was asked to participate in his university's "last lecture" series, he was in a unique situation: He had recently been diagnosed with terminal pancreatic cancer. On September 18, 2007, he gave what would indeed be his last lecture. Pausch, a married father of three young children, was only 46 at the time. Since then, millions of people have watched the video of his lecture, "Really Achieving Your Childhood Dreams" (www.thelastlecture.com). In April 2008, the book The Last Lecture *was published. It contained the information in the lecture, as well as additional insights Pausch wanted to share. The book immediately became a number-one bestseller. The following selection is an excerpt from that book. Although Pausch reports in the book that he "never made it to the NFL"(National Football League), a few months after his lecture, he was invited to participate in a Pittsburgh Steelers practice. So in a different way from what he had envisioned as a boy, Pausch did achieve his childhood dream of "making it to the NFL."*

An award-winning teacher and researcher, Pausch also led the Alice Project (www.alice.org), which uses storytelling and interactive game playing in a 3-D environment to introduce young people to computer programming. The software makes it easy for users to create animation. Professor Pausch has also worked with Google, Adobe, Electronic Arts, and Walt Disney Imagineering—achieving many of his childhood dreams along the way.

1 I love football. *Tackle* football. I started playing when I was nine years old, and football got me through. It helped make me who I am today. And even though I did not reach the National Football League, I sometimes think I got more from pursuing that dream, and not accomplishing it, than I did from many of the ones I did accomplish.

2 My romance with football started when my dad dragged me, kicking and screaming, to join a league. I had no desire to be there. I was naturally wimpy, and the smallest kid by far. Fear turned to awe when I met my coach, Jim Graham, a hulking, six-foot-four wall-of-a-guy. He had been a linebacker at Penn State, and was seriously old-school. I mean, really old-school; like he thought the forward pass was a trick play.

3 On the first day of practice, we were all scared to death. Plus be hadn't brought along any footballs.

4 One kid finally spoke up for all of us. "Excuse me, Coach. There are no footballs."

5 And Coach Graham responded, "We don't need any footballs."

6 There was a silence, while we thought about that . . .

7 "How many men are on the football field at a time?" he asked us.

8 Eleven on a team, we answered. So that makes twenty-two.

9 "And how many people are touching the football at any given time?"

10 One of them.

11 "Right!" he said. "So we're going to work on what those other twenty-one guys are doing."

✓ **Teaching Tips**

- Pausch is pronounced "Powsh."
- At the time Pausch gave the lecture, his sons were 5 years old and 2 years old: his daughter was 1 year old.
- See www.cs.virginia.edu/~robins/Randy/for links to all videos, as well as PowerPoint and PDF versions of slides from Pausch's time management lecture.

Diane Sawyer's *Primetime* interview is an excellent introduction to or follow-up to Selection 8-2. http://video.google.com/videoplay?docid= 265263428002185148. Her interview includes footage from his practice session with the Steelers.

Annotation Practice Exercises

Directions: After you have read the selection, answer the critical reading questions below. This will help you gain additional insights about what you have read.

Practice Exercise

Who is the *author's intended audience*?

the general public: anyone who feels it's not possible to achieve childhood dreams

12 Fundamentals. That was a great gift Coach Graham gave us. Fundamentals, fundamentals, fundamentals. As a college professor, I've seen this as one lesson so many kids ignore, always to their detriment: You've got to get the fundamentals down, because otherwise the fancy stuff is not going to work.

* * *

13 Coach Graham used to ride me hard. I remember one practice in particular. "You're doing it all wrong, Pausch. Go back! Do it again!" I tried to do what he wanted. It wasn't enough. "You owe me, Pausch! You're doing push-ups after practice."

14 When I was finally dismissed, one of the assistant coaches came over to reassure me. "Coach Graham rode you pretty hard, didn't he?" he said.

15 I could barely muster a "yeah."

16 "That's a good thing," the assistant told me. "When you're screwing up and nobody says anything to you anymore, that means they've given up on you."

17 That lesson has stuck with me my whole life. When you see yourself doing something badly and nobody's bothering to tell you anymore, that's a bad place to be. You may not want to hear it, but your critics are often the ones telling you they still love you and care about you, and want to make you better.

18 There's a lot of talk these days about giving children self-esteem. It's not something you can give; it's something they have to build. Coach Graham worked in a no-coddling zone. Self-esteem? He knew there was really only one way to teach kids how to develop it. You give them something they can't do, they work hard until they find they can do it, and you just keep repeating the process.

19 When Coach Graham first got hold of me, I was this wimpy kid with no skills, no physical strength, and no conditioning. But he made me realize that if I work hard enough, there will be things I can do tomorrow that I can't do today. Even now, having just turned forty-seven, I can give you a three-point stance that any NFL lineman would be proud of.

20 I realize that, these days, a guy like Coach Graham might get thrown out of a youth sports league. He'd be too tough. Parents would complain.

21 I haven't seen Coach Graham since I was a teen, but he just keeps showing up in my head, forcing me to work harder whenever I feel like quitting, forcing me to be better. He gave me a feedback loop for life.

* * *

22 When we send our kids to play organized sports—football, soccer, swimming, whatever—for most of us, it's not because we're desperate for them to learn the intricacies of the sport.

23 What we really want them to learn is far more important: teamwork, perseverance, sportsmanship, the value of hard work, an ability to deal with adversity. This kind of indirect learning is what some of us like to call a "head fake."

Practice Exercise

What is the *author's purpose* in writing this?

to persuade (motivate, inspire) readers that they can achieve their childhood dreams

Practice Exercise

What is the *author's tone* in this selection?

motivating, inspirational, encouraging, positive

Practice Exercise

What is the *author's point of view* toward "fundamentals"?

"You've got to get the fundamentals down, because otherwise the fancy stuff is not going to work." (It's possible to do more difficult things only if you have first mastered the basics.)

Practice Exercise

What is the *author's point of view* toward organized sports for kids?

Organized sports are important because indirectly they teach kids teamwork, perseverance, sportsmanship, the value of hard work, and an ability to deal with adversity.

24 There are two kinds of head fakes. The first is literal. On a football field, a player will move his head one way so you'll think he's going in that direction. Then he goes the opposite way. It's like a magician using misdirection. Coach Graham used to tell us to watch a player's waist. "Where his belly button goes, his body goes," he'd say.

25 The second kind of head fake is the really important one—the one that teaches people things they don't realize they're learning until well into the process. If you're a head-fake specialist, your hidden objective is to get them to learn something you want them to learn.

26 This kind of head-fake learning is absolutely vital. And Coach Graham was the master.

Source: From The Last Lecture by Randy Pausch, Professor, Carnegie Mellon with Jeffrey Zaslow, Copyright © 2008 by Randy Pausch. Reprinted by permission of Hyperion. All rights reserved.

SELECTION **8-2**
Memoir
(continued)

Comprehension and Vocabulary Quiz

This quiz has four parts. Your instructor may assign some or all of them.

Comprehension

Directions: Items 1–5 test your comprehension (understanding) of the material in this selection. These questions are much like those that a content-area instructor (such as a business professor) would expect you to know after reading and studying this selection. For each comprehension question below, use information from the selection to determine the correct answer. Refer to the selection as you answer the questions. Write your answers in the spaces provided.

¶1 ___b___ **1.** With regard to his childhood dream of playing football in the NFL, Randy Pausch believes that:

a. he was treated unfairly.
b. he obtained a great deal merely from pursuing the dream.
c. it was the greatest disappointment of his life.
d. he may still have a chance to play.

¶s 18–19 ___b___ **2.** According to the author, people develop self-esteem by:

a. playing organized sports, such as football.
b. achieving increasingly difficult goals by working hard.
c. receiving criticism.
d. experiencing "head-fakes."

¶s 23, 25 ___d___ **3.** "Head-fake learning" refers to:

a. a football player learning how to move his head in one direction to mislead the opposition.
b. a trick learned by magicians.
c. football players learning the direction the ball is actually going to be thrown.
d. learning things without realizing it at first because they are being taught to you indirectly.

¶s 16–17 ___a___ **4.** Coach Graham was hard on Pausch because the coach:

a. cared about Pausch and believed he could become a better football player.
b. didn't like Pausch's quitter attitude.
c. was a difficult man who demanded too much of every player.
d. was frustrated that as a former Penn State linebacker, he was now having to coach a boys' team.

¶s 12, 18, 21 ___d___ **5.** According to the author, Coach Graham:

a. emphasized fundamentals.
b. helped players develop self-esteem.
c. forced him to work harder when he felt like quitting.
d. all of the above.

Vocabulary in Context

Directions: Items 6–10 test your ability to determine the meaning of the word by using context clues. *Context clues* are words in a sentence that allow the reader to deduce (reason out) the meaning of an unfamiliar word in that sentence. Context clues also enable the reader to determine which meaning the author intends when a word has more than one meaning. For each vocabulary item below, a sentence from the selection containing an important word (*italicized, like this*) is quoted first. Next, there is an additional sentence using the word in the same sense and providing another context clue. Use the context clues from *both* sentences to deduce the meaning of the italicized word. *Be sure the answer you choose makes sense in both sentences.* If you need to use a dictionary to confirm your answer choice, remember that the meaning you select must still fit the context of *both* sentences. Write your answers in the spaces provided.

Pronunciation Key: ă **pat** ā **pay** âr **care** ä **father** ĕ **pet** ē **be** ĭ **pit** ī **tie** îr **pier** ŏ **pot** ō **toe** ô **paw** oi **noise** ou **out** ŏŏ **took** ōō **boot** ŭ **cut** yōō ab**use** ûr **urge** th **thin** *th* **this** hw **which** zh vision ə **about** *Stress mark:* ′

¶12 ___c___ **6.** As a college professor, I've seen this as one lesson so many kids ignore, always to their *detriment:* You've got to get the fundamentals down, because otherwise the fancy stuff is not going to work.

Working too many hours a week at a job can be a *detriment* to a student's success.

detriment (dĕt′ rə mənt) means:

a. necessary part

b. confusion

c. something that limits success

d. a strong advantage or benefit

¶12 ___d___ **7.** As a college professor, I've seen this as one lesson so many kids ignore, always to their detriment: You've got to get the *fundamentals* down, because otherwise the fancy stuff is not going to work.

In order to do advanced math, you must first learn math *fundamentals.*

fundamentals (fŭn də mĕn′ təlz) means:

a. concepts that are difficult to understand

b. mathematical calculations

c. procedures understood by only a few

d. basic, essential elements

¶15 ___d___ **8.** I could barely *muster* a "yeah."

We tried to *muster* the energy to visit one more tourist attraction, but after five hours of sightseeing, we were too exhausted.

muster (mŭs′ tər) means:

a. say in a loud voice; shout

b. call forth; summon up

c. hold back

d. ignore; pay no attention to

¶22 a **9.** When we send our kids to play organized sports—football, soccer, swimming, whatever—for most of us, it's not because we're desperate for them to learn the *intricacies* of the sport.

Because of the *intricacies* of the human body, it takes years of training to become a doctor.

intricacies (ĭn′ trĭ kə sēz) means:

a. complexities; fine details

b. confusing aspects

c. unknown nature

d. rules

¶23 a **10.** What we really want them to learn is far more important: teamwork, *perseverance,* sportsmanship, the value of hard work, an ability to deal with adversity.

Through *perseverance* and hard work, the Ortegas were able to expand their business from a single restaurant into a highly successful chain.

perseverance (pûr sə vîr′ əns) means:

a. not giving up

b. luck; good fortune

c. working as a team

d. networking

✓ **Teaching Tips**

• Point out the verb forms of these words in the Word Structure exercise: transmission, *transmit;* emission, *emit,* omission, *omit.*

• Students may also be interested to learn the cognates *remit* (to send back as payment), *missive* (a written message or letter that is sent), *demise* (death; literally, "to let down"), *emissary* (someone sent out on a specific mission), and *intermission* (an interruption or "letting go").

Word Structure

Directions: Items 11–15 below test your ability to use word-structure clues to help determine a word's meaning. *Word-structure clues* consist of roots, prefixes, and suffixes. In these exercises, you will learn the meaning of a word part (a root) and use it to determine the meaning of several other words that have the same word part. If you need to use a dictionary to confirm your answer choice, do so. Write your answers in the spaces provided.

In paragraph 14 of the selection, you encountered the word ***dismissed.*** This word contains the Latin root ***miss,*** which means "to send" or "to let go." (Another form of the root is ***mit.***) The word *dismissed* literally means "sent away." When elementary school students are dismissed at the end of the day, they are "sent away" (free to leave). Use the meaning of the root ***miss*** and the list of prefixes on pages 68–69 to help you determine the meaning of each of the following words that contain the same root.

b **11.** **Transmission** of information via the Internet occurs very rapidly. This means the information is:

a. lost.

b. sent out.

c. rejected.
d. verified.

c 12. The **emission** of radioactive particles from isotopes is sometimes used in treating cancer. This means the radioactive particles are:
a. destroyed.
b. collected from the isotopes.
c. sent out from the isotopes.
d. isolated from the isotopes.

a 13. If a diplomat is given a **mission,** it means the person:
a. is sent to accomplish a specific task.
b. is asked to resign.
c. receives an award or recognition.
d. is given a dangerous job.

c 14. If there is an **omission** of important information in a report, it means the information is:
a. given at the beginning.
b. included at the end.
c. missing.
d. highlighted throughout.

d 15. If a disease is in **remission,** it means the patient's symptoms have:
a. increased slightly.
b. triggered another illness.
c. returned stronger than before.
d. been sent back to lower levels; lessened.

✓ **Teaching Tips**

• Let students know that not all of the skills included in this Reading Skills application section have been introduced yet. This section serves as a valuable preview of these skills, however. Students typically get several of the items correct, and they find this encouraging.

• We suggest that rather than include this section as part of the quiz grade, you use it to give students practice with the skills they have studied and as a helpful preview of upcoming skills. It makes an excellent collaborative activity. All students will find this practice helpful, but especially those who must take course exit tests, standardized reading tests, or state-mandated basic skills tests.

Reading Skills Application

Directions: Items 16–20 test your ability to *apply* certain reading skills to information in this selection. These types of questions provide valuable practice for all students, especially those who must take standardized reading tests and state-mandated basic skills tests. You may not have studied all of the skills at this point, so these items will serve as a helpful preview. The comprehension and critical reading skills in this section are presented in Chapters 3 through 9 of *New Worlds;* vocabulary and figurative language skills are presented in Chapter 2. As you work through *New Worlds,* you will practice and develop these skills. Write your answers in the spaces provided.

¶18 vocabulary in context (Chapter 2)

b 16. Which of the following is the meaning of *no-coddling* as it is used in paragraph 18?
a. referring to the section of the football field near the goal posts
b. not pampering or treating gently
c. relating to defense rather than offense
d. not asking or demanding much

¶12 author's writing pattern (Chapter 7) ___a___ **17.** Which pattern is used to organize the information in paragraph 12?

a. cause-effect
b. list
c. sequence
d. definition

drawing conclusions (Chapter 9) ___c___ **18.** Based on information in the selection, the author would be likely to agree with which of the following statements?

a. Every child should be required to play an organized sport.
b. Coaches should be kinder and more patient with the youngsters they coach.
c. People from our childhood can have a positive influence on us that lasts the rest of our lives.
d. Every learning experience includes both types of head-fakes.

¶17 stated main idea (Chapter 4) ___c___ **19.** Which of the following represents the main idea of paragraph 17?

a. That lesson has stuck with me my whole life.
b. When you see yourself doing something badly and nobody's bothering to tell you anymore, that's a bad place to be.
c. You may not want to hear it, but your critics are often the ones telling you they still love you and care about you, and want to make you better.
d. When people criticize you, it means they have given up on you.

¶3 distinguishing facts from opinions (Chapter 9) ___a___ **20.** Which of the following represents an opinion rather than a fact?

a. On the first day of practice, we were all scared to death.
b. Plus he hadn't brought along any footballs.
c. One kid finally spoke up for all of us.
d. "Excuse me, Coach. There are no footballs."

SELECTION **8-2**
Memoir
(continued)

Writing and Collaborating to Enhance Your Understanding

Option for collaboration: Your instructor may direct you to work with other students or, in other words, to work *collaboratively*. In that case, you should form groups of three or four students as directed by your instructor and work together to complete the exercises. After your group discusses each item and agrees on the answer, have a group member record it. Every member of your group should be able to explain all of your group's answers.

Collaboration Option

1. Reacting to What You Have Read: Randy Pausch describes the impact that Coach Graham had on his life. Think of someone, other than your relatives, who has had a significant impact on your life. Who were they (you do not have to give a name; you can simply say, "a coach," "a neighbor," "a teacher," etc.)? In what way did they help you learn to see yourself or the world differently?

(Answers will vary.)
____
____
____
____

2. **Comprehending the Selection Further:** The author mentions several things he gained from participating in football as a boy. List at least three of those.

- increased physical strength and conditioning
- appreciation of the importance of mastering the fundamentals
- the insight that criticism shows that people care about you and think you can do better
- an understanding of how self-esteem is developed
- an understanding of the importance of hard work

3. **Overall Main Idea of the Selection:** In one sentence, tell what the author wants readers to understand about dreams we pursue, but do not achieve. (Be sure to include "dreams" in your overall main idea sentence.)

Sometimes we gain more from pursuing a *dream,* and not accomplishing it, than we do from dreams we accomplish. (The author uses the rest of the selection to support this by explaining the valuable lessons he learned from playing football, even though he didn't achieve his goal of playing in the NFL.)

Read More about This Topic on the World Wide Web

Directions: For further information about the topic of the selection, visit these websites:

http://video.google.com/videoplay?docid=265263428002185148
Diane Sawyer's *Primetime* interview with Randy Pausch. Her interview includes footage from his practice session with the Steelers.

www.randypausch.com
RandyPausch's website. It contains links to his various presentations and lecture, as well as information about his book, *The Last Lecture,* the Alice Project, and pancreatic cancer.

www.thelastlecture.com
RandyPausch's website, with a link to the videotaped presentation of his last lecture, "Really Achieving Your Childhood Dreams," in September 2007. This uplifting, engaging video runs about an hour and a half.

www.cs.virginia.edu/robins/Randy
This website contains several links related to Randy Pausch's presentations. There are downloads and translations into other languages. Included is his time management lecture, in which Professor Pausch addresses goal-setting, avoiding wasting time, dealing with bosses, delegating, and offers specific tools for time management, as well as for dealing with stress and procrastination. There are links to newspaper articles and Pausch's Wikipedia page.

www.youtube.com/watch?v=RcYv5x6gZTA&feature=related
In May 2008, Professor Pausch gave the commencement address at Carnegie-Mellon's graduation ceremonies. This brief video consists of the advice he gave the graduating class.

You can also use your favorite search engine such as Google, Yahoo!, or Alta-Vista (www.google.com, www.yahoo.com, www.altavista.com) to discover more about this topic. To locate additional information, type in the keywords:

Randy Pausch

or

"The Last Lecture"

Keep in mind that whenever you go to *any* website, it is a good idea to evaluate the website and the information it contains. Ask yourself questions such as:

"Who sponsors this website?"

"Is the information contained in this website up-to-date?"

"What type of information is presented?"

"Is the information objective and complete?"

"How easy is it to use the features of this website?"

READING

SELECTION 8-3

Business

DISPELLING THE MYTHS ABOUT MILLIONAIRES

Part 1: From *Understanding Business*
By William Nickels, James McHugh, and Susan McHugh and
Part 2: "How to Become a Millionaire in 7 Easy (hah!) Steps"
By Laura Bruce, bankrate.com

In 2007, there were approximately 9.2 million U.S. millionaires, more than in any other country. Worldwide, there are 9.5 million millionaires.

Who do you think is the "typical" millionaire in this country? How do most new millionaires acquire their money? Do you think you might someday join the ranks of millionaires? Read this selection and then decide if your answers change after reading it. You may be surprised at what you discover.

Part 1: Think You Could Never Become a Millionaire? Think Again!

1 Let's face it, the chances of becoming a billionaire are not really very good; chances of becoming a millionaire are much better, though. One of the best ways to learn how to become a millionaire is to do what companies do: benchmark those who are successful. That is, you should find out what all those millionaires did to make their money. For over 20 years, Thomas Stanley has been doing just that—studying wealthy people. His research is available in a book called *The Millionaire Next Door: The Surprising Secrets of America's Wealthy,* which he co-authored with William Danko.

2 Stanley and Danko found that the majority of millionaires are entrepreneurs who own one or more small businesses. Self-employed people are four times as likely to be millionaires as people who earn a paycheck working for others. The average income of American millionaires is $131,000 a year. So how did they get to be millionaires? They saved their money. To become a millionaire by the time you are 50 or so, you have to save about 15% of your income every year—starting when you are in your 20s. If you start later, you have to save an even larger percentage. The secret is to put your money in a place where it will grow without your having to pay taxes on it.

3 To save that 15 percent a year, you have to spend less than you earn. Discipline in spending must begin with your first job and stay with you all your life. To save money, the millionaires Stanley studied tended to own modest homes and to buy used cars. In short, becoming a millionaire has more to do with thrift than with how much you earn.

4 Do you want to be a billionaire or, more plausibly, a millionaire? If so, then you need to do what other rich people have done. You need to get an education, work hard, save your money, and make purchases carefully. You need to develop insight into how to manage your finances. Are you ready to do the hard work it takes to become a millionaire? To reach your goal, your final answer must be a "Yes!"

Annotation Practice Exercises

Directions: After you have read this selection, answer the critical reading questions below. This will help you gain additional insight about what you have read.

Practice Exercise

Who is the *authors' intended audience*?

Anyone in the general public who wants to increase his or her wealth, but especially those who are still in their 20s (based, among other things, on information in ¶ 2 and ¶ 6 and this is a college textbook)

Practice Exercise

What is the *authors' purpose* in Part 1 of this selection?

To persuade readers that if they do the right things, they can become wealthier or even become millionaires (based on the title of Part 1 and on ¶ 4)

Part 2: How to Become a Millionaire in 7 Easy (hah!) Steps

5 The road to wealth is not paved with infomercials. Those wee-hour TV staples would have you believe that you'll become "Fantasy Island" rich by placing tiny ads in the classifieds, or by buying up—for no money down—distressed property and selling it for millions. Unfortunately, the only thing you're likely to get from watching those infomercials is dark circles under your eyes from lack of sleep. If you actually go to the seminar or buy the tapes, you'll probably just have more debt.

6 The truth is, unless you're lucky enough to receive a sizeable inheritance, you'll need to navigate your own route to prosperity. But while Bill Gates–style megawealth may be elusive, becoming a millionaire is definitely within reach of those who start young and develop the right habits. And anyone, at any age, can develop the traits that increase wealth and decrease debt.

7 "You can have money or you can have stuff, but seldom do you have both early in life," says Jason Flurry, certified financial planner with Planmark Capital Management LLC, in Alpharetta, Ga. "Part of our culture is, 'Fake it until you make it.' Debt holds people back. They buy liabilities and they make those payments forever. Spend less than you make, live a modest lifestyle and don't live up to every raise. Some people have spent their prosperity for the next 10 years, and they've done it on credit."

Practice Exercise

What is the *author's purpose* in Part 2 of this selection?

To instruct readers in what they must do to increase their wealth or even become millionaires (based on ¶s 11–19)

It's a Matter of Choices

8 Flurry isn't suggesting you decorate your home in plastic lawn furniture, forgo cable TV and dine on macaroni and cheese every night. But do you really need to buy a car that's so expensive that you must stretch the payments out five or more years? Do you have to have that 50-inch widescreen HD-ready TV right now?

9 Many people who choose wealth over "stuff" wouldn't consider spending money on the "latest and greatest" because they know their money can be put to better use elsewhere. Buying a "liability" would probably cause them stress because they'd rather buy an asset—something that will appreciate over time and give them a return on their investment.

10 Flurry says he has a hard time getting some of his older clients to spend their money. "They've been savers all their lives and the thought of spending $5,000 or $10,000 on a vacation is ridiculous; it doesn't matter that they're worth $3 million. The reason? They're the last Depression generation, and it's burned in their memory that they need to squirrel away money."

✓ **Teaching Tip**
You may need to explain the phrase "squirrel away" in ¶10: to hide away or store up for the future (like squirrels hiding nuts so that they will have enough to eat in winter).

7 Steps to Wealth

11 Paring it all down, we've come up with seven steps to becoming wealthy. Remember, wealth is relative; it doesn't necessarily mean "millionaire." The goal for many people is financial independence, says Stewart Welch of The Welch Group in Birmingham, Alabama.

12 "That's the point in time when your cash flow from investments is equal to or greater than your income from work. Look at the statistics: 95 percent of the population never achieves financial independence. For 65 percent of retirees, Social Security is their largest source of retirement income." The No. 1 reason people don't achieve financial independence, says Welch, is they don't have a written financial plan. So, that is our No. 1 rule for becoming wealthy.

1. Develop a Written Financial Plan

13 Saying you want to be wealthy isn't good enough. You need to come up with a workable plan and put it on paper. "The written plan forces you to do something," Welch says. "Calculate what you need to earn and how to invest. The plan isn't just the goal, it's the whole thing—the dream, the goals, the options. The options are scenario planning—all the ways you can accomplish that goal—open a Roth IRA, contribute to a 401(k)."

✓ **Teaching Tip**

You may need to explain these terms that appear in ¶13:

Roth IRA = An individual retirement account in which a person can set aside after-tax income up to a specified amount each year. Earnings on the account are tax-free, and tax-free withdrawals may be made after age 59½.

401(k) = A retirement investment plan that allows an employee to put a percentage of earned wages into a tax-deferred investment account selected by the employer.

2. Save, Save, Save

14 The end result of your financial plan should be systematic investment. Get in the habit of saving money. Build an emergency fund in a money market account so you don't have to raid the rest of your savings and investments when there's an unexpected major expense. Make it a point to save at least half of every pay raise.

3. Live below Your Means

15 Don't be a walking billboard for overpriced designer clothes, shoes, sunglasses or jewelry. Don't allow your house or car payments to be budget-busters.

4. Lay Off the Credit

16 Some people say that if you can eat it or wear it, don't put it on your credit card. That's good advice, but take it further. Try not putting anything on your cards that you can't pay off in two or three months. You need only one or two credit cards. If you have a fistful, pay them off and cancel them. Remember, debt holds you back. "It reduces cash flow for other things, including investing," says Welch. "If no one gave you money to borrow, you'd be better off and the economy would be smaller. If they only let you borrow 75 percent of the value of your home, you'd be a heck of a lot better off."

5. Make Your Money Work for You

17 It takes money to make money, but that doesn't mean you need a lot to invest. Open an account with a mutual fund company that has no-load funds and low expense ratios. Build a diverse portfolio and you can reasonably expect to earn 8 percent to 10 percent annually on your investments over the long haul.

✓ **Teaching Tip**

In ¶17, students may not know the phrase "long haul," meaning a long period of time.

6. Start Your Own Business

18 In the 1969 book *The Millionaire Next Door: The Surprising Secrets of America's Wealthy,* the authors state that two-thirds of the millionaires are self-employed, with 75 percent of them

entrepreneurs, and the remainder professionals such as doctors and accountants. The idea that most people inherit wealth is outdated. A lot is built through businesses. Business creation is the No. 1 driver of wealth in this country.

7. Get Professional Advice

19 If you lack confidence in your own ability to manage your investments, consult with a professional. A good financial planner can help you fill your portfolio with the right investments and dump the wrong ones. You don't need to relinquish control, but you do need to form a good working relationship with someone who has expertise in this complicated area. About 76 percent of those surveyed are actively involved in the day-to-day management of their financial affairs. They get involved; they learn about finances; they're not day traders. They work with advisers but ultimately make their own decisions. If you can't afford to have a financial planner manage your money, many of them will review your portfolio and make recommendations for a one-time fee.

Practice Exercise

What is the *authors' tone*?

Encouraging, supportive but realistic (based on titles of Part 1 and Part 2) (also some humor, as in ¶ 5)

Practice Exercise

What is the *author's point of view* as to whether it is easy or difficult to become a millionaire?

It is difficult to become a millionaire, but if a person has the discipline to do certain things, he or she can become one. (based on the word "hah!" in parentheses after the word "easy" in the title of Part 2, and on ¶ 1 and ¶ 5)

Part 1 Source: William G. Nickels, James M. McHugh, and Susan M. McHugh, *Understanding Business,* 7th ed., p. 669. Copyright © 2005 by The McGraw-Hill Companies, Inc. Reprinted by permission of The McGraw-Hill Companies, Inc. Based on Tom Fetzer, "Never Say Die," *Success,* December/January 2001, p. 60; "The Global Billionaires," *Forbes,* March 18, 2002, pp. 119–52; Thomas J. Stanley. *Fast Company,* October 2002, p. 70; "Women and Wealth," *Fast Company,* October 2002, p. 28; "Survival of the Richest," *Forbes,* March 17, 2003, pp. 87–100; and Muoi Tran, "New Money," *Fortune,* July 7, 2003, p. 34.

Part 2 Source: Adapted from Laura Bruce, "How to Become a Millionaire in 7 Easy (hah!) Steps," posted March 24, 2004, Copyright Bankrate, Inc., N. Palm Beach, FL 33408. Reprinted with permission.

SELECTION 8-3
Business
(continued)

Comprehension and Vocabulary Quiz

This quiz has four parts. Your instructor may assign some or all of them.

Comprehension

Directions: Items 1–5 test your comprehension (understanding) of the material in this selection. These questions are much like those that a content-area instructor (such as a business professor) would expect you to know after reading and studying this selection. For each comprehension question below, use information from the selection to determine the correct answer. Refer to the selection as you answer the questions. Write your answers in the spaces provided.

¶2 b **1.** In general, to become a millionaire by age 50, people in their 20s should start saving what percent of their income?

a. 10
b. 15
c. 20
d. 25

¶3 b **2.** The self-made millionaires Thomas Stanley reports on in *The Millionaire Next Door* tended to:

a. live in apartments and use public transportation.
b. live in modest homes and drive used cars.
c. live in moderate homes and drive mid-level sedans.
d. live in expensive homes and drive luxury automobiles.

¶16 b **3.** In Part 2, the author recommends having no more than:

a. 1 credit card.
b. 2 credit cards.
c. 3 credit cards.
d. 4 credit cards.

¶10 a **4.** The "Depression generation" has difficulty spending money because they:

a. have saved all their lives and are convinced they need to save their money.
b. have their money invested in real estate.
c. do not use credit cards.
d. spent too much money when they were younger.

¶18 c **5.** The majority of self-made millionaires surveyed in *The Millionaire Next Door:*

a. work for small companies.
b. work for large corporations.
c. are self-employed.
d. are unemployed.

Vocabulary in Context

Directions: Items 6–10 test your ability to determine the meaning of the word by using context clues. *Context clues* are words in a sentence that allow the reader to deduce (reason out) the meaning of an unfamiliar word in that sentence. Context clues also enable the reader to determine which meaning the author intends when a word has more than one meaning. For each vocabulary item below, a sentence from the selection containing an important word (*italicized, like this*) is quoted first. Next, there is an additional sentence using the word in the same sense and providing another context clue. Use the context clues from *both* sentences to deduce the meaning of the italicized word. *Be sure the answer you choose makes sense in both sentences.* If you need to use a dictionary to confirm your answer choice, remember that the meaning you select must still fit the context of *both* sentences. Write your answers in the spaces provided.

Pronunciation Key: ă **pat** ā **pay** âr **care** ä **father** ĕ **pet** ē **be** ĭ **pit**
ī **tie** îr **pier** ŏ **pot** ō **toe** ô **paw** oi **noise** ou **out** o͝o **took** o͞o **boot**
ŭ **cut** yo͞o ab**use** ûr **urge** th **thin** *th* **this** hw **which** zh vision
ə **about** *Stress mark:* ′

¶12 ___c___ **6.** Stanley and Danko found that the majority of millionaires are *entrepreneurs* who own one or more small businesses.

Bill Gates, Steven Jobs, and Michael Dell are three of the best known, most successful *entrepreneurs* in the field of software and computers.

entrepreneurs (ŏn trə prə nûrz′) means:

a. people who are skilled with computers
b. people who majored in business in college
c. people who organize, operate, and assume the risk for a business venture
d. people who are award winners

¶13 ___d___ **7.** To save money, the millionaires Stanley studied tended to own *modest* homes and to buy used cars.

Even though he was one of the most prominent attorneys in the city, he preferred an office that was small and *modest.*

modest (mŏd′ ĭst) means:

a. shy
b. likely to attract attention
c. proper in speech, behavior, and dress
d. not showy or extravagant

¶14 ___b___ **8.** Do you want to be a billionaire or, more *plausibly,* a millionaire?

The investigators believe the hiker accidentally fell from the cliff, or less *plausibly,* that he committed suicide.

plausibly (plô′ zə ble) means:

a. dangerously

b. likely

c. interestingly

d. unlikely

¶7 ___c___ **9.** They buy *liabilities* and they make those payments forever.

The Smiths have credit card charges, a large mortgage, two car loans, and several other *liabilities*.

liabilities (lī ə bĭl′ ĭ tēz) means:

a. things that are not truthful

b. things that are essential for daily life

c. things that carry financial obligations or create debt

d. things that create envy in others

¶13 ___a___ **10.** The plan isn't just the goal, it's the whole thing—the dream, the goals, the *options*.

Lynn can work for a year or two, join the military now, or start college in January; at this point, she is considering all of these *options*.

options (ŏp′ shənz) means:

a. choices that are available

b. disadvantages

c. limitations

d. responsibilities that a citizen has

Word Structure

Directions: Items 11–15 test your ability to use word-structure clues to help determine a word's meaning. *Word-structure clues* consist of roots, prefixes, and suffixes. In these exercises, you will learn the meaning of a word part (a root) and use it to determine the meaning of several other words that have the same word part. If you need to use a dictionary to confirm your answer choice, do so. Write your answers in the spaces provided.

In paragraph 19 of the selection, you encountered the word **confidence**. This word contains the Latin root ***fid,*** which means "faith" or "trust." The word *confidence* means "having *faith* or *trust* in someone or something." Use the meaning of ***fid*** and the list of prefixes on pages 68–69 to help you determine the meaning of each of the following words that contain the same root.

___c___ **11.** To **confide** means to:

a. instruct or explain to someone how to do something.

b. give an excuse.

c. tell someone information you do not want repeated to others.

d. consider various options.

d 12. A spouse accused of **infidelity** is accused of:

a. inflexibility.

b. impatience.

c. lack of respect.

d. unfaithfulness.

a 13. A **confidant** is a person:

a. to whom you disclose secrets or private matters.

b. you enjoy talking to.

c. whom you do not know very well.

d. who does not tell the truth.

✓ **Teaching Tip**
Be sure students hear the difference between the pronunciation of confid*e*nt and confid*a*nt.

a 14. A **bona fide** offer is one that is:

a. made in good faith; sincere.

b. sarcastic; cruel.

c. insincere; false.

d. like new; restored.

c 15. The U.S. Marine Corps motto, "**Semper fidelis,**" means:

a. "Always ready."

b. "Always brave."

c. "Always faithful."

d. "Always strong."

✓ **Teaching Tip**
We suggest that rather than include this section as part of the quiz grade, you use it to give students practice with the skills they have studied and as a helpful preview of upcoming skills. It makes an excellent collaborative activity.

Reading Skills Application

Directions: Items 16–20 test your ability to *apply* certain reading skills to information in this selection. These types of questions provide valuable practice for all students, especially those who must take standardized reading tests and state-mandated basic skills tests. You may not have studied all of the skills at this point, so these items will serve as a helpful preview. The comprehension and critical reading skills in this section are presented in Chapters 3 through 9 of *New Worlds;* vocabulary and figurative language skills are presented in Chapter 2. As you work through *New Worlds,* you will practice and develop these skills. Write your answers in the spaces provided.

title; ¶2 inference (Chapter 9) d 16. In the title of Part 2, the author includes the word "hah!" to suggest that becoming wealthy:

a. is a joke.

b. can be achieved by anyone.

c. can be learned from seminars and tapes.

d. is not as easy as it sounds.

¶7 inference (Chapter 9) a 17. In paragraph 7 of this selection, what does the author mean when she says, "Some people have spent their prosperity for the next 10 years and they've done it on credit"?

a. Rather than saving and investing to increase their wealth, some people made purchases they could not have afforded without buying them on credit.

b. Credit can help people achieve prosperity.

c. People will become wealthy if they will stop using credit for 10 years.
d. Some people can achieve wealth within a 10-year period of time.

¶12 conclusion (Chapter 9) ___b___ **18.** Based on the information in Part 2, it can be concluded that most retirees are likely to:
a. start home businesses.
b. have too little income.
c. enjoy their retirement years.
d. stop using credit cards.

¶s 12–13 cause-effect (Chapter 7) ___b___ **19.** According to the selection, the "No. 1 reason" people do not achieve financial independence is that they:
a. live below their means.
b. do not have a written financial plan.
c. start their own businesses.
d. get professional help from a financial planner.

¶10 authors' writing patterns (Chapter 7) ___a___ **20.** The information in paragraph 10 of the selection is organized using which of the following patterns?
a. cause-effect
b. list
c. sequence
d. comparison-contrast

SELECTION **8-3**
Business
(continued)

Writing and Collaborating to Enhance Your Understanding

Option for collaboration: Your instructor may direct you to work with other students or, in other words, to work *collaboratively.* In that case, you should form groups of three or four students as directed by your instructor and work together to complete the exercises. After your group discusses each item and agrees on the answer, have a group member record it. Every member of your group should be able to explain all of your group's answers.

Collaboration Option

1. Reacting to What You Have Read: Which of the guidelines for achieving wealth do you currently follow? If you do not currently follow any of them, which two do you think would help you most? What difference do you think it would make (or would have made) in your life if you were a millionaire by the age of 50?

(Answers will vary.)

2. **Comprehending the Selection Further:** Suppose that you are 24 years old and you understand what it takes to become a millionaire by age 50. Your 20-year-old sister comes to you and tells you that she has $2,000 in credit card debt. She sees that you are managing your finances well and building your savings. She asks you to help her develop a plan for eliminating her debt and dealing with her finances more effectively. What would you advise her to do, and in what order?

   (Answers will vary.)

3. **Overall Main Idea of the Selection:** In one sentence, tell what the authors want readers to understand about who the typical U.S. millionaire is and what it takes to become a millionaire. (Be sure to include the phrase "typical U.S. millionaire" in your overall main idea sentence.)

   The typical U.S. millionaire is a person who saves more than he or she spends, and by starting early and following certain guidelines, a person can become wealthy or even a millionaire.

Internet Resources

Read More about This Topic on the World Wide Web

Directions: For further information about the topic of the selection, visit these websites:

http://goldsea.com/Money/Million/million.html
The article "How to Become a Millionaire by Age 35" appears on the Goldsea Asian American website and explains one strategy for becoming a millionaire through one decade of hard work.

www.soho.org/Finance_Articles/Become_A_Millionaire.htm
Small Office/Home Office (SOHO) America sponsors this website. Dr. Phillip Humbert presents his strategies in the article "The Top 10 Steps to Becoming a Millionaire."

You can also use your favorite search engine such as Google, Yahoo!, or AltaVista (www.google.com, www.yahoo.com, www.altavista.com) to discover more about this topic. To locate additional information, type in combinations of keywords such as:

U.S. millionaires

or

becoming a millionaire

Keep in mind that whenever you go to *any* website, it is a good idea to evaluate the website and the information it contains. Ask yourself questions such as:

"Who sponsors this website?"
"Is the information contained in this website up-to-date?"
"What type of information is presented?"
"Is the information objective and complete?"
"How easy is it to use the features of this website?"

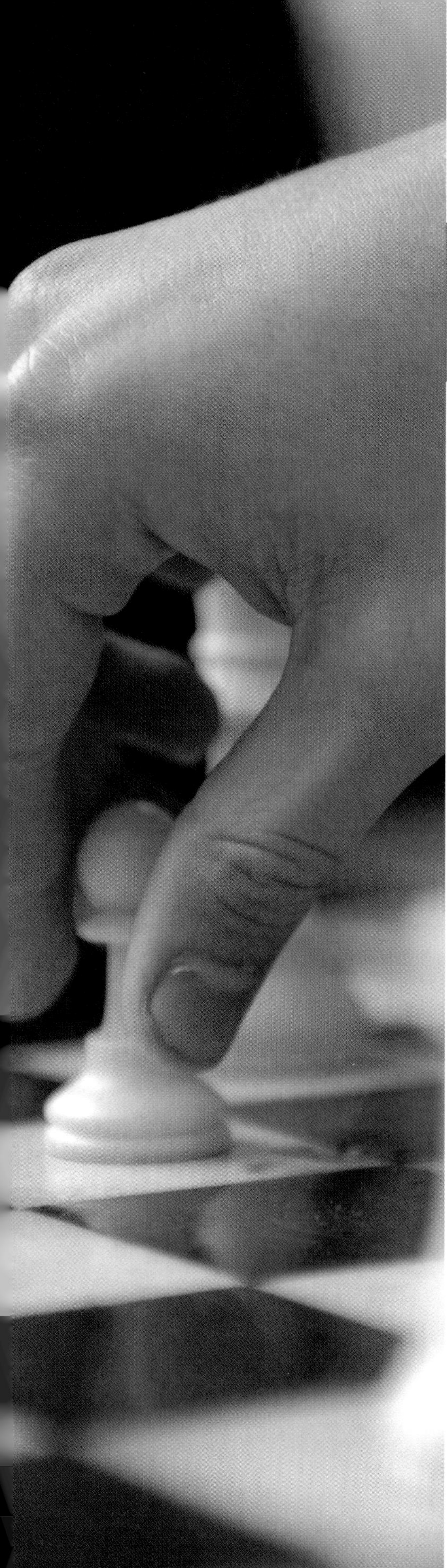

CHAPTER 9

Thinking Critically

CHAPTER OBJECTIVES

In this chapter you will learn the answers to these questions:

- What is thinking critically, and why is it important?
- What are facts and opinions, and why is it important to be able to distinguish between them?
- What are logical inferences, and why is it important to make them?

✓ **Timely Words**

"Too often we enjoy the comfort of opinion without the discomfort of thought."
(John F. Kennedy)

"The fewer the facts, the stronger the opinion."
(Arnold Glasow)

WHAT IS THINKING CRITICALLY, AND WHY IS IT IMPORTANT?

KEY TERM
thinking critically

Thinking in an organized way about material in order to evaluate it accurately.

As you learned in Chapter 8, critical reading means going beyond basic comprehension (such as identifying the topic, main idea, and supporting details) by determining point of view, purpose, intended audience, and tone. This requires rereading and reconsidering the author's message. Sometimes, though, you must go one step further and include **thinking critically:** thinking in an organized way about material in order to evaluate it accurately. To think critically, you can use the skills of:

- Distinguishing between facts and opinions.
- Making inferences and drawing logical conclusions.

WHAT ARE FACTS AND OPINIONS, AND WHY IS IT IMPORTANT TO BE ABLE TO DISTINGUISH BETWEEN THEM?

KEY TERMS
fact

Something that can be proved to exist or to have happened.

opinion

Something that cannot be proved or disproved; a judgment or belief.

Student Online Learning Center (OLC)
***Go to* Chapter 9.**
***Select* Video.**

✓ **Teaching Tip**
Remind students that the student OLC contains an audio and video feature for Chapters 3 through 9 that presents **Key Comprehension Terms** and **Comprehension Monitoring Questions.**

What is the difference between a fact and an opinion? A **fact** is something that can be proved to exist or to have happened. For example, these are facts because the information can be verified: *Alexander the Great, a fourth-century ruler of Greece, conquered most of the ancient world,* and *As a boy, Alexander had as his teacher the philosopher Aristotle.* Proving that something is a fact (that it is true) can be accomplished through research, direct observation or experience, or conducting an experiment. Through research, a person could prove or verify that the statements about Alexander are factual.

An **opinion** is a judgment or belief that cannot be proved *or disproved.* For example, the following statements represent opinions because there is no way to prove or disprove them: *Alexander the Great was the most successful military leader who ever lived,* and *Alexander would never have become an outstanding ruler and military leader if he had not studied with the philosopher Aristotle.* Moreover, these statements contain words that represent judgments ("successful" and "outstanding"). Everyone has a slightly different idea of what words such as "successful" and "outstanding" mean, and people would not agree exactly on their meaning. For this reason, these two statements about Alexander the Great are opinions.

Most statements that refer to events that might happen in the future are opinions. For example, consider the statement "Computer software manufacturing will be the world's largest industry throughout the 21st century." Because this event is a future event and cannot be proved before it happens, this statement represents an opinion. It would remain an opinion until it has happened (or not). That is, it would remain an opinion until it is proved to be a fact or disproved as incorrect information.

When an author includes opinions, it is important for you to evaluate them because not all opinions are valid or useful. It is also important to realize that although opinions cannot be proved, they can nevertheless be supported by valid reasons and reasonable evidence. An opinion is valuable if it is *well supported.* "Well supported" means that the author presents facts and logical reasons for the opinion that he or she holds. Well-supported opinions are based on facts or on the ideas of knowledgeable people. Consequently, well-supported opinions can be as important and useful as facts. Opinions in textbooks typically represent valuable opinions because they are the well-reasoned beliefs of the author or other experts. Scientific theories are also examples of "expert opinions." (Incidentally, if a theory could be proved, it would no longer be a theory. It would become a fact.) Of course, poorly supported or unsupported opinions are not useful, but do not make the mistake of thinking that all opinions are valueless.

Needless to say, an opinion is of little value if it is poorly supported (that is, if the author does not give good reasons for believing it). A warning: Sometimes an author might try to make a poorly supported opinion *seem* believable and valuable by writing very persuasively or emotionally.

To see the difference between a well-supported opinion and a poorly supported one, consider the example below. It presents two sets of reasons (support) for this opinion: *City College makes an excellent, affordable education available to almost everyone.* (This statement is an opinion, of course, because of the judgment words "excellent" and "affordable.") Note the difference between the two sets of support for this opinion, and decide which would more likely cause someone to accept the opinion as valid.

Opinion: *City College makes an excellent, affordable education available to almost everyone.*

Examples of well-reasoned support	Examples of poorly-reasoned support
City College makes an excellent, affordable education available to almost everyone because . . .	*City College makes an excellent, affordable education available to almost everyone because . . .*
• It offers more than 80 programs and majors. (*fact*) • Its tuition is the lowest in the state. (*fact*) • Its financial aid office offers information about more than 200 scholarships, grants, and loans. (*fact*) • Classes are offered days, evenings, weekends, and online. (*fact*) • The computer labs are equipped with more than 500 computers. (*fact*) • The faculty is friendly and supportive. (*opinion*) • More than half of the faculty have earned doctoral degrees. (*fact*)	• It is located less than a mile from the beach. (*fact*) • The campus has beautiful architecture. (*opinion*) • The buildings are attractive and well maintained. (*opinion*) • It has a swimming pool, tennis courts, and a jogging path. (*fact*) • There is plenty of free, convenient parking. (*opinion*) • The food in the cafeteria is good. (*opinion*) • There are a dozen different video games in the student center. (*fact*) • One of its former students is now a major league baseball star. (*fact*)

Clearly, the first set of reasons is stronger than the second. If someone gave you the first set of reasons to explain why he or she believes City College makes an excellent, affordable education available to almost everyone, you would probably agree that it does. However, if someone presented only the second set of reasons, that person probably would not convince you of his or her opinion about City College.

As you now know, opinions represent judgments, beliefs, or interpretations. Authors often use the following words and phrases to indicate that they are presenting an opinion. They typically appear at the beginning of a sentence, although many of them can appear within a sentence as well. They include:

Perhaps	In our opinion
Apparently	Many experts believe
It seems	Many people think that
It appears	It seems likely
Presumably	This suggests

One possibility is | In our view
One interpretation is | In the opinion of

Now look at the following examples and notice the use of those words in these opinions:

- Most Americans, *in our opinion,* do not eat a balanced, nutritious diet.
- *Apparently,* more and more people feel comfortable investing in the stock market.
- Improving one's study habits, *it appears,* can dramatically improve one's self-esteem.
- *It seems likely* that the majority of consumer products companies will eventually sell their products directly over the Internet as well.

In addition, words that indicate someone's *value judgments* can signal opinions. A value judgment is represented by a word that reflects someone's personal evaluation of something or someone. These words signal opinions because they can be interpreted in different ways by different people. Examples of words that signal value judgments are:

greatest	wealthy
best	successful
worst	fascinating
excellent	effective
interesting	humorous
beautiful	pleasant

These words can signal opinions because different people rarely use these words to mean exactly the same thing. For example, people will disagree about what is considered "successful," "fascinating," "beautiful," and so on. Consider the sentence *Students who finish college will be more successful.* The word "successful" could mean successful financially, personally, socially, or in all of these ways. Because there are many interpretations of what "successful" means, it would be impossible to prove this statement (although it could be supported with certain facts about college graduates). Also, many students who do not complete college are "successful" in some or all of these ways. Consequently, this statement expresses the writer's opinion about college graduates. (Even though this may be a widely held opinion, it is still an opinion; *it cannot be proved.*) As you read, then, watch for judgment words that can be interpreted in different ways. They are clues that you are reading an opinion.

Students sometimes confuse incorrect information with opinions because they assume if something is not a fact, it must automatically be an opinion. However, this is not so. There are three possibilities: (1) Information can be a fact (it is correct information), or (2) it can be an opinion (it represents someone's belief), or (3) it can simply be incorrect information. The statements *Alaska has a higher average temperature than Hawaii* and *Water boils at 32°F* are examples of incorrect information. The statement *There have been forty-three U.S. presidents* is an example of out-of-date information. Even though these statements are written without judgment words and may seem factual, they can be proved *incorrect.* Therefore, they are not facts. They are not opinions either. They are simply statements of incorrect information. (Provable facts, of course, are *Hawaii is warmer than Alaska* and *Water freezes—not boils—at 32°F.*)

Finally, do not make the mistake that many students make: They assume that everything that appears in print, especially in textbooks, is a fact. This is incorrect.

Comprehension Monitoring Question for Thinking Critically to Evaluate Whether Statements in Written Material Are Facts or Opinions

"Can the information the author presents be proved or disproved, or does it represent a judgment?"

College textbooks contain countless facts, but they typically include a wealth of valuable expert opinions as well.

To distinguish between facts and opinions when reading critically, ask yourself these questions in this order:

- Can the information in the statement be *proved*? If so, it is correct information and, therefore, a *fact.*
- Can the information in the statement be *disproved*? If so, it is simply *incorrect information.*
- Is the information in the statement something that *cannot be proved or disproved*? If so, it is an *opinion.* (If it is an opinion, consider how well supported it is.)

The chart below summarizes this process for evaluating whether statements are facts or opinions. Use this process to distinguish between facts and well-supported opinions (which are valuable), and incorrect information and unsupported or poorly supported opinions (which are of no value).

To distinguish facts from opinions and, therefore, think critically, you should ask yourself, "Can the information the author presents be proved or disproved, or does it represent a judgment?" If the information can be proved, it represents a fact. If it cannot be proved or disproved, it represents an opinion.

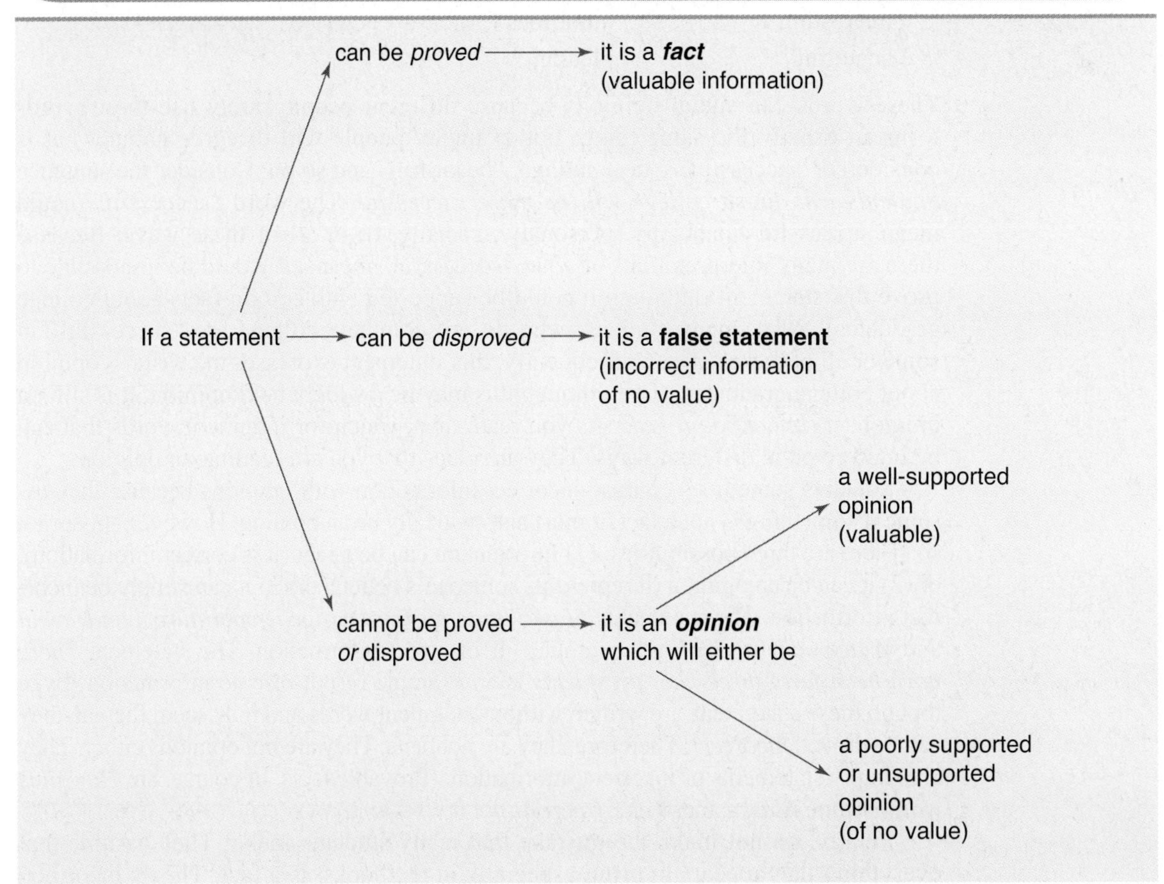
DETERMINING WHETHER A STATEMENT REPRESENTS A FACT, INCORRECT INFORMATION, OR AN OPINION
can be proved → it is a fact
(valuable information)
If a statement → can be disproved → it is a false statement
(incorrect information of no value)
cannot be proved or disproved → it is an opinion which will either be
a well-supported opinion (valuable)
a poorly supported or unsupported opinion (of no value)

To distinguish between facts and opinions, ask yourself these questions in this order:

1. Can the information in the statement be proved? If so, it is a ***fact*** (correct information).
2. Can the information in the statement be disproved? If so, it is a ***false statement*** (incorrect information).
3. Is the information in the statement something that cannot be proved or disproved? If so, it is an ***opinion.***

   When the statement is an opinion, ask yourself these additional questions:

   - Is the opinion *well supported*? (That is, is it based on valid reasons and plausible evidence?) If so, it is a valuable opinion.
   - Is the opinion *poorly supported or unsupported*? If so, it is of little or no value.

✓ **Teaching Tip**
Multimedia refers to computer software that incorporates various "media" such as text, graphics, audio, and video.

Let's apply these steps to a sample passage. The following excerpt is from a computer science textbook. Its topic is *multimedia as a teaching and learning tool.* The formulated main idea of this paragraph is *Multimedia is highly effective as a teaching and learning tool because it allows the learner to use many senses.* The first sentence represents an opinion. The remaining sentences represent facts.

> Multimedia, it seems, is highly effective as a teaching and learning tool. As Computer Technology Research (CTR) reports, people retain only 20% of what they see, and 30% of what they hear. They remember 50% of what they see *and* hear. However, they remember as much as 80% of what they see, hear, and do *simultaneously.*
>
> *Source:* Fred Hofstetter, *Multimedia Literacy,* 2nd ed. Copyright © 1997 by The McGraw-Hill Companies, Inc. Reprinted by permission of The McGraw-Hill Companies, Inc.

Now look at the sentences and the explanations of why each is a fact or an opinion.

Opinion

- Multimedia, it seems, is highly effective as a teaching and learning tool.

This statement represents an opinion because of the words "it seems" and the judgment words "highly effective."

Facts

- "As Computer Technology Research (CTR) reports, people retain only 20% of what they see, and 30% of what they hear."
- "They remember 50% of what they see *and* hear."
- "However, they remember as much as 80% of what they see, hear, and do *simultaneously.*"

These statements represent facts because they report research findings from a company called Computer Technology Research (CTR). Also, it is a fact that CTR reported these findings.

EXERCISE 1

This paragraph comes from a computer science textbook. After you have read the paragraph, decide whether each statement that follows represents a fact or an opinion.

> There has been a continuous demand since the 1950s for people with the skills to design and successfully implement new computer-based systems. Today, the need is for a particular category of specialists—people trained to create and install information systems in business, scientific, manufacturing, and educational organizations. This specialty, ***computer information systems (CIS),*** is now a popular major on many college campuses. The CIS curriculum stresses a sequence of courses in business and management, along with classes in computer programming, application generators, networks, telecommunications, systems development, and decision making. Individuals interested in computers and applications-oriented problem solving will find a CIS program to be both interesting and profitable.

Identify each of these statements from the excerpt as either a fact or an opinion. Write your answer in the space provided.

1. "There has been a continuous demand since the 1950s for people with the skills to design and successfully implement new computer-based systems." fact (can be confirmed by research)
2. "Today, the need is for a newer category of specialists—people trained to create and install information systems in business, scientific, manufacturing, and educational organizations." fact (can be confirmed by research)
3. "This specialty, ***computer information systems (CIS),*** is now a popular major on many college campuses." opinion (judgement word)
4. "The CIS curriculum stresses a sequence of courses in business and management, along with classes in computer programming, application generators, networks, telecommunications, systems development, and decision making." fact (can be confirmed by examining college catalogs)
5. "Individuals interested in computers and applications-oriented problem solving will find a CIS program to be both interesting and profitable." opinion (future event; judgement word)

WHAT ARE INFERENCES, AND WHY IS IT IMPORTANT TO MAKE THEM?

KEY TERM
inference

A logical conclusion based on what an author has stated.

In addition to distinguishing between facts and opinions, it is the responsibility of critical thinkers to make inferences about what they have read. An **inference** is a logical conclusion based on what an author has stated. In other words, a critical thinker understands not only what an author states directly but also what the author *suggests* or *implies.* Inferences go *beyond* what the author states, but they are always *based* on what the author has said. A logical *conclusion* is a decision that is reached after thoughtful consideration of information the author presents.

To repeat: Inferences go beyond what an author has stated directly, but they must always be based on the information the author presents. That means you cannot use as an inference information stated by the author; you must go beyond it. This is logical: If the author has already *stated* something, you cannot infer it. If the author has already stated something, you do not *need* to infer it.

Comprehension Monitoring Question for Critically Evaluating Written Material by Going Beyond What Is Stated

What logical inference (conclusion) can I make based on what the author has stated?

Remember, too, you are not making an inference if you merely restate (paraphrase) information stated in the paragraph: You would simply be retelling information. For example, if the author states, "The *Titanic* sank because it hit an iceberg," you cannot make the inference "The ship sank because it hit an iceberg." You *could,* however, make the inference "The water in which the *Titanic* sank was extremely cold." This is a logical inference because there was an iceberg in the water.

If you are thinking critically as you read, you should ask yourself, "What logical inference or conclusion can I make based on what the author has stated?" Often, an author believes that the conclusion is obvious and does not state it directly. The author expects the reader to make the appropriate inference, that is, draw the logical conclusion.

To make an inference, the reader must *deduce,* or reason out, the author's meaning. Readers must use the evidence and information the author presents in order to arrive at the inference the author wants them to make. They must make the leap from what an author says to what the author wants them to conclude. Sometimes readers conclude that the author wants them to believe or do something. For example, a writer might describe the numerous benefits of regular exercise, yet not state directly, "You should exercise regularly." The author expects *you* to make the inference (draw the conclusion) that you should exercise regularly.

In Chapter 5 you learned about formulating an implied main idea. To formulate an implied main idea, you must make a logical inference. When authors *suggest* a main idea but do not state it directly, they are *implying* it. When readers correctly comprehend an implied main idea, they are *inferring* it. The writer implies the main idea; the reader infers it. Sometimes, formulating an implied main idea is the only inference you need to make about a passage.

Thinking critically, however, may involve making additional inferences. You can make inferences on the basis of longer passages as well as single paragraphs. And sometimes, of course, there are no inferences to be made about the material in a textbook passage. In this case, you need only to understand the topic, stated main idea, and supporting details.

Making inferences is actually something you do every day. In fact, you make them continually. Your ability to understand jokes and cartoons depends on your ability to make correct inferences. Sometimes, when a joke or cartoon does not seem funny, it is because you did not make the right inference. (Look at the two cartoons on pages 504–505 and think about the inferences you must make in order to get each joke.) Every day you draw conclusions on the basis of descriptions, facts, opinions, experiences, and observations. Assume, for example, that another student in your class arrives late. Although he always brings his books to class, he does not have his book bag with him. He seems upset and frustrated, even angry. It would be a logical inference that something has happened to his book bag. He may have accidentally locked it in his car, left it on the bus, or even had it stolen when he momentarily left it unattended. These inferences are logical because they are based on your observations of what you see and the fact that he has always brought his book bag in the past. Based on your observations, it would *not* be logical to assume that he is upset and frustrated today because he broke up with his girlfriend or lost his job.

You also make inferences when you read. For instance, suppose that you wake up and find that your roommate has left you a note saying, "Hope you don't need your car this morning. I have to meet my history study group in the library at 8:00 A.M. I'll be back in time for you to make your 10 o'clock class." After reading the note, you would infer that your roommate is using your car. "I borrowed your car" is your roommate's *intended (implied) meaning,* even though this information is not stated in the note.

MAKING INFERENCES
What inferences must you make in order to understand these two cartoons? In other words, what logical conclusions can you draw about what happened or what is going to happen?

The Far Side® by Gary Larson, "Shark Attack"

✓ **Teaching Tip**
Interences:
- Shark has eaten a diver.
- Shark doesn't like the "tough" parts just as people don't like bones and gristle.

You can learn to make logical inferences by studying examples of correct inferences, such as the ones below. Here is an excerpt from a U.S. history textbook. It presents several details upon which certain inferences can be based. Its topic is *witchcraft in colonial America.* Its main idea is the first sentence: *Colonial communities sometimes responded to assertive women with accusations of witchcraft.* After reading this excerpt, study the details in the paragraph and the logical inferences that are based on them.

✓ **Teaching Tip**
You may have to explain several words in this passage and the one that follows.

Colonial communities sometimes responded to assertive women with accusations of witchcraft. Like most early Europeans during the late 1600s, New Englanders believed in wizards and witches, men and women who were said to acquire supernatural powers by signing a compact with Satan. A total of 344 New Englanders were charged with witchcraft during the first century of settlement. The notorious Salem village episode of 1692 produced the largest outpouring of accusations and 20 executions. More than three-quarters of all accused witches were women. These women were usually middle-aged and older, and most of those accused were regarded as unduly independent. Before they were charged with witchcraft, many had been suspected of heretical religious beliefs. Others were suspected of sexual impropriety. Still others had inherited property or stood to inherit property.

Source: James Davidson, William Geinapp, Christine Heyrman, Mark Lytle, and Michael Stoff, *Nation of Nations,* Vol. 1, 5th ed., p. 97. Copyright © 2005 by The McGraw-Hill Companies, Inc. Reprinted by permission of The McGraw-Hill Companies, Inc.

> ✓ **Teaching Tip**
> In this cartoon, the diagram behind the scientists is a key element. This is a "military" missile. "Warheads" refers to the forward part of a munitions projectile that contains a high explosive system. "Fuel" is also explosive. The explosive nature of the missile and the scientist tapping with a hammer provide the humor. And, of course, it's funny to see a scientist playing a practical joke.

THE FAR SIDE® By GARY LARSON

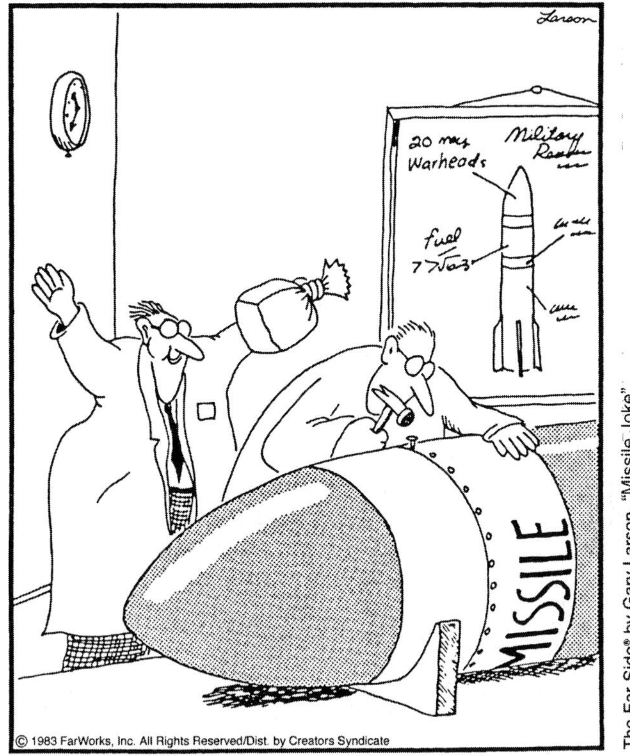

The Far Side® by Gary Larson, "Missile Joke"

Reread these two supporting details from this paragraph:

- "More than three-quarters of all accused witches were women."
- "These women were usually middle-aged and older, and most of those accused were regarded as unduly independent."

Here are some logical inferences that are based on these two details:

- Men were not as likely to be accused of witchcraft.
- Girls and younger women were not as likely to be accused of witchcraft.
- Nonassertive, nonindependent women were not as likely to be accused of witchcraft.

Notice that none of these things is stated in the details, but they are logical conclusions based on what was stated.

Reread these other supporting details from this paragraph:

- "Before they were charged with witchcraft, many women had been suspected of heretical religious beliefs."
- "Others were suspected of sexual impropriety."
- "Still others had inherited property or stood to inherit property."

Here are some logical inferences that are based on these three details:

- Some of the women accused of witchcraft were really being persecuted for other, unrelated reasons.
- Some women were accused of witchcraft because someone wanted to gain control of property they had inherited or were about to inherit.

Again, notice that although these things are not stated in the paragraph, they are logical conclusions.

EXERCISE 2

This paragraph comes from an American history textbook. After you have read the paragraph, study the details listed below it so that you can make logical inferences based on them.

Colonial women suffered legal disadvantages. In 1690, English common law and colonial legal codes allowed married women no control over property. Wives could not sue or be sued. They could not make contracts. They surrendered to their husbands any property they possessed before marriage. Divorce was almost impossible to obtain until the late eighteenth century. Only widows and a few single women had the same property rights as men, but they could not vote in colony elections.

Source: James Davidson, William Geinapp, Christine Heyrman, Mark Lytle, and Michael Stoff, *Nation of Nations,* Vol. 1, 5th ed., p. 97.

✓ **Teaching Tip**
This can be challenging for students, so have them work collaboratively. Some possible answers are given here, but have students try to come up with the answers first.

Here are the six supporting details that are presented in the passage. Reread them, then make logical inferences based on them.

- "English common law and colonial legal codes allowed married women no control over property."
- "Wives could not sue or be sued."
- "They could not make contracts."
- "They surrendered to their husbands any property they possessed before marriage."
- "Divorce was almost impossible to obtain until the late eighteenth century."
- "Only widows and a few single women had the same property rights as men, but they could not vote in colony elections."

1. Write one logical inference about the legal rights and property rights of colonial *men:*
Colonial men possessed nearly all of the legal and property rights.

2. Write one logical inference about the *number* of colonial women who owned property:
Because only unmarried colonial women could own property, there were very few women who owned property.

3. Write one logical inference about the legal rights of colonial women compared with the legal rights of American women *today*:

American women today have considerably more legal rights than colonial women did.

When you read, ask yourself, "Based on what the author has stated, what inference (logical conclusion) can I make?"

The skills of identifying facts and opinions, as well as making inferences (drawing logical conclusions), complement the critical reading skills you learned in the previous chapter. The box below contains the same review of an imaginary CD that you read in Chapter 8. Notice, however, that the critical thinking skills presented in this chapter have been added.

EXAMPLE OF CRITICAL READING AND THINKING SKILLS APPLIED TO A CRITIC'S REVIEW OF A CD

The controversial group The Gate Crashers has just released its first CD, *The Gate Crashers—Live!* Is it a good CD? That depends: Do you like vulgar lyrics that glorify violence? Do you mind listening to painfully bad hip-hop musicians? Do you have any problem sitting through twelve tracks (65 excruciating minutes!) of mind-numbing noise? If not, then you'll surely want to add *The Gate Crashers—Live!* to your collection.

Questions	**Answers**
What is the author's purpose?	To persuade readers not to buy this new CD
Who is the author's intended audience?	People who buy music CDs
What is the author's point of view?	*The Gate Crashers —Live!* CD is awful.*
What is the author's tone?	Sarcastic
Does the author include facts, opinions, or both?	Both facts and opinions
What inference (logical conclusion) does the author expect you to make?	Buying this CD would be a waste of money because you would not like it.

*Notice that this is also the author's main idea, or "argument".

✓ **Teaching Tip**
Have students identify some of the "opinion words" (e.g, *vulgar, painfully bad, excruciating, mind numbing*) and some of the factual information (their first CD, twelve tracks, 65 minutes).

By distinguishing facts from opinions, and by making logical inferences about what you have read, you will be a more critical reader and will evaluate written material more skillfully.

OTHER THINGS TO KEEP IN MIND WHEN THINKING CRITICALLY

Here are three helpful things you should keep in mind about thinking critically:

1. **Facts and opinions may or may not appear together.**
   - Some paragraphs contain facts *only* or opinions *only*.
   - Some paragraphs consist of *both* facts and opinions.
   - Sometimes both facts and opinions are presented in the *same sentence*. For example, consider the sentence "Sidney Smith would make an excellent senator because he has eight years' experience in the House of Representatives." The first part of the sentence presents an opinion: "Sidney Smith would make an excellent senator." The last part presents a fact: "He has eight years' experience in the House of Representatives."
2. **Authors sometimes present opinions in such a way that they *appear* to be facts.**

   An author may intentionally present opinions in ways that make them *appear* to be facts. For example, a writer might introduce an opinion by stating, "*The fact is* . . . " ("The fact is, you need a college degree to get a job in the computer industry.") Stating that something is a fact, however, does not make it a fact. (There are many different jobs in the computer industry. Not all of them require a college degree.)

   Ideally, of course, authors would always express opinions in ways that make it clear that they are opinions. ("In this writer's opinion, you need a college degree to get a job in the computer industry.") But authors do not always do this, and it is your job to think critically and distinguish between facts and opinions. Remember, when you identify an opinion, you should always determine whether or not it is well supported.
3. **Other critical thinking skills, such as *recognizing propaganda devices* and *recognizing fallacies,* can also be used to evaluate written material.**

   You should be aware that, although a full discussion of them is beyond the scope of this textbook, there are additional critical thinking skills that can be used to evaluate written material. These include:
   - Recognizing *propaganda* techniques (such as appeals to emotions, "bandwagoning," presenting either-or false choices, overgeneralizations, appeals to authority, testimonials and endorsements, and "stacking the deck").
   - Recognizing *fallacies* (implausible arguments using false or invalid inferences).

   Here is a brief overview of propaganda devices along with an exercise.

Propaganda Devices

Writers want readers to believe what they say, and sometimes they resort to propaganda devices to try to accomplish this. **Propaganda devices** are techniques authors use to unfairly influence the reader to accept their point of view. "Unfairly" means that propaganda techniques are intended to mislead readers, obscure the truth, or dodge the issue.

Propaganda is designed to manipulate. Some propaganda devices appeal to emotion. Other types rely on flawed reasoning to mislead and manipulate readers. These techniques are often used in advertisements, editorials, and political campaigns.

Columnist and author William Vaughan once observed, "There's a mighty big difference between good, sound reasons and reasons that sound good." If you become aware of these techniques and read critically, you can avoid falling for "reasons that sound good." When you are reading, ask yourself, "Has the author tried to unfairly influence me to accept his or her point of view?"

Now read about these types of propaganda devices, with examples of each.

Circular reasoning. The author restates the argument or conclusion as the truth without ever presenting any evidence or real support. This is also called *circular thinking* or *begging the question* because the author, like a beggar, asks for something (that you accept his or her point of view), but gives nothing (in this case, no proof) in return. The author's premises include the claim that the conclusion is already true (so there is no need to provide proof or support for it).

Examples

- "City College is the best place to start college because there's no place better."
- "You can improve your health by making healthier lifestyle choices."
- "If he were not an effective manager, he would not have been promoted to manager."

Either-or. The author puts everything in one of two mutually exclusive categories and acts as if there are no other possibilities besides one or the other. In other words, the author acts as if there are only two choices when in reality there are other possibilities.

Examples

- "America: Love it or leave it."
- "Either get an education or have an unfulfilling life."
- "Are you among the sophisticated people who drink Bubblemore Champagne or simply an ordinary beer drinker?"

Non sequitur. The author links two ideas or events that are not related; one does not follow from the other.

Examples

- "You should turn your iPod off when it rains. This morning it rained, and after that my iPod stopped working."
- "Maria is wonderful at creative writing and tennis. She'll probably own her own company someday."

Hasty generalization. The author jumps to a conclusion that is based on insufficient proof or evidence.

Examples

- "Forty students polled at the university believe current gun control laws are insufficient. It's clear that today's college students believe the country needs stronger gun control legislation."
- "Yesterday I was nearly run off the road by a truck driver. Truck drivers are reckless."

Appeals to emotion. The author appeals to readers' emotions (such as fear, guilt, sympathy, pity, hate) rather than to reason.

Examples

- "Don't risk your family's life! Install an XYZ Burglar Alarm System today!" (*fear*)
- "Now that you're working, you're embarrassed by your tattoos. Ask your dermatologist about the Laser-Rite tattoo removal procedure." (*embarrassment*)
- "Think how smart you'll look when you drive up in your new hybrid Prius!" (*pride*)
- "Hundreds of abandoned, neglected, and unwanted pets are waiting for loving homes. Call your local animal shelter and adopt a pet today." (*sympathy; pity*)

Red herring. The author presents an irrelevant issue to draw the reader's attention away from the central issue. The name comes from a trick used to throw hunting dogs off the scent of the track: dragging a red herring (a strong-smelling fish) across the tracks.

(continued on next page)

Examples

- "This issue isn't about homeowners' rights; it's actually about whether we're going to allow the city council to tell us how to run our lives."
- "It is often said that many mathematicians and scientists do not write very well, but think about how hard they had to work to become trained in their fields."

Post hoc. The author implies that because one event happened before another, it caused the second event.

Examples

- "After I took Cold-Away tablets, I began to feel better. Cold-Away really works!" (*Maybe it was because time went by, the person got more rest, or some other reason.*)
- "If the troops hadn't ignored the omen of the comet the night before, they would have won the battle." (*The outcome of the battle was not determined by the appearance of a comet.*)

Ad hominem. The author attacks the person rather than the arguments, views, or ideas the person presents.

Examples

- "How can we expect the candidate to be an effective senator when he's had two failed marriages?"
- "The mayor is a liar. How can we believe anything she promises about improving our public schools?"

Bandwagon. The author says that "everyone" believes, accepts, or does what he is describing, and therefore, the reader should also "get on the bandwagon." This is similar to peer pressure; it appeals to people's desire to be part of the crowd and like everyone else. The fact that something is widely accepted does not means it is true.

Examples

- "Join the thousands of Americans who have tripled their income with this simple at-home business. Call today for information about how you, too, can become a successful business owner."
- "All true patriots will urge their government representatives to support the new reform bill."
- "He's the best player in the NFL. Everyone knows that."

Hypostatization. The author treats an abstract concept as if it is a concrete reality.

Examples

- "History has taught us that as long as there are people there will be wars."
- "Government pokes its nose in every aspect of our lives. We have to protect our privacy from this intrusive monster."

False analogy. The author makes a comparison that is either inaccurate or inappropriate. Also called *faulty analogy*.

Examples

- "If the city can prohibit us from talking on cell phones while driving, they are just as likely to prohibit us from listening to the radio while driving."
- "You can't make an omelet without breaking some eggs, and we can't reduce the crime rate without coming down hard on criminals."
- "It's obvious that movie stars are nothing more than spoiled, self-centered children."

Transfer. The author transfers the good or bad qualities of one person or thing to another in order to influence the reader's perception of that person or thing.

Examples

- "He has Jay Leno's sense of humor."
- "This is the kind of project Mother Teresa would have supported."

Plain folks. The author appeals to readers by presenting himself or herself as someone who is just like the readers.

Examples

- "Wealthy people may spend their weekends at their country homes. For the rest of us, there's our backyard. Call Lawn Delight for a consultation about how to transform your backyard into your own little piece of heaven."
- "Crunch-It cereal: No fancy packaging. No exotic ingredients you can't pronounce. No inflated prices. Just plain, good food from a hometown company that takes pride in its products."

Sweeping generalization. The author presents a broad (general) statement that goes far beyond the evidence. (*Stereotyping* is one form of sweeping generalization.)

Examples

- "Student athletes do not excel in academics."
- "Women are too emotional to make good decisions."
- "Men would rather sit and watch television than do anything else."

Straw man. The author misrepresents what an opponent believes, and then attacks that belief.

Examples

- "The senator says that he favors a tax cut, but he has supported numerous spending bills. During these times of economic stress, it's wrong for members of Congress to keep spending money so freely."
- "My professor counts off for late homework. Obviously, he doesn't care about whether or not students are learning. He should be fired and replaced with a faculty member who cares about student success."

Appeal to authority. The author tries to influence the reader to accept his or her argument or point of view by citing some authority who believes it.

Examples

- "To treat occasional heartburn, eight out of ten doctors recommend Acid-Stop."
- "Dr. Milton Vosky, a researcher at Crumpfield University, believes that text messaging and tweeting cause deterioration in students' ability to spell English words properly."

Testimonial. A famous person endorses an idea or a project in order to influence others to believe or buy it. The person's endorsement may mean nothing since he or she may have no special knowledge about it or even any experience with it. Also called *endorsement*.

Examples

- "As a model, I'm often in front of the camera. Soft Touch soap leaves my skin looking younger than ever. It'll do the same for you. Try it and see the difference in just two weeks."
- "Top athletes like Michael Jordan depend on Nike shoes to help make them winners."

EXERCISE 3

Propaganda Devices

Directions: Read each sentence and circle the *letter* that answers the question.

1. Talking on the cell phone while driving endangers your life and the lives of others.

In the sentence above, is the author's argument logically valid or invalid?

a. valid
(b.) invalid (It could, but a careful driver using a hands-free earpiece is unlikely to pose a danger.)

2. More women than men develop breast cancer. If either of my parents develops this form of cancer, my mother is more likely to develop it than my father is.

In the sentence above, is the author's argument logically valid or invalid?

(a.) valid
b. invalid

3. Some college athletes become professional athletes who are paid millions of dollars a year. Because they grew up in poverty, they will not be able to manage their financial affairs wisely once they become wealthy.

In the sentence above, is the author's argument logically valid or invalid?

a. valid
(b.) invalid (Many factors affect how well a person manages financial affairs; growing up poor makes some people more careful with any wealth they attain.)

4. The pond is covered with ice. All ice melts when warmed sufficiently. When the weather becomes warm enough, the ice on the pond will melt.

In the sentence above, is the author's argument logically valid or invalid?

(a.) valid (The ice on the pond is a specific example that follows the general rule.)
b. invalid

5. My sister has been coughing since last night. Either she has allergies or she's coming down with the flu. Which of the following fallacies does the author use in an effort to support the argument?

a. circular thinking
(b.) either-or (Allergies and flu are not the only two conditions indicated by a cough.)
c. non sequitur
d. hasty generalization

6. Four of my teenage son's friends have gotten speeding tickets or been involved in traffic accidents. The high school's driver education course is not doing a good job of preparing young people to drive.

Which of the following fallacies does the author use in an effort to support the argument?

a. circular thinking
b. either-or
c. non sequitur
(d.) hasty generalization (We cannot conclude this on the basis of four teens' experiences.)

7. Astrological horoscopes are scientifically based. After all, most major newspapers and popular magazines publish horoscopes. They wouldn't publish horoscopes if astrology weren't an accurate, reliable way of predicting people's futures.

Which of the following fallacies does the author use in an effort to support the argument?

(a.) circular thinking (They're true because they're published; thery're published because they're true.)
b. either-or
c. non sequitur
d. hasty generalization

8. Bob majored in computer science. That must be why he has such a high-paying job.

Which of the following fallacies does the author use in an effort to support the argument?

a. circular thinking
b. either-or
(c.) non sequitur (Salary depends on many factors; majoring in computer science doesn't guarantee high pay.)
d. hasty generalization

CREATING CHAPTER REVIEW CARDS

Student Online Learning Center (OLC)
***Go to* Chapter 9.**
***Select* Chapter Test.**

Review cards or *summary cards* are a way to select, organize, and summarize the important information in a textbook chapter. Preparing review cards helps you organize the information so that you can learn and memorize it more easily. In other words, chapter review cards are effective study tools.

Preparing chapter review cards for each chapter of *New Worlds* will give you practice in creating these valuable study tools. Once you have learned how to make chapter review cards, you can use actual index cards to create them for textbook material in your other courses and use them when you study for tests.

Now complete the chapter review cards for Chapter 9 by answering the questions or following the directions on each card. Use the type of handwriting that is easiest for you to reread (printing or cursive) and write legibly.

✓ **Teaching Tip**

Remind students that the student OLC contains a 10-item **Chapter Test** for this chapter. After completing the chapter review cards below, students should complete the Chapter Test on the OLC.

Thinking Critically to Evaluate Written Material

1. What is the definition of *thinking critically*? (See page 497.)

   thinking in an organized way about material in order to evaluate it accurately

2. Why is it important to be able to think critically? (See page 497.)

   By taking time to reread and reconsider the author's message, you will be able to understand it accurately and completely.

Card 1 Chapter 9: Thinking Critically

Facts and Opinions

1. What is the definition of a *fact*? (See page 497.)

something that can be proved to exist or have happened

2. What is the definition of an *opinion*? (See page 497.)

a judgment or belief that cannot be proved or disproved

3. List in order the three questions you should ask yourself in order to distinguish between facts and opinions. (See page 500.)

1. Can the information in the statement be proved?
2. Can the information in the statement be disproved?
3. Is the information in the statement something that cannot be proved or disproved?

Card 2 Chapter 9: Thinking Critically

Opinions

1. List at least five *words or phrases* that authors use to indicate that they are presenting an opinion. (See page 498.)

in our opinion — this suggests
apparently — it appears
one possibility is — in our view

2. List at least five *value judgment words* that indicate an opinion is being presented. (See page 499.)

greatest — interesting
worst — effective
best — valuable
excellent — pleasant

Card 3 Chapter 9: Thinking Critically

Making Logical Inferences

1. What is an *inference*? (See page 502.)

   An inference is a logical conclusion based on what an author has stated.

2. Why is it not an inference if a reader simply copies or paraphrases information that the author states? (See pages 502–503.)

   Inferences must go *beyond* what is stated in the paragraph.

Card 4 Chapter 9: Thinking Critically

Things to Keep in Mind When Thinking Critically

List the three additional things you should keep in mind when thinking critically. (See page 508.)

1. Facts and opinions may or may not appear together.
2. Authors sometimes present opinions in such a way that they *appear* to be facts.
3. There are two other critical thinking skills that can be used to evaluate written material: recognizing propaganda techniques and recognizing fallacies.

Define propaganda devices and fallacies. (See page 508)

Propaganda devices: techniques authors use to unfairly influence the reader to accept their point of view.

Fallacies: implausible arguments using false or invalid references.

Card 5 Chapter 9: Thinking Critically

TEST YOUR UNDERSTANDING
CRITICAL THINKING: FACT AND OPINION

REVIEW: **Critical thinking** means thinking in an organized way about material that you have read in order to evaluate it accurately. Critical thinking simply means applying certain reading and thinking skills in a systematic, thorough way. In other words, critical thinking means consistently asking certain additional questions and applying logic when you read. Like critical reading skills, critical thinking skills are *interrelated.* An author's purpose causes him or her to present certain *facts or opinions.*

- **Distinguishing facts from opinions:** A **fact** is something that can be proved to exist or have happened. An **opinion** is a judgment or belief that cannot be proved or disproved. To determine whether statements in written material are facts or opinions, ask yourself, "Can the information the author presents be proved, or does it represent a judgment?"

EXAMPLE: Study the example paragraph below to see how the information you learned in this chapter can be used to think critically. Read the explanations that are given for the correct answers. When you are sure you understand the explanations, complete the five exercises in this section.

This excerpt comes from a music appreciation textbook. Its topic is *the Beatles.* The stated main idea of this paragraph is the first sentence: *The remarkable group that came to be known as the Beatles began as a Liverpool gang more interested in finding trouble than in changing the course of rock and roll.* Read the paragraph, and then distinguish between facts and opinions by asking yourself the comprehension monitoring question: "Can the information the author presents be proved or does it represent a judgment?"

The Beatles

The remarkable group that came to be known as the **Beatles** began as a Liverpool gang more interested in finding trouble than in changing the course of rock and roll. John Lennon formed the group, which included Paul McCartney and soon George Harrison. Music was among the more innocent activities of these three talented, though largely untrained, musicians. They performed their early songs, most of them pleasantly simple and naïve, in a rather primitive style. While Lennon was more inclined to shout than to sing, McCartney had a beautiful voice, and Harrison played the guitar extremely well.

Source: Jean Ferris, *America's Musical Landscape,* 3rd ed. Copyright © 1998 by The McGraw-Hill Companies, Inc. Reprinted by permission of The McGraw-Hill Companies, Inc.

__a__ Which of the following statements is a fact?

a. John Lennon formed the group, which included Paul McCartney and George Harrison.

b. They performed their early songs, most of them pleasantly simple and naïve, in a rather primitive style.

c. While Lennon was more inclined to shout than to sing, McCartney had a beautiful voice, and Harrison played the guitar extremely well.

d. The Beatles were a remarkable group.

Explanation: The correct answer is a. Research would confirm that John Lennon formed the Beatles and that the group included McCartney and Harrison, so this statement is a fact. Answer choice *b* is an opinion, as the judgment words *simple, naïve,* and *primitive* suggest. Answer choice *c* is an opinion, as indicated by the judgment words *beautiful* and *extremely well.* Answer choice *d* is also an opinion, as indicated by the judgment word *remarkable.*

DIRECTIONS: Read each paragraph carefully. Then answer the questions, "Which of the following statements is an *opinion?*" or "Which of the following statements is a *fact?*" (Refer to the chart on pages 500–501 as you evaluate the answer choices.)

1. This paragraph comes from a human development textbook.

On the average, a full-term newborn is between 19 and 22 inches long and weighs 5½ to 9½ pounds. Many newborns give the appearance of a defeated prizefighter. They often have a puffy bluish-red face, a broad, flat nose, swollen eyelids, and ears skewed at odd angles. Their heads are often misshapen and elongated. In most infants the chin recedes and the lower jaw is underdeveloped. Bowleggedness is the rule, and the feet might be pigeon-toed.

Source: Adapted from James Vander Zanden, revised by Thomas Crandell and Corinne Crandell, *Human Development.* Updated 7th ed., p. 115. Copyright © 2003 by The McGraw-Hill Companies, Inc. Reprinted by permission of The McGraw-Hill Companies, Inc.

b Which of the following statements is an *opinion*?

a. On the average, a full-term newborn is between 19 and 22 inches long and weighs 5½ to 9½ pounds.

b. Many newborns give the appearance of a defeated prizefighter.

c. Their heads are often misshapen and elongated.

d. In most infants, the chin recedes and the lower jaw is underdeveloped.

✓ **Teaching Tip**
In the answer choices, have students identify any judgment words or other clues to opinions.

2. This paragraph comes from a public speaking textbook.

Global plagiarism is stealing your speech entirely from another source and passing it off as your own. The most blatant—and unforgivable—kind of plagiarism, it is grossly unethical. Sometimes global plagiarism is the result of deliberate dishonesty. More often, it happens because a student puts off the assignment until the last minute. Then, in desperation, the student downloads a speech from the Internet and delivers it as his or her own. The best way to avoid this, of course, is not to leave your speech until the last minute. If, for some reason, you fail to get your speech ready on time, do not succumb to the lure of plagiarism. Whatever the penalty you suffer from being late will pale in comparison with the consequences if you are caught plagiarizing.

Source: Adapted from Stephen Lucas, *The Art of Public Speaking,* 8th ed., p. 43. Copyright © 2004 by The McGraw-Hill Companies, Inc. Reprinted by permission of The McGraw-Hill Companies, Inc.

a Which of the following statements is a *fact*?

a. Global plagiarism is stealing your speech entirely from another source and passing it off as your own.

b. The most blatant—and unforgivable—kind of plagiarism, it is grossly unethical.

c. If, for some reason, you fail to get your speech ready on time, do not succumb to the lure of plagiarism.

d. Whatever the penalty you suffer from being late will pale in comparison with the consequences if you are caught plagiarizing.

3. This paragraph comes from a political science textbook.

Media has undergone an interesting change. Although traditional outlets such as papers, magazines, radio, and television aimed to broadcast the news to large numbers of people at once, today's abundance of media sources has led to "narrowcasting"—that is, targeting news to individuals who choose only programming that really interests them. Today's media are also characterized by a declining interest in newspapers and, among the young, a declining interest in the news itself. The latter characteristic worries some observers who wonder how the young can fulfill their citizenship responsibilities without adequate information about the world around them.

Source: Adapted from Joseph Losco and Ralph Baker, *Am Gov,* p. 212. Copyright © 2008 by The McGraw-Hill Companies, Inc. Reprinted by permission of The McGraw-Hill Companies, Inc.

a ______ Which of the following statements is an *opinion?*

a. Media has undergone an interesting change.

b. Although traditional outlets such as papers, magazines, radio, and television aimed to broadcast the news to large numbers of people at once, today's abundance of media sources has led to "narrowcasting"—that is, targeting news to individuals who choose only programming that really interests them.

c. Today's media are also characterized by a declining interest in newspapers and, among the young, a declining interest in the news itself.

d. The latter characteristic worries some observers who wonder how the young can fulfill their citizenship responsibilities without adequate information about the world around them.

4. This paragraph comes from an information technology textbook.

E-mail or **electronic mail** is the transmission of electronic messages over the Internet. At one time, e-mail consisted only of basic text messages. Now e-mail includes graphics, photos, and many different types of file attachments. People all over the world send e-mail to each other. You can e-mail your family, your co-workers, and even your senator. All you need to send and receive e-mail is an e-mail account, access to the Internet, and an e-mail program. Two of the most widely used e-mail programs are Microsoft's Outlook Express and Netscape's Mail. E-mail can be a valuable asset in your personal and professional life. However, like many other valuable technologies, there are drawbacks, too. Americans receive billions of unwanted and unsolicited e-mails every year. Unwanted e-mail messages are called **spam.**

Source: Adapted from Timothy J. O'Leary and Linda I. O'Leary, *Computing Essentials, 2005 Introductory Edition,* 16th ed., p. 34. Copyright © 2005 by The McGraw-Hill Companies, Inc. Reprinted by permission of The McGraw-Hill Companies, Inc.

d ______ Which of the following statements is an *opinion*?

a. E-mail or electronic mail is the transmission of electronic messages over the Internet.

b. Unwanted e-mail messages are called spam.

c. Now e-mail includes graphics, photos, and many different types of file attachments. People all over the world send e-mail to each other.

d. E-mail can be a valuable asset in your personal and professional life.

5. This paragraph comes from a music appreciation textbook.

By the mid-1980s, popularity had shifted away from new wave as many bands and several individuals with distinctive sounds became rich and famous. These bands and individuals were variously identified by a string of labels (*new romantics, blitz, punk-jazz, blue wave, techno-pop,* and *techno-funk,* among others). The artist formerly known as Prince, Michael Jackson, Lionel Richie, Madonna, Cyndi Lauper, and Sting (formerly of The Police), among the best-known names of mainstream rock in the late 1980s, maintained various degrees of popularity into the 1990s. "The Boss," Bruce Springsteen, probably the most successful rock star of the late seventies, pointed rock in a new direction in his 1982 album *Born in the U.S.A.* He further revitalized the rock music of the mid-eighties with his stirring songs on socially relevant topics, whose messages were further implemented by Springsteen and other like-minded rock stars in the rock-sponsored benefits for starving masses in Ethiopia, "We Are the World" and "Live Aid." And in 1995, Springsteen commanded new attention and respect with his profoundly moving songs in the film *Philadelphia.*

Source: Jean Ferris, *America's Musical Landscape,* 3rd ed. Copyright © 1998 by The McGraw-Hill Companies, Inc. Reprinted by permission of The McGraw-Hill Companies, Inc.

a ______ Which of the following statements is a *fact*?

a. These bands and individuals were variously identified by a string of labels (*new romantics, blitz, punk-jazz, blue wave, techno-pop,* and *techno-funk,* among others).

b. "The Boss," Bruce Springsteen, probably the most successful rock star of the late seventies, pointed rock in a new direction in his 1982 album *Born in the U.S.A.*

c. Bruce Springsteen further revitalized the rock music of the mid-eighties with his stirring songs on socially relevant topics.

d. And in 1995, Springsteen commanded new attention and respect with his profoundly moving songs in the film *Philadelphia.*

TEST YOUR UNDERSTANDING
CRITICAL THINKING: MAKING LOGICAL INFERENCES

REVIEW: **Critical thinking** means thinking in an organized way about material that you have read in order to evaluate it accurately. Critical thinking simply means applying certain reading and thinking skills in a systematic, thorough way. In other words, critical thinking means consistently asking certain additional questions and applying logic when you read. Like critical reading skills, critical thinking skills are *interrelated.* An author's purpose causes him or her to present certain *facts or opinions.* This allows readers to *make logical inferences* based on what the author has stated.

- **Making logical inferences:** An **inference** is a logical conclusion that is based on what an author has stated. A **conclusion** is a decision that is reached after thoughtful consideration of information the author presents. After you read, you should ask yourself, "What logical inference can I make, based on what the author has stated?"

EXAMPLE: Study the example paragraph below to see how the information you learned in this chapter can be used to think critically. Read the explanations that are given for the correct answers. When you are sure you understand the explanations, complete the five exercises in this section.

This excerpt comes from a management textbook. Its topic is *flextime.* The stated main idea of this paragraph is the first sentence: *Flextime is a work schedule that specifies certain core hours when individuals are expected to be on the job and then allows flexibility in starting and quitting times as long as individuals work the total number of required hours per day.* Read the paragraph, and then ask yourself the comprehension monitoring question: "Based on what the authors have stated, what logical inference can I make?"

Flextime is a work schedule that specifies certain core hours when individuals are expected to be on the job and then allows flexibility in starting and quitting times as long as individuals work the total number of required hours per day. For example, a company may have core hours between 10 A.M. and 3 P.M. (with an hour for lunch). Workers may then choose various schedules, such as 7 A.M. to 4 P.M., that comprise 8 hours of work per day and include the core hours. One recent study showed that the most popular core period is 9 A.M. to 3 P.M.

Source: Kathryn M. Bartol and David C. Martin, *Management,* 3rd ed. Copyright © 1998 by The McGraw-Hill Companies, Inc. Reprinted by permission of The McGraw-Hill Companies, Inc.

Even though a person's eight-hour shift must include the company's "core period," who can you infer might appreciate having flexibility in choosing his or her own starting and quitting times?

- A parent who wants to be home with children in the morning
- A parent who wants to be home when children get out of school
- An employee who wants to avoid rush-hour traffic
- A "morning person" who prefers an early start
- A person who is working two jobs

Explanation: These inferences are logical; they are based on information given in the passage, but they go *beyond* what is stated in the passage.

DIRECTIONS: Read each paragraph carefully and make a logical inference. The italicized words tell what your inference should be about. Remember that you cannot use a sentence from the paragraph (or a restatement of it) as your inference. Your inference must be a logical conclusion *based on* information stated in the paragraph, however. Write your answers in the spaces provided.

1. This paragraph comes from an Internet literacy textbook.

Virtually every computer sold today comes with a microphone and speakers that can be used for audio conferencing. For less than $50, you can add a camera to your computer so others can see as well as hear you during a conference. In *videoconferencing,* each person's PC has a video camera and a microphone attached to the video and audio adapters that digitize what the camera sees and the microphone hears. Because digital audio and video transmissions contain many more bits of information than textual communications, you need a faster connection to the Internet than is required for text-based chat. A lot of research and development is being done on compressing audio and video to make them require less bandwidth, however, and hopefully videoconferencing will become more widespread when the cost of transmitting it decreases. Many corporate intranets have high-speed connections that permit the use of high-quality videoconferencing. If you are fortunate enough to be on such a LAN, you can enjoy today the full benefits of the emerging videoconferencing technology.

Source: Adapted from Fred F. Hofstetter, *Internet Literacy,* 4th ed., p. 151. Copyright © 2006 by The McGraw-Hill Companies, Inc. Reprinted by permission of The McGraw-Hill Companies, Inc.

Based on the information in the passage, write an inference that could be made about *videoconferencing:*

- Videoconferencing can save individuals and companies a great deal of travel time and money.
- It is likely that videoconferencing will increase.

2. This paragraph comes from a marketing textbook.

A product's brand name should be simple (such as Bold laundry detergent, Sure deodorant, and Bic pens) and should be emotional (such as Joy and My Sin perfume). In the development of names for international use, having a nonmeaningful brand name has been considered a benefit. A name such as Exxon does not have any prior impressions or undesirable images among a diverse world population of different languages and cultures. The 7Up name is another matter. In Shanghai, China, the phrase means "death through drinking" in the local dialect, and sales have suffered as a result.

Source: Erin Berkowitz, Roger Kerin, Steven Hartley, and William Rudelius, *Marketing,* 5th ed. Copyright © 1998 McGraw-Hill. Reprinted by permission of The McGraw-Hill Companies, Inc.

Based on the information in the passage, write an inference that could be made about *choosing a brand name for a product:*

A company should choose carefully when selecting or creating a brand name.

3. This paragraph comes from a sociology textbook.

The myth that single parents cannot raise healthy children increases parents' anxiety and guilt. These feelings then may affect their ability to rear children. Single parents—male and female—also must maintain discipline, educate their children, and promote healthy emotional development. Children of divorce experience many difficulties, although in some cases the problems are not as severe as living in a tense household filled with hatred and fighting. Many parents fail to explain to their children why they are separating and what it will mean to the children's future. But most children adapt to their new circumstances within a year of the divorce.

Source: Daniel E. Hebding and Leonard Glick, *Introduction to Sociology,* 4th ed. (New York: McGraw-Hill, 1992).

Based on the information in the passage, write an inference that could be made about *what parents who are divorcing should do to help their children.*

It is important for parents who are divorcing to explain to their children the reason for the divorce and how it will affect the children's lives.

4. This paragraph comes from a geography textbook.

International English

In worldwide diffusion and acceptance, English has no past or present rivals. Along with French, it is one of the two working languages of the United Nations. Two-thirds of all scientific papers are published in it, making it the first language of scientific discourse. In addition to being the accepted language of international air traffic control, English is the sole or joint language of more nations and territories than any other tongue. "English as a second language" is indicated with near-universal or mandatory English instruction in public schools. In Continental Europe, more than 80% of secondary school students study it as a second language and more than one-third of European Union residents can easily converse in it.

Source: Adapted from Arthur Getis, Judith Getis, and Jerome Fellmann, *Introduction to Geography,* 10th ed., p. 241. Copyright © 2006 by The McGraw-Hill Companies, Inc. Reprinted by permission of The McGraw-Hill Companies, Inc.

Based on the information in the passage, write an inference that could be made about *learning English if it is not a person's first language:*

If English is not a person's first language, it is extremely useful to learn it as a second language.

5. This paragraph comes from a public speaking textbook.

The Internet has been called the world's biggest library. Through it you can read electronic versions of the *New York Times,* the *Tokyo Shimbun,* and the *Jerusalem Post.* You can visit the great museums of Europe, browse through the Library of Congress, and get up-to-the-minute bulletins from CNN and Reuters News Service. You can access government agencies and most major corporations. You can read texts of Supreme

Court decisions and of the latest bills proposed in Congress. You can check stock market prices, conduct word searches of the Bible, and find statistics on virtually every topic under the sun.

Source: Stephen Lucas, *The Art of Public Speaking,* 8th ed., p. 147. Copyright © 2004 by The McGraw-Hill Companies, Inc. Reprinted by permission of The McGraw-Hill Companies, Inc.

Based on the information in the passage, write an inference that could be made about *learning to use the Internet:*

Learning to use the Internet opens up a convenient world of information to a person.

SELECTION **9-1**

Child Development

"IT'S *YOUR* TURN TO FEED THE BABY!" HOW INFANTS AFFECT MARRIAGE

From *Childhood*

By Laurence Steinberg and Roberta Meyer

A couple's first baby changes everything—how they spend their time, which friends they see, what seems important, and the way they relate to each other. (Experts say that parents of a newborn lose 450–700 hours of sleep during the baby's first year!) This selection explains what is required for a couple to make a successful transition to parenthood.

1 Couples confront four kinds of problems in adjusting to parenthood. The first involves the physical demands of caring for an infant who needs to be fed and changed at least every 3 to 4 hours. New parents report feeling stressed and fatigued by lack of sleep. Mothers seem to be more susceptible, as they are more likely to feel the strain associated with adding primary caregiver to the role of wife, homemaker, and often employee as well.

2 Strains in the husband-wife relationship create the second problem. New parents complain that they have no time together as a couple anymore and no time for or interest in their sexual relationship. Fathers often feel that their wives pay more attention to their infants' needs than to their own. But for their wives, waking several times each night can easily create a need for sleep stronger than any need for sex or conversation.

3 Becoming parents has direct emotional costs, the third class of problems in the transition to parenthood. The responsibility of caring for an infant can seem overwhelming, and as parents come to realize that being a parent is a lifetime job, doubts about competence can also cause stress.

4 The fourth problem area involves loss of freedom and opportunities. New parents' social lives are constricted, freedom to travel is limited, and doing anything on very short notice is almost impossible. Most new parents discover that life with an infant is far more complicated than they had imagined. They want to go to a movie, but they can't find a babysitter; they take the baby to a restaurant, and he cries through dinner. Some new parents give up and just stay home. In addition to restrictions on mobility, having a child is expensive, and not just in money spent. If one parent stops working, income drops as expenses climb.

5 With all these strains on new parents, marriages can suffer. In fact, overall satisfaction with marriage tends to drop after parenthood begins. Wives become more dissatisfied than husbands, no doubt because women are mainly responsible for child care in most families. But keep in mind that rarely does having a baby ruin a good marriage or improve a bad one. Couples that were happiest before their baby was born tend to continue that way, and those who are least content remain that way as well.

6 Why does having a baby lead to more unhappiness in some couples than in others? Often, the main answer is housework: Who does it, and, more important, who does more of it? Generally, it's the wife who cleans the house, cooks, does the laundry

Annotation Practice Exercises

Directions: For each exercise below, read critically to answer the questions.

✓ **Teaching Tip**

Because paragraphs 1–4 of this selection are so clearly written, these are excellent for marginal annotation practice. Paragraph 1 opens with the overall main idea for this section and then describes the first problem new parents face. Each subsequent paragraph opens with a stated main idea that presents an additional problem.

Practice Exercise

Based on the information in paragraph 6, what *inference* could be drawn about the potential happiness of a couple who has full-time help or a nanny?

Because housework often becomes a major issue once couples have a baby, they are likely to be happier if they can hire full-time help or a nanny.

Taking care of an infant can be exhausting, especially if middle-of-the-night feedings persist for months.

(considerably more than before), and now, additionally, cares for the baby. The more unequally these chores are divided, the more dissatisfied wives become. Women who become most unhappy are those who are more independent and career-oriented. Their lives have become inconsistent with their views of themselves, breeding conflict and dissatisfaction.

7 Another difference among couples affecting their transition to parenthood is how realistic their expectations about the baby have been. Couples often romanticize parenthood, imagining a blissful family unit instead of the combination of joy and stress that being a parent really is. When stresses such as reduced sleep, less frequent sex, and more housework for women are not anticipated, their impact can be quite strong. Unsettling, too, is advice from well-meaning parents, in-laws, friends, and neighbors. When the advice differs from the couple's own views or becomes a source of disagreement, it can increase stress.

8 A couple's age and how long they've been married also affect their adjustment. Older couples and those who have been married longer report fewer problems than newly married and very young couples. And finally, how a baby affects a marriage also depends on the baby. Infants with difficult temperaments, who are fussier, or who are often sick generate more stress for their parents, and this stress can harm a marriage.

9 Before you decide that babies bring nothing but stress to their parents, we will add that they also bring great pleasure. Babies add work, but they also add fun. The love, joy, and happiness that commonly accompany parenthood can be deeply enriching. For many couples, children tighten the bond, both to their own families of origin and to each other. These pleasures most strongly associated with the first child, balance the stress felt by many husbands and wives. Parenthood can also lead to emotional growth for mothers and fathers. It can bring greater maturity, as caring for an infant can enhance feelings of accomplishment and self-enrichment. Parents often report that they feel more like adults, less self-centered, less selfish, and more thoughtful about the future.

Practice Exercise

Does paragraph 9 contain *facts, opinions,* or *both*?

both facts and opinions

SELECTION 9-1 **Child Development** *(continued)*

Comprehension and Vocabulary Quiz

This quiz has four parts. Your instructor may assign some or all of them.

Comprehension

Directions: Items 1–5 test your comprehension (understanding) of the material in this selection. These questions are much like those that a content-area instructor (such as a child development professor) would expect you to know after reading and studying this selection. For each comprehension question below, use information from the selection to determine the correct answer. Refer to the selection as you answer the questions. Write your answers in the spaces provided.

¶s 1–4 ___d___ **1.** Which of the following problems do couples confront in adjusting to parenthood?

a. loss of opportunities and freedom
b. strains in the husband-wife relationship
c. the physical demands of caring for an infant
d. all of the above

¶6 ___c___ **2.** Often, a major issue leading to unhappiness once couples have a baby is:

a. entertainment and recreation.
b. increased freedom and opportunities.
c. the sharing of housework.
d. who will be the primary caregiver.

¶5 ___d___ **3.** According to information in the selection, after a baby is born, women tend to become less satisfied with marriage than men because women:

a. get less sleep than their husbands.
b. have less mobility and lower expectations about the baby.
c. resent no longer being able to work outside the home.
d. are mainly responsible for the care of the child.

¶9 ___c___ **4.** Couples often report that the transition to parenthood:

a. is more difficult if the couple is older and has been married longer.
b. is easier if the couple is newly married and both partners are very young.
c. makes them feel less self-centered and more thoughtful about the future.
d. causes both parents to give in to pressure from family members.

¶9 ___c___ **5.** The authors believe that parenthood is:

a. easier for newly married and very young couples.
b. too demanding for mothers who must balance the demands of primary caregiver, wife, and homemaker.
c. a combination of stress and joy.
d. all of the above

Vocabulary in Context

Directions: Items 6–10 test your ability to determine the meaning of the word by using context clues. *Context clues* are words in a sentence that allow the reader to deduce (reason out) the meaning of an unfamiliar word in that sentence. Context clues also enable the reader to determine which meaning the author intends when a word has more than one meaning. For each vocabulary item below, a sentence from the selection containing an important word (*italicized, like this*) is quoted first. Next, there is an additional sentence using the word in the same sense and providing another context clue. Use the context clues from *both* sentences to deduce the meaning of the italicized word. *Be sure the answer you choose makes sense in both sentences.* If you need to use a dictionary to confirm your answer choice, remember that the meaning you select must still fit the context of *both* sentences. Write your answers in the spaces provided.

Pronunciation Key: ă **pat** ā **pay** âr **care** ä **father** ĕ **pet** ē **be** ĭ **pit**
ī **tie** îr **pier** ŏ **pot** ō **toe** ô **paw** oi **noise** ou **out** o͝o **took**
o͞o **boot** ŭ **cut** yo͞o **abuse** ûr **urge** th **thin** *th* **this** hw **which**
zh **vision** ə **about** *Stress mark:* ′

¶4 b **6.** New parents' social lives are *constricted,* freedom to travel is limited, and doing anything on very short notice is almost impossible.

Those whose mobility is *constricted* by chronic illness find it difficult or even impossible to travel.

constricted (kən strĭk′ təd) means:

a. enlarged
b. restricted
c. characterized
d. enhanced

¶6 a **7.** Their lives have become inconsistent with their views of themselves, *breeding* conflict and dissatisfaction.

The new company president immediately changed several popular policies, thus *breeding* discontent among employees.

breeding (brē′ dĭng) means:

a. causing
b. limiting
c. ending
d. improving

¶7 d **8.** Couples often *romanticize* parenthood, imagining a blissful family unit instead of the combination of joy and stress that being a parent really is.

Many young brides *romanticize* marriage as being like a fairy tale and subsequently are disappointed by everyday married life.

romanticize (rō măn′ tĭ sīz) means:

a. to make tragic
b. to perceive as chronically difficult

c. to view as temporary

d. to view unrealistically by basing on emotion

¶7 ____d____ **9.** *Unsettling,* too, is advice from well-meaning parents, in-laws, friends, and neighbors.

The pilot's announcement that the plane had developed a minor mechanical problem was nevertheless highly *unsettling* to me.

unsettling (ŭn sĕt′ lĭng) means:

a. comforting

b. uninteresting

c. unimportant

d. disturbing

¶9 ____c____ **10.** For many couples, children tighten the bond, both to their own *families of origin* and to each other.

Children who are in foster care still have many feelings about their *families of origin.*

families of origin means:

a. families from their native country

b. foster families they are now part of

c. families into which they were born

d. families they create with children of their own

Word Structure

Directions: Items 11–15 test your ability to use word-structure clues to help determine a word's meaning. *Word-structure clues* consist of roots, prefixes, and suffixes. In these exercises, you will learn the meaning of a word part (a root) and use it to determine the meaning of several other words that have the same word part. If you need to use a dictionary to confirm your answer choice, do so. Write your answers in the spaces provided.

In paragraph 2 of the selection, you encountered the word **conversation.** This word contains the Latin root ***ver,*** which means "to turn" or "to move." In this selection, the word *conversation* refers to a discussion that turns from one person to another; that is, it moves back and forth between two or more people. Use the meaning of ***ver*** and the list of prefixes on pages 68–69 to help you determine the meaning of each of the following words that contain this same root.

____a____ **11.** When a person **converts** to a different religion, he or she:

a. changes religions.

b. stops attending religious services.

c. takes vows to join a religious order.

d. becomes a religious leader.

____b____ **12.** If you try to **divert** a baby's attention so that he will stop crying, you try to:

a. determine the reason he is crying.

b. turn his attention to something else.

c. make him take a nap.
d. rock him to sleep.

d **13.** If you **avert** your eyes when you see a scary scene in a horror movie, you:
a. close your eyes.
b. stare in disbelief at the screen.
c. blink repeatedly.
d. turn your eyes away from the screen.

c **14.** If a person exhibits **perverted** behavior, the person:
a. possesses an unusual sense of humor.
b. socializes with eccentric individuals.
c. deviates greatly from what is considered right or correct.
d. achieves popularity and fame.

a **15.** People who are **extroverts** are:
a. interested in things and people around them.
b. focused in their own thoughts and feelings.
c. preoccupied with learning new information.
d. intensely interested in current events.

Reading Skills Application

Directions: Items 16–20 test your ability to *apply* certain reading skills to information in this selection. These types of questions provide valuable practice for all students, especially those who must take standardized reading tests and state-mandated basic skills tests. Write your answers in the spaces provided.

authors' writing patterns (Chapter 7)

c **16.** The pattern of the overall selection is best described as a:
a. list.
b. comparison-contrast.
c. problem-solution.
d. sequence.

¶1 vocabulary in context (Chapter 2)

d **17.** The meaning of *susceptible* as it is used in paragraph 1 is:
a. accustomed.
b. immune.
c. resilient.
d. affected.

conclusion (Chapter 9)

a **18.** Based on information in the selection, it is logical to conclude that couples:
a. typically face more adjustment difficulties after the birth of the first baby than they do with subsequent children.
b. usually decide after the first baby not to have additional children.

c. should wait to have children until they can afford a live-in nanny.

d. who have twins experience twice as many adjustment problems.

author's intended audience (Chapter 8) ___c___ **19.** Who is the authors' primary audience for this selection?

a. child care providers

b. dissatisfied couples who are trying to understand why becoming parents has had a negative effect on their marriage

c. adults, especially those who are new parents or who are considering becoming parents at some point

d. psychologists, marriage therapists, and other professionals who counsel new parents

¶6 formulated main idea (Chapter 5) ___a___ **20.** Which of the following is the main idea of paragraph 6 of the selection?

a. Having a baby causes more unhappiness in couples who share the housework unequally, especially if the women are independent and career-minded.

b. The more unequally these chores are divided, the more dissatisfied the wives become.

c. Women who become most unhappy are those who are more independent and career-minded.

d. Why does having a baby lead to more unhappiness in some couples than in others?

SELECTION **9-1**
Child Development
(Continued)

Writing and Collaborating to Enhance Your Understanding

Option for collaboration: Your instructor may direct you to work with other students or, in other words, to work *collaboratively*. In that case, you should form groups of three or four students as directed by your instructor and work together to complete the exercises. After your group discusses each item and agrees on the answer, have a group member record it. Every member of your group should be able to explain all of your group's answers.

Collaboration Option

1. **Reacting to What You Have Read:** Do you think the first child has a greater impact on a marriage than subsequent children? Explain why or why not.

(Answers will vary.)

2. **Comprehending the Selection Further:** Based on information in the selection, list at least four factors that would facilitate a couple's successful transition to parenthood.

- The husband and wife share housework equally.
- The couple is older.
- The couple has been married longer.

- The baby is healthy and has a good temperament.
- One parent stays home with the baby and is not employed.
- The couple has a nanny or part-time help to care for the baby.

3. **Overall Main Idea of the Selection:** In one sentence, tell what the authors want readers to understand about how infants affect a marriage. (Be sure to include the words "infant," "marriage," and "parenthood" in your overall main idea sentence.)

   With the birth of their first *infant*, couples experience both problems in their *marriage* and joys, and there are several factors that affect their transition to *parenthood*.

Internet Resources

Read More about This Topic on the World Wide Web

Directions: For further information about the topic of the selection, visit these websites:

www.parenting.org
This website is a service of Girls and Boys Town. It features a variety of articles and FAQs related to parenting.

www.ebabybiz.com/baby/index.htm
This website, sponsored by eBabyBiz, contains links to sites about baby care, parenting, and money-saving tips.

www.urbanext.uiuc.edu/baby
The University of Illinois Extension sponsors this website. It contains information about caring for a new baby.

You can also use your favorite search engine such as Google, Yahoo!, or AltaVista (www.google.com, www.yahoo.com, www.altavista.com) to discover more about this topic. To locate additional information, type in combinations of keywords such as:

new parents

or

parenting infants

Keep in mind that whenever you go to *any* website, it is a good idea to evaluate the website and the information it contains. Ask yourself questions such as:

"Who sponsors this website?"
"Is the information contained in this website up-to-date?"
"What type of information is presented?"
"Is the information objective and complete?"
"How easy is it to use the features of this website?"

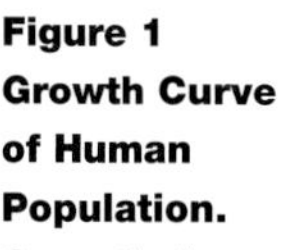

SELECTION 9-2 **Biology**

PLANET UNDER STRESS: CURBING POPULATION GROWTH

From *The Living World: Basic Concepts*
By George B. Johnson

How many people do you think inhabit this planet? A million? A billion? A trillion? In 2009 it was estimated that the global population was more than 6.7 billion! If we were to solve the world's environmental problems caused by pollution, the greenhouse effect, waste disposal, and the loss of biodiversity, we would merely buy time to address the planet's fundamental problem: There are getting to be too many of us.

The rapidly growing human population is at the core of many environmental issues. This selection from a biology textbook presents an overview of the world's population growth and then focuses on solutions—on what can be done to prevent the severe problems that will result from unrestrained population growth. It contains numerous facts about the world's population and invites readers to draw logical conclusions based on the facts that are presented. After reading the selection, you can make some inferences about what must be done to reduce the stress on our planet. What can be done to curb, or restrain, population growth?

1 Humans first reached North America at least 12,000 to 13,000 years ago, crossing the narrow straits between Siberia and Alaska and moving swiftly to the southern tip of South America. By 10,000 years ago, when the continental ice sheets withdrew and agriculture first developed, about 5 million people lived on earth, distributed over all the continents except Antarctica. With the new and much more dependable sources of food that became available through agriculture, the human population began to grow more rapidly. By the time of Christ, 2,000 years ago, an estimated 130 million people lived on earth. By the year 1650, the world's population reached 500 million.

2 The human population has grown explosively for the last 300 years. (See Figure 1.) The average human **birthrate** has

Annotation Practice Exercises

Directions: For each exercise below, read critically to answer the question.

Figure 1 Growth Curve of Human Population. Currently, there are over 6 billion people on Earth.

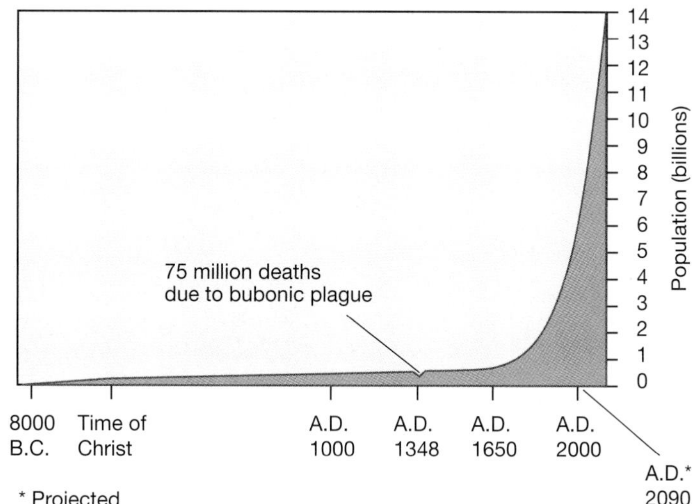

stabilized at about 22 births per year per 1,000 people worldwide. However, with the spread of better sanitation and improved medical techniques, the **death rate** has fallen steadily, to its present level of 9 per 1,000 per year. The difference between birth and death rates amounts to a population **growth rate** of 1.3% per year, which seems like a small number, but it is not, given the large size of the world's population.

3 The world population reached 6.3 billion people in 2003, and the annual increase now amounts to about 80 million people, which leads to a doubling of the world population in about 53 years. Put another way, more than 216,000 people are added to the world population each day, or more than 150 people every minute. At this rate the world's population will continue to grow well over 6.3 billion, and perhaps stabilize at a figure between 8.5 billion and 20 billion, creating a tortuous situation for humanity. Such growth cannot continue, because our world cannot support it. Just as a cancer cannot grow unabated in your body without eventually killing you, so humanity cannot continue to grow unchecked in the biosphere without killing it.

4 One of the most alarming trends taking place in developing countries is the massive movement to urban centers. For example, Mexico City, one of the largest cities in the world, is plagued by smog, traffic, inadequate waste disposal, and other problems; it has a population of about 26 million people. (See Figure 2.) The prospects of supplying adequate food, water, and sanitation to this city's people are almost unimaginable.

5 In view of the limited resources available to the human population, and the need to learn how to manage those resources well, the first and most necessary step toward global prosperity is to stabilize the human population. One of the surest signs of the pressure being placed on the environment is human use of about 40% of the total food-producing productivity of land. Given that statistic, a doubling of the human population in 53 years poses extraordinarily severe problems. The facts virtually demand that we restrain population growth. If and when technology is developed that would allow greater numbers of people to inhabit the earth in a stable condition, the human population can be increased to whatever level might be appropriate.

6 A key element in the world's population growth is its uneven distribution among countries. Of the billion people added to the world's population in the 1990s, 80% to 90% live in developing

✓ **Teaching Tips**

- In 2009 the U.S. population was more than 306 million.
- On a map, point out the Bering Strait between Siberia and Alaska. There was a land bridge there 12,000 to 13,000 years ago that connected the continents. Point out or have students find on a map the places referred to in the selection. Appendix 3 contains maps.
- Our biosphere is all the world's plants, animals, and microorganisms that occur in tropical forests, grasslands, deserts, and marine and freshwater habitats.

Practice Exercise

Does paragraph 3 contain *facts, opinions,* or *both*?

both facts and opinions

Practice Exercise

Does paragraph 5 contain *facts, opinions,* or *both*?

both facts and opinions

Figure 2
The World's Population Is Centered In Mega-Cities.
Mexico City, one of the world's largest cities, has about 26 million inhabitants.

countries and of that number, about 60% of the people in the world live in countries that are at least partly tropical or subtropical. An additional 20% live in China. The remaining 20% live in the so-called developed, or industrialized, countries: Europe, Russia, Japan, the United States, Canada, Australia, and New Zealand. Whereas the populations of the developed countries are growing at an annual rate of only about 0.1%, those of the less developed countries are growing at an annual rate estimated to be about 1.9%.

7 Most countries are devoting considerable attention to slowing the growth rate of their populations, and there are genuine signs of progress. If it continues, the United Nations estimates that the world's population may stabilize by 2100 at a level of 13 to 15 billion people, nearly three times the number living today. No one knows whether the world can support so many people indefinitely. Finding a way to do so is the greatest task facing humanity. The quality of life that will be available for your children and grandchildren in the next century will depend to a large extent on our success.

Population Growth Rate Has Been Declining

8 The world population growth rate has been declining, from a high of 2.0% in the period 1965–1970 to 1.3% in 2003. Nonetheless, because of the larger population, this amounts to an increase of 80 million people per year to the world population, compared to 53 million per year in the 1960s.

9 The United Nations attributes this decline in the population growth rate to family planning efforts and the increased economic power and social status of women. Although the United Nations applauds the United States for leading the world in funding family planning programs abroad, some oppose spending money on international family planning. The opposition states that money is better spent on improving education and the economy in other countries, leading to an increased awareness and lowered fertility rates. The United Nations certainly supports the improvement of education programs in developing countries, but, interestingly, it has reported increased education levels following a decrease in family size as a result of family planning.

10 Slowing population growth will help sustain the world's resources, but per capita consumption is also important. Even though the vast majority of the world's population is in developing countries, the vast majority of the resource consumption occurs in the developed world. The wealthiest 20% of the world's population accounts for 80% of the world's consumption of resources, whereas the poorest 20% is responsible for only 1.3% of consumption. The developed world must lessen the impact each of us makes.

11 It is easy to become discouraged when considering the world's environmental problems, such as pollution, wasting resources, and population growth, but do not lose track of the fact that each problem is solvable. A polluted lake can be cleaned; a dirty smokestack can be altered to remove noxious gas; waste of key resources can be stopped; population growth can be restrained. What is required is a clear understanding of the problem and a commitment to doing something about it.

Practice Exercise

Based on the information in paragraph 6, what *inference* can you make about restraining population growth in less developed countries?

Because 80% to 90% of the world's population lives in less developed countries and their annual growth rate is so high, restraining population growth in these countries is critical.

Practice Exercise

Does paragraph 7 contain *facts, opinions,* or *both*?

both facts and opinions

Practice Exercise

Does paragraph 8 contain *facts, opinions,* or *both*?

facts

Practice Exercise

Based on the information in paragraph 9, what *inference* can you make about why a decrease in family size would result in increased education levels?

Parents who have fewer children (as a result of family planning) are more likely to have resources to pay for their children's education.

Source: Adapted from George B. Johnson, *The Living World. Basic Concepts,* 4th ed., pp. 753, 764–65, 770. Copyright © 2006 by The McGraw-Hill Companies, Inc. Reprinted by permission of The McGraw-Hill Companies, Inc.

SELECTION 9-2
Biology
(continued)

Comprehension and Vocabulary Quiz

This quiz has four parts. Your instructor may assign some or all of them.

Comprehension

Directions: Items 1–5 test your comprehension (understanding) of the material in this selection. These questions are much like those that a content-area instructor (such as a biology professor) would expect you to know after reading and studying this selection. For each comprehension question below, use information from the selection to determine the correct answer. Refer to the selection as you answer the questions. Write your answers in the spaces provided.

¶3 b **1.** The current world population:
- *a.* is about 80 million people.
- *b.* will double in about 53 years.
- *c.* is declining because of the decline in the growth rate.
- *d.* increases by more than 150 people every day.

¶4 b **2.** An alarming and troublesome trend taking place in developing countries is the:
- *a.* decline in the growth rate.
- *b.* increased movement of people from rural areas to urban centers.
- *c.* stabilization of the birth rate.
- *d.* inadequate waste disposal and increases in smog and traffic.

¶9 d **3.** According to the information in the selection, the decline in the worldwide growth rate is caused by:
- *a.* family planning efforts.
- *b.* the increased social status of women.
- *c.* women's increased economic power.
- *d.* all of the above

¶10 d **4.** How much of the total world's resources does the wealthiest 20% of the world population consume?
- *a.* 2%
- *b.* 20%
- *c.* 50%
- *d.* 80%

¶11 d **5.** The author states that the problem of restraining population growth is:
- *a.* dependent on the development of technology for food production.
- *b.* the responsibility of the developing countries.
- *c.* the responsibility of the developed, or industrialized, countries.
- *d.* solvable.

✓ **Teaching Tip**

When you go over the answers, show students where the answer to each comprehension question appears in the selection. Or you may want to have students work in pairs to identify where each answer appears.

Vocabulary in Context

Directions: Items 6–10 test your ability to determine the meaning of the word by using context clues. *Context clues* are words in a sentence that allow the reader to deduce (reason out) the meaning of an unfamiliar word in that sentence. Context clues also enable the reader to determine which meaning the author intends when a word has more than one meaning. For each vocabulary item below, a sentence from the selection containing an important word (*italicized, like this*) is quoted first. Next, there is an additional sentence using the word in the same sense and providing another context clue. Use the context clues from *both* sentences to deduce the meaning of the italicized word. *Be sure the answer you choose makes sense in both sentences.* If you need to use a dictionary to confirm your answer choice, remember that the meaning you select must still fit the context of *both* sentences. Write your answers in the spaces provided.

Pronunciation Key: ă **pat** ā **pay** âr **care** ä **father** ĕ **pet** ē **be** ĭ **pit**
ī **tie** îr **pier** ŏ **pot** ō **toe** ô **paw** oi **noise** ou **out** o͝o **took**
o͞o **boot** ŭ **cut** yo͞o **abuse** ûr **urge** th **thin** *th* **this** hw **which**
zh **vision** ə **about** *Stress mark:* ′

¶3 b **6.** At this rate the world's population will continue to grow well over 6.3 billion, and perhaps stabilize at a figure between 8.5 billion and 20 billion, creating a *tortuous* situation for humanity.

The movie plot was so complicated and *tortuous* that we couldn't make sense of it.

tortuous (tôr′ cho͞o əs) means:

a. very painful

b. extremely complex

c. laborious

d. difficult to comprehend

¶3 a **7.** Just as a cancer cannot grow *unabated* in your body without eventually killing you, so humanity cannot continue to grow unchecked in the biosphere without killing it.

Jasmine's *unabated* use of credit cards eventually forced her to file for bankruptcy.

unabated (ŭn ə bā′ tĭd) means:

a. uncontrolled

b. unseen

c. unaided

d. unplanned

¶4 b **8.** For example, Mexico City, one of the largest cities in the world, is *plagued* by smog, traffic, inadequate waste disposal, and other problems; it has a population of about 26 million people.

We are often *plagued* by telemarketers who call during the dinner hour.

plagued (plāgd) means:

a. interrupted

b. pestered

c. planned

d. covered

¶5 ______ **9.** The facts virtually demand that we *restrain* population growth.

To *restrain* interruptions, choose a quiet place and turn off your cell phone.

restrain (rĭ strān′) means:

a. prevent; avoid

b. maximize; enlarge

c. maintain; preserve

d. restrict; limit

¶9 ______ **10.** The United Nations *attributes* this decline in the population growth rate to family planning efforts and the increased economic power and social status of women.

James *attributes* his love for sports to his father and his older brother, both of whom were professional athletes.

attributes (ə trĭb′ yo͞ots) means:

a. regards as the cause of

b. shows an interest in

c. takes advantage of

d. understands the meaning of

Word Structure

Directions: Items 11–15 below test your ability to use word-structure clues to help determine a word's meaning. *Word-structure clues* consist of roots, prefixes, and suffixes. In these exercises, you will learn the meaning of a word part (a root) and use it to determine the meaning of several other words that have the same word part. If you need to use a dictionary to confirm your answer choice, do so. Write your answers in the spaces provided.

In paragraph 3 of the selection, you encountered the word **tortuous.** This word contains the Latin root ***tort,*** which means "to twist" or "to bend." A *tortuous* mountain road is one that winds, one with many twists and turns. A *tortuous* situation is one that is complex and intricate. Use the meaning of the root ***tort*** and the list of prefixes on pages 68–69 to help you determine the meaning of each of the following words that contain the same root. Write your answers in the spaces provided.

______ **11.** If someone **distorts** the truth, that person:

a. states the facts.

b. twists the facts.

c. distinguishes fact from opinion.

d. presents a personal opinion.

c 12. Clowns and other performers who are **contortionists:**

a. make audiences laugh.

b. wear bright, ridiculous costumes and wigs.

c. twist and bend their bodies in extreme ways.

d. paint on funny, exaggerated faces.

d 13. The Arctic explorers endured *torturous* subzero temperatures, near starvation, and exhaustion. **Torturous** means:

a. slow and time-consuming.

b. requiring extensive, careful planning.

c. done at night.

d. inflicting severe physical and mental anguish or pain.

c 14. This is an example of a famous *retort* given by British Prime Minister Winston Churchill to Lady Astor, a woman who disliked him, and whom he disliked. She said, "If I were married to you, I'd serve you poison tea." His *retort* was, "Madam, if I were married to you, I'd drink it." A **retort** is a:

a. funny comment spoken in public intended to amuse others.

b. cruel reply to a kind comment.

c. clever, quick reply that turns the first speaker's words to his or her disadvantage.

d. thoughtful comment intended to reduce the tension in a social situation.

c 15. Ticket scalpers often make buyers pay four or five times the original amount for tickets, and many people view this as *extortion.* **Extortion** means:

a. a giveaway.

b. an economical service.

c. charging an excessive amount.

d. a sale.

✓ **Teaching Tip**

Point out that *tortuous* and *torturous* come from the same Latin root that means "to twist," but their meanings are very different. *Tortuous* means "twisting" or "winding" (a *tortuous* road) and, by extension, "complex" or "devious" (a *tortuous* plot or legal situation). *Torturous* literally means "full of torture, and refers primarily to torture and the pain associated with it (the *torturous* experience of dying of thirst in the desert).

Reading Skills Application

Directions: Items 16–20 test your ability to *apply* certain reading skills to information in this selection. These types of questions provide valuable practice for all students, especially those who must take standardized reading tests and state-mandated basic skills tests. Write your answers in the spaces provided.

✓ **Teaching Tip**

We suggest that rather than include this section as part of the quiz grade, you use it to give students practice with the skills they have studied and as a helpful preview of upcoming skills. It makes an excellent collaborative activity. All students will find this practice helpful, especially those who must take course exit tests, standardized reading tests, or state-mandated basic skills tests.

all ¶s overall main ideas (Chapters 4 & 5) ___b___

16. Which of the following represents the overall main idea of the selection?

a. It is easy to become discouraged when considering the world's environmental problems.

b. Due to the large human population and the high growth rate in developing countries, serious efforts must be made to restrain population growth because our world cannot support it.

c. A key element in the world's population growth is the 1.9% annual growth rate in developing countries.

d. The human population has grown explosively for the last 300 years, but the growth rate has been declining during the last 35 years due to family planning.

¶5 distinguishing opinions from facts (Chapter 8) ___c___

17. Which of the following represents an opinion rather than a fact?

a. The world population reached 6.3 billion people in 2003.

b. The world population growth rate has declined in the last 35 years.

c. The facts virtually demand that we restrain population growth.

d. Humans now use about 40% of the total food-producing productivity on land.

¶7 supporting details (Chapter 6) ___c___

18. According to information in the selection, which of the following is an accurate statement?

a. By 1650, the world's population had reached 500 billion.

b. The world's population reached 6.3 million people in 2003 and the annual increase now amounts to about 8 million people.

c. The United Nations estimates that the world's population may stabilize by 2010 at a level of 13 to 15 billion people, nearly three times the number living today.

d. Humans first reached North America at least 12,000 years ago, crossing the narrow straits between Siberia and South America.

Conclusion based on figure 1 interpreting graphic material (Chapter 10) ___d___

19. Based on the information presented in Figure 1, which of the following represents a logical conclusion?

a. Currently, there are more than 7 billion people on earth.

b. In 1348 there were 75 million deaths due to bubonic plague.

c. In 2090 there will be approximately 14 billion people on earth.

d. Human population has increased sharply over the past 300 years.

¶6 authors' writing patterns (Chapter 7) ___b___

20. The information in paragraph 6 of the selection is organized by which of the following patterns?

a. cause-effect

b. comparison-contrast

c. sequence

d. list

✓ **Teaching Tip**

When you go over the answers, show students where the answer to each comprehension question appears in the selection. Or you may want to have students work in pairs to identify where each answer appears.

SELECTION 9-2
Biology
(continued)

Collaboration Option

Writing and Collaborating to Enhance Your Understanding

Option for collaboration: Your instructor may direct you to work with other students or, in other words, to work *collaboratively.* In that case, you should form groups of three or four students as directed by your instructor and work together to complete the exercises. After your group discusses each item and agrees on the answer, have a group member record it. Every member of your group should be able to explain all of your group's answers.

1. **Reacting to What You Have Read:** The author presents many facts about global population growth in this selection. List four factual statements about the world's population that were especially surprising to you.

   1. (Answers will vary.)

   2. ___

   3. ___

   4. ___

2. **Comprehending the Selection Further:** The author explains that although the world's population is increasing, the global growth *rate* is declining. List four causes for the decline in the global growth rate suggested by the author.

   1. family planning efforts
   2. increased economic power of women
   3. increased social status of women
   4. improvement of education programs

3. **Overall Main Idea of the Selection:** In one sentence, tell what the authors want readers to understand about the recent changes in immigration to the United States. (Be sure to include the words "human population" and "growth rate" in your overall main idea sentence.)

   Due to the large human population and the high growth rate in developing countries, serious efforts must be made to restrain population growth rates because our world cannot support it.

   OR

   The population growth rate must be curbed because our planet cannot support it.

Read More about This Topic on the World Wide Web

Directions: For further information about the topic of the selection, visit these websites:

http://en.wikipedia.org/wiki/World population
This Wikipedia entry discusses world population growth. It presents information about the population of each continent and includes a map showing worldwide population density.

www.internetworldstats.com/stats8.htm
This site presents data about the current world population and includes a list of the top ten countries with the highest population.

www.census.gov/main/www/popclock.html
This site, sponsored by the U.S. Census Bureau, gives daily estimates of United States and world population. Click on *U.S. POPClock* or *World POPClock* links.

You can also use your favorite search engine such as Google, Yahoo!, or AltaVista (www.google.com, www.yahoo.com, www.altavista.com) to discover more about this topic. To locate additional information, type in combinations of keywords such as:

global population

or

global birthrate

or

population control

Keep in mind that whenever you go to *any* website, it is a good idea to evaluate the website and the information it contains. Ask yourself questions such as:

"Who sponsors this website?"
"Is the information contained in this website up-to-date?"
"What type of information is presented?"
"Is the information objective and complete?"
"How easy is it to use the features of this website?"

SELECTION **9-3**

Human Development

IS IT REALLY WORTH IT? HOW DUAL-EARNER COUPLES COPE

From *Human Development*

By Diane Papalia and Sally Olds

Married couples who work can experience tremendous challenges. In 2008, there were more than 25 million married couples in the United States with children under 18. In more than 65 percent of these households, both parents worked. A study on stress and depression among married couples found that in most marriages women do 70 percent of the housework. The happiest couples, however, were those in which the partners shared the housework equally. This selection from a human development textbook examines both the benefits and the difficulties of a two-income marriage.

---

1 The growing number of marriages in which both husband and wife are gainfully employed presents both opportunities and challenges. A second income raises some families from poverty to middle-income status and makes others affluent. It makes women more independent and gives them a greater share of economic power, and it reduces the pressure on men to be providers; 47 percent of working wives contribute half or more of family income. Less tangible benefits may include a more equal relationship between husband and wife, better health for both, greater self-esteem for the woman, and a closer relationship between a father and his children.

2 However, this way of life also creates stress. Working couples face extra demands on time and energy, conflicts between work and family, possible rivalry between spouses, and anxiety and guilt about meeting children's needs. Each role makes greater or lesser demands at different times, and partners have to decide which should take priority when. The family is most demanding, especially for women, when there are young children. Careers are especially demanding when a worker is getting established or being promoted. Both kinds of demands frequently occur in young adulthood.

3 Men and women tend to be stressed by different aspects of the work-family situation. Among 314 spouses with relatively high income and education, husbands were more likely to suffer from overload (perhaps because they had not been socialized to deal with domestic as well as occupational responsibilities), whereas women were more likely to feel the strain of conflicting role expectations—for example, the need to be aggressive and competitive at work but compassionate and nurturing at home. Temporary withdrawal from social interaction after a busy workday helped settle men down and softened the effects of overload. "Talking things over" seemed to worsen their stress, perhaps because they were uncomfortable expressing feelings or because the outcome of such discussions might be even greater demands. For both men and women, the most successful way of coping was rethinking the way they looked at the situation.

Annotation Practice Exercises

Directions: For each exercise below, read critically to answer the questions.

4 The effects of a dual-earner lifestyle may depend largely on how husband and wife view their relationship. Dual-income couples fall into three patterns: *conventional, modern,* and *role sharing.* In a *conventional* marriage, both partners consider household chores and child care "women's work." The husband may "help," but his career comes first; he earns more than his wife and sees it as "her choice" to add outside employment to her primary domestic role. In *modern* couples, the wife does most of the housework, but the husband shares parenting and wants to be involved with his children. In the *role-sharing* pattern, characteristic of at least one-third of dual-income marriages, both husband and wife are actively involved in household and family responsibilities as well as careers. However, even among such couples, tasks tend to be gender-typed: wives buy the groceries and husbands mow the lawn.

5 In general, the burdens of the dual-earner lifestyle fall most heavily on the woman. While men, on average, earn more and have more powerful positions, women tend to work more hours—20 percent more in industrialized countries and 30 percent more in less developed countries. Women put in a longer "second shift" at home, as well. Although men's participation has been increasing, even husbands in nontraditional marriages still do only one-third of the domestic work. A Swedish study found that working women with three or more children put in 1½ times as many hours as men at home and on the job. A father is most likely to take on child care when his work schedule is different from his wife's.

6 Women's personal activities tend to suffer more than men's, probably due to the disproportionate time they put into domestic work, and in the long run the compromises women make to keep the dual-earner lifestyle afloat may weaken the marriage. An unequal division of work may have contributed to the higher degree of marital distress reported by wives in a study of 300 mostly managerial and professional dual-earner couples. On the other hand, unequal roles are not necessarily seen as inequitable; it may be a *perception* of unfairness that contributes most to marital instability. A national longitudinal survey of 3,284 women in two-income families found greater likelihood of divorce the more hours the woman worked, but only when the wife had a nontraditional view of marriage. Nontraditional wives who work full-time may feel more resentment of their husbands' failure to share equally in household tasks, whereas traditional wives may be more willing to accept additional burdens.

7 What spouses perceive as fair may depend on how much money the wife's earnings contribute, whether she thinks of herself as a co-provider or merely as someone who supplements her husband's income, and what meaning and importance she and her husband place on her work. Whatever the actual division of labor, couples who agree on their assessment of it and who enjoy a harmonious, caring, involved family life are more satisfied than those who don't.

Practice Exercise

Based on the information in paragraph 4, what *inference* could be drawn about a dual-earner marriage in which the husband's view is conventional and the wife's is role sharing?

There is likely to be strife between them.

OR

Their differing views will be a source of stress in their marriage.

Practice Exercise

Does paragraph 6 contain *facts, opinions,* or *both*?

both facts and opinions

8 Family-friendly policies in the workplace can help alleviate the strains experienced by dual-earner families. Parents in a supportive, flexible work environment with family-oriented benefits tend to feel less stress. Such benefits might include more part-time, flex-time, and shared jobs, more at-home work (without loss of fringe benefits), more affordable high-quality child care, and tax credits or other assistance to let new parents postpone returning to work. One encouraging change is the Family and Medical Leave Act of 1993, which requires businesses with 50 or more workers to offer 12 weeks of unpaid leave for the birth or adoption of a child—though this still falls far short of (for example) the 6-month paid leave offered to new parents in Sweden.

Practice Exercise

Based on the information in paragraph 8, what *inference* could be drawn about family-friendly policies in Sweden compared with those in the United States?

U.S. policies are much less family-friendly than Sweden's.

Source: Diane E. Papalia and Sally Olds, *Human Development,* 7th ed., pp. 464–65. Copyright © 1998 by The McGraw-Hili Companies, Inc. Reprinted by permission of The McGraw-Hili Companies, Inc.

SELECTION 9-3 **Human Development** *(continued)*

Comprehension and Vocabulary Quiz

This quiz has four parts. Your instructor may assign some or all of them.

Comprehension

Directions: Items 1–5 test your comprehension (understanding) of the material in this selection. These questions are much like those that a content-area instructor (such as a human development professor) would expect you to know after reading and studying this selection. For each comprehension question below, use information from the selection to determine the correct answer. Refer to the selection as you answer the questions. Write your answers in the spaces provided.

¶1 a **1.** A possible benefit of a two-income marriage is:

a. a more equal relationship between the husband and wife.
b. a lower risk of divorce during the first year of marriage.
c. fewer demands on a husband and wife's time and energy.
d. more time for recreational activities.

¶3 a **2.** When both the husband and wife are employed, the husband's source of stress is most often:

a. feeling overloaded.
b. feeling that he is neglecting his children.
c. dealing with the competition at work.
d. saving enough money for the future.

¶3 c **3.** When both the husband and wife are employed, the wife's source of stress is most often:

a. feeling that she is neglecting her children.
b. feeling overloaded.
c. shifting between acting competative at work and being nurturing at home.
d. saving enough money for the future.

¶4 b **4.** In the *role-sharing* marriage pattern,

a. the husband "helps," but his career comes first.
b. both the husband and wife are actively involved in household and family as well as their careers.
c. the wife does most of the housework, but the husband shares parenting and wants to be involved with his children.
d. the husband does most of the housework, but the wife shares parenting responsibilities and wants to be involved with her children.

¶5 b **5.** In general, the extra burdens of a dual-income lifestyle:

a. often fall most heavily on the husband.
b. often fall most heavily on the wife.
c. are often shared equally by the husband and the wife.
d. often fall most heavily on child care providers and employers.

Vocabulary in Context

Directions: Items 6–10 test your ability to determine the meaning of the word by using context clues. *Context clues* are words in a sentence that allow the reader to deduce (reason out) the meaning of an unfamiliar word in that sentence. Context clues also enable the reader to determine which meaning the author intends when a word has more than one meaning. For each vocabulary item below, a sentence from the selection containing an important word (*italicized, like this*) is quoted first. Next, there is an additional sentence using the word in the same sense and providing another context clue. Use the context clues from *both* sentences to deduce the meaning of the italicized word. *Be sure the answer you choose makes sense in both sentences.* If you need to use a dictionary to confirm your answer choice, remember that the meaning you select must still fit the context of *both* sentences. Write your answers in the spaces provided.

Pronunciation Key: ă **pat** ā **pay** âr **care** ä **father** ĕ **pet** ē **be** ĭ **pit**
ī **tie** îr **pier** ŏ **pot** ō **toe** ô **paw** oi **noise** ou **out** o͝o **took**
o͞o **boot** ŭ **cut** yo͞o **abuse** ûr **urge** th **thin** *th* **this** hw **which**
zh **vision** ə **about** *Stress mark:* ′

¶1 c **6.** The growing number of marriages in which both husband and wife are *gainfully* employed presents both opportunities and challenges.

To keep the prisoners *gainfully* occupied, the prison requires them to work 30 hours a week and allows them to keep a small amount of money that they earn.

gainfully (gān′ fə lē) means:

a. happily and cheerfully
b. continuously; nonstop
c. profitably; providing a gain
d. mindlessly; requiring no thought

¶1 a **7.** A second income raises some families from poverty to middle-income status and makes others *affluent.*

Successful investments in the stock market made the Nguyens *affluent.*

affluent (ăf′ lo͞o ənt) means:

a. wealthy; prosperous
b. well-respected
c. lazy; unwilling to work
d. stingy; unwilling to share

¶3 a **8.** Among 314 spouses with relatively high income and education, husbands were more likely to suffer from overload (perhaps because they had not been socialized to deal with *domestic* as well as occupational responsibilities).

Washing, ironing, and dusting are my least favorite *domestic* chores.

domestic (də mĕs′ tĭc) means:

a. relating to the family or household
b. relating to high pay

c. part-time

d. pertaining to recreation and leisure activities

¶4 ___b___ **9.** In a *conventional* marriage, both partners consider household chores and child care "women's work."

My cousin is very *conventional,* so I am shocked that she got a tattoo.

conventional (kən vĕn′ shə nəl) means:

a. extremely happy

b. traditional; following established standards

c. law-abiding

d. insecure

¶5 ___b___ **10.** While men, on average, earn more and have more powerful positions, women tend to work more hours—20 percent more in *industrialized* countries and 30 percent more in less developed countries.

Establishing U.S. factories and plants in underdeveloped countries can help those nations become more *industrialized.*

industrialized (ĭn dŭs′ trē ə līzd) means:

a. having a strong central government

b. having an economy made up of manufacturing enterprises

c. having profit as the goal

d. internationally respected

Word Structure

Directions: Items 11–15 test your ability to use word-structure clues to help determine a word's meaning. *Word-structure clues* consist of roots, prefixes, and suffixes. In these exercises, you will learn the meaning of a word part (a root) and use it to determine the meaning of several other words that have the same word part. If you need to use a dictionary to confirm your answer choice, do so. Write your answers in the spaces provided.

In paragraph 1 of the selection, you encountered the word **independent.** This word contains the Latin root ***pend,*** which means "to hang." The word *independent* literally means "not *hanging* on to anyone or anything." Use the meaning of ***pend*** and the list of prefixes on pages 68–69 to help you determine the meaning of each of the following words that contain this same root. Write your answers in the spaces provided.

___c___ **11.** In cooperative learning, students are mutually *interdependent* on each other for success. **Interdependent** means each person:

a. operates independently.

b. distrusts the others.

c. depends on the others.

d. checks with the others weekly.

___a___ **12.** A **pendulum** on a grandfather clock consists of the:

a. suspended piece that swings back and forth to regulate the clock.

b. hands that indicate the hour and minutes.

c. chimes that sound at set intervals.
d. mechanism and case of the clock.

b 13. If you invent a new product and the patent is **pending,** it means the patent:
a. has not yet been applied for.
b. has been applied for, but not yet received.
c. has been denied by the patent office.
d. has been issued.

d 14. If you **suspend** a ceiling fan in your den, you:
a. remove it from the ceiling.
b. paint it to match the ceiling.
c. install it above the ceiling.
d. hang it from the ceiling.

b 15. If you give your mother a **pendant** necklace, the necklace is:
a. a strand of pearls.
b. a chain with something that hangs from it.
c. a double chain.
d. an antique.

Reading Skills Application

Directions: Items 16–20 test your ability to *apply* certain reading skills to information in this selection. These types of questions provide valuable practice for all students, especially those who must take standardized reading tests and state-mandated basic skills tests. Write your answers in the spaces provided.

overall main ideas (Chapters 4 & 5)

a 16. Which of the following represents the overall main idea of the selection?
a. The growing number of marriages in which both husband and wife are gainfully employed presents both opportunities and challenges.
b. Dual-earner couples experience more stress than single-earner couples.
c. In general, the burdens of the dual-earner lifestyle fall most heavily on the woman.
d. Family-friendly policies in the workforce can help alleviate the strains experienced by dual-earner families.

¶4 supporting details (Chapter 6)

d 17. According to information in the selection, which of the following is an accurate statement?
a. In all three types of marriages, men actively share in household responsibilities.
b. Neither the men in role-sharing marriages nor the men in modern marriages are particularly involved in household responsibilities.
c. Men in modern marriages and role-sharing marriages have approximately the same level of involvement in household responsibilities.
d. Men in role-sharing marriages share more of the household responsibilities than men in conventional marriages.

¶8 vocabulary in context (Chapter 2) — c

18. As used in paragraph 8 of the selection, *alleviate* means to:

a. encourage to action.

b. change in form.

c. make more bearable.

d. create anew.

conclusion (Chapter 9) — b

19. Based on information in the selection, which of the following could be concluded about the authors' attitude toward the Family and Medical Leave Act of 1993?

a. The Family and Medical Leave Act of 1993 should be repealed.

b. The Family and Medical Leave Act of 1993 is helpful, but more and stronger family-friendly legislation is needed.

c. The Family and Medical Leave Act of 1993 should be modified so that it will apply only to businesses with 100 or more workers.

d. Because the Family and Medical Leave Act of 1993 is so comprehensive, no additional legislation is needed.

author's purpose for writing (Chapter 8) — d

20. The authors' primary purpose in writing this selection is to:

a. describe the three types of marriages and each partner's role in each type.

b. explain why marriage is frustrating for women who are part of a dual-earner couple.

c. tell how the stresses men experience differ from the stresses women experience.

d. explain the opportunities and challenges dual-earner couples face and present ways to reduce some of the strains.

SELECTION **9-3**
Human Development
(continued)

Writing and Collaborating to Enhance Your Understanding

Option for collaboration: Your instructor may direct you to work with other students or, in other words, to work *collaboratively.* In that case, you should form groups of three or four students as directed by your instructor and work together to complete the exercises. After your group discusses each item and agrees on the answer, have a group member record it. Every member of your group should be able to explain all of your group's answers.

Collaboration Option

1. **Reacting to What You Have Read:** The authors describe dual-earner couples as falling into one of three patterns: conventional, modern, or role-sharing. Which one of these patterns do you think will be the most common a decade from now? Why?

(Answers will vary.)

2. **Comprehending the Selection Further:** The authors describe both the opportunities and challenges created when both marriage partners work. In general, do you think the benefits of having a dual income outweigh the challenges and difficulties it creates for the couple? Why do you think this?

(Answers will vary.)

3. **Overall Main Idea of the Selection:** In one sentence, tell what the authors want readers to understand about dual-earner couples. (Be sure to include the phrase "dual-earner couples" in your main idea sentence.)

The number of *dual-earner couples* is growing, and these couples will experience both the benefits and the stresses that result when both partners work.

Read More about This Topic on the World Wide Web

Internet Resources

Directions: For further information about the topic of the selection, visit this website:

archives.cnn.com/2000/CAREER/trends/11/13/dual.earners
This article from CNN's archives is titled "Dual Earners: Double Trouble." The article discusses the findings of a study of dual-earner households conducted by Phyllis Moen, professor of sociology and human development at Cornell University.

You can also use your favorite search engine such as Google, Yahoo!, or AltaVista (www.google.com, www.yahoo.com, www.altavista.com) to discover more about this topic. To locate additional information, type in combinations of keywords such as:

dual earner couples

Keep in mind that whenever you go to *any* website, it is a good idea to evaluate the website and the information it contains. Ask yourself questions such as:

"Who sponsors this website?"
"Is the information contained in this website up-to-date?"
"What type of information is presented?"
"Is the information objective and complete?"
"How easy is it to use the features of this website?"

PART 4

A New World of Studying

Effective and Efficient Study Techniques

CHAPTERS IN PART FOUR

✓ **Related Resources**
See pages IG-11 to IG-15 of the Annotated Instructor's Edition for general suggestions related to the chapters in Part Four.

CHAPTER 10

Studying College Textbooks and Interpreting Visual and Graphic Aids

CHAPTER OBJECTIVES

In this chapter you will learn the answer to these questions:

- What is the three-step process for studying college textbooks?
- What are textbook features?
- How can you interpret visual aids?
- How can you interpret graphic aids?

✓ **Timely Words**

"Reading furnishes the mind only with materials of knowledge. It is thinking that makes what we read ours."
(John Locke)

What Is the Three-Step Process for Studying College Textbooks?

- Step 1: Prepare to Read
  Preview the Material
  Assess Your Prior Knowledge
  Plan Your Reading and Study Time
- Step 2: Ask and Answer Questions to Guide Your Reading
  Ask Questions as You Read
  Answer Questions as You Read
- Step 3: Review by Rehearsing Your Answers

What Are Textbook Features?

- Chapter Introductions and Chapter Objectives
- Chapter Outlines
- Vocabulary Aids and Glossaries
- Boxes
- Chapter Summaries
- Study Questions and Activities
- Other Textbook Features

How Can You Interpret Visual Aids?

- Photographs
- Diagrams
- Maps
- Cartoons

How Can You Interpret Graphic Aids?

- Line graphs
- Pie charts
- Bar graphs
- Flowcharts
- Tables

Other Things to Keep in Mind When Studying Textbook Material:

- You will benefit from examining the features in all of your textbooks at the beginning of the semester.

CREATING CHAPTER REVIEW CARDS

TEST YOUR UNDERSTANDING

Interpreting Graphic Aids

READING

Selection 10-1 *(Student Success)*
"Living with Stress"
from *P.O.W.E.R. Learning: Strategies for Success in College and Life*
by Robert Feldman

WHAT IS THE THREE-STEP PROCESS FOR STUDYING COLLEGE TEXTBOOKS?

KEY TERMS
study-reading process

The three steps of preparing to read, asking and answering questions as you read, and reviewing by rehearsing the answers to your questions.

From the first day of classes, you should read and study your textbooks as if you were preparing for your final exams. If you read and study your textbooks thoroughly the first time, you will not have to start over again and cram when it is time for a test.

As you know, reading your textbooks requires more than casually looking at the pages. Reading and studying take time and effort, but your study time will be more productive if you use a study *process*. An effective **study-reading process** consists of the three steps of preparing to read, asking and answering questions as you read, and reviewing by rehearsing the answers to your questions. The three steps in this process are explained in the next section and summarized in the box on page 563. This study-reading process is similar to the SQ3R study system introduced in Chapter 1 (see page 9).

preparing to read

Previewing the material, assessing your prior knowledge, and planning your reading and studying time.

Step 1: Prepare to Read

The first step of the study-reading process is to prepare to read. Before you begin to read a textbook selection or a chapter, you should spend a few minutes preparing to read. **Preparing to read** involves previewing the material, assessing your prior knowledge, and planning your reading and study time. Let's take a closer look at each of these.

KEY TERM
previewing

Examining reading material before reading it to determine its topic and organization.

Preview the Material

Previewing means to examine reading material before reading it to determine its topic and organization. Previewing gives you a general idea of what a textbook selection will be about, and it allows you to see how the material is organized. This technique is the same as the "survey" step in the SQ3R study system. Previewing not only helps you comprehend what you read, but also improves your concentration, motivation, and interest in what you are about to read.

To preview a section of a textbook or a textbook chapter:

- *First, read the title.* It usually indicates the overall topic.
- *Next, read the introduction.* An introduction (if there is one) usually presents some of the important points to be made in the selection, the organization, or background information that you will need.
- *Read the headings and subheadings of each section.* They tell you the specific topics the author has included, and they provide an outline of how information in the selection or chapter is organized.
- *Read words in special print.* Notice any words that appear in **color,** *italic,* or **bold print.** They are important terms you will be expected to understand and remember.
- *Look at any visuals and graphics,* such as pictures, charts, or diagrams. They provide visual representations of material.

- *Read any questions included in the chapter or the study guide.* They alert you to important information to watch for as you read. The author expects you to be able to answer them when you have finished reading.
- *Finally, read the summary.* A summary presents in brief form many of the most important ideas of the selection or chapter. Like an introduction, it is especially useful. Take advantage of it.

As you preview, you should make predictions: that is, make "educated guesses" about what is in the selection you are about to read. Ask yourself, "What topics does the author seem to be emphasizing?" and "How are the topics organized?"

Assess Your Prior Knowledge

KEY TERM
assessing your prior knowledge
Determining what you already know about a topic.

When you lack background knowledge in a subject—and this is often the case when you are reading college textbook material—you have greater difficulty comprehending the material. **Assessing your prior knowledge** means determining what you already know about a topic. After your preview, take a moment to assess your prior knowledge: How much do you already know about the topic? If the material is largely unfamiliar to you, it is your responsibility to take steps to increase your background knowledge. Try some or all of these strategies:

- Read parts of other, perhaps easier, material on the same subject. These might be other college textbooks or more general study aids, such as an outline of American history or a supplemental book with a title such as *Biology Made Easy*.
- Consult an encyclopedia, a good dictionary, or some other reference book.
- Talk with someone who is knowledgeable about the subject.

These steps require extra effort, but *there are no shortcuts.* Going the extra mile to get necessary background information is part of being a responsible, mature learner and student. As a bonus, you may discover that it is exciting and satisfying to understand new or difficult material through your own efforts. You will also find that when you take increasing responsibility for your own learning, you will feel very good about yourself as a student. (Remember that a *student* is someone who *studies.*)

Plan Your Reading and Study Time

By previewing the material, you can decide whether you can read the entire selection in just one study session or whether you need to study the material in smaller sections over several study sessions.

If you decide that you need more than one study session, divide the assignment into several shorter segments and plan to complete them at times when you know you can concentrate best. For example, a 20-page chapter may be too much for you to read and study effectively all at once. You could divide the assignment into two 10-page segments and read them on two separate days. Or you could divide the assignment into three one-hour study sessions on the same day, perhaps at 1, 5, and 8 P.M. You may find it helpful to paper-clip the smaller sections together or to insert stick-on notes between the sections. In any case, *plan* your study-reading session(s) and follow your plan. Then reward yourself *after* you complete your studying.

Step 2: Ask and Answer Questions to Guide Your Reading

The second step in the study-reading process is guiding your reading by asking and answering questions. To read and study effectively, you need to read and understand *each paragraph or section.* This means you must determine what is important to learn and remember in each section. To put it another way, you need to read for a specific purpose. This will increase your interest and concentration and enable you to monitor (evaluate) your comprehension while you are reading. One of the best ways to learn the material in a reading assignment is to ask and answer questions as you read.

Ask Questions as You Read

Creating one or more questions for each section of a reading assignment can guide you to the important information and help you remember it. When you read to seek answers to questions, you are reading with a specific purpose; in other words, you are reading *selectively and purposefully.*

Turning chapter headings and subheadings into questions is the easiest way to accomplish this. For example, if a section in a history textbook has a heading "The Civil War Ends," you might want to ask, "*Who* won the Civil War?" and "*Why* did it end?" You may also want to ask, "*When and where* did it end?" This technique is the same as the "Question" step in the SQ3R study system.

When a section or paragraph has no heading, it is a good idea to create a question based on what that section or paragraph appears to be about. If you see a term or phrase in **bold print** or *italic,* create a question about it. Create questions about names of people, places, events, and so on. Of course, you will be able to refine your questions later, when you read the material more carefully.

In addition to creating your own questions as you read each section, you may find the author has included questions for you. These may appear at the end of a chapter, at the beginning, throughout a chapter (perhaps in the margins), or in an accompanying study guide. If a textbook chapter contains such questions, read them *before* you read the chapter. Then keep them in mind as you read. When you have finished reading the chapter, you should be able to answer these questions. In fact, you will probably be asked some of these same questions on a test. Chapter questions also enable you to monitor your comprehension. You can tell if you are getting the important information the author and your instructor expect you to know.

Finally, your instructor may give you questions to guide you as you read a chapter. Of course, you should be able to answer these questions by the time you finish reading and studying the chapter.

Answer Questions as You Read

As you read each paragraph or section, look for answers to your questions. Then, *after* you have read that paragraph or section, record the answers by writing them down. An important word of warning: Although you will be answering questions in your head as you read, do not try to write your answers *while* you are reading a section. Switching between reading and writing disrupts your comprehension and greatly slows you down. The time to write your answers is immediately after you *finish* reading a section, not while you are reading it for the first time.

There are several effective ways to record your answers. One is to write the questions and answers on notebook paper. Another is to write them in the margins of your textbook. Some techniques are described in the next chapter. Still another way is to make review cards, like the chapter review cards in this book. In addition, you may want to mark information that answers your questions by highlighting it.

What if you cannot locate or determine the answer to one or more of your questions? In that case, there are several things you can do:

- Read ahead to see if the answer becomes apparent.
- If the question involves an important term you need to know, look the term up in the textbook's glossary or in a dictionary.
- Go back and reread the paragraph.
- Ask a classmate, a tutor, or your instructor.

If you still cannot answer all of your questions after you have read an assignment, note which questions remain unanswered. Put a question mark in the margin, or make a list of the unanswered questions. One way or another, be sure to find the answers.

As you can see, actively seeking answers to questions encourages you to concentrate and focus on *understanding* as you read. Reading for a purpose, that is, to answer specific questions as you read, can help you remember more and ultimately score higher on tests. Often, you will discover that questions on tests are identical to the ones you asked yourself as you studied. When this happens, you will be glad that you took the time to use this technique while you were studying.

Step 3: Review by Rehearsing Your Answers

Experienced college students know that to remember what they read in their textbooks, they need to take certain steps to make this happen. They also know that it is essential to take these steps *immediately* after they finish reading a section or a chapter, while the material is still in short-term memory and fresh in their minds.

Forgetting occurs very rapidly, so you need to rehearse material immediately in order to transfer it into permanent, or long-term, memory. The shocking fact is that unless you take some special action beyond simply reading a textbook assignment, you will forget half of what you read by the time you finish reading it.

One highly effective way to rehearse important points is to *recite* your questions and answers about the material. Simply rereading your answers is not good enough; you must say them aloud until you can do so *without looking at the answers.* It is this simple: If you can't say it (from memory), you don't know it. This technique is the same as the "Recite" step in the SQ3R study system.

Another highly effective way to rehearse important points in a chapter is to *write them from memory.* When you give yourself a "practice test" in this way, you discover what you know and what you still need to learn. And, of course, you are transferring the material into long-term memory. When you check your answers, make corrections and add any information needed to make your answers complete. This technique is the same as the "Review" step in the SQ3R study system.

Take time to review and rehearse immediately after you finish reading a chapter. This not only helps you remember what you learned, but also gives you a feeling of accomplishment that will encourage you to continue learning.

If you use the three-step process just outlined for studying college textbooks, you will learn more from your textbook reading assignments. It also provides the foundation for effective test preparation. Preparing for a test *begins* with reading textbook material effectively. Specific techniques for preparing for tests are discussed in Chapter 11. They include annotating textbooks by writing marginal study notes, outlining, mapping, and writing summaries.

SUMMARY OF THE THREE-STEP PROCESS FOR READING AND STUDYING COLLEGE TEXTBOOKS

Step 1: Prepare to Read

Preview the selection to see what it contains and how it is organized:

- Read the title.
- Read the introduction.
- Read headings and subheadings in each section.
- Read words in italics or bold print.
- Look over illustrations, charts, and diagrams.
- Read any questions that are included in the chapter or a study guide.
- Read the summary.

Ask yourself: "What topics does the author seem to be emphasizing?" and "How are the topics organized?" *Assess your prior knowledge.* Ask yourself: "What do I already know about the topic?" and "How familiar am I with this topic?" *Plan your reading and study time.* Ask yourself: "How can I best allot my time for this assignment?" and "Do I need to divide the assignment into smaller units?"

Step 2: Ask and Answer Questions as You Read

Guide your reading by asking and answering questions:

- Turn chapter headings into questions.
- Create questions based on what the paragraphs or sections appear to be about.
- If the author has included questions, answer them.
- Use questions in a study guide, if there is one.
- Use questions given out by the instructor.

Read actively:

- Look for answers to your questions.

Record the answers to your questions:

- Write the answers on notebook paper or in the margins of the textbook.
- Create notes for the material.
- Emphasize the answers by highlighting or underlining them.

Step 3: Review by Rehearsing the Answers to Your Questions

Review the material and transfer it into long-term memory by rehearsing:

- Recite (say aloud) the answers to your questions.
- Try to write the important points from memory.

WHAT ARE TEXTBOOK FEATURES?

KEY TERM
textbook feature

Any device an author uses to emphasize important material or to show how it is organized. Textbook features are also called *learning aids.*

A **textbook feature** is any device an author uses to emphasize important material or to show how it is organized. Another term for a textbook feature is a *learning aid.*

There are many kinds of textbook features, and in this section you will look at some of the most important ones. Though no single college textbook is likely to include all of these features, your textbooks will have many of them.

Keep in mind that different authors may call the same feature by different names. For example, what one author may call a *Chapter Summary,* another may call *Chapter Review, Chapter Highlights, Key Points, Points to Remember, A Look Back,* or *Summing Up.*

Take advantage of textbook features as you study: They are there to help you locate, select, and organize the material you must learn.

The following sections will introduce you to common textbook features. There is a description of each, the various names by which it might be called, and an explanation of how to use it to full advantage. In addition, you will see examples of each.

Chapter Introductions and Chapter Objectives

KEY TERM
chapter introduction

Textbook feature at the beginning of a chapter that describes the overall purpose and major topics.

A **chapter introduction** is a textbook feature at the beginning of a chapter that describes the overall purpose and major topics of the chapter. It may also describe their sequence or how the chapter is linked to preceding chapters. Or it may set the scene by giving, for instance, a case study or an anecdote. A chapter introduction may be called *Introduction* (such as the one from a business textbook in the example on page 565), or it may be indicated by special type or a large ornamental letter at the beginning of the first word. Read chapter introductions carefully; they are a helpful guide to what lies ahead.

EXAMPLE OF A CHAPTER INTRODUCTION

INTRODUCTION

Every day you read in the newspaper or hear news reports about businesses that are experiencing legal problems because they have violated a law or regulation, failed to honor a contract, acted carelessly, or caused potential damage to a competitor. For example, recent headlines reveal that Microsoft, Visa, and Mastercard have been sued by the government for limiting customer choice and inhibiting competition. Pepsico has sued archrival Coca-Cola, accusing its competitor of unfairly controlling beverages served by restaurants. Most highly respected corporations have a number of legal issues to resolve on a continuous basis. Many of these issues could be avoided if managers had more knowledge of business law and the regulatory environment.

Business law refers to the rules and regulations that govern the conduct of business. Problems in this area come from the failure to keep promises, misunderstandings, disagreements about expectations, or, in some cases, attempts to take advantage of others. The regulatory environment offers a framework and enforcement system in order to provide a fair playing field for all businesses. The regulatory environment is created based on inputs from competitors, customers, employees, special interest groups, and the public's elected representatives. Lobbying by pressure groups who try to influence legislation often shapes the legal and regulatory environment. For example, insurance companies spent $60 million lobbying against a proposed Patient's Bill of Rights for managed health care. This was four times the $14 million-plus that was spent by medical organizations, trial lawyers, unions, and consumer groups pressing for the bill's passage.

An examination of business law and the regulatory environment will not only help you appreciate this important area of the business environment, but also make you aware of your rights in the event that you are wronged in the course of doing business. In this chapter, we will look at the various sources of business law and discuss how disputes may be resolved. Next, we review the administrative agencies that enforce the regulatory environment. We will also examine a number of aspects of the law that affect business, including sales, contracts, agents, property, bankruptcy, and competition. Next, we provide a brief overview of regulatory issues related to the Internet. Finally, we examine the legal pressure for responsible business conduct and organizational compliance programs.

Source: O. C. Ferrell and Geoffrey Hirt, *Business: A Changing World,* 3rd ed. Copyright © 2000 by The McGraw-Hill Companies, Inc. Reprinted by permission of The McGraw-Hill Companies, Inc.

KEY TERMS

chapter objectives

Textbook feature at the beginning of a chapter telling you what you should know or be able to do after studying the chapter.

chapter outline

A list of chapter topics or headings in their order of appearance in the chapter.

Chapter objectives at the beginning of a chapter tell you what you should know or be able to do after studying the chapter. They may also be called *Preview Questions, What You'll Learn, Goals,* and so on. In the example from a public speaking text on page 566, the author states directly, "After studying this chapter, you should be able to . . ." and he has worded the objectives as if they were items on a test. Note the directions such as *describe, define,* and *explain.*

Chapter Outlines

A **chapter outline** is a list of chapter topics or headings in their order of appearance in the chapter. It provides a preliminary overview that helps you see in advance the content and organization of the entire chapter. Reading a chapter without first seeing its outline is like trying to solve a jigsaw puzzle without looking at the picture on the box: It can be done, but it takes longer and is much more difficult.

Chapter outlines may be called by names such as *Chapter Contents, Chapter Topics, Preview, Overview,* or *In This Chapter,* or may have no title at all. They may or may not actually be set up in outline style, and they may be general or detailed.

Chapter outlines in *New Worlds,* for instance, appear at the beginning of each chapter and include headings and subheadings, as well as titles of reading selections. The example from a public speaking text shown below is also in outline style. Notice that next to it, in the second column, is the list of chapter objectives.

EXAMPLE OF CHAPTER OBJECTIVES AND OUTLINE

4

Reaching the Audience

Outline

The Audience-Centered Speaker

Analyzing and Adapting

Getting Information about the Audience
Interviews
Surveys

Audience Diversity
International Listeners
America's Diverse Cultures
Listeners with Disabilities
Gender
Age
Educational Background
Occupation
Religious Affiliation
Economic and Social Status

Audience Knowledge
Analyzing Audience Knowledge
Adapting to Different Levels of Knowledge

Audience Psychology
Interest Level
Attitudes
Needs and Desires

The Occasion
Time Limit
Purpose of the Occasion
Other Events on the Program
Audience Size

Adapting during the Speech

Objectives

After studying this chapter, you should be able to:

1. Describe the difference between a speaker who is audience-centered and one who is not.
2. Define audience analysis and audience adaptation and state why they are important.
3. Use interviews and surveys to gain information about an audience in advance.
4. Explain how speakers can be responsive to diverse audiences.
5. Describe how speakers can adapt to varying levels of audience knowledge, attitudes, interest, and needs and desires.
6. Explain how speakers should adapt to the occasion (time limit, purpose, and size of audience).
7. Describe how a speaker can adapt to the audience during a speech.

Source: Hamilton Gregory, *Public Speaking for College and Career,* 7th ed., p. 65. Copyright © 2005 by The McGraw-Hill Companies, Inc. Reprinted by permission of The McGraw-Hill Companies, Inc.

Vocabulary Aids and Glossaries

KEY TERM
vocabulary aids

Textbook devices that identify important terms and definitions.

Among the most common and helpful textbook features are **vocabulary aids,** devices that identify important terms and definitions. Authors emphasize vocabulary in a variety of ways. Important terms may be set in **boldface,** *italic,* or **color.** They may also be printed in the margins, such as *Key Terms* in *New Worlds* (one of which appears here). There may be a list of terms, perhaps with page numbers, at the end of a chapter (like the example shown below) or after reading a section. These lists can also appear at the beginning of a chapter or a reading. They may be called *Key Terms, Basic Terms, Terms to Know, Vocabulary, Terms to Remember,* and so forth.

EXAMPLE OF END-OF-CHAPTER LIST OF TERMS

KEY TERMS

success (p. 4)	conscious mind (p. 19)	self-presentation (p. 31)
self-direction (p. 7)	subconscious mind (p. 19)	identity (p. 31)
role model (p. 10)	cognition (p. 21)	individual identity (p. 33)
happiness (p. 13)	emotion (p. 22)	relational identity (p. 33)
psychology (p. 17)	self (p. 24)	collective identity (p. 33)
behavior (p. 17)	self-image (p. 24)	culture (p. 34)
nervous system (p. 19)	social role (p. 31)	gender role (p. 38)

Source: Dennis Waitley, *Psychology of Success,* 4th ed., p. 41. Copyright © 2004 by The McGraw-Hill Companies, Inc. Reprinted by permission of The McGraw-Hill Companies, Inc.

KEY TERM
glossary

A list of important terms and definitions from the entire textbook that is located near the end of a textbook.

A list of important terms and definitions from the entire textbook may appear near the end of the book in a **glossary.** A glossary is a minidictionary for the book. (Shown on page 568 as an example is the first page of the glossary of a health textbook.) Pay attention to vocabulary aids: Instructors expect you to know important terms, and they usually include them on tests.

EXAMPLE OF A GLOSSARY

glossary

A

abortion induced premature termination of a pregnancy.

absorption the passage of nutrients or alcohol through the walls of the stomach or intestinal tract into the bloodstream.

abuse any use of a legal or illegal drug in a way that is detrimental to health or well-being.

acquired immunity (AI) the major component of the immune system; forms antibodies and specialized blood cells capable of destroying pathogens.

acupuncture the insertion of fine needles into the body to alter electroenergy fields and treat disease.

acute has a sudden onset and a prompt resolution.

acute alcohol intoxication a potentially fatal elevation of BAC, often resulting from heavy, rapid consumption of alcohol.

acute rhinitis the common cold; the sudden onset of nasal inflammation.

adaptive thermogenesis the physiological response of the body to adjust its metabolic rate to the presence of food.

addiction compulsive, uncontrollable dependence on a substance, habit, or practice to such a degree that cessation causes severe emotional or physiological reactions.

additive effect the combined (but not exaggerated) effect produced by the concurrent use of two or more drugs.

adipose tissue tissue made up of fibrous strands around which specialized cells designed to store liquefied fat are arranged.

aerobic energy production the body's primary means of energy production, used when the respiratory and circulatory systems can process and transport sufficient oxygen to muscle cells to convert fuel energy.

agent the causal pathogen of a particular disease.

agoraphobia a fear of being in situations from which there is no escape or where help would be unavailable should an emergency arise; often associated with panic disorder.

air pollution refers to a wide variety of substances found in the atmosphere that can have adverse effects on human health, crop productivity, and natural communities.

air toxics a class of 188 toxic air pollutants identified by the U.S. Environmental Protection Agency as known or suspected causes of cancer or other serious health effects, such as reduced fertility, birth defects, or adverse environmental effects.

alarm stage the first stage of the stress response involving physiological, involuntary changes which are controlled by the hormonal and nervous system; the fight or flight response is activated in this stage.

alcoholism a primary, chronic disease with genetic, psychosocial, and environmental factors influencing its development and manifestations.

allopathy (ah **lop** ah thee) a system of medical practice in which specific remedies (often pharmaceutical agents) are used to produce effects different from those produced by a disease or injury.

alveoli(al **vee** oh lie) thin, saclike terminal ends of the airways; the site at which gases are exchanged between the blood and inhaled air.

amenorrhea cessation or lack of menstrual periods.

amino acids the building blocks of protein; manufactured by the body or obtained from dietary sources.

anabolic steroids(ann uh **bol** ick) drugs that function like testosterone to produce increases in weight, strength, endurance, and aggressiveness.

anal intercourse a sexual act in which the erect penis is inserted into the rectum of a partner.

anaerobic energy production the body's alternative means of energy production, used when the available oxygen is insufficient for aerobic energy production. Anaerobic energy production is a much less efficient use of stored energy.

androgyny (an **droj** en ee) the blending of both masculine and feminine qualities.

angina pectoris (an **jie** nuh **peck** tor is) chest pain that results from impaired blood supply to the heart muscle.

anorexia nervosa an eating disorder in which the individual weighs less than 85% of their expected weight, and has an intense fear of gaining weight; in females, menstruation ceases for at least 3 consecutive months; people with anorexia perceive themselves as overweight, even though they are underweight.

antagonistic effect the effect produced when one drug reduces or offsets the effects of a second drug.

antibodies chemical compounds produced by the body's immune system to destroy antigens and their toxins.

artificially acquired immunity (AAI) a type of acquired immunity resulting from the body's response to pathogens introduced into the body through immunizations.

asbestos a term used to refer to a class of minerals that have a fibrous crystal structure.

asphyxiation death resulting from lack of oxygen to the brain.

atherosclerosis the buildup of plaque on the inner wall of arteries.

attention deficit hyperactivity disorder (ADHD) an above-normal rate of physical movement; often accompanied by an inability to concentrate on a specified task; also called *hyperactivity.*

Source: Wayne A. Payne, Dale B. Hahn, and Ellen B. Mauer, *Understanding Your Health,* p. G-1.

Boxes

KEY TERM
box

Supplementary material that is separated from the regular text. A box is also known as a *sidebar.*

A **box,** or **sidebar,** is supplementary material that is separated from the regular text. It may appear at the bottom or top of a page of text (such as the example shown on page 569) or on one or more pages by itself. Boxed material may or may not be in an actual box; it may be set off with shading, in columns, in a different typeface, or by color. The example box on the next page, from a marketing text, presents an ethics issue related to information in that chapter.

EXAMPLE OF BOXED MATERIAL

ETHICS AND SOCIAL RESPONSIBILITY ALERT **Coupon Scams Cost Manufacturers $500 Million Each Year**

Coupon fraud has become a serious concern for consumer goods manufacturers. How serious? The Coupon Information Center estimates that companies pay out coupon refunds of more than $500 million a year to retailers and individuals who don't deserve them. That adds a huge cost to promotions designed to help consumers.

The methods used by the cheaters are becoming very sophisticated. For example,

- Some scam artists set up a fake store and send coupons to manufacturers for payment.
- Coupon collectors often sell coupons to retailers who are paid full face value by manufacturers, even though the products were not sold.
- Retailers increase their refunds by adding extra coupons to those handed in by shoppers.
- Counterfeiters print rebate forms and proofs of purchase to collect big cash rebates without buying the products.

One of the newest forms of coupon fraud is the result of Internet coupon sites that allow coupons to be printed at home. The coupon bar code, value, or even the offer can be manipulated and copied with now-common computer equipment and skills.

Some of the steps being taken to reduce coupon and rebate fraud include requiring handwritten redemption requests and requesting a proof of purchase.

What are your reactions to misredemption? Should action be taken against coupon fraud?

Source: Roger Kerin, Steven Hartley, and William Rudelius, *Marketing: The Core,* p. 355. Copyright © 2004 by The McGraw-Hill Companies, Inc. Reprinted by permission of The McGraw-Hill Companies, Inc.

Boxes can contain case studies, research studies, biographical sketches, interviews, excerpts from other works, controversial issues, practical applications—the possibilities are almost endless. Authors use boxes to clarify important points, provide vivid examples, and broaden and deepen your understanding of the material. They choose box titles that describe its purpose: for example, *Points to Ponder, Issues and Debate, Close-Up, Speaking Out, Current Research,* and *What Do You Think?*

Chapter Summaries

KEY TERM
chapter summary
Textbook feature in which the author consolidates most of the main ideas.

A **chapter summary** is one of the most helpful textbook features because it consolidates most of the main ideas. Many students find it useful to read a chapter summary both *before and after* studying a chapter. When you read a summary before you read the chapter, you may not understand it completely, but you will have a general idea about the important material in the chapter.

A summary may also be called *Conclusion, Recapitulation, Looking Back, Summing Up, Key Points, Key Concepts,* and so on. It may be written as paragraphs or lists. Summaries can be very short (as in the example on page 570, from a text for infant and toddler caregivers).

EXAMPLE OF A SUMMARY

Summary

Attachment is a strong, affectional tie that individuals feel toward special people in their lives. It involves closeness and responsiveness to an infant by a caring adult, and it is vital for an infant's healthy development. Current brain research indicates that a secure attachment relationship directly affects the way the brain gets "wired." Warm, positive interactions stabilize connections in the brain, and social and cognitive development have their beginnings in the early attachment experiences.

Secure attachments influence an infant's desire to explore and make sense of the world. For infants and toddlers with special needs, the nurturing support of a knowledgeable child-care provider can make all the difference in their ability to grow and develop.

The more caregivers know about attachment and how to foster it, the more they can respond to the changing needs of infants and toddlers, and their families. Continuity of care, small family groups, and a qualified caregiver are key components to the healthy growth of young children.

KEY TERM
study questions and activities

Exercises, drills, and practice sections that direct your attention to or review information you will be expected to know.

Study Questions and Activities

Many textbooks include **study questions and activities:** exercises, drills, and practice sections that direct your attention to or review information you will be expected to know. These can be among the most important features you use. Take time to do them. They provide valuable practice and give you a way to monitor your comprehension. Also, instructors often use these items or similar items on tests. Generally, if you are able to answer study questions and exercises, you can do well on an actual test.

Study questions and activities may appear at the beginning or end of a chapter, a reading, or other subdivisions of the text. In addition to the terms noted above, questions or activities may be called *Questions for Study and Review, Review, Ask Yourself, Self-Test, Check Your Mastery, Mastery Test, Learning Check, Check Your Understanding, Topics for Discussion, Problems,* and so on. The examples shown on page 571 are typical.

Other Textbook Features

Here are other textbook features that can help you when you study:

Preface: Introductory section in which authors tell readers about the book.

Index: Alphabetical listing of topics and names in a textbook, with page numbers, usually appearing at the end of the book.

Appendix: Section at the end of a book that includes supplemental material or specialized information.

Bibliography: List of sources from which the author of the text has drawn information or a list of recommended reading.

EXAMPLE OF STUDY QUESTIONS AND ACTIVITIES

Questions for Review

Go to the self-quizzes on the CD-ROM and the Online Learning Center to test your knowledge.

1. What are the basic tenets of libertarianism? How do they support the First Amendment?
2. What is the absolutist position on the First Amendment?
3. Name important court cases involving the definition of "no law," "the press," "abridgment," clear and present danger, balancing of interests, and prior restraint.
4. What are libel and slander? What are the tests of libel and slander? How do the rules change for public officials?
5. Define obscenity, pornography, and indecency.
6. What is safe harbor?
7. What is the traffic cop analogy? Why is it important in the regulation of broadcasting?
8. What is copyright? What are the exceptions to copyright? What is DRM?
9. What is normative theory?
10. What are the basic assumptions of social responsibility theory?
11. What are ethics? What are the three levels of ethics?
12. What are some of the individual and group interests that often conflict in the application of media ethics?
13. What is confidentiality? Why is confidentiality important to media professionals and to democracy?
14. What are some examples of personal and professional conflict of interest faced by media practitioners?
15. What are the different grounds on which critics object to media codes of conduct?
16. What are some forms of media self-regulation? What are the strengths and limitations of self-regulation?

Questions for Critical Thinking and Discussion

1. Are you a libertarian? That is, do you believe that people are inherently rational and good and that they are best served by a fully free press? Defend your position.
2. What is your position on pornography? It is legally protected expression. Would you limit that protection? When?
3. How much regulation or, if you prefer, deregulation do you think broadcasters should accept?
4. Of all the groups whose interests must be balanced by media professionals, which ones do you think would have the most influence over you?
5. In general, how ethical do you believe media professionals to be? Specifically, print journalists? Television journalists? Advertising professionals? Public relations professionals? Television and film writers? Direct mail marketers?

Source: Stanley Baran, *Introduction to Mass Communication*, 3rd eds. p. 496. Copyright © 2004 by The McGraw-Hill Companies, Inc. Reprinted by permission of The McGraw-Hill Companies, Inc.

Students often remark that in college textbooks "everything seems important." They also find it hard to get a sense of how the facts and concepts add up to a coherent whole. Taking advantage of textbook features as you read can enable you to identify the essential information in a chapter and to understand its organization. Authors want to help you study and learn from their textbooks. For this reason, they put a great deal of time, effort, and thought into designing the extra textbook features. Use these helpful study tools!

HOW CAN YOU INTERPRET VISUALS AND GRAPHIC AIDS?

If you have ever read a copy of *USA Today,* you know this highly popular newspaper is filled with visuals and graphics. The reason is simple: Attention-grabbing graphics make it easier for readers to understand and remember information. A picture is indeed worth a thousand words.

Because of improved technology, today's textbooks and educational resources abound with visuals and graphics. You must be able to read, interpret, and integrate the information in them with the written explanations of the material. Visual aids include illustrations such as photographs, diagrams, maps, and cartoons. Graphic aids consist of bar graphs, pie charts, line graphs, time lines, flowcharts, and tables.

Don't skip over visuals and graphic aids. They provide visual explanations of concepts and relationships in a way that is often more concise and easier to understand than words alone. They can simplify, clarify, illustrate, and summarize information. They show how things relate to and compare with each other. They emphasize important points and reveal trends and patterns. For visual learners, they make the material more memorable. Sometimes a visual or graphic aid includes information that goes beyond the written explanation, for example, to offer support or proof.

When you preview a reading assignment, notice the type of visuals and graphic aids. Authors refer to them at the point they believe will help readers most, so stop and examine them when the author first mentions it. For example, the author might say, "As Illustration 2.3 shows," or "See Table 4.1." Stop and examine the illustration, or read and interpret the graphic, following the steps described later in the chapter. Move back and forth between the written explanation and the visual or graphic aid as needed. For example, if you are reading about the components of a computer motherboard (system board), refer to the labeled illustration each time a new part is described.

Now find out more about how to use visual and graphics aids to full advantage.

HOW CAN YOU INTERPRET VISUAL AIDS?

KEY TERM
visual aids

Photographs, diagrams, maps, and cartoons that supplement or illustrate narrative information.

In this section, you will learn how to interpret visual aids. **Visual aids** are photographs, diagrams, maps, and cartoons that supplement or illustrate narrative information. Read about each type of visual aid, look at the example, and try the sample exercise.

Photographs

Photographs, images recorded by a camera, serve many purposes.They can bring information to life, make it concrete, and help you visualize it, such as a photo of a wedding ceremony from another culture. They can show an example, such as a photo of a mosaic in an art history book. Sometimes photographs are there to help readers to relate to material on an emotional level. For example, a psychology text discussion of stress might include a photo of Hurricane Katrina victims huddling on the roof of their house, surrounded by rising water. When you encounter photographs in textbooks, study them and read the accompanying captions. Ask yourself questions such as "What are the main elements (people, objects, activities) of the photograph? What does the photo illustrate or exemplify: what is its most important message? How does it fit with the written material? Is the date of the photograph given? The location at which the photograph was taken?"

The photograph below is from a music appreciation textbook. Suppose you had never seen the instrument called chimes and that you had only a written description, such as the one that accompanies the photo: "Chimes are a set of metal tubes hung from a frame. They are struck with a hammer and sound like church bells." Based only on that, would you have had an accurate idea of what chimes look like?

EXAMPLE OF A PHOTOGRAPH

Chimes are a set of metal tubes hung from a frame. They are struck with a hammer and sound like church bells.

Source: R. Kamien, *Music,* 9th ed., p. 36. Copyright © 2008 by The McGraw-Hill Companies, Inc.

EXERCISE 1

Interpreting a Photograph

Directions: Examine the following photograph and then answer the questions about it.

THE UNEMPLOYED, 1930. Thousands of unemployed men wait to be fed outside the Municipal Lodgers House in New York City. *(Library of Congress)*

Source: Alan Brinkley, *The Unfinished Nation,* 5th ed., p. 656. Copyright © 2008 by The McGraw-Hill Companies, Inc.

1. When was the photograph taken and why is this important? In 1930 during the Great Depression. (The photo is black-and-white because that was all that was available in 1930.)
2. What is happening in the photograph? Thousands of unemployed men are waiting to be fed (given a free meal).
3. Where was the photograph taken? New York City
4. What point does the photograph make? During the Great Depression vast numbers of people were unemployed and hungry.

Diagrams

Diagrams are sketches, drawings, or plans that show or explain how something works or shows the relationship between the parts of a whole. The "something" might be an object (a carburetor), a process (the evaporation/condensation cycle of water), or an idea (a proposed solution to the problem of low-cost housing). Flowcharts are a specific type of diagram that shows steps in a process. Diagrams appear in nearly every type of textbook.

When you study any diagram, ask yourself, "What is the purpose of this diagram? Why is it included? What does it show?" A good test preparation strategy is to photocopy any important diagram from your text. In a biology text, for example, it might be a diagram of a cell or of the heart. Cover the labels and make one or more copies. Test yourself to see if you can correctly label the parts. You can also make diagrams or drawings of your own. Creating them is an excellent study strategy.

The environmental science textbook diagram below shows the process of photosynthesis that allows green plants to synthesize carbohydrates by using light as an energy source. For a test, you would need to be able to list the steps. A diagram with a green leaf, the sun, and sky is more effective and memorable than a flowchart of boxes with the same information.

EXAMPLE OF A DIAGRAM

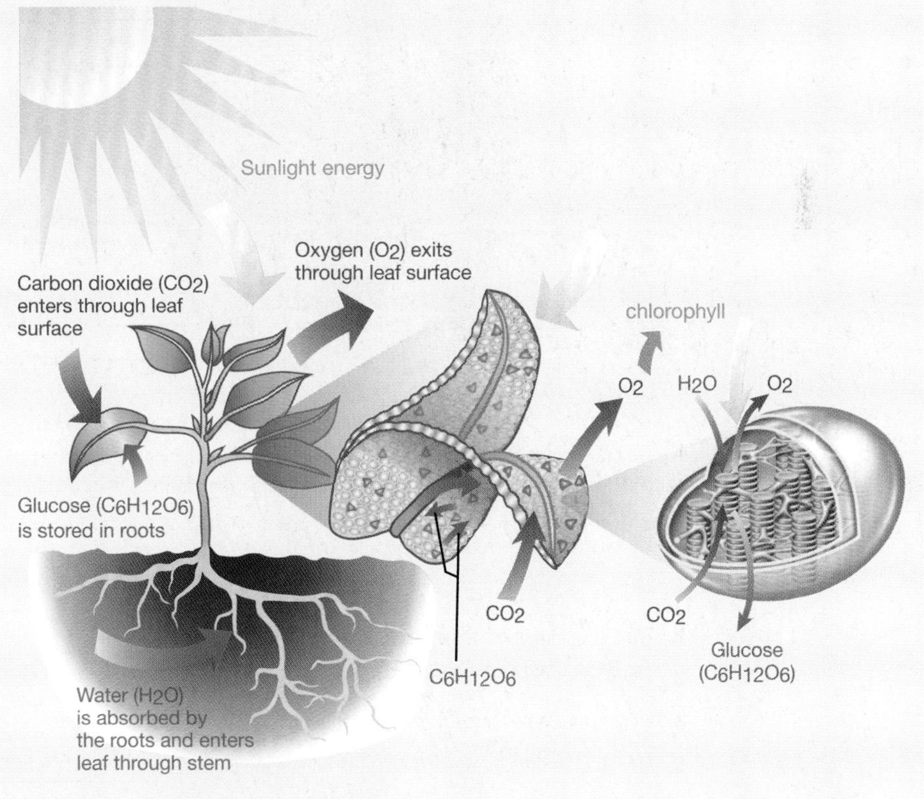

Figure 4.9 Photosynthesis This reaction is an example of one that requires an input of energy (sunlight) to combine low-energy molecules (CO_2 and H_2O) to form sugar ($C_6H_{12}O_6$) with a greater amount of chemical bond energy. Molecular oxygen (O_2) is also produced.

Source: Eldon D. Enger and Bradley F. Smith, *Environmental Science: A Study of Interrelationships* 11th ed., Fig. 4.9, p. 71.Copyright © 2008 by The McGraw-Hill Companies, Inc. Reprinted by permission of The McGraw-Hill Companies, Inc.

EXERCISE 2

Interpreting a Diagram

Directions: Use the diagram of the mouth to answer the questions that follow.

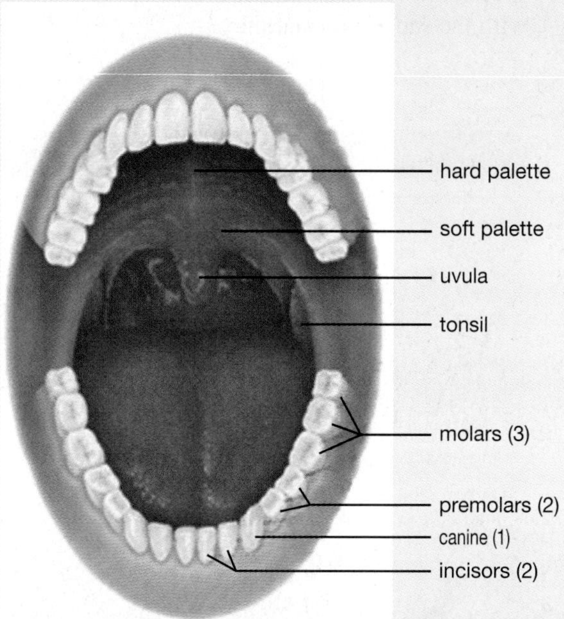

Figure 8.3 Adult Mouth and Teeth The chisel-shaped incisors bite; the pointed canines tear; the fairly flat premolars grind; and the flattened molars crush food.

Source: Sylvia Mader, *Human Biology,* 10th ed., Fig. 8.3, p. 146. Copyright © 2008 by The McGraw-Hill Companies, Inc. Reprinted by permission of The McGraw-Hill Companies, Inc.

1. Which type of teeth occur in the greatest number? molars
2. What structure is located in the top, center of the mouth? uvula
3. Which teeth are located at the front of the mouth? incisors
4. What is the name for the roof (top) of the mouth? hard palate
5. Are the premolars located in front of or behind the molars? in front of

Maps

Maps are representations of regions or other information presented on a flat surface. You've undoubtedly used a *location map:* a road map, atlas, or even a campus map. For any map, ask yourself, "What is the purpose of this map? What important information does it show? What does the date of its creation suggest about the information it contains?"

You will encounter maps in courses such as history, geography, archaeology, anthropology, and astronomy. Some maps are designed to show the exact location of cities, states, countries, battlefields, mountain ranges, rivers, and other physical objects. Pay particular attention to each item's position relative to every other item. For example, a map might indicate that vegetation decreases as regions of the world become colder. In maps such as these, note the following:

- *Title:* the subject matter of the map
- *Legend or key:* an explanatory table or list of symbols in the map and the use of color or shading (such as a star for capital cities, or various colors or shading to indicate different age categories)
- *Scale:* a ratio showing the relationship between the dimensions on the map and the object it represents, such as 1" = 100 miles; enables users to calculate the actual size of features represented on the map
- *Compass:* a symbol indicating the directions north, south, east, and west
- *Source:* the mapmaker; the person, agency, or group that created the map
- *Date:* when the map was created (for example, it might be ancient, from the 1800s, or recent)

Some maps are *thematic* or *special-purpose maps.* They present factual or statistical information for a specific region rather than showing the location of physical objects. For example, a map might use different colors to show voting patterns in parts of the United States during the last presidential election. A map of a coastline might show the amount of erosion in the previous century. In such maps, look for patterns

EXAMPLE OF A THEMATIC MAP

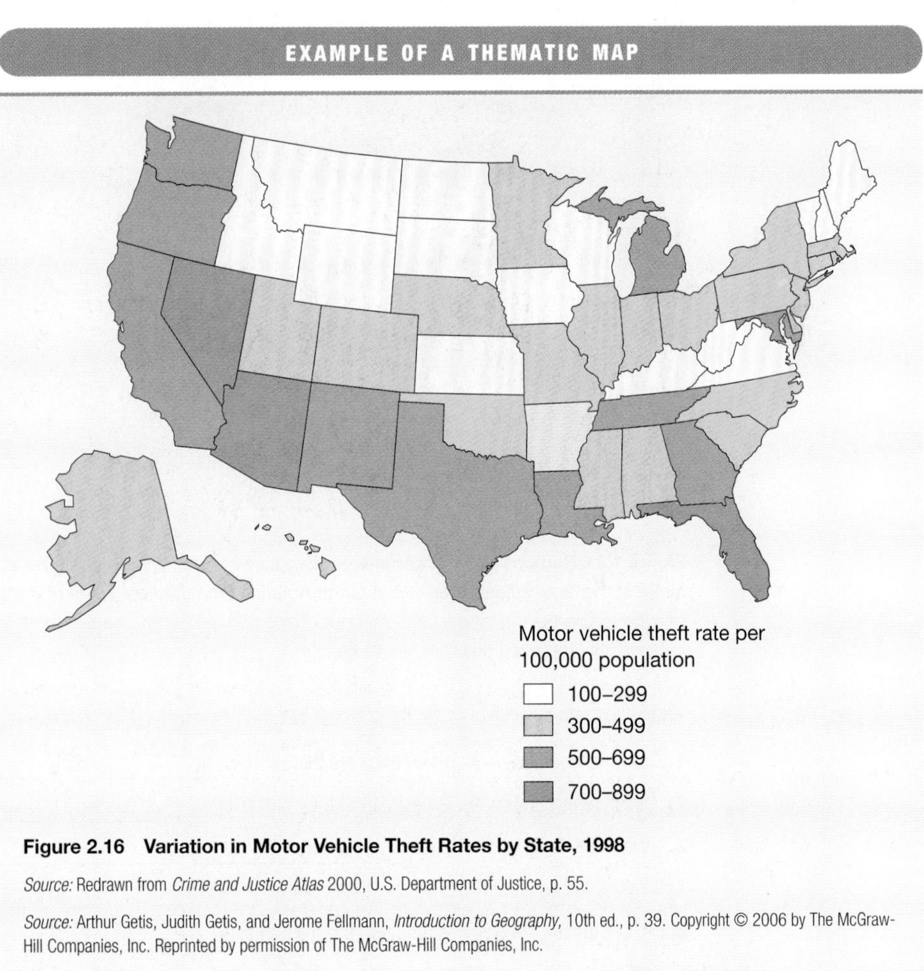

Figure 2.16 Variation in Motor Vehicle Theft Rates by State, 1998

Source: Redrawn from *Crime and Justice Atlas* 2000, U.S. Department of Justice, p. 55.

Source: Arthur Getis, Judith Getis, and Jerome Fellmann, *Introduction to Geography,* 10th ed., p. 39. Copyright © 2006 by The McGraw-Hill Companies, Inc. Reprinted by permission of The McGraw-Hill Companies, Inc.

and trends, in addition to the other aspects noted above. Remember that you can create maps of your own as study aids.

The sample thematic map on page 577 uses color to show for each state the number of stolen motor vehicles per 100,000 people. Theft rates are higher in Florida, near the Great Lakes, and in the southwest and western states. One reasonable conclusion is that vehicles are more likely to be stolen in states with higher populations and/or that border on other countries or in coastal states, in which stolen vehicles can easily be moved offshore. Notice how much more easily the information is visualized in map form than if it were presented in the form of a table.

EXERCISE 3

Interpreting a Map

Directions: Study the following map and then answer the questions about it.

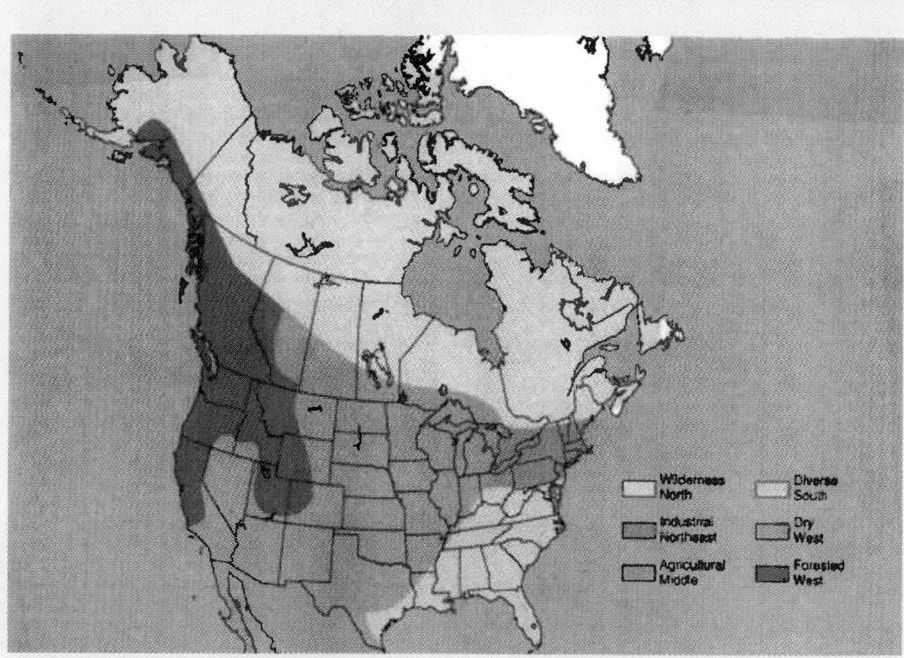

Figure 1.3 Regions of North America Because of natural features of the land and the use people make of the land, different regions of North America face different kinds of environmental issues. In each region people face a large number of specific issues, but certain kinds of issues are more important in some regions than in others.

Source: Eldon D. Enger and Bradley F. Smith, *Environmental Science: A Study of Interrelationships* 11th ed., Fig. 1.3, p 5. Copyright © 2008 by The McGraw-Hill Companies, Inc. Reprinted by permission of The McGraw-Hill Companies, Inc.

✓ **Teaching Tip**
Ask students to find the region in which your college is located.

1. How many regions of North America are there? six
2. Which region covers the largest part of the United States? Agricultural Middle
3. How many regions are there in Texas? three
4. What is the smallest region in the United States? Industrial Northeast
5. Where in the United States are there the most forests? Forested West

EXERCISE 4

Interpreting a Cartoon

"We lost!"

Source: © The New Yorker Collection 2006 Leo Cullum from cartoonbank.com. All Rights Reserved.

What point does the cartoon make? In other words, what is the point of view of the cartoonist about children's participation in sports today?

So that they will "feel good about themselves," children today are rewarded simply for participating in sports, regardless of whether their team won or they actually earned an award or trophy.

✓ **Teaching Tip**

If students read Selection 8-2, the excerpt from "The Last Lecture," ask them if the author, Randy Pausch, would agree with the point of view in this cartoon. He believes children feel better about things they *earn* (and that parents today need to allow children to experience losing).

Cartoons

Cartoons are humorous drawings that may or may not include a caption. Why do authors occasionally include them in textbooks? Well, a cartoon obviously lightens things up, but it can also present a point of view or illustrate a point in a memorable way. (You learned about point of view in Chapter 8.) Look at the cartoon in Exercise 4 and then answer the question that follows.

Political cartoons reflect a newspaper's or magazine's point of view on an issue, often by poking fun at a public figure or current issue. They are also called *editorial* cartoons because they appear on newspapers' editorial pages. These cartoons may contain caricatures, in which a person's distinctive features are exaggerated (such as George W. Bush's ears or Barack Obama's). Cartoonists also use visual metaphors, such as Uncle Sam to represent the United States, an elephant for the Republican Party, and a donkey for the Democrats.

Understanding cartoons depends on your prior knowledge. If a cartoon doesn't make sense, it is usually because you lack background information. For example, in

Exercise 5, the cartoon on the left makes a statement about China, the host of the 2008 Olympics. China is ruled by a Communist dictator and treats political dissidents harshly. The cartoon assigns alternate meanings to the name of Olympic events: "parallel bars" are depicted as prison bars; "rings" refers to torturing and restraining; "vault" suggests an underground burial chamber or perhaps to people trying to escape up the stairs; and "shot put," putting a bullet in someone's head. There also appears to be blood on the stairs.

EXERCISE 5

Interpreting Political or Editorial Cartoons

Source: Copyright © 2008 Creators Syndicate. By permission of John Deering and Creators Syndicate, Inc.

Source: Aislin, *The Montreal Gazette*, 2008.

What does the editorial cartoon on the right suggest?

Polar bears may face extinction due to the melting of polar ice caps by global warming. If their habitat is destroyed, they cannot survive. [Point out again the importance of prior knowledge in comprehending the cartoon. In order to "get" the cartoon, you have to know something about polar bears, polar ice caps, and global warming.]

HOW CAN YOU INTERPRET GRAPHIC AIDS?

KEY TERM
graphic aids

Tables, diagrams, graphs, and charts that present narrative information in an alternative format.

Nearly every textbook contains line graphs, pie charts, bar graphs, flowcharts, and tables. As with visuals, stop and examine **graphic aids** when the author first mentions them. Then return to your reading.

Graphic aids contain important information, but they can appear difficult unless you know how to interpret them. The following steps will enable you to interpret graphic aids more effectively and efficiently.

- First, read the *title* and any *explanation* that accompany the graph. The title tells you what aspect of the author's topic is being clarified or illustrated by the graph or table.
- Next, check the *source* of the information presented in the graphic aid to see if it is current and reliable. Read any footnotes.
- Third, read all the *headings* and *labels* to determine what is being presented or measured. These headings and labels may appear at the top, bottom, and side of a table or graph. For example, in a bar graph that compares the amount of money workers earn and their educational levels, the side of a bar graph may be labeled "Annual Income in Thousands of Dollars" and the bottom may be labeled "Level of Education."
- Then, examine the *units of measurement* in a graph (for example, decades, percents, thousands of dollars, per hour, kilograms, per capita, milliseconds).
- Study the graphic aid. Try to understand how the information on the graphic clarifies, exemplifies, or proves the written explanation. See if there are *patterns* or *trends* in the data. Note any extremes: highs and lows in the data.
- Finally, use the information provided collectively by the title and explanation, source, headings and labels, and units of measurements to determine the *important points* or *conclusions* the author is conveying.

✓ **Teaching Tip**
Explain that *per capita* means "per person" (literally, "per head" in Latin).

Here are explanations and examples of five commonly used graphic aids: line graphs, pie charts, bar graphs, flowcharts, and tables. With bar graphs, line graphs, and tables, look for trends. A trend is important because it means there is a steady, overall increase or decrease. Along with the example of each graphic aid is a summary of its important elements as well as the important conclusions that can be drawn from it.

Line Graphs

A **line graph** is a diagram whose points are connected to show a relationship between two or more variables. There may be one line or several lines, depending on what the author wishes to convey. Watch especially for highs, lows, and trends. The example line graph on page 582 comes from a biology textbook, and it conveys the following:

Title and explanation: "World population growth." (The explanation appears below the title.)

Source: Population Reference Bureau.

Headings and labels: Populations in less-developed countries and more-developed countries (in billions) and dates between 1750 and 2150 given in 50-year increments.

Units of measurement: Billions (population, meaning the number of people) and 50-year periods (of time).

Important points and conclusions: Starting in approximately 1950, the population began to rise dramatically in less-developed countries. This appears to slow down or level off around 2050. However, the world's population will then be approaching 12 billion, with the less-developed countries continuing to contribute overwhelmingly more to world population growth.

EXAMPLE OF A LINE GRAPH

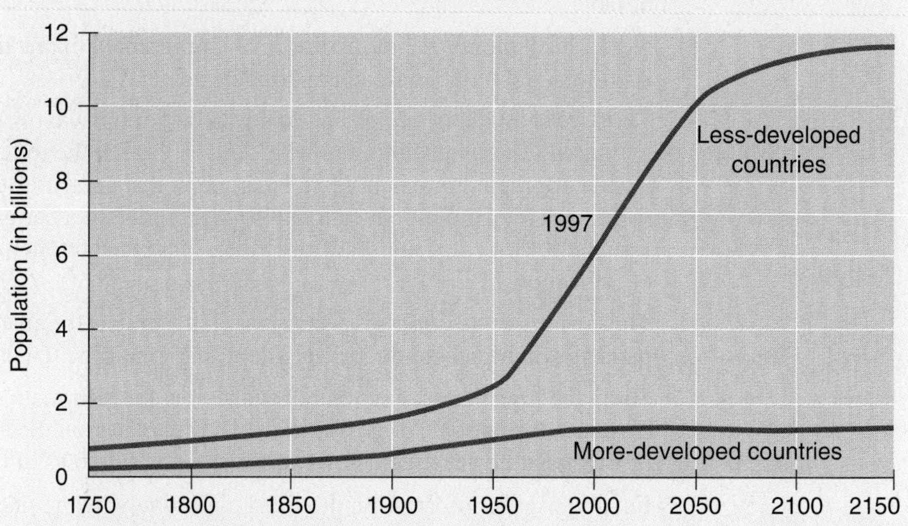

World population growth
The less-developed countries will contribute most to world population growth.
Source: Population Reference Bureau.

Source: Sylvia S. Mader, *Biology*, 8th ed., p. 849. Copyright © 2004 by The McGraw-Hill Companies, Inc. Reprinted by permission of The McGraw-Hill Companies, Inc.

✓ **Teaching Tip**
Although most students do not realize it the answers to these questions are in the explanations that accompany the graphs. Encourage them to base their answers on the graphs. (If done in class, you can duplicate the graphs only and hand them out.) This exercise is a good in-class, collaborative activity.

EXERCISE 6

Studying Line Graphs

1. The populations of which two groups are being compared on the line graph?

less-developed and more-developed countries

2. What is the *total* number of years spanned on the graph?

400 years (1750–2150)

3. In which year did the population of less-developed countries begin to increase sharply?

1950

4. Approximately what is the population of the less-developed countries expected to be in 2050?

slightly more than 10 billion

5. Approximately what is the population of the industrialized countries expected to be in 2050?

slightly more than 1 billion

✓ **Teaching Tip**
On #6 students often try to answer a different question. Urge them to read it carefully and answer it.

6. List at least two logical conclusions that can be drawn about *what life might be like in less-developed countries in 2150.*

- They will be densely populated or overpopulated
- There will be housing shortages.
- There will be more illiteracy.
- There will be food and water shortages.
- Poverty will increase.
- There will be greater health problems, more epidemics, and shorter life spans.

Pie Charts

A **pie chart,** as its name suggests, is a circle graph in which the size of the "slices" represent proportional parts of the whole. Pie charts are a convenient way to show the relationships among component parts as well as the relationship of each part to the whole. The pie chart below comes from a geography textbook and conveys the following information:

Title and explanation: "Sources of primary air pollutants in the United States." The explanation below the title identifies the two largest sources of air pollution.

EXAMPLE OF A PIE CHART

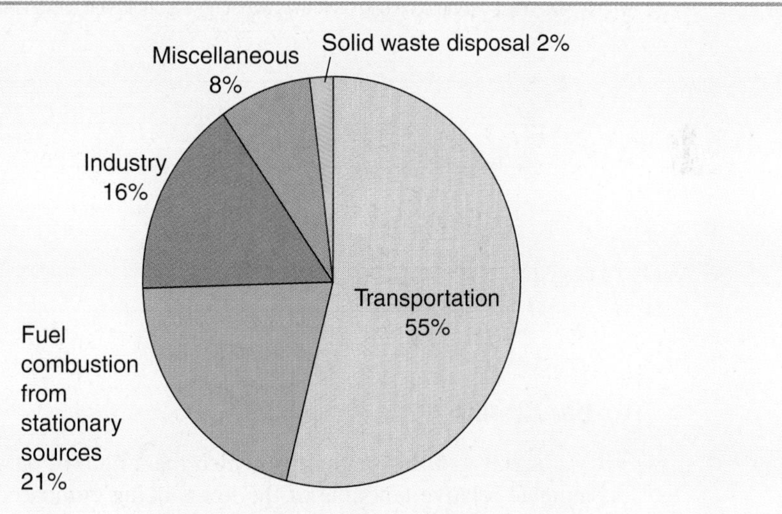

Sources of primary air pollutants in the United States. Transportation is the single largest source of human-caused air pollution. The second largest source is fuel combustion in stationary sources such as power plants and factories.
Redrawn from *Biosphere 2000.* Donald G. Kaufman and Cecilia M. Franz (NY: Harper Collins College Publishers, 1993), Figure 14.4, p. 257.

Source: Arthur Getis, Judith Getis, and Jerome D. Fellmann, *Introduction to Geography,* 10th ed., p. 443. Copyright © 2006 by The McGraw-Hill Companies, Inc. Reprinted by permission of The McGraw-Hill Companies, Inc.

Source: Redrawn from *Biosphere 2000,* Donald G. Kaufman and Cecilia Franz (NY: Harper Collins College Publishers, 1993).

Headings and labels: Transportation, Fuel combustion from stationary sources, Industry, Miscellaneous, and Solid waste disposal.

Units of measurement: Percentages.

Important points and conclusions: As noted in the explanations, transportation is the single largest source of human-caused air pollution. More than half of the air pollution comes from this source. The second largest source is combustion in stationary sources such as power plants and factories.

EXERCISE 7

Studying Pie Charts

1. Which is greater in the pie chart: air pollutants from transportation or air pollution from all other sources combined?

transportation

2. What percentage of air pollutants comes from fuel combustion from stationary sources?

21%

3. What is the smallest source of air pollutants?

solid waste disposal (2%)

4. What conclusions can be drawn about how air pollution could be reduced?

- There is a need to explore ways of minimizing pollution from transportation (such as the increased use of public transportation and the increased use of solar, electric, or natural-gas-powered vehicles).
- Stricter laws could be passed to regulate power plant and factory emissions since they are the second largest source of air pollutants ("Stationary Sources").

Bar Graphs

A **bar graph** is a chart in which the length of parallel rectangular bars is used to indicate relative amounts of the items being compared. The bars in a bar graph may be vertical or horizontal. The bar graph on page 585 comes from a textbook on human development and conveys the following information:

Title and explanation: "Annual incidence of heart attack."

Source: National Center for Health Statistics, 2000.

Headings and labels: Estimated number of persons; age.

Units of measurement: Thousands (in increments of 50,000); age in years.

Important points and conclusions: Among heart attack victims under age 65, men significantly outnumber women. After age 65, women start to catch up.

EXAMPLE OF A BAR GRAPH

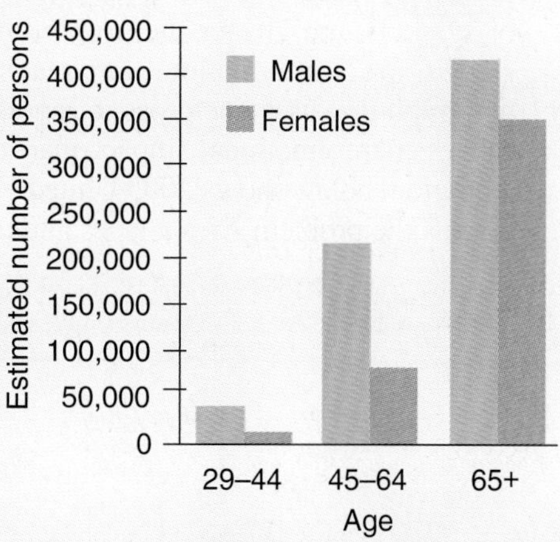

Annual incidence of heart attack.

SOURCE: National Center for Health Statistics, 2000. *Health, United States, 2000.*

Source: Paul Insel and Walton Roth, *Core Concepts in Health*, Brief 9th ed., Copyright © 2002 by The McGraw-Hill Companies, Inc. Reprinted by permission of The McGraw-Hill Companies, Inc.

EXERCISE 8

Studying Bar Graphs

1. Of the gender and age groups represented on the graph, which ones have fewer than 100,000 heart attacks annually?

   men and women aged 29–44: women aged 45–64

2. What are two *trends* across all age groups?

   (1) The incidence of heart attack increases with age for both men and women.

   (2) Men consistently have a higher incidence of heart attack than women do.

3. In which age group is there the greatest difference between the incidence of heart attack in men and in women?

   45–64 years

4. Which gender has the most significant increase in the incidence of heart attack, and between which age groups did this increase occur?

   women, with the increase occurring between the 45–64 age group and the 65+ group (a more than 5-fold increase)

✓ **Teaching Tips**

In #2, take the opportunity to reinforce the meaning of the important term "trend."

Have students draw two trend lines on the graph, one connecting the tops of the bars for men and the tops of the bars for women.

Some graphics, including diagrams and bar graphs, contain *pictograms,* in which a picture or symbol represents numerical data or relationships. The symbols could be dollar signs, stick figures of people, flags, or bushels of grain. The greater the number of symbols, the greater the proportional quantity represented. Pictograms, or *pictographs,* make information more realistic, appealing, and memorable. For example, a bar graph that uses one cross to represent every 1,000 people killed by drunk drivers carries more emotional impact than a plain bar graph with numbers. The example pictogram below shows 2005 United Nations data on HIV/AIDS worldwide. It sharply reveals the problem Africa faces and the growing threat Asia faces from HIV/AIDS.

✓ **Teaching Tip** Sub-Saharan Africa (designated on the pictograph) refers to the region in Africa south of the vast Sahara desert (which covers most of northern Africa).

EXAMPLE OF A PICTOGRAM

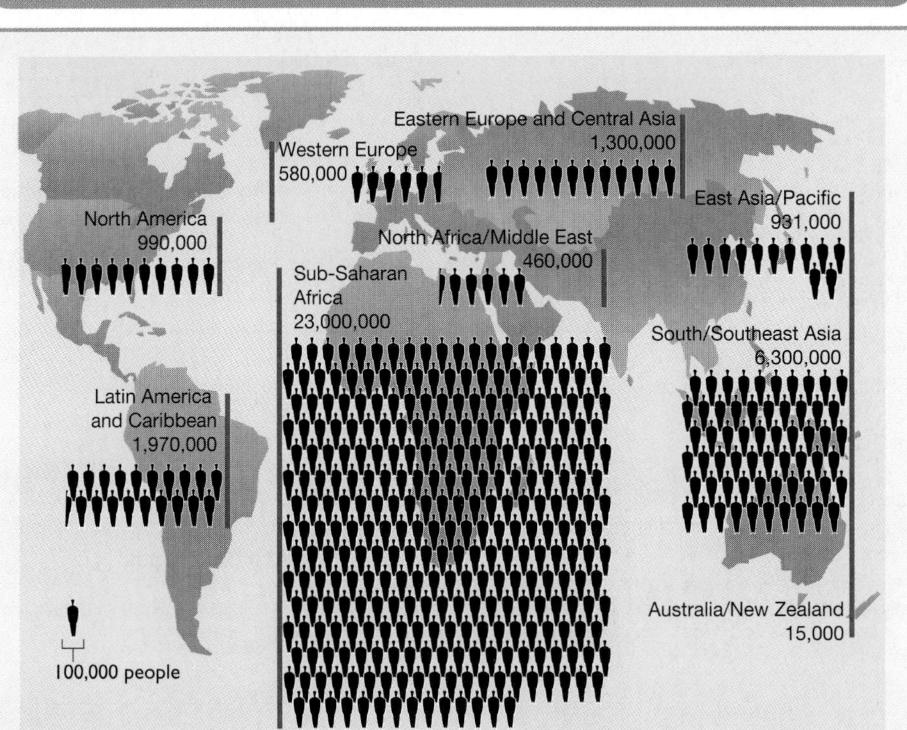

Figure 3 HIV/AIDS has been a significant problem around the world for two decades. According to the United Nations AIDS progam the most cases of the incurable sexually transmitted infection are found in Africa although it is a growing problem in Asia. (*Source:* UNAIDS, 2005.)

Source: Adapted from Robert S. Feldman, *Understanding Psychology,* 8th ed., Fig. 3, p. 391. Copyright © 2008 by The McGraw-Hill Companies, Inc. Reprinted by permission of The McGraw-Hill Companies, Inc.

Flowcharts

A **flowchart** is a type of diagram that shows steps in procedures or processes by using boxes, circles, and other shapes that are connected with lines or arrows. The flowchart on page 587 is from *The New Dictionary of Cultural Literacy* and presents the legislative process of how a bill becomes a law. It conveys the following information:

Title: "How a bill becomes a law."

Source: Presumably the authors of the book, since no other source is given.

Headings and labels: Introduction, Committee action, Floor action, Enactment into law.

Units of measurement: None.

Important points and conclusions: Although bills can be introduced in either the House or the Senate, all bills must go through committee hearings and through floor action in both the House and Senate before the bill is submitted to the president for enactment into law.

EXAMPLE OF A FLOWCHART

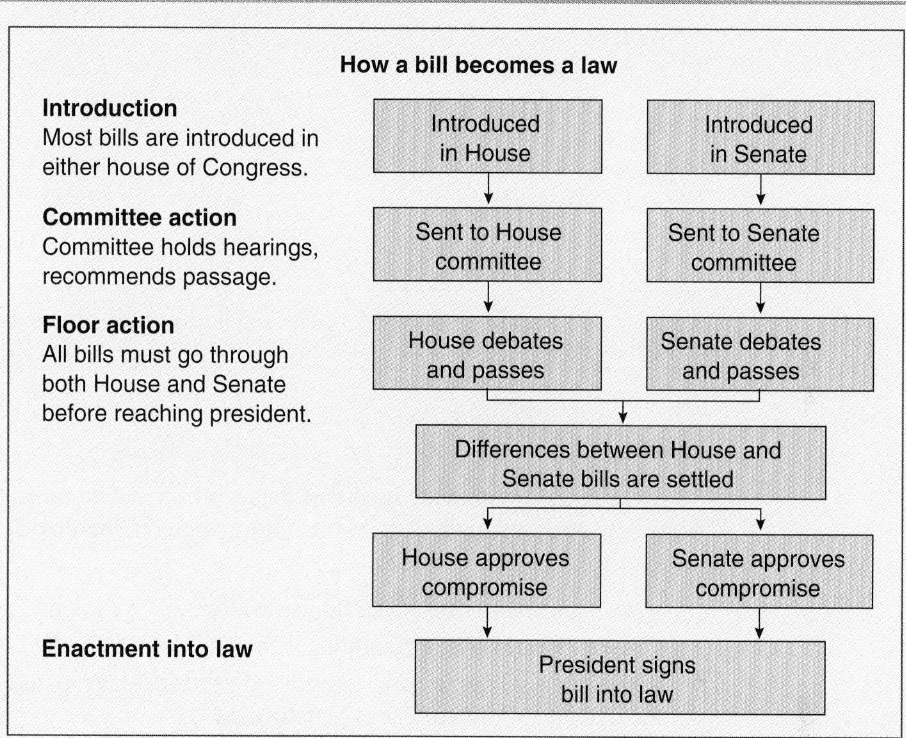

Source: E. D. Hirsch, Jr., Joseph F. Kett, and James Trefil, eds., "How a Bill Becomes a Law" from *The New Dictionary of Cultural Literacy*, p. 344. Copyright © 2002 by Houghton Mifflin Company. Reprinted by permission of Houghton Mifflin Harcourt Publishing Company. All rights reserved.

EXERCISE 9

Studying Flowcharts

1. List the four stages a bill goes through in order to become a law.

- Introduction
- Committee action
- Floor action
- Enactment into law

2. What is the second step in a bill becoming a law? Committee action stage, in which the bill is sent to the House Committee and the Senate Committee

3. In which stage are differences worked out between House and Senate bills?

Floor action

EXAMPLE OF A TABLE

The Supreme Court, 2008

Judge/ Appointing President	Prior Judicial Experience	Law School	Political Party	Senate Vote
John Paul Stevens/Ford	U.S. Court of Appeals	Chicago	R	98–0
Antonin Scalia/Reagan	U.S. Court of Appeals	Harvard	R	98–0
Anthony Kennedy/Reagan	U.S. Court of Appeals	Harvard	R	97–0
Clarence Thomas/G. H. W. Bush	U.S. Court of Appeals	Yale	R	52–48
Ruth Bader Ginsburg/Clinton	U.S. Court of Appeals	Columbia	D	96–3
Stephen Breyer/Clinton	U.S. Court of Appeals	Harvard	D	87–9
John Roberts/G. W. Bush	U.S. Court of Appeals	Harvard	R	78–22
Samuel Alito/G. W. Bush	U.S. Court of Appeals	Yale	R	58–42
Sonia Sotomayor/Obama	U.S. Court of Appeals	Yale	D	68–31

Source: Adapted from Joseph Losco and Ralph Baker, *AM GOV*, p. 330.

Tables

A **table** is a systematic listing of data in rows and columns. The example above, from a government textbook, presents information on Supreme Court Justices and conveys the following information:

Title and explanation: "The Supreme Court." No explanation included.

Source: Presumably the authors of the book, since no other source is given.

Headings and labels: Judge/Appointing President, Prior Judicial Experience, Law School, Political Party, Senate Vote.

EXERCISE 10

Studying Tables

1. Which president nominated Sonia Sotomayor? Obama
2. What is the total number of Supreme Court Justices? 9
3. How many Supreme Court Justices are female? 2 (Ginsberg and Sotomayor)
4. Which president nominated Clarence Thomas? G. H. W. Bush
5. What position did all current justices hold before being nominated to the Supreme Court?

   Judge, U.S. Courts of Appeals
6. How many justices are Republican? 6

Units of measurement: None.

Important points and conclusions: As shown in the table, all nine justices are former U.S. Court of Appeals judges. Three previous presidents have each appointed two justices. The majority of the justices (six) are Republican and were appointed by Republican presidents. There are two female justices. Four justices are graduates of Harvard Law School. The most controversial nominations, according to the Senate vote, were Clarence Thomas (52–48) and Samuel Alito (58–42).

Whenever you see graphic aids in your textbooks, be sure to take advantage of them. Read and study them: They contain valuable information that will enhance your understanding.

OTHER THINGS TO KEEP IN MIND WHEN STUDYING TEXTBOOK MATERIAL

Here is another helpful thing you should know about studying textbook material:

You will benefit from examining the features in all of your textbooks at the beginning of the semester.

It has been estimated that, in college, approximately 80 percent of the material asked on tests comes directly from your textbooks. That means that it will be very important to you to use your textbooks as effectively as possible from the beginning of the semester. Take time at the beginning of every semester to familiarize yourself with the features of each of your textbooks.

Student Online Learning Center (OLC)
***Go to* Chapter 10.**
***Select* Chapter Test.**

Review cards or *summary cards* are a way to select, organize, and summarize the important information in a textbook chapter. Preparing review cards helps you organize the information so that you can learn and memorize it more easily. In other words, chapter review cards are effective study tools.

Preparing chapter review cards for each chapter of *New Worlds* will give you practice in creating these valuable study tools. Once you have learned how to make chapter review cards, you can use actual index cards to create them for textbook material in your other courses and use them when you study for tests.

Now complete the chapter review cards for Chapter 10 by answering the questions or following the directions on each card. Use the type of handwriting that is easiest for you to reread (printing or cursive) and write legibly.

✓ **Teaching Tip**

Remind students that the student OLC contains a 10-item **Chapter Test** for this chapter. After completing the chapter review cards below, students should complete the Chapter Test on the OLC.

Three-Step Process for Studying College Textbooks

List the *steps in the three-step process* of studying college textbooks. (See pages 559–563.)

1. Preparing to read
2. Asking and answering questions as you read and study
3. Reviewing by rehearsing the answers to your questions

Card 1 Chapter 10: Studying College Textbooks and Interpreting Visual and Graphic Aids

Rehearsing Information

1. What is *rehearsing*? (See page 562.)

Saying or writing material to transfer it into long-term memory

2. When should you rehearse the answers to questions from your textbook assignments? Why is it important to do it at that time? (See page 562.)

Immediately after reading a section or chapter because the material is still fresh in mind (in short-term memory)

3. How can you tell when you have rehearsed material sufficiently? (See page 562.)

when you can say or write it from memory

Card 2 Chapter 10: Studying College Textbooks and Interpreting Visual and Graphic Aids

Textbook Features

1. Define the term *textbook feature.* (See page 564.)

Any device used by the author to emphasize important material or to show how it is organized.

2. List at least four types of textbook features. (See pages 564–571.)

- chapter introductions
- chapter objectives
- chapter outlines
- vocabulary aids
- glossary
- boxes
- chapter summaries
- study questions and activities

Card 3 Chapter 10: Studying College Textbooks and Interpreting Visual and Graphic Aids

Interpreting Visual Aids

1. Define *visual aids*. (See page 572.)

photographs, diagrams, maps, and cartoons that supplement or illustrate narrative material

2. List and define on separate lines four types of visual aids. (See pages 572–580.)

photographs—images recorded by a camera

diagrams—sketches, drawings, or plans that show or explain how something works or show the relationship between the parts of a whole

maps—representations of regions or other information presented on a flat surface

cartoons—humorous drawings that may or may not include a caption

Card 4 Chapter 10: Studying College Textbooks and Interpreting Visual and Graphic Aids

Interpreting Graphic Aids

1. Define *graphic aids*. (See page 580.)

tables, diagrams, graphs, and charts that present narrative information in an alternate format.

2. List and define on separate lines five types of graphic aids commonly found in textbooks. (See pages 581–589.)

line graph—diagram with connected points to show relationships

pie chart—circle graph with "slices" to show proportions

bar graph—parallel rectangular bars showing relative amounts

flowchart—diagram showing steps in procedures or processes using boxes, lines, and arrows

table—a systematic listing of data in rows and columns

Card 5 Chapter 10: Studying College Textbooks and Interpreting Visual and Graphic Aids

Directions: Study each graphic aid and answer the questions that follow it.

Line Graph

Exhibit 7–8

U.S. bankruptcies, 1961–2004

Source: Administrative Office of the United States Courts. www.uscourts.gov, April 14, 2005

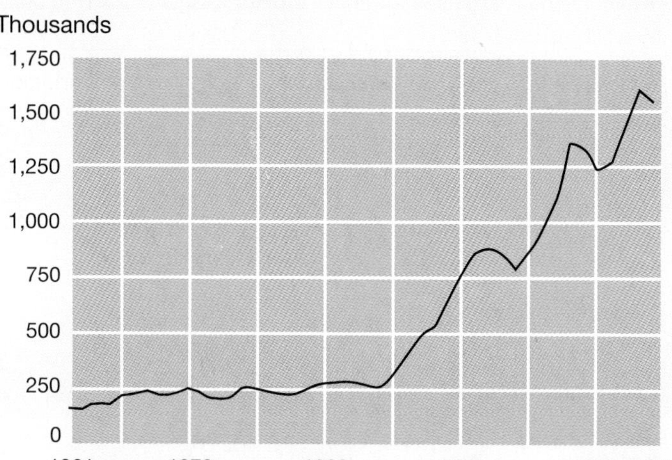

✓ **Teaching Tip**

You may want to mention to students that the economic recession that began in September 2007 caused the number of bankruptcies to escalate dramatically.

1. What is the topic of the line graph? total personal bankruptcies
2. What is the unit of measurement? thousands
3. How many years are covered in the graph? 43 years (1961–2004)
4. How many personal bankruptcies were there in the year 2000? 1,250,000 ("1,250 thousands" = 1,250,000)
5. In which year was there the highest number of personal bankruptcies? 2003

Pie Charts

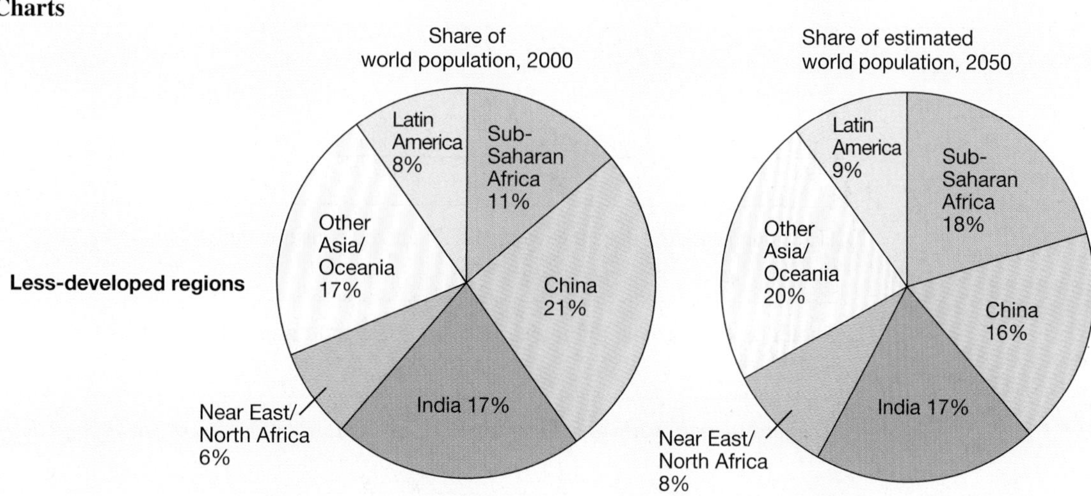

Source: Arthur Getis, Judith Getis, and Jerome Fellmann, *Introduction to Geography,* 10th ed., p.181. Copyright © 2006 by The McGraw-Hill Companies, Inc. Reprinted by permission of The McGraw-Hill Companies, Inc.

1. What amount of time is covered by the two pie charts? 50 years (from 2000 to 2050.)

2. Which less-developed region of the world is projected to have the greatest increase in world population by 2050, and by what percent? Sub-Saharan Africa, by 7% (increasing from 11% to 18%)

3. Which region is expected to show a drop in its share of world population by 2050, and by what percent? China, by 5% (from 21% to 16%)

4. Which region is projected to remain stable in its share of world population? India (at 17%)

Figure 3
How much caffeine do you consume? This chart shows the range of caffeine found in common foods and drinks. (*The New York Times,* 1991). The average person in the United States consumes about 200 miligrams of caffeine each day.

Bar Graph

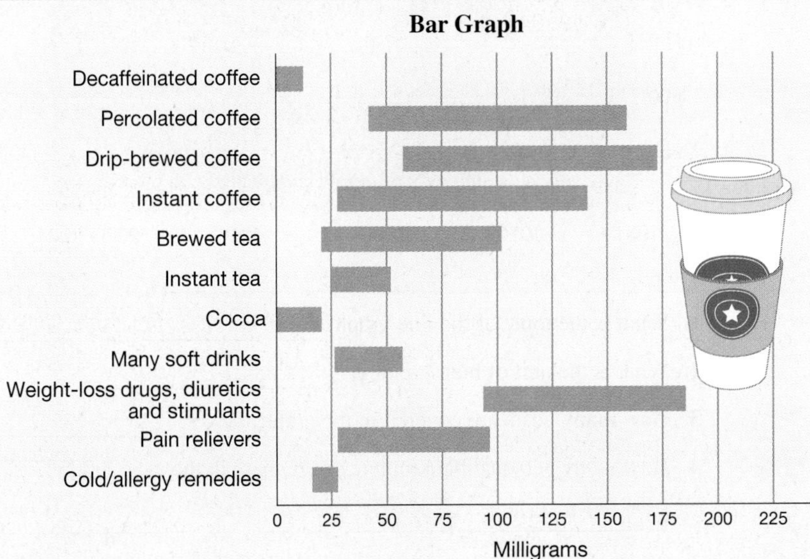

Source: Adapted from Robert S. Feldman, *Understanding Psychology,* 8th ed., Fig. 3, p. 369. Copyright © 2008 by The McGraw-Hill Companies, Inc. Reprinted by permission of The McGraw-Hill Companies, Inc.

1. Which beverage contains the greatest number of milligrams of caffeine? drip-brewed coffee [Weight-loss drugs, diuretics, and stimulants contain more, but they are not beverages.]

2. How much caffeine does the average U.S. citizen consume daily? 200 milligrams (from caption)

3. Should a person trying to limit caffeine choose a soft drink or brewed tea? a soft drink

4. The information in the graph is from 1991. Is that relevant? Why, or why not? It is not relevant because caffeine levels, which are measured scientifically, have not changed.

Flowchart

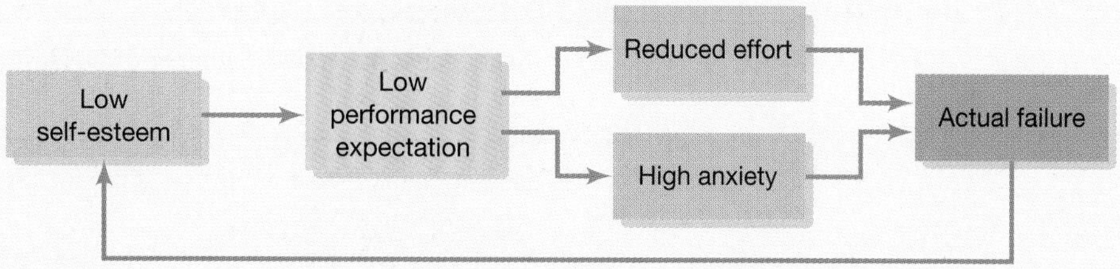

Figure 4 The cycle of low self-esteem begins with an individual already having low self-esteem. As a consequence, the person will have low performance expectations and expect to fail a test, thereby producing anxiety and reduced effort. As a result, the person will actually fail, and failure in turn reinforces low self-esteem.

Source: Adapted from Robert S. Feldman, *Understanding Psychology,* 8th ed., Fig. 4, p. 468. Copyright © 2008 by The McGraw-Hill Companies, Inc. Reprinted by permission of The McGraw-Hill Companies, Inc.

1. What is the topic of this flowchart? The cycle of low self-esteem (example of the effects of low self-esteem on a person preparing for and taking a test)
2. What are the immediate results of low performance expectation? reduced effort and high anxiety
3. What is the result of the person's actually failing the test? sense of low self-esteem is reinforced (causing the cycle to continue)

TABLE 4-1
SOURCES OF DNA EVIDENCE

EVIDENCE	POSSIBLE LOCATION OF DNA ON THE EVIDENCE	SOURCE OF DNA
Baseball bat or similar weapon	Handle, end	Sweat, skin, blood, tissue
Hat, bandanna, or mask	Inside	Sweat, hair, dandruff
Eyeglasses	Nose or ear pieces, lens	Sweat, skin
Facial tissue or cotton swab	Surface area	Mucus, blood, sweat, semen, earwax
Dirty laundry	Surface area	Blood, sweat, semen, vomit
Toothpick	Tips	Saliva
Used cigarette	Cigarette butt	Saliva
Stamp or envelope	Licked area	Saliva
Tape or ligature	Inside or outside surface	Skin, sweat
Bottle, can, or glass	Sides, mouthpiece	Saliva, sweat
Used condom	Inside or outside surface	Semen, vaginal or rectal cells
Blanket, pillow, or sheet	Surface area	Sweat, hair, semen, urine, saliva, dandruff
"Through and through" bullet	Outside surface	Blood, tissue
Bite mark	Person's skin or clothing	Saliva
Fingernail or partial fingernail	Scrapings	Blood, sweat, tissue

Source: "What Every Law Enforcement Officer Should Know about DNA Evidence." National Commission on the Future of DNA Evidence [Washington, D.C.: National Institute of Justice, 1999], pp.3–4.

Source: Charles Swanson, Neil Chamelin, Leonard Territo, and Robert Taylor, *Criminal Investigation,* 9th ed., Table 4-1, p. 120. Copyright © 2006 by The McGraw-Hill Companies, Inc. Reprinted by permission of The McGraw-Hill Companies, Inc.

1. From which types of evidence could saliva be collected? toothpick; used cigarette; stamp or envelope; bottle, can, or glass; blanket, pillow, or sheet; bite mark

2. Which two types of evidence have the greatest number of DNA sources? facial tissue or cotton swab; blanket, pillow, or sheet

3. On a baseball bat or similar weapon, where are the possible locations of DNA evidence? handle, end

READING

SELECTION **10-1**

Student Success

LIVING WITH STRESS

From *P.O.W.E.R. Learning: Strategies for Success in College and Life*
By Robert Feldman

If you're feeling the stress of college on top of everyday living, you're not alone! The author of this selection, psychology professor Robert Feldman, reports that all students experience stress to varying degrees throughout their college careers. In fact, research indicates that almost a third of first-year students report feeling frequently overwhelmed with all they have to do. He continues: "Coping with stress is one of the challenges that college students face. The many demands on your time can make you feel that you'll never finish what needs to get done. This pressure produces wear and tear on your body and mind, and it's easy to fall prey to ill health as a result. However, stress and poor health are not inevitable outcomes of college. In fact, by following simple guidelines for managing stress and deciding to make health a conscious priority, you can maintain good physical and mental health."

The selection below explains more about stress, its effects, and offers strategies for dealing with it effectively. These strategies help you cope with stress in other areas of your life as well, and they will continue to work for you long after you have left college.

---

1 Stressed out? Tests, papers, reading assignments, job demands, roommate problems, volunteer activities, committee work. . . . It's no surprise that these can produce stress. But it may be a surprise to know that so can graduating from high school, starting your dream job, falling in love, getting married, and even winning the lottery.

2 Virtually *anything*—good or bad—is capable of producing stress if it presents us with a challenge. Stress is the physical and emotional response we have to events that threaten or challenge us. It is rooted in the primitive "fight or flight" response wired into all animals—human and nonhuman. You see it in cats, for instance, when confronted by a dog or other threat. Their backs go up, their hair stands on end, their eyes widen, and, ultimately, they either take off or attack. The challenge stimulating this revved-up response is called a *stressor.* For humans, stressors can range from a first date to losing our chemistry notes to facing a flash flood.

3 Because our everyday lives are filled with events that can be interpreted as threatening or challenging, stress is commonplace in most people's lives. There are three main types of stressors:

4 1. **Cataclysmic events** are events that occur suddenly and affect many people simultaneously. Tornadoes, hurricanes, and plane crashes are examples of cataclysmic events. Although they may produce powerful immediate consequences, ironically they produce less stress than other types of stressors. The reason? Cataclysmic events have a clear endpoint, which can make them more manageable. Furthermore, because they affect many people simultaneously, their consequences are shared with others, and no individual feels singled out.

5 2. **Personal stressors** are major life events that produce a negative physical and psychological reaction. Failing

Annotation Practice

Directions: As you read this selection, underline or highlight main ideas and key terms. Use the space in the margins to write out the key terms and their definitions.

✓ **Teaching Tip**
For ease in locating information, numbered items and bullets are numbered as separate paragraphs.

a course, losing a job, and ending a relationship are all examples of personal stressors. Sometimes positive events—such as getting married or starting a new job—can act as personal stressors. Although the short-term impact of a personal stressor can be difficult, the long-term consequences may decline as people learn to adapt to the situation.

6 3. **Daily hassles** are the minor irritants of life that, singly, produce relatively little stress. Waiting in a traffic jam, receiving a tuition bill riddled with mistakes, and being interrupted by noises of major construction while trying to study are examples of such minor irritants. However, daily hassles add up, and cumulatively they can produce even more stress than a single larger-scale event. (Figure 1 indicates the most common daily hassles in people's lives.)

What Is Happening When We Are Stressed Out

7 Stress does more than make us feel anxious, upset, and fearful. Beneath those responses, we are experiencing many different physical reactions, each placing a high demand on our body's resources. Our hearts beat faster, our breathing becomes more rapid and shallow, and we produce more sweat. Our internal organs churn out a variety of hormones. In the long run, these physical responses wear down our immune system, our body's defense against disease. We become more susceptible to a variety of diseases, ranging from the common cold and headaches to strokes and heart disease. In fact, surveys have found that the greater the number of stressful events a person experiences over the course of a year, the more likely it is that he or she will have a major illness (see *Try It 1,* "Assess Your Susceptibility to Stress-Related Illness," pages 602–603).

Figure 1
Daily Hassles

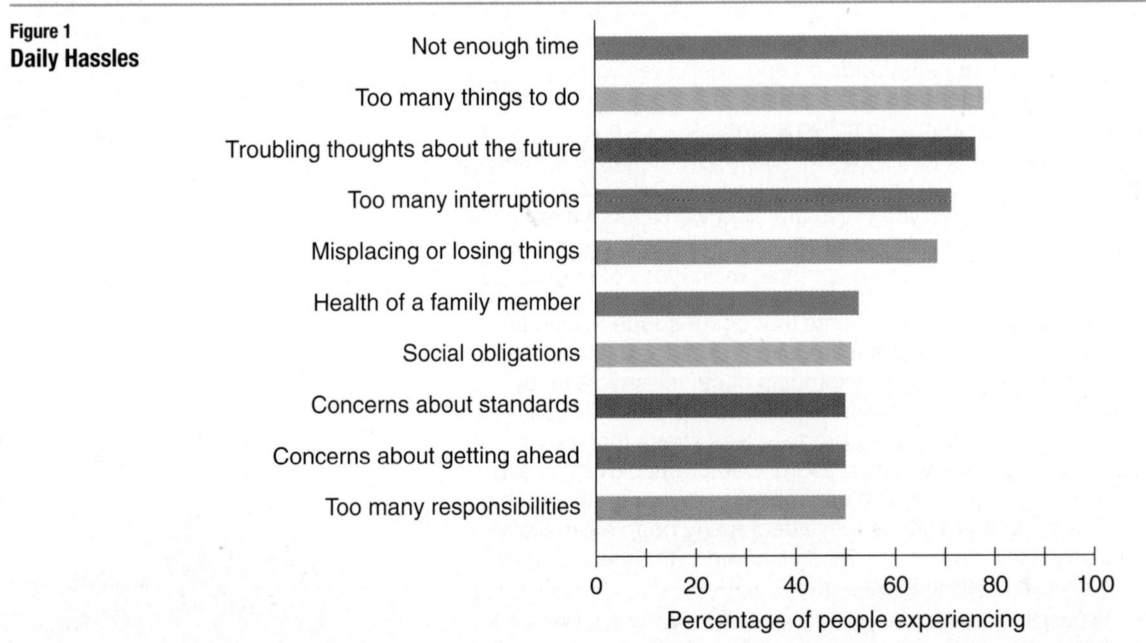

Handling Stress

8 Stress is an inevitable part of life. In fact, a life with no stress at all would be so boring, so uneventful, that you'd quickly miss the stress that had been removed. That doesn't mean, though, that we have to sit back and accept stress when it does arise. **Coping** is the effort to control, reduce, or tolerate the threats that lead to stress. Using the P.O.W.E.R. principles described below can help you ward off stress and actively deal with it. (Each letter in the word "POWER" stands for one of the steps: Prepare, Organize, Work, Evaluate, Rethink.)

Prepare: Readying Yourself Physically

9 Being in good physical condition is the primary way to prepare for future stress. Stress takes its toll on your body, so it makes sense that the stronger and fitter you are, the less negative impact stress will have on you. For example, a regular exercise program reduces heart rate, respiration rate, and blood pressure at times when the body is at rest—making us better able to withstand the negative consequences of stress. Furthermore, vigorous exercise produces endorphins, natural painkilling chemicals in the brain. Endorphins produce feelings of happiness—even euphoria—and may be responsible for the "runner's high," the positive feelings often reported by long-distance runners following long runs. Through the production of endorphins, then, exercise can help our bodies produce a natural coping response to stress.

10 If you now drink a lot of coffee or soda, a change in your diet may be enough to bring about a reduction in stress. Coffee, soda, chocolate, and a surprising number of other foods contain caffeine, which can make you feel jittery and anxious even without stress; add a stressor, and the reaction can be very intense and unpleasant.

11 Eating right can alleviate another problem: obesity. Around one-third of people in the United States are obese, defined as having body weight more than 20 percent above the average weight for a person of a given height. Obesity can bring on stress for several reasons. For one thing, being overweight drags down the functioning of the body, leading to fatigue and a reduced ability to bounce back when we encounter challenges to our well-being. In addition, feeling heavy in a society that acclaims the virtues of slimness can be stressful in and of itself.

Organize: Identifying What Is Causing You Stress

12 You can't cope effectively with stress until you know what's causing it. In some cases, it's obvious—a series of bad test grades in a course, a roommate problem that keeps getting worse, a job supervisor who seems to delight in making things difficult. In other cases, however, the causes of stress may be more subtle. Perhaps your relationship with your boyfriend or girlfriend is rocky, and you have a nagging feeling that something is wrong.

13 Whatever the source of stress, you can't deal with it unless you know what it is. To organize your assault on stress, then, take a piece of paper and list the major circumstances that are

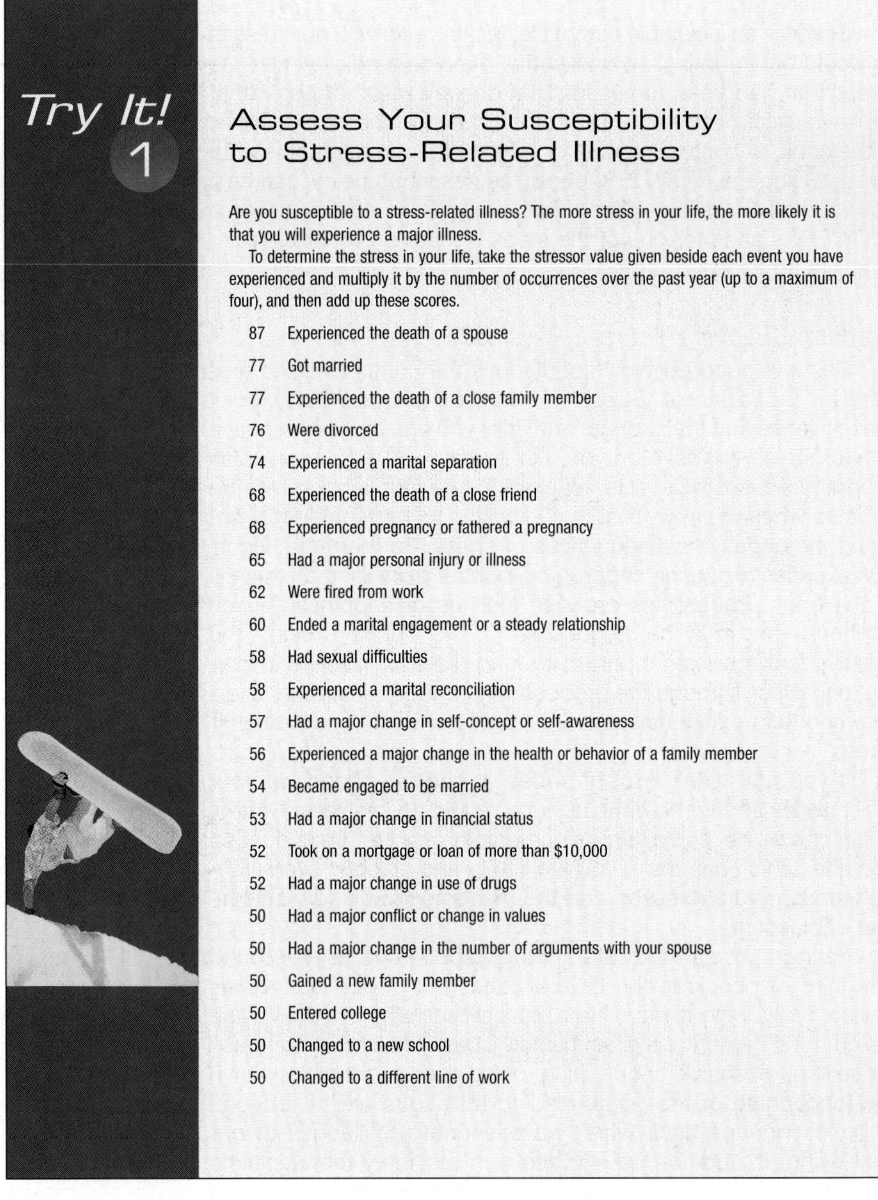

Try It! 1

Assess Your Susceptibility to Stress-Related Illness

Are you susceptible to a stress-related illness? The more stress in your life, the more likely it is that you will experience a major illness.

To determine the stress in your life, take the stressor value given beside each event you have experienced and multiply it by the number of occurrences over the past year (up to a maximum of four), and then add up these scores.

87	Experienced the death of a spouse
77	Got married
77	Experienced the death of a close family member
76	Were divorced
74	Experienced a marital separation
68	Experienced the death of a close friend
68	Experienced pregnancy or fathered a pregnancy
65	Had a major personal injury or illness
62	Were fired from work
60	Ended a marital engagement or a steady relationship
58	Had sexual difficulties
58	Experienced a marital reconciliation
57	Had a major change in self-concept or self-awareness
56	Experienced a major change in the health or behavior of a family member
54	Became engaged to be married
53	Had a major change in financial status
52	Took on a mortgage or loan of more than $10,000
52	Had a major change in use of drugs
50	Had a major conflict or change in values
50	Had a major change in the number of arguments with your spouse
50	Gained a new family member
50	Entered college
50	Changed to a new school
50	Changed to a different line of work

causing you stress. Just listing them will help put you in control, and you'll be better able to figure out strategies for coping with them.

Work: Developing Effective Coping Strategies

14 A wide variety of tactics can help you deal with stress. Among the most effective approaches to coping are these:

15 • **Take charge of the situation.** Stress is most apt to arise when we are faced with situations over which we have little or no control. If you take charge of the situation, you'll reduce the

49	Had a major change in amount of independence and responsibility
47	Had a major change in responsibilities at work
46	Experienced a major change in use of alcohol
45	Revised personal habits
44	Had trouble with school administration
43	Held a job while attending school
43	Had a major change in social activities
42	Had trouble with in-laws
42	Had a major change in working hours or conditions
42	Changed residence or living conditions
41	Had your spouse begin or cease work outside the home
41	Changed your choice of major field of study
41	Changed dating habits
40	Had an outstanding personal achievement
38	Had trouble with your boss
38	Had a major change in amount of participation in school activities
37	Had a major change in type and/or amount of recreation
36	Had a major change in religious activities
34	Had a major change of sleeping habits
33	Took a trip or vacation
30	Had a major change in eating habits
26	Had a major change in the number of family get-togethers
22	Were found guilty of minor violations of the law

Scoring: If your total score is above 1,435, you are in a high-stress category and therefore more at risk for experiencing a stress-related illness. A high score does *not* mean that you are sure to get sick. Many other factors determine ill health, and high stress is only one cause. Other positive factors in your life, such as getting enough sleep and exercise, may prevent illness. Still, having an unusually high amount of stress in your life is a cause for concern, and you may want to take steps to reduce it.

To Try It online, go to **www.mhhe.com/power**.

Encourage students to try this online exercise.

experience of stress. For example, if several assignments are all due on the same day, you might try negotiating with one of your instructors for a later due date.

16 • **Don't waste energy trying to change the unchangeable.** There are some situations that you simply can't control. You can't change the fact that you have come down with a case of mono, and you can't change your performance on a test you took last week. Don't hit your head against a brick wall and try to modify things that can't be changed. Use your energy to improve the situation, not to rewrite history.

17 • **Look for the silver lining.** Stress arises when we perceive a situation as negative and threatening. If we can change how

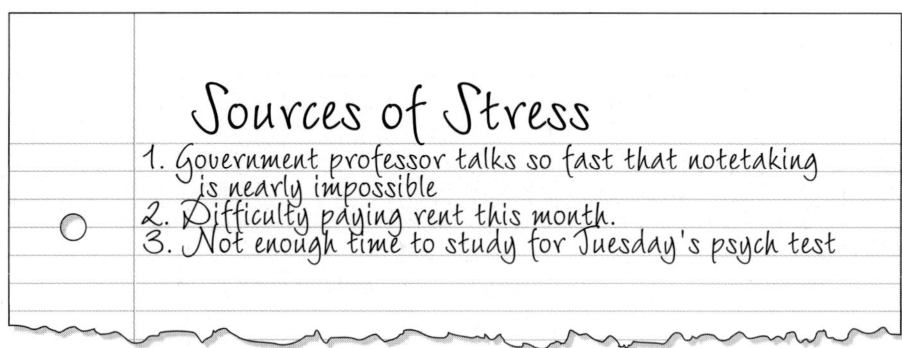

we perceive that situation and find something good about it, we can change our reactions to it. For instance, if your computer science instructor requires you to learn a difficult spreadsheet program in a very short time, the saving grace is that you may be able to use the skill to your advantage in getting a high-paying temporary job during school vacation. (You can practice finding the silver lining in *Try It 2*.)

Sources of Stress
1. Government professor talks so fast that notetaking is nearly impossible
2. Difficulty paying rent this month.
3. Not enough time to study for Tuesday's psych test

18 • **Talk to your friends.** Social support assistance and comfort supplied by others can help us through stressful periods. Turning to our friends and family and simply talking about the stress we're under can help us tolerate it more effectively. Even anonymous telephone hotlines can provide us with social support (The U.S. Public Health Service maintains a master toll-free number that can provide telephone numbers and addresses of many national helplines and support groups. You can reach it by calling 800-336-4794.)

19 • **Relax.** Because stress produces constant wear and tear on the body, it seems possible that practices that lead to the relaxation of the body might lead to a reduction in stress. And that's just what happens. Using any one of several techniques for producing physical relaxation can prevent stress. Among the best relaxation techniques:

20 **Meditation.** Though often associated with its roots in the ancient Eastern religion of Zen Buddhism, meditation, a technique for refocusing attention and producing bodily relaxation, is practiced in some form by members of virtually every major religion. Meditation reduces blood pressure, slows respiration, and in general reduces bodily tension.

21 **How do you meditate?** The process is actually rather simple. As summarized in Table 1, it includes sitting in a quiet room with eyes closed or focused on a point about 6 feet away from you and paying attention to your breathing. Though the specifics of what you do may vary, meditation works by helping you concentrate on breathing deeply and rhythmically, sometimes murmuring a word or sound repeatedly.

22 **Progressive Relaxation.** Progressive relaxation does some of the same things that meditation does, but in a more direct

Look for the Silver Lining

Consider the following list of potentially stressful situations. Try to find something positive—a silver lining—in each of them. The first two are completed to get you started.

Situation	Silver Lining
1. Your car just broke down and repairing it is more than you can afford right now.	1. This is the perfect time to begin exercising by walking and using your bicycle.
2. Your boss just yelled at you and threatened to fire you.	2. Either this is a good time to open an honest discussion with your boss about your job situation, OR this is a good time to get a more interesting job.
3. You have two papers due on Monday and there's a great concert you wanted to go to on Saturday night.	3.
4. You just failed an important test.	4.
5. You're flat broke, you have a date on Saturday, and you wanted to buy some things beforehand.	5.
6. Your last date went poorly and you think your girlfriend/boyfriend was hinting that it was time to break up.	6.
7. Your parents just told you that they can't afford to pay your tuition next semester.	7.
8. You just got cut from a sports team or club activity you loved.	8.
9. Your best friend is starting to turn weird and seems not to enjoy being with you as much as before.	9.
10. You just realized you don't really like your academic major, and you're not even sure you like your college much anymore.	10.

Working in a Group: After you have considered each of these situations individually, discuss each of them in a group. What similarities and differences in others' responses did you find? Evaluate the different responses, and consider whether—and why—some ways of reframing the situations were better than others.

To Try It online, go to **www.mhhe.com/power**.

way. To use progressive relaxation, you systematically tense and then relax different groups of muscles. For example, you might start with your lower arm, tensing it for 5 seconds and then relaxing it for a similar amount of time. By doing the same thing throughout the parts of your body, you'll be able to learn the "feel" of bodily relaxation. You can use the technique when you feel that stress is getting the better of you. (Use *Try It 3* to experience progressive relaxation for yourself.)

23 • **Remember that wimping out doesn't work—so keep your commitments.** Suppose you've promised a friend that you'll help him move, and you've promised yourself that you'll spend more time with your children. You've also been elected to the student body governing board, and you've made a commitment to bring more speakers to campus. Now you are facing all the demands connected to these commitments and feeling stressed.

24 You may be tempted to cope with the feeling by breaking some or all of your commitments, thinking, "I just need to sit

Table 1
Methods of Meditation

Step 1. Pick a focus word or short phrase that's firmly rooted in your personal belief system. For example, a nonreligious individual might choose a neutral word like *one* or *peace* or *love.* A Christian person desiring to use a prayer could pick the opening words of Psalm 23. *The Lord is my shepherd;* a Jewish person could choose *Shalom.*

Step 2. Sit quietly in a comfortable position.

Step 3. Close your eyes.

Step 4. Relax your muscles.

Step 5. Breathe slowly and naturally, repeating your focus word or phrase silently as you exhale.

Step 6. Throughout, assume a passive attitude. Don't worry about how well you're doing. When other thoughts come to mind, simply say to yourself, "Oh, well," and gently return to the repetition.

Step 7. Continue for 10 to 20 minutes. You may open your eyes to check the time, but do not use an alarm. When you finish, sit quietly for a minute or so, at first with your eyes closed and later with your eyes open. Then do not stand for 1 or 2 minutes.

Step 8. Practice the technique once or twice a day.

at home and relax in front of the television!" This is not coping. It is escaping, and it doesn't reduce stress. Ducking out of commitments, whether to yourself or to others, will make you feel guilty and anxious, and will be another source of stress—one without the satisfaction of having accomplished what you set out to do. Keep your promises.

Evaluate: Asking If Your Strategies for Dealing with Stress Are Effective

25 Just as the experience of stress depends on how we interpret circumstances, the strategies for dealing with stress also vary in effectiveness depending on who we are. So if your efforts at coping aren't working, it's time to reconsider your approach. If talking to friends hasn't helped ease your stress response, maybe you need a different approach. Maybe you need to see the silver lining or cut back on some of your commitments.

26 If one coping strategy doesn't work for you, try another. What's critical is that you not become paralyzed, unable to deal with a situation. Instead, try something different until you find the right combination of strategies to improve the situation.

Rethink: Placing Stress in Perspective

27 It's easy to think of stress as an enemy. In fact, the coping steps outlined in the P.O.W.E.R. Plan are geared to overcoming its negative consequences. But consider the following two principles, which in the end may help you more than any others in dealing with stress:

28 • **Don't sweat the small stuff . . . and it's all small stuff.** Stress expert Richard Carlson emphasizes the importance of putting the circumstances we encounter into the proper perspective. He argues that we frequently let ourselves get upset about situations that are actually minor. So what if someone cuts us off in traffic, or does less than his or her

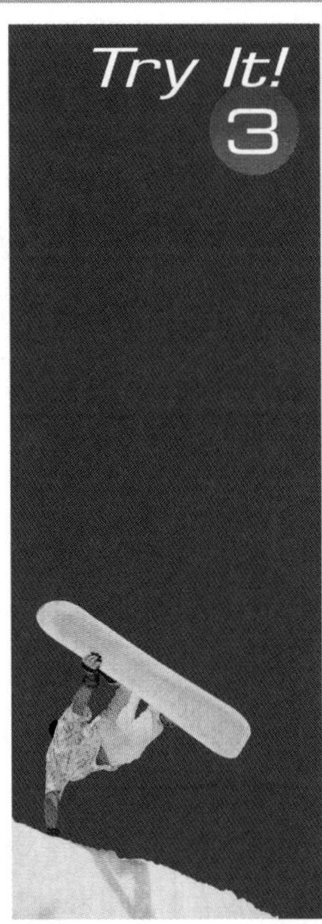

Try Progressive Relaxation

You can undertake progressive relaxation almost anywhere, including the library, a sports field, or a classroom, since tensing and relaxing muscles is quiet and unobtrusive. Although the following exercise suggests you lie down, you can use parts of it no matter where you are.

1. Lie flat on your back, get comfortable, and focus on your toes.
2. Become aware of your left toes. Bunch them up into a tight ball, then let them go. Then let them relax even further.
3. Now work on your left foot, from the toes to the heel. Without tensing your toes, tighten up the rest of your foot and then let it relax. Then relax it more.
4. Work your way up your left leg, first tensing and then relaxing each part. You may move up as slowly or as quickly as you wish, using big leaps (e.g., the entire lower leg) or small steps (e.g., the ankle, the calf, the front of the lower leg, the knee, etc.).
5. Repeat the process for the right leg.
6. Now tense and relax progressively your groin, buttocks, abdomen, lower back, ribs, upper back, and shoulders.
7. Work your way down each arm, one at a time, until you reach the fingers.
8. Return to the neck, then the jaw, cheeks, nose, eyes, ears, forehead, and skull.

By now you should be completely relaxed. In fact, you may even be asleep—this technique works well as a sleep-induction strategy.

To vary the routine, play with it. Try going from top to bottom, or from your extremities in and ending with your groin. Or target any other part of your body to end up at, and take the most circuitous route you can think of.

To Try It online, go to **www.mhhe.com/power**.

share on a group project, or unfairly criticizes us? It's hardly the end of the world, and the behavior of the other people involved in such situations reflects negatively on them, not us. One of the best ways to reduce stress, consequently, is to maintain an appropriate perspective on the events of your life.

29 • **Make peace with stress.** Think of what it would be like to have no stress—none at all—in your life. Would you really be happier, better adjusted, and more successful? The answer is "probably not." A life that presented no challenges would probably be, in a word, boring. So think about stress as an exciting, although admittedly sometimes difficult, friend. Welcome it, because its presence indicates that your life is stimulating, challenging, and exciting—and who would want it any other way?

Source: Robert Feldman, *P.O.W.E.R. Learning,* 2005 ed., pp. 364–74, including figures. Copyright © 2005 by The McGraw-Hill Companies, Inc. Reprinted by permission of The McGraw-Hill Companies, Inc.

SELECTION 10-1 Student Success (continued)

Comprehension and Vocabulary Quiz

This quiz has four parts. Your instructor may assign some or all of them.

Comprehension

Directions: Items 1–5 test your comprehension (understanding) of the material in this selection. These questions are much like those that a content-area instructor would expect you to know after reading and studying this selection. For each comprehension question below, use information from the selection to determine the correct answer. Refer to the selection as you answer the questions. Write your answers in the spaces provided.

¶4 c **1.** Cataclysmic events are:

a. major life events that produce a negative physical and psychological reaction.

b. minor irritants of life that, singly, produce relatively little stress.

c. events that occur suddenly and affect many people at the same time.

d. events that lead to mental and physical problems.

¶7 a **2.** The greater the number of stressful events a person experiences in a year's time:

a. the more likely it is he or she will have a major illness.

b. the faster the heart beats.

c. the more hormones are produced in the body.

d. the more rapid and shallow a person's breathing becomes.

¶5 b **3.** Losing a job is an example of:

a. a cataclysmic stressor.

b. a personal stressor.

c. a daily hassle.

d. bad luck.

¶s 9–11 d **4.** Which of the following can contribute to stress?

a. drinking large amounts of coffee and soda

b. being overweight

c. lack of regular exercise

d. all of the above

¶17 d **5.** The strategy of looking for a silver lining refers to:

a. using your energy to improve a situation, not to rewrite history.

b. seeking assistance in the form of social support.

c. refocusing attention to produce bodily relaxation.

d. changing how you perceive a negative situation to find something good about it.

Vocabulary in Context

Directions: Items 6–10 test your ability to determine the meaning of the word by using context clues. *Context clues* are words in a sentence that allow the reader to deduce (reason out) the meaning of an unfamiliar word in that sentence. Context clues also enable the reader to determine which meaning the author intends when a word has more than one meaning. For each vocabulary item below, a sentence from the selection containing an important word (*italicized, like this*) is quoted first. Next, there is an additional sentence using the word in the same sense and providing another context clue. Use the context clues from *both* sentences to deduce the meaning of the italicized word. *Be sure the answer you choose makes sense in both sentences.* If you need to use a dictionary to confirm your answer choice, remember that the meaning you select must still fit the context of *both* sentences. Write your answers in the spaces provided.

Pronunciation Key: ă **pat** ā **pay** âr **care** ä **father** ĕ **pet** ē **be** ĭ **pit** ī **tie** îr **pier** ŏ **pot** ō **toe** ô **paw** oi **noise** ou **out** o͝o **took** o͞o **boot** ŭ **cut** yo͞o **abuse** ûr **urge** th **thin** *th* **this** hw **which** zh **vision** ə **about** *Stress mark:* ′

¶9 c **6.** Endorphins produce feelings of happiness—even *euphoria*—and may be responsible for the "runner's high," the positive feelings often reported by long-distance runners following long runs.

The wrestler's *euphoria* over winning disappeared when he was later disqualified for an illegal move.

euphoria (yo͞o fôr′ ē ə) means:

a. the "runner's high"

b. feeling of great disappointment

c. feeling of great happiness or well-being

d. feeling of deep anger or hostility

¶11 a **7.** Eating right can *alleviate* another problem: obesity.

There are many over-the-counter medications designed to *alleviate* cold symptoms.

alleviate (ə lē′ vē āt) means:

a. to make less severe

b. to become increasingly unpleasant

c. to assist or aid

d. to intensify

¶11 b **8.** In addition, feeling heavy in a society that *acclaims* the virtues of slimness can be stressful in and of itself.

The series of ads *acclaims* the candidate's achievements without revealing his previous bankruptcies.

acclaims (ə klāmz′) means:

a. mentions or refers to incidentally

b. praises enthusiastically and often publicly

c. directs to a source of help or information

d. pertains to, concerns

¶21 c **9.** Though the specifics of what you do may vary, meditation works by helping you concentrate on breathing deeply and rhythmically, sometimes *murmuring* a word or sound repeatedly.

The breeze was *murmuring* through the trees and made a comforting, soothing sound.

murmuring (mûr′ mər ĭng) means:

a. making a high-pitched sound

b. making a buzzing sound

c. making a low, continuous, indistinct sound

d. making a loud, short sound

¶22 c **10.** To use *progressive* relaxation, you systematically tense and then relax different groups of muscles.

Rather than make sudden, drastic changes in the company, the new owner made *progressive* changes over the course of two years.

progressive (prə grĕs′ ĭv) means:

a. promoting new ideas and better conditions

b. decreasing, diminishing

c. proceeding in steps

d. changing from one position to another

Word Structure

Directions: Items 11–15 test your ability to use word-structure clues to help determine a word's meaning. *Word-structure clues* consist of roots, prefixes, and suffixes. In these exercises, you will learn the meaning of a word part (a root) and use it to determine the meaning of several other words that have the same word part. If you need to use a dictionary to confirm your answer choice, do so. Write your answers in the spaces provided.

In paragraph 18 of the selection, you encountered the word **anonymous.** This word contains the Latin root ***nym,*** which means "name." The word *anonymous* means having an unknown or unacknowledged name (such as an anonymous author or an anonymous donor). Use the meaning of ***nym*** and the list of prefixes on pages 68–69 to help you determine the meaning of each of the following words that contain the same root.

b **11.** If you know that the word part *pseudo* means "false," then a **pseudonym** would be:

a. an author's actual name.

b. a fictitious name an author uses instead of his or her actual name.

c. a nickname.

d. the name of a famous person.

d **12.** "Little" and "small" are examples of synonyms. **Synonyms** are words that:

a. have 5 letters.

b. refer to something that is tiny.

c. appear in the English language.
d. have the same or nearly the same meaning.

a 13. "Big" and "little" are examples of antonyms. **Antonyms** are words that:
a. have opposite meanings.
b. have the same spelling.
c. mean the same thing.
d. have the same sound.

d 14. The words *row* (verb; to propel a boat with oars) and *row* (noun; a straight line) are examples of homonyms. **Homonyms** are words that:
a. look alike.
b. sound alike.
c. mean the same thing
d. have the same sound and spelling, but different meanings.

d 15. *Bow* (noun; a knot with loops) and *bow* (verb; to bend the upper body forward) are examples of heteronyms. **Heteronyms** are words that:
a. sound alike.
b. have the same spelling and pronunciation.
c. mean the same thing.
d. have the same spelling, but different sound and meaning.

✓ **Teaching Tip**
Students may enjoy learning the word *ananym,* a name formed by reversing letters of another name. (For example, talk-show host Oprah Winfrey uses the *ananym* "Harpo" as the name of her production company.) A related word is *aptronym,* a name that's especially suited to one's profession, e.g., Sally Ride, the astronaut.

Reading Skills Application

Directions: Items 16–20 test your ability to *apply* certain reading skills to information in this selection. These types of questions provide valuable practice for all students, especially those who must take standardized reading tests and state-mandated basic skills tests. Write your answers in the spaces provided.

¶s 8–29 authors' writing patterns (Chapter 7)

b 16. The information in the section "Handling Stress" is organized using which overall pattern?
a. list
b. sequence
c. comparison
d. contrast

¶s 27–29 author's tone (Chapter 8)

d 17. In the "Rethink" section, the author's tone is:
a. emotional and opinionated.
b. angry and bitter.
c. apologetic.
d. encouraging and supportive.

¶s 8, 29 author's point of view (Chapter 8) c

18. What is the author's attitude toward stress?

a. Stress is inevitable and can be difficult, but being in good physical health can help you cope effectively with it.

b. Stress is inevitable, and it has harmful mental and physical effects.

c. Stress is inevitable and can be difficult, but it also makes life stimulating, challenging, and exciting.

d. Stress is inevitable, but it also makes life bearable.

¶s 1, 6, 17, 23 author's intended audience (Chapter 8) c

19. The author's intended audience for this selection is:

a. business professionals.

b. people who are coping with health problems.

c. college students.

d. the general public.

¶8 author's assumption (Chapter 9) d

20. Which of the following assumptions does the author make?

a. College students experience a greater number of cataclysmic events than other people.

b. College students should take whatever steps are necessary to avoid experiencing any stress.

c. College students are not capable of recognizing and dealing with stress.

d. College students experience a great deal of stress, but if they are made aware of coping strategies, they will use them.

SELECTION **10-1**
Student Success
(continued)

Collaboration Option

Writing and Collaborating to Enhance Your Understanding

Option for collaboration: Your instructor may direct you to work with other students or, in other words, to work *collaboratively.* In that case, you should form groups of three or four students as directed by your instructor and work together to complete the exercises. After your group discusses each item and agrees on the answer, have a group member record it. Every member of your group should be able to explain all of your group's answers.

1. Reacting to What You Have Read: Which of the strategies in the "Work" section (paragraphs 14–24) do you currently use? If you do not currently use any of them, which ones do you think might work for you? Explain how you use them or how you might use them. In which types of circumstances would they be especially helpful?

(Answers will vary.)
____
____
____
____
____
____
____

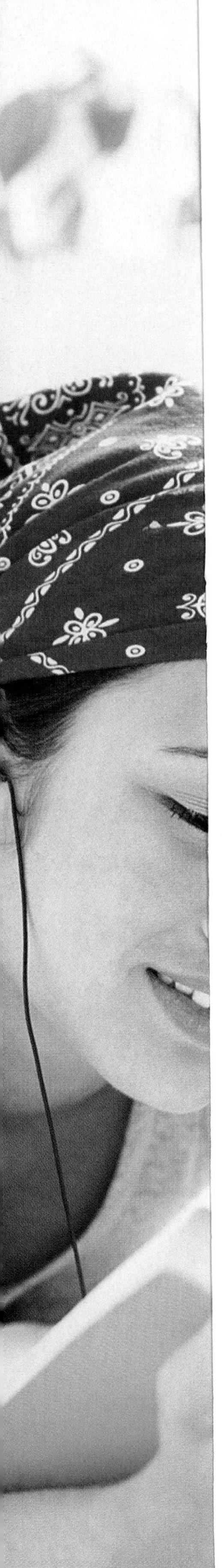

2. **Comprehending the Selection Further:** Based on information in the selection about stress, decide which category each of the following stressors represents. For each stressor, place a check mark in the appropriate column.

	Cataclysmic Event	Personal Stressor	Daily Hassle
1. house fire		✓	
2. flash flooding of region	✓		
3. flu epidemic in a city	✓		
4. losing a computer file			✓
5. becoming engaged		✓	
6. car is stolen		✓	
7. massive hailstorm	✓		
8. misplaced keys			✓
9. flat tire			✓
10. final interview for an important job		✓	

3. **Overall Main Idea of the Selection:** In one sentence tell what the author wants readers to understand about stress. (Be sure to include the word "stress" in your overall main idea sentence.)

Stress is inevitable, yet stimulating, so college students should develop techniques for dealing with it.

Read More about This Topic on the World Wide Web

Internet Resources

Directions: For further information about the topic of the selection, visit these websites:

www.usu.edu/arc/idea_sheets/index.htm
This site is sponsored by the Utah Academic Resource Center. It presents "Idea Sheets" that contain information, strategies, self-assessment, and practice exercises. In the section on "Self-Management," check out the information on "Managing Stress," "C.O.P.E.ing with Problems," and "Change." (Other information on time management, procrastination, test-taking, public speaking, etc., can also reduce stress!)

www.utexas.edu/student/utlc/lrnres/handouts/1439.html
This website is sponsored by the University of Texas at Austin's Learning Center. In the "Tips for Managing Stress" section, you can take a 12-item "Stress Test" and then read some common misperceptions regarding stress, as well as tips for reducing stress. If tests are a particular source of stress, you will find it helpful to click on "How to Survive Exam Week," "Keeping Calm During Tests," "Test Anxiety: Frequently Asked Questions," and "Self-Talk for Reducing Anxiety."

HOW ARE REHEARSAL AND MEMORY RELATED?

As you may have discovered, it is difficult to memorize information that you do not understand. This is why you must focus on understanding material before attempting to memorize it. Thorough comprehension allows you to memorize more efficiently.

Even when you understand material, however, you should not underestimate the time or effort needed to memorize it. To do well on tests, you must study information effectively enough to store it in **long-term memory,** or permanent memory. One serious mistake students make is leaving too little study time before the test to transfer material into long-term memory. Instead, they try to rely on **short-term memory.** However, material remains in short-term memory only temporarily. If you rely on short-term memory only (this is called *cramming*), much of the information will not be there later when you try to recall it on the test.

KEY TERMS
long-term memory
Permanent memory.

short-term memory
Temporary memory.

To understand the difference between long-term and short-term memory, consider a telephone number that you have just heard on the radio. The number is only in your short-term memory and will be forgotten in a matter of seconds *unless you do something to transfer it into long-term memory*. In other words, you will forget the number unless you "rehearse" it in some way.

Rehearsal refers to taking specific steps to transfer information into long-term memory. Typical steps include writing information down and repeatedly reciting it aloud. In the example above, for instance, rehearsing the telephone number would probably involve writing it, saying it aloud several times, or both.

KEY TERM
rehearsal
Steps taken to transfer information into long-term memory.

In Chapter 1, you read about visual, auditory, and tactile/kinesthetic learning styles and about their particular importance to students. It is obvious that rehearsing information by writing and reciting involves all of the senses and addresses all of the learning styles. Rehearsing by writing and reciting involves speaking, hearing, writing, and reading. Writing the information has the added benefit of helping you learn to spell important terms and names that you may have to use in test answers.

Consider how much information you already have stored in long-term memory: the alphabet; the multiplication tables; names of thousands of people, places, and things; and the meanings and spellings of tens of thousands of words. How did these items make it into your long-term memory? You successfully stored these in your long-term memory because you rehearsed them again and again.

Perhaps the greatest mistake students make when trying to memorize information for a test is that they spend their time merely rereading it. You can reread endlessly, but you will not remember the information. Rereading is not the same as rehearsing.

As noted in Chapter 10, rehearsal is the third key to effective studying. When you prepare for a test, spread your studying over several days, enough days to allow you to transfer information from short-term memory into long-term memory. Both sufficient time and ample repetition are needed to accomplish this transfer.

Before you can rehearse textbook information efficiently, you need to *organize* it. The better you organize it, the more efficiently you will be able to memorize it. If you organize the material in your assignments consistently as you study, right from the beginning of the semester, you will be prepared to rehearse and memorize material for each test. You can organize material by using any of these techniques (which are presented later in this chapter):

- Underlining and annotating textbook material
- Outlining or mapping information

- Preparing summaries
- Making review or summary cards (like the ones in each chapter of *New Worlds*)

Underlining, annotating, outlining, mapping, and summarizing have already been discussed. Review cards, which you have been working with throughout *New Worlds,* are another important study tool. The very act of preparing these study tools helps you store information in long-term memory.

After you have organized material, rehearse by doing one or more of the following:

- Reciting from your notes
- Writing out the information again from memory
- Reciting from chapter review cards or test review sheets

As noted earlier, students too often review for a test simply by rereading their notes and their textbook over and over again. But this time-consuming process does not automatically result in remembering. About 80 percent of the time spent studying for a test should be used for memorizing, that is, for transferring information into long-term memory. Here is an example of how you could apply this "80 percent rule." If you need five hours to study for a test, you would spend the first hour organizing the material and getting help with things you do not understand. The remaining four hours would be spent rehearsing the material in order to memorize it.

You may be wondering, "How can I tell when I have successfully transferred information into long-term memory?" The answer is simple: Test yourself. Try to write the information from memory on a blank sheet of paper. If the material is in your long-term memory, you will be able to recall it and write it down. If you cannot write it, or can write only a part of it, then you need to rehearse it further. Until you can write or say the material aloud without looking at your notes, book, or review cards, you haven't mastered it, and you need to keep rehearsing. Isn't it better, though, to make that discovery while there's still time to learn it than to make that discovery when you are taking the test?

These steps may sound like a lot of work, but they are necessary if you want to lock information into long-term memory. It is precisely this type of study effort that leads to mastery.

HOW CAN YOU UNDERLINE, HIGHLIGHT, AND ANNOTATE YOUR TEXTBOOKS?

KEY TERMS

underlining and highlighting

Techniques for marking topics, main ideas, and definitions.

annotating

Writing explanatory notes in the margins of your textbook to organize and remember important information.

It has been estimated that more than three-quarters of the material on college tests comes from the textbooks. For this reason alone, you need to be able to underline, highlight, and annotate the important information in them.

Underlining and **highlighting** are techniques for marking topics, main ideas, and important definitions in textbooks. **Annotating** refers to writing explanatory notes in the margins of your textbook to organize and remember important information. Taking a moment to annotate information (write it down) also helps you concentrate and stay focused on your studying. When you are reading a difficult textbook, you may need to concentrate on it paragraph by paragraph. Effective students combine underlining or highlighting with annotating.

Underlining and highlighting textbook material is a selective process. This means you need to avoid the most common mistake students make in marking textbooks: *overmarking*—underlining or highlighting too much. They generally make this mistake because they underline or highlight while they are reading a paragraph for the first time instead of *after* they have read it. You cannot know what is important until you have *finished* reading. The main idea sometimes does not appear until the end of a paragraph. Also, you may not be able to understand some paragraphs until you have read an entire section. The rule, then, is this: *Read first, and underline only after you have identified the important ideas.* A word of caution: Some students substitute underlining and highlighting for *thinking*. They mistakenly believe that if they have marked a lot in a chapter, they must have read it carefully, found the important information, and understand it. To avoid this error, follow these steps: Read and *think; then* underline or highlight *selectively*.

Second, you need to know the kinds of things you *should* underline or highlight. As mentioned above, underline or highlight the *topic* of a paragraph and the *main idea* of a paragraph if it is stated directly. Keep in mind that you won't always need to underline every word of a main idea sentence to capture the idea it is expressing. Underline or highlight important *terms* and *definitions*.

Third, you need to know the kinds of things you should *not* underline or highlight. Do not underline or highlight examples or other supporting details because this results in overmarking. (As you will learn below, annotation can be used effectively for supporting details.)

Once you have underlined and highlighted topics, main ideas, and important terms, you will want to *annotate:* that is, write explanatory notes and symbols in the margins. If a textbook has narrow margins, you may prefer to use notebook paper or even stick-on notes. You may be wondering what types of annotations are helpful and why it is necessary to annotate as well as to underline or highlight. Of course, you can jot the *topic* in the margin beside each paragraph. This is especially helpful with complex material and with passages on standardized reading tests. In addition, writing out an important *term* and its *definition* in the margin helps you remember it. When your instructor uses those terms in class, you will recognize them and be able to use them in your lecture notes. And, of course, you will need to know terms for tests.

Also, you may choose to list essential *supporting details* in shortened (paraphrased) form in the margin. Annotating is an effective, convenient, concise way to organize details, and jotting details in the margin helps you connect them with the main ideas they support.

Formulated main ideas are another type of helpful annotation. Write them in the margin next to the paragraph.

Symbols and *abbreviations* are still another helpful type of annotation. They enable you to locate important material quickly and find passages that need further study. Here are examples of abbreviations and symbols you can use in the margins:

def	*Definition*. Use *def* when an important term is defined.
1, 2, 3 . . .	*Numbers*. Use numbers when an author gives items in a list or series, or when you want to make the primary supporting details stand out.
*	Use an *asterisk* to mark important information, such as information the instructor has indicated will be on a test.
?	*Question mark*. Use this when you do not understand something and need to come back to it for further study or get help with it.
ex	Use *ex* to identify helpful examples.

✓ **Teaching Tip**
Point out that the name of this symbol (*) is pronounced asteri*sk* (not asteri*ck*). The starburst shape gets its name from the Latin word *aster*, meaning "star."

The box on page 620 shows how a passage from a human development textbook (about different forms of marriage) could be underlined and annotated. Notice how helpful these markings would be when reviewing for a test on the material.

AN EXAMPLE OF UNDERLINING AND ANNOTATION

A lifestyle practice that apparently exists in all societies is marriage—a socially and/or religiously sanctioned union between a woman and a man with the expectation that they will perform the mutually supportive roles of wife and husband. After studying extensive cross-cultural data, anthropologist George P. Murdock (1949) concluded that ① reproduction, ② sexual relations, ③ economic cooperation, and the ④ socialization of offspring are functions of families throughout the world. We now recognize that Murdock overstated the matter, ? because in some societies, such as Israeli kibbutz communities, the family does not perform all four of these functions (Spiro, 1954; Gough, 1960). What Murdock describes are commonly encountered tendencies in family functioning in most cultures.

def marriage: socially and/or religiously sanctioned union of a woman and a man with the expectation they will perform the mutually supporting roles of wife and husband

4 tendencies in functions of families:*
—reproduction
—sexual relations
—economic cooperation
—socialization of offspring

Societies differ in how they structure marriage relationships. Four patterns are found: monogamy, one husband and one wife; polygyny, one husband and two or more wives; polyandry, two or more husbands and one wife; and group marriage, two or more husbands and two or more wives. Although monogamy exists in all societies, Murdock discovered that other forms are not only allowed but preferred. Of 238 societies in his sample, only about one-fifth were strictly monogamous.

Four patterns of marriage:*
—monogamy: 1 husband/1 wife
—polygyny: 1 husband/2+ wives
—polyandry: 2+ husbands/1 wife
—group marriage: 2+ husbands/2+ wives

Polygyny has been widely practiced throughout the world. The Old Testament reports that both King David and King Solomon had several wives. In his cross-cultural sample of 238 societies, Murdock found that 193 (an overwhelming majority) permitted husbands to take several wives. In one-third of these polygynous societies, however, less than one-fifth of the married men had more than one wife. Usually only the rich men in a society can afford to support more than one family.

Ex:
Old Testament kings with several wives:
—Solomon
—David
—Murdock study: 193/238 societies permitted polygyny
—Usually only rich were polygynous

In contrast with polygyny, polyandry is rare among the world's societies. And in practice, polyandry has not usually allowed freedom of mate selection for women—it has often meant simply that younger brothers have sexual access to the wife of an older brother. For example, if a father is unable to afford wives for each of his sons, he may secure a wife for only his oldest son.

—women not usually allowed to choose mates

—often simply means younger brothers have sexual access to wife of older brother

Source: James Vander Zanden, revised by Thomas Crandell and Corrine Crandell, *Human Development,* Updated 7th ed., p. 476.

HOW CAN YOU TAKE NOTES FROM TEXTBOOKS?

In addition to underlining, highlighting, and marginal annotations, *taking notes from textbooks* is another important study skill. Three very useful forms of textbook note-taking are outlining, mapping, and summarizing.

Guidelines for Outlining

KEY TERM
outlining

Formal way of organizing main ideas and supporting details to show the relationships among them.

Outlining is a formal way of organizing main ideas and supporting details to show the relationships among them. Even if you underline main ideas in your textbook and annotate supporting details in the margin, there may be times when it is helpful to outline a section or chapter. Outlines are especially useful for organizing complex material. Outlining is best done on separate paper rather than written in the textbook.

Obviously, you will not need to outline every section or every chapter, so when should you outline? Besides organizing complex material, outlining is helpful when you need to condense a lengthy section or chapter in order to gain an overview. Seeing how an entire section or chapter is organized makes the material easier to study and remember.

How do you create an outline of textbook material? To outline a paragraph, you first write its main idea. Then, on separate, indented lines below the main idea, write each supporting detail that goes with it, like this:

I. Main idea sentence
   A. Supporting detail
   B. Supporting detail
   C. Supporting detail
   D. Supporting detail

For longer passages consisting of several paragraphs, continue your outline in the same way:

I. First main idea sentence
   A. Supporting detail for main idea I
   B. Supporting detail for main idea I
   C. Supporting detail for main idea I
   D. Supporting detail for main idea I

II. Second main idea sentence
   A. Supporting detail for main idea II
   B. Supporting detail for main idea II

III. Third main idea sentence
   A. Supporting detail for main idea III
   B. Supporting detail for main idea III
   C. Supporting detail for main idea III

The purpose of your study outline is to show how the ideas are related. Making your outline look perfect is not as important as making sure that the relationships are clear to *you.* Main ideas should stand out, however, and it should be obvious which details go with each main idea. Roman numerals (I, II, III, etc.) are often used for main ideas, and uppercase letters (A, B, C, D, etc.) are used for the major supporting details below them. Arabic numerals (1, 2, 3, etc.) are used for minor supporting details. The indentation shows how ideas are related: The farther an item is indented (to the right), the less important it is. When the information you are writing is longer than a single line, indent the second line below the first word in the line above it. Do not go any farther to the left: The goal is to make the numbers and letters stand out clearly.

An outline can consist of phrases or sentences. However, when you have complex material, a sentence outline works well because it gives complete thoughts.

Use the same title for your outline as the one that appears in the original material. Do not title your outline "Outline." It will be obvious from the way the information

SAMPLE OUTLINE

Good Boss? Bad Boss? Three Leadership Styles

I. The results of most leadership studies have been neither statistically significant nor reliable, which indicates how difficult it is to pin down leadership traits.
   A. Nothing has challenged researchers in the area of management more than the search for the "best" leadership traits, behaviors, or styles.
   B. Thousands of studies have been made to find leadership traits (characteristics that make leaders different from other people).

II. Although there is no one set of traits that can describe a leader and no best style of leadership that works in all situations, there are some commonly recognized leadership styles that are effective in certain situations.
   A. Autocratic leadership involves making managerial decisions without consulting others, and this style is effective in emergencies and when absolute followership is needed, and with new, relatively unskilled workers.
      1. L.A. Lakers coach Phil Jackson used this style to transform a group of individuals into a winning team.
   B. Participative (democratic) leadership consists of managers and employees working together to make decisions.
      1. Employee participation in decisions may not always increase effectiveness, but it usually increases job satisfaction.
      2. Many new, progressive organizations are highly successful with this style that values flexibility, good listening skills, and empathy.
      3. Examples of organizations that have successfully used this style include Walmart, FedEx, IBM, Xerox, AT&T, and most smaller firms.
      4. At meetings, employees discuss management issues and resolve them in a democratic manner (in which everyone has an equal say).
      5. Many firms have meeting rooms throughout the company and allow employees to request a meeting.
   C. Free rein leadership involves managers setting objectives and employees being relatively free to do whatever it takes to accomplish those objectives.
      1. In certain organizations in which managers deal with doctors, engineers, and other professionals, this is often the most successful style.
      2. Free rein managers need warmth, friendliness, and understanding.
      3. More and more firms are adopting this style with at least some of their employees.

III. Individual leaders rarely fit neatly into just one of these categories.
   A. Leadership is a continuum with varying amounts of employee participation.

IV. The "best" leadership style depends largely on who's being led and in what situations.
   A. Any leadership style can be successful depending on the people and the situation.
   B. The same manager may use different styles depending on the person with whom he or she is working and the specific circumstances.

V. There's no single leadership trait that is effective in all situations, nor is there a leadership style that always works best.
   A. A successful leader is able to use the leadership style most appropriate to the situation and the employees involved.

is organized on the page that it is an outline. The box on page 622 shows a sentence outline of the passage from a business textbook entitled "Good Boss? Bad Boss? Three Leadership Styles," which appears as Reading Selection 4-1. Notice that the actual outline has been given the same title as the selection itself.

Guidelines for Mapping

KEY TERM
mapping

Informal way of organizing main ideas and supporting details by using boxes, circles, lines, arrows, etc.

Another form of textbook note-taking is mapping. **Mapping** is an informal way of organizing main ideas and supporting details by using boxes, circles, lines, arrows, and the like. The idea is to show information in a way that clarifies relationships among ideas. Like outlining, mapping is done on a separate sheet of paper rather than in the textbook. With some maps, it works better to turn the page sideways.

One simple type of map consists of the topic in a circle or box in the middle of the sheet of paper, with main ideas written on lines radiating out from it, or with the main idea in the center with the supporting details radiating out. Another type has the main idea in a box at the top of the page, with the supporting ideas in smaller boxes below it and connected to it by arrows or leader lines. If the information is sequential (for instance, significant events in World War I), a map can take the form of a flowchart. Samples of these kinds of maps are shown below.

Three Examples of Mapping

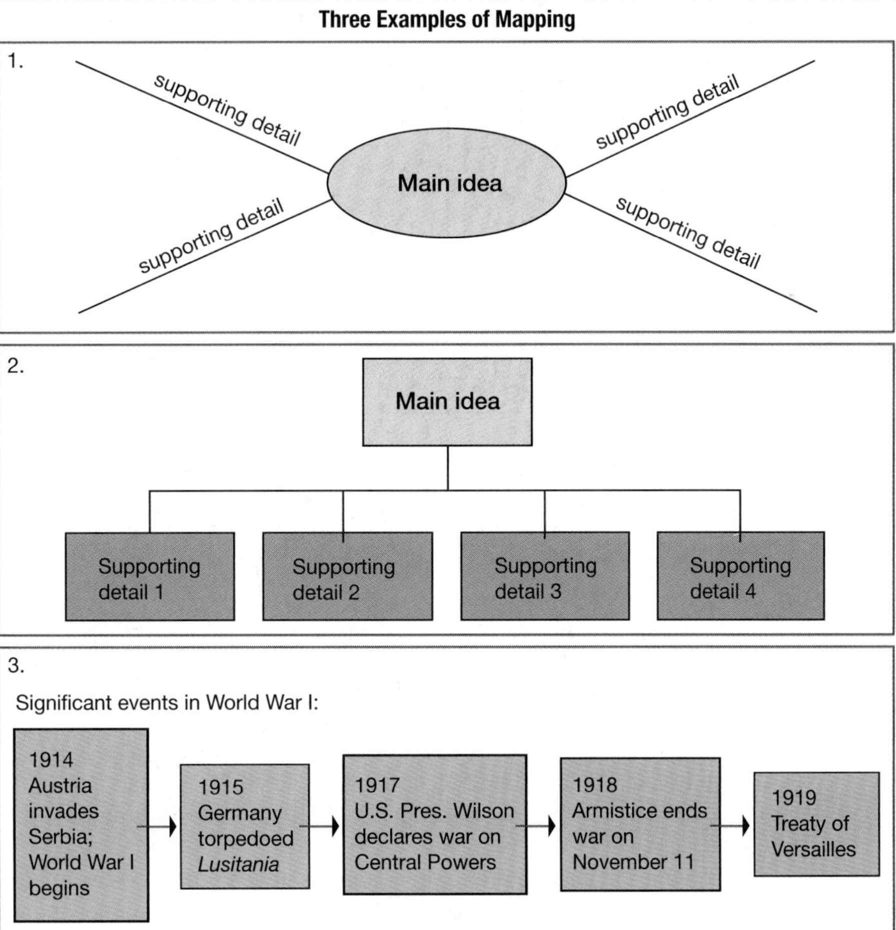

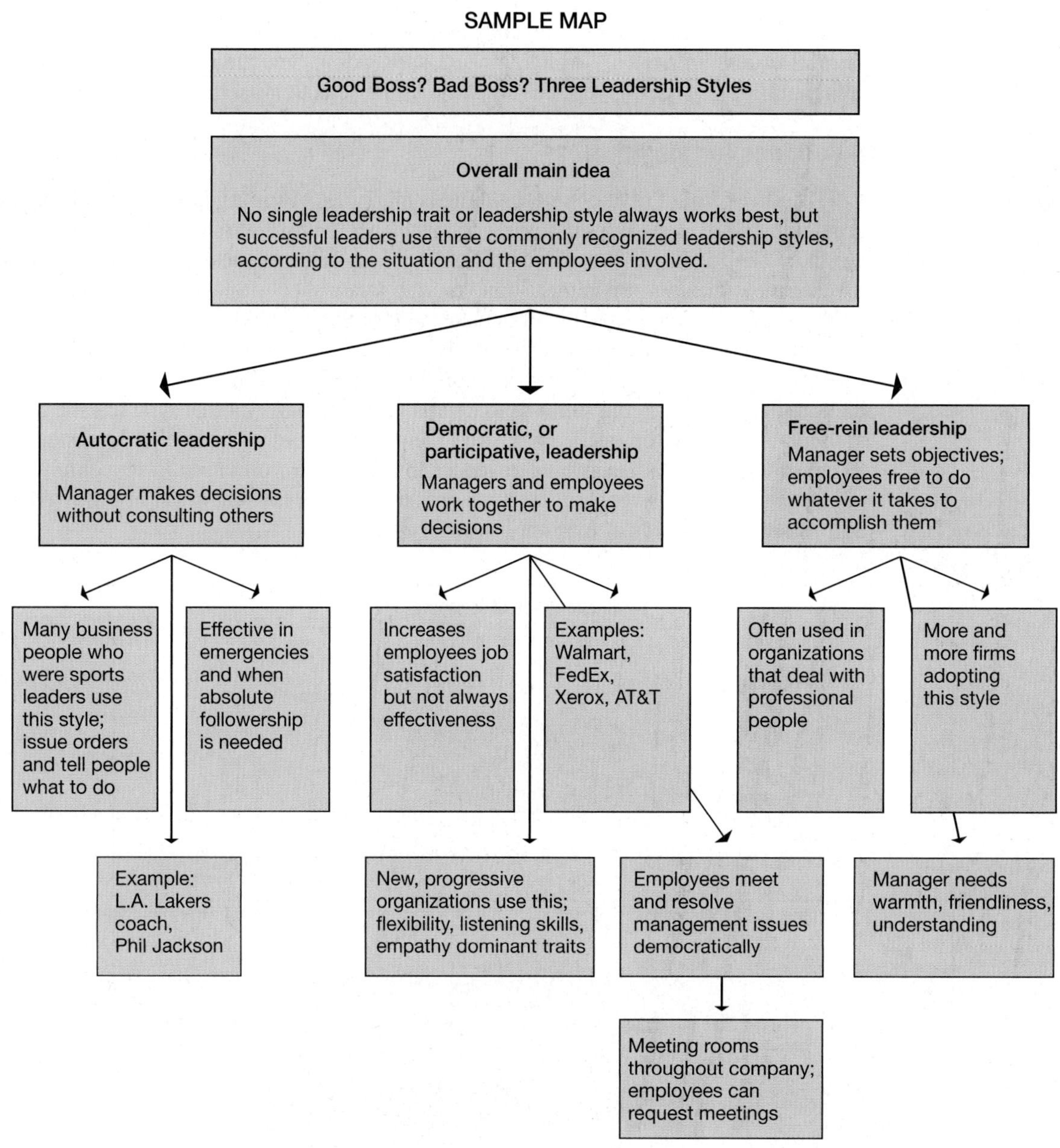
SAMPLE MAP
Good Boss? Bad Boss? Three Leadership Styles
Overall main idea
No single leadership trait or leadership style always works best, but successful leaders use three commonly recognized leadership styles, according to the situation and the employees involved.
Autocratic leadership
Manager makes decisions without consulting others
Democratic, or participative, leadership
Managers and employees work together to make decisions
Free-rein leadership
Manager sets objectives; employees free to do whatever it takes to accomplish them
Many business people who were sports leaders use this style; issue orders and tell people what to do
Effective in emergencies and when absolute followership is needed
Increases employees job satisfaction but not always effectiveness
Examples: Walmart, FedEx, Xerox, AT&T
Often used in organizations that deal with professional people
More and more firms adopting this style
Example: L.A. Lakers coach, Phil Jackson
New, progressive organizations use this; flexibility, listening skills, empathy dominant traits
Employees meet and resolve management issues democratically
Manager needs warmth, friendliness, understanding
Meeting rooms throughout company; employees can request meetings

A study map for Reading Selection 4-1, "Good Boss? Bad Boss? Three Leadership Styles," is shown above. It condenses the important information in the selection onto a single page.

It is obvious that a complete study map like this requires considerable thought and effort. The very process of *creating* a map, however, helps you understand and transfer the information into your long-term memory. And, of course, you have created a valuable study aid to refer to when you prepare for a test.

Since outlines and study maps both show relationships among important ideas in a passage, how can you decide which to use for a particular passage? Your decision will depend on how familiar you are with each technique, how the passage itself is written, and your own personal preference. Keep in mind that mapping is an informal study technique, whereas outlining can be formal or informal. When you are asked to prepare a formal outline in a college course, do not assume that you can substitute an informal outline or a study map.

Guidelines for Summarizing

KEY TERM
summary
Single-paragraph condensation of all the main ideas presented in a longer passage.

A third technique of textbook note-taking is summarizing. A **summary** is a way of condensing into one paragraph all the main ideas an author has presented in a longer selection (such as an essay or article) or a section of a chapter. When you have identified the main ideas in a passage, you have identified the information for the summary.

Summarizing is an effective way to check your comprehension. Writing a summary also helps you transfer the material into your long-term memory. You learn key terms and how to spell them correctly. Summarizing is particularly helpful when you know you will be answering essay questions on a test: Summarizing allows you to "rehearse" an answer you may have to write on a test.

Here are guidelines for writing a summary:

- **Include all the main ideas.** Include a supporting detail only if a main idea cannot be understood without it.
- **Do not add anything beyond what appears in the selection itself.** Do not add your own opinions, information you know about the subject, or anything else that is not one of the author's ideas.
- **Keep the author's original sequence of ideas.** Present the ideas in your summary in the same order that the author presents them. Do not rearrange them.
- **Reword as necessary, providing transitions between main points.** You can paraphrase (reword) the main ideas if you like. Include clear transitions so that you or your reader will understand the connections among the author's ideas.
- **Give your summary the same title as the selection you are summarizing.** Do not title your summary "Summary."

✓ **Teaching Tip**
Remind students that they learned about transition words in Chapter 7. You will find it helpful to review pages 352–355 with them.

Look at the box on page 626 for a sample summary of Selection 4-1, "Good Boss? Bad Boss? Three Leadership Styles." Notice that it has the same title as the original selection. It contains all of the main ideas in the same order as they appeared in the selection. The transition words *second* and *final* have been added. No details are included.

SAMPLE SUMMARY

Good Boss? Bad Boss? Three Leadership Styles

The results of most leadership studies have been neither statistically significant nor reliable, which indicates how difficult it is to identify leadership traits. Although there is no one set of traits that can describe a leader and no style of leadership that works best in all situations, there are some commonly recognized leadership styles that are effective in certain situations. The first is autocratic leadership, which involves making managerial decisions without consulting others. This style is effective in emergencies and when absolute followership is needed, as well as with new, relatively unskilled workers. A second commonly recognized leadership style is participative (democratic) leadership, which consists of managers and employees working together to make decisions. The third style, free rein leadership, involves managers setting objectives and employees being relatively free to do whatever it takes to accomplish those objectives. Individual leaders rarely fit neatly into just one of these three categories. The "best" leadership style depends largely on who is being led and in what situations. There is no single leadership trait that is effective in all situations, nor is there one leadership style that always works best.

Source: From William G. Nickels, James M. McHugh, and Susan McHugh, *Understanding Business,* 7th ed. Copyright © 2005 by The McGraw-Hill Companies, Inc. Reprinted by permission of The McGraw-Hill Companies, Inc.

PRACTICE EXERCISES

Creating Outlines, Summaries, and Study Maps

✓ **Teaching Tip**
For the topic outline in item 2, students should use the major and minor headings.

1. On notebook paper, write a *summary* of paragraphs 1–4 of Selection 9-1, "It's *Your* Turn to Feed the Baby." Use the first sentence of the selection as the overall main idea of your summary.
   Each paragraph has a clearly stated main idea sentence. Use the main ideas to create your summary. Be sure to give your summary the correct title.
2. On notebook paper, write a topic *outline* of paragraphs 8–29 of Selection 10-1, "Living with Stress." Be sure to give your outline the correct title.
3. Use the information in your outline to write a *summary* of paragraphs 2–6 of Selection 10-1, "Living with Stress." Write your summary on notebook paper. Be sure to give your summary the correct title.
4. On notebook paper, create a study map for paragraphs 6–18 of Selection 11-1, "Information Technology, the Internet, and You." Be sure to label your map with the correct title.

HOW CAN YOU FOLLOW DIRECTIONS?

An important part of college reading is following written directions. You need to understand directions in order to do assignments correctly, carry out procedures in classes and labs, and earn high grades on tests.

You know from experience that problems can arise from misunderstanding or failing to follow directions. Perhaps you once answered an entire set of test questions instead of the specific number stated in the directions ("Answer any *five* of the following seven essay questions"). Or perhaps you lost points on a report because you did not follow the correct format ("Double-space your paper and number the pages"). When you do not follow directions, you waste time and might lower your grade.

✓ **Teaching Tip**
Employers report that employees' failure to follow directions costs them thousands of dollars every year. Employers value employees who can read and follow directions.

Guidelines for Following Directions

There are a few simple things to remember about following written directions:

- **Read the entire set of directions carefully before doing any of the steps.** It is tempting to assume you know what to do and to plunge in without reading the directions. That's a mistake. This is one time when you should slow down and pay attention to every word.
- **Make sure you understand all the words in the directions.** Although directions may include words you see often, you may still not know precisely what some words mean. For example, on an essay test you might be asked to *compare* two poems or *contrast* two pieces of music. Do you know the difference between *compare* and *contrast*? Unless you do, you cannot answer the question correctly. Words in test questions, such as *enumerate, justify, explain,* and *illustrate,* each have a specific meaning. General direction words include *above, below, consecutive, preceding, succeeding, former,* and *latter*. Directions in textbooks and assignments often include specialized terms that you must understand. For example, in a set of directions for a biology lab experiment, you might be instructed to "stain a tissue sample on a slide." The words *stain, tissue,* and *slide* have specific meanings in biology.
- **Circle signal words that announce steps in directions and underline key words.** Not every step in a set of directions will have a signal word, but steps in sets of directions frequently are introduced by letters or numbers (*a, b, c,* or *1, 2, 3,* etc.) or words such as *first, second, third, next, then, finally,* and *last* to indicate the order of the steps.
- **Mark directions before you begin following them, since you must understand what you are to do before you try to do it.** Find and number steps if they are not already numbered. A single sentence sometimes contains more than one step (for example, "Type your name, enter your I.D. number, and press the Enter key"). When you are working on a test or an assignment, it is easy to become distracted and leave a step out or do the steps in the wrong order. Another reason to number the steps is that even though the steps may not include signal words, you are still responsible for finding each step. Especially on tests, then, you should number each step and mark key words in directions.

Look at the box on page 628 that shows a set of directions from a computer textbook titled *Getting Started with the Internet.* The directions explain "How to Log On," that is, establish a connection with a network. (It is necessary to log on in order to use e-mail, visit Internet websites, and access certain software programs.) Notice that the steps are not numbered. If you were actually following these directions, you would read the entire set first, number each step, then mark keywords. Notice also that before you could carry out the directions, you must understand certain terms (such as *system, host name, alpha,* and *numeric*) and know certain information (such as your assigned *username* and the last four digits of your Social Security number). Notice also that step 4 is followed by a paragraph that gives special information about logging on for the first time. It is a small set of directions within the larger set. It may be helpful to insert small letters by the steps. This makes it clear that there are two important parts in this step: After typing your password the first time, you must verify it by typing it again.

How to Log On

The method for logging on may vary by site. The following steps are very general. Check with your instructor for specific steps at your site.

Turn on system.

Choose Host Name: **LOCAL**

Username: Enter your assigned username.

Password: Enter the last four digits of your Social Security number.

The first time, you may have to change the password to something of your choice.

It should be at least 6 characters (alpha, numeric, or a combination of both).

Enter your selection and then verify it by entering the same password again.

Remember it or you will not be able to log in again!

A > prompt will appear. You are now logged on to the network.

When you are finished, log out of the system by typing **lo.**

Source: Joan Lumpkin and Susan Durnbaugh, *Getting Started with the Internet,* pp. 12–13.

Here is the same set of directions after they have been marked. Notice how much more clearly each step stands out.

How to Log On

The method for logging on may vary by site. The following steps are very general. Check with your instructor for specific steps at your site.

① Turn on system.

② Choose Host Name: **LOCAL**

③ Username: Enter your assigned username.

④ Password: Enter the last four digits of your Social Security number.

- Ⓐ The first time, you may have to change the password to something of your choice.
- Ⓑ It should be at least 6 characters (alpha, numeric, or a combination of both).
- Ⓒ Enter your selection and then verify it by entering the same password again.
- Ⓓ Remember it or you will not be able to log in again!

⑤ **A >** prompt will appear. You are now logged on to the network.

⑥ When you are finished, log out of the system by typing **lo.**

Source: Joan Lumpkin and Susan Durnbaugh, *Getting Started with the Internet,* pp. 12–13.

OTHER THINGS TO KEEP IN MIND AS YOU PREPARE FOR TESTS BY APPLYING CORE COMPREHENSION SKILLS

Here are two helpful things you should know as you prepare for tests by applying core comprehension skills.

1. **When you study, choose the study techniques (underlining, highlighting, annotating, outlining, mapping, summarizing, making review cards or test review sheets) that (*a*) are appropriate to the type of material you are studying, (*b*) correspond with how you will be tested on the material, and (*c*) best suit your learning style.**

   For example, if you are dealing with complex material, you may prefer to use an outline to organize the information. If you are enrolled in a course in which the tests include essay questions, you may find it helpful to write summaries of important points in a chapter. You may want to use different techniques in different courses.

   Think about how you learn best. (See the section in Chapter 1 on learning styles.) If you are a visual or kinesthetic learner you will find maps and outlines especially helpful. If you are an auditory learner, you may want to rehearse the material by reading it or saying it aloud after you have written it down.

2. **Learn how to handle outline, summary, and mapped notes questions on standardized reading tests.**

   When you are taking a standardized reading test, you may be asked to choose the correct *outline* for all or part of a reading selection. You should rule out as incorrect answers that (*a*) have the information in the wrong order, (*b*) list main ideas or details at the wrong level (such as putting a detail at the level of importance of a main idea), (*c*) leave out main ideas, or (*d*) include incorrect information or information that did not appear in the passage. Compare the first item in each answer choice. If they are the same, drop to the next level. As soon as you encounter incorrect information in an answer choice, you can rule it out. This approach is more effective and efficient than reading each complete answer choice.

   When you are taking a standardized reading test, you may be asked to choose the correct *summary* for all or part of a reading selection. You should rule out as incorrect answers that (*a*) have the information in the wrong order, (*b*) include examples or other details, (*c*) leave out main ideas, or (*d*) include incorrect information or information that did not appear in the passage. A helpful strategy is to rule out answer choices that begin or end with the wrong information.

   When you are taking a standardized reading test, you may be asked to choose the correct *set of mapped notes* for all or part of a reading selection. You should rule out as incorrect answers that (*a*) have the information in the wrong order, (*b*) list details with a main idea that they do not support, (*c*) leave out main ideas or important details, or (*d*) include incorrect information or information that did not appear in the passage. Use the same strategy as for outlines: compare the answer choices level by level, and rule out an answer choice as soon as you encounter the first bit of incorrect information.

CREATING CHAPTER REVIEW CARDS

Student Online Learning Center (OLC)
***Go to* Chapter 11.**
***Select* Chapter Test.**

Review cards or *summary cards* are a way to select, organize, and summarize the important information in a textbook chapter. Preparing review cards helps you organize the information so that you can learn and memorize it more easily. In other words, chapter review cards are effective study tools.

Preparing chapter review cards for each chapter of *New Worlds* will give you practice in creating these valuable study tools. Once you have learned how to make chapter review cards, you can use actual index cards to create them for textbook material in your other courses and use them when you study for tests.

Now complete the chapter review cards for Chapter 11 by answering the questions or following the directions on each card. Use the type of handwriting that is easiest for you to read (printing or cursive) and write legibly.

✓ **Teaching Tip**
Remind students that the student OLC contains a 10-item **Chapter Test** for this chapter. After completing the chapter review cards below, students should complete the Chapter Test on the OLC.

Rehearsing Textbook Material (See pages 617–618.)	
Rehearsing—steps taken to transfer information from short-term to long-term memory.	
To rehearse effectively, information must be ORGANIZED.	
To organize material, use:	
• outlines	• test review sheets
• maps	
• summaries	
• review cards	
After you have organized material, rehearse by:	
• reciting from the study tool you created	
• writing out the information again from memory	
LTM memory check: "If you can't say it, you don't know it!"	
Card 1 Chapter 11: Preparing for Tests: Study-Reading, Rehearsal, and Memory	

Underlining and Highlighting Textbook Material (See page 618.)

Use underlining and highlighting for marking topics, main ideas, and important terms and definitions.

Rule: *Read first, and underline only after you have identified the important ideas.*

Underlining and highlighting should be *selective:*

- Avoid overmarking (underlining or highlighting too much).
- Underline only topics, stated main ideas, and important terms and definitions. (You won't always need to underline or highlight every word of a main idea sentence.)
- Do not underline or highlight supporting details or examples.

Card 2 Chapter 11: Preparing for Tests: Study-Reading, Rehearsal, and Memory

Guidelines for Annotating Textbook Material (See pages 618–619.)

Annotating—writing explanatory notes in the margins of your textbook to organize and remember important information.

Rule: *Read first, and annotate only after you have identified the important ideas.*

Helpful annotations:

- Jot the *topic* in the margin beside each paragraph (helpful with complex material).
- Writing *important terms and definitions* in the margin.
- List *essential supporting details* (paraphrased) in the margin.
- Write the *formulated main idea* next to the paragraph.
- Use symbols and abbreviations: *def* 1, 2, 3 . . . * ? *ex*

Annotating information (writing it down) helps you concentrate and stay focused on your studying.

Card 3 Chapter 11: Preparing for Tests: Study-Reading, Rehearsal, and Memory

Guidelines for Outlining (See pages 621–623.)

Outlining—a formal way to organize main ideas and supporting details to show relationships among them.

- Outlining is best done on a separate piece of paper rather than in your textbook.
- Write main ideas on separate lines.
- Write supporting details on separate, indented lines below the main idea.
- An outline can consist of sentences or phrases.
- Use the same title for outline as the one in the original material.

Card 4 Chapter 11: Preparing for Tests: Study-Reading, Rehearsal, and Memory

Guidelines for Mapping (See pages 623–625.)

Mapping—informal way of organizing main ideas and supporting details by using boxes, circles, lines, arrows, etc.

✓ **Teaching Tip**
Students may want to include small sketches of types of maps.

Guidelines:

- Done on a separate piece of paper
- Can be box or circle in middle of page with topic or main idea in it with details radiating from it
- Can be main idea in box at top linked to details in boxes below it
- Can be a flowchart for sequential information

Card 5 Chapter 11: Preparing for Tests: Study-Reading, Rehearsal, and Memory

Guidelines for Summarizing (See pages 625–626.)

Summary—single-paragraph condensation of all the main ideas in a longer passage

Guidelines:

- Include all main ideas.
- Don't add anything beyond what appears in the selection.
- Keep author's original sequence of ideas.
- Reword as necessary, providing transitions between main points.
- Give your summary the same title as the selection you are summarizing.

Card 6 Chapter 11: Preparing for Tests: Study-Reading, Rehearsal, and Memory

Guidelines for Following Written Directions (See pages 626–628.)

Procedure:

- Read the entire set of directions before doing any of the steps.
- Make sure you understand all the words in the directions.
- Circle signal words that announce steps in directions and underline key words.
- Mark directions before you begin following them.

Card 7 Chapter 11: Preparing for Tests: Study-Reading, Rehearsal, and Memory

SELECTION **11-1**

Information Technology

INFORMATION TECHNOLOGY, THE INTERNET, AND YOU

From *Computing Essentials*

By Timothy O'Leary and Linda O'Leary

In today's world, almost everyone needs to know how to operate a computer for work, for school, even for communicating and entertainment. This introductory chapter from an information technology textbook presents an overview of information systems, types of computers, the Internet, and the World Wide Web. The chapter also introduces the notion of computer competency—having the skills to be a knowledgeable end user of computer technology.

Annotation Practice

Directions: As you read this selection, underline or highlight main ideas and key terms. Use the space in the margins to write out the key terms and their definitions.

1 Today, it's vitally important for you to become competent in computer-related skills. In other words, you must have **computer competency.** This notion may not be familiar to you, but it's easy to understand. Put another way, it means being able to walk into a job and immediately be valuable to an employer because you are knowledgeable about information technology and are comfortable using computers.

2 In this chapter we first present an overview of an information system: people, procedures, software, hardware, and data. Competent end users need to understand these basic parts and how connectivity through the Internet and the Web expands the role of information technology (IT) in our lives. Question # 1

3 Fifteen years ago, most people had little to do with computers, as least directly. Of course, they filled out computerized forms, took computerized tests, and paid computerized bills. But the real work with computers was handled by specialists—programmers, data entry clerks, and computer operators.

✓ **Teaching Tip**

Notations to the right of paragraphs indicate the answer to a particular question appears in that paragraph.

4 Then microcomputers came along and changed everything. Today it is easy for nearly everybody to use a computer. Today, microcomputers are common tools in all areas of life. Writers write, artists draw, engineers and scientists calculate—all on microcomputers. Students and businesspeople do all this, and more. New forms of learning have developed. People who are homebound, who work odd hours, or who travel frequently may take courses on the Web. A college course need not fit within the usual time of a quarter or a semester. Because of computers, there are also new ways to communicate, to find people with similar interests and to buy all kinds of merchandise. People are using electronic mail, electronic commerce, and the Internet to meet and to share ideas and products. Question #20

5 What about you? How are you using information technology? Many interesting and practical uses have recently surfaced to make our personal lives richer and more entertaining. These applications range from recording digital video clips to creating personalized Web sites.

Information Systems

6 When you think of a microcomputer, perhaps you think of just the equipment itself. That is, you think of the monitor or the

keyboard. Yet, there is more to it than that. The way to think about a microcomputer is as part of an information system. An **information system** has five parts: *people, procedures, software, hardware,* and *data*. Question #8

- **People:** It is easy to overlook people as one of the five parts of a microcomputer system. Yet this is what microcomputers are all about—making **people,** or **end users,** more productive.
- **Procedures:** The rules or guidelines for people to follow when using software, hardware, and data are **procedures.** These procedures are typically documented in manuals written by computer specialists. Software and hardware manufacturers provide manuals with their products. These manuals are provided in either printed or electronic form.
- **Software:** A **program** consists of the step-by-step instructions that tell the computer how to do its work. **Software** is another name for a program or programs. The purpose of software is to convert **data** (unprocessed facts) into **information** (processed facts). For example, a payroll program would instruct the computer to take the number of hours you worked in a week (data) and multiply it by your pay rate (data) to determine how much you are paid for the week (information). Question #11
- **Hardware:** The equipment that processes the data to create information is called **hardware.** It includes the keyboard, mouse, monitor, system unit, and other devices. Hardware is controlled by software. Question #2 Question #4
- **Data:** The raw, unprocessed facts, including text, numbers, images, and sounds are called **data.** Processed, data yields information. Using the example above, the data (number of hours worked and pay rate) are processed (multiplied) to yield information (weekly pay).

7 Almost all of today's computer systems add an additional part to the information system. This part, called **connectivity,** allows computers to connect and to share information. These connections, including Internet connections, can be via telephone lines, by cable, or through the air. Connectivity allows users to greatly expand the capability and usefulness of their information systems.

8 In large computer systems, there are specialists who write procedures, develop software, and capture data. In microcomputer systems, however, end users often perform these operations. To be a competent end user, you must understand the essentials of **information technology (IT),** including software, hardware, and data.

Software

9 Software, as we mentioned, is another name for programs. Programs are the instructions that tell the computer how to process data into the form you want. In most cases, the words software and programs are interchangeable. There are two major kinds of software—*system software* and *application software.* You can think of application software as the kind you use. Think of system software as the kind the computer uses.

System Software

10 The user interacts primarily with application software. **System software** enables the application software to interact with the computer hardware. System software is "background" software that helps the computer manage its own internal resources.

11 System software is not a single program. Rather, it is a collection of programs:

- **Operating systems** are programs that coordinate computer resources, provide an interface between users and the computer, and run applications. **Windows XP** and the **Mac OS X** are two of the best-known operating systems for today's microcomputer users. Question #3
- **Utilities,** also known as **service programs,** perform specific tasks related to managing computer resources. For example, the Windows utility called Disk Defragmenter locates and eliminates unnecessary file fragments and rearranges files and unused disk space to optimize computer operations. Question #10
- **Device drivers** are specialized programs designed to allow particular input or output devices to communicate with the rest of the computer system.

Application Software

12 **Application software** might be described as end user software. These programs can be categorized as either *general-purpose* or *special-purpose applications.*

13 **General-purpose applications,** or **basic applications,** are widely used in nearly all career areas. They are the kinds of programs you have to know to be considered computer competent. One of these basic applications is a browser to navigate, explore, and find information on the Internet. The two most widely used browsers are Microsoft's Internet Explorer and Netscape's Navigator.

14 **Special-purpose applications,** also known as **specialized applications,** include thousands of other programs that are more narrowly focused on specific tasks, disciplines, and occupations. Some of the best known special-purpose applications are word processing, spreadsheets, graphics, audio and video, multimedia, and Web authoring. Question #5

Hardware

15 Computers are electronic devices that can follow instructions to accept input, process that input, and produce information. Today, most end users use microcomputers, but it is almost certain that you will come into contact, at least indirectly, with other types of computers.

Types of Computers

16 There are four types of computers: supercomputers, mainframe computers, minicomputers, and microcomputers. **Supercomputers** are the most powerful type of computer. These machines are special high-capacity computers used by very large organizations. For example, NASA uses supercomputers to track Question #17

and control space explorations. **Mainframe computers** occupy specially wired, air-conditioned rooms. Although not nearly as powerful as supercomputers, mainframe computers are capable of great processing speeds and data storage. For example, insurance companies use mainframes to process information about millions of policyholders. **Minicomputers,** also known as mid-range computers, are refrigerator-sized machines. Medium-sized

Figure 1
Four types of microcomputers: desktop, notebook, tablet PC, and handheld computers.

companies or departments of large companies typically use them for specific purposes. For example, production departments use minicomputers to monitor certain manufacturing processes and assembly line operations. **Microcomputers** are the least powerful, yet the most widely used and fastest-growing type of computer. There are four types of microcomputers: *desktop, notebook, tablet PC, and handheld computers.* (See Figure 1.) Question #9 Question #7

Data

17 Data are raw, unprocessed facts, including text, numbers, images, and sounds. As mentioned earlier, processed data becomes information. When stored electronically in files, data can be used directly as input for the information system. Question #18

18 Four common types of files are: (See Figure 2.) Question #12

- **Document files,** created by word processors to save documents such as memos, term papers, and letters.
- **Worksheet files,** created by electronic spreadsheets to analyze things like budgets and to predict sales.
- **Database files,** typically created by database management programs to contain highly structured and organized data. For example, an employee database file might contain all the workers' names, social security numbers, job titles, and other related pieces of information. Question #15
- **Presentation files,** created by presentation graphics programs to save presentation materials. For example, a file might contain audience handouts, speaker notes, and electronic slides.

Connectivity, the Wireless Revolution, and the Internet

19 **Connectivity** is the capability of your microcomputer to share information with other computers. The single most dramatic change in connectivity in the past five years has been the widespread use of mobile or wireless communication devices. (See Figure 3.) Many experts predict that these wireless applications are just the beginning of the **wireless revolution,** a revolution that is expected to dramatically affect the way we communicate and use computer technology. Question #13 Question #14 Question #19

20 Central to the concept of connectivity is the **network** or **computer network.** A network is a communications system connecting two or more computers. The largest network in the world is the **Internet.** It is like a giant highway that connects you to millions of other people and organizations located throughout the world. The **Web,** also known as the **World Wide Web** or **WWW,** provides a multimedia interface to the numerous resources available on the Internet. Question #6 Question #16

A Look to the Future

Using and Understanding Information Technology Means Being Computer Competent

21 Being computer competent involves understanding how information technology is used today and anticipating how technology

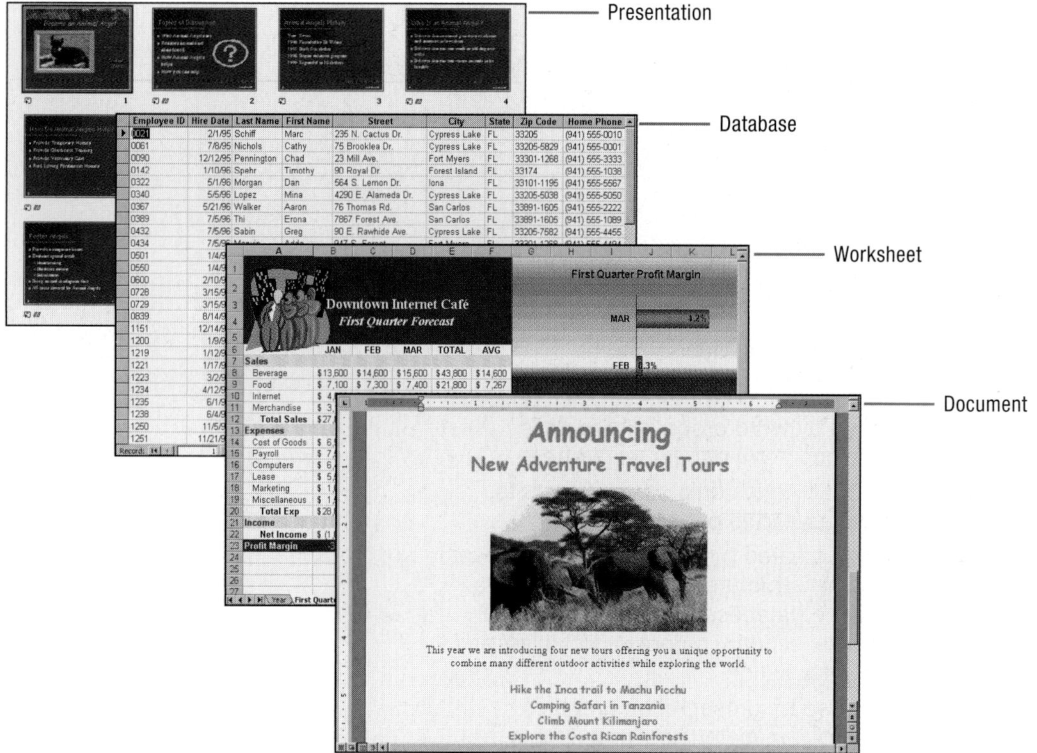

Figure 2
Four types of files: presentation, database, worksheet, and document

will be used in the future. This will enable you to benefit from important information technology developments as they occur.

The Internet and the Web

22 The Internet and the Web are considered by most people to be the two most important technologies for the 21st century. Understanding how to efficiently and effectively use the Internet to browse the Web, communicate with others, and locate information are indispensable computer competencies.

Powerful Software

23 Software that is now available can do an extraordinary number of tasks and help you in an endless number of ways. You can create professional looking documents, analyze massive amounts of data, create dynamic multimedia Web pages, and much more. Today's employers are expecting the people they hire to be able to effectively and efficiently use a variety of different types of software.

Powerful Hardware

24 Microcomputers are more powerful than they used to be. New communication technologies such as wireless networks are dramatically changing the ways to connect to other computers, networks, and the Internet.

Figure 3
The widespread use of mobile or wireless communication devices has dramatically increased microcomputer connectivity capabilities.

Privacy and Security

25 What about people and privacy? Experts agree that we as a society must be careful about the potential of technology to negatively impact our personal privacy and security. Additionally, we need to be aware of potential physical and mental health risks associated with using technology. Finally, we need to be aware of negative effects on our environment caused by the manufacture of computer-related products.

Source: Adapted from Timothy J. O'Leary and Linda I. O'Leary, *Computing Essentials, 2005 Introductory Edition,* 16th ed., pp. 3–16, including Fig. 2. Copyright © 2005 by The McGraw-Hill Companies, Inc. Reprinted by permission of The McGraw-Hill Companies, Inc.

SELECTION **11-1**

Information Technology

(continued)

Practice Chapter Quiz

This quiz differs from ones in previous chapters. It is a 20-item practice quiz that consists of questions like those an information technology professor would expect you to be able to answer after you have read and studied the selection. It is designed to give you the experience of taking an actual test. For each question below, refer to the selection to determine the correct answer.

¶1 c **1.** Computer competency means that you are:

a. interested in learning about computers.

b. trained to program mainframe computers and minicomputers.

c. knowledgeable about and competent in computer-related skills.

d. eligible for training by an employer.

¶6 b **2.** Equipment such as a system unit, monitor, keyboard, and mouse is called:

a. software.

b. hardware.

c. operating systems.

d. information systems.

¶11 a **3.** One type of system software program is:

a. an operating system, such as Windows XP.

b. a special-purpose application, such as multimedia.

c. a general-purpose application, such as Internet Explorer.

d. user software.

¶6 d **4.** Hardware is controlled by:

a. procedures.

b. data.

c. end users.

d. software.

✓ **Teaching Tip**
Be sure to go over the directions with students so they understand how this culminating quiz differs from the quizzes that accompany reading selections in previous chapters.

¶14 c **5.** Word processors and spreadsheets are types of:

a. system software.

b. general-purpose applications.

c. special-purpose applications.

d. navigation devices.

¶20 b **6.** The largest network in the world is called the:

a. World Wide Web.

b. Internet.

c. WWW.

d. all of the above

¶16 b **7.** Handheld computers, tablet PCs, desktop computers, and notebooks are known as:

a. minicomputers.

b. microcomputers.

c. PDAs.
d. operating systems.

¶6 ___d___ **8.** The five parts of an information system are:
a. system unit, monitor, keyboard, mouse, and printer.
b. application software, system software, operating system, device driver, and utilities.
c. computer, connectivity, network, Internet, and the World Wide Web.
d. people, procedures, software, hardware, and data.

¶16 ___c___ **9.** The least powerful type of computer is the:
a. mainframe computer.
b. supercomputer.
c. microcomputer.
d. minicomputer.

¶11 ___a___ **10.** Utilities, also known as service programs,
a. perform specific tasks related to managing a computer's resources.
b. allow output devices to communicate with the rest of the computer system.
c. coordinate computer resources.
d. provide an interface between the end users and the computer.

¶6 ___a___ **11.** The purpose of a software program is to:
a. convert data into information.
b. process data.
c. allow computers to connect and share information.
d. run applications.

¶18 ___d___ **12.** Four common types of files are document files, worksheet files, presentation files, and:
a. word processing files.
b. graphic files.
c. multimedia files.
d. database files.

¶19 ___d___ **13.** Connectivity refers to:
a. the giant "highway" that connects you to millions of other people and organizations located throughout the world.
b. connections among the five parts of an information system.
c. converting data into information.
d. the capability of a computer to share information with other computers.

¶19 ___c___ **14.** The most dramatic change in computer connectivity in the past five years has been the:
a. availability of microcomputers.
b. use of the Internet.
c. use of mobile or wireless communication.
d. increased concerns about security and privacy.

¶18 ___c___ **15.** A company's database files might contain:

a. documents, letters, and memos.

b. budgets and spreadsheets.

c. workers' names, addresses, social security numbers, job titles, salaries, and other related information.

d. materials such as electronic slides and multimedia presentations.

¶20 ___b___ **16.** The World Wide Web:

a. allows microcomputers to share information with other computers.

b. provides an interface to the numerous resources available on the Internet.

c. is the largest network in the world.

d. supplies "background" software to computers to help them manage their own internal resources.

¶16 ___b___ **17.** The most powerful type of computer is the:

a. mainframe computer.

b. supercomputer.

c. microcomputer.

d. minicomputer.

¶17 ___d___ **18.** Examples of raw data are:

a. numbers.

b. images.

c. text.

d. all of the above

¶19 ___c___ **19.** Many experts have predicted that, in the future, the way we communicate and use computer technology will be dramatically changed by the increase in the use of:

a. the Internet.

b. the Web.

c. wireless applications.

d. more powerful software and hardware.

¶4 ___d___ **20.** Today, microcomputers make it possible to:

a. take college courses on the Web.

b. find people with similar interests.

c. buy all kinds of merchandise online.

d. all of the above

SELECTION 11-1
Information Technology
(continued)

Writing and Collaborating to Enhance Your Understanding

Option for collaboration: Your instructor may direct you to work with other students or, in other words, to work *collaboratively*. In that case, you should form groups of three or four students as directed by your instructor and work together to complete the exercises. After your group discusses each item and agrees on the answer, have a group member record it. Every member of your group should be able to explain all of your group's answers.

Collaboration Option

1. **Reacting to What You Have Read:** In the last paragraph of this selection, the authors ask the question "What about people and privacy?" Do you have any concerns about how computers affect our personal lives and our privacy? What are some of the negative effects of computer technology?

   (Answers will vary.)

2. **Comprehending the Selection Further:** This selection is organized into six subsections. Create a topic outline for this selection using the six subsections as the major points in your outline. Be sure to give your outline a title.

   Using Information Technology

   I. Information systems
      A. People (end users)
      B. Procedures (rules and guidelines)
      C. Software (a program to convert data into information)
      D. Hardware (keyboard, mouse, monitor, system unit, etc.)
      E. Data (raw, unprocessed facts)

   II. Software
      A. System software
         1. Operating systems
         2. Utilities
         3. Device drivers
      B. Application software
         1. General-purpose applications (basic applications)
         2. Special-purpose applications (specialized applications)

III. Hardware
  A. Types of computers
    1. Supercomputers
    2. Mainframe computers
    3. Minicomputers
    4. Microcomputers
IV. Data
  A. Document files
  B. Worksheet files
  C. Database files
  D. Presentation files
V. Connectivity and the Internet
  A. Sharing information with other computers
  B. Internet: largest network in the world
  C. World Wide Web: a multimedia interface
VI. Information technology in the future
  A. Internet and World Wide Web: most important technologies
  B. More powerful hardware and software
  C. Privacy and security

3. **Overall Main Idea of the Selection:** In one sentence, tell what the authors want readers to understand about computer competency, that is, knowing about and being able to use computers. (Be sure to include the phrase "computer competency" in your overall main idea sentence.)

Today, *computer competency* is vitally important because so many areas of life require knowledge about computers and computer-related skills.

OR

Computer competency requires knowledge about information systems, software, hardware, data, connectivity, and the Internet, and the ability to use computers.

Internet Resources

Read More about This Topic on the World Wide Web

Directions: For further information about the topic of the selection, visit this websites:

http://netforbeginners.about.com
This site, sponsored by About.com, is an "Internet Primer" containing a collection of Internet tutorials, tips, help, and advice for new Internet users. The site lists the fundamentals every Internet user should know.

You can also use your favorite search engine such as Google, Yahoo!, or AltaVista (www.google.com, www.yahoo.com, www.altavista.com) to discover more about this topic. To locate additional information, type in combinations of keywords such as:

information technology
or
types of computers
or
Internet
or
World Wide Web

Keep in mind that whenever you go to *any* website, it is a good idea to evaluate the website and the information it contains. Ask yourself questions such as:

"Who sponsors this website?"
"Is the information contained in this website up-to-date?"
"What type of information is presented?"
"Is the information objective and complete?"
"How easy is it to use the features of this website?"

A P P E N D I X 1

Glossary of Key Terms

IN THIS APPENDIX

Appendix 1 lists key terms from *New Worlds* with definitions. This listing will help you review material from this textbook and monitor your understanding of the concepts you have studied. The listing is alphabetical, and the chapter(s) in which the key term is presented is indicated.

affixes Word parts that are added to roots. Prefixes and suffixes are affixes. (*Chapter 2*)

annotating Writing explanatory notes in the margins of your textbook to organize and remember important information. (*Chapter 11*)

assessing your prior knowledge Determining what you already know about a topic. (*Chapter 10*)

audience (See *intended audience.*)

auditory learner One who prefers to hear material to be learned. (*Chapter 1*)

average reading rate 200–300 wpm. Used for textbooks, newsmagazines, journals, and literature. (*Chapter 1*)

bar graph Chart in which the length of parallel rectangular bars is used to indicate relative amounts of the items being compared. (*Chapter 10*)

being selective as you read and study Focusing on main ideas and important supporting details. (*Chapter 1*)

box Supplementary material that is separated from the regular text. A box is also known as a *sidebar.* (*Chapter 10*)

cause-effect pattern Reasons (causes) and results (effects) of events or conditions are presented. (*Chapter 7*)

chapter introduction Textbook feature at the beginning of a chapter that describes the overall purpose and major topics. (*Chapter 10*)

chapter objectives Textbook feature at the beginning of a chapter, telling you what you should know or be able to do after studying the chapter. (*Chapter 10*)

chapter outline A list of chapter topics or headings in their order of appearance in the chapter. (*Chapter 10*)

chapter review cards Study tool and special textbook feature in *New Worlds;* a way to select, organize, and review the most important information in a chapter. (*Chapters 1–11*)

chapter summary Textbook feature in which the author consolidates most of the main ideas. (*Chapter 10*)

comparison-contrast pattern Similarities (comparisons) between two or more things are presented, differences (contrasts) between two or more things are presented, or both. The comparison-contrast pattern is also known as *ideas in opposition.* (*Chapter 7*)

comprehension Understanding what you read. (*Chapters 3–6*)

comprehension monitoring Evaluating your understanding as you read and correcting the problem whenever you realize that you are not comprehending. (*Chapter 1*)

conclusion A logical outcome or judgment; often stated by the author at the end of a paragraph or a selection as the main idea. (*Chapter 9*)

context clues Words in a sentence or paragraph that help the reader deduce (reason out) the meaning of an unfamiliar word. (*Chapter 2*)

critical reading Gaining additional insights and understanding that go beyond comprehending the topic, main idea, and supporting details. Critical reading is also referred to as *critical reasoning* or *critical thinking.* (*Chapter 8*)

definition pattern Pattern presenting the meaning of an important term discussed throughout the paragraph. (*Chapter 7*)

details (See *supporting details.*)

etymology The origin and history of a word. (*Chapter 2*)

fact Something that can be proved to exist or to have happened. (*Chapter 9*)

fallacies Implausible arguments using false or invalid inferences. (*Chapter 9*)

figurative language Words that create unusual comparisons or vivid pictures in the reader's mind. Figurative language is also called *figures of speech.* (*Chapter 2*)

flowchart A chart that shows steps in procedures or processes by using boxes, circles, and other shapes that are connected with lines or arrows. (*Chapter 10*)

formulated main idea (See *implied main idea.*)

glossary A list of important terms and definitions from the entire textbook that is located near the end of a textbook. (*Chapter 10*)

graphic aids Tables, diagrams, graphs, and charts that present narrative information in an alternate format. (*Chapter 10*)

highlighting Technique for marking topics, main ideas, and definitions. (*Chapter 11*)

hyperbole Figure of speech using obvious exaggeration for emphasis or effect. (*Chapter 2*)

implied main idea A sentence formulated by the reader that expresses the author's main point about the topic. An implied main idea is also known as an *unstated main idea,* an *indirectly stated main idea,* and the *formulated main idea.* (*Chapter 5*)

inference A logical conclusion based on what an author has stated. (*Chapter 9*)

intended audience People an author has in mind as his or her readers. (*Chapter 8*)

intermediate goal Goal you want to accomplish within the next three to five years. (*Chapter 1*)

learning style The modality through which an individual learns best. (*Chapter 1*)

line graph A diagram whose points are connected to show a relationship between two or more variables. There may be one line or several lines, depending on what the author wishes to convey. (*Chapter 10*)

list pattern A group of items presented in no specific order since the order is unimportant. The list pattern is also known as *listing pattern.* (*Chapter 7*)

long-term goal Goal you want to accomplish during your lifetime. (*Chapter 1*)

long-term memory Permanent memory. (*Chapter 11*)

main idea A sentence that expresses both the topic and the author's single most important point about this topic. (*Chapters 4–5*)

major details Details that directly support the main idea. Major details are also known as *primary details.* (*Chapter 6*)

mapping Informal way of organizing main ideas and supporting details by using boxes, circles, lines, arrows, etc. (*Chapter 11*)

metaphor Figure of speech suggesting a comparison between two seemingly dissimilar things, usually by saying that one of them *is* the other. (*Chapter 2*)

minor details Details that support other details. Minor details are also known as *secondary details.* (*Chapter 6*)

mixed pattern A combination of two or more patterns in the same paragraph. (*Chapter 7*)

monitoring your comprehension Evaluating your understanding as you read and correcting the problem whenever you realize that you are not comprehending. (*Chapter 1*)

opinion A judgment or belief that cannot be *proved.* (*Chapter 9*)

organizational patterns (See *writing patterns.*)

organizing as you read and study Arranging main ideas and supporting details in a meaningful way. (*Chapter 1*)

outlining Formal way of organizing main ideas and supporting details to show relationships among them. (*Chapter 11*)

overall main idea The general point of an entire selection (such as a section of a textbook chapter, a short reading selection, or an essay). (*Chapters 4–5*)

paraphrasing Restating an author's material in your own words. (*Chapter 6*)

patterns (See *writing patterns.*)

personification Figure of speech in which nonhuman or nonliving things are given human traits. (*Chapter 2*)

pie chart A circle graph in which the size of the "slices" represents proportional parts of the whole. (*Chapter 10*)

point of view An author's position (opinion) on an issue. Point of view is also known as the *author's argument.* (*Chapter 8*)

predicting Anticipating what is coming next as you read. (*Chapter 1*)

prefix Word part attached to the beginning of a word that adds its meaning to that base word. (*Chapter 2*)

preparing to read Previewing the material, assessing your prior knowledge, and planning your reading and studying time. (*Chapter 10*)

previewing Examining reading material (before reading it) to determine its topic and organization. (*Chapters 1 and 10*)

prior knowledge What you already know about a topic. Prior knowledge is also known as *background knowledge.* (*Chapter 1*)

propaganda devices Techniques authors use to unfairly influence the reader to accept their point of view. (*Chapter 9*)

purpose An author's reason for writing. (*Chapter 8*)

rapid reading rate 300–500 wpm. Used for fairly easy material; when you want only important facts or ideas; for leisure reading. (*Chapter 1*)

rehearsal Steps taken to transfer information into long-term memory. (*Chapter 11*)

rehearsing to remember information Saying or writing material to transfer it into long-term memory. (*Chapter 1*)

root Base word that has a meaning of its own. (*Chapter 2*)

scanning 1,500 wpm (words per minute) or more. Used to find a particular piece of information (such as a name, date, or a number). (*Chapter 10*)

sequence pattern A list of items presented in a specific order because the order is important. The sequence pattern is also known as *time order, chronological order, a process,* or *a series.* (*Chapter 7*)

short-term goal Goal you want to accomplish within three to six months. (*Chapter 1*)

short-term memory Temporary memory. (*Chapter 11*)

signal words Words that indicate the author's writing pattern. (*Chapter 7*)

simile Figure of speech presenting a comparison between two seemingly dissimilar things by saying that one of them is *like* the other. (*Chapter 2*)

skimming Reading at 800–1,000 wpm. Used to get an overview of material. (*Chapter 1*)

SQ3R study system Textbook study system consisting of five steps: Survey, Question, Read, Recite, and Review. (*Chapter 1*)

stated main idea sentence The sentence in a paragraph that contains both the topic and the author's single most important point about this topic. A stated main idea sentence is also known as the *topic sentence.* (*Chapter 4*)

study map (See *mapping.*)

study questions and activities Exercises, drills, and practice sections that direct your attention to or review information you will be expected to know. (*Chapter 10*)

study-reading process The three steps of preparing to read, asking and answering questions as you read, and reviewing by rehearsing the answers to your questions. (*Chapter 10*)

study-reading rate 50–200 wpm. Used for new vocabulary, complex concepts, technical material, and retaining details (such as material to be memorized, legal documents, and material of great interest or importance). (*Chapter 1*)

suffix Word part attached to the end of a root word. (*Chapter 2*)

summary Single-paragraph condensation of all the main ideas presented in a longer passage. (*Chapter 11*)

summary review cards Study cards that help you select, organize, and review the important information in a textbook chapter. (*Chapters 1–11*)

supporting details Additional information in the paragraph that helps you understand the main idea completely. Supporting details are also known as *support* or *details.* (*Chapter 6*)

table A systematic listing of data in rows and columns. (*Chapter 10*)

tactile learner One who prefers to write information to be learned or to manipulate materials physically. (*Chapter 1*)

test review sheets Single sheet of paper consolidating and summarizing, on its front and back, the most important information to be covered on a test. (*Chapter 11*)

textbook feature Any device used by the author to emphasize important material or to show how it is organized. Textbook features are also called *learning aids.* (*Chapter 10*)

thinking critically to evaluate written material Using the additional skills of distinguishing between facts and opinions, and drawing logical inferences about what you have read. (*Chapter 9*)

three-step process for reading and studying college textbooks Step 1: Prepare to read; Step 2: Ask and answer questions as you read; Step 3: Review by rehearsing the answers to your questions. (*Chapter 10*)

tone Manner of writing (choice of words and writing style) that reveals an author's attitude toward a topic. (*Chapter 8*)

topic Word, name, or phrase that tells whom or what the author is writing about. The topic is also known as the *subject* or the *subject matter.* (*Chapter 3*)

transition words Words and phrases that show relationships among ideas in sentences, paragraphs, and longer selections. (*Chapter 7*)

underlining Technique for marking topics, main ideas, and definitions. (*Chapter 11*)

visual aids Photographs, diagrams, maps, and cartoons that supplement or illustrate narrative information. (*Chapter 10*)

visual learner One who prefers to see or read material to be learned. (*Chapter 1*)

vocabulary aids Textbook devices that identify important terms and definitions. (*Chapter 10*)

word-structure clues Roots, prefixes, and suffixes that help you determine a word's meaning. Word-structure clues are also known as *word-part clues.* (*Chapter 2*)

writing patterns Ways authors organize the information they present. Writing patterns are also known as *organizational patterns, patterns of development,* and *thinking patterns.* (*Chapter 7*)

APPENDIX 2

Master Vocabulary List

IN THIS APPENDIX

Appendix 2 lists vocabulary words in the Vocabulary in Context and Word Structure quizzes that accompany the chapter reading selections. It will enable you to locate the vocabulary exercise in which each word appears. Vocabulary in Context words are in black; Word Structure ones are in red. Numbers in parentheses indicate the reading selection in which the vocabulary word occurs and are followed by the page numbers on which the word appears. In ***Part One,*** vocabulary words are ordered by reading selection. In ***Part Two,*** vocabulary words are listed alphabetically.

✓ **Teaching Tip**

This list can be used to make vocabulary tests on the words in the Vocabulary in Context Quizzes and/or Word Structure quizzes.

Part One

dictate (1-1) 29
dilapidated (1-1) 29
coalesce (1-1) 29
spewing (1-1) 30
consternation (1-1) 30
dictate (1-1) 30
predictable (1-1) 30
contradicts (1-1) 30
diction (1-1) 31
dictator (1-1) 31
edict (1-1) 31

prompts (1-2) 41
concise (1-2) 41
constitutes (1-2) 41
flawless (1-2) 42
rote memorization (1-2) 42
visual (1-2) 42
revise (1-2) 42
provisions (1-2) 43
visionary (1-2) 43
visionless (1-2) 43
visualizes (1-2) 38

systematic (1-3) 53
outweigh (1-3) 53
dredge (1-3) 53
vigilant (1-3) 54
fueling (1-3) 54
portable (1-3) 54
transporting (1-3) 54
reporters (1-3) 55
import-export (1-3) 55
deported (1-3) 55
support (1-3) 55

conforms (2-1) 98
derived (2-1) 98
menial (2-1) 98
undermine (2-1) 99
cynical (2-1) 99
factors (2-1) 99
factory (2-1) 100
satisfaction (2-1) 100
manufacture (2-1) 100
malefactors (2-1) 100
benefactor (2-1) 100

adapts (2-2) 108
tout (2-2) 108
reaps (2-2) 109
derived (2-2) 109
anthropologist (2-2) 109
promotions (2-2) 109
demoted (2-2) 110
remote (2-2) 110
commotion (2-2) 110
emotion (2-2) 110
motive (2-2) 110

per se (2-3) 119
tactics (2-3) 119
anonymity (2-3) 120
inflict (2-3) 120
engaging (2-3) 120
aggressive (2-3) 120
regresses (2-3) 121
digress (2-3) 121
progress (2-3) 121
egress (2-3) 121
progression (2-3) 121

temperament (3-1) 150
authoritarian (3-1) 150
permissive (3-1) 150
authoritative (3-1) 151
competence (3-1) 151
impose (3-1) 151
reposition (3-1) 151
transpose (3-1) 151
compose (3-1) 152
proposes (3-1) 152
repository (3-1) 152

mortified (3-2) 161
groundless (3-2) 161
unrelenting (3-2) 161
diffused (3-2) 162
assailed (3-2) 162
rejection (3-2) 162
ejects (3-2) 163
dejected (3-2) 163
interject (3-2) 163
projector (3-2) 163
injection (3-2) 163

lunar (3-3) 171
robust (3-3) 171
cessation (3-3) 172
hordes (3-3) 172
bouts (3-3) 172
spectrum (3-3) 172
spectacle (3-3) 173
retrospect (3-3) 173
spectator (3-3) 173
prospector (3-3) 173
specimen (3-3) 173

progressive (4-1) 203
empathy (4-1) 203
resolve (4-1) 204
adopting (4-1) 204
fostered (4-1) 204
autocratic (4-1) 204
automatically (4-1) 205
autopilot (4-1) 205
autonomous (4-1) 205
autodidact (4-1) 205
autobiography (4-1) 206

Eastern (4-2) 212
tended (4-2) 212
matchmaker (4-2) 213
betrothal (4-2) 213
nuclear family (4-2) 213
prescribed (4-2) 213
transcribes (4-2) 214
subscribe (4-2) 214
scribe (4-2) 214
scribble (4-2) 214
inscribed (4-2) 214

congregations (4-3) 224
ostracized (4-3) 224
tolerant (4-3) 225
adamant (4-3) 225
curtailed (4-3) 225
advocates (4-3) 226
vocal (4-3) 226
vocabulary (4-3) 226
vocation (4-3) 226
vociferous (4-3) 226
avocation (4-3) 226

commemorate (5-1) 259
flouted (5-1) 259
stark (5-1) 260
fitting (5-1) 260
incomparably (5-1) 260
commemorate (5-1) 260
memorial (5-1) 260
memorialize (5-1) 261
remembrance (5-1) 261
memorize (5-1) 261
memorandum (5-1) 261
memoir (5-1) 261
memorable (5-1) 261

species (5-2) 269
lethal (5-2) 269
strain (5-2) 269
unprecedented (5-2) 270
contain (5-2) 270
evolving (5-2) 270
revolves (5-2) 270
devolves (5-2) 271
involve (5-2) 271
convoluted (5-2) 271
revolt (5-2) 271

erotic (5-3) 284
reserved (5-3) 284
repel (5-3) 284
disdain (5-3) 285
prowess (5-3) 285
repel (5-3) 285
propeller (5-3) 285
dispels (5-3) 286
compelled (5-3) 286
expelled (5-3) 286
impels (5-3) 286

innovative (6-1) 321
incentives (6-1) 321
mandatory (6-1) 322
banned (6-1) 322
glut (6-1) 322
innovative (6-1) 322
novice (6-1) 323
novel (6-1) 323
renovate (6-1) 323
novelty (6-1) 323
nova (6-1) 323

material (6-2) 330
ascetic (6-2) 330
enlightened (6-2) 331
intrinsically (6-2) 331
pacifist (6-2) 331
mortification (6-2) 332
mortuary (6-2) 332
post mortem (6-2) 332
mortician (6-2) 332
moribund (6-2) 332
mortal (6-2) 332

turmoil (6-3) 343
emigration (6-3) 343
hour glass (6-3) 344
metropolitan (6-3) 344
transient (6-3) 344
generation (6-3) 344
genetics (6-3) 345
genealogy (6-3) 345
generate (6-3) 345
ingenious (6-3) 345
progeny (6-3) 345

acute (7-1) 400
listless (7-1) 400
onset (7-1) 400
subside (7-1) 401
prolonged (7-1) 401
temporary (7-1) 401
extemporaneous (7-1) 401
contemporaries (7-1) 401
temporal (7-1) 402
tempo (7-1) 402
contemporary (7-1) 402

ratification (7-2) 412
disenfranchised (7-2) 412
barred (7-2) 112
prevalent (7-2) 413
disparity (7-2) 413
include (7-2) 413
excluded (7-2) 413
occluded (7-2) 413
secluded (7-2) 413
precludes (7-2) 413
conclude (7-2) 413

consumption (7-3) 424
yielding (7-3) 424
foes (7-3) 425
conventional (7-3) 425
altered (7-3) 425
manipulate (7-3) 426
manual (7-3) 426
manuscripts (7-3) 426
manage (7-3) 426
manacles (7-3) 426
maneuver (7-3) 426

eclipsing (8-1) 468
guffawed (8-1) 468
sashay (8-1) 468
hoisted (8-1) 469
doused (8-1) 469
intending (8-1) 469
extends (8-1) 469
tenacious (8-1) 469
untenable (8-1) 470
distends (8-1) 470
attention (8-1) 470

detriment (8-2) 477
fundamentals (8-2) 477
muster (8-2) 477
intricacies (8-2) 478

Part Two

APPENDIX 3

Maps of the World and the United States

IN THIS APPENDIX

Appendix 3 contains maps of the world and the United States.

ARCTIC OCEAN
GREENLAND (Denmark)
RUSSIA
ALASKA (United States)
CANADA
ICELAND
UNITED STATES
NORTH PACIFIC
NORTH ATLANTIC OCEAN
Azores
Midway I.
Hawaiian Islands
Wake I.
Marshall Islands
Equator
NAURU
KIRIBATI
TUVALU
SAMOA
VANUATU
FIJI
TONGA
New Caledonia
NEW ZEALAND
MEXICO
BAHAMAS
CUBA
DOMINICAN REPUBLIC
Puerto Rico
ST. KITTS AND NEVIS
ANTIGUA AND BARBUDA
DOMINICA
JAMAICA
BELIZE
HONDURAS
HAITI
Virgin Is.
GUATEMALA
NICARAGUA
ST. GRENADA
BARBADOS
ST. VINCENT AND THE GRENADINES
TRINIDAD AND TOBAGO
EL SALVADOR
COSTA RICA
PANAMA
VENEZUELA
GUYANA
FRENCH GUIANA
COLOMBIA
SURINAME
Galapagos
ECUADOR
PERU
BRAZIL
BOLIVIA
PARAGUAY
CHILE
URUGUAY
ARGENTINA
Easter Is.
SOUTH PACIFIC
SOUTH ATLANTIC
Falkland Is.
165°E
180
165°
150°
135°
120°
105°
90°
75°
60°
45°
30°
15°
75°N
60°N
45°N
30°N
0°
15°S
30°S
45°S
60°S

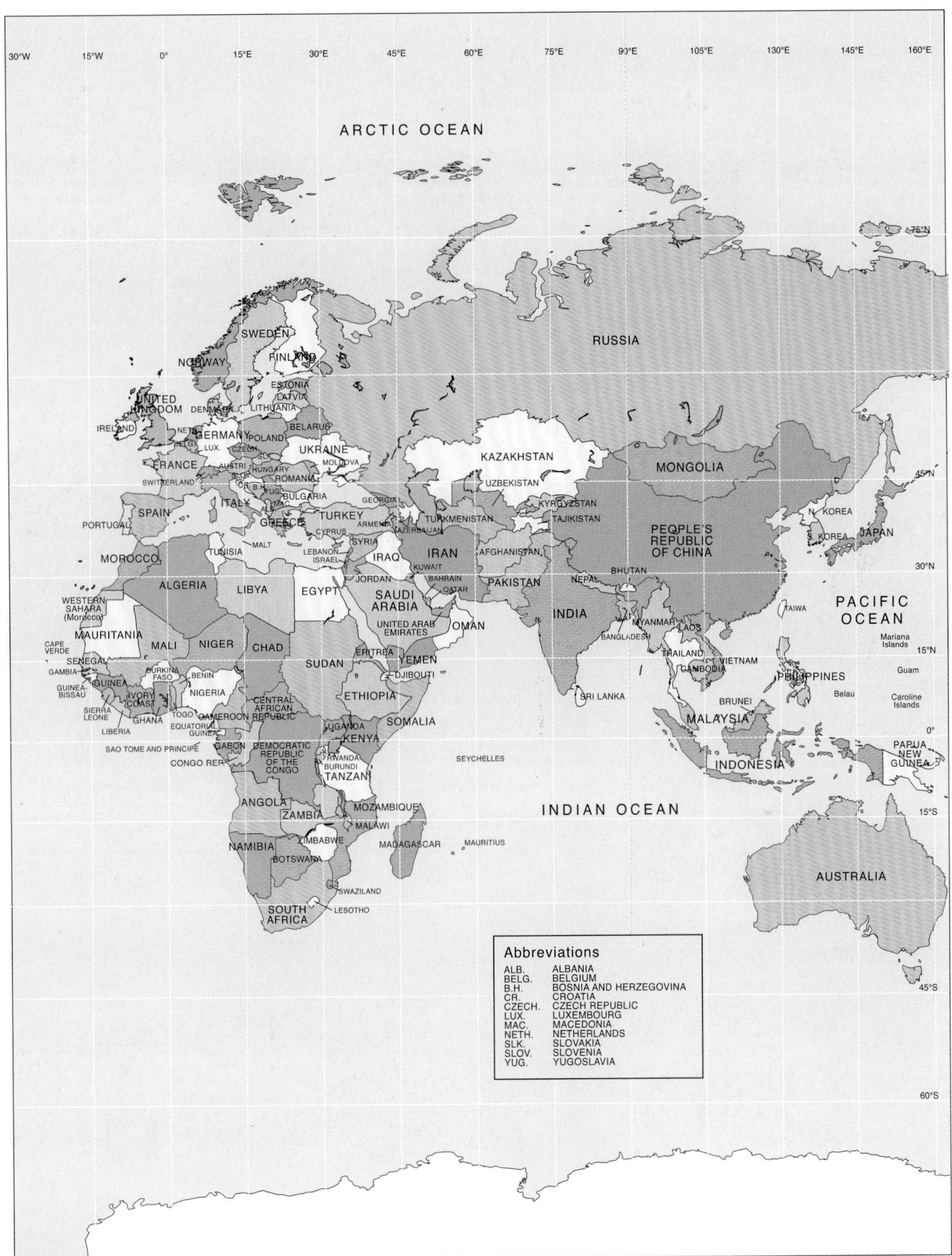
30°W
15°W
0°
15°E
30°E
45°E
60°E
75°E
90°E
105°E
130°E
145°E
160°E
ARCTIC OCEAN
75°N
RUSSIA
SWEDEN
FINLAND
NORWAY
ESTONIA
LATVIA
LITHUANIA
UNITED KINGDOM
DENMARK
IRELAND
NETH.
BELG.
GERMANY
POLAND
BELARUS
LUX.
CZECH.
UKRAINE
FRANCE
AUSTRIA
SLK.
MOLDOVA
HUNGARY
SWITZERLAND
ROMANIA
B.H.
YUG.
BULGARIA
ITALY
SPAIN
PORTUGAL
GEORGIA
TURKEY
ARMENIA
AZERBAIJAN
GREECE
CYPRUS
SYRIA
MALT
TUNISIA
LEBANON
ISRAEL
IRAQ
IRAN
KUWAIT
JORDAN
BAHRAIN
QATAR
MOROCCO
ALGERIA
LIBYA
EGYPT
SAUDI ARABIA
UNITED ARAB EMIRATES
OMAN
WESTERN SAHARA (Morocco)
MAURITANIA
MALI
NIGER
CHAD
SUDAN
ERITREA
YEMEN
CAPE VERDE
SENEGAL
GAMBIA
BURKINA FASO
BENIN
DJIBOUTI
GUINEA-BISSAU
GUINEA
NIGERIA
ETHIOPIA
IVORY COAST
SIERRA LEONE
GHANA
TOGO
CENTRAL AFRICAN REPUBLIC
CAMEROON
LIBERIA
EQUATORIAL GUINEA
SOMALIA
UGANDA
KENYA
SAO TOME AND PRINCIPE
GABON
CONGO REP.
DEMOCRATIC REPUBLIC OF THE CONGO
RWANDA
BURUNDI
TANZANIA
SEYCHELLES
ANGOLA
ZAMBIA
MOZAMBIQUE
MALAWI
NAMIBIA
ZIMBABWE
MADAGASCAR
MAURITIUS
BOTSWANA
SWAZILAND
SOUTH AFRICA
LESOTHO
KAZAKHSTAN
UZBEKISTAN
KYRGYZSTAN
TAJIKISTAN
TURKMENISTAN
AFGHANISTAN
PAKISTAN
MONGOLIA
PEOPLE'S REPUBLIC OF CHINA
NEPAL
BHUTAN
INDIA
BANGLADESH
MYANMAR
LAOS
THAILAND
VIETNAM
CAMBODIA
SRI LANKA
N. KOREA
S. KOREA
JAPAN
45°N
30°N
TAIWAN
PACIFIC OCEAN
Mariana Islands
15°N
Guam
PHILIPPINES
Belau
Caroline Islands
BRUNEI
MALAYSIA
0°
INDONESIA
PAPUA NEW GUINEA
INDIAN OCEAN
15°S
AUSTRALIA
45°S
60°S
Abbreviations
ALB. ALBANIA
BELG. BELGIUM
B.H. BOSNIA AND HERZEGOVINA
CR. CROATIA
CZECH. CZECH REPUBLIC
LUX. LUXEMBOURG
MAC. MACEDONIA
NETH. NETHERLANDS
SLK. SLOVAKIA
SLOV. SLOVENIA
YUG. YUGOSLAVIA

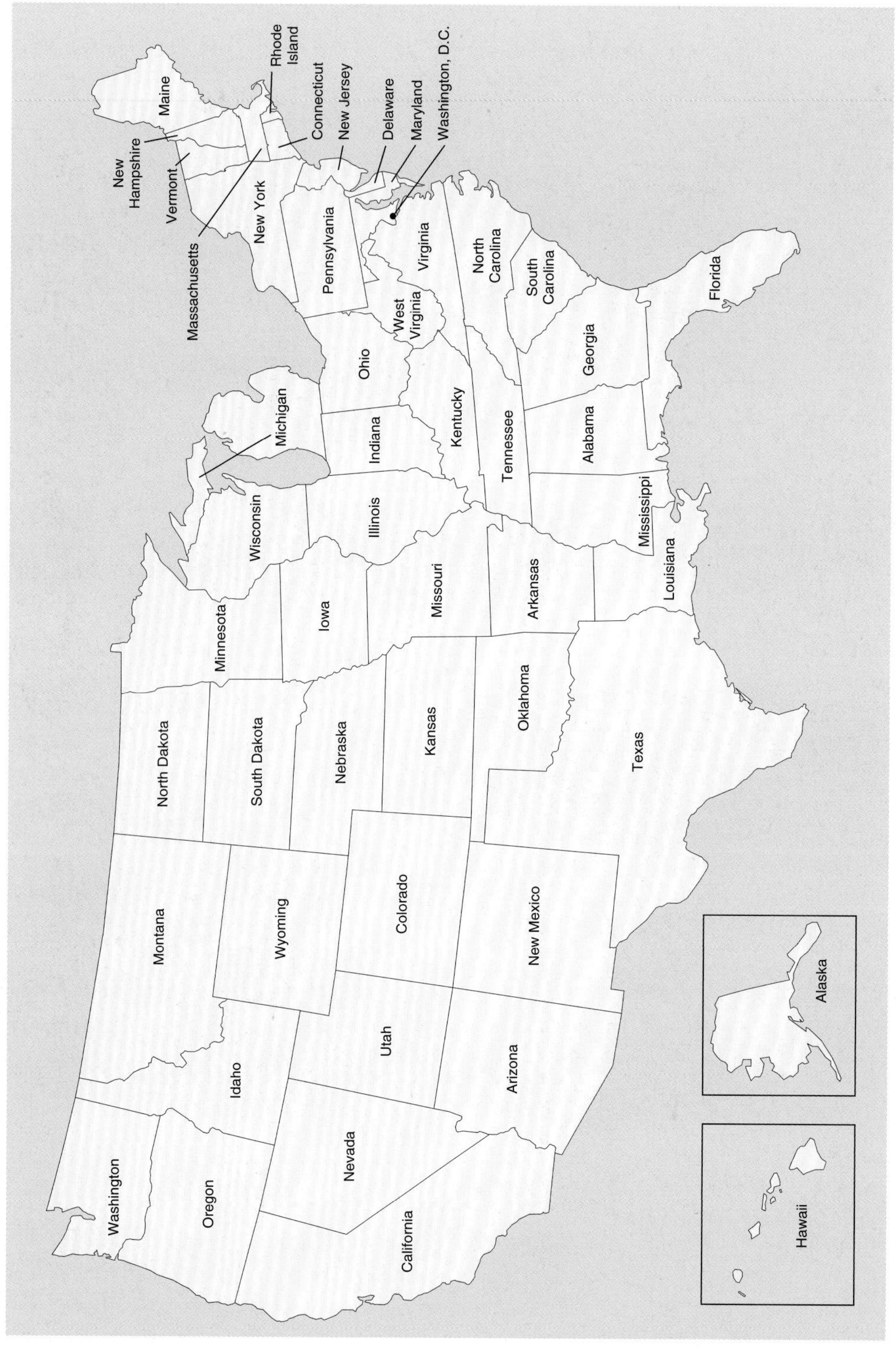

Maine
New Hampshire
Vermont
Massachusetts
Rhode Island
Connecticut
New York
New Jersey
Pennsylvania
Delaware
Maryland
Washington, D.C.
Virginia
West Virginia
North Carolina
South Carolina
Georgia
Florida
Ohio
Michigan
Indiana
Kentucky
Tennessee
Alabama
Mississippi
Louisiana
Illinois
Wisconsin
Missouri
Arkansas
Iowa
Minnesota
Oklahoma
Texas
North Dakota
South Dakota
Nebraska
Kansas
Montana
Wyoming
Colorado
New Mexico
Idaho
Utah
Arizona
Washington
Oregon
Nevada
California
Alaska
Hawaii

Index

T

U

V

W

COMPREHENSION MONITORING QUESTIONS PRESENTED IN *NEW WORLDS*

Monitoring your comprehension means *evaluating your understanding as you read and correcting the problem whenever you realize that you are not comprehending.* You should monitor your comprehension whenever you read and study college textbooks. Asking yourself comprehension monitoring questions as you read will guide your reading and enhance your understanding. The comprehension monitoring questions that are presented throughout *New Worlds* are listed below.

Reading Comprehension Chapters 3–7

Determining the Topic: *"Who or what is this paragraph about?"*

Stated Main Idea: *"What is the single most important point the author wants me to understand about the topic of this paragraph?"*

Implied Main Idea: *"What is the single most important point the author wants me to infer about the topic of this paragraph?"*

Identifying Supporting Details: *"What additional information does the author provide to help me understand the main idea completely?"*

Recognizing Authors' Writing Patterns: *"What pattern did the author use to organize the main idea and the supporting details?"*

Critical Reading and Thinking Chapters 8–9

Determining an Author's Purpose: *"Why did the author write this?"*

Determining an Author's Intended Audience: *"Who did the author intend to read this?"*

Determining an Author's Point of View: *"What is the author's position on this issue?"*

Determining an Author's Tone: *"What do the author's choice of words and style of writing reveal about his or her attitude toward the topic?"*

Determining an Author's Intended Meaning: *"What is the author's real meaning"*

Evaluating Whether Statements in Written Material Are Facts or Opinions: *"Can the information the author presents be proved, or does it represent a judgment?"*

Making Inferences: *"What logical inference (conclusion) can I make, based on what the author has stated?"*

Instructor's Guide

OUTLINE

- The Format of *New Worlds*
- Direct Instruction in Comprehension
- "Comprehension Core" Emphasis
- Methodology and Approach
- The Demands of College-Level Reading
- Alternative Teaching Sequences
- Chapter Teaching Tips
- General Suggestions for Reading Selections and Accompanying Exercises
- Roots and Sample Words
- Comparison of *Entryways into College Reading and Learning, New Worlds,* and *Opening Doors*

The Format of *New Worlds*

New Worlds takes a four-part approach to introducing students to college reading:

1. In **Part 1, A New World of Learning: Reading and Studying in College,** students learn what successful college students do when they study and specific ways to approach college textbook assignments effectively. (Chapters 1–2)
2. In **Part 2, A New World of Understanding: Using Core Comprehension Skills When You Read College Textbooks,** students are guided through the "comprehension core" of the text. This section features an integrated, recursive presentation of essential reading comprehension skills that students must learn in order to be successful in college courses. (Chapters 3–7)
3. In **Part 3, A New World of Reading and Thinking Critically,** students are introduced to a variety of skills they must have in order to read and evaluate critically material they are reading. (Chapters 8–9)
4. In **Part 4, A New World of Studying: Effective and Efficient Study Techniques,** students learn study skills and test-preparation skills that can help them become even more successful students. (Chapters 10–11)

In all four parts of *New Worlds,* students gain experience with college-level material, acquire useful background knowledge in a variety of subjects, and gain the confidence they need to deal with the "real thing"—college textbooks.

Direct Instruction in Comprehension

As the term "direct instruction" suggests, the instructor plays an important role in explaining each comprehension skill to students. *Although full explanations of each skill are provided in each chapter, most students need the instructor to go over the section in class.* We have taken care to arrange the explanations and examples in a logical manner. Carefully guiding students through these sections will make it easier for them to grasp each reading comprehension skill.

Your favorite instructional materials and media can be used to complement *New Worlds,* and we encourage you to integrate these materials whenever appropriate. In our own classes, we supplement *New Worlds* with computer software programs that provide instruction and practice on the comprehension skills presented in the comprehension core (Chapters 3–7).

"Comprehension Core" Emphasis

New Worlds truly emphasizes *comprehension,* the heart of the reading process. Part Two, "A New World of Understanding: Using Core Comprehension Skills When You Read College Textbooks," contains five chapters that present a thorough explanation of each reading comprehension skill.

New Worlds provides an extensive, *recursive application of reading skills.* There is ample opportunity for students to practice the skills presented in each chapter: Chapters 1 through 9 each contain three selections, and Chapters 10 and 11 each contain a chapter-length selection from a content-area textbook. These practice selections are accompanied by a broad range of exercises featuring:

- Within-chapter exercises providing immediate application and practice of skills presented. (Chapters 2–10)

- Test Your Understanding exercises requiring objective responses as well as exercises requiring written responses. (Chapters 2–10)
- Structured marginal annotation exercises for students to complete. (Chapters 3–9)
- Comprehension exercises and quizzes with questions of the type that content-area instructors ask on tests. (Chapters 1–11)
- Vocabulary exercises that present *two* word-in-context examples for each word as well as the word's pronunciation. (Chapters 1–10)
- Word-structure exercises that present the meanings of important Latin roots. (Chapters 1–10)
- Reading Skills Application exercises that present types of questions that appear on standardized reading tests. (Chapters 1–10)
- Writing and Collaborating to Enhance Your Understanding exercises that call for written responses and offer collaborative options for completion. (Chapters 1–11)
- *Read More about This Topic on the World Wide Web* exercises to encourage students to find additional related material and read further.

With *New Worlds,* students gain experience with introductory college-level material, acquire useful background knowledge in a variety of subjects, and gain the confidence they need to deal with the "real thing"—college textbooks.

Methodology and Approach

- Focus on reading as a *thinking* process.
- Focus on *"core" of essential comprehension skills* (Part 2: Chapters 3–7) and a *cumulative review* of these essential skills.
- Emphasis on teaching students to *ask questions* in order to become interactive readers and monitor their comprehension as they read.
- *Exclusive use of college textbook excerpts, articles, and other material of the type that college students would be likely to encounter,* in order to
  - broaden background knowledge.
  - learn college-level vocabulary in context.
  - learn important Latin and Greek roots.
  - create a "transferability bridge" to other content-area courses.
- *A variety of reading comprehension exercises:*
  - *Comprehension and Vocabulary Practice Exercises*
  - *Annotation Practice Exercises*
- *Comprehension and Vocabulary Quizzes* with four subsections:
  - Content-Area Comprehension
  - Vocabulary in Context
  - Word Structure
  - Reading Skills Application
- *Writing and Collaborating to Enhance Your Understanding Exercises* to
  - employ writing-to-learn strategies.
  - increase involvement in learning.
  - provide group support.
  - permit peer evaluation of responses.

The Demands of College-Level Reading

Text-Related Demands

College textbooks are typically the most difficult reading adults ever encounter. There are several reasons textbooks are so demanding.

1. *Difficulty of Content*
   Typically, college textbooks present the most difficult reading adults ever encounter. Students need to know that at times every undergraduate feels frustrated or discouraged by a textbook. It can be reassuring to students to learn that this happens to everyone, that they can improve their reading and study skills, and that they can learn to deal successfully with these feelings.
2. *Idea Density*
   In college material, even a single paragraph can contain a wealth of information. Students may feel overwhelmed and complain that "there's too much to learn!" and "everything seems important!" Mastering the core comprehension skills helps students identify and remember essential information.
3. *Vocabulary Level*
   In addition to the high general vocabulary level of college textbooks, there is a great deal of specialized and technical vocabulary. Students are not always aware that instructors expect them to learn these terms and be able to use them.
4. *Patterns of Organization*
   Teaching students to recognize the organizational patterns commonly used in college textbooks can help students comprehend and recall information more effectively and efficiently.

Reader-Related Demands

5. *Prior Knowledge*
   What appears to be a reading comprehension problem may in reality be a more general comprehension problem. Students simply may not have enough background knowledge to understand the new material—regardless of whether it is presented orally or in print. Nor do students always realize that it is their responsibility to fill in the gaps in their knowledge. They can be directed to talk to a knowledgeable person or to read a simpler explanation first. Then they are often able to deal successfully with the "difficult" textbook.
6. *Comprehension Monitoring*
   College material is complex. Consequently, students must learn to stop at regular intervals to monitor their comprehension. They should be taught that when they feel they are not understanding (or not understanding enough), they should apply the comprehension monitoring questions taught in *New Worlds.* (In other words, they should begin by asking themselves, "Who or what is this passage about?" in order to determine the topic.) A complete list of the comprehension monitoring questions appears on page 660.

Alternative Teaching Sequences

If circumstances require you to deviate from the recommended sequence of chapters, we suggest one of the three alternative sequences below.

ALTERNATIVE TEACHING SEQUENCE I (BEGINNING WITH STUDY SKILLS)

Chapter 1	Introduction to Reading and Studying: Being Successful in College
Chapter 10	Studying College Textbooks and Interpreting Visual and Graphic Aids
Chapter 11	Preparing for Tests: Study-Reading, Rehearsal, and Memory
Chapter 2	Developing a College-Level Vocabulary: A New World of Words
Chapter 3	Determining the Topic
Chapter 4	Locating the Stated Main Idea
Chapter 5	Formulating an Implied Main Idea
Chapter 6	Identifying Supporting Details
Chapter 7	Recognizing Authors' Writing Patterns
Chapter 8	Reading Critically
Chapter 9	Thinking Critically

ALTERNATIVE TEACHING SEQUENCE II (BEGINNING WITH CORE COMPREHENSION SKILLS)

Chapter 3	Determining the Topic
Chapter 4	Locating the Stated Main Idea
Chapter 5	Formulating an Implied Main Idea
Chapter 6	Identifying Supporting Details
Chapter 7	Recognizing Authors' Writing Patterns
Chapter 2	Developing a College-Level Vocabulary: A New World of Words
Chapter 8	Reading Critically
Chapter 9	Thinking Critically
Chapter 1	Introduction to Reading and Studying: Being Successful in College
Chapter 10	Studying College Textbooks and Interpreting Visual and Graphic Aids
Chapter 11	Preparing for Tests: Study-Reading, Rehearsal, and Memory

ALTERNATIVE TEACHING SEQUENCE III (READING FOLLOWED BY STUDY SKILLS)

Chapter 2	Developing a College-Level Vocabulary: A New World of Words
Chapter 3	Determining the Topic
Chapter 4	Locating the Stated Main Idea
Chapter 5	Formulating an Implied Main Idea
Chapter 6	Identifying Supporting Details
Chapter 7	Recognizing Authors' Writing Patterns
Chapter 8	Reading Critically
Chapter 9	Thinking Critically
Chapter 1	Introduction to Reading and Studying: Being Successful in College
Chapter 10	Studying College Textbooks and Interpreting Visual and Graphic Aids
Chapter 11	Preparing for Tests: Study-Reading, Rehearsal, and Memory

CHAPTER TEACHING TIPS

Part 1 A New World of Learning: Reading and Studying in College

Chapter 1 Introduction to Reading and Studying: Being Successful in College

- The "It's Your Call" feature will remind students that more extensive information about studying textbooks and preparing for tests appears in Chapters 10 and 11 of *New Worlds*.

  Take time to preview Chapters 10 and 11 with students. They can use some of the information from the start of the semester, although it will make much more sense after they have completed the chapters that precede them. The main goal in doing this is for students to see where they are going, and how they will actually use—and benefit from—the important reading skills they learn in the comprehension core of *New Worlds* (Chapters 3–9). Highly motivated students in particular will appreciate these "It's Your Call" opportunities to explore and examine certain skills in more depth.
- When you introduce students to the SQ3R Study System, let them know that Part 4 of this text elaborates on this system in relation to organizing and preparing for a test. The "It's Your Call" feature encourages students who have an interest (or who feel the need) to read the material in Part 4 ahead of time. We do, however, stress that mastery of the basic comprehension skills is a prerequisite for most study skills.
- Underprepared readers are often eager to speed up their rate, though that is not their primary need. (They do not understand that speed is a *by-product* of comprehension.) Recognizing students' interest in rate, however, we have included a brief explanation of the various reading rates in Chapter 1.
- Selection 1-1, "A Mother's Answer" from Ben Carson's *The Big Picture,* is a great read-aloud activity and a wonderful way to start the semester. (The Test

✓ **Teaching Tip**
See www.scantronforms.com

Bank includes another selection from *The Big Picture.* It is titled "To Students, I Say: Your Dreams, Your Choice." It makes a great way to *end* the semester.) "A Mother's Answer" is an easily comprehended and highly motivating piece. You can read it aloud to your class or, if you prefer, have students read it to each other in groups of three or four, with students taking turns reading a few paragraphs to each other. (Ask students not to read ahead while others are reading.) Even if you choose the "group read," you may wish to begin this activity by reading aloud the introduction and perhaps the first few paragraphs to the class.

- If you have access to a Scantron® machine, you may wish to ask students to purchase packages of machine-scorable answer sheets (such as Scantron® Form 2020) to use with the four-part "Comprehension and Vocabulary Quiz." To reduce the paper flow, instruct students to answer items in their text and then transfer their answers to a machine-scorable sheet. Have them hand in only the machine-scorable sheet. That way, you can discuss the quizzes without having to return their machine-scorable answer sheets; students will know from the class discussion which items they answered correctly. They can check the answers they've written in their books against the correct ones you give in class. You may prefer to go over only items students have questions about. (This also helps keep the answers a bit more "secure" over succeeding semesters.) You may find it helpful to do an item analysis on each class's answers. If you have your students record their answers on Scantrons, you can use Scantron Form 9702, the Item Analysis, to identify quickly and easily items that caused difficulty for a large number of students.
- If you do not want to grade students on the Reading Skills Application section of the quiz (or even on the Word Structure section), instruct them to transfer *only* the Comprehension and Vocabulary in Context answers to the Scantron. Students can write the answers for the other sections in their books and check their answers when you go over them in class.
- Most students greatly enjoy the Writing and Collaborating to Enhance Your Understanding sections. For example, this section for Reading Selection 1-1, "A Mother's Answer" from *The Big Picture,* typically elicits strong responses from students. For each selection, we have deliberately included an item that allows students to connect their own experience with material in the selection. Remember that you do not have to grade (or correct the mechanics in) any of these exercises that you assign. Focus on the correctness of content, reasonableness of conclusions, and so forth, and simply give students credit for completing them. You can use them as a springboard for a class discussion. And, of course, you can always choose to assign only part of the Respond in Writing exercises or omit the section altogether when you are short on time.
- Students are always pleased when we bring to class copies of the books or textbooks from which a reading selection has been taken. You may already own some of the books that the literary and non-textbook selections come from, or be able to check them out from the library. If your college uses any of the textbooks from which reading selections have been drawn, borrow a copy to take to class. Developmental students feel great pride in knowing they have read an excerpt from a well-known work or from a textbook used in a college-level content area course.

Chapter 2 Developing a College-Level Vocabulary: A New World of Words

- Remind students that although vocabulary is important, they must ultimately shift their attention from the meaning of individual *words* to the author's *thoughts.* Developmental students and English-as-a-second-language speakers, in particular, often lock in at the word level. They do this because it is easier to deal with individual words than with an author's more complex thoughts. Also, many students believe that if they can memorize the definitions of enough words, comprehension will somehow magically occur. In reality, good readers do the reverse: They use their understanding of the sentence or paragraph to determine the meaning of any unfamiliar words (that is, they use the context). For this reason, we always present vocabulary in context rather than presenting words and definitions in isolation.
- That having been said, you will need to caution students that not every sentence that contains an unfamiliar word also contains context clues. (Both this point and the one above are noted in the text, but you will need to emphasize them.)
- Remind students that although this is the only chapter that deals exclusively with vocabulary, they will have many opportunities throughout the book to apply the important skill of using the context. The first 28 reading selections contain a five-item vocabulary-in-context activity.
- Using the context involves inferring the meaning of a word. Using word-structure clues (affixes and roots) is quite a different skill: The meaning of the word parts must first be learned (memorized), then applied to the unknown word. Word-structure clues and context clues can often be used together to confirm a word's meaning. (The Word Structure sections of the first 28 reading selection quizzes introduce students to 28 important roots.)

Part 2 A New World of Understanding: Using Core Comprehension Skills When You Read College Textbooks

Chapter 3 Determining the Topic

- As you present this chapter and read each example passage aloud, have students write the topic beside each passage. In other words, they should follow the "Stop and Annotate" directions. Students need to get into the habit of making annotations, and this activity provides a structured introduction to it.
- At this point, it is an excellent idea to have students begin memorizing the comprehension monitoring questions. (For example, the question they should ask themselves to help determine the topic is, "Who or what is this paragraph about?") Have them repeat the question aloud as a group, or turn to the person next to them and say it aloud. Eventually, students should memorize the comprehension monitoring question for each comprehension skill.
- Emphasize the *within-chapter exercises* throughout the comprehension core chapters. They provide immediate application and practice of the skills presented.

Chapter 4 Locating the Stated Main Idea

- When trying to locate the main idea, students often select a sentence that does not contain the topic of the passage and therefore cannot be the main idea. Emphasize that the main idea sentence must *always* contain the topic. If a sentence expresses the most important point about the topic, but does not explicitly mention the topic, we view the passage as having an implied main idea. This is because the *reader* must make the connection and reformulate the sentence so that it includes the topic.

- Students often select a supporting detail as a main idea. Remind them that "main" means "most important." (Give them some familiar examples, such as the "main character" in a novel or the "main source" of stress.) In a paragraph, they are looking for the one main—that is, *most important*—idea.
- Be sure students can define "main idea" and learn the comprehension monitoring question a stated main idea.

Chapter 5 Formulating an Implied Main Idea

- Plan to spend some additional time on this chapter: students find it challenging. Formulating main idea sentences is a higher-level cognitive skill that requires time, practice, and patience. Work carefully through the example passages.
- Many students are unclear about what a sentence is, so be sure to review this. A simple exercise or demonstration that distinguishes sentences from fragments will help students. Also, students find this formula helpful:

Subject	+	Something said about the subject (predicate)	=	*Sentence*

- Students must understand that the topic of a passage is the subject of the main idea sentence as well. Since they already know how to determine the topic, all they need to do is combine it with *the one most important point* the author is making about the topic. In other words, the general formula is

Topic of passage	+	Most important point author is making about the topic	=	*Implied main idea sentence*

- When students realize that formulating main ideas is merely a matter of combining the topic with the author's most important point about it, the task seems more manageable to them.
- When you present the chapter, read each example passage aloud. Insist that students *write out* the formulated main idea sentence for each example passage as indicated in the "Annotate" instructions. Although the answers follow the examples in the text, it helps to show them on a transparency or a PowerPoint slide. Writing complete sentences strengthens students' language development. This is especially important for underprepared students.
- Plan to devote at least one class period to working with example passages in the chapter. Demonstrate a few formulations of main idea sentences and/or have students complete a few of the exercises in pairs or small groups.
- The two major errors students make in formulating main idea sentences (as the exercises will reveal) are (1) writing fragments—often simply a better version of the topic—rather than sentences and (2) formulating sentences that do not include the topic.

- Be sure students can define "implied main idea," that they memorize the comprehension monitoring question, and learn the three formulas.
- When introducing selections that refer to specific places (such as Mexico City in Selection 9-2), have students locate them on the maps in Appendix 3.

Chapter 6 Identifying Supporting Details

- Remind students that, in a sense, they have already been working with supporting details as they completed exercises in Chapters 4 and 5. They had to "screen" supporting details in the passages in order to identify and formulate main ideas.
- Emphasize that supporting details often lead the reader to the paragraph's main idea. Readers must determine what the supporting details "add up to" and then create a general main idea (Formula 3). Advise students to use this technique if they are having difficulty determining the main idea. When a paragraph has a stated main idea, the details explain more about that one most important sentence.
- This chapter also provides an opportunity for more practice in determining the topic, as well as identifying and formulating main ideas. Many students who have difficulty with Chapters 3, 4, and 5 discover that determining main ideas becomes easier in this chapter as they "sort out" the details from the main ideas.
- Be sure students can define what a supporting detail is and can write from memory the comprehension monitoring question, "What additional information does the author want me to know so that I can understand the main idea fully?"

Chapter 7 Recognizing Authors' Writing Patterns

- Besides presenting paragraph patterns, this chapter is a good *review* of what students have learned in Chapters 3–6 (recursive practice!). This ongoing practice on topic, main idea, and supporting detail is just as crucial and beneficial as the new skills they are learning.
- Research on memory suggests it is critical for readers to recognize some pattern that is meaningful to *them.* Students may sometimes disagree as to which pattern an author is using. This is fine as long as each student can give a plausible rationale for his or her choice of pattern.
- A problem you will probably encounter is that many students initially describe every paragraph as having a list pattern. Teach them that whenever they tentatively identify a passage as having a list pattern, they should ask themselves the additional question, "A list of *what*?" If the answer is "a list of causes," "a list of effects," "a list of events in order," "a list of differences," or "a list of similarities," then one of those patterns (cause-effect, sequence, comparison-contrast) is the primary pattern. In other words, they should use the simple list pattern only when they have ruled out all other choices. (Refer students to the chapter's "Other Things to Keep in Mind" section for a description of this problem.)
- You may wish to have students work in pairs to develop a chart (perhaps without referring to the text) with the pattern names, a description of each, and clues and signal words for each pattern. Or you can assign one pattern per group. Have each group present its pattern on a transparency. Have the other groups make any corrections or add anything that is missing.

- Be sure students can define "authors' writing patterns" and that they learn the comprehension monitoring question, the pattern names, and some signal words and clues associated with each pattern.

Part 3 A New World of Reading and Thinking Critically

Chapter 8 Reading Critically

- Be sure students can define the areas of critical reading covered in this chapter:
  author's point of view,
  author's purpose,
  author's intended audience, and
  author's tone.
- Ask students (individually or in groups) to write from memory the definitions of the critical reading terms. Call on them to read their definitions aloud. Spend class time discussing the definitions.
- Be sure students learn the definition and corresponding comprehension monitoring question for each critical reading skill.

Chapter 9 Thinking Critically

- Be sure students can define the critical reading terms presented in this chapter ("fact," "opinion," and "inference") and that they know the comprehension monitoring question for each.
- Students rarely have had previous practice determining whether a statement is a fact or an opinion. Carefully review "judgmental words" (*better, successful,* etc.) that indicate an opinion. Enlarge the list of these terms that appears in the chapter and make a transparency or PowerPoint slide for a class discussion.
- Some students may select a sentence verbatim from the passage and call it an inference. Explain that although some sentences may indeed represent inferences or express conclusions of the author, they are being asked to go *beyond* what is stated in the passage and think of *other* inferences that are logically based on the passage. Information stated in the passage is just that: stated information. Information that is already stated obviously cannot be inferred by the reader. (For example, if the author *states* he believes in equal pay for equal work, the reader cannot infer this is what the author believes.) This is emphasized in the chapter, but it seems to elude many students at first.
- Note that the new section in this chapter on propaganda devices includes exercises for immediate application and practice.

Part 4 A New World of Studying: Effective and Efficient Study Techniques

Chapter 10 Studying College Textbooks and Interpreting Visual and Graphic Aids

- Most students do not take full advantage of the features in their textbooks. Teaching students to use textbook features is an important starting point for teaching them to become selective and organized in their reading and studying.
- Keep a set of various content area textbooks on hand or have students bring some of their other texts to class and examine the features available in them. For example, ask students to determine which texts have chapter summaries and the

forms these summaries take. (Because many developmental students are not yet enrolled in actual college-level courses, we keep on hand a supply of content-area texts for this discussion. Ask colleagues in other disciplines to donate any extra or unused books they might have.)

Chapter 11 Preparing for Tests: Study-Reading, Rehearsal, and Memory

- You will find it beneficial to make transparencies or PowerPoint slides of some of the examples of textbook features that appear in this chapter.
- This is a long chapter. A discussion on taking notes from a textbook chapter (by outlining, mapping, and summarizing) makes a complete lesson by itself.
- Remind students that they have been using another study tool, review cards, all semester long.
- Students need to understand the term "rehearsing." Be explicit: *Rehearsing* means saying the material *out loud* or *writing it down.* (Point out that this is the reason you ask them to repeat the comprehension monitoring questions aloud.) Many students mistakenly think that reading material once is sufficient. They do not believe they need to do anything else to learn (remember) it. Of course, when they take a test, they discover that they cannot recall the information.
- Incidentally, sometimes students assume that when they study, they must apply every technique presented in Chapters 10 and 11, and they feel overwhelmed. Assure them that it is not necessary to use *all* the techniques presented; rather, they should experiment and then adopt the strategies or combination of strategies that work best for them.

GENERAL SUGGESTIONS FOR READING SELECTIONS AND ACCOMPANYING EXERCISES

1. To "set up" a reading selection we assign, we typically read aloud the italicized introduction that precedes it. This creates interest and provides an opportunity to relate the content to students' lives, other selections, or current events. Sometimes students are able to contribute knowledge they have about a topic. Taking a minute to introduce the selections is well worthwhile because it also builds students' confidence in dealing with the material. Moreover, your sense of intellectual curiosity and enthusiasm for learning new things will profoundly influence your students. How you introduce a selection sets the stage.

2. As part of introducing chapter reading selections in the core comprehension skills and critical reading skills chapters, we often complete the first Annotation Practice Exercise of a reading selection with the class. (The Annotation Exercises are the exercises that appear in the margin to the right of a reading selection.) If an annotation item is unusually challenging, we complete it as a demonstration and have students copy the correct answer(s) in the blanks in their books. (If you use transparencies, you can write in the answers ahead of time on the page. Stick-on notes are an easy way to cover/uncover the answer blanks. Also, a yellow transparency pen works as a highlighter on transparencies.) Completing the first annotation exercise in class not only gives students a model answer, but also is a great motivator: You can then talk in terms of "finishing" the rest of the exercises for homework. (If a skill seems very challenging, such as formulating the implied main idea, we sometimes do one annotation exercise as a demonstration, then have students complete the rest in class and go over them. The students complete the rest of the selection and its activities for homework.)

3. Reading aloud part (or occasionally all) of a reading selection generally helps students understand it better. As a rule, it is better for you to read the selection than to call on a student to read it. If your voice gives out, however, an equally effective alternative is to divide students into groups and have students take turns reading paragraphs aloud. Reading aloud in a small group is less daunting to students than reading in front of the whole class.

4. Another technique we use is to "talk through" a reading selection, giving our thoughts aloud as we read and interact with the material. Students are often surprised that even experienced readers make false starts, get "lost" while reading, or encounter unknown words. You can also ask students to bring challenging passages from their other textbooks. Students are fascinated at the opportunity to peek in on an experienced reader's metacognitive and comprehension monitoring processes.

5. We always indicate in *New Worlds* not only the actual source but the content area of each sample passage used in the chapters and the exercises. In class, we make it a point to describe academic disciplines that may be new to students. Beginning college students are often not sure, for example, what sociology, human development, art appreciation, or other content areas entail. Remind students that the information in the example passages and reading selections helps build their fund of general knowledge, and that this will enhance their future comprehension as they make connections between their existing knowledge and new information they are learning.

6. For the exercises that ask students to create an overall main idea for the entire selection, have groups of students write a "group answer." Have each group share its answer with the class using a whiteboard or document camera. Then discuss which are the best answers and why.

7. As noted earlier, class sessions are energized by periodically having students work together in small groups on the reading selections.

8. Go over the directions for the Vocabulary in Context quiz to be sure students understand that the definition they choose must fit the context of *both* sentences.

9. We occasionally have students share in small groups their answers to the four-part multiple-choice Comprehension and Vocabulary quiz. Then we have each group list its "group answers" on a grid on the board. We discuss only items on which the groups disagree.

10. Whenever possible, go over the corrected Comprehension and Vocabulary quiz. *Unless students understand what they missed and why, they lose the opportunity to learn.* Feedback is crucial. If several students miss the same items, you may want to discuss only those. Another option is to allot a specific amount of time (for example, 10 minutes) for questions. Finally, you can allow them to ask questions about items they did not understand even *after* finding out the correct answers.

11. Review the use of the dictionary pronunciation key, pronunciations are always included with the vocabulary words in the Comprehension and Vocabulary quiz. When students inquire about which dictionary to purchase, we recommend the *Merriam-Webster Dictionary* and/or *Student Notebook Dictionary,* or the most recent edition of *American Heritage Pocket Dictionary.*

12. Some selections offer opportunities to contrast the information in them. For example, the selections on parenting styles and leadership styles present information that can be logically related.
13. We make a big production of discussing the Annotation Practice Exercises that accompany the reading selection. Working in small groups, students discuss their answers and arrive at consensus. Then a representative from each group writes, for example, the topic and the formulated main idea sentence for the *same* item on the board or on transparency strips. Seeing the variations in formulated main ideas for the same paragraph is a revelation to students. We lead a class discussion about which answers they think are the best and why, and the reason the incorrect ones are incorrect.
14. Some concepts and individuals mentioned in this book are so important that they should be a part of any educated person's general knowledge. We periodically use the following technique to provide the class with additional information about a topic, while at the same time lifting a student's self-esteem and prestige in the class. Identify any student who is very shy or quiet, not yet involved, is performing marginally, or is discounted by his or her classmates. Tell the student in private that we need some assistance: Ask him or her to locate information about an important person or concept that will be discussed in an upcoming chapter reading selection. Ask the person to look up the information before the next class session. When you introduce the reading selection, ask if anyone in the class happens to know anything about [whatever the topic is]. Check ahead of time to be sure the student has the information, "happen" to call on that person. He or she has a chance to shine—and classmates are often dazzled. The positive effects of this simple technique can be striking.
15. At the end of the exercises for each reading selection is a "Webliography" titled "Read More about This Topic on the World Wide Web." It is a brief list of websites that pertain to the author or topic of the selection. (Although each website was rechecked immediately prior to publication, websites change, so some sites may no longer be active.) The hope is that these websites can be used as starting points for finding additional information on the topic. Emphasize to students what we note in the text: As with other types of material they read, they should evaluate Internet material critically. Just as many students mistakenly believe that anything that appears in print must be true, many mistakenly assume that if information appears on the Internet, it must be true.
16. Another reason for including the websites is to introduce students to the idea of going beyond the minimum for an assignment (the essence of true scholarship). Many students think in terms of just getting by or doing the minimum, but we want them to discover the joy of learning for its own sake. Your own pleasure in learning new things, your own intellectual curiosity, and your own enthusiasm make a powerful statement to students.
17. We included a world map and a map of the United States in Appendix 3 because most students, especially underprepared ones, have a tenuous grasp of geography. Some even have trouble indicating which way on a map is north. If your students have access to the Internet in your classroom or in a computer lab, have them look at a map and locate some of the places mentioned in the chapter reading selections (see www.worldatlas.com). If you do not have computer access for your students, a full-color classroom map is helpful. (A "globe" beachball or pillow is also a fun

teaching aid to use for this!) Any effort to help your students expand their background knowledge will be worthwhile.

18. The Online Learning Center for *New Worlds* (www.mhhe.newworlds4e.com) contains excellent review material, including comprehension quizzes, web links, journal writing prompts, and supplemental activities. It also contains helpful information for instructors, such as answer keys, indexes of excerpt topics and reading selection topics, and supplemental reading selections.

ROOTS AND SAMPLE WORDS

The roots and example words presented in the Word-Structure Quizzes are listed below.

Selection 1-1, pp. 30–31

dict *say; tell*

dictate
predictable
contradicts
diction
dictator
edict

Selection 1-2, pp. 42–43

vis *to see*

visual
revise
provisions
visionary
visionless
visualizes

Selection 1-3, pp. 54–55

port *to carry; to bear*

portable
transporting
reporters
import-export
deported
support

Selection 2-1, p. 100

fac *make; do*

factors
factory
satisfaction
manufacture
malefactors
benefactor

Selection 2-2, p. 110

mot *to move; motion*

promotions
demoted
remote
commotion
emotion
motive

Selection 2-3, p. 121

gress *go; step*

aggressive
regresses
digress
progress
egress
progression

Selection 3-1, pp. 151–152

pos *put; place*

impose
reposition
transpose
compose
proposes
repository

Selection 3-2, p. 163

ject *to throw*

rejection
ejects
dejected
interject
projector
injection

Selection 3-3, p. 173

spec *to look; to see*

spectrum
spectacle
retrospect
spectator
prospector
specimen

Selection 4-1, p. 205

auto *self*

autocratic
automatically
autopilot
autonomous
autodidact
autobiography

Selection 4-2, p. 214

scrib *to write; to record*

prescribed
transcribes
subscribe
scribe
scribble
inscribed

Selection 4-3, p. 226

voc *to say; to call*

advocates
vocal
vocabulary
vocation
vociferous
avocation

Selection 5-1, p. 261

mem *memory*

commemorate
memorial
memorialize
remembrance
memorize
memorandum
memoirs
memorable

Selection 5-2, pp. 270–271

volvere *to roll; turn; twist*

evolving
revolves
devolves
involve
convoluted
revolt

Selection 5-3, pp. 285–286

pel *to drive; to push*

repel
propeller
dispels
compelled
expelled
impels

Selection 6-1, p. 323

nov *new*

innovative
novice
novel
renovate
novelty
nova

Selection 6-2, p. 332

mort *death*

mortification
mortuary
post mortem
mortician
moribund
mortal

Selection 6-3, p. 345

gen *birth; origin*

generations
genetics
genealogy
generate
ingenious
progeny

Selection 7-1, pp. 401–402

tempor *time*

temporary
extemporaneous
contemporaries
temporal
tempo
contemporary

Selection 7-2, pp. 413–414

clude *to close; to shut*

include
excluded
occluded
secluded
precludes
conclude

Selection 7-3, p. 426

man *hand*

manipulate
manual
manuscripts
manage
manacles
maneuver

Selection 8-1, pp. 469–470

ten *to stretch; to hold or grasp*

intending
extends
tenacious
untenable
distends
attention

Selection 8-2, pp. 478–479

mis *to send; to let go*

dismissed
transmission
emission
mission
omission
remission

Selection 8-3, pp. 489–490

fid *faith; trust*

confidence
confide
infidelity
confidant
bona fide
Semper Fidelis

Selection 9-1, pp. 531–532

ver *to turn; to move*

conversation
converts
divert
avert
perverted
extroverts

Selection 9-2, pp. 540–541

tort *to twist; to bend*

tortuous
distorts
contortionists
torturous
retort
extortion

Selection 9-3, pp. 550–551

pend *to hang*

independent
interdependent
pendulum
pending
suspend
pendant

Selection 10-1, pp. 610–611

nym *name*

anonymous
pseudonym
synonyms
antonyms
homonyms
heteronyms

COMPARISON OF *ENTRYWAYS INTO COLLEGE READING AND LEARNING*, *NEW WORLDS*, AND *OPENING DOORS*

	Entryways into College Reading and Learning (Beginning & lowest-level; first generation to college)	***New Worlds: Introduction to College Reading*** (Beginning and lower-level developmental)	***Opening Doors: Understanding College Reading*** (Intermediate or upper-level developmental)
Parts and Their Contents	**Part 1: Adopting Success Behaviors** Success behaviors in and out of class (Ch. 1–2) **Part 2: Acquiring Basic Vocabulary-Building Tools** Context clues, dictionary usage, and commonly confused and misused words (Ch. 3–5) **Part 3: Acquiring Basic Comprehension Tools** Understanding sentences, introduction to basic comprehension skills (topic, stated and implied main ideas, supporting details, and paragraph patterns), and reading and marking textbook assignments (Ch. 6–12)	**Part 1: A New World of Learning: Reading and Studying in College** Introduction to study skills and college-level vocabulary (Ch. 1–2) **Part 2: A New World of Understanding: Using Core Comprehension Skills When You Read College Textbooks** Introduction to essential comprehension skills—the basic "comprehension core" (Ch. 3–7) **Part 3: A New World of Reading and Thinking Critically** Introduction to critical reading skills (Ch. 8–9) **Part 4: A New World of Studying: Effective and Efficient Study Techniques** Introduction to study skills (Ch. 10–11)	**Part 1: Orientation: Preparing and Organizing Yourself for Success in College** Introduction to college, college vocabulary, and the reading & studying process (Ch. 1–3) **Part 2: Comprehension: Understanding College Textbooks by Reading for Ideas** Essential comprehension skills: determining the topic, stated and implied main ideas, primary and secondary supporting details, and paragraph patterns. Two chapters devoted to critical reading and critical thinking skills. A comprehensive "comprehension core" (Ch. 4–9) **Part 3: Systems for Studying Textbooks: Developing a System That Works for You** Study skills, including information about selecting, organizing and rehearsing textbook material to prepare for tests (Ch. 10–11)
Chapter Review Technique	• 12 sets of 15-item Chapter Checks (fill-in-the-blank) • My Toolbox (students record important information in ways meaningful to them)	11 sets of chapter review cards students complete to create their own summary of essential information	11 sets of chapter review cards students complete to create their own summary of essential information

(continued on next page)

	Entryways into College Reading and Learning (Beginning & lowest-level; first generation to college)	***New Worlds: Introduction to College Reading*** (Beginning and lower-level developmental)	***Opening Doors: Understanding College Reading*** (Intermediate or upper-level developmental)
Reading Selections (number and types)	10 reading selections (grouped at the end of the text) Selections are excerpted or adapted from introductory college textbooks, newspapers; and other popular publications, Web sources, and include an essay and a memoir.	29 reading selections (3 each in Ch. 1–9; 1 chapter-length selection in Ch. 10–11) Selections are excerpted from widely used introductory college textbooks or other nonfiction or literary material typical of that used in freshman-level courses. Selections within each chapter have varying lengths.	29 reading selections (3 each in Ch. 1–9; 1 chapter-length selection in Ch. 10–11) Selections are excerpted from widely used introductory college textbooks or other nonfiction or literary material typical of that used in freshman-level courses. Selections within each chapter have varying lengths. Most are more challenging than those in *New Worlds*.
Reading Selection Apparatus (quizzes, writing prompts, Web resources, etc.)	Two 10-item multiple-choice quizzes: • Vocabulary Check • Comprehension Check 10 sets of additional activities: • Connecting with What You Already Know (preparing to read) • Writing to Make Connections • Web Resources	28 four-part quizzes that consist of 20 multiple-choice questions (5 questions of each type): • Comprehension • Vocabulary in Context • Word Structure • Reading Skills Application 1 practice chapter quiz (accompanying the chapter-length reading selection) consisting of 20 questions designed to simulate a chapter quiz a content area professor would give (Ch. 11) 29 sets of additional activities: • Reacting to What You Read • Comprehending Further • Overall Main Idea • Read More about This Topic on the World Wide Web	27 three-part quizzes that consist of 25 multiple-choice questions (10 comprehension; 10 vocabulary, 5 reading skills application): • Comprehension • Vocabulary in Context • Reading Skills Application 2 practice chapter quizzes (to accompany the chapter-length reading selections in Ch. 10–11) consisting of 25 questions designed to simulate a chapter quiz a content area instructor would give (included in the Instructor's Edition of the Online Learning Center) 29 sets of additional activities: • Reacting to What You Read • Comprehending Further • Overall Main Idea • Read More about This Topic on the World Wide Web These are similar to those in *New Worlds*, but many are longer and more sophisticated.

Chapter Exercises	79 Stop and Process exercises (multiple exercises throughout each chapter for immediate application of skills) 21 sets of Review Exercises (2–4 sets per chapter, depending on the skill presented)	57 brief within-chapter exercises providing immediate application and practice of skills presented (Ch. 2–10) 18 sets of Test Your Understanding exercises on vocabulary, comprehension, critical reading, critical thinking, and interpreting graphic aids. (These follow the Chapter Review Cards in Ch. 2–10.) 29 sets of Annotation Practice, Exercises on predicting, comprehension, critical reading, and critical thinking appear in the margins of each reading selection (Ch. 1–11)	8 Test Your Understanding exercises providing immediate feedback on student understanding of chapter concepts (Ch. 4–9) 24 sets of Annotation Practice Exercises on predicting, formulating study-reading questions, comprehension, critical reading, and critical thinking appear in the margins of 24 reading selections (Ch. 2–9)
Special Features	• Inductive approach (students figure out the "rules" for themselves) • 2 full-color Visual Summaries (recap key concepts and learning style tips) • Super Student Tips (shared by other successful students) • Jumpstart Your Brain! (chapter starter that taps various learning styles) • Brain-Friendly Tip boxes (tips for easier, more efficient learning) • Bonus Tips (memory, pegs, practical suggestions) • Cross-Chapter Connections boxes (pointing out interrelatedness of skills) • Listen Up! boxes ("raps" in the comprehension chapters that capture key points) • Comprehension-Monitoring Question for each skill • Marginal notes about related Online Reading Center (ORL) and Catalyst material • Assess Your Understanding (students' metacognitive assessment of their understanding of a chapter)	• Putting Your Goals in Writing exercise (identifying short-term, intermediate, and long-term goals) • Identifying Your Learning Style exercise (informal assessment of preferred learning style) • Key Terms given in the margins • Comprehension-Monitoring Questions given in the margins • Marginal Annotation boxes ("Stop and Annotate" exercises giving directions for applying to sample excerpts skills being introduced) • Other Things to Keep in Mind sections (tips and reminders about skills that were introduced) • Creating Chapter Review Cards (chapter review card exercises with structured practice)	• Putting Your Goals in Writing exercise (identifying short-term, intermediate, and long-term goals) • Identifying Your Learning Style exercise (informal assessment of preferred learning style) • Key Terms given in the margins • Comprehension-Monitoring Questions given in the margins • Marginal Annotation boxes ("Stop and Annotate" exercises giving directions for applying to sample excerpts skills being introduced) • A Word about Standardized Reading Tests sections (tips and strategies for taking assessment tests, exit tests, and state-mandated "basic skills" tests) • Creating Your Summary—Developing Chapter Review Cards (chapter review card exercises with structured practice) • Propaganda Techniques exercise (identifying propaganda types) • Interpreting Graphic Aids exercises (application of specific skills from Ch. 10)

(continued on next page)

	Entryways into College Reading and Learning (Beginning & lowest-level; first generation to college)	***New Worlds: Introduction to College Reading*** (Beginning and lower-level developmental)	***Opening Doors: Understanding College Reading*** (Intermediate or upper-level developmental)
Appendixes	• Master Vocabulary List • Glossary of Key Terms	• Glossary of Reading and Study Skills Terms • Master Vocabulary List • United States and World Map	• Glossary of Key Reading and Study Skills Terms • List of Roots, Prefixes, and Suffixes • United States and World Map with list of World Capitals • Master Vocabulary List
Student Online Resources	Online Reading Lab (ORL), www.mhhe.com/entryways, includes • supplemental chapter activities • 15 full-length reading selections with apparatus • 15 "Small Bites," shorter selections with abbreviated apparatus • material on phonics, pronunciation, and syllabication, on spelling, test taking, and learning styles • chapter-length module on word structure • chapter-length module on outlining, mapping, and review cards • chapter-length module on summarizing • Catalyst 2.0 links (online resources for writing that includes interactive tutorials, and thousands of articles)	Online Learning Center (OLC), www.mhhe.com/newworlds, includes • video and audio clips • flashcards • comprehension quizzes • quizzes on chapter content • reading selection quizzes • Internet exercises • writing prompts • glossary	Online Learning Center (OLC), www.mhhe.com/openingdoors, includes • video and audio clips • flashcards • comprehension quizzes • quizzes on chapter content • reading selection quizzes • Internet exercises • writing prompts • crossword puzzles • glossary
Annotated Instructor's Edition	Annotated Instructor's Edition includes answers, Teaching Tips, and an Instructor's Guide	Annotated Instructor's Edition includes answers, Teaching Tips, and an Instructor's Guide	Annotated Instructor's Edition includes answers, Teaching Tips, and an Instructor's Guide

Instructor Online Resources	Instructor's Edition of Online Learning Center (OLC), www.mhhe.com/entryways, includes • Supplemental chapter-related downloads and resources • Master lists of text and ORL reading selections • Master vocabulary lists • Thematic grouping of reading selections • Webliography of additional instructor resources Resources include information and techniques related to • informal, ongoing assessment • end-of-class activities • brain-friendly teaching and learning • classroom instruction and management • cooperative (collaborative) learning	Instructor's Edition of Online Learning Center (OLC), www.mhhe.com/newworlds, includes • information center • instructor resources • alternative teaching sequences • PowerPoint slides • Internet Primer • annotated answer keys • Test Bank of supplemental reading selections and quizzes • comprehensive review test	Instructor's Edition of Online Learning Center (OLC), www.mhhe.com/openingdoors, includes • information center • instructor resources • alternative teaching sequences • PowerPoint slides • Internet Primer • annotated answer keys • Test Bank of supplemental reading selections and quizzes • comprehensive review test • annotation, outlining, study map, summarizing, Cornell notetaking, test review sheet, test study card, exercises to accompany chapter-length reading selections • practice chapter quizzes for chapter-length reading selections

Exercise Your College Reading Skills: Developing More Powerful Comprehension

The Cortina/Elder continuum also includes *Exercise Your College Reading Skills,* a supportive, clearly written text that capitalizes on brain-friendly strategies and incorporates the motivating metaphor of sports. As the title suggests, it emphasizes the *application* of skills to college-textbook material, giving developmental students the extensive practice they need. Each chapter includes three sets of exercises of increasing difficulty. The text is intermediate-level, but because instructors can choose some or all of the exercises, it can be used flexibly in a variety of courses. Three full review chapters provide students with recursive application of all skills. The second edition contains "A User's Guide to the Brain," "The 'Secrets' of Success," "Handling Textbooks and Textbook Assignments Like a Pro," more than 200 new and updated passages and photos, expanded coverage of authors' writing patterns, a new chapter on analyzing word structure, and 12 longer and full-length reading selections in the final chapter. Chapter sections consist of the "Skill" (a concise explanation), the "Trainer" (showing an effective reader's thoughts as he/she applies the skill), the "Edge" (additional pointers from the "coach"), the "Replay" (review section), and "Practice" (three sets of exercises: two multiple-choice and one open-ended). Appendixes include a comprehensive list of word parts, material on test taking, on recognizing propaganda and fallacies, conducting research on the Internet and evaluating websites, learning style tips, and common figures of speech. The dedicated Online Learning Center includes additional material and quizzes for each chapter, supplemental readings, PowerPoint presentations, information on test taking and spelling, a chapter-length unit on (1) commonly confused and misused words, (2) interpreting literature, and (3) interpreting figurative language. The AIE gives every answer (along with explanations of why incorrect answers are incorrect), as well as a wealth of brain-friendly teaching suggestions.

Notes

Notes